Second Edition

LESSONS ABOUT THE STRUCTURE OF FINANCE

Thomas W. Downs
University of Alabama

PEARSON

Custom
Publishing

Cover photo courtesy of Photodisc/Getty Images.

Printed in the United States of America

10 9 8 7 6 5 4 3

ISBN 0-536-91515-6

2005160102

BK/LS

Please visit our web site at *www.pearsoncustom.com*

PEARSON CUSTOM PUBLISHING
75 Arlington Street, Suite 300, Boston, MA 02116
A Pearson Education Company

PREFACE

Every science has its golden age, and today is the golden age for finance. Perhaps 50 years ago was the age of the economist and everyone benefited by discovery of key insights on how government policies affect business and household behavior. It must have been exciting a century ago, too, as physicists and chemists discovered fundamental laws describing the behavior of atoms and molecules, of light and energy. Biologists have been at work for centuries, and their accumulated efforts are providing bigger dividends today than ever-dreamed possible. These historic sciences have shaped today's world, and promise to change the future even more.

Finance is a relatively new but rapidly growing science. The rapid growth in financial science is due to dramatic increases in financial applications. Each day more than a trillion dollars flow through global financial transactions. Explosive growth in the volume of financial market transactions is possible because technological innovations teem with maturing political economies to create a world ready for finance. And as the volume of transactions explodes, the characteristics of markets and securities evolve further and faster. The increasing sophistication of financial applications reveals novel and sometimes puzzling observations about financial relations. The existence of unexplained observations drives scientific discovery. In today's world financial observations abound. Financial science is quickly evolving because the world demands answers to financial questions.

A single unifying theme underlies all topics in finance: the creation and sustenance of value. Everything in finance has something to do with value! Financial science reveals three sources of value: time value, transformation value, and arbitrage value.

Time value is the simple worth of an asset and is sustained as the present value of future cash flow streams.

Transformation value is the value-added by combining different inputs to produce a unique output. A special case of transformation value is the diversification benefit from combining security cash flow streams.

Arbitrage value exists when prices or rates in different markets misalign, thereby providing a temporary opportunity for instantaneous profit.

Valuation principles underlying the three sources of value follow a natural progression from simple to complex. Time value is the simplest yet most common source of value because all economic assets at a given moment possess time value. Entrepreneurs have known for millennia that a sure dollar in the hand is worth more than a probable dollar in the future. In primitive economies, such as today's third world countries and yesteryear's major pre-industrial economies, the exclusive source of value often relates to simple time value concepts. Austrian economists in the mid-nineteenth century intent on explaining the determination of interest rates formally describe time value relationships.

As economies grew more complex the need to understand economic principles of production grew, too. Industrial companies add value by transforming land, labor, and capital into a product that clients demand. Transportation companies, likewise, add value by transforming a product at location A into a product at location B. Hairdressers transform a bad-hair day into a proud moment. Clients willingly pay a price to providers of goods and services that equals the transformation value plus production cost. Competitive forces assure fair compensation to companies that add value.

Growth of financial markets in the second half of the twentieth century revealed a perplexing situation. Institutions became dominant forces in financial markets, collecting money from investors, buying securities, and passing profits back to investors. Often investors had the same access as institutions to investment opportunities. Often, too, investors had as much skill as institutions picking investments. Apparently rapidly growing institutions were adding value to the world, yet how? Institutions in many cases were paper-shufflers providing few incremental services or insights.

Financial economists discovered that even though institutions do not produce tangible goods and sometimes their services are nil, they nonetheless garner transformation value. Combining securities generally reduces risk even when expected cash flows remain constant. Institutional investors provide clients with diversification benefits. Clients willingly pay for diversification benefits a price that equals the transformation value of combining cash flow streams. Transformation value accrues when inputs are combined to form a unique product. Sometimes the inputs are tangible land, labor, and capital; sometimes the inputs are intangible expected cash flow streams from securities. Transformation value accrues in either case. Insights about diversification benefits learned through financial science apply universally to many situations, even non-financial ones. Companies today routinely use diversification principles to manage bundles of assets and multiple product lines.

Events of the past quarter-century reveal the existence of arbitrage value, the most complex and powerful financial force of all. Technological possibility of instantaneous information flow throughout global markets means that financial rates and prices must align within certain tolerance limits. Movement outside those limits creates arbitrage value. Multinational investors have a keen sense for arbitrage opportunities. When investors see arbitrage profit they instantly capture it. They prudently spend money going after it, too, hiring knowledgeable workers and setting up offices and computer lines to disparate parts of the globe. The strong attractive force of arbitrage value causes development of markets and economies in ways unthinkable a generation ago.

Movement toward a unitary financial science coincides with curriculum changes at business colleges. Ten years ago most business students were required to study two finance courses. One course was "Corporate Finance" and the other was "Financial Markets and Institutions." Finance textbooks of that era reflect the two-course curriculum. Today, however, the requirement generally is one finance course. And this one required course is the only one about four-fifths of all business students will ever take. Today's finance textbook, instead of focusing exclusively on corporate finance or financial markets, must instruct on the intrinsic structure of finance. Maturation of the discipline now makes possible such a presentation. This book delivers it.

FOCUS OF THE *LESSONS*

The structure of finance builds upon foundations of economics and accounting. Underlying concepts are so complex and far-ranging that intuition becomes exceedingly important. Students often ask "will it be on the test." The question annoys some instructors who know that lesson importance lies in understanding underlying intuition. Surveys routinely show that students include introductory finance among the more difficult college courses, like an advanced foreign language course. Reason for this is many students direct study efforts toward memorizing solutions for different problems. Exclusive reliance on memorization is unwise in finance and often leads to failure. Instead, mastering finance requires, like a foreign language, internalizing underlying intuition well enough to think in *finance!* Presentations in *Lessons about the Structure of Finance* focus on intuition of underlying concepts—the many, many different finance problems tend to rely on surprisingly few basic ideas.

Nonetheless, "will it be on the test" is a well-founded query, an *acid-test* of importance, because problems and questions define the subject. Too often we may wave our hands at a topic and claim to understand the underlying ideas yet when it comes to solving specific problems we encounter difficulty. Indeed, the devil is in the details and failure to solve a problem often results from failure to fully understand underlying relationships. Problem solving repetition reinforces understanding relationships.

Presentations in *Lessons about the Structure of Finance* also focus on problem solving. Throughout each chapter examples or questions solve a problem from one direction and then from another in order to reinforce underlying concepts. At the end of most subsections find *Exercises*. Chapter 4, for example, presents five sections with a total of twelve subsections. Following each is a set of exercises offering a total of 67 unique questions. While 12 exercise sets appear throughout this one chapter, *answers* for all always appear at end-of-chapter.

Exercises ask conceptual as well as numerical questions. End-of-chapter answers for all are written in paragraph form with varying degree of explanation. Written answers sometimes expound on chapter lessons with new insights, details, or shortcuts important for student and teacher alike that may otherwise be overlooked. Throughout *Lessons* the answers also provide opportunity for instructors to buttress class presentations and drive home important intuitive insights.

Numerical problems obviously are important for finance. Numerous and frequent problems with written paragraph answers assist student learning. Also assisting students and teachers is algorithmic study software, *Algogen©*, that accompanies *Lessons*. Most textbook problems contain a code that *Algogen©* uses for repetitively generating problems with new numbers.

Exercise 4.1, #4, for example, looks like this:

4. Two years ago you purchased a stock for $40. One year ago the price had moved to $19. Today it is at $60. What are the arithmetic and geometric average annual rates of return? ©ROR3c .

Algogen for Students© allows students to checkmark question *ROR3c* and make, say, five different versions, each with different numbers (*Algogen©* gives answers and clues, too). *Algogen©* allows an unprecedented teaching tool for directing student study efforts. The teacher may announce, for example, "next class starts with a quiz on Exercise 4.1, #4, so study it!" or "here are codes for one-third of the questions on the exam." Students use *Algogen©* and with a few simple mouse-clicks create documents containing selected questions, as many versions of as many problems as desired. Students appreciate direction for studying. It's great when they study— repetitions build strength. And algorithmic questions appearing on the quiz or exam have different numbers than the ones studied.

The *Algogen©* library that accompanies *Lessons* contains about 700 questions. Some questions are very simple, some very complex, some are multi-part, some are conceptual, most are numerical. And every one looks different with each recalculation. All questions pertain to *Lessons about the Structure of Finance*.

CHAPTER ORGANIZATION OF *LESSONS*

Valuation principles underlying the three sources of value dictate a natural organization for topics. Figure 1 on the following page lists chapter titles in *Lessons about the Structure of Finance* pertinent to each source. Chapter 1 contains important introductory information. Then Part 1 presents lessons in chapters 2–8 that all pertain to time value relationships. Part 2 presents lessons in chapters 9–11 pertinent to diversification benefits and determination of equilibrium rates of return. Part 3 comprises one chapter with important lessons on risk management and financial arbitrage. Find below a synopsis of lesson objectives found in each chapter. Mention is made of novel features that render *Lessons* unique among introductory finance textbooks.

Chapter 1 introduces the field of finance. Lessons include a definition for *finance*, descriptions of financial functions within the company, and discussion of finance sub-disciplines and certifications. Attention turns to the *Cash flow cycle* wherein the company obtains financing from capitalists in financial markets for purchasing factors of production from stakeholders in real asset markets. The company adds value when the equilibrium amount that clients pay for the company's goods and services exceed economic production and capital costs. Source of the created wealth is transformation value. Subsequent discussion details different kinds of capitalists and financial markets. Between sources and

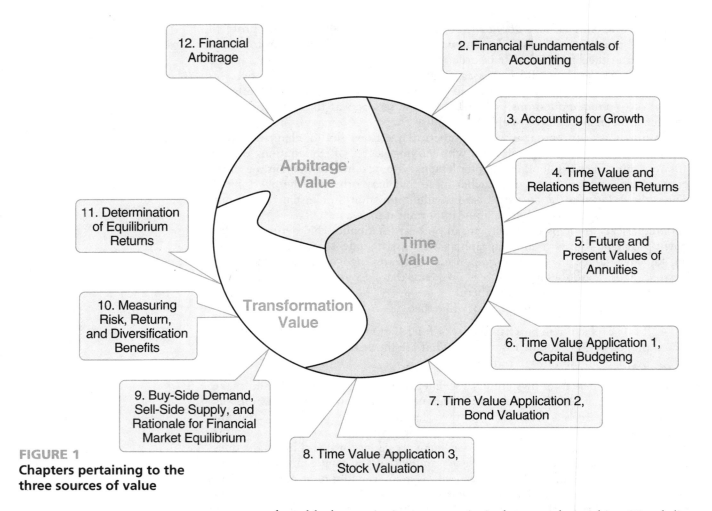

FIGURE 1

Chapters pertaining to the three sources of value

The figure shows a circle divided into three regions labeled "Arbitrage Value," "Time Value," and "Transformation Value," with chapter callouts:

- 12. Financial Arbitrage
- 2. Financial Fundamentals of Accounting
- 3. Accounting for Growth
- 4. Time Value and Relations Between Returns
- 11. Determination of Equilibrium Returns
- 5. Future and Present Values of Annuities
- 10. Measuring Risk, Return, and Diversification Benefits
- 6. Time Value Application 1, Capital Budgeting
- 9. Buy-Side Demand, Sell-Side Supply, and Rationale for Financial Market Equilibrium
- 7. Time Value Application 2, Bond Valuation
- 8. Time Value Application 3, Stock Valuation

users of wealth there exist important principal-agent relationships. Novel discussion explains the employee versus management/shareholder agency problem that arises from pension liabilities. Another important lesson teaches about wealth creation and the company goal. *Lessons* presents a novel argument that the objective for company management is pursuit of policies maximizing capitalized value of wealth creation irrespective of distribution of economic profit. Stock price maximization is an indicator variable for managerial effectiveness not a bonafide managerial objective. The chapter concludes with lessons about different definitions for the "company." Companies in the corporate sector, noncorporate sector, and even consideration of households as companies, shows that all make financial decisions that depend on common underlying concepts.

Chapters 2 and 3 offer in-depth lessons about flows, balances, and financial fundamentals of accounting. The first lesson explains that a flow is a wealth transfer whereas a balance is a wealth accumulation. Mention is made of difficulties arising because generally accepted financial statements mix realized with accrued flows and balances. Balance sheets exist as a snapshot in time. Mergers provide a wonderful opportunity devoid of time to combine balance sheets for *Raider* and *Target* companies. Presentations infer financial effects of mergers on equity book value, price-to-book ratio, earnings per share, and shareholder wealth. Problems created for this setting are unique to *Lessons* and availability of algorithmic capability is an added bonus. Discussion turns next to the income statement and ratio analysis. Included within ratio analyses are problems and explanations about DuPont decomposition and breakeven ratios. *Lessons* formula 2.7 is new to the literature and reveals relation between return-on equity, stockholder rate of return, and price-to-book ratio. Resultant financial problems also are new and of interest to the literature. Discussions next explain how an income statement encompasses a time window. Formulas show that the income statement connects with balance sheets at beginning and end of the time window through differential processes for *Stockholder's equity* and for *Plant, property, and equipment*. Chapter 2 closes with lessons determining shareholder rates of return with information from balance sheets, income statements, and price multiples. Chapter 3 focuses on financial accounting effects of growth. Initial lessons forecast financing needs given *pro forma* balance sheets or income statements. Subsequent lessons examine characteristics of natural growth rates. Formulas for the internal and sustainable growth rates are unique to *Lessons* and enable reconciliation of conflicting presentations apparent across other textbooks. Subsequent lessons introduce cash flow formulas. Underlying intuition is that cash flow residually reconciles adjacent balance sheets. Novel problems compute and interpret price-to-cash flow ratios. Chapters 2 and 3 introduce many novel and interesting *financial* applications for important accounting fundamentals.

Chapters 4 and 5 teach time value relationships. Lessons introduce time value by measuring the average periodic rate of return. Start at $100, drop a period later to $60, and return a period later to $100. The arithmetic average of periodic returns is biased whereas the geometric average is accurate. Rearrange the formula for geometric average and obtain lump-sum time value formula 4.6. Subsequent lessons examine return components such as periodic interest, interest-on-principal, interest-on-interest, etc. Especially useful are frequent *Calculator Clues* that teach keystrokes on the Texas Instruments BA2Plus calculator. Standard lessons on intraperiod compounding and annual and effective interest rates appear. Lessons subsequently rely on the additive property of present value to motivate general time value formula 4.11 for mixed cash flows. Numerical problems may be relatively complex because (a) *Calculator Clues* raise the level of acceptable complexity by simplifying computations, and (b) algorithmic capability simplifies problem creation, study, and learning assessment. The section on inflation and time value is unique to *Lessons*. Teachers and financial planners know importance of inflation and this section offers simple yet complete lessons integrating its effect. Chapter 5 introduces the constant annuity formula. Standard lessons appear for using the lump-sum and annuity formulas together in two-stage problems. Novel is generalization of the *Rule of 72* for constant annuities. Explanations and examples offer extensive lessons on amortization mechanics and loan re-pricing.

Chapter 6 introduces capital budgeting as a time value application. Standard discussions explain profitability assessment measures and NPV as a measure of economic profit. The lesson on significance of NPV as a measure of economic profit is novel. Explanations, graphs, and *Calculator clues* show the relation between NPV and IRR for ranking projects. The lesson for finding the cross-over rate for two NPV profiles is unique to *Lessons*. Discussion about incremental cash flows includes examples on mortgage refinancing. Discussion on importance of salvage value, recapture taxes, and depreciation tax savings is standard. Extensive problems take advantage of *Calculator clues*, paragraph answers at end-of-chapter, and algorithmic capability of problem creation.

Chapter 7 introduces bond valuation as a time value application. Lessons instruct on the price-to-yield relation. Strong emphasis is given to partitioning the promised yield into current and capital gains yield. Problems examine the scientific amortization time path for evolution of bond price given constant yield-to-maturity. *Calculator clues* teach "which buttons to push" and consequently complexity is rigorous relative to the typical introductory textbook. Unique to *Lessons* is inclusion of bond horizon analysis and effect of yield changes on *ex post* rate of return. Also unique is inclusion of lessons on riding the yield curve.

Chapter 8 pertains to stock valuation. The chapter opens by comparing technical with fundamental analysis. Lessons examine the moving average trading rule and present novel formulas for determining cross-over prices at which signal reversals from buy or sell occur. An excerpt from Graham and Dodd points us back to fundamental analysis and discussion of intrinsic value. Examples and problems reaffirm that fundamental analysis is a time value application. A *Street-bite* describes the distribution of equities among U.S. households and summarizes the different markets providing trade execution. Attention turns to preferred stocks and a novel problem finding rate of return when the preferred dividend yield reverts over time to a normal spread. *Calculator clues* simplify computations. Subsequent lessons examine common stocks with growing dividends. Unique to *Lessons* is estimation from a time series dividend history of the dividend growth rate using an exponential fit. *Calculator clues* simplify the procedure. Next appears discussion about the standard constant growth valuation model. Novel problems ask to find the shareholder rate of return when at the end of a horizon the stock price converges to intrinsic value. Reliance on prior financial accounting lessons about sustainable growth allows pretty interesting and synthesizing questions. The chapter concludes with examination of price multiples. A novel formula for the *intrinsic price-to-earnings ratio* provides a lesson that P/E ratios may vary even in the absence of pricing errors.

Chapter 9 is totally descriptive and contains no problems or computations. This chapter commences Part 2 of *Lessons* and describes the market backdrop for determining financial equilibrium. Instead of focusing on time value relations with largely exogenous financing rates, as in Part 1, lessons now focus on factors driving endogenous market financing rates. Discussion explains that primary market supply and demand for financial securities is a determinant of equilibrium security prices. Investigation proceeds with market participants that demand securities: *buy-side* institutional investors plus households. *Lessons* discuss household demand for securities and interaction between demographics, educational attainment, and life-cycle effects. Next is discussion of pension funds and dramatic changes in recent decades due to shifts from defined benefit to defined contribution plans. Mutual funds are the next buy-side participant and discussions explain major categories and characteristics. Final discussions of buy-side participants pertain to insurance companies, non-profit institutions, and commercial banks. Interesting characteristics for each are described as well as discussion on bank sector history and regulation. Subsequent discussion explains characteristics of security supply on the *sell-side* such as open market paper, asset backed securities, government securities, and convertibles, preferred, and common equities. Finally, find important lessons explaining the rationale for financial market equilibrium. Lessons clearly distinguish between expected and required rates of return. $ROR^{expected}$ is the internal rate of return that equates the actual security price to the discounted sum of expected cash flows. $ROR^{required}$ is the minimum discount rate that an investor willingly accepts for computing intrinsic value. Discussion explains why required returns equal the risk-free interest rate plus a risk premium. Further discussion explains why the efficient market hypothesis implies that expected returns vibrate around required returns. Learning about factors driving endogenous market financing rates therefore necessitates study of factors driving risk premia.

Chapter 10 presents lessons on risk, return, and diversification benefits. The chapter opens with discussion on dominance and the risk-for-return trade-off. Next appears explanation that at the limit there exist two primal types of risk: *idiosyncratic* risk that can be managed or eliminated through diversification and *systematic* risk that can't. Different sources of idiosyncratic risk include liquidity risk, term risk, default risk (this discussion links back to operating and financial breakeven ratios from chapter 3), political risk, and cross-border exchange rate risk. Attention turns toward investigating how diversification affects portfolio risk and return. Explanations and problems rely on standard statistical specification of probabilities and outcome rates of return. Problems examine individual securities and then two-security portfolios. Subsequent lessons assume outcomes are equally likely in which case *Calculator clues* teach keystrokes for easily finding risk and return measurements for a two-security portfolio. Frequent exercises, *Calculator clues*, and algorithmic problems simplify teaching and learning these invaluable lessons. Explanations and examples describe easy methods for graphing the parabola representing a two-security risk-return profile. This graphic technique vividly illustrates that portfolio risk often diminishes when one sells a low risk and buys a high risk investment. Definition 10.6 is unique to *Lessons* and states that *diversification benefit* ("DB") equals the difference between average component risk and actual portfolio risk. Illustrations show that DB equals the horizontal distance between the risk-return profile and the *line-of-averages*. Lessons emphasize that correlation between component securities determines inflection in the risk-return profile, hence correlation influences diversification benefits. Final lessons pertain to investment advice that the preceding analyses suggest.

Chapter 11 uses concepts from preceding lessons to explain determination of equilibrium rates of return. A simple graphical illustration provides intuitive support for the *Capital market line* and the equilibrium market price for risk. A general formula specifies that the required rate of return equals the risk-free rate plus a risk premium. Lessons introduce a simplified *loanable funds theory of interest* for a top-down explanation of the short-term risk free rate of return. The role of inflation as a component of the term risk premium is explicit. Other discussions suggest ad hoc procedures for determining risk premia for other credit market securities. Explanations then focus on risk premia for equity securities. When idiosyncratic risk is completely diversifiable and only one source of systematic risk exists then the risk premium for security A equals the market price for risk times $\sigma_A \times \rho_{A,market}$. The lesson reinforces importance of diversification benefits because the correlation coefficient between security and market measures the proportion of σ_A that merits the market price for risk. Figure 11.6 showing rays of correlation overlaid on the *Capital market line* and *Efficient frontier* is new to the literature. Next is introduction of β as a risk measure. The chapter closes with lessons about the company weighted average cost of capital.

Chapter 12 is sole contributor to Part 3 of *Lessons* on the third source of value: arbitrage. Opening discussion examines simple futures contracts and explains why market equilibrium requires that arbitrage profit vibrates within a narrow tolerance range around zero. Simple examples with gold and stock indexes show how spot and futures prices depend more on today's prices and interest rate within a time value relationship and less on expectations about tomorrow's prices. Futures contracts allow companies an opportunity to restrict outcome prices and profits within a narrow range. Problems and examples show how companies use futures contracts to hedge and manage risk. *Lessons* next introduce currencies prevalent in global commerce. Examples and formulas show effects of currency appreciation and depreciation on revenues and profits. Simple examples illustrate how companies use currency futures contracts to hedge exchange rate risk. Subsequent lessons examine risk management applications of options. Simple examples of portfolio insurance with call and put options introduce students to this important derivative security mentioned frequently in the media. Last section of the chapter explains triangle arbitrage with currencies. Next is explanation of purchasing power parity ("PPP") and the relation between inflation and currency depreciation. The text explains that PPP does not give rise to arbitrage opportunity because of market incompleteness. For currencies and interest rates, however, interest rate parity constitutes a powerful force that binds the largest financial market in the world, the foreign exchange market. Formulas in this chapter are simple and problems are straightforward and content is important. The intuition is powerfully fundamental and merits coverage in *Lessons about the Structure of Finance*.

THE *ALGOGEN* SUPPORT SYSTEM FOR *LESSONS*

Lessons about the Structure of Finance supports students and teachers with a free **algorithmic** problem **gen**erator. *Algogen for Students* is an easy to use point-and-click *Windows* software that automatically creates numerically distinct versions of questions in the textbook (plus many more that are not in the book). *Algogen* allows students to create additional practice problems as study aids. Download and freely install *Algogen* onto any computer with *Microsoft Office* (requires *Word* and *Excel*). Within minutes make new documents containing problems with new numbers and new answers. Point your internet browser to this website to obtain *Algogen* from the author and install the software on your computer: http://bama.ua.edu/~fi302/algogen_install_structure.htm. Follow installation instructions <u>very</u> carefully. Almost all causes for improper execution of *Algogen* occur because the student (or teacher) fails to properly follow installation instructions.

Algogen allows teachers an unprecedented tool for creating exams and for directing student study efforts. The system contains seven different algorithms that drive randomization. The algorithms make powerful <u>verbal</u> questions in addition to quantitative ones. For example, Table 12.3 compares hedging and speculative motives for trading in derivative contracts. The *Lessons* testbank includes a question about Table 12.3. Here is how one recalculation of the question appears:

> Two motives drive trading of commodity contracts in the futures and options markets: hedging and speculating. Choose the statement that best describes characteristics of speculators.
> a. they expect or already have a position in the underlying commodity
> b. movements in the commodity price have modest effect on the overall outcome
> c. the outcome depends exclusively on whether the futures contract makes a profit or a loss
> d. Two choices, A and C, are correct
> e. The three A-B-C choices are all correct

For convenience the random fields are colored blue for this discussion (they usually are indistinguishable). For each recalculation there is a 50% chance the question asks about speculators, 50% chance it's about hedgers. There is a one-in-five chance that the correct answer appears in any location a-to-e. Underlying each a-to-c selection is one true and one false statement. When the correct answer appears in location a, b, or c then that location shows a correct statement and the others show false statements. When the correct answer appears in location d then there is a one-in-three chance that the two correct choices are A and B, or A and C, or B and C. When the correct answer appears in location e then there is a 50% chance that all choices are correct and 50% chance that all are false. Bottom-line is that for this one question there are 52 possible permutations!

Teachers may easily make several versions of exams and, because they are standard *Word* documents, editing and adding supplemental questions is simple. With algorithmically generated exams students sitting side-by-side obtain no advantage looking at neighboring papers. Question orderings on neighboring papers are identical but certainly question content is unique.

Biggest strength of the enhanced software *Algogen for Teachers* is capability for any teacher to customize the testbank by adding new questions. Fully automated wizards drive question creation and completely handle all programming details. The teacher simply launches *Word* and types in the new question-body leaving blank the value of random fields such as prices, rates, modifies (increase vs. decrease), etc. Then launch *Excel* and use standard procedures to make a setup for the problem containing prices, rates, etc. Then start the wizard that appears on the main *Excel* toolbar. The wizard adds the new question that forevermore becomes a permanent part of the teacher's *Algogen* library.

Built into *Algogen* is capability for the teacher to share new questions with students. The teacher simply selects "Export questions to students" from the *Excel* toolbar and the application creates a file for distribution to students. Students obtain the file from the teacher and in *Algogen for Students* click the button "Import the teacher questions." Immediately they can begin studying and building strength with that specific question.

Every teacher has favorite topics and questions. By integrating personal favorites into an algorithmic generator the teacher possesses an incredibly powerful course development tool. And students love the guidance and direction that study with algorithmic questions provides. Contact the author, tdowns@cba.ua.edu, to obtain a free copy of *Algogen for Teachers*.

CONTENTS

LIST OF FIGURES

Lecture 1: Intro & Cash Flow Cycle (handwritten)

CHAPTER 1

Introduction to the Study of Finance

CHAPTER CONTENTS

1. SO JUST WHAT IS "FINANCE" ANYWAY?

Finance is an unusually rich subject. Notice it is one of the few college courses for which the course name has two definitions, one as action verb and the other as noun.

DEFINITION 1.1 Usage of "finance" in common vocabulary

(verb):   To *finance* means the act of borrowing money.
Example: How did you finance your car?
(noun):   *Finance* is the study of wealth management.
Example: This book explains basic principles of finance.

Although many types of wealth exist, society and history seem to suggest that money is a very important type. *Finance*, accordingly, has a lot to do with money regardless of whether the word usage is as verb or noun. Because everyone somewhat relies on money, everyone benefits from understanding basic principles of finance. Every lesson in this book applies directly to some aspect of wealth management.

    Finance is a relatively new science. At most universities the Finance department is fairly new. The majority of academic finance journals started less than 25 years ago. Furthermore, most big discoveries in finance have been made in the last few decades! Perhaps finance evolved from baby to toddler only in 1990. This is the year that, for the first time, the Nobel Prize in Economic Science was awarded for discoveries taught exclusively in finance courses. The prize was shared by three American professors: Harry Markowitz from the City University of New York, William Sharpe at Stanford University, and Merton Miller at the University of Chicago. Again in 1997, a finance discovery won the Nobel Prize in Economic Science.

    The fact that discoveries in finance sometimes win the Nobel Prize is significant. Financial principles rest upon a strong scientific foundation; they are not whimsical conjectures. The intuition and mathematics of financial theories often match the rigor associated with hard-core sciences such as engineering, chemistry, and physics. For example, the discovery that won the 1997 Nobel Prize by Myron Scholes (Stanford) and Robert Merton (Harvard) uses insights from heat transfer physics to model the valuation of financial stock options! There is, nonetheless, a strong practical side for most financial principles. The application of finance often requires strong familiarity with accounting fundamentals. In short, *finance* is a wonderful science because it uses the pragmatism of accounting to apply the rigor of economics to the study of wealth management.

People use financial knowledge everyday to make personal wealth management decisions. But exactly how, and who, uses finance? Glean insight from several perspectives.

1.A. Finance in the corporate pyramid

Figure 1.1 takes a perspective focusing on the "finance group" within the corporate pyramid. This particular hierarchy is for IBM, but the layout is fairly typical of any large corporation.

The finance group generally reports to the Chief Financial Officer ("CFO"). The CFO reports directly to the Chief Executive Officer ("CEO"). The figure shows that eleven different groups at IBM report to the CEO. The finance group headed by the CFO is very important, but equally important is the Strategy group that ponders question of corporate mission, the Marketing group that creates a positive corporate image, the Sales & Service group that generates revenues, the General Counsel group that keeps the company compliant, etc. There is a lot more to business than simply finance, but finance is essential.

The CEO is the most senior employee. The CEO reports to the Board of Directors. The Board of Directors hires and fires the CEO. Persons on the Board of Directors typically are not employees of the company. Directors are individuals with careers unrelated to IBM's mission. The figure shows that on IBM's board is a president of a publishing empire, several university presidents, oil company presidents, etc. Presumably, external Directors see the big picture and assess the sensibility of the company's efforts. But who hires and fires the Board of Directors? Shareholders, that's who! Shareholders of a corporation elect Directors from a slate of nominees. Typically one share of common stock casts one vote. The chain-of-command is thus: shareholders elect or oust the Board of Directors; the Board of Directors hires and fires the CEO, the CEO hires and fires senior management, senior management hire and fire middle management, and middle management hire (seldom fire, hopefully) college graduates that are just starting-out. When you buy common stock, you get more than hoped-for profits; you get control over management (don't get too excited, though, IBM has over half-billion shares outstanding and it's one vote per share!)

Figure 1.2 shows typical units within the finance group.

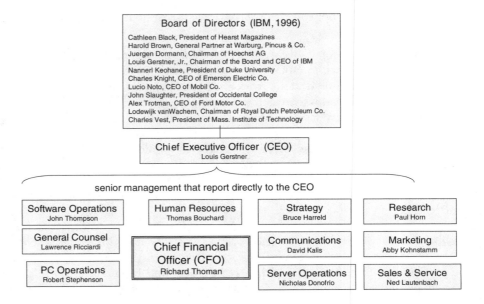

FIGURE 1.1
Finance in the corporate hierarchy

Board of Directors (IBM, 1996)

Cathleen Black, President of Hearst Magazines
Harold Brown, General Partner at Warburg, Pincus & Co.
Juergen Dormann, Chairman of Hoechst AG
Louis Gerstner, Jr., Chairman of the Board and CEO of IBM
Nannerl Keohane, President of Duke University
Charles Knight, CEO of Emerson Electric Co.
Lucio Noto, CEO of Mobil Co.
John Slaughter, President of Occidental College
Alex Trotman, CEO of Ford Motor Co.
Lodewijk vanWachem, Chairman of Royal Dutch Petroleum Co.
Charles Vest, President of Mass. Institute of Technology

Chief Executive Officer (CEO)
Louis Gerstner

senior management that report directly to the CEO

Software Operations
John Thompson

Human Resources
Thomas Bouchard

Strategy
Bruce Harreld

Research
Paul Horn

General Counsel
Lawrence Ricciardi

Chief Financial Officer (CFO)
Richard Thoman

Communications
David Kalis

Marketing
Abby Kohnstamm

PC Operations
Robert Stephenson

Server Operations
Nicholas Donofrio

Sales & Service
Ned Lautenbach

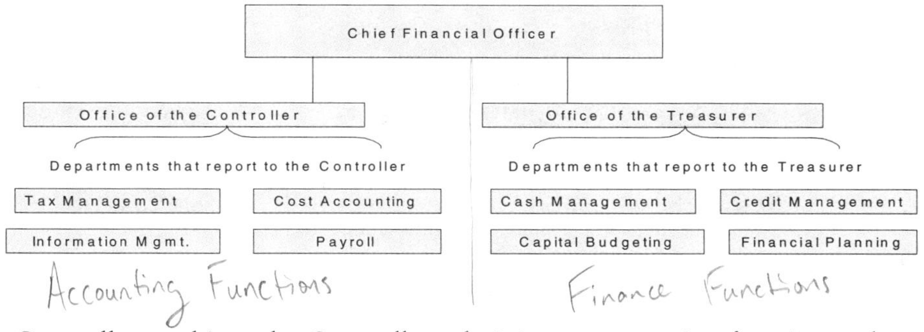

FIGURE 1.2
Typical finance group in the company

```
                        ┌─────────────────────────┐
                        │  Chief Financial Officer │
                        └─────────────────────────┘
              ┌────────────────────┴────────────────────┐
    ┌──────────────────────┐                  ┌──────────────────────┐
    │ Office of the Controller │              │ Office of the Treasurer │
    └──────────────────────┘                  └──────────────────────┘
  Departments that report to the Controller   Departments that report to the Treasurer

  ┌──────────────┐  ┌──────────────┐    ┌──────────────┐  ┌──────────────┐
  │ Tax Management │  │ Cost Accounting │  │ Cash Management │  │ Credit Management │
  └──────────────┘  └──────────────┘    └──────────────┘  └──────────────┘
  ┌──────────────┐  ┌──────────────┐    ┌──────────────┐  ┌──────────────┐
  │ Information Mgmt. │ │ Payroll │      │ Capital Budgeting │ │ Financial Planning │
  └──────────────┘  └──────────────┘    └──────────────┘  └──────────────┘
```

Accounting Functions   *Finance Functions*

Generally speaking, the Controller administers accounting functions whereas the Treasurer administers finance functions. The Cash management department assures that checks don't bounce and that a prudent amount of cash is on-hand. Credit management pertains to customer loan policies, collections, and payments. Capital budgeting pertains to long-term decisions about investing or financing of plant, property, and equipment. Financial planning assesses current and future financial health given likely trends. Basic finance functions in the Office of the Treasurer generally monitor how the company's wealth is or should be allocated, where the wealth is coming from, and where the wealth is going. These essential business functions use financial science.

1.B. Finance sub-disciplines

Glean another perspective of finance by examining traditional sub-disciplines:

Corporate Finance—topics include working capital management, capital budgeting, obtaining financing, capital structure decisions, and dividend payout policies;

Investments—topics include company and security analysis, portfolio theory and management, futures and options;

Markets and Institutions—topics include banking, analysis of interest rates, and financial market microstructure;

Specialty Areas—topics include real estate, insurance, law and financial economics, personal financial planning, enterprise finance, risk management, etc.

Many universities offer one or more courses organized around these sub-disciplines. Until the mid-1990's, in fact, the accrediting agency "American Assembly of College Schools of Business" (AACSB) required that undergraduate business programs include two finance courses. Typically one course was "Corporate Finance" and the other was "Markets and Institutions." The AACSB rescinded the two-finance-course rule and as a result most undergraduate business students today study only one finance course. The curriculum for today's singular introductory course overviews all traditional sub-disciplines of finance. The maturation of financial science blurs lines separating traditional sub-disciplines and a continuous discipline is emerging.

1.C. Finance certifications

One final perspective about finance comes from inspecting professional certifications. Perhaps most widespread is the Chartered Financial Analyst ("CFA"). The CFA designation for finance is analogous to the CPA designation that accountants earn (the "Certified Public Accountant"). Earning the CFA title requires taking a series of exams, as well as satisfying on-the-job experience requirements. Other designations often are seen following individual names on office doors or in professional advertisements. Each certification suggests that the individual satisfies the

TABLE 1.1
Professional Certifications in Finance

Certificate Title	Description	Contact
Chartered Financial Analyst (CFA)	The CFA is a recognized standard of competency for financial analysts in more than 70 nations worldwide	**www.aimr.com** Association for Investment Management and Research
NASD Stock Broker's License	NASD brokers represent more than 5,500 securities firms with more than 82,000 branch offices across the U.S. Acquiring the license requires multiple applications and qualifications	**www.nasd.com** National Association of Securities Dealers
Certified Financial Consultant (CFC)	Recognized by institutions and individuals as a sign of integrity and professional excellence. Many employers require the CFC designation when hiring or promoting	**www.ifcusa.com** Institute of Financial Consultants
Certified in Financial Management (CFM)	The CFM is for students, practitioners, and academicians that understand techniques defining the field of finance	**www.fma.org** Financial Management Association
Certified Financial Planner (CFP)	Holders of the CFP meet rigorous requirements in banking, estate, insurance, investment, and tax planning	**www.cfp-board.org** Certified Financial Planner Board of Standards
Chartered Financial Consultant (ChFC)	Granted to individuals completing a comprehensive 10-course practical that includes economics, taxes, insurance	**www.financialpro.org** Society of Financial Services Professionals and investing
Chartered Life Underwriter (CLU)	This is the undisputed professional credential for persons involved in the protection and preservation of financial wealth through life insurance	**www.amercoll.edu** The American College
Commodity Trading Advisor (CTA)	A registered adviser regarding the value of securities or of the advisability of investing in securities.	**www.securitiesexam.com** Securities Exam Preparation, Inc.
Financial Risk Management (FRM)	Earned by individuals who have been qualified to legally give clients financial planning service and advice	**www.rims.org** Risk and Insurance Management Society

stringent criteria promulgated by the respective professional organization. Many of the more visible certifications appear in Table 1.1.

2. THE COMPANY CASH FLOW CYCLE

There are many types of wealth, just as there are many types of businesses, markets, or human wants. All wealth, however, possesses a common characteristic:

DEFINITION 1.2 Wealth (noun)
Wealth is any capital or asset that provides returns over time.

Typical examples include: (a) This IBM common stock represents a lot of her *wealth*; or (b) This building represents a lot of the company's *wealth*. Clearly a building is a useful asset that provides services for many years, so a building is a type of wealth. Likewise, the IBM stock promises to return money in the future, so it too is a type of wealth. Of course, a building made from bricks and mortar is quite different than a security made from paper. Both assets, nonetheless, represent wealth because they promise future returns.

   Markets transfer ownership of wealth. There are as many different markets as there are asset types. Yet at the broadest level a market is either (a) a financial market, or (b) a real asset market. Financial markets trade exclusively paper claims and obligations. Paper claims and obligations represent contracts that promise either implicitly or explicitly to deliver returns through time. These pieces of paper are called "securities," and examples include stocks, bonds, and loan obligations. The

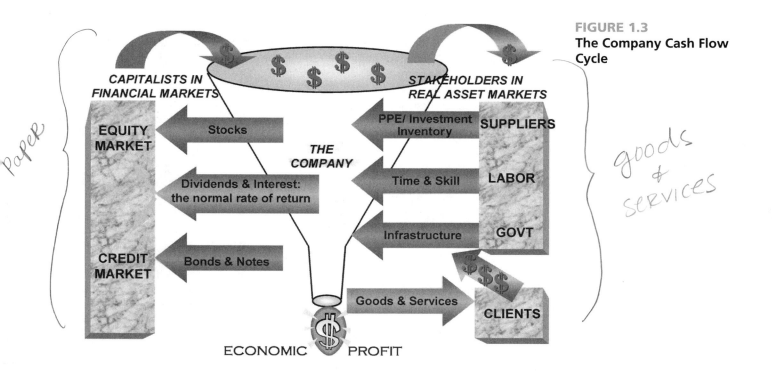

FIGURE 1.3
The Company Cash Flow Cycle

[Handwritten annotations: "Paper", "goods & services"]

paper itself does not possess intrinsic traits that endear it; you can't eat the paper or use it for anything useful. Instead, the paper represents wealth because it promises future returns (usually more paper!). Real asset markets trade goods and services. The market that trades buildings is a real asset market. Other examples of real asset markets include the markets for books, automobiles, steel, groceries, and haircuts or massages. Real goods provide economic utility. Real goods are real things!

Financial securities and real assets represent wealth because both provide returns over time. Some economists argue that financial markets are like a veil lying on top of the economy's real assets. They question the extent to which financial wealth leads to creation of real assets. This is a complex issue. Inspection of economies around the globe reveals that nations possessing the most real assets also have the most highly developed financial markets. Whether financial markets lead to sophistication of real asset markets, or vice versa, is like asking whether the chicken or egg came first. Regardless, the cash flow cycle in Figure 1.3 illustrates the relation between financial and real asset markets:

The company lies at the heart of the cash flow cycle. The company brings together resources from diverse sectors of the economy in order to produce goods and services. The company deals with capitalists in the financial markets, and with stakeholders in the real asset markets.

2.A. Stakeholders

[Handwritten annotation: "→ almost all that come in contact w/ physical goods."]

A stakeholder is an economic entity in the real asset markets that exchanges goods and services with the company. There are four major classes of stakeholders: suppliers, labor, government, and clients. Suppliers provide the company with inventory, raw materials, and plant, property, and equipment. Those factors of production are real goods and services that the company needs to make its product. The company exchanges money with the suppliers. Labor includes management and employees. These individuals provide the labor services that the company needs to function. The company exchanges wages, salaries, and bonuses for labor services. The government is another major stakeholder with the company. The government provides highways and airports, they protect property and maintain civil obedience with police, firefighters, and military. The government also educates the workforce, and they maintain a regulatory environment that is politically responsive to the company.

[Handwritten annotation: "stakeholders: ① suppliers ② labor ③ gov. ④ clients"]

The company in return pays taxes to local, state, and federal governments. Clients, too, are stakeholders with the company. Notice in the cash flow diagram that the direction of money flow is different for the client than the other stakeholders. The company delivers goods and services to the client. The client exchanges revenues with the company.

Why does the company exist? Some people claim that the client is the sole reason for the company to exist. The argument has merit because the company stays financially healthy only as long as clients continue to buy the goods and services that the company produces.

Employees often claim that they sacrifice a lot for their company and, therefore, the company owes them a decent wage and reasonable job security. The claim that companies exist to provide people a way to make a living has merit, too.

At times in history, government has claimed that some particular company is so vital to the national interest that the government nationalizes the company. That is, the government forces the company to work toward a specific public objective. The claim that companies exist to promote national welfare has merit, too.

Between the company and each stakeholder there is a relationship. For example, a company may hire and train labor in expectation that labor will grow to become loyal and productive workers. Or a supplier may expect to make future sales to the company as long as the cost and quality of its supplies is best. Or a government may invest in infrastructure and expect the company to employ the populace. Stakeholders and the company often make decisions with the expectation of continuing a relationship. When a stakeholder relationship unexpectedly ends, then sometimes a stakeholder, the company, or both, seem to lose something valuable. So to whom does the company owe its highest allegiance? That is, what is the goal of the company? Before answering this question, let's examine the relation between the company and financial markets.

2.B. Financial markets

Companies receive money by selling securities to capitalists in financial markets. Financial securities do not provide real goods and services. Securities, just like money, are paper. More than likely, however, securities represent an ownership claim on assets or goods and services.

There are many types of financial markets, and there are many schemes for categorizing them. Table 1.2 summarizes three common schemes. One scheme is *primary* versus *secondary* financial market. In the "primary financial market" companies receive money by selling or issuing securities to capitalists. Sometimes capitalists re-sell securities to other investors in "secondary financial markets" and, in turn, the security may pass from hand-to-hand many times. IBM stock exists because once, and only once, the company issued that particular stock in a primary market transaction. Every subsequent trade between two different financial investors is a secondary market transaction. Most exchanges of marketable securities occur in the secondary market because one investor simply sells to another without direct involvement of the company.

A second scheme for categorizing financial markets is by the length of the financial contract's time horizon: *money market* versus *capital market*. The "money market" includes financing that is repayable within one year. Examples of money market transactions include short-term bank loans, overnight repurchase agreements, installment loans, and trade credit from suppliers. When a company obtains a short-term loan (or any other credit agreement) they sign a legal contract stipulating terms of repayment. The loan contract is a financial security. Sometimes the loans can be re-sold to other investors in a secondary market transaction, sometimes they can't. As the arrows in the cash flow cycle show, the company receives money from the financial market - the financial market receives a security from the company. Money market securities have a relatively short life because the financing is totally repaid within one year. "Capital markets" are at the other extreme of the time horizon because they represent long-term financing arrangements. The prominent types of capital market

TABLE 1.2

Common schemes for categorizing financial markets

distinguishing criterion	category 1 & description	category 2 & description
new vs. seasoned security	*primary market,* stocks & bonds issued by company to investor	*secondary market,* stocks & bonds sold by one investor to another investor
length of financial contract	*money market,* financing repayable within one year	*capital market,* financing repayable in more than one year
type of repayment promise	*credit market,* trade credit, notes, and bonds that stipulate specific payments and/or interest	*equity market,* stocks that do not specify repayment but instead represent a claim on residual cash flows

securities include stocks, bonds, and mortgages. Perhaps some bonds may stipulate repayment, say, in five or ten years. Stocks, in principle, possess infinite life.

A third scheme for categorizing financial markets is by type of repayment promise: *credit markets* versus *equity markets*. Credit markets include all short-term financing arrangements available in the money market. Credit markets also include all long-term debt arrangements such as bonds and mortgages. A common characteristic of credit market financing is a promise by the company to repay to the creditor all principal plus interest. Typically credit market contracts specify exact repayment terms and conditions. If the company encounters financial difficulties and is unable to satisfy the promised repayment schedule then bankruptcy may occur. Conversely, if the company strikes it rich there is no upward adjustment to the scheduled repayment. Credit markets do not receive the windfall gains that a company may earn—the repayment schedule is fixed.

Windfall gains and losses earned by the company flow to equity. Equity markets are sometimes called *stock markets*. Companies issue stocks to capitalists in exchange for money. The company does not make a legally binding promise about repaying stockholders. Instead, the motivation for stock investing is to have a controlling interest in the corporation (usually 1 vote per share of common stock), or because the investor anticipates financial gains such as dividends or share price appreciation. Stockholders may own the stocks for a reasonable length of time, after which they may sell the stocks to other investors. The company has no legal obligation to pay dividends to shareholders. Because shareholders control the Board of Directors and therefore can fire top management, however, the company likes to treat shareholders as fairly as possible.

The income statement, as the next chapter explains, shows how a company's revenues pay for the various factor costs of production. The profit, that is net income, either is paid-out as dividends to shareholders or else is plowed-back into the company to support growth. Company growth helps push-up the stock price, and that benefits shareholders. Shareholders are *residual claimants* on company cash flows because they get that which is leftover after all costs have been paid. Shareholders sometimes are beneficiaries of unexpected windfall gains when the company strikes it rich, but they bear the burden of windfall losses when things unexpectedly go sour. Windfalls accrue to equity!

2.C. Agency problems

An agency problem potentially exists when a source of financing delegates decision-making authority for using the funds. The source that owns the funds is called the *principal,* and the decision-maker controlling the funds is called the *agent*. A principal-agent relationship exists when the owner of wealth is different from the controller of wealth.

An agency problem exists when objectives of the principal and agent are different. The resulting misalignment of interests may result in sub-optimal company performance. The direct and indirect decline in wealth resulting from a principal-agent problem is called an *agency cost*. The company expends substantial resources to minimize agency costs. There are three important principal-agent relationships within a company.

C1. Shareholders versus management

Shareholders supply, as the next chapter explains, a source of financing called "stockholders equity." Stockholders lend money to the company yet management decides how to use the money. Managerial decisions generally advance the interests of shareholders because, after all, shareholders can pressure the Board of Directors to fire management. Yet managers naturally pursue their own self-interests. Sometimes, for example, management may buy a company jet or spruce up the office unnecessarily. Determining the proper amount of perquisite consumption by managers is a difficult but largely managerial decision. Perhaps managers over-invest in assets, product lines, or empire building, simply because managerial salaries tend to correlate directly with company size. Sometimes managers in pursuit of self-interest may make decisions that reduce the amount of residual wealth available to shareholders. That is an agency problem!

Several *control mechanisms* help align management and shareholder interests.

1. shareholders can lobby to fire management
2. managers can be given clever incentive compensation contracts
3. shareholders can closely monitor and/or restrict managerial decisions
4. languishing stock prices can increase the threat of take-over
5. managers wish to maintain pristine reputations for the next job

Operation of the first control mechanism is clear. Management cannot ignore shareholder interests too much lest they be terminated.

The second control mechanism links compensation with stock price performance. In today's world a significant fraction of management compensation depends on movement in the company stock price. These clever contracts ring similar to professional athlete contracts wherein, for example, there may be bonuses for making the all-star game or winning the conference title, etc. Managers earn big bonuses when during their tenure the company stock price rises. So managers have an incentive to make decisions maximizing the stock price. Clever compensation contracts align shareholder and managerial interests because both parties benefit from stock price increases.

Compensation contracts unexpectedly introduce agency costs when the company stock price rises for reasons unrelated to managerial actions. Strong bull markets tend to raise all share prices and, like a boat with the tide, a particular manager may be the beneficiary of an unanticipated windfall gain. The windfall would flow to equity if not for the compensation package. Instead, however, management gets more than its fair share of the windfall. Certainly hiring good managers is expensive. But when top management earns, for example, $60 million from executive stock options, then surely shareholders are paying more than management's reservation wage. Management would have performed the same services for less. The excess compensation, that is the amount above the manager's reservation wage, represents a drain from shareholder wealth and is an indirect agency cost.

The third control mechanism consists of financial audits and constraints on managerial decision-making. Audits ascertain that shareholders have full information about the company's financial actions. When management knows shareholders are watching, management is more responsive to shareholder interests. Constraints on managerial decision-making take many forms. There may be a requirement, for example, that major strategic decisions require presentation and approval at the annual shareholder meeting. This control mechanism introduces direct and indirect agency costs.

The fourth control mechanism is not written in any contract but instead is a naturally occurring market mechanism. When management does a bad job that results in a low share price the company assets become relatively cheap to acquire. Outside entrepreneurs may sense an opportunity to gain control of the company assets by purchasing the relatively cheap stock. Attainment of majority stock ownership allows the takeover group to oust extant management. The new shareholders install new management and set a new direction for the company. This control mechanism does not introduce obvious agency costs. Instead, managers have a natural incentive to maximize stock price in order to avoid being a takeover target.

The fifth control mechanism recognizes that managers have careers that evolve over time. Maintenance of reputation and dignity are important incentives. Being a good manager with one company naturally opens doors for advancement with other companies. Shareholders surely will not hire an executive who screwed shareholders at his or her previous job.

C2. Creditor versus management/shareholder

Creditors are a financing source for the company. Management decides how to use the money. The creditor is a principal, management is an agent, and there is a problem due to misalignment of interests. Because management is directly responsive to shareholders, however, we also may view this as an agency problem between creditors and shareholders. Several control mechanisms help align creditor and management/shareholder interests.

1. threat of bankruptcy induces fiduciary responsibility
2. restrictive covenants stipulate precise uses for creditor financing
3. managers wish to maintain a good reputation so they can borrow again

Operation of the first control mechanism is clear. If management misuses credit then the creditor can force bankruptcy and everybody loses.

Operation of the second control mechanism is less obvious. Credit agreements vary by the degree to which they restrict the use of borrowed funds. At one extreme is the line-of-credit agreement that basically allows the company to borrow money for any purpose whatsoever. At the other extreme is the mortgage bond that lends money for purchase of a specific property, perhaps ties the repayment schedule to revenues the company realizes from the property, and further disallows additional borrowing against the property. The essence of this principal-agent problem is that the creditor lends money to managers at a fixed interest rate. The manager, however, is first-most responsive to shareholders. By pursuing high-risk high-return investments the manager potentially obtains windfalls that flow through to shareholders (and perhaps his/her own bonus, too). Creditors do not want managers to invest low-cost financing in high-risk investments. Sometimes creditors may impose covenants restricting the uses of the funds.

The third control mechanism recognizes the existence of a long-term relationship between company and creditor that transcends a single credit arrangement. Irresponsible company behavior by the manager may signal to the creditor irreconcilable differences. Companies, just like households, need financing and burning a bridge with a creditor diminishes future financing opportunities.

C3. Employee versus management/shareholder

Balance sheets show, as the next chapter explains, that employees are a significant financing source for many companies. Employees usually do not give direct loans to the company. Instead, employees provide financing by deferring compensation. Under guidelines for traditional pension plans, for example, an employee may provide labor services to the company that are worth $60,000 but accept immediate compensation for only $50,000. The company retains the $10,000 of deferred compensation and promises to pay the employee a pension in the remote future. Employees for many companies are an important financing source and own the wealth, but manager/shareholders control the wealth. This is an agency problem!

Several control mechanisms help align employee and management/shareholder interests.

1. threat of litigation induces fiduciary responsibility
2. assignment of pension contributions to third parties

Dozens of court cases about pension assets dot the legal landscape. When the manager/shareholder reneges on promises it made to employees about pension benefits, employees often sue. The threat of litigation helps align the interests of employees and manager/shareholders.

Many companies are disbanding traditional pension plans and instead offer a novel type called a "defined contribution plan." With this type of plan the employee is not a financing source for the company because all deferred compensation is typically transferred to a third party. Ownership of the funds clearly belongs to the employee, and fund management is not by company managers. Instead, the company (usually) hires an independent management company such as Scudder Management Co., or Merrill Lynch, etc. The pension management company communicates with employees to make sure employee interests are pursued.

2.D. Wealth creation and the company goal

The cash flow cycle in figure 1.3 shows the many wealth transfers that exist between the company, stakeholders in real asset markets, and capitalists in financial markets. The next chapter explains that wealth transfers represent a flow per time period, and later chapters explain the crucial relation between time and the valuation process. The occurrence in the real world every period of all the flows in the diagram creates a very complicated mosaic of wealth transfers between capitalists, stakeholders and company.

Glean insight on wealth creation by imagining this simplistic situation. During one period the company receives money from capitalists and, from stakeholders, the company receives supplies, labor, and infrastructure services. The company does its thing, transforming productive inputs into final goods and services. Then during the next period the company delivers the final goods and services to clients, receives sales revenues, and passes all revenues on to capitalists and stakeholders.

Assume for the moment that the revenues exactly equal the economic costs of production. That is, assume economic profit equals zero.

> ### DEFINITION 1.3 Economic profit
> Economic profit equals the difference between company revenue and total economic costs of production. Economic profit (or loss) exists when the company passes revenues on to capitalists and stakeholders that is greater (or less) than the minimum amount they were willing to receive for providing that good or service.

The cash flow cycle in figure 1.3 illustrates economic profits as the golden droplet coming out of the funnel. For this simplistic case there is no drip.

Participants in real asset and financial markets compete for compensation from the company. Suppliers want to charge the highest possible price for plant, property, and equipment, but the company wants to pay the least possible purchase price (all else equal). Labor wants the highest possible wages, but the company pays only what the market will bear. Governments collect taxes to build infrastructure in response to political pressures, and companies hire lobbyists to inform politicians about constraints on business. Capitalists look for investments providing the highest risk-adjusted rate of return, yet companies search for the best available financing terms. And of course, clients and customers always are on the lookout for the best deal and, in competitive markets, pay a price exactly equal to their perceived value of the good or service. Economic theory suggests *in the long-run you get what you pay for and equilibrium economic profits equal zero!*

The company adds value by transforming real factors of production into a good or service that clients demand. The sales transaction between company and client consummates wealth creation. The real value of the sales revenue exceeds the real value of the inputs from stakeholders and capitalists by the amount of real wealth created. The wealth created equals the transformation value from production. The company subsequently distributes the new wealth to stakeholders and capitalists. This simplistic scenario in which economic profits equal zero is not as bad as it

to act all trying pockible deal for possible deal for themselves

sounds—stakeholders and capitalists receive fair prices, wages, and rates of return and wealth accumulates through time.

Economic theory establishes that in realistic and dynamic situations, economic profits (and losses) exist because of population and demand growth, technological innovation, market maturation, product development, and myriad other phenomena such as fads, changing preferences, or plain old luck. Company management, too, potentially creates economic profit through superior foresight and decision-making.

Consider the distribution of economic profit in the cash flow cycle. One fact is clear: residual wealth flows to equity. If no stakeholders or creditors lobby for the economic profit then surely it accrues to equity. But when stakeholders and creditors see the wealth droplet forming, mouths move toward the funnel. Competition and market structure determines who sips from the font of economic profit.

For example, perhaps suppliers make technological breakthroughs that reduce economic costs of production. Surely in the long run, and in the absence of barriers, the company pays a lower price for supplies and clients pay a lower price for goods and services. In the short-run, however, suppliers and company management negotiate the distribution of economic profit. Suppliers want to pocket the profit by charging the same price for supplies as before. Management, under the shadow of an agency problem, tries to pay lower costs but charge the same price for the final product and pass the economic profit on to capitalist shareholders. So who gets it? Well, it depends on who has the strongest negotiating position. Capitalists and stakeholders most likely share economic profit.

Other examples abound. Clients respond to fads and willingly pay a higher price for a good even though the company's economic costs of production remain the same. Or a company is venturing into a new production process for which there is a scarcity of labor with exactly the right skill package. Who gets the economic profit? Skilled and highly sought labor tries to get it, or possibly even managers lobby for bonuses claiming superior foresight for product development. Clearly in the absence of action the residual flows to equity. But don't count on inaction by stakeholders. They are just as smart and greedy as capitalists!

The creation of wealth in a competitive economy helps the world, irrespective of who gets it (as long as no one is made worse off in which case the situation is maddeningly complex), and irrespective of whether economic profit is zero. This leads to statement of a proper and ethical objective for company management:

RULE 1.1 The objective for company management
Management should pursue policies that maximize net wealth creation by the company, irrespective of the distribution of economic profit.

The management job is tough. A good manager faces the difficult challenge of ascertaining fair and competitive prices and wages for stakeholders. Sometimes those payments include economic profit, but not always. Sometimes equity receives all economic profit, sometimes economic profit is zero. Yet as long as managers transfer wealth to creditors, labor, and suppliers at competitive market prices, and likewise sell final goods and services to clients at competitive market prices, the company maximizes wealth creation for capitalists and stakeholders alike.

The change through time of the equity stock price is a useful indicator of managerial effectiveness. A later chapter explains that stock prices depend on market assessments of long-run company profitability. A rising stock price indicates (all else equal) a rising forecast of residual cash flows to equity. A rising stock price (all else equal) generally confirms that management pursues wealth-creating projects. In cases when stakeholders with inelastic competitive positions capture a share of economic profits, the stock price still rises because the fair rate of return to capitalists includes a real increase in wealth. The stock price would rise even faster, of course, if the manager could negotiate lesser payments for stakeholders and divert all economic profit toward equity. That cannot always be accomplished because stakeholders sometimes control scarce factors of production. Still, employing scarce factors of production and getting shareholders half of something is better than getting them all of nothing.

In the rare case where a stakeholder holds all the cards and receives all economic profit, management should pursue a policy that creates incremental wealth for the stakeholder, even though none flows to the shareholder. The fair rate of return to shareholders excludes economic profit yet still provides a wealth-increasing risk-adjusted rate of return. The world becomes a better place when the company pursues policies that maximize wealth creation, irrespective of the distribution of economic profit, as long as all capitalist and stakeholder exchanges with the company occur at competitive prices and rates.

A falling stock price (all else equal) is an indication that management either is overpaying stakeholders or is selling the final good or service for less than the economic cost of production. Once again, running a company is a tough balancing act and the stock price is an indicator variable for managerial effectiveness.

3. CLONES OF THE COMPANY CASH FLOW CYCLE

The cash flow cycle in figure 1.3 depicts economic activity applicable for many different scenarios. Minor interpretive changes allow the cash flow cycle to depict scenarios in which the company is (1) a corporate business, (2) a noncorporate business, and (3) a household or individual. Principles of financial science pertain to all these economic entities with surprising uniformity. It behooves us to discuss these alternative scenarios.

3.A. Corporate business

The preceding sections identify the company as a corporation. Understanding basic characteristics of the corporate sector is important and generally eye opening. The corporate sector in the U.S.A. contains business names that almost every citizen recognizes: General Electric, AT&T, Microsoft, Disney, etc. Table 1.3 presents information about several of these American corporate icons.

Every corporation has common stock. The common stocks that trade on a stock exchange have a company identifier called the "ticker symbol". The table shows, for example, that the ticker for Exxon Mobil is XOM, and for Ford it simply is F. Armed with a ticker symbol one can easily find on the internet a recent stock price and other news for exchange-traded companies.

The range in number of full-time employees is huge. Over 1.1 million walk the floors of Wal-Mart. At Ford Motor Company, which has roughly the same amount of annual sales (just over $160 billion dollars), the number of employees (365,000) is about one-third as large. Ford has three times more total assets than Wal-Mart, too. Clearly, sales per employee and sales per dollar of asset is three times higher at Ford than Wal-Mart. But the automotive and retail industries differ so significantly that this comparison is little more than amusing trivia.

The rightmost column of table 1.3 lists company market capitalization. Market "cap," as the next chapter explains, measures the company's value in the stock mar-

TABLE 1.3

American corporate icons. All dollars in millions. Data are from the American Association of Individual Investors, February 2001.

Corporation Name	Ticker symbol	Number of full-time employees	Annual sales	Total assets	Annual net income	Market cap
AOL-Time Warner, Inc.	AOL	15,000	$6,886	$10,673	$1,232	$203,958
AT&T Corporation	T	147,800	62,391	169,406	5,450	87,755
Exxon Mobil Corporation	XOM	123,000	185,527	144,521	7,874	288,489
Ford Motor Company	F	364,550	162,558	276,229	7,222	53,113
General Electric Company	GE	340,000	111,630	405,200	10,717	458,579
General Motors Corp.	GM	388,000	176,558	274,730	6,018	31,637
IBM	IBM	307,401	88,396	88,349	8,073	193,455
Microsoft Corporation	MSFT	39,100	22,956	52,150	9,408	324,275
Pfizer Inc.	PFE	94,900	27,601	31,379	4,959	283,276
Wal-Mart Stores, Inc.	WMT	1,140,000	166,809	70,349	5,377	244,595
Walt Disney Company	DIS	120,000	25,402	45,027	1,196	63,931

% of exchange-traded nonfinancial corporations with less than number at right	Number of full-time employees	Annual sales	Total assets	Market cap
100%	1,140,000	$185,527	$405,200	$458,579
75%	2,077	402	496	507
50%	388	76	100	80
25%	94	13	21	13

TABLE 1.4
Quartile breakpoints on key variables for 6,954 public companies. All dollars in millions, total assets reported at book values. Data are from the American Association of Individual Investors, February 2001, and include 509 companies from Amex, 3515 from NASDAQ, 1600 from NYSE, and 1330 over-the-counter. The sample of 6,954 represents nonfinancial (and non-ADR) companies with available data (> 0) for all 4 variable fields.

ket. General Electric has the largest stock market value of any company in the U.S.A., $458 billion. Next highest is Microsoft at $324 billion. Notice that GE has almost ten times more employees and sales than Microsoft. Yet the net incomes in year 2000 for the two companies are within 15 percent ($10.7 billion versus $9.4 billion; the next chapter explains that net income is the company profit from the income statement). And compare AOL with IBM. The two have roughly the same stock market value but comparison of employees, assets, and sales shows differences of incredible magnitude.

The corporate icons in table 1.3 are not typical corporations. Public stock exchanges in the U.S.A. trade stocks for more than 9,000 different corporations. Table 1.4 shows quartile breakpoints for a large sample of these listed companies circa year-end 2000.

While true that Wal-Mart has over 1 million employees, 75% of exchange-traded nonfinancial companies have less than 2,077 employees. One-fourth have fewer than 94 full-time employees. The American corporate icons are huge compared to average.

Similar tendencies apply to the other variables in table 1.4. The maximum annual sales of any corporation in the U.S.A. is $185,527 million yet over 50% of all exchange-traded nonfinancial companies have annual sales less than $76 million. Total assets and market cap are skewed even more. Comparing the biggest company to the median is like comparing Jane and John Doe's wealth to Microsoft's Bill and Melinda Gates. Yet the same financial principles apply to all.

The biggest companies may be atypical, and there may be few of them, but they command huge influence in the financial and real asset markets. Table 1.5 lists the sum for all companies in the sample within each quartile.

There are 33.5 million full-time employees for this sample of exchange-traded non-financial corporations. Rank all companies by number of employees and count the total employees in the biggest 25 percent. The table shows that the biggest 25% employ 93.6 percent of all employees in the sample. Combine the smallest two quartiles to see a more startling fact: 50 percent of companies in the sample employ only 1.3 percent of all employees working for exchange-traded nonfinancial corporations.

Glean insight on the size of the sample relative to the entire US economy. According to the Bureau of Census there are 108.1 million full-time employees in the USA in 1998 working for all business forms of organization. The sample of 33.5 million (which is for early year 2000) represents about 31% of total US employment

table entry is sum for all nonfinancial corporations in sample quartile	Number of full-time employees	Annual sales	Total assets	Market cap
biggest quartile	31,389,532 (93.6%)	$7,044,269 (94.6%)	$8,906,717 (96.5%)	$12,797,552 (94.5%)
upper middle	1,703,520 (5.1%)	331,640 (4.5%)	413,709 (4.4%)	395,534 (3.0%)
lower middle	361,195 (1.1%)	64,489 (0.9%)	91,086 (1.0%)	65,376 (0.5%)
smallest quartile	69,085 (0.2%)	8,044 (0.1%)	14,438 (0.2%)	8,870 (0.1%)
TOTAL	33,523,332	$ 7,448,443	$ 9,425,950	$ 13,267,331

TABLE 1.5
Aggregate distribution of resources for 6,954 public companies (quartiles rebalanced by sorting on each variable). All dollars in millions, assets reported at book values, and parentheses list percent of sample total. See table 1.4 for a description of the data source.

(inclusion of exchange-traded financial corporations pushes this to 34%). The number of employees that work with companies employing more than 94 full-time workers ("big" companies) is 69.0 million for the entire USA and 33.4 million for the sample. The sample represents 48% of total employment at big companies. The upshot is that our sample of exchange-traded nonfinancial corporations primarily includes companies bigger than average. And within our sample, already tilted toward large companies, employment tends to tilt toward the largest among the large.

The tendency is true for all variables in the table. Consider this: almost 96 1/2 percent of stock market wealth in the U.S.A. is due to only 25 percent of listed companies; 75 percent of corporations represent 3 1/2 percent of stock market wealth. (The clustering is true even with inclusion of financial corporations.)

Perhaps small corporations represent a relatively trivial proportion of corporate employment, sales, total assets, and stock market value, but do not trivialize the small company. Any individual is a big-time success who can establish a corporation that grows to employ 94 people, generates $13 million in annual sales, has $21 million of total assets, and has a value in the stock market of $13 million. You can bet, too, that this successful entrepreneur owns a big share of that $13 million and, to 94 different families and countless stakeholders, he or she is a very important person. Furthermore, 39.1 million full-time employees in the USA work for companies that employ fewer than 94 employees (although many of those companies are noncorporate businesses).

About ten thousand different corporate stocks trade on stock exchanges in the U.S.A. Each active corporation in the nation files a tax return. The Internal Revenue Service receives about 2.8 million corporate tax returns a year (form 1120). This suggests that exchange-traded corporations represent less than one percent of all corporations. The apparent motivation for organizing a company as a corporation is **not** so that its stocks can trade on an exchange. Rather, the corporate form of business organization offers other **advantages**. These include:

1. limited liability for the owner(s)
2. easy transferability and sharing of ownership
3. potentially infinite life (at least it might surpass the owner's lifespan)
4. easier access to the financial markets

Several significant **disadvantages** include:

5. legal obligations for corporations are sometimes quite complex
6. corporate income is subject to "double taxation"

Shareholders are the corporation owners. Limited liability for the owners implies that the maximum shareholder wealth at risk equals the value of the shares. The shareholder of a corporation protects personal wealth (house, car, savings, etc.) from litigation against the company. Someone suing a corporation may receive, in an extreme case, a judgment bankrupting the company, and perhaps sometimes an unscrupulous manager may be thrown in jail because of actions on-the-job. But the personal wealth of shareholders is untouchable, as though shielded behind a firewall.

Advantages 2 and 3 occur because every corporation has common stock and whoever owns the common stocks possesses control over management and has claims on residual cash flows. The owner/manager of a small company cannot sell company shares on stock exchanges without satisfying many government and exchange rules. But the owner/manager may privately sell (or give) shares to key employees, family members, or capitalists. Selling or sharing common stock implies sharing of corporate control and profits. The transferability of shares gives the company a lifespan that potentially is infinite.

Advantage 4, access to financial markets, largely occurs because advantages 1–3 encourage purchase of shares by outside investors. Furthermore, government regulations place stringent requirements on corporate financial reporting. These information disclosures, even though they impose a burden on corporations because preparing reports takes time and money, increase the company's attraction to capitalists.

Tax policies for corporate income are interesting and controversial. Imagine that a man-on-the street generates sales and profits from goods in his shopping cart. The personal tax on the profit is the same as if the income for the man were from wages instead of business profit. Suppose instead that the man-on-the street is organized as a corporation. The man pays corporate tax on the profit, distributes the profit to himself since he is the owner, and then as a capitalist he pays personal tax on the distribution. This is "double-taxation." Both the corporation and capitalist pay taxes on the same income stream.

Economists persuasively argue that double-taxation biases the allocation of capital and makes the economy less wealthy. Politicians, conversely, argue for popular votes by pointing fingers at mighty corporations that pay few taxes. Politicians generally ignore the claim by economists that if double-taxation were abolished, corporations would either (a) pass along the tax savings to capitalists where it would incur personal taxes, or (b) pass along the tax savings to stakeholders in the form of higher wages or purchases. The U.S.A. is the only major economy on the globe that has not abolished double-taxation of corporate income.

3.B. Noncorporate business

Companies often operate in an organization that is **not** a corporation. There are two primary forms of noncorporate business: sole proprietorship and partnership. Table 1.6 provides insight by listing number of tax returns received by the Internal Revenue Service.

The sole proprietorship is, by number, the most prevalent type of business organization. Any individual may operate a business as a sole proprietorship so long as the company is compliant with local and state regulations. The federal government does not require that sole proprietors obtain IRS permission to operate. Sole proprietors file individual income tax returns (form 1040) and attach a Schedule C summarizing business income and expenses.

Almost half of all business receipts for nonfarm sole proprietorships lie within three industry groups. Retail trade is the largest industry for sole proprietors, garnering 19.1% of the total. Construction is second (15.9%), and Professional Services third (11.0%). Individuals in these industries pursue an entrepreneurial dream by setting-up shop as sole proprietor. Advantages of the sole proprietorship form of business organization include:

1. relatively easy start-up and record-keeping requirements
2. there is no double-taxation

Disadvantages generally are that the sole proprietor does not have the corporate advantages:

3. the sole proprietor has unlimited liability and his/her personal wealth is at risk
4. ownership is not easily transferred so company lifetime is somewhat limited
5. access to financial markets is linked to collateral provided by the proprietor

A hybrid form of sole proprietorship is the "S-corporation." The Internal Revenue Service allows companies meeting certain conditions, such as fewer than 75 shareholders, to organize as S-corporations. An S-corporation files form 1120S but

	Approximate number of tax returns received by the IRS from the economic entity at left
nonfarm sole proprietorship	17.6 million
partnership	2.1 million
corporation (form 1120)	2.8 million
S-corporation (form 1120S)	3.1 million
individuals	127.9 million

TABLE 1.6

Relative prevalence of economic entities in U.S.A., circa 1999–2000. Source: "Projections of returns to be filed in calendar years 2000–2007" by Frank Zaffino; and "Sole proprietorship returns, 1999" by Brian Balkovic and Michael Parisi. Both articles are published by the Internal Revenue Service

does not pay any corporation taxes. Instead, all profits pass through to shareholders. The shareholders file a Schedule E with their individual tax form 1040. Profits earned by S-corporations incur personal taxes but avoid double-taxation.

Partnerships are the least common form of business organization. There are two types: general partnerships and limited partnerships. The general partnership has the same advantages and disadvantages as the sole proprietorship. The income and profits of the partnership are distributed among the partners, and each partner declares his/her share on an individual tax return. The partnership also files a tax return (form 1065), but double-taxation does not exist.

The limited partnership allows each partner to insulate personal wealth from litigation against the partnership. This attribute is similar to the limited liability enjoyed by corporate shareholders.

The cash flow cycle in figure 1.3 is a fair depiction for sole proprietorships and partnerships. The only difference occurs in definition of the equity market. These two forms of business organizations do not have shareholders as a financing source. The source of equity financing for these business forms is, respectively, the sole proprietor or partner.

3.C. Households as companies

Many people realize that running a household may be as complex as running a small company. Households, like corporate and noncorporate companies, bring together resources from financial markets and stakeholders in order to create real goods and services. Households are the largest economic entity in the U.S.A. Financial forecasts of economic recession or expansion often begin by stating the importance of household financial behavior on aggregate spending, employment and production. Table 1.7 compares corporate and household wealth.

Total assets are three times larger in the household sector ($43.6 trillion) than in the nonfinancial corporate sector ($14.3 trillion). The two largest types of assets for households include real estate and pension assets. Pensions assets are financial assets, and households own a lot of financial assets ($26.3 trillion). A lot of the financial assets that households own include equities issued by the nonfinancial corporate sector. People living in households are, after all, the shareholders that own corporations.

Perhaps you are surprised how much wealth households own compared to businesses. But drive around town and notice all the real goods and services that you see. Businesses undeniably have a lot of stuff: stores and service stations seemingly are everywhere. Keep driving, though, and begin to notice that people own so much

TABLE 1.7

Balance sheets for the nonfarm nonfinancial corporate sector and for households (including nonprofit organizations), year-end 1998, dollars in billions, all entries at market value or replacement cost. Source: "Flow of Funds Accounts of the United States", Board of Governors of the Federal Reserve System, tables B100 and B102.

Nonfarm nonfinancial corporations		Household (and nonprofit) economic entities	
total assets	$14,262	total assets	$43,637
real estate	4,203	real estate	10,238
trade receivables	1,322	durable goods	2,688
equipment & inventories	4,045	deposits	4,142
other financial assets	4,692	corporate equities	6,338
		equity in noncorporate business	4,395
		pension fund reserves	9,161
		other financial assets	6,675
total liabilities $ 7,361		total liabilities	$ 6,208
credit market securities	3,852	credit market debt	5,910
trade payables	982	other liabilities	298
other liabilities	2,527		
net worth	$ 6,901	net worth	$37,429
market value of equity $	11,561	market value of equity	not traded

Houses don't issue stock

more: houses, cars, plus $26 trillion in financial assets causing a feeding frenzy by institutions competing for management of household financial assets!

The wealthiest households, just like the biggest companies, are atypical and there are few of them. Yet they command huge influence in politics and financial and real asset markets. Recent statistics from the Internal Revenue Service report that the top 1 percent of taxpayers now furnishes more than one-third of income tax receipts. The top 50 percent pay 96 percent of revenues that the government receives in personal income taxes.

The company cash flow cycle in figure 1.3 depicts households, too. The funnel represents the household acting as a company. Managing households requires many of the same functional skills as managing companies. Households depend on credit markets as a financing source for buying homes, cars, and college education. Households, like noncorporate companies, do not have shareholders. Still, the household inhabitants are a source of equity financing, and households accumulate net worth. Net worth equals total assets minus total liabilities. Household net worth of $37.4 trillion is more than five times larger than corporate net worth of $6.9 trillion.

Households also develop stakeholder relationships in real asset markets. Households go to suppliers such as grocery stores, clothiers, car dealers, etc. Households hire labor such as carpenters, carpet cleaners, baby sitters, etc. Certainly households pay taxes; table 1.6 shows that households are filing over 120 million tax returns annually (and census data show 105 million total households in year 2000).

Clients of households are of two types. First, employers are clients because the household sells its labor services in exchange for wages (revenue). Second, household inhabitants are clients to themselves. Individuals and/or family units realize benefits of the goods and services that households create. And the objective of the household is to maximize the wealth that it creates. That is, the household maximizes the enjoyment and utility of the goods and services created from transformation of capitalist and stakeholder resources.

Several important components of national wealth are not in table 1.7. Most significant is government wealth. The government owns schools, fire stations, parks, aircraft carriers, and on and on. It almost is incomprehensible to consider how much wealth the local, state, and federal governments own. And in almost every way, the citizenry are the shareholders and owners of government wealth.

Financial science is about the study of wealth management. Irrespective of where wealth exists, and regardless of who owns it or how it is distributed, there is benefit for all of us to understand basic principles about the structure of finance.

PART ONE

Many sciences recognize important differences between flows and balances. In hydrology, for example, predicting floods crucially depends on measuring reservoir water capacities and rainfall/runoff rates. The quantity of standing water is a balance whereas rainfall and runoff are flows. Finance, too, crucially depends on measuring quantities and transfers of wealth. The quantity of wealth is a balance whereas wealth transfers are flows. Part 1 of *Lessons about the Structure of Finance* examines in chapters 2 and 3 how financial statements provide information about flows and balances of wealth. Then in chapters 4 and 5 the focus narrows to how flows and balances pertain to time value relationships. Recall this definition from the preface.

> *Time value* is the simple worth of an asset and is sustained as the present value of future cash flow streams.

Time value is one of the most important concepts in finance. Chapters 6, 7, and 8 use time value relationships to examine how companies analyze capital budgeting decisions, how bond prices behave, and how stock prices are sustained.

CHAPTER 2

Financial Fundamentals of Accounting

CHAPTER CONTENTS

"Accounting is the language of business." This phrase is well known to people in business. Accounting and accountants play an important role in our economy. Large corporations have their own accounting staff, and most businesses and many households often seek the advice of accountants. Professional accountants sometimes are ridiculed as "bean-counters" yet, at the same time, they are admired and envied for their skill and mastery of the business language.

Accounting is important to finance because it forces exactness—accountants insist on documenting expenditures and revenues. Records help a company, or a potential investor in the company, analyze the financial situation and anticipate or solve money problems. Knowing and using accounting is important for companies and investors, large and small.

A good financial analysis requires a lot more than accounting skills, however. Simply keeping good records is no assurance that a business or individual makes sound financial decisions. A thorough understanding of financial principals helps assure financial success. For better or for worse, finance and accounting form the foundations of business sciences. Learning finance requires familiarity with accounting fundamentals.

This chapter presents fundamental accounting information necessary for understanding finance. There are four sections. The first discusses conceptual foundations about flows and balances. Section 2 elaborates on basic financial statements and section 3 looks at financial ratios. The last section links the income statement to balance changes through time.

1. THE RELATION BETWEEN FLOWS AND BALANCES

Accounting and finance recognize differences between cash flows and balances. Cash flows represent transfers of wealth. Balances represent accumulations of wealth. Cash flows and balances obviously are related because they both pertain to wealth. There are differences, however, in the way cash flows and balances relate to time.

1.A. The relativity of time

A cash flow is a transfer of wealth per unit of time. Consider, for example, a $2,000 loan payment that is due on the 15th of every month. This $2,000 expense is a cash flow and, even though it occurs at a specific moment, like 2PM on the 15th, it is a payment "per month". Even if one were to talk collectively about payments for the last 12 months, the payments represent a cash flow because they measure a transfer of wealth per unit of time: the payments equal $24,000 per year.

A company's profit is akin to a cash flow. Consider a company that earns $1,000,000. Maybe the time that it took the company to make a million dollars was a day, a month, a year, or a decade. We don't really know the pertinent "unit of time." The information is incomplete without the time period. Nonetheless, the profit accrues throughout some time interval and therefore this sum is a cash flow. A cash flow **always** embodies a time period, albeit the period might be very short (e.g., an hourly wage) or very long (e.g., career earnings).

Businesses generally realize a cash inflow when they make a sale and receive income, or perhaps when they take out a loan and receive money from the bank. Conversely, a cash outflow for the business may be the wages it pays workers, or perhaps a payment the business makes to a bank, or to a supplier from whom it's buying a new machine. Notice that with cash flows there is a type of "duality": one concern's outflow is at the same time another concern's inflow. A loan payment, for example, is an outflow for the company but an inflow for the bank. Measuring and monitoring cash flows is important because cash flows signal **changes** in wealth.

Balances embody time differently than cash flows. A balance is *not* a *transfer* of wealth per unit of time—a balance is the accumulation of wealth at a point in time. In this regard, a balance is like a snapshot at a single point in time; it pictures the momentary status of an account. Companies, and households too, typically have many different types of balances. There is a balance in a checking account, another for a savings account and also there is a balance representing the value of investments in marketable securities. All the preceding balances are financial balances, but likewise there are many types of nonfinancial balances such as Inventories, or Plant, Property, and Equipment.

The balances in the preceding paragraph represent wealth that the company owns—they are asset balances. Also, however, the company owes wealth to other market participants. The wealth that a company or individual owes to other market participants are liability balances. For example, a loan balance is an amount the company owes the bank, and so the loan is a liability. Other common liabilities include Accruals that represent wages owed to labor, Payables that represent sums owed to suppliers, and Stockholders' equity that represents the claim to company wealth by shareholders.

As time passes, of course, balances probably change. The snapshot of a company's balances nonetheless provides substantial information about the company or individual. For example, every morning the company conceivably can call the bank and ask for the outstanding balance on a loan. The balance from day-to-day equals the previous day's balance, plus any new accrued interest expense, minus any credits for loan payments. The loan balance represents the wealth that the company owes. The loan balance also is the wealth that the bank owns. This exemplifies the duality property for balances: one concern's asset is another concern's liability. For any economic entity, whether it represents a single household, a business, or an entire economy, the following financial identity always is true: *the sum of all asset balances equals the sum of all liability balances.*

1.B. Cash flows accumulate to form balances

Balances and cash flows are interrelated because they both pertain to wealth. As an illustration of the interrelation, consider a savings account balance. Suppose that at the beginning of the week the balance is $12,000. During the next few days say that two thousand dollars is deposited, twenty dollars of interest is credited, and one thousand dollars is withdrawn. The balance at the end of the week obviously is $13,020. Each deposit, addition of interest, and withdrawal represents a cash flow; the cash flows for the savings account are $+2,000, $+20, and $-1000. The sum of the cash flows is $1,020. Also, the balance changes by exactly $1,020. This illustrates an important rule of finance.

The difference between balances at different times equals the sum of the cash flows occurring during the time interval.

1.C. Accrued versus realized flows and balances

When a business sends its loan payment to the bank there is an obvious transfer of wealth from the business to the bank. This exemplifies a *realized* cash flow: a realized cash flow is a transfer of wealth accompanied by a flow of funds. There is an alternative way, however, by which wealth transfers. On an outstanding loan, for example, the bank may assess a daily interest charge against the company. The accrual of this interest charge in the loan account represents a transfer of wealth per unit of time; according to the definition, therefore, the accrual of interest is a cash flow. Yet because funds do not transfer, this is not a realized cash flow. Instead, this is an *accrued* cash flow. An accrued cash flow is a transfer of wealth per unit of time that is not accompanied by a flow of funds. All wealth transfers per unit of time are cash flows, and all cash flows are either realized or accrued.

Some events transfer wealth while other events create or destroy wealth. Consider, for example, a change in the value of a company's land. As the land becomes more valuable then obviously the company owners become wealthier. There has been a transfer of wealth to the company, but from where? Unlike other cash flows for which the duality principal requires that the increase in one participant's wealth equals the decrease in another participant's wealth, the creation (or destruction) of economic wealth is a net gain (or loss) to the economy. It is as though a wealth transfer occurs between an active market participant and the omnipresent "invisible hand."

The company owns the land before its value goes up, and they own it afterwards. Wealth in this case *accrues* but if the company wishes to *realize* the increased wealth, they must take action. To realize the new wealth they must realize a cash inflow, which they might do by selling the land, or using the land as loan collateral. Regardless, all changes in wealth are either realized or accrued cash flows and fundamental rule 2.1 still holds true, albeit with clarification: (1) The difference between realized balances at different times equals the sum of the realized cash flows occurring during the time interval; and (2) the difference between accrued balances at different times equals the sum of the accrued cash flows occurring during the time interval. Traditional financial statements are hybrids that contain both accrued and realized line items.

2. REPRESENTING FLOWS AND BALANCES ON FINANCIAL STATEMENTS

The purpose of financial statements is two-fold. First, the statements provide the company with information for monitoring or analyzing its financial situation. Second, the statements provide external analysts with information for gleaning insight about the company's financial health. Most descriptions in this chapter apply directly to corporate financial statements. The previous chapter explains, however, that many companies are not corporations. The principals herein also apply to situations in which the company is a noncorporate company or a household. Indeed, many households construct personal financial statements.

Several organizations in the USA promulgate procedures for preparing financial statements. The most influential organization is the "Financial Accounting Standards Board" (FASB). FASB issues rules followed by almost all preparers of financial statements. These "generally accepted accounting principles" (GAAP) result primarily in two types of statements showing flows (the income statement and the statement of cash flows), and one type of statement showing balances (the balance sheet). The following discussion elaborates about balance sheets and income statements. Discussion on cash flows appears in the next chapter.

2.A. The Balance Sheet

Balance sheets summarize the many different types of wealth that the company owns (assets) and owes (liabilities). Large companies prepare a quarterly balance sheet every 3 months. Each one shows the company's financial position at that particular moment. Companies almost always also report a year-end balance sheet. The year-end balance sheet does **not** equal the sum of the line items for the four separate quarterly balance sheets. Instead, the year-end balance sheet is identical to the year's last quarterly balance sheet. The table below presents the IBM balance sheet for December 31, 1996, followed by a discussion on main line items.

A1. Liabilities are financing sources

The balance sheet's right-hand side shows the liabilities from which the company already has obtained its financing. In that regard, the right-hand side lists wealth that the company owes to its historical sources of financing. These sources have financial claims on the firm's wealth and are called "claimants." It is conventional to separate claimants into two groups. *Current liabilities* include claims that tend to be repaid in the near term, such as one or two years. *Long term liabilities* include claims generally outstanding over longer periods of time.

Current Liabilities   The sum of all short term claims is *Current liabilities*. *Current liabilities* represent financing already made available to the company. Analogously, though, *Current liabilities* portend the amount of future payments that the company must repay in the near future. The discussion below elaborates on the more significant *Current liabilities*.

Payables are financing, or trade credit, made available by suppliers for purchasing *Inventory* and other assets. *Payables* rise, for example, whenever a delivery truck backs up to the company's receiving dock, unloads supplies, and the warehouseman signs a docket attesting to delivery. The receiving company owes the deliverer money for the shipment—the increase in *Payables* represents a loan made to the company by the supplier. *Payables*, just like any other liability, represent wealth that the company owes to another concern.

The *Payables* entry on the balance sheet is not a cash flow. The value of all deliveries within a particular week, for example, is a cash flow. But the balance sheet entry shows the sum of all deliveries ever made, minus all payments ever sent by the company to the suppliers—the balance sheet entry is the sum of all previous cash flows for the *Payables* account.

Another *Current liability* on the balance sheet is *Accruals*. This is money the company owes its workers for jobs they have completed but not received pay. *Short term notes* typically represents short-term bank loans; longer term notes usually appear under *Long term liabilities*.

Long term Liabilities   *Long term liabilities* represent wealth the company repays in the remote future. *Long term debt* typically includes financing from banks or other capitalists that are repayable over three years, five years, ten years or even longer. The specific details for each loan stipulate the company's obligations

TABLE 2.1

International Business Machines Corporation and Subsidiary Companies. Consolidated Balance Sheet, December 31, 1996. (Dollars in millions)

Assets		Liabilities and Stockholders' Equity	
Cash	$ 7,687	$ 4,767	Payables
Inventories	5,870	2,950	Accruals
Receivables	16,515	12,957	Short Term Notes
Other Current Assets	10,623	13,326	Other Current Liabilities
Total Current Assets	*$40,695*	*$34,000*	*Total Current Liabilities*
Net PP&E	17,407	9,872	Long Term Debt
Other Long Term Assets	23,030	21,628	Total Stockholders' Equity (509,070,542 shares)
	_____.	15,632	Other Long Term Liabilities
Total Assets	$81,132	$81,132	Total Liabilities & SE

regarding the amount of interest, and timing of principal payments. Quite often banks are the sources of long term loans. Companies, just like individual households, sometimes take out a 30-year mortgage from a bank for purchasing a building. Such a loan is a component of *Long term debt*.

Another common component of *Long term debt* is *Bonds*. The bond is simply a financial security that the company sells to capitalists in exchange for money. The bond is like an "I-O-U" in which the company promises to repay money in the future. Between time of issuance and time of maturity, the company agrees to pay interest. Each bond owner has a claim on part of the company, and the category *Long term debt* documents the claim.

The IBM balance sheet lists significant *Other long term liabilities*. This line item represents claims on IBM's wealth largely by retired or nearly-retired employees. According to generally accepted accounting principles (GAAP), the company computes future retirement benefits that already it has promised employees. Some of these employees currently are in retirement whereas others may be a decade or more from retirement. The employees presumably exchanged with the company labor services that exceeded the value of wages received. IBM promised future retirement benefits.

The pension obligation is, according to GAAP, a *Long term liability*. Even though employees did not give a cash loan to IBM, they contributed wealth to the company in the guise of labor services. IBM in exchange transfers wealth to its employees. Some of the wealth transfer is a realized cash flow that employees receive as wages. The rest of the wealth transfer is an accrued cash flow. It accrues when IBM signs contracts promising employees future retirement benefits. The balance sheet clearly shows, for all to see, that IBM owes its retirees a substantial chunk of change.

Perhaps the most important of all long term liabilities is *Stockholders' equity*. Stockholders are the owners of the corporation. By voting and appointing management, shareholders determine the company mission and the actions by which the company pursues its mission. In a simplistic setting, *Stockholders' equity* measures all the cash lent to the firm by the stockholders. There are several ways that cash flows occur between stockholders and the corporate treasury.

Stockholders may provide the firm with cash inflow by directly purchasing shares from the company. As a result of this primary market transaction the investor receives a share of stock and the corporation realizes a cash inflow. In effect, the company borrows money from the shareholder and the share of stock represents an I-O-U that the investor owns and safeguards. The liability on the balance sheet labeled *Stockholders' equity* rises when the company issues new shares.

STREET-BITE A thrilling financing source: initial public offerings

The Internal Revenue Service receives more than 5 million corporate tax returns each year (see table 1.6). Yet fewer than one percent of these corporations raise money by selling shares to the public. When finally, however, a corporation grows to a certain level of maturity the natural next step is "going public."

An *initial public offering* ("IPO") occurs when a corporation sells its shares for the very first time to the public markets. The main reason for going public is to expand possible financing sources by tapping into the huge public financial markets. IPOs represent a relatively small fraction of trading volume but they nonetheless receive fantastic media coverage. Table 2.2 hints why.

The far right column is fantastic. The initial return for an IPO is the percentage change from the offer price early in the day until trading ends later the same day. The average one-day return for the 2,439 IPOs in the sample is 20.7%. That huge sum exceeds the return that most stocks earn in an entire year—yet this accrues in one day. This column explains media hype about IPOs!

Do issuing companies view huge initial returns as a sign that their going-public process was a success? The answer is: not totally. Consider the case of MarketWatch.com offered in the primary market at $17 a share on January 15, 1999. The company issued

TABLE 2.2 Data on initial public offerings.

Annual sales of issuing firm ($ millions)	Number of IPOs	Average initial return
$0	386	42.9%
< $1 million	678	31.4%
$1-$5 million	353	14.3%
$5-$10 million	347	10.7%
$15-$25 million	182	6.5%
> $25 million	493	5.3%
All	2,439	20.7%

Source: Roger Ibbotson, Jody Sindelar, and Jay Ritter, "Initial Public Offerings" *Journal of Applied Corporate Finance* (Summer 1988).

2.7 million shares at $17 each and raised $46.8 million of financing (=$17 x 2.7 million). On the liability side of the balance sheet *Stockholders' equity* rises to reflect the $46.8 million financing source. The asset side also rises by $46.8 million; probably *Cash* is the account which first receives all monies.

Two hours after MarketWatch.com's IPO the stock was trading in the secondary market at $130 a share. That represents an incredible increase of 665%. And what happened to the company during that time? Nothing. The balance sheet did not change at all during those two hours. To the contrary, managers at MarketWatch.com watched as some investors who bought shares for $17 were able to sell them hours later for $130. Investors made money from the price run-up, but not the corporation (maybe managers personally owned some stock that became worth millions). MarketWatch.com managers were wondering why they offered the stock for only $17. The company arguably sold underpriced stock and "left money on the table."

The going-public process is complex with many tasks. Generally, however, tasks fall into one or more of three functional categories.

1. *Regulatory* Transition from a privately-held to a publicly-traded corporation involves huge changes in regulatory responsibilities. Once a company goes public they are required to disclose a lot of information that perhaps previously manager/owners considered confidential. The "Securities Act of 1933" and "Securities Exchange Act of 1934" impose strong reporting requirements. The "Corporate Accountability Act of 2002" imposes strong penalties for fraudulent statements (that Act, also known as the Sarbanes-Oxley law, created the "Public Company Accounting Oversight Board" that inspects, registers, and disciplines companies that prepare accounting statements). Companies going public submit to the SEC (Securities and Exchange Commission) a detailed registration statement as well as a preliminary prospectus. The company hopes to eventually distribute the prospectus to potential investors. The prospectus informs investors about the company, its mission and management, and other financial information useful for analyzing the company. SEC approval is required before a company goes public. After going public, the company must forevermore frequently file forms with the SEC (www.sec.gov is an interesting government website allowing online viewing of corporate filings and forms).

2. *Underwriting* Companies going public most likely are already successfully delivering a product that customers want. The managers, however, probably don't know much about successfully delivering stocks to the public financial markets. So they hire an investment banker to advise the company on procedural and financial tasks. Especially interesting is the underwriting process. Underwriting by an investment banker(s) is the analysis of new security issuances in order to properly assign prices and collect fees. Several investment bankers may join together for relatively large deals and form an "underwriter syndicate." Two extreme fee structures exist. (a) With a "firm commitment" contract the investment banker purchases the security from the issuing company for a mutually agreeable price. The issuing company receives a spec-

ified sum of money and the underwriter (that is, the investment banker or syndicate) receives the security. The underwriter subsequently sells the security in the primary market. The underwriter's income depends on the spread between the price paid to the issuing company and the price received upon resell. The underwriter has relatively high risk exposure with a firm commitment contract because, for example, the IPO may not sell-out. Perhaps the underwriter gets stuck with a lot of stock that nobody values. The issuing company has relatively low risk exposure because they receive a firm commitment of capital. (b) With a "best efforts" contract the investment banker receives a mutually agreeable fee from the issuing company and sells the security for them in the primary market at the best possible price. The underwriter has relatively low risk exposure with a best efforts contract because they never take ownership of the stock. The issuing company, however, has relatively high risk exposure. Perhaps they do not raise as much money as desired due to lackluster investor interest.

3. *Distribution* Perhaps the most difficult task is setting the offer price for issuing stocks in the primary market. The underwriter compares existing public companies to the IPO company and sets a preliminary price range for the new issue. They then gauge potential investor interest by conducting pre-market activities: roadshows tell institutional investors about the company; order books fill with tentative purchase agreements; allocation agreements stipulate which underwriters, brokers, and customers get the IPO stocks. Underwriters set the final offer price the day before shares begin trading. Then, like horses out of the gate, the shares flow out of the primary market and begin trading in the secondary market. The stock price moves up or down in response to supply and demand forces.

The annual sales for more than 70% of all companies in table 2.2 is less than $1 million. Not all IPOs, however, are small companies. Shares for well-known Kraft Foods, Inc., began trading through an IPO on June 13, 2001. Prior to the IPO the company was a wholly owned subsidiary of Philip Morris. Kraft Foods booked almost $35 billion in sales for the year preceding the IPO. Phillip Morris spun off Kraft and gave it an identity of its own. They offered and sold 280 million shares at $31 per share, thereby raising $8.7 billion of cash for Phillip Morris. By the way, Phillip Morris retained ownership of 1.4 billion shares in Kraft Foods that represent a potential financing source for the future. Other examples of large IPOs abound.

History reveals that IPOs are especially popular during strong bull markets when prices are rising and investors seem to like anything resembling stock. IPO volume drops off during downturns and bear markets.

Contrary to the impression given by the fantastic initial returns in table 2.2, most investments in IPO stocks underperform market averages in the long-run. This excerpt from the *Wall Street Journal* says it best:

"When the history of the 1990s bull market is written, one of the more intriguing postscripts will be that it has given birth to so many new companies that created so little wealth. From May 1988 through the market's record high on July 17 of this year [1998], stocks of America's blue-chip companies rose more than fourfold. In that period, about 4,900 companies had initial public offerings. Their fate? Just 71% are still trading regularly, and of those, on July 17 fully 44% were below their offering prices . . . the median annual return as of the July market peak was a minuscule 2.4%, not even beating Treasury bills."

Greg Ip, "Bull market has sired a lot of new stocks, but few become stars", *Wall Street Journal,* September 15, 1998.

The bottom-line is that on average IPOs are great investments for investors making the purchase in the primary market and selling the stock within a day or two in the secondary market. But late-comers watch out! And, by the way, the SEC found that many investment bankers and brokers pursued illegal and unethical allocation agreements during the 1990s and millions of dollars of fines were levied. The Google IPO in 2004 allowed investors to sign-up for IPO shares on the internet. That may have broke the mold and make IPOs even more thrilling.

Another way that a cash flow passes between the firm and stockholder is through share repurchases. A share repurchase occurs when the company buys shares of its own stock from its shareholders. The company either inventories or shreds the stock they repurchase. Share repurchases occur for a variety of reasons and by a variety of methods. Most share repurchases occur when a company's managers believe that their shareprice is too "cheap." A stock repurchase cancels a liability owed to the shareholder and is reflected on the balance sheet as a decline in *Stockholders' equity*.

Technically speaking, the sale and repurchase of stock by the company affects two components of *Stockholders' equity*: *Paid-in-equity capital* and *Equity capital surplus*. We ignore the distinction between these two subcategories, however. Instead we lump these subcategories together into the broader entry called *Stockholders' equity*.

Stockholders' equity sometimes is called *Net worth*. Recall the discussion from the previous chapter about the company cash flow cycle. *Net worth* for nonfinancial corporations ($6,901 billion in 1998) was compared to household *Net worth* ($37,429 billion). In both cases the *Net worth* equals *Total assets* minus *Total liabilities*. A section below discusses *Total liabilities* in more detail. Equity is the residual claimant on company wealth, and *Net worth* measures the value of the claim. *Net worth* belongs to stockholders for a corporate company, to sole proprietors and partners for noncorporate companies, and to families for "household companies."

Corporations issue many shares of stock to put money on the balance sheet. Dividing total *Stockholders' equity* by the number of shares outstanding gives the equity book value per share:

FORMULA 2.1 Equity book value per share

The equity book value per share is how much each share of common stock is worth according to the financial statements:

$$\left(\begin{array}{c} equity \\ book\ value \\ per\ share \end{array} \right) = Stockholders'equity \Big/ number\ of\ shares\ outstanding$$

Equity book value per share is an important number. If accounting statements properly reflect true values, and if the stock market properly prices shares, then market shareprices should equal equity book value per share. Indeed, market analysts often compare market shareprice to equity book value per share in order to assess whether a stock seems fairly priced. The ratio of stock market shareprice to equity book value is the "equity price-to-book" ratio:

FORMULA 2.2 Equity price-to-book ratio

The equity price-to-book ratio is the common stock's shareprice relative to book value:

$$\left(\begin{array}{c} equity \\ price-to-book \\ ratio \end{array} \right) \equiv \left(P \Big/ B \right)$$

$$= market\ shareprice \Big/ equity\ book\ value\ per\ share$$

This important financial ratio is referred to as the "*P/B* ratio."

A *P/B* ratio equal to 1.0 has a special meaning. For a company with *P/B* at unity a dollar of company assets has a price in the sharemarket of exactly one dollar. When *P/B* differs from unity, a dollar of assets according to the books has a stock market price different from $1. There is not, of course, any "law" that requires equality between market shareprice and balance sheet book value. Shareprices are forward-looking assessments of value that are supported by expectations about future profits. Book values are backward-looking allocations of historical expenditures.

For a very small *P/B*, for example say 0.50, the stock market trades a dollar of company assets for only 50 cents. If an individual believes that book value correctly measures the "true value" of the company's assets, then the implication is that the sharemarket undervalues the assets. An investor finding an undervalued company probably thinks the shares are a good investment. They think that when the market corrects its mistake, the share price should rise and *P/B* should go towards unity. Conversely, if an individual believes that the sharemarket reflects true value, the implication is that book value overstates true value. Perhaps the very small *P/B* is not a result of market undervaluation as much as inaccurate accounting of book value. There always is uncertainty whether a small P/B implies market undervaluation or accounting overstatement.

A relatively large *P/B* means that a dollar of company assets trades in the sharemarket for more than its accounting value. Once again, two interpretations of an anomalous *P/B* are plausible. Maybe it is the stock price, or maybe it is the book value, that is a more accurate measure of true value. Unfortunately, one never knows for sure whether a relatively large *P/B* signifies that the stock market is overvaluing a share, in which case the share represents a bad investment that should be avoided. Alternatively, perhaps the large *P/B* occurs because the stock market properly prices the share whereas book value understates assets.

Many investors examine company *P/B* ratios before buying stocks. Generally speaking, the rumor on the street is that a company with a relatively low *P/B* signifies an undervalued stock, a good prospect for investment. Conversely, according to the rumor, relatively high *P/B* stocks might be overvalued shares that are ripe for a major market correction. Careful studies on this issue find some support for this conjecture. The situation is cloudier than the discussion implies, however, because *P/B* ratios distribute around a number that generally is not 1.0. Inferring that a target *P/B* is relatively small (or large) requires identifying the proper benchmark for comparison. That is tricky.

Before concluding that *P/B* ratios contain a secret for successful stock-picking, be forewarned. Stock prices are very "noisy"—they jump all over the place. No single ratio or statistic does a good job predicting whether a particular stock price will rise or fall. Among all the many poor measures that one can examine, however, the *P/B* ratio is among the best. There is statistical evidence that, in the long-run and on-average, *P/B* ratios vibrate around long-run steady state values.

Substitute formula 2.1 for equity book value per share into formula 2.2 for the *P/B* ratio. Rearrange and obtain a formula

$$\begin{pmatrix} equity \\ price-to-book \\ ratio \end{pmatrix} = market\ shareprice \div \left(\frac{Stockholders'equity}{number\ of\ shares\ outstanding} \right)$$

$$= \frac{(market\ shareprice \times number\ of\ shares\ outstanding)}{Stockholders'equity}$$

The product in the numerator of the lower line equals the company's current stock price times the number of shares outstanding. This number represents the company's market capitalization:

FORMULA 2.3 Market capitalization

Market capitalization (also known as "market cap") is the total stock market value for all outstanding common stocks at the current shareprice:

$$\begin{pmatrix} company \\ market \\ capitalization \end{pmatrix} = market\ share\ price \times number\ of\ shares\ outstanding.$$

A table in the previous chapter lists market capitalization for several American corporate icons. The market cap of General Electric, for example, is over $400 billion. The formulas above establish that *P/B* actually measures two algebraically identical ratios: (i) share price over equity book value per share, and (ii) total company market capitalization over *Stockholders' equity*.

The financial press often reports with fanfare about corporate mergers. Mergers are one mechanism that chapter 1 discusses for controlling principal-agent problems. Besides the real-world importance of mergers, however, mergers also provide a wonderful setting to work with balance sheets. A merger is like a marriage of balance sheets—two snapshots pulled together at a moment devoid of time. Before working with the financial effects of mergers, however, read the accompanying *Street-bite* for background information.

STREET-BITE Mergers, acquisitions, and contests for corporate control

Common stockholders are the company owners. Whoever owns the common stock controls the Board of Directors and sets the company strategic mission. Inspect any *Wall Street Journal* and likely there is an article about one company taking control of another. That's what mergers and acquisitions are all about: one company, call them the *Raider*, getting a controlling amount of common stock in another company, call them the *Target*.

Before two companies merge they each possess their own unique common stock and company name. After the merger perhaps the name of the combined company is a blend of the individual company names, perhaps not. Almost surely, however, where there used to be two unique common stocks there is, after the merger, only one. In most situations a large *Raider* assimilates the smaller *Target* and consequently the *Target* loses its independent identity.

While every deal is different, figure 2.1 shows typical steps in the merger process. Initial discussions lead *Raider* management to tender an offer for acquiring *Target* company common stock. This "tender offer" may specify (1) the cash price or number of *Raider* shares that is offered in exchange for a share of *Target* stock, (2) a deadline at which the offer becomes void, and (3) other conditions such as withdrawal of the offer if the *Raider* fails to obtain a majority of *Target* shares. The *Target* Board of Directors **must** obtain approval of its shareholders. After all, the *Target* shares will cease to exist so this surely affects *Target* shareholders.

FIGURE 2.1 Typical managerial steps for mergers and acquisitions

1. Raider and Target management commence negotiations about becoming a conglomerate company under one common stock

2. Raider management presents Target Board of Directors with an official offer to merge.

3A. Target Board of Directors recommends that Target shareholders approve merger.

3B. Target Board of Directors rejects offer.

Negotiations recommence or cease

4A. Target shareholders approve merger.

4B. Target shareholders reject merger.

5. Raider and Target companies become one; only one common stock continues to exist.

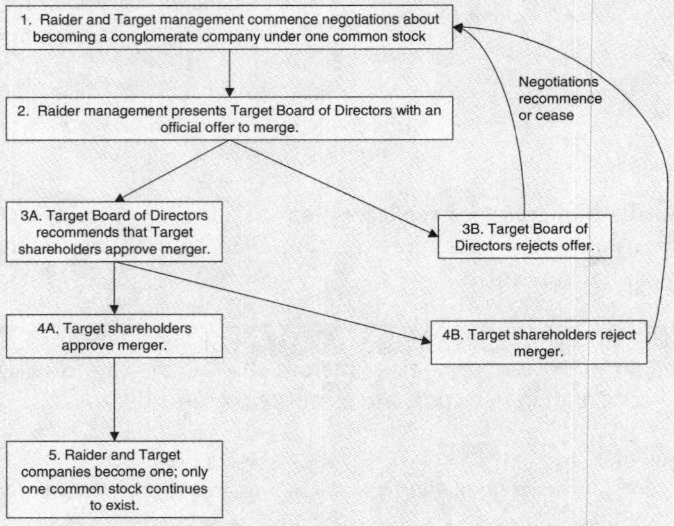

Summary statistics about recent mergers and acquisitions activity in the USA appear in table 2.3. Data over longer horizons are cyclical yet the ones here are somewhat typical. Thousands of mergers occur each quarter-year representing hundreds of billions of dollars of corporate wealth. Notice that there are two methods by which the *Raider* pays for *Target* stock. One, perhaps the *Raider* pays cash to *Target* shareholders. Two, perhaps the *Raider* offers shares of *Raider* stock as payment. These stock swaps are very common, especially when *Raider* management perceives their own stock is highly valued. Many *Raiders* pay with a combination ("combo") of cash and stocks.

TABLE 2.3 Recent activity on mergers and acquisitions activity in the USA

Year and quarter	Total completed transactions		Mode of payment (M&A subsample)			Average stock price premium
	Number	Value ($ bil.)	Cash	Stock	Combo	
1997Q2	1,793	$209	54%	29%	18%	32.9%
1997Q3	2,034	214	57%	26%	17%	33.5%
1997Q4	2,448	231	59%	26%	15%	25.4%
1998Q1	2,419	233	60%	24%	17%	24.5%
1998Q2	2,619	272	56%	27%	17%	25.6%
1998Q3	2,754	376	57%	25%	18%	23.1%
1998Q4	2,315	464	61%	28%	11%	35.2%
1999Q1	2,410	292	60%	27%	14%	31.0%
1999Q2	2,260	362	59%	26%	14%	37.2%
1999Q3	2,340	271	61%	26%	13%	33.6%
1999Q4	2,191	498	57%	29%	14%	31.3%
2000Q1	2,206	287	53%	31%	16%	33.6%
2000Q2	2,207	723	51%	33%	16%	34.0%
2000Q3	1,866	258	52%	32%	16%	33.3%

Source: *Mergers and Acquisitions,* various issues.

The rightmost column shows the average stock price premium that the *Raider* pays to *Target* shareholders. The average premium is about 30%. This implies, for example, that a *Target* shareholder whose stock is trading at $50 before the merger announcement receives an offer from the *Raider* in cash or stock worth $65 per share [= $50 x (1 + 0.30)]. The *Raider* pays more for *Target* stock than its current trading price in order to entice *Target* shareholders to approve the deal. This hefty premium motivates some investors to be on the lookout for potential target companies. Irrespective of the *Target's* profit from operations, buying stock in a company that subsequently attracts a *Raider* leads to big stock returns. Identifying potential *Targets,* however, is tricky, too.

Raider management explains to its own shareholders that overpayment to *Target* shareholders is sensible due to the existence of long-run benefits. Statistical studies show, conversely, one generally cannot reject the hypothesis that post-merger sales, net income, and market capitalization for the conglomerate equal the sum of the pre-merger items for the *Raider* and *Target.* That is, the whole equals the sum of the parts—mergers generally do not create value, they simply transfer wealth from *Raider* to *Target* shareholders.

Typically, but not always, both companies welcome the merger. Sometimes *Target* managers believe the merger is a bad idea. Several common anti-takeover measures thwart *Raider* intentions.

1. *Golden parachutes* are compensation contracts in which *Target* management is guaranteed huge bonuses in event of termination due to takeover. This is analogous, in some ways, to wage contracts for coaches and athletes that specify a huge sum payable in event of firing or trading. The existence of golden parachutes for *Target* management diminishes the attraction to the *Raider* of the merger.

Tax effects and accounting policies for mergers are in reality complex and controversial. Hordes of lawyers, politicians, and accountants debate proper policy. The regulatory environment is ever changing, too. Our objective is simply to focus on financial effects. Consequently, we adopt simplifying assumptions that tax effects and synergisms are nil. In other words, the sales, costs, profits, and market caps of the *Raider* and *Target* sum to that of the *Conglomerate*. We assume the merger does not create wealth—the whole simply equals the sum of parts. Even in this simplistic setting, though, interesting insights about mergers emerge. The example below uses a hypothetical merger to provide practice working with balance sheets and *P/B* ratios.

EXAMPLE 1 Merger mechanics

The Raider Company's balance sheet at year-end 2525 is below.

RAIDER COMPANY BALANCE SHEET, 12/31/2525

	Assets		Liabilities
Cash	$ 400	$ 600	Debt
PP&E	2,460	2,260	Stockholders' Equity
Total Assets	$2,860	$2,860	Total Liabilities & Equity

The Raider Company has 550 common shares outstanding and their equity price-to-book ratio is 0.54. The Raider Company plans to take over the Target Company whose balance sheet appears below.

TARGET COMPANY BALANCE SHEET, 12/31/2525

	Assets		Liabilities
Cash	$ 410	$ 350	Debt
PP&E	1,400	1,460	Stockholders' Equity
Total Assets	$1,810	$1,810	Total Liabilities & Equity

The Target has 220 common shares outstanding and their equity price-to-book ratio is 1.23 . The Raider Company offers 9 shares of Raider stock to Target shareholders that tender 2 Target shares. Suppose synergistic and tax effects are nil. After the Raider takes control of all Target shares, find (i) the *P/B* ratio for the new Conglomerate Company, and (ii) the effect of the merger on each shareholders' wealth?

SOLUTION

Our simplifying assumptions mean that the balance sheet for the Conglomerate Company simply equals the sum of each line item for the separate companies.

CONGLOMERATE COMPANY BALANCE SHEET, 12/31/2525

	Assets		Liabilities
Cash	$ 810	$ 950	Debt
PP&E	3,860	3,720	Stockholders' Equity
Total Assets	$4,670	$4,670	Total Liabilities & Equity

Recall that *P/B* equals the ratio of company market cap to *Stockholders' equity*. The problem gives each company's *P/B* and *Stockholders' equity*. Solve for the unknown market cap as follows:

P/B = market capitalization / Stockholders' equity ,

so for the Raider

0.54 = market capitalization / $2,260

or

market capitalization = $1,220.

For the target,

market capitalization = $1,460 x 1.23

$$= \$1,796 .$$

Market capitalization for the Conglomerate Company is $3,016 , the sum of the component company market values (= $1,220 + $1,796). The *P/B* ratio for the Conglomerate Company equals its market capitalization divided by total *Stockholders' equity*, which is 0.81 (= $3,016 ÷ $3,720). This is the answer for part (i) of the question.

The wealth effects for each shareholder depend on the Conglomerate shareprice after conclusion of the merger. Already we have found the total stock market value of the Conglomerate (its market cap) equals $3,016. Market cap equals price per share times number of shares, so a necessary step is finding the total number of Conglomerate shares outstanding. Each share of Raider stock outstanding before the merger remains intact even after the merger. For the Target Company, however, its shares cease to exist because the Raider absorbs the Target's shares. Each Target shareholder receives 9 shares of Raider stock for every 2 Target shares he/she tenders. The 220 Target shares outstanding before the merger exchange into 990 new Raider shares (= 220 x (9 / 2)). The Conglomerate Company therefore consists of the 550 Raider shares outstanding prior to the merger, plus the 990 Raider shares that the merger creates:

$$\begin{pmatrix} \text{number of} \\ \text{Conglomerate} \\ \text{shares} \end{pmatrix} = \begin{pmatrix} \text{number of} \\ \text{original} \\ \text{Raider shares} \end{pmatrix} + \begin{pmatrix} \text{number of} \\ \text{new Raider} \\ \text{shares issued} \\ \text{to Target shareholders} \end{pmatrix}$$

$$= \quad 550 \quad + \quad 220 \times \left(\frac{9}{2}\right)$$

$$= \quad 1,540$$

In total, therefore, the Conglomerate Company comprises 1,540 shares. Now use the definition of market capitalization to find the Conglomerate's shareprice:

$3,016 = (price per share) x 1,540 shares,

or *price per share = $1.96*

One share in the Conglomerate Company is worth $1.96 after the merger. A Conglomerate share after the merger is physically identical to a Raider share before the merger, albeit the company name printed on each share may (or may not) be different than before. The merger affected the shareprice, however. Compute the shareprice before the merger with formulas 2.1 and 2.2:

$$P/B = (\text{ price per share }) / (\text{ Stockholders' equity / \#shares outstanding})$$

so for the Raider

$$0.54 = (\text{ price per share }) / (\$2,260 / 550)$$

$$(\text{ price per share }) = \$2.22$$

The Raider has a share worth $2.22 before the merger and $1.96 afterwards. The capital loss is 26 cents per share (a loss of almost 12 percent).

For the Target shareholder before the merger:

$$1.23 = (\text{ price per share }) / (\$1,460 / 220)$$

$$(\text{ price per share }) = \$8.16$$

A target stockholder tenders two Target shares worth $16.32 (= 2 x $8.16) and receives nine Conglomerate shares worth $17.64 (= 9 x $1.96). Wealth increases by $1.32 for every two shares tendered, or $0.66 per share, or about 8 percent. This is much less than the average premium shown in table 2.3.

The assumption that the merger neither creates nor destroys wealth, together with a scheme in which the Raider overpays Target shareholders, implies that Target shareholders gain at the expense of Raider shareholders. The total wealth transfer from Raider to Target shareholders is about $143 (= 550 x (2.22–1.96)).

EXERCISES 2.2A

Conceptual

1. The Company has Stockholders Equity equal to $7,100 and there are 250 shares outstanding. The market shareprice for their stock is $24.30. The price-to-book ratio for this company's peer group equals 0.67. How does the company's price-to-book ratio compare to its peer group, and what might this possibly mean? ©FA4

Numerical quickies

2. The company share price in the stock market is $41. The equity book value per share according to the balance sheet is $35. There are 490 million shares outstanding. Find the company market capitalization and equity price to book ratio. ©FA5

3. The company stock price yesterday was $23 a share. Suppose that today the share price increases by 3.2%. There are 260 million shares outstanding. Find the change in company market capitalization. ©FA10

Challengers: problems 4-8 refer to these balance sheets and setup
The balance sheets for the Raider Company and the Target Company appear below:

Raider Balance Sheet

$3,900 Curr. assets	$3,900 Debt
$9,500 PP&E	$9,500 Stockholders Equity
$13,400 Total Assets	$13,400

Target Balance Sheet

$2,000 Curr. assets	$2,600 Debt
$4,200 PP&E	$3,600 Stockholders Equity
$6,200 Total Assets	$6,200

The Raider Company plans to takeover the Target Company. The Raider Company has 820 common shares outstanding and their equity price-to-book ratio is 3.80. The Target Company has 770 common shares outstanding and their equity price-to-book ratio is 1.50. The Raider Company offers 1 shares of Raider stock to Target shareholders that tender 5 Target shares (the exchange ratio is 0.20; assume fractional shares can be exchanged). Suppose tax effects and synergistic gains and losses equal zero; that is, sales and profits remain the same.

4. Find the market capitalization for the new conglomerate company. ©FA3jm
5. Find the shareprice for the new conglomerate company. ©FA3cm
6. Find the equity price-to-book ratio for the new conglomerate company. ©FA3am
7. Find the total transfer of wealth between Raider and Target shareholders. ©FA3gm
8. Find the percentage change in wealth for each shareholder. ©FA3fm

A2. Assets are financing uses

The balance sheet's left-hand side shows the assets on which the company has used its resources. In that regard, the left-hand side lists wealth that the company owns. It is conventional to separate assets into two groups. *Current assets* include ones that tend to be liquidated or sold within the near term. *Long term assets* include items generally owned by the firm for longer periods of time. Discussion below elaborates on the more important asset accounts.

Current Assets   The *Cash* line item includes funds in the checking and savings account, and possibly other short-term demand deposits or liquid interest-earning securities. Quite often, a separate line item labeled *Marketable securities* may appear on the balance sheet. *Inventories* represent items the company uses for making goods and services. Perhaps there are inventories in many different stages of progress. There may be, for example, unfinished goods as well as finished goods. Regardless, the balance sheet entry for *Inventory* lists the funds that already the company has used for purchasing and finishing the goods; the value of inventory includes product costs but does not include hopeful profits.

Receivables represent sales for which money remains uncollected. Many businesses find that issuing credit to customers increases the client base. When a credit sale is made, the customer effectively signs an IOU to the company that legally defines the customer's obligations regarding eventual payment. Until paid, however, credit sales remain on the balance sheet as *Receivables* because they represent wealth that the company owns.

Long term Assets   The most significant long term asset that a company typically owns is its buildings, factories, furniture, computers, etc. These fixed assets are measurable and their aggregate value goes on the balance sheet as "Net Plant, Property, & Equipment", referred to as *PP&E*. *PP&E* changes when old assets lose value or new assets are acquired. There are many well-known problems with assessments of *PP&E*. Consider the difficulties for the simpler problem of measuring the value of a house and all of its contents. When one gets down to the nitty-gritty, there are many different defensible ways for defining a used asset's value and, without selling it, there are very few ways for verifying such a valuation estimate. For the more complex problem of valuing an entire company, vagaries abound.

IBM lists a line item, *Other Long Term Assets,* that actually is larger than *PP&E*. These other assets predominantly include the capitalized value of long term leases that IBM makes available to its customers. This line item illustrates the basic yet important relation between leases and the balance sheet. Suppose that a university wishes to use a large, $12 million mainframe computer made and sold by IBM. The university may not be in a position to purchase outright such an expensive machine. IBM finds, like many other companies, that the customer base expands by making leases available to customers. The customer signs a long term contract in which they agree to pay IBM for usage of the machine throughout the next 3 or 5 years. Before leased, the unsold mainframe computer appears on the IBM balance sheet as *Inventory*. While leased, however, the asset really is not inventory. Yet IBM definitely owns something—they own a university's commitment to provide IBM with future cash flows. The value of the lease on the balance sheet relates directly to the future cash flows the contract promises to deliver to IBM.

Net Working Capital Financial statements sometimes list a line item, net working capital ("NWC"), as an asset on the balance sheet. NWC actually represents the difference between current assets and current liabilities:

> **FORMULA 2.4 Net working capital**
> Net working capital equals current assets minus current liabilities and is an indicator of the company's short term financial solvency.
>
> *Net working capital = Current assets – Current liabilities.*

An increase in any asset represents a use of funds, whereas an increase in a liability represents a source of funds. Typically with a growing company both current assets and current liabilities increase over time. There consequently is an increase in net working capital.

EXERCISES 2.2B
Conceptual
1. The Company balance sheet lists Stockholders' Equity at $12 million. Does this necessarily imply that the company has cash available for paying its bills?

Numerical quickies
2. The Company had quite a few changes during the past year. On the balance sheet, for example, Cash is $6,800 at year-end 2525, and $7,900 at year-end 2526. Explain whether this change represents a source or use of funds.
3. The Company had quite a few changes during the past year. The changes for their different balance sheet items from last year to this year were (the changes in parentheses are declines; otherwise the changes are increases) : ($4,400) for Receivables; $6,800 for Payables; $6,100 for Cash; $5,600 for Short-term Notes; $6,000 for Plant, Property, & Equipment; and ($6,800) for Long-Term Debt. Was the change in net working capital a source or use of funds? @FA1

2.B. The Income Statement

An income statement summarizes many types of flows that occur throughout a specific time period. The time period may be a month, quarter, year, etc. A quarterly income statement reflects activity occurring only during the specified quarter, for example, whereas an annual income statement reflects activity for a specified year. An annual income statement could be constructed by summing line-by-line all items on 4 consecutive quarterly income statements.

The table following shows an income statement for the IBM Company. The actual statement in IBM's annual report is very complicated because IBM is a huge, complex company. The table shows a condensed version that summarizes the main line items from the income statement. Notice the income statement clearly shows that the relevant unit of time is calendar year 1996. This statement summarizes activity occurring between January 1st and December 31st of 1996.

This income statement documents all wealth transfers occurring during the year, and the balance sheet in the previous section represents a snapshot taken at the exact moment that the income statement concludes. The discussion below explains several of the significant line items from the income statement.

Sales represents the company's only cash inflow on the above statement. Above all else, a company must make sales to survive. Financial statements often list *Net revenues* instead of *Sales*; *Net revenues* equals *Sales* minus returned items and dis-

Sales	$76,654	*realized*
– Cost-of-goods sold *(COGS)*	46,815	
– Selling, general, and administrative expenses	16,854	
– Depreciation	3,676	– *accrued*
= Operating income (EBIT)	$9,303	
– Interest expense	716	– *tax shield*
= Taxable income	$8,587	
– Taxes	3,158	
= Net income *(NI)*	$5,429	– *earnings*
– Dividends	706	– *realized*
= New retained earnings	$4,723	

Belongs to Shareholders

counts. All lessons in this book refer to the top-line as *Sales*. The *Cost-of-goods sold* represents the company's primary cash outflow associated with production costs, while *Selling, general, and administrative expenses* represent periodic overhead expenses such as advertising, marketing analyses, coffee and copying costs, etc. Generally, these expenses are realized cash flows representing payments to stakeholders for factors of production.

Depreciation represents a cost related to Plant, Property, and Equipment ("*PP&E*"). Notice that the income statement does not show a line item associated with purchase of *PP&E*. The company, nonetheless, often purchases *PP&E*. Instead of subtracting from *Sales* the full purchase price of *PP&E,* however, the company only subtracts *Depreciation*: an amount roughly equal to the periodic decline in the value of *PP&E*. *Depreciation* is an accrued cash flow (that is, a cash flow *unaccompanied* by a flow of funds), also sometimes called a non-cash charge.

As the statement shows, *Operating income* equals *Sales* minus the traditional costs of business. Financial statements sometimes list *Operating revenues* instead of *Operating income* but these two are synonyms. Financial analysts sometimes apply the acronym *EBIT* to *Operating income*; *EBIT* stands for "earnings before interest and taxes." The items beneath *Operating income* are outflows pertaining to financing costs and taxes. *Interest* is the cost paid for borrowing money from creditors. Notice that the income statement does not show as an inflow the principal a company borrows. Neither does the income statement show the principal that a company repays. Only shown is *Interest,* the amount repaid in excess of principal.

Subtract *Interest* from *Operating income* to compute *Taxable income*. This implies that *Interest,* just like *Depreciation* and *Cost of-goods sold*, is a tax deduction; every dollar of *Interest* reduces *Taxable income* by one dollar. *Interest* and *Depreciation* are two of the larger ways that businesses shield income from taxes: *Interest* and *Depreciation* are tax shields.

The *Taxes* that the business owes the federal government are based on tax tables contained in laws passed by the U.S. Congress. Congress delegates responsibility for collecting taxes to the Internal Revenue Service, a division in the Treasury Department. The tax rate often exceeds 30%, which implies that *Taxes* often are a fairly significant cash outflow for business. Sometimes, in fact, a business finds it easier to increase profits through thoughtful tax planning rather than changes in production or pricing policies.

Subtract *Taxes* from *Taxable income* in order to compute *Net income*. Sometimes financial statements also refer to *Net income* as "earnings after taxes." *Net income* represents wealth available for shareholders. Shareholders take possession of *Net income* either of two ways. First, some *Net income* might be paid directly to shareholders as a dividend. Companies record shareholder mailing addresses and typically pay out dividends quarterly. Second, some *Net income* might be kept by the business in order to finance growth and operations. The funds kept by the business, that is, *Net income* minus *Dividends*, equals *New retained earnings*. Sometimes *New retained earnings* is called "additions to retained earnings", or "internal financing", or "plowback", because it represents funds accessible to the corporation without explicitly borrowing from financial markets.

3. FINANCIAL RATIOS

A financial ratio compares in fraction form two different financial measures. Ratios typically convey important information about financial health. Contrast the insight gleaned about financial health in the following illustration. Suppose that two companies in the same line of business each have annual sales of $100,000. This fact conveys information about company size but little else. Suppose you learn that the "asset turnover ratio" equals five for the first company and 1/2 for the second company. The definition of the asset turnover ratio is *Sales* divided by *Total assets*. Knowing that the asset turnover ratio for the first company is five implies the company generates $5 of sales for every $1 of assets. The second company's asset turnover ratio of 1/2 implies a half-dollar of sales per dollar of assets. Even though the *Sales* figures for these two companies may be equal and suggestive of similar health, inspection of the asset turnover ratio suggests extremely different situations.

Ratio analysis is extremely important in the real world, even for you. When you apply for a personal bank loan, for example, the loan officer generally analyzes several of *your* ratios in order to decide whether or not to authorize the loan. The loan officer computes, for example, the ratio of monthly fixed expenses divided by monthly income. She then compares your ratio to a standard declared by the bank's policy committee. If your ratio exceeds the standard then you do not qualify for the loan because your expenses are too high relative to income. Alternatively, if your ratio is low then the bank determines that your financial health is good and you qualify for the loan.

3.A. Ratio categories

There are five broad categories of financial ratios. Table 2.5 lists well-known ratios in each category and offers a few anecdotal examples.

For some ratios the numerator and denominator are from the same financial statement. The current ratio, for example, equals current assets divided by current liabilities. Both obviously are from the same balance sheet. The net profit margin divides net income by sales and both of these obviously are from the (same) income statement. Consider the asset turnover ratio, however: divide sales from the income statement by total assets from the balance sheet. But which balance sheet? There is one balance sheet at the beginning of the income statement's horizon and another one at its end. For any financial ratio that relates a flow with a balance three plausible definitions exist. Consider three widely used definitions for asset turnover:

$$\frac{Sales_t}{Total\ assets_{t-1}} \qquad \frac{Sales_t}{Total\ assets_t} \qquad \frac{Sales_t}{(Total\ assets_{t-1} + Total\ assets_t)/2}$$

Suppose that *Sales* is from the Income statement for year 2525. The first formula divides with *Total assets* from the year-end 2524 balance sheet. The middle formula divides with *Total assets* from the year-end 2525 balance sheet. The rightmost formula divides by average *Total assets*. All three formulations are defensible definitions. Different books quite often use different formulas for financial ratios. The point is to exercise care and awareness when comparing a flow with a balance. In order to eliminate ambiguities this book always presents time subscripts for ratios that relate a flow with a balance.

The discussion below elaborates on general importance of the five ratio categories.

Liquidity ratios enable insights about the ability to pay bills as they come due. Perhaps you have heard the phrase "land rich but cash poor." This phrase sometimes applies to businesses or households that own a lot of long term assets (in this way they are "rich"), but they don't have enough money to pay the bills (this is the "poor" part). The balance sheet for this unfortunate concern probably lists ample assets for *PP&E* or *Land*, but very little for current assets such as *Cash* or *Marketable securities*. This household or business has a "liquidity" problem.

It is relatively difficult and time-consuming to convert *PP&E* or *Land* into a form useful for paying bills; such long term assets are "illiquid." *Cash* or *Marketable secu-*

TABLE 2.5

Ratio categories, formulas, and company examples

Ratio category	ratio name and formula	company examples (February 2001)
liquidity ratios	*current ratio* current assets / current liabilities	Coca Cola 0.7 IBM 1.2 GAP, Inc. 1.3
	quick ratio (cash + marketable securities + receivables) / current liabilities	Southern Co. 0.4 Gateway, Inc. 1.3 Daimler Chrysler 1.4
	times interest earned (pretax income + total interest expense) / total interest expense	Anheuser-Busch 7.9 Ann Taylor Stores 10.8 Men's Wearhouse 38.8
debt management ratios	*debt to capital* debt due more than a year later / (debt due more than a year later + stockholders' equity)	Pier One 5% Honda Motor Co. 23% Georgia Pacific 57%
	debt to equity total liabilities / stockholders' equity	Qualcomm, Inc. 0.1 3M Co. 1.2 Quaker Oats 10.1
	debt to assets total liabilities / total assets	Qualcomm, Inc. 9% 3M Co. 55% Quaker Oats 91%
	equity multiplier total assets / stockholders' equity	Qualcomm, Inc. 1.1 3M Co. 2.2 Quaker Oats 11.1
profitability ratio	*gross margin* (sales—cost of goods sold) / sales	Halliburton Co. 10% Best Buy Co. 16% Litton Industries 22%
	operating margin (sales—total operating expenses) / sales	7-Eleven, Inc. 1% Hertz Corp. 9% AG Edwards 21%
	net margin net income / sales	Walt Disney, Inc. 5% General Mills, Inc. 9% Bristol-Myers Squibb 21%
	return on assets net income / total assets	Brunswick Corp. 1% Black & Decker 7% T. Rowe Group 18%
	return on equity net income / stockholders' equity	Viacom, Inc. 3% Chevron Corp. 12% Proctor & Gamble 33%
	payout ratio dividends / net income	Circuit City 8% Wal-mart 16% Electronic Data Systems 43%
	retention ratio new retained earnings / net income	Circuit City 92% Wal-mart 84% Electronic Data Systems 57%
asset management ratios	*asset turnover* sales / total assets	Lucent Technology 0.7 Goodyear Tire & Rubber 1.0 Office Depot, Inc. 2.4
	inventory turnover annual cost-of-goods sold / inventory	Dollar General 3.9 Intel 15.0 Six Flags, Inc. 39.3
	average age of inventory 365 x inventory / annual cost-of-goods sold	Dollar General 94 days Intel 24 days Six Flags, Inc. 9 days
	average collection period 365 x receivables / annual sales	
	average payment period 365 x payables / annual cost-of-goods sold	
market-based ratios	*price-to-book* stock price / equity book value per share	Saks, Inc. 0.88 Phelps Dodge, Inc. 1.17 Texas Instruments 5.94
	price-to-earnings stock price / net income per share	Ford Motor Co. 9.8 Caterpillar, Inc. 14.7 Clorox Corp. 20.9

continued

TABLE 2.5
(Continued)

Ratio category	ratio name and formula	company examples (February 2001)
	price-to-cash flow stock price / {(net income + depreciation) ÷ # shares}	Sears, Roebuck, & Co. 5.2 Bear Stearns Co. 12.0 International Speedway 44.3
	price-to-free-cash flow stock price / {(net income + depreciation − dividends − capital expenditures) ÷ # shares}	General Motors, Inc. 6.6 Service Master Co. 15.6 Johnson Controls, Inc. 49.0
market-based ratios	*price-to-sales* stock price / sales	Boeing Co. 0.9 Harley-Davidson, Inc. 4.6 Applied MicroCircuits 50.0
	dividend yield annual dividend per share / stock price	Motorola Inc. 0.8% E.I. Dupont de Nemours 3.3% Host Marriott 8.1%
	stockholders' rate-of-return (ending stock price + dividend per share − beginning stock price) / beginning stock price	Walt Disney -38% Exxon Mobil Co. 6% Pfizer Inc. 139%

rities, on the other hand, are very liquid. An individual or business with a lot of liquid assets might only be a phone call away from obtaining cash for paying bills.

Liquidity ratios often focus on the relation between *Current assets* and *Current liabilities*. For example, the "current ratio" equals *Current assets* divided by *Current liabilities* (recall that *Net working capital* equals *Current assets* minus *Current liabilities*; the current ratio conveys a relative sense of scale that NWC does not convey). A high current ratio implies the company is likely to have sufficient cash on hand throughout the near term for paying bills. A reasonably high liquidity ratio is, generally speaking, a sign of good short term health.

Debt management ratios enable insights about the company's ability to take out new loans. Businesses sometimes face unexpected crises, or perhaps opportunities, and effective handling of the situation might require borrowing money. "Excess debt capacity" refers to the amount of additional debt that firms can safely borrow without endangering financial health. A company with zero excess debt capacity is already stretched to the limit—they have not managed their debt very well—and any unexpected crisis might push them into bankruptcy.

Debt management ratios often focus on the amount of debt relative to assets or net worth. A large debt-to-equity ratio, for example, implies the company already has a lot of debt, and perhaps not much excess debt capacity remains. When the debt-to-equity ratio gets too high, the company's financial health is in jeopardy. When the debt-to-equity ratio is too low, conversely, the company may not be taking prudent advantage of its interest tax shield.

Many lessons in corporate finance discuss debt ratios. Often it is convenient to recall that three unique ratios in the debt-management category are algebraic reformulations of each other: "debt-to-assets" equals *Total liabilities* divided by *Total assets*; "debt-to-equity" equals *Total liabilities* divided by *Stockholders' equity*; and "equity multiplier" equals *Total assets* divided by *Stockholders' equity*. Given a number for any one of these three ratios than the other two must take on specific values as shown below:

> **FORMULA 2.5 Alternative specifications for debt ratios**
>
> $$equity\ multiplier = 1 + (debt-to-equity)$$
>
> $$equity\ multiplier = \frac{1}{1 - (debt-to-assets)}$$
>
> $$(debt-to-equity) = \frac{(debt-to-assets)}{1 - (debt-to-assets)}$$

Suppose, for example, the debt-to-assets ratio is 0.40. The debt-to-equity ratio *must* therefore equal 0.67, and the equity multiplier *must* equal 1.67.

Profitability ratios enable insights about the company's pricing or cost containment policies. Profitability ratios are large when the gap between sales revenues and production costs is large. For example, the "net profit margin," defined as *Net income* divided by *Sales*, measures net income per dollar of sales. Managers probably prefer the largest possible profit margin for the business. The ratio rises by increasing sales revenue while holding constant costs, or equivalently, by decreasing costs while holding constant sales revenues. Several sources exert downward pressure on profit margins. First, customers want the lowest possible prices. Second, stakeholders and creditors want the most from the company they can get. The previous chapter discusses the goal of the firm and suggests that perhaps the most essential yet difficult managerial responsibility is balancing revenues and costs.

Asset management ratios enable insights about the efficiency of operations. The "asset turnover ratio" (= *Sales* ÷ *Total assets*) is one of the more important ratios in this category. The asset turnover ratio is analogous to the amount of "blood squeezed from stone"—the blood is the sales, and the stone is the assets. For a given bundle of assets, call it a pile of bricks and mortar, the company prefers to extract as many sales as possible. It is possible, of course, to run assets so intensely in pursuit of short-run sales that long-run prospects are damaged. As almost every student knows, if you run an engine too fast for too long it is more likely to break too soon. The same goes for factories and workers!

Market-based ratios often relate the company's common stock price to an item from the balance sheet or income statement. The most common include: price-to-book (*P/B*), price-to-earnings (*P/E*), price-to-sales, and price-to-cash flow (*P/CF*). A previous section discusses *P/B*, and the next chapter looks at *P/CF*. The *P/E* ratio equals the stock price divided by earnings per share ("*eps*"). A company's *eps* simply equals net income from the income statement divided by the number of common shares outstanding. The financial press focus on *eps* because it represents the profit (that is, earnings) per share of common reported by the company.

There is, as the table below shows, substantial variation in market-based ratios. In all cases the ratio measures the equity market valuation for one dollar of the variable in the denominator. The *P/E* is 76.1 for Pfizer pharmaceuticals, for example, and 9.1 for General Motors. A dollar of earnings may be "purchased" in the stock market for $9.10 if the company is General Motors, but the dollar of earnings costs $76.10 from Pfizer. The rumor on the street is that a high *P/E* ratio signifies stock overvaluation. A low *P/E* signifies, some argue, a bargain stock. As the chapter on stock valuation explains, however, there are a lot of legitimate reasons why *P/E* ratios vary from company to company, and most of those reasons shed no insight on whether a stock is under or overvalued.

The example below combines the balance sheet with several financial ratios in

---

FORMULA 2.6 Shareholders' rate of return

The shareholder rate of return ("ROR") for time period *t* represents the percentage change in wealth and equals the stock price change plus dividend relative to beginning price.

$$\text{shareholders' } ROR_t = \frac{P_t + \text{dividend per share}_t - P_{t-1}}{P_{t-1}},$$

where P_t is the stock price at end of period *t*.

Corporation name	P/B	P/E	P/Sales	P/CF
AOL-Time Warner, Inc.	17.0	108.6	14.2	72.4
AT&T Corporation	0.8	24.4	1.3	4.8
Exxon Mobil Corporation	4.2	17.9	1.2	13.6
Ford Motor Company	2.5	9.8	0.3	3.4
General Electric Company	9.6	36.4	3.5	23.7
General Motors Corp.	1.0	9.1	0.2	2.9
IBM	9.4	24.7	2.2	24.8
Microsoft Corporation	7.0	33.6	13.6	33.8
Pfizer Inc.	17.3	76.1	9.5	63.2
Wal-Mart Stores, Inc.	8.4	39.1	1.3	26.8
Walt Disney Company	2.7	53.9	2.5	11.3

TABLE 2.6
Market-based financial ratios for American corporate icons. P/B is price-to-book, P/E is price-to-earnings, and P/CF is price-to-cash flow from operations. Data are from the American Association of Individual Investors, February 2001.

order to find the stockholders' expected rate of return over the next year. The stockholder rate of return formula appears in the bottom row of table 2.5, reprinted below:

EXAMPLE 2 Find the stockholders' rate of return given ratios and balance sheet
At year-end 2525 the company has Total assets of $4,900 financed by Debt of $2,400 and Stockholders' equity of $2,500. For 800 common shares outstanding, the equity price-to-book ratio at year-end 2525 is 1.8. During 2526, the company expects an asset turnover ratio (= $Sales_t \div Total\ assets_{t-1}$) of 3.5 and an operating margin of 16%. Interest charges will equal 12% of Debt. Corporate taxes equal 34% of taxable income and the payout ratio always is 40%. Your analyst tells you that at year-end 2526 the company price-to-earnings ratio will equal 7. Find the shareholders' rate of return for year 2526.

SOLUTION
We must find all information for computing the shareholder rate of return ("ROR") from formula 2.6. Find first the stock price at the beginning of the horizon, that is, at year-end 2525. Use formulas 2.1 and 2.2 for P/B and equity book value per share:

$$1.8 = (\ price\ per\ share_{2525}\ )\ /\ (\$2,500\ /\ 800)$$

$$(\ price\ per\ share_{2525}\ ) = \$5.62$$

The shareholder owns a stock at end-of-year 2525 worth $5.62. During year 2526 she expects to receive a dividend plus a capital gain equal to the change in stock price.
Use the ratios from the problem to construct the income statement for year 2526:

sales	$17,150	(=$4,900 x 3.5)
– total operating costs	14,406	(=$17,150 x (1 – 0.16))
= operating income	2,744	(=$17,150 x 0.16)
– interest	288	(=$2,400 x 0.12)
= taxable income	2,456	
– taxes	835	(=$2,456 x 0.34)
= net income	1,621	
– dividends	648	(=$1,621 x 0.40)
= new retained earnings	973	

All line items are straightforward. The 800 common shares outstanding receive total company dividends of $648, implying a dividend per share of $0.81. Earnings per share ("eps") equals net income divided by number of shares, thereby implying

$$(P/E)_t = price\ /\ eps_t$$

$$= price_t\ /\ (net\ income\ /\ \#shares)_t.$$

The P/E for year-end 2526 relates to eps as:

$$7 = price_{2526}\ /\ (\$1,621\ /\ 800)$$

$$price_{2526} = \$14.18$$

The stock at year-end 2526 garners a dividend of 81 cents and has a price of $14.18. All information needed for computing the shareholder ROR is ready for substitution into formula 2.6 :

$$shareholder's\ ROR_{2526} = \frac{\$14.18 + \$0.81 - \$5.62}{\$5.62}$$

$$= 167\%$$

The scenario describes a fairly hefty rate of return for shareholders equal to 167% for year 2526!

EXERCISES 2.3A

Conceptual
1. Identify the ratios in table 2.5 that relate a flow with a balance and so are subject to alternative definitions differing only because of time subscripts.

2. Your company's latest financial statements list annual *Net income* of $132,500 and *Stockholders' equity* of $980,000. On last year's balance sheet *Stockholders' equity* was $905,000. Your boss informs you that the return-on-equity ("*ROE*") for this company's peer group equals 14.0%. Find whether your company's *ROE* is larger or smaller than its peer group's *ROE*.

Numerical quickies

3. The company balance sheet lists *Total liabilities* of $85,000 and *Stockholders' equity* of $114,000. Find the company equity multiplier, debt-to-assets, and debt-to-equity ratios. ©FA11

4. Today the company announces net income equals $42 million. They have 20 million shares outstanding, and today's share price is $136.80. Find the company's price-to-earnings ratio. ©FA8

5. The company reports that sales equal $129,000 and the net profit margin is 6.4%. How much is net income? ©FA9

6. During year 2526 company expects sales of $32,000 and a gross margin of 26%. Depreciation is expected to equal $1,030 and interest charges will equal $2,500. Corporate taxes equal 34% of taxable income. What is net income for 2526? ©FA12

7. How much was the company's *Total assets* if they just announced earnings per share of $1.25, there are 2,500 shares outstanding, the net profit margin is 11.5%, and the asset turnover ratio (= $Sales_t \div$ Total assets$_t$) is 3.6? ©FA13

Challengers

8. Shareholders had a good year, earning a 32% annual rate of return. The P/E ratio today is 26.4 and the company just announced earnings per share of $4.50. The company has a 35% payout ratio. How much did the stock price rise over the past year? ©FA14

9. The company last year had annual cost-of-goods sold equal to $50,000 and a 9.5 inventory turnover ratio (= *Annual cost-of-goods sold$_t$* $\div Inventory_t$). The company wants to decrease the average age of inventory by 5 days. If everything else remains exactly the same, how much is the resultant source of funds? ©EFN7

Problems 10-12 refer to this setup

At year-end 2525 the company has Total assets of $6,400 financed by Debt of $2,600 and Stockholders' equity of $3,800. For 325 common shares outstanding, the equity price-to-book ratio at year-end 2525 is 3.60. During 2526, the company expects an asset turnover ratio (= $Sales_t \div$ Total assets$_{t-1}$) of 3.2 and an operating margin of 12%. Interest charges will equal 8% of Debt. Corporate taxes equal 30% of taxable income and the payout ratio always is 35%. Your analyst tells you that at year-end 2526 the company price-to-earnings ratio will equal 11 1/2.

10. What is net income for 2526? ©FA15am
11. What is the expected stock price at year-end 2526? ©FA15bm
12. What is the shareholders' rate of return for year 2526? ©FA15cm

3.B. Ratio Relationships

Interpreting financial ratios is art as much as science. There are several elementary situations, though, when the importance of ratio analysis is apparent. The discussion below explains ratios within these useful contexts.

B1. Ratio norms

Financial ratios are especially useful in either a "time series" or "cross-sectional" analysis. A time series analysis examines movement over time in a ratio. The table below shows the operating margin for Home Depot, Inc. throughout a six-year window:

1996	1997	1998	1999	2000	2001
7.6%	7.8%	7.8%	8.8%	9.9%	9.8%

The steady increase in operating profit margin may lead Home Depot management to conclude that price-cuts are allowable because costs seem under control. Likewise, an external analyst may conclude that Home Depot stock merits a buy recommendation because the company looks healthy.

A cross-sectional analysis compares for a specific time period one company's ratio to other companies or averages. Table 2.8 shows a cross-section of operating margins for "retail home improvement" companies around end-of-year 2000.

The operating margin is substantially larger for Home Depot than its competitors. This implies that Home Depot's costs are small relative to revenues. Perhaps management of its competitors should sneak into the nearest Home Depot and glean insight on their operations.

Ratio averages differ by industry. Table 2.9 lists the average for selected ratios and industries. The current ratio, which equals *Current assets* divided by *Current liabilities*, ranges from 0.6 for Fast Foods to 2.1 for Department Stores. This is consistent with the observation that fast food businesses maintain little inventory compared to department stores. The high debt-to-equity ratio for Fast Food indicates heavy reliance on debt financing. Once again this contrasts starkly with Department Stores, which have the lowest debt-to-equity ratio. Grocery Stores possess a very high asset turnover ratio. Perhaps this is not surprising because some supermarkets that are little more than a warehouse generate huge amounts of sales. This contrasts with Electric Services, where multibillion dollar power plants generate relatively little revenue. Profit margins vary widely, from about 1% for grocery stores to over 10% for Electric Services.

B2. Return on equity and the DuPont analysis

The return on equity ("ROE"), a profitability ratio, is a key financial ratio for shareholders. Obviously shareholders care about stock prices, but there is a lot about stock prices beyond anyone's control. The company's books, on the other hand, are under management's control, and ROE is the book measure of shareholder returns.

The ROE equals *Net income* divided by *Stockholders' equity*. The denominator equals the book value of stockholder claims on the company. The numerator equals the earnings available to shareholders. The ROE consequently represents the rate of return, according to the books, that shareholders earn. Notice that because ROE is the ratio of a flow to a balance several alternative definitions exist that differ only by time subscripts.

The shareholders' ROR from formula 2.6 represents the rate of return based on prices from the stock market. Glean important insights on the relation between ROE ($NI_t \div SE_{t-1}$) and shareholders' ROR for the special case when the equity P/B ratio is constant.

> **FORMULA 2.7 Numerical Relation between ROE and shareholders' ROR**
> The shareholder rate of return ("ROR") for time period *t* relates to the reported return-on-equity ("ROE") as shown below only when the equity P/B ratio is constant and the company does not issue any new shares:
>
> $$\text{shareholder's } ROR_t = \left\{ 1 - \frac{\left(\dfrac{payout}{ratio}\right)\left(P/B - 1\right)}{P/B} \right\} ROE_t$$

Services of America	Building Materials Hldg	Calloway's Nursery Inc.	D.I.Y. Home Warehouse	Home Depot	HomeBase, Inc.	Lowes, Inc.	Wickes Inc.
3.7%	4.5%	5.4%	–9.0%	9.8%	–1.3%	7.2%	2.8%

	LOW	MEDIUM	HIGH
Liquidity category Current ratio	Fast Food (0.6) Electric Services (0.9) Mortgage Bankers (1.2) Petroleum (1.3) Groceries (1.3)	Soft Drinks (1.4) Motor Vehicles (1.4) Brokers (1.5)	Computers (1.8) Clothing (1.9) Department Stores (2.1)
Debt Management Category Debt-to-Equity	Department Store (1.0) Brokers (1.5) Clothing (1.6)	Steel (1.7) Computers (1.7) Petroleum (1.8) Electric Services (2.1) Groceries (2.3)	Soft Drinks (2.5) Motor Vehicles (2.7) Mortgage Bankers (3.2) Fast Food (3.7)
Asset Utilization Category asset turnover	Mortgage Bankers (0.4) Electric Services (0.5) Brokers (0.7)	Steel (1.9) Computers (2.0) Soft Drinks (2.1) Department Stores (2.1) Clothing (2.4) Petroleum (2.5) Motor Vehicles (2.7)	Fast Food (3.3) Groceries (5.8)
Profitability Category Net profit margin (%)	Groceries (1.0) Clothing (1.2) Motor Vehicles (2.0) Department Stores (2.4) Computers (2.7)	Petroleum (3.0) Soft Drinks (3.3) Fast Food (3.3) Steel (4.2)	Mortgage Bankers (8.2) Brokers (10.0) Electric Services (10.5)

The formula simplifies even further for two limiting cases. Inspect the formula and notice that if always P/B were unity then always shareholders' ROR would equal book ROE . The rate of return according to the books equals the market rate of return when P/B equals 1! Next, suppose that always the company pays out 100% of net income as dividends. Simplify the formula to see:

$$shareholder's\ ROR = ROE \left(P/B \right)^{-1}$$

The shareholders' ROR equals ROE times the reciprocal of P/B.

For a given ROE, a relatively small P/B ratio causes a relatively large ROR. Vice versa, a large P/B causes a smaller ROR. With a 14% ROE (and 100% payout ratio), for example, the shareholder ROR is doubled (28%) for a company with P/B of 1/2, and ROR is halved (7%) for a company with P/B of 2. The P/B ratio inversely amplifies stockholder rates of return. The inverse amplification occurs because P/B measures the relative size of the equity base that receives net income—small P/B implies big ROR because net income distributes over a relatively small equity base (and vice versa). We return to this issue later, after studying the connection between *Stockholders' equity* and the income statement.

The example below shows a simple application of formula 2.7.

EXAMPLE 3 Find the shareholders' ROR given expected ROE and constant P/B
Company X reports that next year they expect a 22% return-on-equity. Company Z expects exactly the same ROE. Both companies also have a 40% dividend payout ratio. You figure the best assumption is that the equity P/B ratios are likely to stay constant. The current P/B equals 0.75 for company X and 2.25 for company Z. Find the expected shareholder rates of return for each company.

SOLUTION
Substitute the numbers for company X into the formula:

$$shareholder's\ ROR = \left\{ 1 - \frac{0.40\ (0.75 - 1)}{0.75} \right\} 0.22$$

$$= 24.9\%$$

The market rate of return for shareholders in company X includes dividends plus stock price capital gains and equals 24.9%. A similar computation for company Z shows that their shareholder rate of return equals 17.1%. Even though the accountants proclaim the two companies provide equal returns on equity, differences in P/B ratios translate into almost an eight percentage-point gap in stockholder rates of return.

The ROE varies substantially across time or across companies. The "DuPont analysis" is a technique that enables insight about the source of variation in ROE. The DuPont analysis partitions the ROE into three components:

FORMULA 2.8 The DuPont decomposition

The DuPont decomposition breaks the ROE into three components:

$$Return-on-equity = \frac{Net\ income}{Stockholders'equity}$$

$$= \left(\frac{Net\ income}{Sales}\right)\left(\frac{Sales}{Total\ assets}\right)\left(\frac{Total\ assets}{Stockholders'equity}\right)$$

$$= (net\ profit\ margin)(asset\ turnover)(equity\ multiplier)$$

The ROE is the ratio of a flow to a balance so the caveat about timing raised in section 3A applies. That is, some applications may define ROE as $Net\ income_t \div Stockholders'\ equity_{t-1}$, whereas others may define as $Net\ income_t \div Stockholders'\ equity_t$, etc.

The DuPont analysis decomposes the ROE into the multiplicative product of three financial ratios. The "net profit margin" is from the profitability category, the "asset turnover ratio" is from the asset management category, and the "equity multiplier" is from the debt management category. We obtain an advantage by computing the ROE as the product of these three ratios, even though we certainly obtain the identical answer if we compute ROE directly as *Net income* divided by *Stockholders' equity*. The advantage occurs, as the example below illustrates, because the decomposition helps identify the source of variation in the ROE.

EXAMPLE 4 Apply the Dupont analysis to IBM
Use a DuPont analysis to explain why IBM's return-on-equity differs from the industry average.

SOLUTION
The IBM balance sheet (table 2.1) and income statement (table 2.4) contain the numbers to plug into the DuPont formula:

$$Return-on-equity = \left(\frac{Net\ income}{Sales}\right)\left(\frac{Sales}{Total\ assets}\right)\left(\frac{Total\ assets}{Stockholders'equity}\right)$$

$$= \left(\frac{\$5,429}{\$76,654}\right)\left(\frac{\$76,654}{\$81,132}\right)\left(\frac{\$81,132}{\$21,628}\right)$$

$$= (7.1\%)(0.9)(3.8)$$

$$= 25.1\%$$

The DuPont analysis for the industry depends on numbers for the computer industry contained in the table 2.9. Notice the table does not present the ROE. It presents, however, the industry net profit margin (2.7%), the asset turnover ratio (2.0), and debt-to-equity ratio (1.7). According to formula 2.5, the equity multiplier equals one plus the debt-to-equity ratio, we write for the industry that:

$$ROE = (2.7\%) \ (2.0) \ (1.7 + 1)$$

$$= \quad 14.6\%.$$

The ROE in 1996 is 25.1% for IBM and 14.6% for the computer industry. The relatively high ROE for IBM stems from two sources. First, IBM's profit margin is much larger than the industry average (7.1% vs. 2.7%), suggesting that IBM either controls its costs very effectively or receives a premium price for its product. Second, IBM relies on debt more than the average computer company (3.8 vs. 2.7). The reliance on debt amplifies the ROE. It is interesting to point out that even though IBM's ROE is relatively high, its asset turnover ratio is much smaller than the industry average (0.9 vs. 2.0). If IBM could increase their productive efficiency up to the norm, its ROE would be even higher.

EXERCISES 2.3B
Conceptual
1. Suppose that the company P/B ratio is constant. Is the shareholders' rate of return smaller or larger than the reported return-on-equity?

Numerical quickies
2. The return on equity (= net income ÷ Stockholders equity) is one of the more important measures of company performance. Suppose a company's net profit margin (= net income ÷ sales) is 9.1%, asset turnover (= sales ÷ total assets) is 1.7, and debt-to-assets ratio is 60%. What is this company's return on equity? ©BA7
3. Company X reports that next year they expect a 26% return-on-equity. Company Z expects exactly the same ROE. Both companies also have a 30% dividend payout ratio. You assume that the equity P/B ratios are likely to stay constant. The current P/B equals 1.35 for company X and 2.75 for company Z. What is the difference between expected shareholder rates of return for each company? ©FA16

Challengers
4. The P/B ratio is 0.8 for company X and 2.75 for company Z. Both have 25% dividend payout ratios. Company X expects an 18% return-on-equity. What ROE for company Z provides its shareholders with exactly the same rate of return that company X shareholders receive? ©FA17
5. The DuPont formula relates return on equity to the company's net profit margin , asset turnover (= $sales_t$ ÷ total $assets_t$), and equity multiplier. This Company is in an industry where the average net profit margin is 5.10%, the debt-to-asset ratio is 37.8%, and return on equity is 30.90%. Find below the Company's financial statements for year 2525.

Balance Sheet, 12/31/2525				Income, 1/1—12/31/2525	
$1,750	Current assets	$2,450	Debt	Sales	$24,130
$4,600	PP&E	$3,900	Stockholders equity	all costs	$22,470
$6,350	Total assets	$6,350	Liabilities & equity	net income	$1,660

Contrast the company and industry ROE and explain the source of differences. ©BA6

3.C. Breakeven ratios

Breakeven analysis relies on the stylized income statement below to estimate the amount of sales required for realizing specific income targets.

Sales revenue	pQ
- Total fixed costs	F
- <u>Total variable costs</u>	<u>vQ</u>
= Earnings before interest & taxes	$EBIT$
- Interest	I
- Taxes	T
- <u>Preferred dividends</u>	<u>PD</u>
= Earnings available for common	EAC

The variable Q represents the quantity of product that the company sells, p is the unit sales price of the product (p times Q equals total *Sales revenue*), and v is the variable cost per unit. The preceding income statement categorizes operating costs as either "fixed" or "variable." This simplification, favored by economics textbooks and models (as you may dare remember!), is very useful even though somewhat inconsistent with financial reporting practices. Actual income statements do not list line items labeled "fixed costs" and "variable costs." Cost analysis reveals, however, that some production costs (like wages) rise proportionately with sales whereas other costs (like depreciation) are somewhat independent of short-run sales fluctuations. This stylized model allows incredible insights!

The "operating breakeven point" occurs when company *Sales revenue* equals fixed plus variable operating costs. That is, a company at the operating breakeven point has *EBIT* equal to zero. Usually, however, companies prefer a target *EBIT* that is bigger than zero. The operating breakeven ratio allows computation of any target *EBIT*.

FORMULA 2.9a and 2.9b Operating breakeven ratio

The "operating breakeven ratio" equals the amount of sales that generates a target *Earnings before interest and taxes (EBIT^{target})*.

$$\left(\begin{array}{c}\text{Sales Revenue}\\ \text{@}EBIT^{target}\end{array}\right) = \frac{\text{Total fixed costs} + EBIT^{target}}{1 - \dfrac{\text{Total variable costs}}{\text{Sales revenue}}}$$

$$\left(\begin{array}{c}\text{Sales quantity}\\ \text{@}EBIT^{target}\end{array}\right) = \frac{F + EBIT^{target}}{p - v}$$

where p is the unit price of the product, v is the variable cost per unit, and F is *Total fixed costs*. The upper and lower formulas compute, respectively, sales in <u>dollars</u> and sales in number of <u>units</u>. This model assumes the ratio of *Total variable costs* to *Sales revenue* is constant. At the operating breakeven point $EBIT^{target}$ equals zero.

Consider this example.

EXAMPLE 5 Find the operating breakeven point

The most recent annual report lists company *Sales revenue* at $175,000. Cost analysis suggests that annual *Total fixed costs* equal $42,000 and *Total variable costs* equal $108,000. Find the company's operating breakeven *Sales revenue*.

Notice that the company's annual report lists total operating costs of $150,000 (= $42,000 + $108,000) and *Sales revenue* of $175,000. Their actual *EBIT* therefore is $25,000 (= $175,000 − 150,000). The operating breakeven point is the amount of sales at which *EBIT* equals zero. To find the *Sales revenue* that generates *EBIT* of zero, plug numbers into formula 2.9a:

$$\begin{pmatrix} Sales\ Revenue \\ @EBIT = \$0 \end{pmatrix} = \dfrac{\$42,000 + \$0}{1 - \dfrac{\$108,000}{\$175,000}}$$

$$= \$109,701$$

Sales revenue at the operating breakeven point is $109,701. If the company were at the operating breakeven point then the upper half of the income statement looks like this (notice that the ratio of *Total variable costs* to *Sales revenue* equals 61.71%):

Sales revenue	$109,701
- Total fixed costs	42,000
- <u>Total variable costs</u>	<u>67,701</u> (= 0.6171 × $109,701)
= Earnings before interest & taxes	$0

At the operating breakeven point the *Sales revenue* pays operating costs but nothing else. Fortunately, the company at $175,000 annual sales is far beyond breakeven.

The preceding example solves for the amount of *Sales revenue* that pays all operating costs but nothing else. The same formula, however, also is useful for finding the amount of sales that provide a specific amount of operating income. Consider this example.

EXAMPLE 6 Find sales quantity that provides target operating income

The company computes that each unit of production incurs variable operating costs of $36 and sells for $48. The company's fixed costs are $74,000 per year. How many units per year must the company sell to earn $35,000 of operating income?

SOLUTION

The company must generate sufficient sales to cover the $74,000 fixed costs to suppliers plus the $35,000 operating income to them self. Use formula 2.9b and find the quantity of production at the operating breakeven point.

$$\begin{pmatrix} Sales\ Quantity \\ @EBIT = \$35,000 \end{pmatrix} = \dfrac{\$74,000 + \$35,000}{\$48 - \$36}$$

$$= 9,083\ units$$

Reconstruct the income statement and verify that Sales revenue is $436,000 (= 9,083 x $48) and Total fixed costs equal $74,000 and Total variable costs equal $327,000 (= 9,083 x $36). *EBIT*, also known as operating income, equals the desired target of $35,000 (= $436,000 - $74,000 - $327,000).

Economic theory finds (as you may dare forget!) that equilibrating forces depend on relationships between marginal revenue and marginal costs. The denominator for the preceding problem, $p - v$ from formula 2.9b, provides significant economic insights about market equilibrium. Suppose with the stylized income statement above, for example, that the company uses only labor and capital to create its product. The marginal revenue is the income from selling one extra unit of production and equals p. The marginal cost of labor is the variable cost of making one extra unit and equals v. The difference $p - v$ is the pre-tax revenue, net of variable costs, from selling one extra unit of production. Equilibrating forces link $p - v$ to user costs of capital. In other words, $p - v$ is an important determinant of capital market equilibrium. A large literature of economic research measures and models $p - v$ in order to make inferences about producer behavior toward capital expenditures.

For purposes, herein, however, simply note the intuition underlying the breakeven ratio in formula 2.9b. The upstairs term is the sum of fixed costs and target *EBIT*. The downstairs term, $p - v$, is the revenue net of variable costs that each unit provides. Breakeven ratio 2.9b basically divides "total money required" by "money provided per unit."

Breakeven ratio 2.9a relies on similar intuition. Divide each term of $(p - v)$ by p and obtain $(1 - v/p)$, an expression that appears in the denominator of formula 2.9a. This expression represents operating income per dollar of sales. Hence, breakeven ratio 2.9a basically divides "total money required" by "money provided per dollar of sales." Consider this example.

EXAMPLE 7 Find sales that generate a target operating margin
The company computes that each unit of production incurs variable operating costs of $28 and sells for $35. The company's fixed costs are $44,000 per year. How many units per year must the company sell to attain a 15% operating margin [= *(Sales revenue – Total operating costs) ÷ Sales]* ?

SOLUTION
Solving this problem requires a little algebra. Realize that Total operating costs equals $F + vQ$. Write the definition for the operating margin with variables from the stylized income statement:

$$\binom{operating}{margin} = \frac{pQ - (F + vQ)}{pQ}$$

$$= 1 - \frac{F}{pQ} - \frac{v}{p}$$

Now solve for Q:

$$Q = \frac{F}{p\left(1 - \dfrac{v}{p} - \binom{operating}{margin}\right)}$$

Insert numbers from the problem setup to find Q, the quantity sold when the operating margin equals 15%:

$$Q = \frac{\$44,000}{\$35\left(1 - \dfrac{\$28}{\$35} - 0.15\right)}$$

$$= \$25,143 \ units$$

Reconstruct the income statement and verify that with sales at 25,143 units the *Sales revenue* equals $880,000 (= 25,143 x $35); *Total variable costs* equal $704,000 (= 25,143 x $28); *Total fixed costs* equal $44,000; *EBIT* equals $132,000 (= $880,000 - $704,000 - $44,000); and the operating margin equals 15% [= {$880,000 – ($704,000 + $44,000)} ÷ $880,000]. Ain't algebra wonderful!

The bottom-half of the income statement documents cash flows from company to capitalists in financial markets. The company sends interest to creditors and dividends to shareholders. Analysis of the preceding stylized income statement allows further insights on how breakeven ratios allow computation of sales needed to reach specific targets.

The *Earnings available for common (EAC)* equals *EBIT*, minus *Interest (IE)*, *Interest (I)*, minus *Taxes*, minus *Preferred dividends (PD)*. When *Taxes* are proportional to taxable income we may write:

$$EAC = (EBIT - IE)(1 - tax\ rate) - PD.$$

The "total breakeven point" occurs when the *Sales revenue* pays all operating costs, interest to creditors, taxes, and preferred dividends, and *EAC* equals zero.

FORMULAS 2.10a and 2.10b Total breakeven ratio

The "total breakeven ratio" equals the amount of sales that generates a target *Earnings available for common (EAC^{target})*:

$$\begin{pmatrix} Sales\ Revenue \\ @EAC^{target} \end{pmatrix} = \frac{Total\ fixed\ costs + IE + \left(\dfrac{PD + EAC^{target}}{1 - tax\ rate} \right)}{1 - \dfrac{Total\ variable\ costs}{Sales\ revenue}}$$

$$\begin{pmatrix} Sales\ quantity \\ @EAC^{target} \end{pmatrix} = \frac{Total\ fixed\ costs + IE + \left(\dfrac{PD + EAC^{target}}{1 - tax\ rate} \right)}{p - v}$$

where p is the unit price of the product, v is the variable cost per unit, *IE* is periodic *Interest expense*, and *PD* equals periodic *Preferred dividends*. The upper and lower formulas compute, respectively, sales in <u>dollars</u> and sales in number of <u>units</u>. This model assumes the ratio of *Total variable costs* to *Sales revenue* is constant. At the total breakeven point *EAC^{target}* equals zero.

Consider this example.

EXAMPLE 8 Find how far beyond the total breakeven point are sales

The most recent annual report lists company *Sales revenue* at $175,000. Cost analysis suggests that annual *Total fixed costs* equal $42,000 and *Total variable costs* equal $108,000. The company has annual *Interest* expense of $8,500 and pays $2,000 in *Preferred dividends*. They pay taxes equal to 30% of taxable income. Find how far company sales must fall if the company unfortunately were to fall to its total breakeven point.

SOLUTION

At the total breakeven point *EAC^{target}* equals zero. To find the *Sales revenue* that generates *EAC* of zero, plug numbers into formula 2.10a:

$$\begin{pmatrix} Sales\ Revenue \\ @EAC\ \$0 \end{pmatrix} = \frac{\$42,000 + \$8,500 + \$2,000/(1-0.30)}{1 - \dfrac{\$108,000}{\$175,000}}$$

$$= \$139,366$$

If *Sales revenue* were at the total breakeven point then the income statement looks like this:

Sales revenue	$139,366
- *Total fixed costs*	42,000
- *Total variable costs*	86,009 (= 0.6171 x $139,366)
= *Earnings before interest & taxes*	11,357
- *Interest*	8,500
- *Taxes (@30% tax rate)*	857
- *Preferred dividends*	2,000
= *Earnings available for common*	$ 0

The actual *Sales revenue* of $175,000 surpasses by a good amount the total breakeven point of $139,366. Sales would have to decline by 20.4% [= ($139,366 - $175,000) ÷ $175,000] for the company to fall to its total breakeven point.

The final example in this section shows that breakeven analysis dovetails with DuPont analysis to provide insight about company profitability.

EXAMPLE 9 Find sales increase required to reach target ROE

The most recent annual report lists company *Sales revenue* at $56,125. Cost analysis suggests that annual *Total fixed costs* equal $21,375 and *Total variable costs* equal $25,375. The annual *Interest* expense is $2,550 and there is no preferred stock. The company pays 35% of taxable income as taxes. The annual report also shows ROE, that is return on equity *(= Net income$_t$ ÷ Stockholders' equity$_t$)*, equals 12.8%. The company wants to increase ROE to a target of 19.0%. They plan to hold constant *Stockholders' equity, Total assets, Total fixed costs, Interest,* and the ratio of *Sales revenue* to *Total variable costs*. Find the target *Sales revenue* that provides the target ROE.

SOLUTION

Reconstruct the stylized income statement from the annual report:

Sales revenue	$56,125
- *Total fixed costs*	21,375
- *Total variable costs*	25,375
= *Earnings before interest & taxes*	9,375
- *Interest*	2,550
- *Taxes (@35% tax rate)*	2,389
= *Earnings available for common (=Net income)*	$4,436

When there is no preferred stock then *Earnings available for common* is synonymous with *Net income*; it equals $4,436 in the most recent annual report. The ROE is 12.8% but the company wants to increase it to 19%.

Because *Stockholders' equity* remains constant we easily find *Net income* at the target ROE. Recall that ROE = *Net income$_t$ / Stockholders' equity$_t$*. Thus, in the annual report

$0.128 = \$4,436 / $ *Stockholders' equity* so *Stockholders' equity* = $34,658.

With a target ROE of 19% find the target *Net income:*

$$0.19 = \text{target Net income} / \$34,658 \quad \text{so} \quad \text{target Net income} = \$6,585.$$

With *Net income* of $6,585 the ROE equals 19%. Plug numbers into formula 2.10a to find the *Sales revenue* that generates *EAC* of $6,585:

$$\left(\begin{array}{c} \text{Sales Revenue} \\ @EAC\ \$6,585 \end{array}\right) = \frac{\$21,375 + \$2,550 + 6,585/_{(1-0.35)}}{1 - \dfrac{\$25,375}{\$56,125}}$$

$$= \$62,159$$

If the company increases sales to $62,159 then the ROE rises to its target 19%. This is a $6,034 sales increase.

And what's the effect on company profitability? In the most recent annual report the net profit margin *(= Net income ÷ Sales revenue)* equals 7.90% (= $4,436 ÷ $56,125). At the target ROE of 19% the net profit margin is 10.59% (= $6,585 ÷ $62,159). The company obtains a higher ROE by pursuing policies that result in a larger profit margin.

The larger profit margin occurs because average costs decline as sales increase. Notice that *Total variable costs* in the annual report equal 45.21% of *Sales revenue* – this ratio presumably is constant. Every extra dollar of sales contributes 54.79 cents (= $1 – 0.4521) to pre-tax revenue. Taxes attract 35% of revenue, implying that net income rises by 35.61 cents [= 54.79 x (1 – 0.35)] for every extra dollar of sales. Analysts sometimes refer to this number as the "after-tax contribution margin". It measures the change in net income per dollar increase in sales. Easily compute the after-tax contribution margin as *(1 – tax rate) x (1 – (Total variable costs ÷ Sales revenue)}*.

Total fixed costs, of course, do not increase with sales. As sales increase then fixed costs as a proportion of sales diminishes and the net profit margin increases (and ROE increases, too). For the preceding example the company finds that raising ROE to 19% requires extra net income of $2,149 (= $6,585 – $4,436). Divide the extra net income by the after-tax contribution margin of $0.3561 and compute that the company requires $6,034 of extra sales to reach its target.

The DuPont analysis establishes that a rising net profit margin, all else equal, pushes up the ROE. But in our stylized example is all else equal? The answer is *no*. The company expects to increase sales while holding constant *Total assets*. The ratio of *Sales* to *Total assets* is the asset turnover ratio, a key component in the DuPont decomposition. The implication is that in order to achieve a higher return on equity the company in our stylized example increases both its net profit margin <u>and</u> asset turnover ratio (but the equity multiplier is constant).

EXERCISES 2.3C

Conceptual

1. Inspection of the breakeven ratios shows that the role of taxes is limited. For example, when the company has no preferred stock then the total breakeven point at which *Earnings available for common* equals zero does not depend at all on the tax rate. Yet all companies (and households) know the importance of taxes. Why does the total breakeven ratio appear to assign limited importance to taxes?

Numerical quickies

2. The company computes that each unit of production incurs variable operating costs of $7 and sells for $12. The company's fixed costs are

$12,000 per year. Find the number of units per year the company must sell to exactly cover operating costs. ©BE1a

3. The company computes that each unit of production incurs variable operating costs of $16 and sells for $22. The company's fixed costs are $34,000 per year. How many units per year must the company sell to earn $15,000 of operating income? ©BE1b

4. The most recent annual report lists company *Sales revenue* at $83,195. Cost analysis suggests that annual *Total fixed costs* equal $38,250 and *Total variable costs* equal $40,400. The company believes that the ratio of *Sales revenue* to *Total variable costs* is constant. Find the company's operating breakeven *Sales revenue*. ©BE2a

5. The most recent annual report lists company *Sales revenue* at $95,525. Cost analysis suggests that annual *Total fixed costs* equal $42,500 and *Total variable costs* equal $50,500. The company believes that the ratio of *Sales revenue* to *Total variable costs* is constant. Find the target *Sales revenue* per year at which the company earns $6,300 of operating income. ©BE2b

6. The most recent annual report lists company *Sales revenue* at $97,450. Cost analysis suggests that annual *Total fixed costs* equal $34,000 and *Total variable costs* equal $50,500. The company believes that the ratio of *Sales revenue* to *Total variable costs* is constant. The annual *Interest* expense is $3,825 and the company pays *Preferred dividends* of $500 per year. They also pay 30% of taxable income as taxes. Find the *Sales revenue* and *EBIT* at the total breakeven point. ©BE5b

7. The most recent annual report lists company *Sales revenue* at $91,350. Cost analysis suggests that annual *Total fixed costs* equal $29,750 and *Total variable costs* equal $50,500. The company believes that the ratio of *Sales revenue* to *Total variable costs* is constant. The annual *Interest* expense is $2,550 and the company pays *Preferred dividends* of $350 per year. They also pay 25% of taxable income as taxes. Find the target annual *Sales revenue* at which the company has $7,900 of *Earnings available for common*. ©BE6

8. The most recent annual report lists company *Sales revenue* at $745,200 and *Net income* at $125,000. Cost analysis suggests that *Total variable costs* equal $475,000. The company pays 30% of taxable income as taxes and there is no preferred stock. The ROE currently is 14%, but the company wants to increase *Net income* so that ROE rises to 18%. They plan to hold constant *Stockholders' equity*, *Total assets*, *Total fixed costs*, *Interest*, and the ratio of *Sales revenue* to *Total variable costs*. By how much must *Sales revenue* increase?

Challengers

9. The most recent annual report lists company *Sales revenue* at $66,900 . Cost analysis suggests that annual *Total fixed costs* equal $34,000 and *Total variable costs* equal $25,250. The company believes that the ratio of *Sales revenue* to *Total variable costs* is constant. Find the percentage decline in annual *Sales revenue* that would cause the company to fall to its operating breakeven point. ©BE3

10. The company computes that each unit of production incurs variable operating costs of $33 and sells for $45. The company's fixed costs are $25,500 per year. Find the number of units per year the company must sell to attain a 18% operating margin [= (Sales revenue − total operating costs) ÷ Sales]. ©BE4a

11. The company computes that each unit of production incurs variable operating costs of $21 and sells for $30 . The company's fixed costs are $34,000 per year. Find the annual *Sales revenue* at which the company attains a 20% operating margin [= (Sales revenue − total operating costs) ÷ Sales]. ©BE4b

12. The most recent annual report lists company *Sales revenue* at $107,175. Cost analysis suggests that annual *Total fixed costs* equal $42,750 and *Total variable costs* equal $45,675. The annual *Interest* expense is $3,825 and there is no preferred stock. The company pays 30% of taxable income as taxes. The annual report also shows ROE, that is return on equity (=*Net income*$_t$ ÷ *Stockholders' equity*$_t$), equals 15.7%. The company wants to increase its ROE to a target of 24.0%. They plan to hold constant *Stockholders' equity, Total assets, Total fixed costs, Interest,* and the ratio of *Sales revenue* to *Total variable costs*. Find the target *Sales revenue* and net profit margin (=*Net income* ÷ *Sales revenue*) that provides the target ROE. ©BE7b

4. THE INCOME STATEMENT LINKS ADJACENT BALANCE SHEETS

The balance sheet is a momentary snapshot of the company assets and liabilities. After the snapshot is taken, time elapses and the income statement records all cash flows that occur. Then, at the end of the period, another snapshot captures the balance sheet showing the new amounts for all assets and liabilities. As rule 2.1 states, the change in balances from one snapshot to the next equals the sum of intervening cash flows.

Two processes link the income statement with the two adjacent balance sheets. These differential processes are given below:

FORMULAS 2.11 and 2.12 Differential processes for Stockholders' Equity and PP&E

Two formulas link the income statement with its adjacent balance sheets.

$$\left(\begin{array}{c} Stockholders' \\ equity \end{array}\right)_t = \left(\begin{array}{c} Stockholders' \\ equity \end{array}\right)_{t-1} + Net\ equity\ issues_t + \left(\begin{array}{c} New \\ retained \\ earnings \end{array}\right)_t.$$

$$PP\&E_t = PP\&E_{t-1} + Capital\ expenditure_t - Depreciation_t.$$

For each formula the left-hand-side represents a line item on the balance sheet from the snapshot taken at the end of the reporting period. *Stockholders' equity* is on the liability side of the balance sheet, and *PP&E* is on the asset side. The first right-hand-side term for each formula represents the line item from the balance sheet at the beginning of the reporting period (that is identical to the end of the previous period). The rightmost right-hand-side terms (*New retained earnings* and *Depreciation*) in each formula appear on the income statement. The middle terms represent realized cash flows that affect the respective balance but do not appear on the income statement.

The formulas show that the balance this period equals the balance last period plus adjustments for cash flows. The process is analogous to the water level of a lake. The water level this period equals the level last period, minus evaporation and runoff, plus rain and inflow. For the *PP&E* account the *Depreciation* is analogous to the evaporation. *Depreciation* causes the balance of *PP&E* to fall. *Capital expenditure* is like the rainfall and causes the balance of *PP&E* to rise.

The explanation for *Stockholders' equity* is similar. The term *Net equity issues* equals the value of shares sold by the company to the public, minus the value of shares that it repurchases. The term *New retained earnings* equals *Net income* minus *Dividends*. Suppose, for example, that a company makes $100,000 of *Net income*. The company certainly can payout all of the $100,000 as *Dividends*. These dividends represent a return to shareholders for investing in the company's stock. The company may choose, however, that instead of paying out 100% of *Net income* as *Dividends* they will retain some, say 60%, within the firm. This *New retained earnings* of $60,000 represents internal financing for the company. Managers plowback earnings into the company when they believe they can put the money to good use.

A company that keeps *New retained earnings* incurs a liability to shareholders. The money could have been paid-out as a dividend to shareholders but, instead, the company implicitly borrows money from shareholders. Consequently, the appearance on the income statement of *New retained earnings* causes an increase on the balance sheet of *Stockholders' equity*.

Some balance sheets partition *Stockholders' equity* into several components: Accumulated retained earnings, paid-in-equity capital, equity capital surplus, etc. Throughout this book we lump these components together into the broader category called *Stockholders' equity*.

The differential processes in formula 2.11 shape evolution of the balance sheet through time. Examples below provide practice linking the income statement with its adjacent balance sheets. First, use the relation for *Stockholders' equity*.

EXAMPLE 10 Use the differential process for *Stockholders' equity* to find next period's book value
At year-end 2525 the company has Total assets of $4,400 financed by Debt of $1,700 and Stockholders' equity of $2,700. For year 2526 the company forecasts an asset turnover ratio (= $Sales_{2526} \div Total\ assets_{2525}$) of 3.9, a net profit margin of 6.4%, and a dividend payout ratio of 45%. There are 270 shares outstanding. If no additional shares are issued, what is the equity book value per share at year-end 2526?

SOLUTION
Use formula 2.11 to find *Stockholders' equity* at year-end 2526:

$$\left(\begin{array}{c}Stockholders'\\equity\end{array}\right)_{2526} = \left(\begin{array}{c}Stockholders'\\equity\end{array}\right)_{2525} + Net\ equity\ issues_{2526} + \left(\begin{array}{c}New\\retained\\earnings\end{array}\right)_{2526}$$

$$= \$2,700 + 0 + \left(\begin{array}{c}New\\retained\\earnings\end{array}\right)_{2526}$$

Necessary information is *New retained earnings* from the income statement for year 2526. Reconstruct the income statement from the information given: sales equals 3.9 x $4,400; net income equals 0.064 x sales; and *New retained earnings* equals 0.55 times net income (45% of net income is paid-out as dividends, 55% is retained). Thus, *New retained earnings* for year 2526 equals $604 (= 3.9 x $4,400 x 0.064 x 0.55). Substitute this amount above to find that *Stockholders' equity*$_{2526}$ equals $3,304. Divide by the 270 shares outstanding to find equity book value per share of $12.24.

PP&E differential process in formula 2.12 offers one more lesson about *Capital expenditures*. There exist two motivations for company management to invest in real capital: *replacement investment* to offset effects of depreciation or obsolescence and *expansion investment* to increase the asset base. Rearrange and relabel formula 2.12 to find:

$$Capital\ expenditure_t = \underbrace{PP\&E_t - PP\&E_{t-1}}_{expansion\ investment_t} + \underbrace{Depreciation_t}_{replacement\ investment_t}$$

Lessons in chapter 6 examine assessment tools for determining whether capital investments create, maintain, or destroy wealth. For current purposes, however, learn to compute the difference between replacement and expansion investment.

EXAMPLE 11 Find and partition *Capital expenditures* into replacement and expansion investment

The balance sheet shows $PP\&E_{2525}$ equals \$46,400 and *Total assets*$_{2525}$ equal \$64,000. *Sales*$_{2526}$ are \$86,000. The company sets its target asset turnover ratio (= *Sales*$_{2526}$ ÷ *Total assets*$_{2526}$) at 1.20. *PP&E* is the only asset that increases during 2526. Suppose *Depreciation*$_{2526}$ equals 18% of beginning of year *PP&E*. Find the *Capital expenditures* in 2526. Partition the expenditure into two components: that which replaces depreciating assets and that which expands the asset base.

SOLUTION

Because *Sales*$_{2526}$ ÷ *Total assets*$_{2526}$ equals 1.20 and *Sales*$_{2526}$ equals \$86,000 then *Total assets*$_{2526}$ equals \$71,667 (= \$86,000 ÷ 1.20). Between year-ends 2525 and 2526 the increase in *Total assets* is \$7,667 (= \$71,667 – \$64,000). Because *PP&E* is the only asset that increases during 2526 then *PP&E* also increases by \$7,667. Rearrange formula 2.12 to find *Capital expenditures*$_{2526}$ and substitute that *Depreciation* equals 18% of beginning of year *PP&E*.

$$Capital\ expenditure_{2526} \quad = \Delta PP\&E + Depreciation_{2526}$$

$$= \$7,667 + (0.18\ x\ \$46,400)$$

$$= \$7,667 + \$8,352$$

$$= \$16,019.$$

The company spends a total of \$16,019 purchasing *PP&E*. Of that expenditure, more than half (\$8,352) is replacement investment with sole purpose of replacing depreciating assets. Expansion investment, that is the net increase in the fixed asset stock, equals \$7,667. This example highlights the realistic fact that a large proportion of the economy's investment in fixed capital assets does not expand the asset base, but simply replaces that which is obsolete, out-of-favor, or just plain wears out.

Linking *Stockholders' equity* from one year to the next provides an opportunity to strengthen understanding of the relation between book and market measures of the shareholders' rate of return.

EXAMPLE 12 Contrast market ROR with book ROE given financial ratios and constant P/B

For year 2526 the company forecasts sales of \$70,000 , an asset turnover ratio (= *Sales*$_t$ ÷ *Total assets*$_{t-1}$) of 2.9, a net profit margin (= *Net income* ÷ *Sales*) of 4.2%, a dividend payout ratio (= *Dividends* ÷ *Net income*) of 70%, and a debt-to-equity ratio (= *Total debt* ÷ *Stockholders' equity*) of 135%. The company expects the equity price-to-book ratio to remain constant and they do not intend to issue any new shares. Contrast for year 2526 the shareholders' book and market rates-of-return given the P/B ratio is (a) 1.00, or (b) 0.60, or (c) 1.40.

SOLUTION

The book return-on-equity does not depend on the P/B ratio, so ROE is the same number for case a-b-c. Define ROE for this example as *Net income*$_{2526}$ ÷ *Stockholders' equity*$_{2526}$. Multiply *Sales* of \$70,000 by the net profit margin of 4.2% to obtain that

Net income is \$2,940. Obtain *Stockholders' equity*$_{2525}$. by combining information about the asset turnover and debt-to-equity ratios:

$$\frac{Sales_{2526}}{Total\ assets_{2525}} = 2.9\ ;\ \ or\ \ \frac{\$70,000}{Total\ assets_{2525}} = 2.9\ ;\ \ so\ Total\ assets_{2525} = \$24,318$$

$$\frac{Total\ debt_{2525}}{Stockholders'\ equity_{2525}} = 1.35\ \ or\ \ Total\ debt_{2525} = 1.35\ x\ Stockholders'\ equity_{2525}$$

$$\left(Total\ debt_{2525} + Stockholders'\ equity_{2525}\right)\ = \$24,318$$

$$\left(1.35\ x\ Stockholders'\ equity_{2525} + Stockholders'\ equity_{2525}\right)\ = \$24,318$$

$$Stockholders'\ equity_{2525}\ = \$24,318\ /\ 2.35\ ;\ \ = \$10,271$$

$$ROE = \frac{\$2,940}{\$10,271}\ ;\ = 28.6\%$$

ROE is the book measure for the shareholders' rate-of-return and equals 28.6%. Notice that the DuPont decomposition in formula 2.8 arrives at the identical answer [that is, 28.6% = 4.2% x 2.9 x (1+1.35)].

The market ROR depends on the shareprice. The ROR differs between cases a-b-c because the P/B ratio differs and B, the equity book value, is constant. Formula 2.6 shows the ROR on a per share basis. The identical number is found, however, on the accumulated basis when number of shares outstanding is constant.

$$ROR_t = \frac{market\ capitalization_t + total\ dividends_t - market\ capitalization_{t-1}}{market\ capitalization_{t-1}}\ ,$$

Already we have found that *Net income*$_{2526}$ is \$2,940 which, combined with a pay-out ratio of 70%, implies that *Total dividends*$_{2526}$ equals \$2,058 and *New retained earnings*$_{2526}$ equals \$882.

Now let's examine cases a-b-c.

case a: P/B =1.0 Previous examples have taught us that the company's market capitalization equals its *Stockholders' equity* times the P/B ratio. Already we computed that *Stockholders' equity*$_{2525}$ is \$10,271. Formula 2.11 shows that *Stockholders' equity*$_{2526}$ equals *Stockholders' equity*$_{2525}$ plus *New retained earnings*$_{2526}$. Thus, let's find *ROR* with P/B = 1 as follows:

$$ROR_t = \frac{\{1.0\ x\ (\$10,271 + \$882)\} + \$2,058 - (1.0\ x\ \$10,271)}{1.0\ x\ \$10,271}$$

$$= \frac{\$2,058 + (1.0\ x\ \$882)}{1.0\ x\ \$10,271}\ ;\ = \frac{\$2,940}{\$10,271}\ ;\ = 28.6\%$$

The ROR of 28.6% is identical to the ROE found previously. That's because the P/B was 1.0.

case b: P/B =0.60 Recompute the above expression:

$$ROR_t = \frac{\{0.60\ x\ (\$10,271 + \$882)\} + \$2,058 - (0.60\ x\ \$10,271)}{1.0\ x\ \$10,271}$$

$$= \frac{\$2,058 + (0.60\ x\ \$882)}{0.60\ x\ \$10,271}\ ;\ = 42.0\%$$

The market ROR of 42.0% is substantially greater than the ROE of 28.6%. This result is expected because the P/B is less than one.

case c: P/B =1.40 Recompute the above expression, but this time let's jump to the second line showing the numerator equals *Dividends* plus the product of P/B times *New retained earnings*:

$$ROR_t = \frac{\$2,058 + (1.40 \times \$882)}{1.40 \times \$10,271} \quad ; \quad = 22.9\%$$

The market ROR of 22.9% is smaller than the ROE of 28.6%. This result is expected because the P/B is bigger than one.

The above illustration reaffirms formula 2.7 showing how ROE and ROR relate to each other. The findings easily summarize into a rule that always is true when P/B is constant.

Rule 2.2 Qualitative relation between ROE and shareholders' ROR when P/B is constant

The shareholder rate of return ("ROR") for time period t relates to the reported return-on-equity ("ROE") as shown below only when the equity P/B ratio is constant and the company does not issue any new shares:

$$\text{shareholders' } ROR_t \quad \begin{Bmatrix} > \\ = \\ < \end{Bmatrix} \quad ROE_t$$

$$\text{whenever} \quad P/B_t \quad \begin{Bmatrix} < \\ = \\ > \end{Bmatrix} \quad 1.0$$

The P/B ratio inversely amplifies stockholder rates of return—small P/B implies big ROR because net income distributes over a relatively small equity base (and vice versa).

The example below further brings *Depreciation* into the analysis. This complexity typically arises in the real world. This means that usually you have to work simultaneously with the PP&E and SE relations.

EXAMPLE 13 Use the PP&E relation to find next period's
Stockholders' equity and ROR
Find below the Company balance sheet for year-end 2525.

Balance Sheet, 12/31/2525

Current Assets	$1,700	$3,200	Debt
PP&E	$6,200	$4,700	Stockholders equity (500 shares)
	$7,900	$7,900	Total

For year 2526 the company forecasts an asset turnover ratio (= sales$_{2526}$ ÷ total assets$_{2525}$) of 2.8, a net profit margin (= net income ÷ sales) of 7.7%, a dividend pay-out ratio (=dividends ÷ net income) of 55%, and depreciation that is 21% of beginning-of-year PP&E. Throughout year 2526 Debt remains unchanged, and the P/B ratio of 1.4 is expected to remain constant. The company expects to make *Capital expenditures* such that for the year-end 2526 balance sheet PP&E is $400 larger than on the 2525 balance sheet. Suppose the *Capital expenditure* is financed *exclusively* by issuing new shares at the stock price of year-end 2525. Find (i) Stockholders' equity at year-end 2526, and (ii) the shareholders' ROR for year 2526.

Realize that $Depreciation_{2526}$ equals $1,302 (=.21 \times \$6,200)$. Furthermore, the company wants PPE_{2526} to equal $6,600 (=\$6,200 + 400)$. Use formula 2.12 to find the *Capital expenditure* that occurs during year 2526:

$$PP\&E_{2526} = PP\&E_{2525} + Capital\ expenditure_{2526} - Depreciation_{2526}$$

$$\$6,600 = \$6,200 + Capital\ expenditure_{2526} - \$1,302$$

$$Capital\ expenditure_{2526} = \$1,702$$

By investing $1,702 in plant and equipment the company more than offsets effects of depreciation and *PP&E* rises to $6,600 on the year-end 2526 balance sheet.

The company pays a supplier $1,702 for the PP&E. The setup tells us they obtain this financing by selling new stock. *Stockholders' equity* increases by $1,702 plus the amount of *New retained earnings*$_{2526}$. Use the logic from the previous example to compute that *New retained earnings* equals $766 (= 2.8 \times \$7,900 \times 0.077 \times 0.45)$. Thus,

$$\left(\begin{array}{c} Stockholders' \\ equity \end{array}\right)_{2526} = \left(\begin{array}{c} Stockholders' \\ equity \end{array}\right)_{2525} + Net\ equity\ issues_{2526} + \left(\begin{array}{c} New \\ retained \\ earnings \end{array}\right)_{2526}$$

$$= \$4,700 + \$1,702 + \$766$$

The answer to question (i) is that Stockholders' equity at year-end 2526 is $7,168.

Find the answer to question (ii) by using formula 2.6 for shareholders' ROR. The stock price at year-end 2525 uses the definition for the P/B ratio:

$$1.4 = (price\ per\ share)_{2525} / (\$4,700 / 500)$$

$$(price\ per\ share)_{2525} = \$13.16$$

The company raises $1,702 by selling new stock at $13.16 a share. The company issues 129 shares (= $1,702 ÷ $13.16), thereby bringing to 629 shares (= 500 + 129) the total outstanding at year-end 2526. Now use the P/B definition again:

$$1.4 = (price\ per\ share)_{2526} / (\$7,168 / 629)$$

$$(price\ per\ share)_{2526} = \$15.95$$

The shareholder has a stock worth $13.16 at the beginning and $15.95 at the end, plus they receive a dividend. The dividend per share is $1.49 (= 2.8 \times \$7,900 \times 0.077 \times 0.55 ÷ 629)$.

$$shareholder's\ ROR_{2526} = \frac{\$15.95 + \$1.49 - \$13.16}{\$13.16}$$

$$= 32.5\%$$

The scenario describes a fairly hefty rate of return for shareholders equal to 32.5% for year 2526! By the way, notice that formula 2.7 relating ROR and ROE does not exactly apply to situations when the company issues new stock.

The last example in this chapter simply illustrates how an income statement connects two adjacent balance sheets.

EXAMPLE 14 Balance sheet dynamics

The Company's balance sheet for December 31, 2525, and its income statement for the year 2526 appear on the following page.

COMPANY BALANCE SHEET, 12/31/2525

	Assets	Liabilities	
Cash	$50,000	$100,000	Debt
PP&E	250,000	200,000	Stockholders' Equity (10,000 shares)
Total Assets	$300,000	$300,000	Total Liabilities & Equity

COMPANY INCOME STATEMENT, JAN. 1–DEC. 31, 2526

Sales	$500,000
– expenses (includes depreciation of $40,000)	450,000
= Net Income	$50,000
– Dividends	20,000
= New Retained Earnings	$30,000

The company does not plan to acquire new assets nor change their *Debt* or shares outstanding. Based solely on this information, what does the balance sheet look like on December 31, 2526?

SOLUTION

The balance sheet at year-end 2526 reflects an increased *Stockholders' equity* due to *New retained earnings*. Recall formula 2.11 that governs how Stockholders' equity changes over time. We are told that the company does not repurchase nor issue shares, so substitution shows:

$$SE_{2526} = \$200,000 + \$30,000$$
$$= \$230,000$$

On the balance sheet's right-hand side, *Debt* is unchanged and *Stockholders' equity* rises to $230,000. On the balance sheet's left-hand-side, *PP&E* falls due to the effects of *Depreciation*. We are told the company does not acquire new assets. Use formula 2.12 that governs the relation between depreciation and capital expenditures.

$$PP\&E_{2526} = \$250,000 - \$40,000$$
$$= \$210,000$$

Summarizing our results shows the year-end 2526 balance sheet as follows:

COMPANY BALANCE SHEET, 12/31/2526

	Assets	Liabilities	
Cash	$?	$100,000	Debt
PP&E	210,000	230,000	Stockholders' Equity (10,000 shares)
Total Assets	$330,000	$330,000	Total Liabilities & Equity

Properly accounting for the information from the problem setup leads to the balance sheet above. Yet what do we know about the proper amount for the *Cash* line item. The answer: *everything*. Because Total assets must equal Total liabilities and equity, and all other items are specified, *Cash* **must** equilibrate the balance sheet—cash must rise to $120,000!

This example utilizes the bottom-line identity of balance sheets: the sum of the right-hand-side always equals the sum of the left-hand-side. The problem gives sufficient information in the setup for determining the balance sheet's right-hand-side: the only change is *Stockholders' equity*. On the left-hand-side, *PP&E* falls because of *Depreciation*. The question that undoubtedly pops-up, though, is how and why does *Cash* rise?

Inspection of the income statement shows that *Depreciation* was subtracted in order to compute *New retained earnings*. The company, though, never had to "pay" or write a check for *Depreciation*; this is a non-cash charge. So the company actually has cash "flowing" into the checking account equal to the $30,000 *New retained earnings* plus the $40,000 *Depreciation*. If the company does not spend this $70,000 then the *Cash* account on the balance sheet increases by $70,000 and closes the year at $120,000. Lessons in the next chapter explain that the distinction between "cash flow" and income is important.

EXERCISES 2.4
Numerical quickies

1. At year-end 2525 the company has total assets of $3,700 financed by Debt of $1,100 and Stockholders' equity of $2,600. For year 2526 the company forecasts an asset turnover ratio (= sales$_{2526}$ ÷ total assets$_{2525}$) of 3.8, a net profit margin of 7.80%, and a dividend payout ratio of 45%. There are 260 shares outstanding. If no additional shares are issued, what is the equity book value per share at year-end 2526?

2. On January 1, the company has total assets of $4,800 financed by debt of $1,670 and *Stockholders' equity* of $3,130; for 900 common shares outstanding, the equity price-to-book ratio is 0.80. During the subsequent year the company does not issue new shares. They also expect an asset turnover ratio (= *Sales$_t$* ÷ Total assets$_{t-1}$) of 3.5; a 9% net profit margin; and a 30% payout ratio. If the year-end equity price-to-book ratio were 0.90, what year-end shareprice is forecast? ©BA13

3. At year-end 2525, Stockholders' Equity is $4,000 and there are 170 common shares outstanding. For 2526, sales should equal $18,800, the net profit margin is 4.70%, the payout ratio is 55%, and no shares are issued or repurchased. If the equity price-to-book ratio at year-end 2525 is 0.80, and it moves to 0.90 at year-end 2526, what is the shareprice at year-end 2526? ©BA12a

Challengers

4. At year-end 2525, Stockholders' Equity is $3,800 and there are 100 common shares outstanding. For 2526, sales should equal $12,540, the net profit margin is 6.40%, the payout ratio is 60%, and no shares are issued or repurchased. If the equity price-to-book ratio at year-end 2525 is 0.67, and it moves to 0.84 at year-end 2526, what is the shareholders' annual rate of return for 2526? ©BA12b

5. At year-end 2525 the company has total assets of $5,800 financed by Debt of $2,400 and Stockholders' equity of $3,400. For 500 common shares outstanding, the equity price-to-book ratio is 1.25. During 2526, they expect sales equal to $25,500 and a gross margin (=operating income before depreciation ÷ sales) of 22%. Depreciation is expected to equal $1,280 and interest charges will equal 12% of Debt. Corporate taxes equal 32% of taxable income, and the dividend payout ratio (=dividends ÷ net income) is 58%. Suppose the company has no intention of borrowing more money or buying more assets. What would be the percentage change in shareprice for 2526 that could be supported if the equity price to book ratio were to remain constant? ©BA2dm

6. At year-end 2525 the company has total assets of $3,100 financed by Debt of $1,500 and Stockholders' equity of $1,600. For year 2526 the company forecasts an asset turnover ratio (= sales$_{2526}$ ÷ total assets$_{2525}$) of 4.5, a net profit margin of 7.60%, and a dividend payout ratio of 40%. There are 150 shares outstanding and, at year-end 2525, the price-to-earnings ratio is 14.1. Throughout year 2526 no additional shares are issued, and the price-to-earnings ratio remains unchanged. Suppose that the net income is 7.3% larger in 2526 than in 2525. Find the shareholder annual rate of return for year 2526. ©BA14

7. At year-end 2525 the company has total assets of $4,900 financed by Debt of $1,000 and Stockholders' equity of $3,900. For year 2526 the company forecasts an asset turnover ratio (= sales$_{2526}$ ÷ total assets$_{2525}$) of 3.5, a net profit margin (= net income ÷ sales) of 6.50%, and a dividend payout ratio (=dividends÷net income) of 55%. There are 390 shares outstanding and, at year-end 2525, the price-to-earnings ratio is 14.5. If no additional shares are issued, and the price-to-earnings ratio remains unchanged, what is the shareprice at year-end 2526? ©BA1c

Problems 8 & 9 pertain to this setup
Find below the Company balance sheet for year-end 2525.

BALANCE SHEET, 12/31/2525

Current Assets	$1,800	$3,600	Debt
PP&E	$7,300	$5,500	Stockholders equity (700 shares
	$9,100	$9,100	Total

For year 2526 the company forecasts an asset turnover ratio (= sales$_{2526}$ ÷ total assets$_{2525}$) of 3.1, a net profit margin (= net income ÷ sales) of 8.7%, a dividend payout ratio (=dividends ÷ net income) of 55%, and depreciation that is 22% of beginning-of-year PP&E. Throughout year 2526 Debt remains unchanged, and the P/B ratio of 0.8 is expected to remain constant. The company expects to make capital expenditures such that for the year-end 2526 balance sheet PP&E is $400 larger than on the 2525 balance sheet. Suppose the *Capital expenditure* is financed *exclusively* by issuing new shares at the stock price of year-end 2525.

8. Find Stockholders' equity at year-end 2526. ©BA9am
9. Find the stockholders' rate of return for year 2526. ©BA9cm
10. For year 2526 the company forecasts sales of $40,000, an asset turnover ratio (= sales$_{2526}$ ÷ total assets$_{2525}$) of 1.5, a net profit margin (= net income ÷ sales) of 6.1%, a dividend payout ratio (=dividends ÷ net income) of 60%, and a debt-to-equity ratio (= total debt ÷ stockholders equity) of 111%. The company expects the equity price-to-book ratio of 1.40 to remain constant. Contrast for year 2526 the shareholder's book return-on-equity (= net income$_{2526}$ ÷ stockholder's equity$_{2525}$) and market rate of return. ©BA11a

ANSWERS TO CHAPTER 2 EXERCISES

EXERCISES 2.2A
1. Equity book value per share is ($7,100 ÷ 250), or $28.40. The company *P/B* therefore equals ($24.30 ÷ $28.40), or 0.86. *P/B* for the peer group is 0.67. The company *P/B* is a little higher than the peer group's, and to the extent that comparing their ratios is valid (the chapter on stock valuation discusses this more fully), the following inferences apply: the price the stock market assigns to a dollar of assets is larger for the company than for peer group, so either (i) the company stock is over-valued relative to the peer group, or (ii) the peer group is undervalued relative to the company.
2. Company market capitalization equals $41 x 490 million, or $20,090 million (just over $20 billion). The company *P/B* equals ($41 ÷ $35), or 1.17.
3. The stock price today is $23(1+.032), and today's market capitalization is $23(1+.032)(260 million), or $6.17 billion. Today's *change* in market cap is $23(032)(260 million), or $191.6 million.

4. Market cap for the Raider equals $9,500 x 3.80, or $36,100. Target market cap is $3,600 x 1.50, or $5,400. Conglomerate market cap therefore equals ($36,100 + $5,400), or $41,500.

5. The Conglomerate shareprice equals its market cap divided by total number of shares outstanding. Total number of shares equals {820 + 770x(1/5)}, or 974. Conglomerate shareprice consequently equals ($41,500 ÷ 974), or $42.61.

6. Conglomerate *Stockholders' equity* equals ($9,500 + $3,600), or $13,100. Conglomerate *P/B* therefore equals ($41,500 ÷ $13,100), or 3.17.

7. The value of 820 Raider shares before the merger equals its market cap, or $36,100. The value of those 820 shares after the merger is ($42.61 x 820), or $34,940. The total Raider loss on all shares is ($36,100 – $34,940), or $1,160. This sum also equals the total gain by Target shareholders.

8. Raider shareprice before the merger is ($9,500 x 3.80 ÷ 820), or $44.02. The loss for each Raider share due to the merger is ($44.02 – $42.61), or $1.41. This represents a 3.2 percent decline in wealth {= ($42.61 – $44.02) / $44.02; also equals $1,160 ÷ $36,100}. Target shareprice before the merger is ($3,600 x 1.50 ÷ 770), or $7.01. Target shareholders tender 5 Target shares worth $35.05 and receive one Conglomerate share worth $42.61, so their wealth increases 21.5 percent {= ($42.61 – $35.05) / $35.05; also equals $1,160 ÷ $5,400}.

EXERCISES 2.2B

1. No! Appearance on the balance sheet of a liability means that the company already has received financing from that source. For this problem, shareholders have been an historical source of $12 million. As to the future, well that is different. Maybe the company put the money in the cash account, in which case the funds are available for paying bills. If the company bought plant and equipment that over the next few decades should return profits, then right now maybe the money for paying bills is unavailable. The bottom line: insights about sources of funds provides little insight about uses of funds. Paying bills is a use of funds, *Stockholders' equity* is a source of funds, and one implies little about the other.

2. Cash is $6,800 on the balance sheet for 12/31/2525 and $7,900 for 12/31/2526. An increase in an asset is a use of funds. Maybe during year 2525 the company took out a loan for $1,100 and put the money into its cash account. The increase in the liability (loans) would have been a source of funds. Realize the importance of temporal perspective, here. The increase in *Cash* was a use of funds during year 2526. As for the future, well because more money is in the account then potentially the company can withdraw more *Cash* than otherwise. When that draw-down occurs, the decline in *Cash* (or any asset) will represent a source of funds. Financial statements document history, the increase in *Cash* represents a historical use of funds. But more *Cash* means more potential future sources—financial statements, however, do not document the future!

3. *Net working capital* equals *Current assets* minus *Current liabilities*. Components of *Current assets* include *Receivables* (decreases $4,400) and *Cash* (increases $6,100). Components of *Current liabilities* include *Payables* (increases $6,800) and *Short-term notes* (increases $5,600). Long-term accounts such as *PP&E* and *Long-term debt* do not affect *Net working capital*. The *Current assets* increase $1,700 (= $6,100 – $4,400), while *Current liabilities* increases $12,400 (= $6,800 + $5,600). Because *Current liabilities* increases more than *Current assets* there is a decline in *Net working capital*. The change in *NWC* equals $-10,700 (= $1,700 – $12,400) and is a source of funds.

1. When F and B represent a flow and balance variable, respectively, the plausible definitions for a financial ratio include F_t and either B_t or B_{t-1}. Perhaps the ratio, for example, equals F_t/B_t or F_t/B_{t-1} or $F_t \div \{(B_t + B_{t-1})/2\}$, or B_t/F_t, etc. Ratios in table 2.5 that are a flow divided by a balance include return-on-assets, return-on-equity, asset turnover, inventory turnover, and dividend yield. Ratios that are a balance divided by a flow include average age of inventory, average collection period, average payment period, price-to-earnings, price-to-cash flow, price-to-free cash flow, and price to sales.

2. Table 2.5 shows the formula for return-on-equity is *Net income ÷ Stockholders' equity*. Because this formula relates a flow to a balance, however, three defensible computations for your company's *ROE* exist: 13.5% (= $132,500 ÷ $980,000); or 14.6% (= $132,500 ÷ $905,000); or 14.1% {= $132,500 ÷ (($980,000 + $905,000)/2)}. While you know the peer group *ROE* is 14.0%, you do not know which formula they use. So you cannot say with certainty whether your company's *ROE* is larger or smaller than the peer group's. They are pretty close, though, irrespective of formula.

3. *Total assets* equals the sum of *Total liabilities* ($85,000) and *Stockholders' equity* ($114,000), so *Total assets* is $199,000. The equity multiplier equals *Total assets ÷ Stockholders' equity*, which is 1.75. The debt-to-assets ratio is 43% (=$85,000/$199,000), and debt-to-equity ratio is 0.75 (=$85,000/$114,000).

4. *Earnings per share* equals $42 million divided by 20 million shares, or $2.10. The P/E ratio is $136.80 / $2.10, or 65.1. This is much larger than the traditional average P/E that ranges between 10 and 15.

5. *Net income* equals $129,000 x 0.064, or $8,256.

6. The income statement looks like this:

sales	$32,000	
– cost of goods good	not needed	
= earnings before depreciation	8,320	(= $32,000 x 0.26)
– depreciation	1,030	
= operating income	7,290	
– interest	2,500	
= taxable income	4,790	
– taxes	1,629	(= $4,790 x 0.34)
= net income	3,161	

7. *Net income* equals $3,125 (= $1.25 x 2,500). *Net income* divided by *Sales* is 0.115, so *Sales* equals $27,174 (= $3,125 ÷ 0.115). Therefore *Total assets* equals $7,548 (= $27,174 ÷ 3.6).

8. A P/E of 26.4 with earnings of $4.50 implies that the shareprice is $118.80 (= 26.4 x $4.50). The end-of-period shareprice is $118.80 and the dividend is $1.57 (= $4.50 x 0.35). The ROR of 32% equals ($118.80 + $1.57 – P_{t-1}) / P_{t-1}. Solve the preceding for P_{t-1} and find that the previous price was $91.19 [= ($118.80 + $1.57) / (1 + 0.32)]. The shareprice capital gain to $118.80 from $91.19 equals $27.61.

9. An inventory turnover at 9.5 with annual cost-of-goods sold of $50,000 implies that (a) *Inventory* equals $5,263 (= $50,000 ÷ 9.5), and (b) the average age of inventory is 38.4 days (= 365 ÷ 9.5). The average age of inventory decreases by 5 days to become 33.4 days. The new inventory turnover becomes 10.9 (= 365 ÷ 33.4), suggesting that the company turns over inventory more frequently than before. Compute that *Inventory* therefore equals $4,578 (= $50,000 ÷ 10.9). The decline in *Inventory* on the balance sheet to $4,578 from $5,263 suggests a source of funds equal to $685 (= $5,263 – $4,578).

10. Find *Net income* from the ratios in the setup. *Sales* equals 3.2 x $6,400; *Taxable income* equals *Sales* x 0.12 – (0.08 x $2,600). *Net income* equals *Taxable income* x (1 – 0.30). Thus, *Net income* equals $1,575 [= { (3.2 x $6,400 x 0.12) – (0.08 x $2,600) } x 0.70].

11. The P/E of 11÷ given *Net income* of $1,575 and 325 shares outstanding implies a stock price of $55.72 (= 11.5 x $1,575 ÷ 325).

12. The P/B at year-end 2525 of 3.6 with *Stockholders' equity* of $3,800 and 325 shares outstanding implies a stock price of $42.09 (= 3.6 x $3,800 ÷ 325). The stock price begins at $42.09 and a year later equals $55.72. Also, the share receives a dividend of $1.70 (= $1,575 x 0.35 ÷ 325). The stockholders' rate of return therefore equals 36.4% {= ($55.72 + $1.70 – $42.09) ÷ $42.09}.

EXERCISES 2.3B

1. When P/B is constant then P and B are changing at the same rate: the capital gains rate equals the percentage change in book value. The explanation therefore can focus on the role of the dividend yield ($Dividend_t \div P_{t-1}$ and $Dividend_t \div B_{t-1}$). When the P/B < 1 then the shareholders' ROR ≥ ROE because $Dividend_t \div P_{t-1} > Dividend_t \div B_{t-1}$. With a relatively small stock price the market dividend yield exceeds the book dividend yield (a relatively small price buys a relatively large dividend). Conversely, when the P/B > 1 then the shareholders' ROR ≤ ROE because $Dividend_t \div P_{t-1} < Dividend_t \div B_{t-1}$, The equality for both cases occurs when the payout ratio is zero.

2. The ROE equals 9.1% x 1.7 x (equity multiplier). The debt-to-asset ratio of 60% means the equity-to-asset ratio is 40%, and the reciprocal of 40% is the equity multiplier (2.5). Now multiply the three parts together and find that the ROE equals 38.7%.

3. Use formula 2.7. For company X find the unknown ROR:
   ROR = 26% { 1 – (0.30)(1.35 – 1)/1.35 }; ROR = 24.0%.
   Now for company Z use the formula:
   ROR = 26% { 1 – (0.30)(2.75 – 1)/2.75 }; ROR = 21.0%.
   The difference between ROR equals 3 percentage points.

4. Use formula 2.7. For company X find the unknown ROR:
   ROR = 18% { 1 – (0.25)(0.8 – 1)/0.8 }; ROR = 19.1%.
   Now for company Z use the formula to find the unknown ROE (given the ROR of 19.1%).
   19.1% = ROE { 1 – (0.25)(2.75 – 1)/2.75 }; ROE = 22.7%.
   The ROE must be 4.7% bigger for company Z than company X in order for the two to provide the same shareholders' ROR.

5. Compute the company numbers directly from the financial statements. The table below summarizes everything:

	ROE	NI/Sales	Sales/TA	TA/SE
company	42.6%	6.9%	3.8	1.6
industry	30.9%	5.1%	??	1.6

Find the industry equity multiplier from the debt-to-assets ratio as follows using formula 2.5 [or reason that if debt-to-assets is 37.8% then equity-to-assets is 62.2% and equity multiplier equals (62.2%)⁻¹.] Find the unknown industry Sales/TA as 0.309 x (5.1%)⁻¹ x 62.2%; that equals 3.8. The company ROE is larger than the industry average because the company net profit margin is larger (and all else is equal).

EXERCISES 2.3C

1. The basic reason that the tax rate does not enter the total breakeven point when *Preferred dividends* equal $0 is due to the assumption that taxes are a constant proportion of taxable income. With taxable income of zero the *Taxes due* equal zero, the *EAC* equals zero, and the company

is at the total breakeven point. Taxes matter when the company is beyond the total breakeven point. Suppose, for example, that the tax rate is 25%. To earn an extra $1 of *EAC* the company must earn an extra $1.33 of taxable income [=$1/(1 – 0.25)]. Taxes are a big deal, only not at the breakeven point.

2. Straightforward application of formula 2.9b shows that the quantity of production at the operating breakeven point equals 2,400 units [= $12,000 ÷ ($12 - $7)].

3. The company must cover the $34,000 fixed costs to suppliers plus the $15,000 operating income to them self, so they must net $49,000 (= $34,000 + $15,000). Use formula 2.9b and find that the quantity of production at the operating breakeven point equals 8,167 units [= $49,000 ÷ ($22 - $16)]. Reconstruct the income statement and verify that *EBIT*, also known as operating income, equals $15,000 when *Sales revenue* is $179,667 (= 8,167 x $22) and *Total fixed costs* equal $34,000 and *Total variable costs* equal $130,667 (= 8,167 x $16).

4. Use formula 2.9a and find that the *Sales revenue* at the operating breakeven point equals $74,359 [= $38,250 ÷ (1 - $40,400/$83,195)]. Verify that *EBIT* equals $0 when *Sales revenue* is $74,359 and *Total variable costs* is $36,109 (= $74,359 x $40,400/$83,195).

5. Use formula 2.9a and find that with $EBIT^{target}$ = $6,300 the *Sales revenue* equals $103,534 [= ($42,500 + $6,300) ÷ (1 - $50,500/$95,525)]. Verify that *Total variable costs* equal $54,734 (= $103,534 x $50,500/$95,525).

6. Use formula 2.10a and find that the *Sales revenue* at the total breakeven point equals $79,993 [= ($34,000 + $3,825 + (500/(1-0.30))) ÷ (1 - $50,500/$97,450)]. *EBIT* equals $4,539 and may be computed as $79,993 x (1 - $50,500/$97,450) - $34,000.

7. Use formula 2.10a and find that the *Sales revenue* is $96,829 when EAC^{target} = $7,900 [= ($29,750 + $2,550 + (350+$7,900)/(1-0.25))) ÷ (1 - $50,500/$91,350)]. *EBIT* equals $13,550 and may be computed as $96,829 x (1 - $50,500/$91,350) - $29,750.

8. Find the after-tax contribution margin is 0.2538 [= (1 – 0.30) x (1 – $475,000/$745,200)]. This means that each extra dollar of sales contributes 25.38 cents to *Net income*. Find that *Net income* must increase by $35,714 to reach the ROE of 18% [= .19($125,000/0.14) - $125,000]. Consequently, sales must rise by $140,712 (= $35,714 ÷ 0.2538) to reach the 18% ROE.

9. Use formula 2.9a and find that the *Sales revenue* at the operating breakeven point equals $54,612 [= $34,000 ÷ (1 - $25,250/$66,900)]. This is a decline relative to the original *Sales revenue* of –18.4% [= ($54,612 - $66,900) ÷ $66,900].

10. Example 7 shows the relation between quantity sold when the operating margin is
Q = F / [p (1 – v/p – operating margin)]
Insert the numbers to find Q, the quantity sold when the operating margin equals 18%:
Q = $25,500 / [$45 (1 – 33/45 – 0.18)]
  = 6,538 units
Verify that with sales at 6,538 units the *Sales revenue* equals $294,231 (= 6,538 x $45); *Total variable costs* equal $215,769 (= 6,538 x $33); *Total fixed costs* equal $25,500; and the operating margin equals 18%, as requested [= ($294,231 - $215,769 - $25,500) ÷ $294,231].

11. Like the previous problem, find the quantity sold when the operating margin is 20%:
Q = $34,000 / [$30 (1 – 21/30 – 0.20)]
  = 11,333 units

With sales at 11,333 units the *Sales revenue* equals $340,000 (= 11,333 x $30).

12. Reconstruct the stylized income statement from the annual report and find that *Net income* equals $10,448. The ROE of 15.7% with *Net income* of $10,448 implies that *Stockholders' equity* is $66,545. To get an ROE of 24% the *Net income* must rise to $15,971 (an increase of $5,523). Compute the requisite *Sales revenue* either of two ways. Method 1: Plug numbers into formula 2.10a and find that *Sales revenue* is $120,925 [= ($42,750 + $3,825 + ($15,971)/(1-0.30)) ÷ (1 - $45,675/$107,175)]. Method 2: Divide the after-tax contribution margin of 0.4017 [= (1 − 0.30) x (1 - $45,675/$107,175)] into the extra *Net income* to find the extra *Sales revenue* is $13,750 (= $5,523 / 0.4017). Thus, sales must rise to $120,925 (= $107,175 + $13,750).

EXERCISES 2.4

1. *Sales* equals 3.8 x $3,700; *Net income* equals 0.078 x *Sales*; *New retained earnings* equals (1 − 0.45) x *Net income*; SE_{2526} equals *New retained earnings* plus $2,600; equity book value per share equals SE_{2526} ÷ 260. Thus, equity book value per share = { (3.8 x $3,700 x 0.078 x 0.55) + $2,600 } ÷ 260; which is $12.32.

2. *Sales* equals 3.5 x $4,800; *Net income* equals 0.09 x *Sales*, *New retained earnings* equals (1 − 0.30) x *Net income*; SE_{2526} equals *New retained earnings* plus $3,130; $price_{2526}$ equals SE_{2526} x 0.90 ÷ 900. Thus, $price_{2526}$ = { (3.5 x $4,800 x 0.09 x 0.70) + $3,130 } x 0.90 ÷ 900; which is $4.19.

3. *Net income* equals $18,800 x 0.047; *New retained earnings* equals (1 − 0.55) x *Net income*; SE_{2526} equals *New retained earnings* plus $4,000; equity book value per share equals SE_{2526} ÷ 170; $price_{2526}$ equals 0.90 x equity book value per share. Thus, $price_{2526}$ = { ($18,800 x 0.047 x 0.45) + $4,000 } ÷ 170 x 0.90; which is $23.28.

4. *Net income* equals $12,540 x 0.064; *New retained earnings* equals (1 − 0.60) x *Net income*; SE_{2526} equals *New retained earnings* plus $3,800; equity book value per share equals SE_{2526} ÷ 100; $price_{2526}$ equals 0.84 x equity book value per share. Thus, $price_{2526}$ = { ($12,540 x 0.064 x 0.40) + $3,800 } ÷ 100 x 0.84; which is $34.62. The beginning shareprice, $price_{2525}$, equals ($3,800 ÷ 100) x 0.67, which is $25.46. The dividend per share equals {($12,540 x 0.064 x 0.60) ÷ 100, which is $4.82. The shareholders' ROR equals ($34.62 + $4.82 − $25.46) ÷ $25.46, which is 55%.

5. With a constant P/B ratio the percentage changes in P and B are equal. Finding the percentage increase in shareprice therefore requires finding the percentage increase in *Stockholders' equity*. SE_{2525} is given as $3,400. SE_{2526} equals $3,400 plus *New retained earnings*$_{2526}$. Find *New retained earnings* by reconstructing the income statement. *Taxable income* equals $25,500 x 0.22 − $1,280 − (0.12 x $2,400); *Net income* equals (1 − 0.32) x *Taxable income*; *New retained earnings* equals (1 − 0.58) x *Net income*. Thus, *New retained earnings* = { $25,500 x 0.22 − $1,280 − (0.12 x $2,400) } x 0.68 x 0.42; which is $1,154. SE_{2526} equals $4,554; the percentage increase is $1,154 ÷ $3,400; which is 34%.

6. With a constant P/E ratio the percentage changes in P and E are equal. The setup states that E increases 7.3% during 2526, so therefore the stock price increases 7.3%, too. The shareholders' ROR equals ($price_{2526}$ + $dividend_{2526}$ − $price_{2525}$) ÷ $price_{2525}$, which also may be written as %Δprice + ($dividend_{2526}$ ÷ $price_{2525}$). Find $dividend_{2526}$ and $price_{2525}$ as follows. *Sales* equals 4.5 x $3,100; *Net income* equals 0.076 x *Sales*; *Dividends per share* equals *Net income* x 0.40 ÷ 150. Thus, $dividend_{2526}$ = 4.5 x $3,100 x 0.076 x 0.40 ÷ 150, which is $2.83. Notice that $price_{2526}$ equals 14.1 x *earnings per share*$_{2526}$; thus $price_{2526}$ = 14.1 x 4.5 x $3,100 x 0.076 ÷ 150; which is $99.66. We know

price$_{2526}$ is 7.3% larger than *price*$_{2525}$. Thus, *price*$_{2525}$ = $99.76 ÷ (1 + 0.073); which is $92.88. Therefore, *dividend*$_{2526}$ ÷ *price*$_{2525}$ equals $2.83 ÷ $92.88; which is 3.0%. The shareholders' ROR equals 7.3% + 3.0%, which is 10.3%.

7. *Sales* equals 3.5 *x* $4,900; *Net income* equals 0.065 *x Sales*; *Earnings per share* equals *Net income* ÷ 390; *price*$_{2526}$ equals 14.5 *x Earnings per share* . Thus, *price*$_{2526}$ = { (3.5 *x* $4,900 *x* 0.065 ÷ 390) *x* 14.5 }, which is $41.45.

8. *Sales* equals 3.1 *x* $9,100; *Net income* equals *Sales x* 0.087; *New retained earnings* equals (1 − 0.55) *x Net income*; *SE*$_{2526}$ equals $5,500 plus *New equity issues* plus *New retained earnings*; *New equity issues* equals the *Capital expenditure*, (0.22 *x* $7,300 + 400), which equals $2,006. Therefore, *SE*$_{2526}$ = { (3.1 *x* $9,100 *x* 0.087 *x* 0.45) + $5,500 + $2,006}; which is $8,610.

9. The beginning shareprice, *price*$_{2525}$, equals ($5,500 ÷ 700) *x* 0.80, which is $6.29. The ending shareprice, *price*$_{2526}$, equals ($8,610 ÷ #*shares*) *x* 0.80. The #*shares* equals the 700 original shares plus the new issues. Issuing equity to finance the *Capital expenditure* of $2,006, at $6.29 per share, means that 319 shares were issued. Therefore, *price*$_{2526}$ = ($8,610 ÷ 1,019) *x* 0.80; which is $6.76. The dividend per share equals {(3.1 *x* $9,100 *x* 0.087 *x* 0.55) ÷ 1,019, which is $1.32. The shareholders' ROR equals ($6.76 + $1.32 − $6.29) ÷ $6.29, which is 29%.

10. There are two ways to solve this. First, let's use the memory intensive approach. Use the DuPont decomposition to find ROE (recall that the equity multiplier equals 1 plus debt-to-equity).

ROE = net profit margin x asset turnover x equity multiplier
     = 6.1% x 1.5 x (1 + 1.11)
     = 19.3%

Now use formula 2.7 that relates ROR to ROE when the P/B is constant. Realize that because P/B is bigger than one we expect that the ROR is smaller than 19.3%.

ROR = 19.3% { 1 − (0.60)(1.4 − 1)/1.4 }
     = 16.0%.

The market ROR, as expected, is 16% and is somewhat smaller than the book ROE of 19.3%.

  The second approach for solving this problem is not memory intensive, it is more intuitive, but it takes more steps. Find net income$_{2526}$ is $2,440 (= $40,000 x .061); total dividends$_{2526}$ is $1,464 (= $2,440 x 0.60); new retained earnings$_{2526}$ is $976 (= $2440 − $1,464). Next combine the asset turnover and debt-to-equity ratios to find SE$_{2525}$ is $12,638 (D/SE = 1.11; D = 1.11 x SE; then D + SE = $40,000; 1.11SE + SE = $40,000/1.5; then solve for SE$_{2525}$); find that SE$_{2526}$ is $13,614 (= $12,638 + $976). Compute ROE as the ratio of net income$_{2526}$ to SE$_{2525}$, which is 19.3% (= $2,440 / $12,638). Compute market cap as SE x P/B for the ROR formula and find ROR is 16.0% {= ($1,464 + 1.4x$13,614 − 1.4x$12,638)/ (1.4x$12,638)}.

CHAPTER 3

Accounting for Growth

It is almost impossible for a company to remain unchanged from one year to the next. Some changes occur because of overt management actions, while other changes seem to happen all by themselves. Changes that occur over time, planned or otherwise, include "growth".

Growth is as natural to businesses as to households and individuals. Growth is a complex yet important phenomenon. Companies sometimes grow too slow—they may fail if they do not take advantage of opportunities. Alternatively, sometimes companies grow too fast—they may fail as a result of ill-advised explosive growth. Growth is just like many other phenomena: there can be too much as well as too little. The table below illustrates that company growth rates vary widely.

TABLE 3.1

Growth rates for selected variables of American corporate icons. Each number is the annual average percentage change in the respective variable for three years, 1998-2000 (stock price adjusted for splits). Data are from the American Association of Individual Investors, February 2001.

Corporation Name	%Δ Total assets	%Δ Annual sales	%Δ net income	%Δ dividend / share	%Δ stock price
AOL-Time Warner, Inc.	93%	46%	66%	0%	102%
AT&T Corporation	67	7	−2	0	−8
Exxon Mobil Corporation	2	−4	9	3	n.a.
Ford Motor Company	−1	3	18	8	7
General Electric Company	15	12	6	15	23
General Motors Corp.	9	3	9	8	6
IBM	1	4	10	9	35
Microsoft Corporation	53	24	40	0	33
Wal-Mart Stores, Inc.	25	16	21	22	41
Walt Disney Company	4	4	−15	7	−21

There are many ways to measure company growth: percentage change in total assets, net income, stock price, or even number of employees. The table reveals that huge growth in total assets usually relates to huge revenue and stock price growth, but not always. At more moderate levels of growth, the relations are even more confused. Surely growth matters, as every business and household knows, but what are its effects and how can we plan for it?

Understanding the relation between growth and financial statements assists the planning process. This chapter contains lessons examining how growth affects flows and balances. Section 1 focuses on the effect of growth on financing needs. Section 2 looks for insights about growth rates that financial statements may reveal. Section 3 examines effects of growth on cash flows.

1. FINANCIAL FORECASTING

A successful company anticipates financing needs long before it requires funds. Once the company identifies the need, management arranges financing just in case the need eventuates. For any business, as for any household too, it's stressful to learn today that a large sum of money is needed tomorrow. Planning financial needs is critically important.

There are two general approaches for forecasting financing needs. One relies primarily on cash flow analysis and the other primarily on balance sheets. The objective of both approaches is identical: determine whether the company in the future expects sources of funds to satisfy requisite uses. Results of the analysis suggest that the company expects either a surplus or a shortfall.

DEFINITION 3.1 Surplus and shortfall

Management should forecast future financing needs long before funds are needed.

When forecast sources of funds $\begin{Bmatrix} > \\ < \end{Bmatrix}$ forecast uses of funds

then the company expects a $\begin{Bmatrix} surplus \\ deficit\ or\ shortfall \end{Bmatrix}$.

When the company forecasts a surplus then management is in the fortunate position of debating prudent uses of surplus funds. Conversely, when the company faces an expected shortfall then management must take strategic action to avoid financial misfortune.

1.A. Cash budgeting

In a *cash budgeting* analysis the company sums expected revenues (sources of funds) and subtracts expected cash costs (uses of funds). A surplus occurs when more money comes in than goes out. Conversely, a deficit occurs when more money goes out than comes in. An advantage of the cash flow approach is its directness. Most students intuitively understand cash budgeting, and most routinely conduct one: estimate tuition and costs of living, estimate likely revenue sources, and make arrangements to cover shortfalls. The company analysis is analogous, as the example below simply illustrates.

EXAMPLE 1 Find the surplus or shortfall

The third quarter just concluded. September's monthly sales were $60,000 and the company paid shareholders quarterly dividends totaling $8,000. The end-of-September quarterly balance sheet lists *Cash* at $10,500. The company never wants the cash account to drop below $10,000 because the cash buffer provides protection against forecasting errors. The company forecasts the following events during the next four months (October–January):

    a. monthly sales forecasts equal $64,000; $80,000; $95,000; and $60,000; 40% of all sales revenue is collected in month of sale and the remainder is collected the subsequent month

b. cash variable costs for taxes and supplies equal 78% of the previous month's sales
c. cash fixed costs equal $12,000 per month
d. an extraordinary debt payment of $14,000 is due in November
e. quarterly dividends payable in December will be 4% larger than September's dividends

Find the company's pre-tax net cash flow each month and determine financing needs.

SOLUTION

Summarize numbers from the setup into tabular form.

	October	November	December	January
S_t, sales	$64,000	$80,000	$95,000	$60,000
collections from S_{t-1}	$36,000	$38,400	$48,000	$57,000
collections from S_t	$25,600	$32,000	$38,000	$24,000
variable costs	$46,800	$49,920	$62,400	$74,100
fixed costs	$12,000	$12,000	$12,000	$12,000
extraordinary costs		$14,000	$8,320	
Beginning of month cash	$10,500	$13,300	$7,780	$11,060
cash inflows	$61,600	$70,400	$86,000	$81,000
cash outflows	$58,800	$75,920	$82,720	$86,100
pretax net cash flow	$2,800	-$5,520	$3,280	-$5,100
End of month cash	$13,300	$7,780	$11,060	$5,960

All entries are straightforward. During October the company has collections equal to 60% of September's sales (S_{t-1}), plus 40% of October's sales (S_t). The other 60% of October's sales is collected in November. Variable costs equal 78% of the previous months sales, and fixed costs always equal $12,000 per month. Extraordinary costs include the debt payment in November and dividends in December ($8,320 = $8,000 x 1.04).

The bottom panel presents the beginning of month cash balance. Cash inflows (that is, the sum of collections) increase the balance, whereas cash outflows (that is, the sum of variable plus fixed and extraordinary costs) decrease the balance. Pretax net cash flow equals the sum of inflows minus outflows—net cash flow equals sources minus uses of cash and measures that month's surplus or shortfall. In October the net cash flow of $2,800 raises the end of month cash balance to $13,300 (=$10,500 + $2,800). The company expects a surplus in October, and its cash balance exceeds the target minimum of $10,000.

In November the company expects a deficit of $5,520. Furthermore, the ending cash balance of $7,780 is less than the allowable minimum. To raise the balance to $10,000 the company must borrow an additional $2,220 (=$10,000 – $7,780). In December the company expects a surplus, however, and the short-term loan could be partially repaid. Finally, in January there is a deficit of $5,100. January's ending cash balance is $4,040 less than the desirable minimum (=$10,000 – $5,960), suggesting that management has a few months to arrange for financing or to institute pricing or cost polices that lessen the shortfall.

The most difficult task with a cash budgeting analysis is getting good forecasts. Otherwise, cash budgeting is mechanical. Few financial exercises, however, are as important as cash budgeting—figuring whether checks are going to bounce because of a cash shortfall is, as we all intuitively know, necessary for financial health.

One temporal trait of cash budgeting merits mention. It is impossible to detect a surplus or deficit at a frequency that is shorter than the cash flow period. The example above employs a monthly frequency for tabulating cash flows. This means that daily or weekly deficits are undetectable. Consider the October scenario, for example. The monthly surplus is $2,800. It is possible, though, that the cash outflows of $58,800 may occur during the first half of the month whereas the inflows of $61,600 occur during the latter half. Because the checking account begins with $10,500 then the checks written to suppliers may start bouncing before the money from customers arrives. The key point is that monthly cash budgets detect monthly shortfalls, but are incapable of detecting weekly shortfalls. For that, construct a weekly cash budget!

With cash budgeting the details overwhelm the analysis. Forming long range plans with cash budgets is difficult because detailed forecasts of cash flows are difficult to obtain. For long-run planning, balance sheets come to the rescue!

1.B. Balance sheet forecasts

This section examines a method for forecasting financing needs that depends on the balance sheet identity that *Total assets* equals *Total liabilities & Stockholders' equity*. The balance sheet approach shines because of its stark simplicity and irrefutable logic: make a forecast of (a) expected *Total assets*, and (b) expected *Total liabilities & Stockholders' equity*. The "External Financing Needs" (*EFN*) equals the difference

---

FORMULA 3.1 External financing needs

EFN is a positive number when expected uses of cash exceed expected sources.

$$\begin{pmatrix} External \\ Financing \\ Needs \end{pmatrix} = \begin{pmatrix} expected \\ Total \ assets \end{pmatrix} - \begin{pmatrix} expected \\ Total \ liabilities \\ \& \ Stockholders' \\ equity \end{pmatrix}$$

When *EFN* is positive, there are insufficient funds to finance the company's expected assets and the company should arrange additional financing to cover the shortfall. A negative *EFN*, conversely, implies a surplus—the company expects to have more than enough financing to support expected assets.

B1. Fundamentals of forecasting with reliance on balance sheets

This example illustrates fundamental principles about forecasting financing needs with reliance on balance sheets.

EXAMPLE 2 Find EFN in a static setting

Suppose a company's balance sheet looks as follows:

COMPANY BALANCE SHEET

	Assets		Liabilities
Cash	$ 100	$ 200	Current Liabilities
Inventory	400	350	Long term Debt
PP&E	500	450	Stockholders' Equity
Total Assets	*$1,000*	*$1,000*	*Total Liabilities & Equity*

Also suppose that *Sales* equal $2,500 and that *Cost-of-goods sold* equal $1,875. The company realizes that if they cut by 30 days the length of time that inventory stays on the shelf before sold, and all else remains the same, the company reduces the amount of inventory required. If the company proceeds with this inventory policy change, what is the effect on external financing needs?

SOLUTION

The first step in solving this problem is to compute the length of time inventory stays on the shelf before sold. The definition from table 2.5 for the "average age of inventory" is:

$$\begin{pmatrix} average \\ age \ of \\ inventory \end{pmatrix} = \frac{365 \times (Balance \ Sheet \ Inventory)}{(Annual \ Cost-of-goods \ sold)}$$

$$= \frac{365 \times \$400}{\$1,875}$$

$$= 77.8 \ days$$

Reducing by 30 the number of days that inventory remains on the shelf lowers the average age of inventory to 47.8 days.

In the preceding definition, set average age of inventory to 47.8 and hold cost-of-goods-sold the same as before at $1,875. Solve for the new balance sheet *Inventory* as:

$$47.8 \text{ days} = \frac{365 \times (Balance\ Sheet\ Inventory)}{\$1,875}$$

$$Balance\ Sheet\ Inventory = \$245$$

The balance sheet after the policy change lists *Inventory* at $245. The original balance sheet lists Inventory at $400. This policy change decreases the amount of inventory that the company keeps on hand.

What does the new balance sheet look like, and how much is *EFN*? This elementary yet important question deserves discussion. So far, we deduce the following:

FORECAST COMPANY BALANCE SHEET (PRELIMINARY)

Assets			Liabilities
Cash	$ 100	$ 200	Current Liabilities
Inventory	245	350	Long term Debt
PP&E	500	450	Stockholders' Equity
Total Assets	*$845*	*$1,000*	*Total Liabilities & Equity*

EFN is found as

$$\begin{pmatrix} External \\ Financing \\ Needs \end{pmatrix} = \begin{pmatrix} expected \\ Total\ assets \end{pmatrix} - \begin{pmatrix} expected \\ Total\ liabilities \\ \&\ Stockholder's \\ equity \end{pmatrix}$$

$$= \quad \$845 - \$1,000$$

$$= \quad \$-155$$

The analysis shows the policy change results in a surplus of $155.

The preceding analysis finds that the company expects a surplus. The analysis has not yet finalized a prediction about the appearance of the forecast balance sheet. The actual balance sheet that eventuates depends on the policy choice that management pursues. Carefully consider the company's options if they adopt the policy change.

The final balance sheet cannot look like the preliminary one forecast above. The forecast one does not equalize the right and left-hand side bottom-lines. The reason a balance sheet must "balance" is not because it is a federal law, nor because it is the ethical thing to do. Instead, the balance sheet balances because it is **impossible** for it to be unbalanced. It is just as likely to have a coin with only one side as it is to have an unbalanced balance sheet. It just won't happen!

Consider the company with its surplus of $155. What can it do? While there are many possibilities, consider the following three.

Case 1: Maybe the company chooses to hold the surplus as cash, in which case the final balance sheet appears as follows:

FORECAST COMPANY BALANCE SHEET (FINAL, CASE 1)

Assets			Liabilities
Cash	$ 255	$ 200	Current Liabilities
Inventory	245	350	Long term Debt
PP&E	500	450	Stockholders' Equity
Total Assets	*$1,000*	*$1,000*	*Total Liabilities & Equity*

Cash increases by $155. That is, *Total as*sets rises to equilibrate with *Total liabilities & Stockholders' equity* and now everything balances.

Case 2: Perhaps the company uses the surplus to pay an extraordinary dividend to its shareholders. For this choice, the final balance sheet is:

FORECAST COMPANY BALANCE SHEET (FINAL, CASE 2)

Assets			Liabilities
Cash	$ 100	$ 200	Current Liabilities
Inventory	245	350	Long term Debt
PP&E	500	295	Stockholders' Equity
Total Assets	*$845*	*$845*	*Total Liabilities & Equity*

Notice that *Stockholders' equity* decreases by $155. This occurs because the company income statement lists *Dividends* that are $155 larger than otherwise, and *New retained earnings* (and *Stockholders' equity*) are lower by $155. That is, *Total liabilities & Stockholders' equity* falls to equilibrate with *Total assets*. Everything balances.

Case 3: Finally, suppose that the company uses the surplus to pay off some debt, in which case the final balance sheet is:

FORECAST COMPANY BALANCE SHEET (FINAL, CASE 3)

Assets			Liabilities
Cash	$ 100	$ 200	Current Liabilities
Inventory	245	195	Long term Debt
PP&E	500	450	Stockholders' Equity
Total Assets	*$845*	*$845*	*Total Liabilities & Equity*

Debt decreases by $155 and everything balances.

Financial planning determines whether a surplus or deficit is likely. Once the outcome is determined, management pursues strategic decisions that advance the corporate mission: namely, maximize wealth creation for stakeholders and capitalists. Typically, long-range forecasts with balance sheets are the best analysis for seeing "the forest", whereas to see "the trees" employ the always-essential cash budgeting.

Growing a company often requires access to capital. For comparative purposes imagine how growing a household requires access to capital. Buying a car usually involves borrowing money. And certainly buying a house requires borrowing money. Paying for college, as you may already know, too often requires access to capital from financial markets. Before continuing lessons on forecasting external financing needs, learn a little about the premier forum for raising capital: the *New York Stock Exchange*.

STREET-BITE The New York Stock Exchange

The New York Stock Exchange traces origins to 1792 when two dozen New York City stockbrokers and merchants signed an agreement for trading securities. For years the trading forum was on Wall Street, so-named after a 12-foot high stockade fence constructed in 1653 as protection for the fledgling village of New Amsterdam (apparently the wall was ineffective because in 1664 England captured the town from the Netherlands and renamed it New York). The NYSE moved operations a few blocks south to Broad Street in 1865 and still is there today in their glorious building constructed in 1903.

The NYSE is a privately-held corporation. Its owners include member firms that own or lease a "seat" on the NYSE. Only members may buy and sell securities on the trading floor. Members meet rigorous professional standards set by the Exchange. The number of seats has remained constant at 1,366 since 1953. To get a seat you must buy or lease it from someone that already owns it. About 18 seats changed ownership in 2003. The highest price ever paid for a seat was $2.65 million in 1999. Going-price for a NYSE seat in summer 2004 was about $1.2 million. Wall Street companies such as Merrill-Lynch or Goldman-Sachs own several seats in order to trade securities for themselves and their clients. Some wealthy individuals also own seats – probably get quite a few thrills from it, too.

The NYSE, Inc., earned revenues of $1.1 billion in 2003 from several activities: they collect a fee for every trade that executes (2003 trading fees for the NYSE totaled $0.2 billion); the NYSE provides data processing services and sells proprietary information ($0.4 billion); they collect various fees from members ($0.2 billion); and the NYSE collects fees ($0.3 billion) from companies like IBM that pay for the privilege to have their stocks traded at the prestigious New York Stock Exchange! The NYSE earns revenues, pays expenses, and earns *Net income* that is fully retained, thereby increasing the *Stockholders' equity* of its members.

About 2,750 different companies list stocks at the NYSE; roughly 450 are foreign-based while the rest have headquarters in the U.S. Each company pays fees to list its stock, perhaps as much as half-million dollars per year. The exchange sets standards that companies must satisfy to qualify for listing. For example, aggregate pretax earnings over the previous three years for domestic companies must equal $10 million or market capitalization must exceed $100 million. Companies listed at the NYSE are basically big-to-huge. The total market cap in the summer of 2004 for all U.S. corporations listed on the NYSE is $11.4 trillion. The table below shows that by far the NYSE has the largest market cap of any stock exchange in the world (in 1990 the Tokyo Stock Exchange briefly was bigger than the NYSE). About one-third of the entire world's stock market value resides at the Big Board.

TABLE 3.2 GLOBAL STOCK MARKET CAPITALIZATION ($ TRILLIONS)

	World Total	NYSE	NYSE %world	NASDAQ	Tokyo	London	Deutsche Börse	Euronext
2004	$31.4	$11.4	36%	$2.7	$3.2	$2.4	$1.0	$2.0
2003	$31.3	$11.3	36%	$2.8	$3.0	$2.4	$1.0	$2.1
2002	$23.1	$9.4	41%	$2.2	$2.1	$1.8	$0.7	$1.6
2001	$26.8	$11.0	41%	$2.9	$2.3	$2.1	$1.1	$1.8
2000	$30.9	$11.4	37%	$3.6	$3.2	$2.6	$1.3	$2.3
1999	$35.6	$11.8	33%	$5.8	$4.0	$2.8	$1.4	$2.4
1998	$26.3	$10.3	39%	$2.5	$2.4	$2.3	$1.1	$1.8
1997	$22.3	$8.9	40%	$1.7	$2.1	$2.1	$0.8	$1.3
1996	$20.1	$6.8	34%	$1.5	$3.0	$1.7	$0.7	$1.1
1995	$17.5	$5.7	33%	$1.2	$3.5	$1.3	$0.6	$0.9
1990	$9.6	$2.7	28%	$0.3	$2.8	$0.9	$0.4	$0.5
1980	$2.9	$1.2	41%	. . .	$0.4	$0.2	$0.1	$0.1

Excludes investment companies (closed-end funds, etc.). All figures are year-end, except for 2004 which is end of June. The "World Total" includes the 50 exchanges that are members of the World Federation of Exchanges. Source: www.nyse.com > About the NYSE > Factbook.

The NYSE is the premier forum for on-going companies to raise capital. For example, an on-going listed company such as IBM (they originally listed with the NYSE in 1915) decided that they needed external financing for their pension obligations. In November 2002 IBM registered with the Securities and Exchange Commission the intention to sell up to $1.5 billion of new stock (about 19.3 million shares). The stocks were to be distributed at prevailing market prices on the NYSE (among others; IBM also is listed on the Chicago Stock Exchange and the Pacific Stock Exchange in Seattle). The NYSE is so large and liquid that the market (fairly) easily absorbed the stocks allowing IBM to raise capital successfully securing its employee's pension plans.

The NYSE also is the premier forum for initial public offerings. Companies with IPOs on the NYSE are of course already large and well-established. In late 2001, for example, Aramark Inc. decided to raise capital through an IPO on the NYSE. This previously privately held company is a leading provider of food and support services, uniform and career apparel services and childcare and early education — they have a big presence on college campuses. Aramark reported sales during fiscal 2001 of approximately $7.8 billion and net income of approximately $176 million. Aramark sold 30 million shares on the NYSE and raised almost $700 million of external financing in order to support their growth. NYSE IPOs during 2004 raised more than $30 billion of capital.

Most stock exchanges in today's world are purely electronic trading systems ("ETS") in which traders click on computer screens to execute trades. The NYSE offers several ETS alternatives. For example, NYSE Direct+ automatically matches buy and sell orders up to 1,099 shares, enabling users anonymity and speed. Between 2002 and 2004 the number of NYSE Direct+ orders increased 140 percent. Another ETS alternative, SuperDot, transmits orders up to specified sizes (depending on the stock) to the proper trading floor position. These orders execute on the floor as quickly as market interest and activity permit.

Daily trading at the NYSE in 2004 averages about 1.4 billion shares worth $46 billion. About 80 percent of all trades execute on the floor where members meet face-to-face in an open-outcry auction. Every listed security is assigned to a specific trading position. Furthermore, every listing company assigns its stock to a specialist that acts as auctioneer for, typically, between 5 and 10 different listed stocks. Specialists are NYSE members empowered to *maintain a fair and orderly market for the trading of securities at their assigned positions* (there are about 450 specialists employed by 7 different firms working 18 trading posts; each post has about 2 dozen trading positions). The trading crowd around a post includes floor-brokers that are members offering either to buy stocks at the "bid-price" or to sell stocks at the "ask-price." The specialist records bid and ask prices, directing floor brokers to the best price in the crowd. About 85 percent of all floor trades occur between floor brokers. For the other 15 percent, however, the trade typically occurs between the specialist and one floor broker. The specialist, for example, takes one side of all orders coming to the floor by SuperDot. Also, the specialist steps in as middleman when imbalance between buy and sell orders spreads apart the bid and ask prices so far that trading stalls. Specialists supposedly do not affect direction of stock price movements, they simply keep the stock trading.

The NYSE must follow government regulations, most notably the Securities Exchange Act of 1934. That federal law was passed in response to public out roar about the stock market crash of 1929 and its seemingly deleterious effect on the economy. Politicians in the U.S. Congress responded by establishing the Securities Exchange Commission ("SEC"). Ever since then the NYSE has reported significant activities to the SEC. For some actions the NYSE must seek prior permission. Generally, however, the NYSE is "self-regulating" and devotes significant resources to maintain a fair and orderly stock market.

The U.S.A. is unique among nations for the nature of relations between the government and private sector organizations such as the NYSE, the Financial Accounting Standards Board, the American Medical Association, etc. Basically, the government pursues a hands-off approach unless the organization screws up and public pressure pushes Congress into action. Such an event occurred in summer 2003 when members of the NYSE voted a $138 million compensation package for their President and CEO Richard Grasso. The loud out roar from Main Street sent Wall Street into damage-control mode; after all, the NYSE got the $138 million from its captive audience — Main Street investors. NYSE members responded by forcing out Mr. Grasso, by revoking some of his compensation package, and most significantly, by reorganizing so as to satisfy the SEC and dissipate political pressure on Congress. The NYSE governance structure adopted in 2004 creates an independent Board of Directors ("BoD") and a Board of Executives comprised of representatives from the securities industry. The NYSE believes that independence of the BoD will enable the exchange to address issues objectively and intelligently so that, once again, the public may put its trust in the New York Stock Exchange.

B2. Forecasting external financing needs when internal financing is available

This method for estimating future financing needs assumes the availability of a forecast for expected future sales. The forecast sales revenue, combined with reasonable assumptions about profit margins, enables an estimate about the availability of *New retained earnings*. *New retained earnings* represents internal financing available to the company and diminishes the amount of External Financing Needs.

The number "future Sales Revenue" is incredibly important. It is hard to get, too. Regardless, we assume that perhaps the marketing staff conduct surveys, the MBAs run numbers, make phone calls, or take clients to lunch, and that somehow the company obtains a forecast for expected sales. Given the sales forecast, the basic procedure for finding EFN is given below:

(1) Forecast the *Total assets* required for sustaining desired future sales. Most likely, use a financial ratio to link future sales with specific asset categories and then estimate *Total assets*.

(2) Forecast the future *Total liabilities & Stockholders' equity* that you expect to accumulate. There are 3 reasons these might change from current values:
   a. Some liabilities such as *Payables* often increase spontaneously and proportionately with *Sales*
   b. *Stockholders' equity* increases because expected *Sales* creates *New retained earnings*
   c. Pre-commitments might cause *Notes* and *Long term debt* to change. Otherwise, these should remain constant for forecasting.

(3) Compute *EFN* as the difference between expected *Total assets* from step 1 and expected *Total liabilities & Stockholders' equity* from step 2. A summary formula for this general procedure is:

FORMULA 3.2 External financing needs, concise version

Let $\triangle A$ equal the change in *Total assets* (that is, $A_t - A_{t-1}$) expected throughout the next period, let $\triangle L$ equal the forecast change in spontaneous liabilities, and let R_t equal the forecast internal financing from *New retained earnings*. The company must arrange for financing during period t equal to EFN_t, where:

$$EFN_t = \triangle A - \triangle L - R_t$$

Examples for applying the above procedure are given below for two common situations.

EFN when balances change proportionately with sales

Consider the situation in which a company at end-of-year t-1 expects sales growth at rate g during year t, while at the same time it expects to remain unchanged the following ratios: the asset turnover ratio, net profit margin, and dividend payout ratio. For this situation, the summary formula specializes to become:

$$EFN_t = g\,A_{t-1} - \triangle L - (1+g)\,R_{t-1}$$

EXAMPLE 3 Find EFN when all ratios except debt-to-equity stay constant

The Company's balance sheet for December 31, 2525, and its income statement for the year 2525 appear below:

COMPANY BALANCE SHEET, 12/31/2525

Assets	Liabilities		
		$ 200	Payables
		150	Short term notes
		225	Long term Debt
		325	Stockholders' Equity
Total Assets	$900	$900	Total Liabilities & Equity

COMPANY INCOME STATEMENT, JAN. 1–DEC. 31, 2525

Sales	$2,500
– expenses	2,250
= Net Income	$250
– *Dividends*	200
= *New Retained Earnings*	$ 50

The company plans to increase sales by 12% during 2526. They hope, however, to hold constant at 2.78 the asset turnover ratio ($=Sales_t \div A_t$), the net profit margin at 10%, and the dividend payout ratio at 80%. If *Payables* rise proportionately with sales, how much are external financing needs?

SOLUTION

The situation is a perfect match for application of the formula:

$$EFN_t = g\, A_{t-1} - \Delta L - (1 + g)\, R_{t-1}$$
$$= (0.12 \times \$900) - (0.12 \times \$200) - (1.12 \times \$50)$$
$$= \$28$$

The company forecasts a shortfall of $28; this sum must be borrowed in order to support required *Total assets*.

Even though the answer for the above problem is $28, further inspection of the outcome is instructive. Consider first the income statement for 2526. *Sales* grow 12% to become $2,800; application of the 10% net profit margin and 80% payout ratio yield the following:

COMPANY INCOME STATEMENT, JAN. 1—DEC. 31, 2526

Sales	$2,800
– expenses	2,520
= Net Income	$280
– Dividends	216
= New Retained Earnings	$ 56

The balance sheet for year-end 2526 reflects the $56 internal financing as an increase in *Stockholders' equity*. The only other liability to increase is *Payables*, which rise spontaneously with sales (12%) to become $224. On the left-hand-side side, *Total assets* increases proportionately with sales ($900 x 1.12 = $1,008). The preliminary balance sheet appears here:

COMPANY BALANCE SHEET, 12/31/2526 (PRELIMINARY)

	Assets		Liabilities
		$224	Payables
		150	Short term notes
		225	Long term Debt
		381	Stockholders' Equity
Total Assets	$1,008	$980	Total Liabilities & Equity

Expected *Total assets* is $28 more than expected *Total Liabilities & Stockholders' equity*. This shortfall identifies a financing need of $28 during the year 2526. The company should make arrangements for obtaining this financing in case the need eventuates. If the funds are not raised, *Total assets* cannot grow as required.

EFN for flexible cases

The procedure outlined above easily adapts to variations in the business situation. Variations might occur, for example, as a result of the following circumstances: (1) perhaps only some *Total assets* increase proportionately with sales; (2) perhaps profit margins change. Regardless, the procedure remains the same as in formula 3.2. The two examples below illustrate the flexibility of this procedure for finding *EFN*.

The first example analyzes a company that currently underutilizes its *PP&E*. The company believes that if it works its *PP&E* harder, maybe by running an extra labor shift, the existing *PP&E* can support the sales growth.

EXAMPLE 4 Find EFN when PP&E is constant

The Company's balance sheet for December 31, 2525, and its income statement for the year 2525 appear below:

COMPANY BALANCE SHEET, 12/31/2525

	Assets		Liabilities
Cash	$ 40	$ 210	Payables
Inventory	170	120	Short term notes
Receivables	60	250	Long term Debt
PP&E	900	590	Stockholders' Equity
Total Assets	$1,170	$1,170	Total Liabilities & Equity

COMPANY INCOME STATEMENT, JAN. 1–DEC. 31, 2525

Sales	$3,600
– expenses	3,130
= Net Income	$280
– Dividends	220
= New Retained Earnings	$ 60

The company plans to increase sales by 6% during 2526. They hope, however, to hold constant the net profit margin and dividend payout ratio. *Payables* rise proportionately with sales. All assets also rise proportionately with sales, except for *PP&E* which currently is underutilized and can support fully the sales growth. How much external financing is needed?

SOLUTION

The situation implies that all assets except *PP&E* rise by 6%. Thus, the change in *Total assets* equals 16.2 {= 0.06 x ($1,170 – 900) }. Because the profit margin and payout ratios remain the same, however, the *New retained earnings* simply equals the previous year's *New retained earnings* multiplied by one plus the growth rate. *New retained earnings* for 2526 equal the 2525 value times 1.06. Substitution into formula 3.2 shows:

$$EFN = \{ 0.06 \times (\$1{,}170 - 900) \} - (0.06 \times \$210) - (1.06 \times \$60)$$

$$= \${-}60$$

The company forecasts a surplus of $60. This sum will be available for repaying debt or acquiring new assets.

Verify for the previous example that the income statement for 2526 shows *Sales* of $3,816 and *New retained earnings* of $63.6. Also verify that the preliminary balance sheet for year-end 2526 appears as below:

COMPANY BALANCE SHEET, 12/31/2526 (PRELIMINARY)

	Assets		Liabilities
Cash	$ 42.4	$ 222.6	Payables
Inventory	180.2	120	Short term notes
Receivables	63.6	250	Long term Debt
PP&E	900	653.6	Stockholders' Equity
Total Assets	$1,186.2	$1,246.2	Total Liabilities & Equity

EFN equals the difference between the left and right-hand-side bottom-lines. The final balance sheet depends on the strategic decisions by management for equating the bottom lines.

The next example analyzes a company that increases its profit margin. The change in profit margin affects the availability of internal financing. The computation of *New retained earnings* should properly reflect the new profit margin, as the example on the following page illustrates:

EXAMPLE 5 Find EFN when the profit margin changes

The Company's balance sheet for December 31, 2525, and its income statement for the year 2525 appear below:

COMPANY BALANCE SHEET, 12/31/2525

	Assets		Liabilities
Cash	$ 60	$ 170	Payables
Inventory	200	230	Short term notes
Receivables	90	350	Long term Debt
PP&E	950	550	Stockholders' Equity
Total Assets	$1,300	$1,300	Total Liabilities & Equity

COMPANY INCOME STATEMENT, JAN. 1–DEC. 31, 2525

Sales	$4,200
– expenses	3,850
= Net Income	$350
– Dividends	275
= New Retained Earnings	$ 75

The company plans to increase sales by 7% during 2526. They plan to hold constant the dividend payout ratio. *Payables* rise proportionately with sales. All assets also rise proportionately with sales. The company intends, however, to institute cost cutting measures so that the net profit margin rises by one percentage point. For this scenario, how much external financing is needed?

SOLUTION

The situation implies that all assets rise by 7%. Thus, the change in *Total assets* equals { 0.07 x ($1,300) }. *New retained earnings* for 2526 is based upon the new *Sales* figure of $4,494 (= 1.07 x $4,200), the new net profit margin of 9.33% (= .01 + $350/$4,200), and the retention ratio of 21.43% (= 100% – $275/$350). Substitution into formula 3.2 shows:

$$EFN = \{ 0.07 \times (\$1,300) \} - (0.07 \times \$170) - (1.07 \times \$4,200 \times .0933 \times .2143)$$

$$= \$-10.8$$

The company forecasts a surplus of $10.8 . This sum will be available for repaying debt or acquiring new assets.

EXERCISES 3.1

Numerical quickies

1. Analysts report that the company has *Total assets* of $287,000. Over the next year the *Total assets* should increase 5.4%, spontaneous financing should equal $3,870 and *New retained earnings* should equal $9,530. Other liabilities are unchanged. What is the forecast EFN ("external financing needed")? ©EFN5a

Challengers

2. Company *Sales* equal $58,000 for the year ending December 31, the *Costs-of-goods sold* (cogs) equal 75% of *Sales*, and *Inventory* was replaced about every 65 days (inventory turnover in days = 365 ÷ inventory turnover ratio; inventory turnover ratio = annual cogs ÷ *Inventory*). The Company is considering a change in their inventory ordering policy. As a result, they believe that *Sales* would remain constant in the forthcoming year, yet the length of time that *Inventory* stays on the shelf would increase by 33 days. If the financing rate for inventories is 14% per year, by how much would they change their annual inventory financing costs? ©EFN1a

3. For year 2525 the company's *Sales* were $360,000 and annual *Cost-of-goods-sold* equaled 75% of *Sales*. The company followed a policy that set the average payment period (= *Payables* ÷ daily-cost-of-goods-sold) at 56 days. The company realizes that relying on *Payables* as a financing source is free, whereas relying on *Debt* costs 19% per annum. Suppose they institute a policy that causes the average payment period to increase by 30 days. Further, suppose the policy has no effect on the firm's *Total Assets* or *Sales*. Based on the numbers for year 2525, how much would the new policy affect annual financing costs due to the company's switch between high-cost *Debt* and low-cost (free) *Payables*? ©EFN3a

4. Find below the Company's financial statements for year 2525.

Balance Sheet, 12/31/2525				Income, 1/1 – 12/31/2525	
$525	Cash & securities`	$540	Current liabilities	Sales	$16,600
$735	Inventory	$620	Debt	total costs	*$16,200*
$1,700	PP&E	$1,800	Stockholders' equity	Net income	$400
$2,960	Total assets	$2,960		Dividends	$140
				New retained earnings	$260

For 2526 the company plans 17.50% sales growth. They plan to hold constant the asset turnover (=*Sales*÷*Total assets*) and payout ratio (=*Dividends*÷*Net income*). They plan to increase *Current liabilities* spontaneously with *Sales*, while holding *Debt* constant. Suppose the company holds constant their net profit margin (=*Net income* ÷ *Sales*). Given the above plan, how much external financing is needed for year 2526? ©EFN2am

5. Find below the Company's financial statements for year 2525.

Balance Sheet, 12/31/2525				Income, 1/1–12/31/2525	
$635	Cash & securities	$310	Current liabilities	Sales	$19,500
$655	Inventory	$620	Debt	total costs	$18,800
$1,790	PP&E	$2,150	Stockholders' equity	Net income	$700
$3,080	Total assets	$3,080		Dividends	$340
				New retained earnings	$360

For 2526 the company plans 12% sales growth. They plan to hold constant the asset turnover (=*Sales*÷*Total assets*) and payout ratio (=*Dividends*÷*Net income*). They plan to increase *Current liabilities* spontaneously with sales, while holding *Debt* constant. Suppose the company institutes cost-cutting measures that should increase the net profit margin (=*Net income* ÷ *Sales*) by 2.60% above its value of year 2525. Given the above plan, how much external financing is needed for year 2526? ©EFN2bm

6. Find below the Company's financial statements for year 2525.

Balance Sheet, 12/31/2525				Income, 1/1–12/31/2525	
$420	Cash & securities	$740	Current liabilities	Sales	$18,000
$720	Inventory	$1,000	Debt	total costs	$17,700
$2,700	PP&E	$2,100	Stockholders' equity	Net income	$300
$3,840	Total assets	$3,840		Dividends	$170
				New retained earnings	$130

For 2526 the company plans 12.30% sales growth. They plan to hold constant the asset turnover (=*Sales*÷*Total assets*) and payout ratio (=*Dividends* ÷ *Net income*). They plan to increase *Current liabilities* spontaneously with *Sales*, while holding *Debt* constant. Suppose the company holds constant their net profit margin (=*Net income* ÷ *Sales*). How much is *Total assets* for year 2526 if the forecast shortfall is not financed with external borrowing? ©EFN2cm

7. The Company balance sheet on 12/31/2525 contains the following:

Balance Sheet, 12/31/2525

$1,700	Current liabilities		
$2,100	Current assets	$1,300	Debt
$3,000	PP&E	$2,100	Stockholders' equity
$5,100	Total assets	$5,100	

From the income statement for 2525, *Sales* equal $21,930 and *Net income* is $1,645 and *Dividends* equal $1,234. The Company expects sales growth during year 2526 of 10.7%. They expect *Current assets* and *Current liabilities* will increase spontaneously and proportionately with *Sales*. They believe, however, that they can better utilize existing *PP&E*. Consequently, they expect *PP&E* to remain constant. Also expected to remain constant are the net profit margin (= *Net income* ÷ *Sales*) and the payout ratio (= *Dividends* ÷ *Net income*). The company anticipates running a surplus during year 2526. Given that *Debt* is unchanged, how large is the forecast surplus? ©EFN4

8. Find below the Company financial statements for year 2525.

Balance Sheet, 12/31/2525				Income, 1/1–12/31/2525	
Current assets	$2,100	$1,200	Current liabilities	Sales	$16,500
		$1,700	Debt	total costs	$15,741
PP&E	$5,400	$4,600	Stockholders equity	Net income	$759
	$7,500	$7,500	Total	Dividends	$569

For year 2526 the company forecasts sales growth of 8.8% with constant net profit margin (= *Net income* ÷ *Sales*) and dividend payout ratio (=*Dividends*÷ *Net income*). The company expects that due to more efficient asset management they can increase the asset turnover ratio (= $Sales_t$ ÷ Total assets$_t$) to 2.70. They expect *Current liabilities* will rise spontaneously with *Sales*. According to these forecasts, find the surplus external financing needed in 2526. ©EFN6

2. NATURAL GROWTH RATES

What amount of growth is just right? This is a complex question and the answer always depends on the specific business situation. While there are no golden rules, there are two baseline cases that provide insight about natural growth rates.

Gain understanding of growth rates by examining simplified financial statements. Suppose that the left-hand side of the balance sheet contains *Total assets*, denoted A. The right-hand-side lists *Debt* and *Stockholders' equity*, denoted D and SE, respectively. The right and left-hand-sides are of course equal; that is, A = D + SE. Further suppose that the income statement lists only *Sales*, *Total expenses*, *Net income*, and *Dividends*. The bottom-line of the income statement is *New retained earnings*, denoted R, which represents internal financing available for growth.

2.A. Growth exclusively with internal financing

A natural question arises: *How fast can a company grow by relying exclusively on internal financing?* Believe it or not, obtain a straightforward answer for this question by adopting the reasonable assumption that several of the company's most important financial ratios are stable. The answer appears in the formula on the following page.

A company with constant asset turnover ratio, net profit margin, and dividend payout ratio that relies exclusively on internal financing grows at the "internal growth rate":

$$g^{internal} = \frac{R_t}{A_t - R_t}$$

$$= \frac{(retention\ ratio)(ROA)}{1 - (retention\ ratio)(ROA)} \qquad when\ ROA = \frac{Net\ income_t}{Total\ assets_t}$$

$$= (retention\ ratio)(ROA) \qquad when\ ROA = \frac{Net\ income_t}{Total\ assets_{t-1}}$$

The variables R and A denote *New retained earnings* and *Total assets*, respectively. The "ROA" is the return-on-assets.

Derivation of formula 3.3 assumes that the following ratios are constant: asset turnover ratio; net profit margin; and dividend payout ratio. As the discussion in the previous chapter suggests, these ratios often tend toward constants.

The numerical example in table 3.3 illustrates the dynamics of this growth story. During year 2525 this company generates $90 of *New retained earnings*. The end-of-year balance sheet lists total assets of $1,000. The balance sheet bottom-line, however, already includes this $90 of *New retained earnings*. Because end-of-year total assets equal $1,000 but internal financing contributes $90 toward that total,

TABLE 3.3
Natural growth rate dynamics

PANEL A: Status Quo for year 2525

Balance Sheet, 12/31/2525			Income Statement, 1/1 to 12/31/2525	
	400	Debt (D)	Sales	$3,000
	600	Equity (SE)	total expenses	2,850
Total (A) $1,000	$1,000	Liabilities & Equity	Net Income	150
			Dividends	60
			New Retained Earnings (R)	90

PANEL B: Effect on year 2526 of growth at rate g^internal

Balance Sheet, 12/31/2526			Income Statement, 1/1 to 12/31/2526	
	400	Debt (D)	Sales	$3,297
	699	Equity (SE)	total expenses	3,132
Total (A) $1,099	$1,099	Liabilities & Equity	Net Income	165
			Dividend	66
			New Retained Earnings (R)	99

PANEL C: Effect on year 2526 of growth at rate g sustainable

Balance Sheet, 12/31/2526			Income Statement, 1/1 to 12/31/2526	
	471	Debt (D)	Sales	$3,530
	706	Equity (SE)	total expenses	3,354
Total (A) $1,177	$1,177	Liabilities & Equity	Net Income	176
			Dividends	70
			New Retained Earnings (R)	106

PANEL D: End-of-year financial ratios

	12/31/2525 status quo	12/31/2526 growth @ $g^{internal}$	12/31/2526 growth @ $g^{sustainable}$
asset turnover ratio: (sales ÷ total assets)	3.0	3.0	3.0
net profit margin: (net income ÷ sales)	5.0%	5.0%	5.0%
payout ratio: (dividends ÷ net income)	40%	40%	40%
debt-to-equity ratio: (debt ÷ Stockholders' equity)	0.67	0.57	0.67

the beginning-of-year total assets would equal $910 if all else were equal. If $910 of total assets were to generate $90 of internal financing, the company is growing 9.89% with exclusive reliance on *New retained earnings*:

$$g^{internal} = \frac{\$90}{\$1000 - \$90}$$

$$= 9.89\%$$

Panel B shows the outcome in year 2526 when the company grows at the internal growth rate of 9.89%. *Sales* become $3,297 (= $3,000(1.089)). *Net income*, too, is up 9.89% to become $165. Likewise, *Dividends* become $66. The *New retained earnings* of $99 flow into *Stockholders' equity*, thereby bringing the balance sheet's bottom line for year-end 2526 to $1,099.

Notice in Panel D that with growth at rate $g^{internal}$ the asset turnover ratio remains at 3.0 in year 2526, exactly as it was in 2525. The net profit margin remains constant, too, at 5.0%, and the dividend payout ratio remains constant at 40%. This particular sales growth rate of 9.89% is the only rate at which exclusive reliance on internal financing holds constant these three ratios.

2.B. The sustainable growth rate

Businesses typically target a particular debt-to-equity ratio as desirable. A shortcoming of growth at rate $g^{internal}$ is that the debt-to-equity ratio declines over time. Inspect the numerical illustration above, for example. In year 2525, the debt-to-equity ratio equals 0.67; in 2526 it equals 0.57. If the company initially were at its target debt-to-equity ratio, growth at rate $g^{internal}$ moves the company away from its target.

Slight modification of the preceding formula leads to the following result:

FORMULA 3.4a, 3.4b, and 3.4c The sustainable growth rate

A company with constant asset turnover ratio, net profit margin, dividend payout ratio, and debt-to-equity ratio grows at the "sustainable growth rate":

$$g^{sustainable} = \frac{R_t(1 + D_t/SE_t)}{A_t - R_t(1 + D_t/SE_t)}$$

$$= \frac{(retention\,ratio)(ROE)}{1 - (retention\,ratio)(ROE)} \qquad when\ ROE = \frac{Net\ income_t}{Stockholders\ equity_t}$$

$$= (retention\,ratio)(ROE) \qquad when\ ROE = \frac{Net\ income_t}{Stockholders\ equity_{t-1}}$$

The variables *R*, *A*, *D*, and *SE* denote *New retained earnings*, *Total assets*, *Total debt*, and *Stockholders' equity*, respectively.

These three formulations are algebraically equivalent. The top line (formula 3.4a) uses from the income statement *New retained earnings* (R_t) and from the contemporaneous balance sheet *Total assets* (A_t), *Total debt* (D_t), and *Stockholders equity* (SE_t). The middle and bottom lines (3.4b and 3.4c, respectively) use the retention ratio (that is, *1 − dividends/Net income*) and return-on-equity (*ROE*). The *ROE* is the ambiguous ratio of a flow and a balance with different definitions in-use. The two *ROE* definitions above differ because *Net income* is divided by *Stockholders equity* at either the end or beginning of period.

For the illustration begun in Panel A, we use formula 3.4a to easily compute the sustainable growth rate.

$$g^{sustainable} = \frac{\$90(1 + 400/600)}{\$1000 - \$90(1 + 400/600)}$$

$$= 17.65\%$$

Panel C shows the outcome in year 2526 when the company grows at 17.65%. *Sales* are up 17.65% to become $3,530 (= $3,000(1.1765)), *Net income* becomes $176, and *Stockholders' equity* becomes $706. Because the asset turnover ratio is constant, *Total assets* also are up 17.65% to $1,177. One other aspect changes, too. *Debt* on the balance sheet rises to $471, an increase of 17.65%, which implies the company takes out additional loans of $71 (that is, external financing equals $71). Confirm that all ratios, including the debt-to-equity ratio, are the same in Panels A and C when sales grow at the sustainable growth rate.

EXAMPLE 6 Contrasting growth rates for IBM

For the IBM financial statements presented in tables 2.1 and 2.3, find both $g^{internal}$ and $g^{sustainable}$.

SOLUTION

The actual financial statements contain a lot of detail absent in the growth rate formulas. Consolidation consequently must occur. Partition all right-hand-side balance sheet line items into *Stockholders' equity* and *Debt*. Similarly simplify the income statement (all dollars in millions) and see

IBM CORPORATION FINANCIAL STATEMENTS

Balance Sheet, 12/31/1996			Income Statement, 1/1 to 12/31/1996	
	59,504	Debt (D)	Sales	$76,654
	21,628	Equity (SE)	total expenses	71,225
Total (A) $81,132	$81,132	Liabilities & Equity	Net Income	5,429
			Dividends	706
			New Retained Earnings (R)	4,723

Application now of the growth rate formulas is straightforward:

$$g^{internal} = \frac{R_t}{A_t - R_t}$$

$$= \frac{\$4,723}{\$81,132 - \$4,723}$$

$$= 6.18\%$$

and

$$g^{sustainable} = \frac{R_t(1 + D_t/SE_t)}{A_t - R_t(1 + D_t/SE_t)}$$

$$= \frac{\$4,723(1 + \$59,504/\$21,628)}{\$81,132 - \$4,723(1 + \$59,504/\$21,628)}$$

$$= 27.94\%$$

Computations indicate that if IBM holds constant its asset turnover ratio, net profit margin, and payout ratio, the resultant *New retained earnings* support a growth rate of 6.18%. If they also issue more debt such that the debt-to-equity ratio is constant, growth at 27.94% is supported. We note parenthetically, however, that IBM already relies on debt much more than the average computer company (see the discussion in the previous chapter about the DuPont analysis). Consequently, IBM probably should tend toward lower growth so that their debt ratio diminishes.

EXERCISES 3.2

Numerical quickies

1. Find below items from the company's income statement.

Income, 1/1 – 12/31/2525

Sales	$10,000
all costs	$9,400
Net income	$600
Dividends	$390
New retained earnings	$210

Total assets at 12/31/2525 equal $2,635. If the company is growing at their internal growth rate, what are *Total assets* at 12/31/2526? ©GR4

2. Find below items from the company's income statement.

Income, 1/1–12/31/2525

Sales	$12,000
all costs	$10,800
Net income	$1,200
Dividends	$920
New retained earnings	$280

Total assets at 12/31/2525 equal $3,650 and the debt-to-assets ratio is 45%. If the company is growing at their sustainable growth rate, what are *Total assets* at 12/31/2526? ©GR1

3. Analysts report that the company successfully grows at their sustainable growth rate of 7.4%. Today the company's total assets equal $105,600 and this past year their sales were $48,000 . What is the likely increase over the next year in the company's sales? ©GR5

4. Find below the Company's financial statements for year 2525.

Balance Sheet, 12/31/2525				**Income, 1/1–12/31/2525**	
$450	Current assets	$1,650	Debt	Sales	$21,500
$3,200	PP&E	$2,000	Stockholders' equity	total costs	$21,100
$3,650	Total assets	$3,650		Net income	$400
				Dividends	$250
				New retained earnings	$150

For 2526 the asset turnover (*Sales÷Total assets*), net profit margin (=*Net income ÷ Sales*), and payout ratio (=*Dividends÷Net income*) will be constant. The number of shares outstanding is 100. The firm seeks maximum growth by relying exclusively on retained earnings; external financing will be zero. What is the sales growth rate? ©GR2a

Challengers

5. Find below the Company's financial statements for year 2525.

Balance Sheet, 12/31/2525				**Income, 1/1–12/31/2525**	
$300	Current assets	$1,600	Debt	Sales	$14,100
$3,400	PP&E	$2,100	Stockholders' equity	total costs	$13,700
$3,700	Total assets	$3,700		Net income	$400
				Dividends	$275
				New retained earnings	$125

For 2526 the asset turnover (=*Sales÷Total assets*), net profit margin (=*Net income ÷ Sales*), payout ratio (=*Dividends÷Net income*) and price-to-earnings ratio (now 14.6) will be constant. The number of shares outstanding is 110. The firm seeks maximum growth by relying exclusively on retained earnings; external financing will be zero. What is the equity book value per share at year-end 2526? ©GR2c

6. Find below the Company's financial statements for year 2525.

Balance Sheet, 12/31/2525

$375	Current assets	$875	Debt			
$2,400	PP&E	$1,900	Stockholders' equity			
$2,775	Total assets	$2,775				

Income, 1/1–12/31/2525

Sales	$8,900
total costs	$8,200
Net income	$700
Dividends	$380
New retained earnings	$320

For 2526 the asset turnover (=*Sales÷Total assets*), net profit margin (=*Net income ÷ Sales*), payout ratio (=*Dividends÷Net income*) and price-to-earnings ratio (now 20.4) will be constant. The number of shares outstanding is 100. The firm seeks maximum growth by relying exclusively on retained earnings; external financing will be zero. What is the equity price-to-book ratio at year-end 2526? ©GR2d

7. Find below the Company's financial statements for year 2525.

Balance Sheet, 12/31/2525

$450	Current assets	$1,650	Debt
$3,200	PP&E	$2,000	Stockholders' equity
$3,650	Total assets	$3,650	

Income, 1/1–12/31/2525

Sales	$21,500
total costs	$21,100
Net income	$400
Dividends	$250
New retained earnings	$150

For 2526 the asset turnover (=*Sales÷Total assets*), net profit margin (=*Net income ÷ Sales*), payout ratio (=*Dividends÷Net income*) and price-to-earnings ratio (now 24.6) will be constant. The number of shares outstanding is 100. The firm seeks maximum growth by relying exclusively on retained earnings; external financing will be zero. What is the debt-to-equity ratio at year-end 2526? ©GR2e

8. Find below the Company's financial statements for year 2525.

Balance Sheet, 12/31/2525

$360	Current assets	$960	Debt
$2,500	PP&E	$1,900	Stockholders' equity
$2,860	Total assets	$2,860	

Income, 1/1–12/31/2525

Sales	$13,200
total costs	$12,600
Net income	$600
Dividends	$220
New retained earnings	$380

For 2526 the asset turnover (=*Sales÷Total assets*), net profit margin (=*Net income ÷ Sales*), payout ratio (=*Dividends÷Net income*) and price-to-earnings ratio (now 14.3) will be constant. The number of shares outstanding is 100. The firm seeks maximum growth by relying exclusively on retained earnings; external financing will be zero. For the shareholder that buys a share at year-end 2525 and holds the stock through year-end 2526, what is the rate of return? ©GR2b

9. Find below the Company's financial statements for year 2525.

Balance Sheet, 12/31/2525

$4,350	Current assets	$8,350	Debt
$21,000	PP&E	$17,000	Stockholders' equity
$25,350	Total assets	$25,350	

Income, 1/1–12/31/2525

Sales	$76,100
total costs	$72,000
Net income	$4,100
Dividends	$2,870
New retained earnings	$1,230

For 2526 the asset turnover (=*Sales÷Total assets*), net profit margin (=*Net income ÷ Sales*), and payout ratio (=*Dividends÷Net income*) will be constant. The price-to-earnings ratio, 29.2 at year-end 2525, is expected to equal 22.5 at year-end 2526. The number of shares outstanding is 8500. The firm seeks maximum growth by relying exclusively on retained earnings; external financing will be zero. For the shareholder that buys a share at year-end 2525 and holds the stock through year-end 2526, what is the rate of return? ©GR3a

10. Find below the Company's financial statements for year 2525.

Balance Sheet, 12/31/2525				Income, 1/1–12/31/2525	
$450	Current assets	$1,650	Debt	Sales	$21,500
$3,200	PP&E	$2,000	Stockholders' equity	total costs	$21,100
$3,650	Total assets	$3,650		Net income	$400
				Dividends	$250
				New retained earnings	$150

For 2526 the asset turnover (=*Sales÷Total assets*), net profit margin (=*Net income ÷ Sales*), and payout ratio (=*Dividends÷Net income*) will be constant. The number of shares outstanding is 100. The firm seeks maximum growth by relying on internal and external financing such that the debt-to-equity ratio remains constant. What is the equity book value per share at year-end 2526? ©GR2g

11. Find below the Company's financial statements for year 2525.

Balance Sheet, 12/31/2525				Income, 1/1–12/31/2525	
$375	Current assets	$1,275	Debt	Sales	$8,900
$2,600	PP&E	$1,700	Stockholders' equity	total costs	$8,000
$2,975	Total assets	$2,975		Net income	$900
				Dividends	$560
				New retained earnings	$340

For 2526 the asset turnover (=*Sales÷Total assets*), net profit margin (=*Net income ÷ Sales*), payout ratio (=*Dividends÷Net income*) and price-to-earnings ratio (now 29.5) will be constant. The number of shares outstanding is 90. The firm seeks maximum growth by relying on internal and external financing such that the debt-to-equity ratio remains constant. What is the equity price-to-book ratio at year-end 2526? ©GR2h

12. Find below the Company's financial statements for year 2525.

Balance Sheet, 12/31/2525				Income, 1/1–12/31/2525	
$510	Current assets	$910	Debt	Sales	$16,000
$2,400	PP&E	$2,000	Stockholders' equity	total costs	$15,600
$2,910	Total assets	$2,910		Net income	$400
				Dividends	$180
				New retained earnings	$220

For 2526 the asset turnover (=*Sales÷Total assets*), net profit margin (=*Net income ÷ Sales*), payout ratio (=*Dividends÷Net income*) and price-to-earnings ratio (now 22.0) will be constant. The number of shares outstanding is 100. The firm seeks maximum growth by relying on internal and external financing such that the debt-to-equity ratio remains constant. For the shareholder that buys a share at year-end 2525 and holds the stock through year-end 2526, what is the rate of return? ©GR2j

13. Find below the Company's financial statements for year 2525.

Balance Sheet, 12/31/2525				Income, 1/1–12/31/2525	
$4,050	Current assets	$9,450	Debt	Sales	$245,400
$39,000	PP&E	$33,600	Stockholders' equity	total costs	$233,100
$43,050	Total assets	$43,050		Net income	$12,300
				Dividends	$8,490
				New retained earnings	$3,810

For 2526 the asset turnover (=*Sales÷Total assets*), net profit margin (=*Net income ÷ Sales*), and payout ratio (=*Dividends÷Net income*) will be constant. The price-to-earnings ratio, 19.4 at year-end 2525, is expected to equal 21.8 at year-end 2526. The number of shares outstanding is 16,800. The firm seeks maximum growth by relying on internal and external financing such that the debt-to-equity ratio remains constant. For the shareholder that buys a share at year-end 2525 and holds the stock through year-end 2526, what is the rate of return? ©GR3b

3. FOCUS ON CASH FLOW

Accounting earnings on the income statement equals *Net income*. Quite often, however, analysts want other flow measures. The rate of return to capitalists, for example, relates directly to cash flow the company provides investors. Perhaps higher cash flow correlates with higher *Net income,* but perhaps not. The fact is, cash flows signal wealth changes and many different stakeholders or capitalists want information about distribution of the company's wealth. This section offers insights about measuring cash flow.

3.A. Cash Flow from the corporation to the financial markets

The Cash Flow Cycle from chapter 1 diagrams flows between the corporation and the financial markets. Straightforward definitions stem from this diagram. Focusing first on shareholders:

FORMULA 3.5 Cash flow to shareholders

$CF^{\text{to shareholders}}$ = Dividends – Net equity issues

---

$CF^{\text{to shareholders}}$ measures the net amount of wealth the company transfers to shareholders. It increases as *Dividends* rise. Conversely, $CF^{\text{to shareholders}}$ falls when the company sells shares, and rises when the company repurchases shares.

Focus now on all other financial market participants that lend money to the corporation. Group these lenders together under the label *Creditors,* and define $CF^{\text{to creditors}}$ as follows:

FORMULA 3.6 Cash flow to creditors

$CF^{\text{to creditors}}$ = Interest – Net debt issues

Net debt issues equals the change in principal of all the company's outstanding credit obligations. $CF^{\text{to creditors}}$ diminishes when the company takes out new loans because the company is the recipient of a wealth transfer from the financial markets. Conversely, the repayment of loans causes an increase in $CF^{\text{to creditors}}$. Finally, $CF^{\text{to creditors}}$ rises when the company pays interest. In short, $CF^{\text{to creditors}}$ measures the net wealth transfer from the company to its financial market creditors.

The sum of cash flows to shareholders and creditors is the total wealth transfer from the corporation to the financial markets. This summation is the cash flow to capitalists:

FORMULA 3.7 Cash flow to capitalists

$CF^{\text{to capitalists}} = CF^{\text{to shareholders}} + CF^{\text{to creditors}}$

Company value in the financial markets depends exclusively on the cash flows that the company is forecast to deliver to capitalists throughout the foreseeable future.

Financial markets supply financing to companies because of expectations about future cash flows. If cash flows promise to be "big enough", then capitalists choose to be a source of funds for the company: the funds enable the purchase of factors of production required for producing goods and services. Capitalists in pursuit of profit determine which companies to finance, which industries to nurture, and which goods and services to produce—successful capitalists predict the types of goods and services the clients want.

EXAMPLE 7 Compute cash flow measures for IBM

Find below simplified financial statements for IBM. Definitions of *PP&E* and *Total debt* for this illustration have been expanded so that these line items contain the "Other Long Term" balance sheet entries (all dollars in millions). From the statements, find these three cash flow measures for 1996: $CF^{\text{to creditors}}$, $CF^{\text{to shareholders}}$, and $CF^{\text{to capitalists}}$.

IBM CONSOLIDATED BALANCE SHEET, 12/31/1995

Assets			Liabilities
Cash	$ 7,259	$ 31,648	Current liabilities
Other current assets	33,432	26,221	Total Debt
PP&E	39,601	22,423	Stockholders' Equity
Total Assets	*$80,292*	*$80,292*	*Total Liabilities & Equity*

IBM INCOME STATEMENT, JAN. 1–DEC. 31, 1996

Sales revenue	$76,654
– Cost-of-goods-sold	46,815
– Selling and general expenses	16,854
– Depreciation	3,676
= Operating income	$9,303
– Interest expense	716
= Taxable income	$8,587
– Taxes	3,158
= Net income	$5,429
– Dividends	706
= *New Retained Earnings*	$4,723

IBM CONSOLIDATED BALANCE SHEET, 12/31/1996

Assets		Liabilities	
Cash	$ 7,687	$ 34,000	Current liabilities
Other current assets	33,008	25,504	Total Debt
PP&E	40,437	21,628	Stockholders' Equity
Total Assets	*$81,132*	*$81,132*	*Total Liabilities & Equity*

SOLUTION

$CF^{to\ creditors}$ equals the net wealth transfer to long term debt. Notice from the income statement that IBM pays interest to creditors of $716 million. Also notice from the two balance sheets that during 1996 the outstanding balance of long term debt (expanded definition) changes by $–717 million (= $25,504 – $26,221); that is, debt declines. Both of these items represent a transfer of wealth from IBM to creditors. Substitution of the above into the cash flow definition shows that $CF^{to\ creditors}$ is $1,433 million (= $716 – ($–717)).

$CF^{to\ shareholders}$ equals the net wealth transfer to shareholders. Notice from the income statement that IBM pays *Dividends* to shareholders of $706 million. Also notice from the definition of *Stockholders' equity* that *Net equity issues* must equal $–5,518 million (= $21,628 – $22,423 – $4,723). Once again, both of these items represent a transfer of wealth from IBM to shareholders. Substitution of the above into the cash flow definition shows that $CF^{to\ shareholders}$ equals $6,224 million (= $706 – ($-5,518)).

The total transfer of wealth from IBM to capitalists in 1996, $CF^{to\ capitalists}$, equals the sum of $CF^{to\ shareholders}$ and $CF^{to\ creditors}$, which is $7,657 million (= $1,433 + $6,224). IBM transfers over $7.6 billion to the financial markets in this one year alone. This huge sum represents about 9.5% of total assets. In addition to this realized cash flow to capitalists, financial market investors in IBM also accrued wealth increases because stock and bond prices rose substantially in 1996.

3.B. Other Cash Flow Measures

Modern capitalist theory purports that in perfectly fluid and competitive markets the principal and profit from assets ultimately returns to financial markets. This gives rise to the following definition.

FORMULA 3.8 The link between assets and capitalists

$$CF^{from\ assets} = CF^{to\ capitalists}$$

Cash flow from assets identically equals *Cash flow to capitalists*. This identity **assumes** that stakeholder cash flows wash out and do not create value. The discussion on the importance of $CF^{\text{to capitalists}}$ for allocating resources applies to $CF^{\text{from assets}}$ too. For an asset investment to receive financing, capitalists must believe that the venture promises to deliver sufficient future *Cash flow from assets* to justify the investment.

The right-hand-side of the above equation contains items (*Interest* and *Dividends*) that appear on the income statement. Substitution and rearrangement of several formulas results in a very useful alternative expression for $CF^{\text{from assets}}$.

FORMULA 3.9 Cash flow from assets, expanded version

$CF^{\text{from assets}}$ = EBIT + Depreciation − Taxes − ΔNWC − Capital expenditures

---

where *EBIT* represents "earnings before interest and taxes". Sometimes *EBIT* also is called "operating income" or "operating revenue."

EBIT = *Sales* − *COGS* − *SGA* − *Depreciation*,

COGS represents *Cost-of-goods-sold* and *SGA* represents *Selling, general, and administrative expenses*. NWC represents net working capital (*NWC* is *Current assets* minus *Current liabilities*; ΔNWC is its change), and *Capital expenditures* represent spending on *PP&E*.

Publicly traded corporations generally report *Net income* every 3 months. This bottom line number often reflects effects extraordinary activity. Often, however, analysts want a measure of cash flow resulting directly from the company's ordinary operations:

FORMULA 3.10 Cash flow from operations

$CF^{\text{from operations}}$ = EBIT + Depreciation − Taxes
= EBITDA − Taxes

EBITDA, "earnings before interest, taxes, depreciation and amortization," is increasingly popular in the press:

EBITDA = *EBIT* + *Depreciation*

The difference between *EBITDA* and $CF^{\text{from operations}}$ is *Taxes*. When the analyst believes that a company's particular tax bill is unusual, she may choose to focus on *EBITDA* since it is unaffected by taxes. Regardless, $CF^{\text{from operations}}$ often portrays a better picture than *Net income* of financial health and wealth creation.

Comparison of formulas 3.9 and 3.10 reveals that the *Cash flow from assets* equals *Cash flow from operations* when the company spends absolutely nothing on *Net working capital* and *PP&E*. Usually, though, some funds get used on *Net working capital* or *PP&E* so not all *Cash flow from operations* immediately returns to capitalists. Combining several of the preceding formulas yields a key expression.

FORMULA 3.11 Cash flow from assets, summary version

$CF^{\text{from assets}}$ = $CF^{\text{from operations}}$ − ΔNWC − capital expenditures

---

Besides cash flow, many analysts watch the company's *Cash surplus*. The *Cash surplus* is simply the change in *Cash* from one balance sheet to the next. Rearrangement of the above definitions shows:

FORMULA 3.12 Cash surplus

cash surplus = Δcash = $CF^{\text{from operations}}$ − ΔNWC(excluding Cash)
− Capital expenditures − $CF^{\text{from assets}}$

The example below applies cash flow definitions to IBM.

EXAMPLE 8 Get detailed cash flow measures for IBM

From the financial statements for IBM presented for example 7, find the following for 1996: (i) CF $^{from\ operations}$; (ii) ΔNWC; (iii) *Capital expenditures*; (iv) CF $^{from\ assets}$; and (v) the *Cash surplus*.

SOLUTION

(i) Compute CF $^{from\ operations}$ as *EBIT* ($9,303), plus *Depreciation* ($3,676), minus *Taxes* ($3,158). *Cash flow from operations* is $9,821 million.

(ii) NWC$_{1995}$ equals total current assets minus total current liabilities, and is $9,043 million (= $7,259 + $33,432 – $31,648); NWC$_{1996}$ equals $6,695 million (= $7,687 + $33,008 – $34,000). From year-end 1995 to 1996, the ΔNWC is $–2,348 million. The decline in net working capital represents a source of funds for IBM in 1996 of over $2.3 billion.

(iii) Apply formula 2.12 and find that *Capital expenditures* equals $4,512 million (= $40,437 – $39,601 + $3,676). This sum represents a use of $4.5 billion for increasing the balance of long term assets (recall that the simplified balance sheet for this example consolidates *PP&E* with *Other Long Term Assets*).

(iv) CF $^{from\ assets}$ equals CF $^{from\ operations}$ ($9,821), minus ΔNWC ($–2,348), minus *Capital expenditures* ($4,512). The *Cash flow from assets* is $7,657 million. Notice that this answer is identical to CF $^{to\ capitalists}$ from example 7.

(v) The *Cash surplus* equals the change in *Cash* on the balance sheet. From year-end 1995 to 1996, the *Cash surplus* is $428 million (= $7,287 – $7,259). The increase in *Cash* represents a use of funds by IBM during 1996 to pad their checking account. Reliance on formula 3.12 obtains the identical answer:

$$Cash\ surplus = CF\ ^{from\ operations} - \Delta NWC(excluding\ Cash)$$
$$- Capital\ expenditures - CF\ ^{from\ assets}$$

$$= \$9,821 - \{\ (\$33,008 - \$34,000) - (\$33,432 - \$31,648)\ \}$$

$$- \$4,512 \qquad - \$7,657$$

$$= \$428\ million$$

IBM has a cash surplus in 1996 and the amount in their checking account increases even though they return a huge sum to capitalists.

The next example combines many different formulas from chapters 2 and 3 and hones basic accounting skills to the degree required for doing well at finance.

EXAMPLE 9 Combine the balance sheet with income
statement items to find cash flows

Find below the Company's balance sheet at year-end 2525.

BALANCE SHEET, 12/31/2525			
Cash	$ 90	$200	Current liabilities
Other current assets	300	180	Debt
PP&E	680	690	Stockholders equity (80 shares)
	$1,070	$1,070	Total

For year 2526 the following are forecast: the stock price should end the year at $7.50 per share; *Sales* equal $2,100; operating margin (= *EBIT* ÷ *Sales*) is 14%; *Depreciation* is 15% of *PP&E*; *Interest* is 10% of debt; *Taxes* are 35% of taxable income; *Dividends* are 60% of *Net income*. Suppose the company makes sufficient *Capital expenditures* during 2526 so that it holds *PP&E* constant. It finances these *Capital expenditures* by issuing 10 shares during 2526 for $7 per share. The remainder of the *Capital expenditures* is financed internally. All else remains the same. Find all the different cash flow measures as well as the price-to-earnings, price-to-book, and price-to-cash flow.

SOLUTION

For convenience forecast the income statement from the preceding facts.

COMPANY INCOME STATEMENT, JAN. 1–DEC. 31, 2526

Sales revenue	$2,100
– Other costs (see discussion)	. . .
– Depreciation (@ 15% of PPE)	102
= EBIT (@ 14% of sales)	$294
– Interest (@ 10% of debt)	18
= Taxable income	$276
– Taxes (@ 35% tax rate)	97
= Net income	$179
– Dividends (@ 60% payout)	108
= New Retained Earnings	$ 71

The operating margin allows computation of EBIT from Sales. It is unnecessary to compute *Other costs*. Notice that the income statement does not show in any way the *Capital expenditures* nor equity issues. These latter items, however, affect the balance sheet for year-end 2526. Apply formula 2.11 to compute that SE_{2526} equals $832 (= 690 + 72 + 70). For convenience show all that is known about the balance sheet for year-end 2526:

BALANCE SHEET, 12/31/2526

Cash	$?	$200	Current liabilities
Other current assets	300	180	Debt
PP&E	680	832	Stockholders equity (80 shares)
	$1,212	$1,212	Total

Cash is found such that it equalizes the bottom line. That is, $Cash_{2526}$ equals $232 (= $1,212 – 300 – 680). Now apply the cash flow formulas and find that $CF^{\text{to creditors}}$ equals interest paid on debt and equals $18 (no new loans are taken out); $CF^{\text{to shareholders}}$ equals *Dividends* minus new issues and equals $38 (= $108 – $70); $CF^{\text{from assets}}$ equals the sum of $CF^{\text{to creditors}}$ plus $CF^{\text{to shareholders}}$ and is $56. The *Cash surplus* is the change in *Cash* on the balance sheet and is $142 (= $232 – $90). As an aside, confirm that $CF^{\text{from assets}}$ and *Cash surplus* are consistent with formulas 3.9 and 3.12, respectively.

One final comment about this example pertains to the source of the $102 *Capital expenditure* that the Company pays to the capital goods supplier. The Company sells new shares and raises $70; the remaining $32 is paid in cash. Confirm that if *Capital expenditures* were zero and no shares were issued, *Cash* is $32 higher at $264, and *Total assets* is $1,142.

The next example uses accounting skills to answer a very relevant financial question.

EXAMPLE 10 Construct and interpret the price-to-operating cash flow multiple
Find below the Company's balance sheet for year-end 2525.

BALANCE SHEET, 12/31/2525

Cash	$455	$490	Current liabilities
Inventory	$725	$870	Debt
PP&E	$3,800	$3,620	Stockholders equity
	$4,980	$4,980	Total

For 2525 the Company's asset turnover ratio ($Sales_{2525} \div Total\ assets_{2525}$) is 3.2. *Depreciation* equals 15% of *PP&E*, and the operating profit margin (= earnings before interest and taxes ÷ Sales) is 12.40%. *Interest* expense equals 8.20% of *Debt*. *Taxes* equal 35% of taxable income, and the payout ratio (=*Dividends*÷*Net income*) is 40%. There are 180 shares outstanding and the price-to-earnings ratio at year-end 2525 equals 21.4. There are no other items on the income statement for 2525.

As a prospective investor in the Company's shares, you are especially interested in their financial ratios. You know that the ratio of price-to-operating cash flow for this company's peer group is 6.2. What is the company's price-to-operating cash flow ratio, and does it make the company's stock look cheap or expensive?

SOLUTION

First, work down the income statement in order to compute components necessary for applying formula 3.10 to find $CF^{from\ operations}$. *Sales* equals $15,936 (= 3.2 x $4,980). Next use the operating profit margin of 12.40% to find that *EBIT* equals $1,976 (= 0.1240 x $15,936). Notice that *EBIT* subtracts from *Sales* expenses that include *Cost-of-goods sold*, *Depreciation*, and *Selling, general, and administrative expenses*. Formula 3.10 requires knowledge that *Depreciation* equals $570 (= $3,800 x 0.15). Subtract *Interest* from *EBIT* to compute that *Taxable income* equals $1,904 (= $1,976 – (.0820 x $870)). With a 35% tax rate the *Taxes* equal $667 (= $1,904 x 0.35)). Now use formula 3.10 to find $CF^{from\ operations}$

$$CF^{from\ operations} = EBIT + Depreciation - Taxes$$

$$= \$1,976 + 570 - \$667$$

$$= \$1,879$$

Second, recognize that the ratio of price to operating cash flow for one share is identical to the ratio of the entire company's market capitalization to total operating cash flow. Find market capitalization by using the price-to-earnings ratio of 21.4. Earnings, that is *Net income*, equals *Taxable income* minus *Taxes* and is $1,237 (= $1,904 – $667). Thus,

$$\frac{market\ capitalization}{Net\ income} = 21.4$$

and market cap equals $26,472 (= 21.4 x $1,237). The numerical answer is:

$$\frac{price\ per\ share}{operating\ cash\ flow\ per\ share} = \frac{market\ capitalization}{total\ operating\ cash\ flow}$$

$$= \frac{\$26,472}{\$1,879}$$

$$= 14.1$$

The qualitative interpretation is this. For the peer group the price-to-cash flow averages 6.2. This means that the stock market pays $6.20 for a dollar of cash flow from this type of company. For this specific company, however, the stock market pays $14.10 for a dollar of cash flow. A possible inference is that the company's stock price is expensive relative to the other companies in the peer group. Perhaps the stock is *too* expensive for the cash flows that the company creates. Chapter 8 explores in more detail the use of price multiples for making valuation inferences.

The final example for this chapter shows a simplified setting for a company that obtains financing from a venture capitalist. The venture capital industry is an alternative financing source for many companies.

STREET-BITE An American invention: venture capitalists

Companies need money to grow and quite often venture capitalists are a tremendous financing alternative. Table 3.4 summarizes U.S. venture capital financing during the recent past.

TABLE 3.4 VENTURE CAPITAL FINANCING

Year	Number of companies	Average per company ($ millions)	Sum of venture capital financing ($ millions)
1990	1,471	1.95	2,862
1991	1,279	1.79	2,285
1992	1,415	2.54	3,593
1993	1,209	3.20	3,868
1994	1,239	3.39	4,200
1995	1,901	4.04	7,683
1996	2,656	4.36	11,582
1997	3,250	4.66	15,160
1998	4,203	5.11	21,473
1999	5,684	9.68	54,995
2000	8,208	12.96	106,391
2001	4,691	8.76	41,082
2002	3,028	6.99	21,155
Sum and/or average	40,234/ 3,095	7.4	296,329/ 22,795

Source: National Venture Capital Association, *www.nvca.org/ffax.html,* March 2003.

Companies receiving venture capital financing number in the low thousands. This number is small relative to the millions of corporations that operate and/or receive business loans from commercial banks or other sources. The run-up in technology stock prices during the latter 1990s induced huge inflows of venture capital, however. In year 2000 the average venture capital deal of almost $13 million was spread over 8,200 companies. All in all, however, venture capital is a relatively small but extremely important financing source for economic innovation and growth. This financing source is insignificant in every other country on planet earth, although in Europe venture capital firms are beginning to appear.

Venture capital firms, like banks, lend money. When banks lend, however, they loan to well-established companies, they give the company a payment book, and they collect interest over the life of the loan. Here are several ways that venture capitalists differ.

1. Venture capital firms take an equity stake in the company. That is, when the venture capitalist lends money they actually purchase shares directly from the company. The venture capitalist is not pursuing a fixed interest rate of return. Instead, they expect the stock eventually to rise in value.
2. The company may have reached its debt capacity as far as bank loans go, yet venture capital still may be available. Banks tend to rely on historical records for lending decisions, whereas venture capitalists look toward the future. "Seed investing" occurs for companies that are at very early stages before there is a real product. Venture capitalists also invest in rapidly growing companies in their "expansion stage." And sometimes venture capitalists invest in "later stage" companies that are on the verge of going public. In rare occasions, too, venture capitalists may invest in companies that already are publicly traded.
3. Venture capitalists are activists. They use their experience to help managers of growing companies make sound decisions about strategic marketing, planning, and development. Venture capitalists are like farmers who love to grow successful companies. They are entrepreneurs first and financiers second.
4. Venture capitalists grow the company but eventually intend to liquidate their equity stake. The average venture capital investment lasts between 4 and 7

years. The different ways that the venture capitalist liquidates the investment include: (a) the venture capitalist sells the stock back to the company at a negotiated repurchase price; (b) the company is taken-over or merges with an established company and the venture capitalist swaps their equity for cash or acquiring-company stock; (c) the company goes public and the venture capitalist sells their equity through an IPO; (d) the company goes bankrupt or reorganizes and the venture capitalist's stock becomes worthless.

The success story for a venture capital deal occurs when the company grows to a level of maturity that an IPO occurs (see the *Street-bite* on initial public offerings in chapter 2). Table 3.5 provides information about venture-backed IPOs during the recent past.

TABLE 3.5 VENTURE-BACKED INITIAL PUBLIC OFFERINGS

Year	Number of U.S. IPOs	Number of U.S. venture-backed IPOs	Average venture-backed offer size ($ millions)	Average venture-backed post-offer value ($ millions)
	-1-	-2-	-3-	-4-
1997	537	131	35.9	159.1
1998	329	75	48.3	224.5
1999	480	233	76.4	493.0
2000	354	226	93.3	470.5
2001	88	35	82.6	383.4
2002	94	22	86.8	373.6
Sum and/ or average	1,882	722	70.6	350.7

Source: National Venture Capital Association, www.nvca.org, March 2003.

About 38% of all companies going public from 1997 to 2002 received venture capital financing before the IPO. Column 3, "offer size", is the amount of financing that the company raises by selling stock during the IPO. Column 4, "post offer value", is the amount the stock is worth one-day later in secondary market trading. The huge gap between offer size and post offer value suggests that venture capitalists grow companies in which public markets have a lot of interest. The gap suggests, too, that these companies underprice their stock during the IPO and leave a lot of money on the table!

Other important non-bank sources of financing for young companies include the Small Business Administration (read about "small business investment companies" at www.sba.gov/INV/overview.html) and angel investors (see www.angeldeals.com, for example).

Consider this example for finding the cash flows for a venture capitalist.

EXAMPLE 11 Find cash flows for venture capitalist

A venture capitalist lends a start-up company $100,000 at year-end 2525 and acquires 500 shares. The company also obtains $200,000 by selling its owner/manager 1000 shares, and by borrowing for 2-years a balloon loan of $40,000 on which it pays 10% annual interest. The company's net profit margin (= *Net income* ÷ *Sales*) is forecast at 12%. Sales should equal $400,000 during year 2526, and they should grow 18% for year 2527. The Company sets a 20% dividend payout ratio (= *Dividends* ÷ *Net income*). They promise to repurchase the shares from the venture capitalist at year-end 2527 for 140% of their book value. For this scenario, sketch the cash flows to equity and to creditors.

SOLUTION

The first stage for solving this problem is to sketch the initial balance sheet. For clarity, partition *Stockholders' equity* into several components.

COMPANY BALANCE SHEET, 12/31/2525

Assets		Liabilities	
	$ 40,000	Debt	
	300,000	Total Stockholders' Equity	
		200,000	manager/owner (1,000 shares)
		100,000	venture capitalist (500 shares)
		0	accumulated retained earnings
$340,000		$340,000	

Notice the original equity book value per share is $200 (= $300,000 / 1,500 shares). *Stockholders' equity* changes over subsequent years as a result of *New retained earnings*. *New retained earnings* simply equals *Net income* (12% of *Sales*) minus *Dividends* (20% of *Net income*). For year 2526 when *Sales* equal $400,000 *Net income* is $48,000 and *Dividends* are $9,600 and *New retained earnings* are $38,400. For year 2527 when *Sales* are 18% higher at $472,000 *Net income* is $56,640 and *Dividends* are $11,328 and *New retained earnings* are $45,312. The balance sheet at year-end 2527, before the loan and venture capitalist are repaid, appears as follows:

COMPANY BALANCE SHEET, 12/31/2527 (BEFORE RESTRUCTURE)

Assets		Liabilities	
	$ 40,000	Debt	
	383,712	Total Stockholders' Equity	
		200,000	manager/owner (1,000 shares)
		100,000	venture capitalist (500 shares)
		83,712	accumulated retained earnings
$423,712		$423,712	

At this point in time, the balloon loan of $40,000 is repaid. Presumably the firm liquidates an asset, say money in its cash account, to pay off the loan. Both assets and liabilities decline by $40,000. Furthermore, the equity book value per share equals $255.81 (= $383,712 / 1,500 shares). Equity book value increases over the two-year horizon primarily because the company earns profits and plows back for growth. This is the ideal situation for start-ups. They are a lot like seeds that store their energy so that when eventually they sprout, they survive and thrive.

The company repurchases shares from the venture capitalist at 140% of book value. The repurchase price is therefore $358.13 per share (= $255.81 x 1.4). For 500 shares, the total payment to the venture capitalist is $179,066 (= $358.13 x 500). The company repurchases the shares from the venture capitalist, further drawing down their cash account. Repayment of loan and venture capitalist reduces company cash by a total of $219,066 (=$40,000 + $179,066). *Total assets* declines by exactly this amount, and it falls to $204,646 (=$423,712 − $219,066). The balance sheet after restructuring appears as follows:

COMPANY BALANCE SHEET, 12/31/2527 (AFTER RESTRUCTURE)

Assets		Liabilities	
	$ 0	Debt	
	204,646	Total Stockholders' Equity	
		200,000	manager/owner (1,500 shares)
		0	venture capitalist (0 shares)
		4,646	accumulated retained earnings
$204,646		$204,646	

The *Stockholders' equity* was derived so that it equaled the known *Total assets* of $204,646. Notice that *Accumulated retained earnings* is less after the restructuring than before. In effect, the company took a charge against retained earnings because they used equity to pay off the venture capitalist.

What did the bank and venture capitalist obtain from the company? The answer, of course, is **cash flow**. For the bank, the cash flows are given by

12/31/2525	12/31/2526	12/31/2527
$−40,000	+$4,000	+$44,000

The rate of return for this cash flow stream, as the next chapter explains, is 10%. The bank's rate of return equals the interest rate that it charges.

Cash flows for the venture capitalist equal their share of *Dividends* (500/1500, or 1/3rd of total dividends, which equals $3,200 in 2526 and $3,776 in 2527) plus the repurchase sum:

12/31/2525	12/31/2526	12/31/2527
$-100,000	$3,200	$182,842

The rate of return for this cash flow stream, as the next chapter explains, is about 37% per year. While this certainly is higher than the rate earned on savings accounts, the venture capitalist finances a lot of projects, and some of them fail. The high earnings on winners compensate the venture capitalists for the losses suffered on losers.

EXERCISES 3.3
Numerical quickies

1. The Company balance sheet for year 2525 shows that *Total assets* of $4,300 are financed by *Debt* of $400 and *Stockholders' equity* of $3,900. There are 430 shares outstanding at year-end 2525. The company plans to obtain venture capital by selling 140 additional shares at their current book value to a venture capitalist. The company agrees to repurchase the shares at year-end 2526 at a price equal to 146% of that year's book value. For year 2526 the company forecasts *Sales* of $29,240 and a net profit margin (= *Net income* ÷ *Sales*) of 9.20% and a dividend payout ratio (= *Dividends* ÷ *Net income*) of 30%. Assume *Debt* remains unchanged. How much total cash flow (*Dividends* plus repurchase price) does the venture capitalist receive at year-end 2526? ©BA3am

2. The Company balance sheet for year 2525 shows that *Total assets* of $3,800 are financed by *Debt* of $600 and *Stockholders' equity* of $3,200. There are 270 shares outstanding at year-end 2525. The company plans to obtain venture capital by selling 120 additional shares at their current book value to a venture capitalist. The company agrees to repurchase the shares at year-end 2526 at a price equal to 125% of that year's book value. For year 2526 the company forecasts *Sales* of $25,080 and a net profit margin (= *Net income* ÷ *Sales*) of 10.50%, and a dividend payout ratio (= *Dividends* ÷ *Net income*) of 35%. Assume *Debt* remains unchanged. How much is the equity repurchase shareprice at year-end 2526? ©BA3bm

Challengers

3. The Company balance sheet for year 2525 shows that *Total assets* of $4,900 are financed by *Debt* of $400 and *Stockholders' equity* of $4,500. There are 640 shares outstanding at year-end 2525. The company plans to obtain venture capital by selling 240 additional shares at their current book value to a venture capitalist. The company agrees to repurchase the shares at year-end 2526 at a price equal to 130% of that year's book value. For year 2526 the company forecasts *Sales* of $25,400 and a net profit margin (= *Net income* ÷ *Sales*) of 7.50%, and a dividend payout ratio (= *Dividends* ÷ *Net income*) of 25%. Assume *Debt* remains unchanged. What is the rate of return for the venture capitalist on this investment? ©BA3cm

4. The Company balance sheet for year 2525 shows *Total assets* of $3,500 financed by *Debt* of $400 and *Stockholders' equity* of $3,100. There are 340 shares outstanding at year-end 2525. The company plans to obtain venture capital by selling 70 additional shares at their current book value to a venture capitalist. The company agrees to repurchase the shares at year-end 2527 at a price equal to 120% of that year's book value. For year

2526 the company forecasts *Sales* of $21,700 , a net profit margin (= *Net income ÷ Sales*) of 13.50%, and a dividend payout ratio (= *Dividends ÷ Net income*) of 35%. For year 2527, *Sales* should be higher by 19% but the net profit margin and payout ratio should remain constant. Also, assume that *Debt* always remains unchanged. How much total cash flow (*Dividends* plus repurchase price) does the venture capitalist receive at year-end 2527? ©BA4am

5. The Company balance sheet for year 2525 shows *Total assets* of $4,900 financed by *Debt* of $300 and *Stockholders' equity* of $4,600. There are 660 shares outstanding at year-end 2525. The company plans to obtain venture capital by selling 260 additional shares at their current book value to a venture capitalist. The company agrees to repurchase the shares at year-end 2527 at a price equal to 124% of that year's book value. For year 2526 the company forecasts *Sales* of $38,710 and a net profit margin (= *Net income ÷ Sales*) of 7.80%, and a dividend payout ratio (= *Dividends ÷ Net income*) of 20%. For year 2527, *Sales* should be higher by 22% but the net profit margin and payout ratio should remain constant. Also, assume that Debt always remains unchanged. How much is the equity repurchase shareprice at year-end 2527? ©BA3bm

6. Find below the Company's balance sheet at year-end 2525.

BALANCE SHEET, 12/31/2525

Cash	$555	$1,255	Debt
PP&E	$3,100	$2,400	Stockholders equity
	$3,655	$3,655	Total

For the year 2526, the following items are forecast: *Depreciation* is $430; *Capital expenditures* equal $360; *Interest* expense is $110; *Net income* is $480; *Dividends* equal $154; *Cash flow from assets* is –$114; *Net debt issues* is $138 (that is, debt increases). There is no preferred stock or extraordinary items, and there are no other non-cash expenses. The balance sheet for year-end 2526 contains only the same line items as appear above. For year 2526, how much is *Net equity issues*? ©CF1e

7. Find below the Company's balance sheet at year-end 2525.

BALANCE SHEET, 12/31/2525

Cash	$555	$1,055	Debt
PP&E	$1,600	$1,100	Stockholders equity
	$2,155	$2,155	Total

For the year 2526, the following items are forecast: *Depreciation* is $130; *Capital expenditures* equal $110; *Interest* expense is $90; *Net income* is $320; *Dividends* equal $157; *Cash flow from assets* is $185; *Net debt issues* is $95 (that is, *Debt* increases). There is no preferred stock or extraordinary items, and there are no other non-cash expenses. The balance sheet for year-end 2526 contains only the same line items as appear above. For year 2526, how much is the *Cash flow to shareholders*? ©CF2

8. Find below the Company's balance sheet at year-end 2525.

BALANCE SHEET, 12/31/2525

Cash	$495	$1,095	Debt
PP&E	$2,000	$1,400	Stockholders equity
	$2,495	$2,495	Total

For the year 2526, the following items are forecast: *Depreciation* is $200; *Capital expenditures* equal $170; *Interest* expense is $100; *Net income* is $400; *Dividends* equal $132; *Cash flow from assets* is $264; *Net debt issues* is $66 (that is, *Debt* increases). There is no preferred stock or extraordinary items, and there are no other non-cash expenses. The balance sheet for year-end 2526 contains only the same line items as appear above. For year-end 2526, how much is *Stockholders' equity*? ©CF1cm

9. Find below the Company's balance sheet at year-end 2525.

BALANCE SHEET, 12/31/2525

Cash	$420	$1,120	Debt
PP&E	$3,100	$2,400	Stockholders equity
	$3,520	$3,520	Total

For the year 2526, the following items are forecast: *Depreciation* is $430; *Capital expenditures* equal $360; Interest expense is $80; Net income is $490; Dividends equal $162; Cash flow from assets is $280; *Net debt issues* is $34 (that is, debt increases). There is no preferred stock or extraordinary items, and there are no other non-cash expenses. The balance sheet for year-end 2526 contains only the same line items as appear above. For year 2526, how much is the *Cash surplus?* ©CF1am

10. Find below the Company's balance sheet for year-end 2525.

BALANCE SHEET, 12/31/2525

Cash	$435	$435	Current liabilities
Inventory	$780	$780	Debt
PP&E	$3,000	$3,000	Stockholders' equity
	$4,215	$4,215	Total

For 2525 the Company's asset turnover ratio ($Sales_{2525} \div Total\ assets_{2525}$) is 3.8. *Depreciation* equals 17% of *PP&E*, and the operating profit margin (= earnings before interest and taxes ÷ *Sales*) is 10.70%. *Interest* expense equals 9.40% of *Debt*. Taxes equal 35% of taxable income, and the payout ratio (=*Dividends÷Net income*) is 35%. There are no other items on the income statement for 2525. There are 150 shares outstanding.

As a prospective investor in the Company's shares, you are especially interested in their ability to generate cash flow. How much is *Cash flow from operations* for year 2525? ©CF3b

11. Find below the Company's balance sheet for year-end 2525.

BALANCE SHEET, 12/31/2525

Cash	$345	$750	Current liabilities
Inventory	$795	$790	Debt
PP&E	$4,000	$3,600	Stockholders equity
	$5,140	$5,140	Total

For 2525 the Company's asset turnover ratio ($Sales_{2525} \div Total\ assets_{2525}$) is 3.6. *Depreciation* equals 18% of *PP&E*, and the operating profit margin (= earnings before interest and taxes ÷ *Sales*) is 9.70%. *Interest* expense equals 9.60% of *Debt*. Taxes equal 35% of taxable income, and the payout ratio (=*Dividends÷Net income*) is 45%. There are no other items on the income statement for 2525. There are 180 shares outstanding.

As a prospective investor in the Company's shares, you are especially interested in their financial ratios. You know the price-to-earnings ratio at year-end 2525 equals 28.3. More significant to you, however, is the price-to-cash-flow ratio (= shareprice ÷ operating cash flow per share). What is the company's price-to-cash-flow ratio? ©CF3a

ANSWERS TO CHAPTER 3 EXERCISES

EXERCISES 3.1

1. The increase in *Total assets* equals $15,498 (= .054 x $287,000). The change in *Total liabilities and Stockholders' equity* equals $13,400. Applying formula 3.2 shows that EFN equals $2,098 (= $15,498 –

$13,400). The company must borrow $2,098 or else the assets cannot grow as required.

2. The first step is finding original *Inventory*. The inventory turnover ratio is 5.6154 (= 365 / 65) and original *Inventory* therefore is $7,747 (= 0.75 x $58,000 / 5.6154). After the policy change the inventory turnover ratio becomes 3.7245 (= 365 / (65+33)). The new balance of *Inventory* therefore is $11,679 (= 0.75 x $58,000 / 3.7245). The rise in *Inventory* of $3,933 (= $11,679 – $7,747) incurs additional annual financing costs of $551 (= $3,933 x 0.14).

3. Find that original *Payables* equals $41,425 (= 56 x $360,000 x 0.75 / 365). Then find that new *Payables* equals $63,616 (= (56+30) x $360,000 x 0.75 / 365). The annual financing costs that the company avoids from increasing the average payment period equals $4,216 (= 0.19 x ($63,616 – $41,425)).

4. *Total assets* increases by $518 (= 0.175 x $2,960). *Current liabilities* rises by $94 (= 0.175 x $540). *New retained earnings* for 2526 grows to $306 (= (1+0.175) x $260). Use formula 3.2 to find that EFN is $118 (= $518 – $94 – $306).

5. *Total assets* increases by $370 (= 0.12 x $3,080). *Current liabilities* rises by $37 (= 0.12 x $310). *New retained earnings* for 2526 grows to $695 (= [($700 /$19,500)+0.026)] x (1+0.12) x $19,500 x ($360/$700)). Use formula 3.2 to find that EFN is –$363 (= $370 – $37 – $695). The negative sign means the company will run a surplus.

6. This question asks that if EFN equals zero how much is the allowable increase in *Total assets*. *Current liabilities* rises by $91 (= 0.123 x $740). *New retained earnings* for 2526 grows to $146 (= (1+0.123) x $130). Internal and spontaneous financing sum to $237 (= $91 + $146). In the absence of external financing, *Total assets* can rise to become $4,077 (= $3,840 + $237).

7. *Total assets* increases by $225 (= 0.107 x ($5,100 – $3,000). *Current liabilities* rises by $182 (= 0.107 x $1,700). *New retained earnings* for 2526 grows to $455 (= (1+0.107) x ($1,645 – $1,234). Use formula 3.2 to find that EFN is –$412 (= $225 – $182 – $455); that's the surplus.

8. The company increases *Sales* to $17,952 (= (1+.088) x $16,500). *Total assets* for year 2526 with the new asset turnover ratio becomes $6,649 (= $17,952 / 2.70). The change in *Total assets* is –$851 (= $6,649 – $7,500). The negative sign means *Total assets* decreases. Remember that a decline in an asset is a source of financing. *Current liabilities* rises by $106 (= 0.088 x $1,200). *New retained earnings* for 2526 grows to $207 (= (1+0.088) x ($759 – $569). Use formula 3.2 to find that EFN is –$1,163 (= –$851 – $106 – $207); that's a surplus.

EXERCISES 3.2

1. Apply formula 3.3a and find that $g^{internal}$ equals 8.66% (= $210 / ($2,635 – $210)). *Total assets* at 12/31/2526 therefore equals $2,863 (= $2,635 x (1 + .0866)).

2. Use formula 2.5 to find that the debt-to-equity ratio equals 0.8182 (= 0.45 / (1 – 0.45)). Apply formula 3.4a and find that $g^{sustainable}$ equals 16.21% (= $280 x (1 + 0.8182) / [$3,650 – $280 x (1 + 0.8182)]). *Total assets* at 12/31/2526 therefore equals $4,241 (= $3,650 x (1 + .1621)).

3. The increase in sales equals $4,241 (= $48,000 x 0.074).

4. Because the company relies exclusively on retained earnings and the key ratios (except for the debt ratio are constant) the company grows at $g^{internal}$. Apply formula 3.3a and find that $g^{internal}$ equals 4.29% (= $150 / ($3,650 – $150)). That's the sales growth rate!

5. Apply formula 3.3a and find that $g^{internal}$ equals 3.50% (= $125 / ($3,700 – $125)). Because of constant ratios find that *New retained earnings*$_{2526}$ equals $129 (= $125 x (1 + .035)). *Stockholders' equity*$_{2526}$ therefore

becomes \$2,229 (= \$2,100 + \$129), and equity book value per share is \$20.27 (= \$2,229 / 110).

6. Apply formula 3.3a and find that $g^{internal}$ equals 13.03% (= \$320 / (\$2,775 – \$320)). Because of constant ratios find that $Net\ income_{2526}$ equals \$791 (= \$700 x (1 + .1303)). Market capitalization at year-end 2526 becomes \$16,141 (= 20.4 x \$791). $New\ retained\ earnings_{2526}$ equals \$362 (= \$320 x (1 + .1303)) and $Stockholders'\ equity_{2526}$ therefore becomes \$2,262 (= \$1,900 + \$362). The ratio of $Market\ cap_{2526}$ to $Stockholders'\ equity_{2526}$ therefore equals 7.14.

7. Apply formula 3.3a and find that $g^{internal}$ equals 4.29% (= \$150 / (\$2,775 – \$150)). Because of constant ratios find that $New\ retained\ earnings_{2526}$ equals \$156 (= \$150 x (1 + .1303)) and $Stockholders'\ equity_{2526}$ therefore becomes \$2,156 (= \$2,000 + \$156). $Debt$ is constant, so the ratio of $Debt_{2526}$ to $Stockholders'\ equity_{2526}$ therefore equals 0.77.

8. We find the rate of return to equity as the increase in market capitalization plus total dividends (the rate of return to one share is identical to the rate of return to all equity; this approach works when no shares are issued). Market capitalization at year-end 2525 equals \$8,580 (= 14.3 x \$600). Apply formula 3.3a and find that $g^{internal}$ equals 15.32% (= \$380 / (\$2,860 – \$380)). Because of constant ratios find that $Net\ income_{2526}$ equals \$692 (= \$600 x (1 + .1532)). Market capitalization at year-end 2526 becomes \$9,895 (= 14.3 x \$692). $Dividends_{2526}$ equals \$254 (= \$220 x (1 + .1532)). The stockholder rate of return therefore equals 18.28% (= (\$9,895 + \$254 – \$8,580) / \$8,580)).

9. This problem is the same as the previous one except that there is a change in the price-to-earnings ratio. Market capitalization at year-end 2525 equals \$119,720 (= 29.2 x \$4,100). Apply formula 3.3a and find that $g^{internal}$ equals 5.10% (= \$1,230 / (\$25,350 – \$1,230)). Because of constant ratios find that $Net\ income_{2526}$ equals \$4,309 (= \$4,100 x (1 + .0510)). Market capitalization at year-end 2526 becomes \$96,954 (= 22.5 x \$4,309). $Dividends_{2526}$ equals \$3,016 (= \$2,870 x (1 + .0510)). The stockholder rate of return therefore equals –16.50% (= (\$96,954 + \$3,016 – \$119,720) / \$119,720)).

10. This problem applies formula 3.4a to find $g^{sustainable}$; it equals 8.11% (= {\$150 x (1 + \$1,650 / \$2,000)} / (\$3,650 – {\$150 x (1 + \$1,650 / \$2,000)})). Because of constant ratios find that $New\ retained\ earnings_{2526}$ equals \$162 (= \$150 x (1 + .0811)). $Stockholders'\ equity_{2526}$ therefore becomes \$2,162 (= \$2,000 + \$162), and equity book value per share is \$21.62 (= \$2,162 / 100).

11. Apply formula 3.4a and find that $g^{sustainable}$ equals 25.00% (= {\$340 x (1 + \$1,275 / \$1,700)} / (\$2,975 – {\$340 x (1 + \$1,275 / \$1,700)})). Because of constant ratios find that $Net\ income_{2526}$ equals \$1,125 (= \$900 x (1 + .25)). Market capitalization at year-end 2526 becomes \$33,187 (= 29.5 x \$1,125). $New\ retained\ earnings_{2526}$ equals \$425 (= \$340 x (1 + .25)) and $Stockholders'\ equity_{2526}$ therefore becomes \$2,125 (= \$1,700 + \$425). The ratio of $Market\ cap_{2526}$ to $Stockholders'\ equity_{2526}$ therefore equals 15.6.

12. Find the rate of return to equity as the increase in market capitalization plus total dividends. Market capitalization at year-end 2525 equals \$8,800 (= 22.0 x \$400). Apply formula 3.4a and find that $g^{sustainable}$ equals 12.36% (= {\$220 x (1 + \$910 / \$2,000)} / (\$2,910 – {\$220 x (1 + \$910 / \$2,000)})). Because of constant ratios find that $Net\ income_{2526}$ equals \$449 (= \$400 x (1 + .1236)). Market capitalization at year-end 2526 becomes \$9,888 (= 22.0 x \$449). $Dividends_{2526}$ equals \$202 (= \$180 x (1 + .1236)). The stockholder rate of return therefore equals 14.66% (= (\$9,888 + \$202 – \$8,800) / \$8,800)).

13. This problem is the same as the previous one except that there is a change in the price-to-earnings ratio. Market capitalization at year-end 2525 equals $238,620 (= 19.4 x $12,300). Apply formula 3.4a and find that $g^{sustainable}$ equals 12.79% (= {$3,810 x (1 + $9,450 / $33,600)} / ($43,050 – {$3,810 x (1 + $9,450 / $33,600)})). Because of constant ratios find that *Net income*$_{2526}$ equals $13,873 (= $12,300 x (1 + .1279)). Market capitalization at year-end 2526 becomes $302,434 (= 21.8 x $13,873). *Dividends*$_{2526}$ equals $9,576 (= $8,490 x (1 + .1279)). The stockholder rate of return therefore equals 30.76% (= ($302,434 + $9,576 – $238,620) / $238,620)).

EXERCISES 3.3

1. The venture capitalist purchases 140 shares for a total of $1,270 (= 140 x $3,900 / 430). *Stockholders' equity* therefore rises immediately to $5,170 (= $3,900 + $1,270) and there are 570 shares outstanding (= 430 + 140). Then throughout year 2526 there is *Net income* of $2,690 (= .0920 x $29,240); *Dividends* of $807 (= $2,690 x 0.30); and *New retained earnings* of $1,883 (= $2,690 x 0.70). *Stockholders' equity*$_{2526}$ consequently equals $7,053 (= $5,170 + $1,883). Equity book value per share at year-end 2526 is $12.37 (= $7,053 / 570). The company repurchases shares from the venture capitalist for $18.07 each (= $12.37 x 1.46). The total repurchase amount is $2,529 (= $18.07 x 140). The venture capitalist's total *Dividends* equal $198 (= $807 x 140 / 570). Total cash flow to the venture capitalist at year-end 2526 equals $2,727.

2. Collapse the logic for the previous problem into fewer steps. The venture capitalist purchases 120 shares and *Stockholders' equity* therefore rises immediately to $4,622 (= $3,200 + 120 x $3,200 / 270). Then throughout year 2526 there is *New retained earnings* of $1,712 (= .1050 x $25,080 x (1 – 0.35)). *Stockholders' equity*$_{2526}$ consequently equals $6,334 (= $4,622 + $1,712). The company repurchases shares from the venture capitalist for $20.30 each (= $6,334 x 1.25 / (120 + 270)).

3. Collapse the logic for the previous problems into fewer steps. The venture capitalist purchases 240 shares for $1,837 and *Stockholders' equity* therefore rises immediately to $6,737 (= $4,900 + 240 x $4,900 / 640). Then throughout year 2526 there is *New retained earnings* of $1,429 (= .0750 x $25,400 x (1 – 0.25)) and *Dividends* of $476 (= .0750 x $25,400 x 0.25). *Stockholders' equity*$_{2526}$ consequently equals $8,166 (= $6,737 + $1,429). The company repurchases 240 shares from the venture capitalist for $2,784 (= $8,166 x 1.25 x 240 / (240 + 640)). The venture capitalist's rate of return is 58.6% (= {$2,784 + [$476 x 240 / (240 + 640)] – $1,837 } / $1,837).

4. *Stockholders' equity* rises immediately to $3,738 (= $3,100 + 70 x $3,100 / 340). *Stockholders' equity*$_{2526}$ rises to $5,642 (= $3,738 + .1350 x $21,700 x (1 – 0.35)). *Stockholders' equity*$_{2527}$ rises to $7,908 (= $5,642 + .1350 x $21,700 x (1 + .19) x (1 – 0.35)). The venture capitalist at year-end 2527 receives *Dividends* of $208 (= .1350 x $21,700 x (1 + .19) x 0.35 x 70 / (70 + 340)) and a repurchase amount of $1,620 (= $7,908 x 1.20 x 70 / (70 + 340)), for total cash flow of $1,828 (= $208 + $1,620).

5. *Stockholders' equity*$_{2527}$ rises to $11,775 (= $4,600 + {$4,600 x 260 / 660} + {.0780 x $38,710 x (1 – 0.20)} + {.0780 x $38,710 x (1 + .22) x (1 – 0.20)}). The venture capitalist at year-end 2527 receives a repurchase price per share of $15.87 (= $11,775 x 1.24 / (260 + 660)).

6. Use the formula $CF^{from\ assets}$ = Interest – Net debt issues + Dividends – Net equity issues. Substitute values from the set-up: –$114 = $110 – $138 + $154 – *Net equity issues*. Compute that *Net equity issues*$_{2526}$ equals 240 (the positive sign means the sells stock in the primary market).

7. Use the formula $CF^{\textit{from assets}} = \textit{Interest} - \textit{Net debt issues} + \textit{Dividends} - \textit{Net equity issues}$. Substitute values from the set-up: $185 = \$90 - \$95 + \$157 - \textit{Net equity issues}$. Compute that $\textit{Net equity issues}_{2526}$ equals –33 (the negative sign means the company repurchases equity). $CF^{\textit{to}}_{\textit{shareholders}}$ is $190 (= \$157 - (-33))$.

8. Use the formula $CF^{\textit{from assets}} = \textit{Interest} - \textit{Net debt issues} + \textit{Dividends} - \textit{Net equity issues}$. Substitute values from the set-up: $264 = \$100 - \$66 + \$132 - \textit{Net equity issues}$. Compute that $\textit{Net equity issues}_{2526}$ equals –98. Now find that $\textit{New retained earnings}_{2526}$ is $268 (= \$400 - \$132)$. SE_{2526} consequently equals $1,570 (= \$1,400 + \$268 - \$98)$.

9. Use the formula $CF^{\textit{from assets}} = \textit{Interest} - \textit{Net debt issues} + \textit{Dividends} - \textit{Net equity issues}$. Substitute values from the set-up: $280 = \$80 - \$34 + \$162 - \textit{Net equity issues}$. Compute that $\textit{Net equity issues}_{2526}$ equals –\$72. Now find that $\textit{New retained earnings}_{2526}$ is $328 (= \$490 - \$162)$. SE_{2526} consequently equals $2,656 (= \$2,400 + \$328 - \$72)$. Also, $PP\&E_{2526}$ equals $3,030 (= \$3,100 - \$430 + \$360)$. Construct the balance sheet for year-end 2526 by entering the known values for $Debt_{2526}$ and SE_{2526} and $PP\&E_{2526}$.

   Balance Sheet, 12/31/2526

Cash	?	$1,154	Debt
PP&E	$3,030	$2,656	Stockholders equity
$3,810		$3,810	Total

   Compute that *Cash* equals $780 (= \$3,810 - \$3,030)$. The *Cash surplus* equals the change in *Cash*, which equals $360 (= \$780 - \$420)$.

10. Work down the income statement and apply formula 3.10. *Sales* equals $16,017 (=3.8 \times \$4,215)$; *EBIT* is $1,714 (= 0.1070 \times \$16,017)$; *Taxable income* is $1,640 (= \$1,714 - (.0940 \times \$780))$; *Taxes* equal $574 (= \$1,640 \times 0.35)$; and $CF^{\textit{from operations}}$ equals $1,650 (= \$1,714 + (.17 \times \$3,000) - \$574)$.

11. Collapse the logic for the previous problems into fewer steps in order to find $CF^{\textit{from operations}}$. *EBIT* is $1,795 (= 3.6 \times \$5,140 \times 0.0970)$; *Taxes* equal $601 (= \{\$1,795 - (.0970 \times \$790)\} \times 0.35)$; and $CF^{\textit{from operations}}$ equals $1,913 (= \$1,795 + (.18 \times \$4,000) - \$601)$. Now find market capitalization: *Net income* is $1,117 (= \{\$1,795 - (.0970 \times \$790)\} \times \{1 - 0.35\})$; market cap equals $31,607 (= 28.3 \times \$1,117)$. The ratio of market cap to $CF^{\textit{from operations}}$ is identical to the ratio of shareprice to operating cash flow per share and equals 16.5 (= \$31,607 / \$1,913).

CHAPTER 4

Time Value and Relations Between Returns

CHAPTER CONTENTS

Financial decisions generally require relating cash flows occurring at different times. This section explains that a dollar today is not the same as a dollar yesterday or tomorrow. Cash flows occurring at different times, even though apparently the same amount, possess different time values. Combining cash flows from different times requires adjusting for time value differences. This chapter explains time value relations.

1. FRAMEWORK FOR PROPERLY MEASURING AVERAGE RATES OF RETURN

Financial decisions often require recognition about rates of return that different cash flow streams offer. Measuring rates of return can be tricky, and it's important to carefully consider what really is meant by "rate of return". ROR is the abbreviation for rate of return.

When you invest $100 and get back $120, it seems intuitively obvious that the cumulative rate of return is 20 percent. This gives rise to the following definition for the cumulative rate of return:

> **FORMULA 4.1 The cumulative rate of return**
>
> $$ROR^{cumulative} = \frac{W^{end} - W^{beginning}}{W^{beginning}}.$$

The variables $W^{beginning}$ and W^{end} denote beginning and ending wealth. With the numbers above, for example, you begin with $100 and end with $120, so $ROR^{cumulative}$ easily is found as

$$ROR^{cumulative} = \frac{\$120 - \$100}{\$100}$$

$$= 20\%.$$

The cumulative rate of return represents the percentage change in wealth between the beginning and ending times, regardless of how much time elapses. With the numbers above, for example, the cumulative ROR is 20 percent regardless of whether the $20 increase in wealth accrues overnight, over a month, or over two years. Sometimes $ROR^{cumulative}$ also is called the holding period rate of return. Later we adjust the formula for $ROR^{cumulative}$ to account for dividends and other distributions. The current discussion, however, assumes zero dividends and distributions in order to focus on the basic relation between rates of return and wealth changes.

Formula 4.1 is easily rewritten to show several equivalent and often used cumulative rate of return versions:

$$ROR^{cumulative} = \frac{W^{end} - W^{beginning}}{W^{beginning}}$$

$$= \frac{\Delta W}{W^{beginning}}$$

$$= \frac{profit}{W^{beginning}}$$

$$= \frac{W^{end}}{W^{beginning}} - 1.$$

The first alternative version computes ROR as change in wealth relative to beginning wealth. The middle formulation recognizes that the change in wealth equals profit, so the ROR equals profit over beginning wealth. Finally, the last version divides ending wealth by beginning wealth, and subtracts 1. Convince yourself that the different versions are equivalent, and that they always give the same answer. Use the one that best matches your problem's information.

Often institutions and individuals express a rate of return per period of time. Banks quote interest rates, for example, as annual rates—the relevant period of time for these is a year. Many institutions present quarterly rates of return that they earn on investments or offer on accounts. Some mutual funds report monthly or even daily returns. Irrespective of the period's length, the formula for the periodic ROR during period t is:

FORMULA 4.2 The periodic rate of return

$$ROR_t = \frac{W_t - W_{t-1}}{W_{t-1}}.$$

W_t denotes the price, value, or wealth for an investment at time t. ROR_t is the periodic rate of return for period t, and simply represents the percentage change in asset value during the time period. If one uses year-end security prices, for example, formula 4.2 computes an annual ROR; if one uses end-of-month prices, then periodic ROR are monthly rates of return; etc.

Suppose you invest $100 in a security today; in one year the security price is $60; and in two years you sell the security for $100, the original price. For the first year the periodic ROR is:

$$ROR_1 = \frac{\$60 - \$100}{\$100}$$
$$= -40\%$$

Wealth diminishes 40 percent the first year. The second year, however, the security price climbs back to $100. The second year's periodic ROR is:

$$ROR_1 = \frac{\$100 - \$60}{\$60}$$
$$= -67\%$$

Wealth increases two-thirds the second year.

The annual ROR is −40 percent for the first year and 67 percent for the second year. What is the average annual ROR? This seemingly simple yet important question has two plausible answers. The first answer uses the "arithmetic average periodic ROR" definition below:

FORMULA 4.3 The arithmetic average rate of return

$$ROR^{arithmetic\,average} = \sum_{t=1}^{N} \frac{ROR_t}{N}.$$

ROR_t is the periodic rate of return for period t, and N is the number of terms added together. $ROR^{arithmetic\,average}$ simply adds together all periodic ROR and divides by the number of periods; it is a simple average.

$$ROR^{arithmetic\,average} = \frac{-40\% + 67\%}{2}$$
$$= 13.5\%$$

The average annual ROR for our example is found by adding together the two annual ROR of –40 percent and 67 percent, and dividing by two:
The average annual ROR of 13.5 percent suggests to a casual reader that the investor earns 13.5 percent per year. The more astute reader realizes, though, that $W^{beginning}$ is $100, W^{end} two years later is $100, and $ROR^{cumulative}$ is 0 percent. In other words, the investor ends and begins with the same wealth, yet the arithmetic average annual ROR implies earnings of over 13 percent per year.

This curious situation motivates introduction of a second definition for the average ROR. We use this definition to get the second answer for our simple question "what is the average annual ROR?"

FORMULA 4.4 The geometric average rate of return, expanded version

$$ROR^{geometric\,average} = \sqrt[N]{(1+ROR_1)(1+ROR_2)\ldots(1+ROR_N)} - 1$$

The geometric average periodic rate of return adds 1 to each periodic ROR, multiplies together all N of the "1 plus ROR's", takes the Nth root of the product, and subtracts one. For our example, the periodic ROR equal –40 percent and +67 percent for the first and second years, respectively. Thus,

$$ROR^{geometric\,average} = \sqrt[2]{(1+(-.40))(1+0.67)} - 1$$
$$= \sqrt[2]{(0.60)(1.67)} - 1$$
$$= \sqrt[2]{1.00} - 1$$
$$= 0.0\%$$

Notice the formula for geometric average ROR requires entry of the periodic ROR as their decimal equivalents. That is, enter sixty-seven percent as 0.67.

The geometric average ROR accurately relates beginning and ending wealth. A little bit of algebra and rearrangement of equation 4.4 provides a simpler definition:

FORMULA 4.5 The geometric average rate of return, concise version

$$ROR^{geometric\,average} = \sqrt[N]{\frac{W^{end}}{W^{beginning}}} - 1$$

To compute the geometric average rate of return divide ending wealth by beginning wealth, take the Nth root, and subtract 1!

The geometric average rate of return depends only on the ending and beginning wealth. Whatever happens in the middle is irrelevant. For this reason more information about financial outcomes often is given by the geometric average instead of the arithmetic average. The important outcome in a poker game, for example, is not how much you win or lose on each hand. Rather, the significant financial information is how much you begin and end with!

Two commonly used procedures for computing an average rate of return include the arithmetic and the geometric procedures (formulas 4.3 and 4.4). Table 4.1 confirms that the alternative procedures lead to extremely different estimates. The table shows the monthly average rate of return for the respective company's common stock throughout the stated sample period. All companies trade on either the New

TABLE 4.1

Differences between geometric and average rates of return for selected NYSE and AMEX stocks
Source: Author's computations with data from the Center for Research in Security Prices (1998). Each entry is the maximum among all NYSE+AMEX firms of the difference between arithmetic and geometric average monthly rates of return for the respective sample period.

Description	ROR arithmetic average	ROR geometric average	Difference
January–December 1997 Saf T Lok, Inc.	41.12%	−1.41%	42.53%
January 1990–December 1997 O C G Technology, Inc.	26.94	1.01	25.93
January 1980–December 1997 Venus Exploration, Inc.	2.44	−1.00	3.44
January 1960–December 1997 United Park City Mines, Co.	1.39	0.15	1.24
January 1940–December 1997 Sunshine Mining & Refining, Co.	1.14	0.24	0.90
December 1927–December 1997 Texas Instruments, Inc.	2.26	0.72	1.54

STREET–BITE Mistaken Measures: Case of the Beardstown Ladies

It seems like it should be pretty simple to correctly measure the rate of return. The issue actually can be pretty complicated. It becomes even more confusing when cash infusions, withdrawals, taxes, and other factors come into play.

One relatively well-known debacle involving mismeasurement of the rate of return is the Case of the Beardstown Ladies. In 1999 the Beardstown ladies were reaping profits from their New York Times Bestseller entitled *How to Win Big in the Stock Market*. These dozen senior ladies had formed an investment club a decade and a half earlier. Each contributed money, researched and analyzed possible purchases, and made buy and sell recommendations at club meetings. The fortunate women began amassing quite a fortune from their stock picks. After a while people started talking. The Beardstown ladies loved to talk, too, and became popular guests on daytime talk shows. The business press began a full-court press, tracking down the ladies, interviewing them, and critically analyzing claims. Time magazine describes what happened next.

"The lovable ladies were unmasked as frauds—unintentional, mind you—but frauds nonetheless. Five books, hundreds of speeches and dozens of national-TV appearances later, Chicago Magazine challenged their claim of earning compound annual average returns of 23.4% in the 10 years ending in 1993. Undeterred but under pressure, the ladies went to Price Waterhouse for an audit and discovered that their actual return was a sickly 9.1%—far less, according to Lipper Analytical Services, than the Standard & Poor's 500 average annual return of 14.9% or even the average general-stock-fund return of 12.6% during that same period." [*Time*, March 30, 1998. Vol. 151, No. 12, found @ www.pathfinder.com/time]

The lovable ladies unfortunately made an honest mistake measuring the rate of return. As you can see, measuring it correctly can be very important!

York Stock Exchange or American Stock Exchange, and consequently represent rather large, liquid securities with substantial investor interest.

The first row shows that in 1997 the average of the twelve monthly rates of return for Saf T Lok common stock is 41.12 percent by the arithmetic procedure. This implies a hugely profitable investment, especially since this represents a monthly rate of return. The implication is false, however. The geometric average rate of return is –1.41 percent per month. Shareholders in this company actually lose wealth during the year. The arithmetic average overstates the geometric average rate of return by 42.53 percent per month.

The table illustrates extreme differences between these rates of return measures for long time horizons, too. For Texas Instruments common stock over the 70 years concluding with year-end 1997, the monthly average rate of return is 2.26 percent by the arithmetic procedure, and 0.72 percent by the geometric procedure. The difference exceeds 1 3/4 percent per month. Applying an incorrect rate in the time value relation grossly misstates wealth accumulation—ask any one of the Beardstown Ladies.

The table also highlights an important rule regarding the relation between arithmetic and geometric average returns:

RULE 4.1 The ranking of average ROR

The arithmetic average rate of return always exceeds or equals the geometric average rate of return, that is

$$ROR^{arithmetic\ average} \geq ROR^{geometric\ average}.$$

EXAMPLE 1 Find the average ROR

You bought a stock three years ago for $48. Today the stock is worth $120. What has been your average annual rate of return?

SOLUTION

The question doesn't specify whether to find the arithmetic average, or the geometric average. Consider both answers.

Use formula 4.5 to find the geometric average annual ROR:

$$ROR^{geometric\ average} = \sqrt[3]{(\$120/\$48)} - 1$$
$$= \sqrt[3]{2.50} - 1$$
$$= 1.3572 - 1$$
$$= 35.72\%$$

That's not bad, 35.72 percent a year for three years!

CALCULATOR CLUE

Many calculators use the [y^x] key in order to compute the xth root of a term. Recall that taking the 3rd root is the same as raising to the 1/3 power. Solve the above problem on the BAII Plus© with the following keystrokes:

2.5 [y^x] 3 [1/x] [=] [–] 1 [=]

The answer of 0.3572 appears on the display.

Now consider the arithmetic annual average rate of return. Inspect equation 4.3 and notice that the computation requires each year's performance. ROR^arithmetic average depends on the pattern between beginning and ending prices. The problem set-up only tells us that the beginning price is $48 and, three years later, the ending price is $120. There is not enough information to compute the arithmetic average ROR. Furthermore, there are many plausible answers. For example, the two scenarios below show plausible price histories:

	W_0	W_1	W_2	W_3	ROR$^{\text{arithmetic average}}$
Scenario 1	$48	$72	$96	$120	36.1%
Scenario 2	$48	$29	$35	$120	75.0%

In each case the price begins at $48 and ends at $120. In between, however, the price histories differ and consequently the arithmetic averages differ. There exist infinite plausible arithmetic annual averages for this problem because there are an infinite number of plausible price histories. The geometric average depends only on the beginning and ending wealth, not the price history, and at 35.72 percent is smaller than every one of those infinite arithmetic averages. The time value framework requires that uniqueness.

EXERCISES 4.1
Concept quiz
1. Suppose an asset price rises during the first period. The second period the price falls to its original value. Is the second period's absolute percentage change larger or smaller than the first period's? What does this suggest about the relation between arithmetic and geometric average rates of return?
2. True or False: A column of three prices can make one and only one column of rates of return, but a column of three rates or return can make an infinite number of columns of prices.

Numerical quickies
3. Two years ago you purchased a stock for $40 . One year ago the price had moved to $19. Today it is at $60. What are the arithmetic and geometric annual average rates of return? ©ROR3c
4. Two years ago the stock price was $20. The periodic rates of return during the subsequent two years are –15% and 65%. What is today's stock price? ©ROR5

Numerical challenger
5. Your broker correctly tells you that your portfolio's average annual rate of return for the past two years is 20%. You know the portfolio value today of $9,150 is $850 less than when you started the account two years ago. What was the portfolio's value one year ago? ©ROR6

2. THE LUMP-SUM TIME VALUE FORMULA: ONE INFLOW, ONE OUTFLOW

The definition for the geometric average periodic rate of return yields a measure with intuitively pleasing properties. The definition easily rearranges to express the beginning wealth as a function of the ending wealth, the rate of return, and the number of periods:

$$W^{\text{beginning}} = \frac{W^{\text{end}}}{(1 + ROR^{\text{geometric average}})^N} .$$

The variables above are given new names for the lump-sum time value formula, but they represent identical ideas:

> **FORMULA 4.6 The lump-sum time value relation**
>
> $$PV = \frac{FV}{(1 + r)^N}$$

PV is the beginning wealth, abbreviated as PV to denote "present value". FV is the ending wealth N periods later, abbreviated as FV to denote "future value". The rate of return r is, of course, the investment's geometric average periodic rate of return.

Equation 4.6 is the lump-sum time value formula. The relation involves one cash flow at the beginning, one cash flow at the end, and none in the middle.

"Compounding" is the process by which beginning wealth, PV, grows to become ending wealth, FV. Perhaps you have heard about the magic of compounding. Sometimes a beginning amount accumulates such a large sum that magic seems involved. It's not, of course. The explanations below elaborate on this issue.

The lump-sum time value formula implicitly contains several other important members of the relationship: periodic interest, total accumulated interest, and interest-on-interest.

$$periodic\ interest = \left(\begin{array}{c} periodic\ interest \\ rate \end{array}\right)\left(\begin{array}{c} beginning\ of \\ period\ balance \end{array}\right)$$

$$\left(\begin{array}{c} total\ accumulated \\ market\ interest \end{array}\right) = \left(\begin{array}{c} account \\ balance \end{array}\right) - \left(\begin{array}{c} total\ contributed \\ principal \end{array}\right),$$

$$\left(\begin{array}{c} total\ accumulated \\ market\ interest \end{array}\right) = \left(\begin{array}{c} total\ interest\text{-} \\ on\text{-}interest \end{array}\right) + \left(\begin{array}{c} total\ interest\text{--} \\ on\text{--}principal \end{array}\right)$$

Formula 4.7 computes the periodic interest that an asset earns, or likewise that a liability owes, by multiplying the periodic interest rate times the beginning of period balance. The total market interest that accumulates in an account, specified in equation 4.8, is the difference between the account balance and the principal contributed by the depositor or investor. The concept of total accumulated market interest is broad. It includes interest paid on an account by a bank, and also it includes the price appreciation accruing to a security's market value. Formula 4.9 shows that total accumulated market interest also equals the sum of total interest-on-interest plus total interest-on-principal.

Suppose, for example, a bank receives at time 0 a deposit of $1,000 into an account that earns interest at an annual rate of 4.75 percent. The lump-sum time value formula allows us to determine the account balance one year later immediately after the bank credits the account with the first year's interest. Set PV equal to $1,000 and r to 0.0475. N equals 1. Substitute into formula 4.6 and solve for FV, the account's ending balance.

$$\$1,000 = \frac{FV}{(1+0.0475)^1}$$

$$\$1,000(1+0.0475)^1 = FV$$

$$\text{or} \quad FV = \$1,047.50$$

The account grows because the bank contributes interest to the account. The amount of periodic interest obviously equals $47.50, a sum consistent with equation 4.7:

$$periodic\ interest = (0.0475)(\$1,000)$$
$$= \$47.50$$

The account balance increases each year by the same proportion, 4.75 percent, but every passing year's periodic interest gets larger and larger. For example, the account ending balance after two years is $1,097.26:

$$\$1,000 = \frac{FV}{(1+0.0475)^2}$$

or $FV = \$1,097.26$. The second year's periodic interest is

Problems that use the lump-sum time value formula sometimes are easier to solve by using the basic arithmetic keys. The time value functions, however, also may be used. These pre-programmed functions are especially useful for solving complex time value calculations. Before using time value functions prepare the *BAII Plus©* calculator as follows:

(1) clear existing values from the time value memories by typing $\boxed{2^{nd}}$ $\boxed{FV}$.

(2) verify the compounding frequency is set to the appropriate number. For this problem, compounding frequency is once per year (a later section discusses intraperiod compounding) so type $\boxed{2^{nd}}$ $\boxed{I/Y}$ 1 $\boxed{ENTER}$ $\boxed{2^{nd}}$ $\boxed{CPT}$.

Time value functions now are ready to use. Type the following keys to solve the preceding problem.

1000 $\boxed{PV}$ 4.75 $\boxed{I/Y}$ 1 $\boxed{N}$ $\boxed{CPT}$ $\boxed{FV}$

The answer of $-1,047.50 appears on the display. The negative sign in front of the number simply means that FV is available to flow out of the account. PV and FV must have opposite signs on the BAII Plus© in all lump-sum problems.

$$periodic\ interest = (0.0475)(\$1,047.50)$$
$$= \$49.76$$

The second year's periodic interest of $49.76 exceeds the first year's $47.50. It's important to realize why. Recall that the bank adds $47.50 to the account at time 1, and so during the second year the interest earns its own interest. The second year's periodic interest, in other words, results from two sources: interest-on-principal plus interest-on-interest. During the second year the interest-on-principal is $47.50 and the interest-on-interest is $2.26.

At the close of the third year the account's future value, given by equation 4.6, is $1,149.38:

$$\$1,000 = \frac{FV}{(1 + 0.0475)^3}$$

or $\quad FV = \$1,149.38$.

Prepare the *BAII Plus©* calculator by typing to $\boxed{2^{nd}}$ $\boxed{FV}$ clear the time value memories, and $\boxed{2^{nd}}$ $\boxed{I/Y}$ 1 $\boxed{ENTER}$ $\boxed{2^{nd}}$ $\boxed{CPT}$ to set for annual compounding. Find the ending wealth after 3 years by typing:

1000 $\boxed{PV}$ 4.75 $\boxed{I/Y}$ 3 $\boxed{N}$ $\boxed{CPT}$ $\boxed{FV}$

The answer of $-1,149.38 appears on the display.

Total accumulated market interest, given by equation 4.8, is $149.38:

$$\binom{total\ accumulated}{market\ interest} = \binom{account}{balance} - \binom{total\ contributed}{principal},$$

$$= \quad \$1,149.38 - \$1,000$$

$$= \quad \$149.38$$

Because the principal earns interest each year of $47.50, the total interest-on-principal equals $142.50 (that is, $142.50 = $47.50 x 3). The total interest-on-interest, given by rearrangement of equation 4.9, therefore equals $6.88:

$$\begin{pmatrix} total\ interest\ - \\ on\text{-}interest \end{pmatrix} = \begin{pmatrix} total\ accumulated \\ market\ interest \end{pmatrix} - \begin{pmatrix} total\ interest\ - \\ on\text{-}principal \end{pmatrix},$$

$$= \quad \$149.38 - \$142.50$$

$$= \quad \$6.88.$$

The preceding story allows the easy computation of all the important concepts implicit in the lump-sum time value relation. The story is so simplistic, though, that interest-on-interest seems trivial. The example below illustrates the magical power of seemingly trivial interest-on-interest.

EXAMPLE 2 Powerful magic of interest-on-interest.

Two twins each receive an inheritance of $20,000 which they dutifully invest in an exceptional account that earns 12.25 percent per year. Andraya leaves each year's interest in the account so that she earns interest-on-interest. Zarcog is content to earn only interest-on-principal, so every year he goes to the bank and withdrawals all interest-on-interest. After 20 years, how much wealth has each sibling accumulated?

SOLUTION

Principal of $20,000 that earns 12.25 percent per year accumulates periodic interest during the first year equal to $2,450:

$$1^{st}\ year\ periodic\ interest\ = (0.1225)(\$20,000)$$
$$= \$2,450$$

At the end of the first year neither sibling takes money out of the account. At the end of the second year, however, Zarcog notices that the periodic interest is $300.12 larger than a year earlier:

$$2^{nd}\ year\ periodic\ interest\ = (0.1225)(\$22,450)$$
$$= \$2,750.12$$

Instead of leaving this extra interest-on-interest of $300.12 in the bank, Zarcog withdraws it. He figures, hey, $300.12 out of $2,750.12 isn't much and he might as well enjoy some of it! (By the way, notice that the interest-on-interest of $300.12 equals $2,450 x 0.1225). So every year Zarcog withdraws from the account any annual interest exceeding $2,450 per year. Throughout twenty years the account earns total interest-on-principal of $2,450x20, or $49,000. Zarcog began with $20,000 and the account rose by $49,000 to end at $69,000. Along the way, of course, Zarcog withdrew all interest-on-interest.

Andraya resists the temptation to spend and leaves in the account all interest-on-interest. The account's ending wealth consequently is easily deduced from the lump-sum time value equation. Set N equal to 20, r equal to 0.1225, and PV to $20,000. Solve for FV:

$$\$20,000 = \frac{FV}{(1 + 0.1225)^{20}}$$

or FV = $201,724 . The lump-sum time value formula gives an answer that automatically includes interest-on-interest plus interest-on-principal.

CALCULATOR CLUE

Prepare the *BAII Plus*© calculator by typing **2nd** **FV** to clear the time value memories, and **2nd** **I/Y** 1 **ENTER** **2nd** **CPT** to set for annual compounding. Find the ending wealth after 20 years by typing:

20000 **PV** 12.25 **I/Y** 20 **N** **CPT** **FV**

The answer of $–201,724 appears on the display.

Total accumulated market interest for Andraya is found with equation 4.8:

$$\begin{pmatrix} total\ accumulated \\ market\ interest \end{pmatrix} = \begin{pmatrix} account \\ balance \end{pmatrix} - \begin{pmatrix} total\ contributed \\ principal \end{pmatrix},$$

$$= \$201,724 - \$20,000$$

$$= \$181,724 .$$

Total accumulated market interest equals the sum of interest-on-principal plus interest-on-interest. Andraya's account earns interest-on-principal throughout 20 years totaling $49,000. The interest-on-interest for Andraya therefore equals $132,724 (that is, $132,724 = $181,724 – $49,000).

Andraya ends up with $201,724 and Zarcog ends up with $69,000; Andraya's account balance is larger by $132,724. For Andraya the interest earned interest, then the interest-on-interest earned interest, too, and the whole process compounded immensely. Zarcog spent his interest-on-interest, so the interest itself never earned more. Sure Zarcog benefited by spending money along the way (don't worry about finding the sum of withdrawals, but it equals $57,022 (=$300.12 x (1+2+ . . . +19)). He sure paid for it, though, because he ended with $132,724 less than Andraya. Allowing seemingly trivial interest-on-interest to accumulate increases wealth accumulation almost magically.

The lump-sum time value formula contains four variables: PV, FV, r, and N. The basic formula contains PV on the left-hand side. Arguably, PV is the most important variable because good financial decisions typically increase present value. Yet the formula contains four variables, and given any three, the fourth one comprises the unknown variable and takes on a value that satisfies the equality. The discussions below consider different scenarios in which each variable is the unknown answer.

2.A. Ending wealth, FV, as the unknown

Many situations require knowledge about ending wealth. For example, suppose exactly eight years ago relatives placed $10,000 in an account that earns 7.25 percent annually. How much is the account balance today? Equation 4.6 easily solves this equation, but first decisions must be made about the different variable settings. Clearly N equals 8 and r equals 0.0725. What about PV and FV, though? The beginning wealth is $10,000 and PV represents beginning wealth. The unknown variable is FV, the ending wealth. Just because we are finding today's account balance, PV is not automatically the unknown variable. Instantly recognize that the words tell us beginning wealth, and the formula expects PV to take on a value equal to beginning wealth. PV equals $10,000 and FV is the unknown variable. Getting the answer requires finding FV.

Rearrangement of formula 4.6 shows:

$$FV = PV(1 + r)^N .$$

For this particular problem,

$$FV = \$10,000(1 + .0725)^8$$

$$= \$17,506$$

If $10,000 earns seven and a quarter percent for eight years, it grows to $17,506. The problem below combines a few of the preceding concepts.

EXAMPLE 3 Find total interest.
Today you invest $4,500 in a security on which you expect to earn a 12.5 percent average annual rate of return (and of course, this is the geometric average, not the arithmetic average). How much total market interest will have accumulated exactly 5 years from today?

SOLUTION

The first step once again is to set the variables that equation 4.6 requires. Set N equal to 5, r equal to 0.125, and set PV equal to the beginning wealth of $4,500. Solve for the ending wealth, FV:

$$FV = \$4,500 \ (1 + .125)^5$$

$$= \$8,109.$$

Because the ending wealth is $8,109 and the investor's contribution is $4,500 then the remainder is market interest.

Total account balance = Total principal + Total market interest,

$8,109 = $4,500 + Total market interest,

or *Total market interest = $3,609.*

The market interest accruing to this investment represents a transfer of wealth to you from the market's invisible hand.

EXERCISES 4.2A

Concept quiz

1. What typically has the biggest impact on ending wealth: doubling the initial wealth, doubling the investment horizon, or doubling the rate of return?

Numerical quickies

2. Exactly 375 years ago immigrants purchased the island of Manhattan from native Americans for $24. If that sum were invested at 6.25% compounded annually, and the account left alone, what would be the accumulation today? ©LS3

3. A deposit of $1,000 five years ago earns an annual average return of 5.5%. Otherwise, the account has been left alone. As of today, how much total interest has accumulated on the deposit? ©LS4b

4. Ten years ago a $5,000 stock fund was established. The account will be closed eight years from now. The account always earns an average annual geometric rate of return of 12%. Otherwise, the account will have been left alone. At the time the account is closed, how much is the total accumulated interest-on-principal and interest-on-interest? ©LS4c and ©LS4d

Numerical challengers

5. A $3,500 savings account was established 4 years ago. The account earns 8.75% compounded annually. Otherwise, the account has been left alone. When the annual interest is credited to the account today, how much is credited? ©LS6a

6. An account established four years ago is today credited with annual interest of $2,500. The interest rate is 6.75% compounded annually. Otherwise, the account has been left alone. How much is the end-of-day balance? ©LS7a

7. Saf T Lok, Inc. had a volatile year in 1997. Their shareprice on December 31, 1996, was $12.50. During January, 1997, their shareprice was up 43.75 percent. The monthly rates of return throughout 1997 are shown below:

Jan.	Feb.	Mar.	Apr.	May	June
43.75	−13.04	70.00	−45.59	22.97	−28.57
July	Aug.	Sept.	Oct.	Nov.	Dec.
−49.23	−21.21	−50.00	607.69	−5.43	−37.93

Compute the arithmetic and geometric average monthly rates of return for Saf T Lok in 1997. For 1,000 shares of the stock, use the lump-sum time value relation to find the value at year-end 1997. Find FV by using as r both the arithmetic and geometric averages. How much are the differences in computed ending wealth, and which is correct?

2.B. Beginning wealth, PV, as the unknown

Financial decisions often require computing how much beginning wealth ventures require. For example, suppose a venture capitalist wants to make a deposit today that, given the interest rate, finances a series of planned future withdrawals. The unknown variable is beginning wealth, PV. For many asset management decisions, the future returns and target rate of return may be fairly known. The unknown variable is PV, the proper allocation to finance the investment.

Consider a simple illustration in which 4 years from today you wish to withdraw $80,000 from an account. The account earns 6.25 percent compounded annually, and you withdraw the money immediately after the 4th year's interest is credited to the account. You establish the account today by making a deposit. How much is today's deposit?

The answer for this question requires setting N equal to 4, r equal to 0.0625, and FV equal to $80,000. Substitution into equation 4.6 shows

$$PV = \frac{FV}{(1+r)^N}$$

$$= \frac{\$80,000}{(1+.0625)^4}$$

$$= \$62,773.$$

The answer of $62,773 is the amount which, if deposited today, grows at an annual rate of six and one-quarter percent to become equal to $80,000 in four years. The investment earns total market interest equal to $17,227 (Total market interest = $80,000 − $62,773).

CALCULATOR CLUE

Prepare the *BAII Plus*© calculator by typing `2nd` `FV` to clear the time value memories, and `2nd` `I/Y` 1 `ENTER` `2nd` `CPT` to set for annual compounding. Solve the preceding problem by typing:

80000 `FV` 6.25 `I/Y` 4 `N` `CPT` `FV`

The answer of $−62,773 appears on the display.

Finding present value requires dividing the future sum by one plus the rate raised to an exponent. Dividing $80,000 by a number greater than one gives an answer smaller than $80,000. The answer is smaller by exactly the amount of interest accruing over the investment horizon. This process of dividing a future sum by $(1+r)t$ is called "discounting". Finding a present value requires discounting future cash flows. The rate r often is called the "discount rate". Common conversation relies on similar word usage, as in the phrase "you have to discount what you hear on TV." The accompanying Street-Bite illustrates importance of discounting.

The following example illustrates that measurements for periodic and total market interest from equations 4.7 and 4.8 also pertain to PV computations.

STREET-BITE The Fed, the Discount Rate and the Stock Market

The present value of a future cash flow equals the cash flow divided by one-plus-the-discount rate raised to the tth power. This discount rate is important.

> **DEFINITION 4.1 Discount rate**
>
> The discount rate is the periodic percentage return subtracted from the future cash flow for computing present value.

The discount rate is important because it constitutes a link between present values and future returns.

There are many different ways to measure the economy's discount rate. One important measure is the official U.S. government discount rate managed by the Federal Reserve System. The Fed is historically the most important bank in the USA. It is called the nation's "central bank" and most nations have one. Often activities of central banks are extremely politicized. Even in the USA appointment of the Fed's top management requires approval of the United States Congress. Because of influences by men such as Alexander Hamilton, appointed Treasurer by George Washington in 1789-1795 and killed in duel by Aaron Burr in 1804 arguing about bank policy (either that or money), the Fed today represents the interests of a broad band of participants in the US political economy.

The Federal Reserve Board of Directors, today led by ~~Alan Greenspan~~ BEN BERNAKE from Washington University (St. Louis), uses several tools to influence market activity. These include:

- the Federal Reserve Board votes whether to raise or lower the official government discount rate; this is the interest rate charged by federal district banks to member public and private banks.
- the Fed sets the reserve requirement on member bank accounts; this regulates the amount of loans that banks may lend to business and individual borrowers.
- the Fed buys and sells marketable currencies and government securities in the global financial marketplace; this affects supply and demand conditions.

The Fed meets fairly regularly. The markets have grown accustomed to paparazzi hoopla about Fed actions and inactions. So called "Fed watching" is a popular pastime to many regular viewers of CNBC and CNN. The table below shows how the stock market has responded when the Fed changed the official discount rate.

Each row's date is the actual day on which the Fed executes an order to change the discount rate. Each column's entry represents the cumulative rate of return (see formula 4.1) for a big basket of stocks. For each date the cumulative rate of return is collected for different investment holding periods. The upper left number, 0.95 percent, indicates that cumulative stock returns were a little less than one percent for the two days following the Fed discount rate change on January 31, 1996. On this date the rate was lowered to 5 percent from 5.25%. Over the 7 trading days subsequent to the announcement, cumulative returns equaled 2.00 percent. Over the subsequent 180 trading days (until late summer of 1996) aggregate share values rose 14.76 percent.

That nearly 15 percent return is rather healthy. Money doubles in about five years at 15 percent per year. Still, this return is less than the overall sample average of 19.91 percent per 180-day horizon. The bottom row lists average returns in the entire sample period for different investment horizons. This sample period contains one of the most remarkable sustained bull markets in financial history.

Nine of the twelve Fed announcements are followed over the next seven days by above average stock returns. Seemingly this gives rise to conjecture that perhaps stock returns after Fed action are bigger than average. Contrary evidence exists for the 30 day horizon returns, however. In this column, eight of twelve announcement period returns lag the average. Such flip-flops in comparisons make generalization difficult. Indeed, predicting share price responses to anything, even the powerful visible hand of the Fed, seems for many the mother of all mysteries.

TABLE 4.2
Stock returns after changes to the Fed's discount rate. Source: Compiled by author.

Announcement date and rate change	Stock index returns during the days after announcement of a discount rate change by the Federal Reserve Board's Open Market Committee			
	next 2 days	next 7 days	next 30 days	next 180 days
January 31, 1996 lowered to 5%	0.95%	2.00%	2.44%	14.76%
February 1, 1995 raised to 5.25%	0.45	2.32	2.98	23.37
Nov. 15, 1995 raised to 4.75%	0.03	−2.39	−1.99	20.79
August 16, 1994 raised to 4%	0.45	1.43	1.62	9.41
May 17, 1994 raised to 3.5%	0.96	1.79	−0.45	4.49
July 2, 1992 lowered to 3%	0.09	0.79	2.10	26.82
Dec. 20, 1991 lowered to 3.5%	2.16	8.57	21.52	26.74
Nov. 6, 1991 lowered to 4.5%	1.21	2.14	−3.35	19.80
Sept. 13, 1991 lowered to 5%	−0.10	0.51	2.31	25.81
April 30, 1991 lowered to 5.5%	0.61	1.43	3.68	23.30
February 1, 1991 lowered to 6%	3.30	9.53	19.44	36.37
Dec. 19, 1990 lowered to 6.5%	0.41	−0.14	12.32	48.81
average return for entire sample period	0.20	0.71	3.07	19.91

EXAMPLE 4 Find the initial deposit given this year's periodic interest.

Your uncle marvels at the power of compound interest. Twelve years ago he deposited money into an account that earns 6 5/8 percent per year. Otherwise he never has deposited nor withdrawn money from the account. Just today the most recent year's interest of $4,000 was credited to the account. How much was your uncle's initial deposit?

SOLUTION

The first step is finding the account balance at the beginning of the most recent year by manipulating (1) this year's periodic interest, and (2) the periodic interest rate. Use equation 4.7:

$$periodic\ interest = \left(\begin{array}{c} periodic\ interest \\ rate \end{array}\right)\left(\begin{array}{c} beginning\ of \\ period\ balance \end{array}\right)$$

$$\$4,000 = (0.06625)\left(\begin{array}{c} beginning\ of \\ period\ balance \end{array}\right)$$

$$\left(\begin{array}{c} beginning\ of \\ period\ balance \end{array}\right) = \$60,377$$

If an account earning 6 5/8 percent per annum has a balance one year ago equal to $60,377 then how much was deposited in the account twelve years ago? Determine the answer to this question with the lump-sum time value formula. Set r to 0.06625, N to 11 (from twelve years ago until 1 year ago is 11 years), and FV to $60,377:

$$PV = \frac{\$60,377}{(1 + .06625)^{11}}$$

$$= \$29,814.$$

Your uncle's initial deposit 12 years ago was $29,814.

EXERCISES 4.2B

Concept quiz

1. In the lump-sum time value relation, is *PV* always less than *FV*? Explain.

Numerical quickies

2. Today you sell your stock fund for $19,500. You bought it 4 years ago and otherwise the account has been left alone. The stocks have earned a 16% average annual rate of return. How much did you buy the stocks for? ©LS8

3. Eight months from now a bill of $3,500 is due. Today you deposit money such that if the account earns 1.25% per month, the bill is perfectly financed. How much do you deposit? ©LS9

Numerical challengers ⟨Exam 2   Quiz 9⟩

4. In exactly 14 months a bill of $6,200 is due. Today you deposit money such that if the account earns 1.25% per month, the bill is perfectly financed. Unfortunately, your account earns only 1.05% per month. When the bill is due, how much money do you lack? ©LS10a

5. Exactly 18 years ago your uncle deposited money into an account that earns 6.25% per year. Otherwise, he has left the account alone. Just today the most recent year's interest of $2,200 was credited to the account. How much was the initial deposit? ©LS11

2.C. The investment horizon, N, as the unknown

When known variables include the rate and the beginning and ending wealth, the unknown variable N adjusts to satisfy the lump-sum time value equation. Recall the formula:

$$PV = \frac{FV}{(1 + r)^N} .$$

The variable N appears on the right-hand-side only as the exponent in $(1+r)^N$. Getting N out of the exponent requires taking the logarithm of both sides of the equation. Rearranging to isolate N by itself on the left-hand side yields:

$$N = \frac{\log\left(FV/PV\right)}{\log\left(1 + r\right)} .$$

EXAMPLE 5 Find the investment horizon.

If you invest $1,000 today in a security that you expect to earn 12⅛ percent per year, how many years does it take to accumulate $2,500.

SOLUTION

Use the preceding formula, set *r* to 0.12125 , *PV* to $1,000 and *FV* to $2,500:

$$N = \frac{\log\left(\$2,500/\$1,000\right)}{\log\left(1 + 0.12125\right)}$$

or *N* = 8.01. In about 8 years the investment's value increases to $2,500.

EXERCISES 4.2C
Numerical quickies

1. Today you purchase some international mutual funds for $2,400. You read that they should earn a 14% average annual rate of return throughout the foreseeable future. If you leave the account alone, how long should it take to accumulate $6,000? ©LS12

2. A newspaper reports that a particular mid-level manager today has stocks worth $100,000. The person bought the stocks with $2,660 from a summer job while in college. The stocks have earned an average annual return of 12%. How along ago did she buy the stocks? ©LS13

Numerical challengers

3. Today your account was credited with its annual interest of $1,100. The account was established some time ago with a $7,000 initial deposit. Otherwise, the account has been left alone. The account earns 7.25% annual interest. How long ago was the account established? ©LS14

4. Some time ago a $7,000 initial deposit opened an account. Today the annual interest was credited to the account. Total lifetime interest now equals $7,095. The account earns 7.25% annual interest. How long ago was the account established? ©LS15

5. You are entering a creative financing arrangement that involves two different transactions. For the first transaction you will borrow $15,300 at an annual interest rate of 8.70%. For the second transaction you will invest the borrowed money today in a security that promises a future pay-off of $29,800. Upon receiving the pay-off from the second transaction, you will repay in-full the loan from the first transaction. It is certain that these cash flows actually will happen, but the timing of the pay-off isn't clear. What determines whether or not this is a good deal? ©LS2

2.D. The rate of return, r, as the unknown

Recall that r is the geometric average periodic rate of return that links the beginning and ending wealth across N periods. When r is the only unknown variable, simple rearrangement of the lump-sum time value formula shows an easy solution:

$$r = \sqrt[N]{FV/PV} - 1 .$$

This is identical to the definition of $ROR^{geometric\ average}$ from equation 4.6.

EXAMPLE 6 Find initial deposit and subsequent rate of return.
Today Ben needs $15,000 to make a deposit on a house. He invested enough money 8 years ago so that if he earned his target rate of return of 10 percent, his accumulation today would exactly equal $15,000. Instead, however, the investment did better than expected so today Ben has $19,000. By how much does the actual average rate of return exceed the target rate of return?

SOLUTION
The problem set-up states that N equals 8, and the ending wealth, *FV*, equals $19,000. Also we need the beginning wealth, yet *PV* is not explicitly stated. To find the beginning wealth, though, take away eight years of ten percent interest from $15,000:

$$PV = \frac{\$15,000}{(1 + .10)^8}$$

$$= \$6,998.$$

Ben invested $6,998 eight years ago with the expectation that it would grow to $15,000. Given that eight years later it actually grows to $19,000 then r is found as:

$$r = \sqrt[8]{\$19,000\big/\$6,998} - 1,$$

$$= \quad 13.30\%.$$

Ben's actual rate of return, 13.30 percent, exceeds the 10 percent target by 3.30 percent. The investment earns 330 basis points more than expected, so Ben has $4,000 more than expected.

The preceding paragraph introduces the phrase "basis point."

DEFINITION 4.2 Basis point

A basis point is one-hundredth of a percentage point.

For example: (1) the difference between 6 percent and 7 percent is 100 basis points; (2) the difference between 6.25 percent and 6.50 percent is 25 basis points; (3) the difference between 6¾ percent and 6⅞ percent is 12.5 basis points. In the real world, basis points count. Some investors win or lose thousands of dollars when interest rates move even three basis points!

EXERCISES 4.2D

Numerical quickies

1. Exactly 5 years ago you put $1,350 in an investment account. Today the account was credited with its annual interest so that its balance now is $2,750. What is the annual average rate of return for the account? ©LS16

2. Today you are buying some stocks for $900. In 8 years you would like the account to have accumulated $2,700. What is the desired annual average rate of return for the account? ©LS17

3. A sum of money doubles in 24 years. What is the annual average rate of return? ©LS19

4. Today your account was credited with its annual interest of $800, thereby bringing the balance to $9,000. What is the account's annual interest rate? ©LS20

Numerical challengers

5. In exactly 18 months a bill of $5,300 is due. Today you deposit money such that if the account earns 1.25% per month, the bill is perfectly financed. Unfortunately, your actual monthly rate of return was less than the target, so your account accumulates $5,080. What was the actual average monthly rate of return? ©LS21a

6. Investment A returns $8,000 in 11 years. Investment B costs $6,800 today and $10,000 in 7 years. If your sole objective is to buy the one investment with the largest annual average rate of return, what is the decision rule? ©LS1.

2.E. Approximations with the rule of 72

Doing time value calculations in your head is sometimes useful. Perhaps it's useful because you want to check whether an answer on your calculator or spreadsheet seems reasonable. Perhaps it's useful because you don't walk around with a calculator and, on a rare occasion, need to know a time value answer. Fortunately, there is a very useful rule-of-thumb that often helps: the rule of 72.

> **RULE 4.2 The rule of 72**
> The approximate number of periods in which a sum of money doubles equals 72 divided by the periodic rate of return.

Consider the following application for the rule of 72. Suppose a savings account earns interest at 6 percent per year. The doubling period, according to the rule of 72, equals 72 divided by 6, which is 12. That is, at a six percent rate money doubles in about twelve years. Notice that the interest rate in the Rule of 72 formula is not a decimal.

To find the exact doubling-period, use the lump-sum time value formula. In equation 4.6 set the ratio FV/PV to 2.0 since wealth doubles and FV is twice as large as PV, set r to 0.06, and solve for N:

$$N = \frac{\log(2)}{\log(1 + 0.06)},$$

or $N = 11.9$ years. The rule of 72 is wrong by only one-tenth a year. Not bad for a rule of thumb!

EXAMPLE 8 Find approximate doubling period
You hear from your friend that for the past four years the stock market has averaged about 20 percent per year. You wonder approximately how much has your friend's stock fund increased?

SOLUTION
Divide 72 by 20 and get about three and-a-half. According to the rule of 72 money doubles in 3 1/2 years at 20 percent. Thus, if the funds earned twenty percent for four years, the balance more than doubled. The exact answer is found with the lump-sum formula with FV as the unknown: $FV = PV (1 + .20)^4$; $FV = PV \times 2.07$; this means the ending value equals 2.07 times beginning value.

EXERCISES 4.2E
Concept quiz
1. Long-run averages suggest corporate bonds return 8% and the stock market returns 12% per year. Sketch a table with two columns pertaining to the two preceding rates. Insert 3 rows corresponding to the investor's age at time of making a $10,000 deposit: 25 years of age, 40 years of age, and 55 years of age. Use the rule of 72 to approximate in each cell the ending wealth at age 70 given the respective investor age and rate of return. Comment on the relative importance of investment horizon and rate of return. {HINT: The bottom row of the first column, 8% and 55 years when saving begins, is about $35,000.}

3. INTRAPERIOD COMPOUNDING OF INTEREST

The horizon for accruing periodic interest almost always is less than a year. Corporations pay interest every 6 months to investors in corporate bonds. Credit unions pay interest every quarter to savings account deposits. Credit cards and consumer loans charge interest every month on outstanding balances. There is even an overnight market between banks, and interest accrues at an overnight interest rate. The lump-sum time value formula from the previous section properly compounds intraperiod interest regardless of period length.

3.A. The relationship between periodic components

The lump-sum time value formula with intraperiod compounding is

$$PV = \frac{FV}{(1+r)^N}$$

Still PV is the beginning wealth, FV is the ending wealth N periods later, and r is the geometric average periodic rate of return. Intraperiod compounding enters through the definition for r,

$r = i / m.$

The rate i is the annual percentage rate ("APR") and m is the number of compounding periods per year. For semiannual situations, for example, m equals 2. For monthly situations, such as credit cards or car loans, m equals 12. For daily compounding, m equals 365.

Compounding frequency affects the time value relation. Consider, for example, a depositor that puts $1,000 in an account earning interest at an annual percentage rate of 8.4 percent. Table 4.3 shows the account balance after one year for alternative compounding frequencies.

When interest accrues once a year then m equals 1 and the formula is

$$FV = \$1000\left(1 + \frac{.084}{1}\right)^1$$

$$= \quad \$1,000\ (1.084)$$

$$= \quad \$1,084.00$$

The bank credits the account at the end-of-year with interest-on-principal equal to $84. There is no interest-on-interest.

Suppose, however, the bank credits interest every half-year. For this case, m equals 2. The periodic interest rate now is a semiannual rate of 0.084_2, or 4.2 percent per semiannum. Substitution into the formula shows that the ending wealth after 2 semiannual periods is:

$$FV = \$1000\left(1 + \frac{.084}{2}\right)^2$$

$$= \quad \$1,000\ (1.042)^2$$

$$= \quad \$1,085.76$$

,

compounding frequency m	period description	future value of $1,000 after one year at 8.4%
1	annual	$1,084.00
2	semiannual	$1,085.76
4	quarterly	$1,086.68
12	monthly	$1,087.31
365	daily	$1,087.62

TABLE 4.3

Ending wealth of a $1,000 deposit at an 8.4 percent APR for different compounding frequencies

The ending wealth is higher with intraperiod compounding because interest earns interest. After six months the bank credits the savings account with a half-year of interest. The periodic interest after six months is:

$$periodic\ interest = \left(\begin{array}{c} periodic\ interest \\ rate \end{array} \right) \left(\begin{array}{c} beginning\ of \\ period\ balance \end{array} \right)$$

$$= (0.084 / 2)(\$1,000)$$

$$= \$42$$

The first half-year's periodic interest equals exclusively the $42 interest-on-principal. The bank credits periodic interest to the account and brings the account balance at the beginning of the second half-year to $1,042. During the second six months periodic interest equals:

$= (0.084 / 2) (\$1,042)$

$= \$43.76.$

During this second half-year the principal once again earns interest of $42. The interest from the first six months earns its own interest, too. Interest-on-interest is $1.76 (notice that $42 x 0.084/2 is $1.76).

Ending wealth increases as compounding frequency increases. With daily compounding, m equals 365. The lump-sum time value formula shows the ending wealth after 365 days is:

$$FV = \$1000 \left(1 + \frac{.084}{365} \right)^{365}$$

$$= \$1,000\ (1.0002301)^{365}$$

$$= \$1,087.62.$$

A $1,000 deposit with an 8.4 percent annual percentage rate earns interest-on-principal in one year of $84. Because the account balance indicates total market interest of $87.62, the interest-on-interest with daily compounding is $3.62 (that is, $3.62 = $87.62 – $84.00).

CALCULATOR CLUE

Prepare the *BAII Plus©* calculator by typing `2nd` `FV` to clear the time value memories. Now access the intraperiod compounding setting by typing `2nd` `I/Y`. To set for daily compounding, for example, type 365 `ENTER`. Once the compounding frequency is properly set, exit this loop by typing `2nd` `CPT`. The N key refers to the number of periods, not number of years.

Suppose you wish to find the future value after 1 year of a $1,000 investment given an 8.4 percent APR and daily compounding. Type:

`2nd` `I/Y` 365 `ENTER` `2nd` `CPT` 1000 `PV` 8.4 `I/Y` 365 `N` `CPT` `FV`

The answer $–1,087.62 appears on the display.

Simply knowing the annual percentage rate is not enough to know how much interest actually accrues per dollar per year. Compounding frequency matters, too. Suppose the deposit is $10 million, instead of $1,000. The difference in annual interest at an 8.4 percent annual percentage rate ranges from $840,000 with annual compounding, to $876,184 with daily compounding. As you can imagine, that extra $36,184 is pretty significant to someone. Compounding frequency is important. Its importance increases, too, as the investment horizon lengthens or size of the pot grows.

EXAMPLE 9 Find the benefit of switching compounding frequency
Ms. Williams just made a $10,000 investment that promises to pay 8.25 percent compounded semiannually for 8 years. She just learned that on 8-year investments an alternative bank offers 8.15 percent compounded monthly. She can switch out of her original deal and reinvest in the alternative. She might have to pay a penalty to the original bank, however. To switch or not to switch, that is the question!

SOLUTION
The question really asks which alternative accumulates the most wealth. Compute first the ending wealth for the original investment if Ms. Williams sticks with it for 8 years. There are 16 half-years in 8 years, so N is 16. PV is $10,000. The semiannual interest rate r is $0.0825 \div 2$. Use the lump-sum time value formula:

$$\$10,000 = \frac{FV}{\left(1 + \frac{.0825}{2}\right)^{16}}$$

$$FV = \$10,000 \, (1.04125)^{16}$$

$$= \$19,093 \, .$$

Ms. Williams receives $19,093 if she sticks with the original investment.

Now compute for the alternative investment how much she needs to invest today in order to receive $19,093 in eight years. That is, use the lump-sum time value equation with FV at $19,093 and r at $0.0815 \div 12$ (monthly compounding), and N at 96 (eight years is 96 months):

$$PV = \frac{\$19,093}{\left(1 + \frac{.0815}{12}\right)^{96}}$$

$$= \$9,970$$

Ms. Williams gets the same ending wealth as the original investment if, in the alternative, she invests $9,970. As long as she gets back $9,970 or more from her original $10,000 investment, she should cancel and reinvest in the alternative. In other words, $30 is the maximum penalty at which switching is profitable.

Many asset management decisions involve finding an alternative with the best present value. For an outflow the best alternative has the smallest possible present value. For an inflow, however, the best alternative has the largest present value. This is true regardless of compounding frequency. The following example illustrates that different capital costs must be discounted before choosing the cheapest alternative.

EXAMPLE 10 Which cost has the cheapest present value.
Quickie.Dot purchases inventory from one of three suppliers. The suppliers offer different prices and payment plans for exactly the same item. Quickie.Dot must choose the least expensive alternative. The following table summarizes the choices. Suppose that Quickie.Dot finances its operations at a 12 percent annual financing rate (compounded daily). Which supplier and payment plan is cheapest?

TABLE 4.4

Payment & discount plans for purchasing inventory

Supplier	Base price	Payment plan	Grace period for full price sales	Percent discount for prompt payment
Alpha Inc.	$17,500	"1.5 in 5 or net 60"	60 days	1.5% if paid within 5 days
Kappa Inc.	$17,400	"0 net 90"	90 days	Never a discount
Zeta Inc.	$17,350	"2 in 10 or net 30"	30 days	2% if paid within 10 days

SOLUTION

First understand data in the table. The base price of the item from Alpha Inc. is $17,500. When Quickie.Dot buys from Alpha, they can pay the full base price any time within 60 days without falling delinquent. Quickie.Dot wisely plans to stay away from delinquency. Yet if they buy from Alpha at full price the prudent strategy delays payment as long as practical. If Quickie.Dot pays for the item within 5 days, however, they receive a 1.5 percent discount. The discount price is $17,237 {= $17,500 x (1 – 0.015)}. Consequently, the alternative payment plans for Quickie.Dot if they purchase from Alpha include (1) pay $17,500 after 60 days, or (2) pay $17,237 after 5 days. The present values of these two alternatives at a 12 percent annual rate (compounded daily over 365 days) is:

$$PV(\text{full price from Alpha}) = \frac{\$17,500}{\left(1+\frac{.12}{365}\right)^{60}}$$

$$= \$17,158.$$

$$PV(\text{discount price from Alpha}) = \frac{\$17,237}{\left(1+\frac{.12}{365}\right)^{5}}$$

$$= \$17,209.$$

The least expensive purchase is one with the lowest present value of cost. The prudent payment plan if Quickie.Dot purchases inventory from Alpha Inc. is to pay the full price after 60 days.

Perhaps it seems strange that paying $17,500 at day 60 is cheaper than paying $17,237 at day 5. Those prices, however, occur at different times. Consequently, comparing them is like comparing apples and oranges. Time value relations require discounting all cash flows before making comparisons. Paying more to Alpha later has a smaller discounted cost than paying less sooner. It actually is cheaper for Quickie.Dot to **forgo the discount** and pay the full base price later.

The cost of forgoing the discount equals the rate of return connecting the later higher price (FV= $17,500) and sooner lower price (PV= $17,209) . That is,

$$\$17,209 = \frac{\$17,500}{\left(1+\frac{i}{365}\right)^{60-5}}$$

$$i = 11.13\%.$$

The percentage cost of forgoing the discount, 11.13 percent, is less than the 12 percent financing rate that Quickie.Dot pays on its operations. Suppose the sooner purchase were financed with a $17,209 loan at 12 percent interest for 55 days. Repayment of the loan incurs an ending principal and accumulated interest balance of

$$\$17,209 = \frac{FV}{\left(1+\frac{.12}{365}\right)^{60-5}}$$

$$FV = \$17,523.$$

The lower purchase price on day 5 has a time value of $17,523 at day 60. This exceeds the full base price of $17,500. The cost of forgoing the discount from Alpha is less expensive than the cost of paying the full price.

Quickie.Dot also might choose to purchase from Kappa and pay $17,400 after 90 days. The present value of this cost is

$$PV(full price from Kappa) = \frac{\$17,400}{\left(1+\frac{.12}{365}\right)^{90}}$$

$$= \$16,893.$$

Purchase from Kappa is less expensive than any payment plan that Alpha offers.

Alternative purchase plans from Zeta Inc. include (1) pay $17,350 after 30 days or (2) pay $17,003 {= $17,350 x (1 − 0.02)} after 10 days. The present values of these costs equal

$$PV(full price from Zeta) = \frac{\$17,350}{\left(1+\frac{.12}{365}\right)^{30}}$$

$$= \$17,179.$$

$$PV(discount price from Zeta) = \frac{\$17,003}{\left(1+\frac{.12}{365}\right)^{10}}$$

$$= \$16,947.$$

The payment plan offering Zeta's customers the best deal is payment at 10 days of the discount price.

Five alternative payment plans exist for Quickie.Dot. The best of the lot has the smallest present value; it might also have the smallest price, but not necessarily. Sometimes paying less now is better than paying more later, sometimes it's not. Periodic cash flows from different times must be discounted before comparisons with other cash flows are meaningful. Quickie.Dot looks at its choices and quickly finds that the best deal is purchase of inventory at full base price from Kappa with deferral of payment for 90 days.

EXERCISES 4.3A
Numerical quickies

1. A deposit five years ago of $1,200 earns 5.5% annual interest compounded monthly. Otherwise, the account has been left alone. As of today, how much total interest has accumulated on the deposit? ©CY6b.

2. Today you plan to cash in savings bonds for $15,000. You bought them exactly 10 years ago. The savings bonds have earned a 6.25% annual rate of return compounded semiannually. How much did you pay for the savings bonds? ©CY7.

3. In 4 years you must transfer $4,200 to associates. Today you invest money such that if it earns 12.5% per annum, compounded monthly, you'll accumulate the required funds. How much do you invest? ©CY8.

4. Today you invest $3,100 that earns 9% per annum compounded quarterly. If you leave the account alone, how long should it take to earn $2,550 of total interest? ©CY9

Numerical challengers

5. In exactly 14 months you expect to receive $6,200 from an investment. Today you borrow money from an associate such that if interest accrues at an annual rate of 8.25% compounded monthly, the investment exactly repays the loan. Unfortunately, the associate charges you 250 basis points more than expected. In 14 months when the investment returns $6,200 and you repay the loan, how much money do you lack? ©CY12

6. Exactly 14 years ago your uncle deposited money into an account with a 5.50% annual percentage rate that compounds quarterly. Otherwise, he has left the account alone. Just today the most recent quarter's interest of $350 was credited to the account. How much was the initial deposit? ©CY13

7. In exactly 18 months a bill of $5,300 is due. Today you deposit money such that if the account earns the target APR of 7.25%, compounded monthly, the bill is perfectly financed. Otherwise, there are no other deposits or withdrawals. When the bill is due, the account actually has $5,080. What was the actual average APR? ©CY10a

8. A $1,200 savings account was established 42 months ago. Otherwise, there are no other deposits or withdrawals. The account earns a 7.75% annual percentage rate, compounded monthly. When the monthly interest is credited to the account today, how much is credited? ©CY14a

9. An account established four years ago is today credited with quarterly interest of $620. The interest rate is a 5.25% APR, compounded quarterly. Except for the initial deposit, there are no other deposits or withdrawals. How much is the end-of-day balance? ©CY15a

10. Today your account was credited with semiannual interest of $608. The account was established some time ago with a $9,000 initial deposit. Otherwise, there are no other deposits or withdrawals. The account earns a 7.5% APR, compounded semiannually. How long ago was the account established? ©CY16

11. Some time ago a $3,200 initial deposit opened an account. Today the monthly interest was credited to the account. Total lifetime interest now equals $1,321. The account earns a 6.5% APR, compounded monthly. How long ago was the account established? ©CY17

12. Suppliers X and Z are competing to sell your company supplies. The full price of supplies from supplier X is $2,200 and they offer these payment plans: 4.4% discount if you pay within 30 days, otherwise pay full price within 140 days. The full price with supplier Z is $2,060 and they offer these payment plans: 3.6% discount if you pay within 30 days, otherwise pay full price within 115 days. Your company financing rate is 12.8% compounded daily. Find the supplier and payment plan that represent the lowest present value of cost. ©CY21

3.B. Annual percentage rate (APR) vs. effective annual rate (EAR)

The periodic interest rate for computing actual interest income or interest expense equals the annual percentage rate divided by the number of periods in a year. The annual percentage rate, abbreviated APR for convenience, gives rise to differing amounts of annual interest. This motivates introduction of the effective annual rate (EAR).

DEFINITION 4.3 Effective Annual Rate
The effective annual rate is the amount of interest that accrues on one dollar in one year.

Annual Percentage Rate	compounding frequency, m			
	2	4	12	365
4%	4.04%	4.06%	4.07%	4.08%
6%	6.09%	6.14%	6.17%	6.18%
8%	8.16%	8.24%	8.30%	8.33%
10%	10.25%	10.38%	10.47%	10.52%
12%	12.36%	12.55%	12.68%	12.75%
14%	14.49%	14.75%	14.93%	15.02%
16%	16.64%	16.99%	17.23%	17.35%
18%	18.81%	19.25%	19.56%	19.72%

Compute the *EAR* from the *APR* with the following formula.

FORMULA 4.10 Relation between Effective Annual Rate and Annual

$$\begin{pmatrix} effective \\ annual \\ rate \end{pmatrix} = \left(1 + \frac{APR}{m}\right)^m - 1 \, .$$

Table 4.4 shows the effective annual rate for different combinations of APR and compounding frequencies. The EAR for a 4 percent APR, for example, is 4.04 percent with semiannual compounding, and 4.27 percent with daily compounding. Thus, a deposit of $100 that earns a 4 percent APR accrues interest of $4.00 with annual compounding, $4.04 with semiannual compounding, and $4.27 with daily compounding.

The table reveals a few general tendencies.

- The *EAR* always exceeds the *APR*. For this reason, institutions advertising loans tend to state the *APR*. The *APR* is smaller than the *EAR* and the institution wants to make the rate appear small. On the other hand, institutions advertising savings rates tend to state the bigger *EAR*.
- The EAR always increases with compounding frequency. This naturally occurs because interest-on-interest increases with compounding frequency.
- The gap between the *EAR* and *APR* is bigger for high interest rates. When a credit card charges an *APR* of 18 percent, for example, the effective annual rate might be higher by 415 basis points!

Because the same *APR* on different offerings may provide varying amounts of interest, *APRs* generally cannot be compared to find the best one. Instead, valid comparisons involve the *EAR*.

EXAMPLE 11 Choose the lowest effective annual rate.
Which of the following loans is least expensive: an 8 3/4 percent loan compounded monthly, or an 8⅝ percent loan compounded quarterly.

SOLUTION
Find the *EAR* for each deal. The smallest *EAR* is the cheapest rate. For the *APR* of 8¾ percent, *m* equals 12:

$$\begin{pmatrix} effective \\ annual \\ rate \end{pmatrix} = \left(1 + \frac{.0875}{12}\right)^{12} - 1$$

$$= \quad 9.11\% \, .$$

For the *APR* of 8 5/8 percent, *m* equals 4:

$$\begin{pmatrix} effective \\ annual \\ rate \end{pmatrix} = \left(1 + \frac{.08625}{4}\right)^4 - 1$$

$$= \quad 8.91\%.$$

The quarterly loan has the lowest *EAR* and is the cheapest choice.

EXERCISES 4.3B

Concept quiz

1. For a given APR, do savers prefer increased or diminished compounding frequency? How about borrowers?

Numerical quickies

2. What is the effective annual rate (EAR) for a credit card whose annual percentage rate (APR) is 15.70% compounded monthly? ©CY1

3. Is it better to invest in a Certificate of Deposit that pays 9.34% compounded monthly, or 9.24% compounded daily? ©CY18

Numerical challenger

4. Exactly 32 months ago you put $3,250 in a cash management account. Otherwise, you have left the account alone. Today the account was credited with its monthly interest so that its balance now is $3,860. What is the account's APR? How about its EAR? ©CY19

4. INFLATION AND TIME VALUE

Prices of goods change over time. The U.S. government collects information about prices and publishes the *consumer price index* ("CPI"). Think of the CPI as the price for an imaginary shopping basket full of food, clothing, transportation and housing services, and myriad other things that consumers purchase. The annual *inflation rate* measures the percentage price changes that occur during a year. The government estimates that consumer prices during 2004 increased about 2½ percent. This number is relatively small compared to other years during the past century. In 1990, for example, consumer prices increased over 6 percent, in 1979 they were up more than 13 percent, and for the previous 50 years the inflation rate averages 4 percent per year!

A primary reason that companies and households save is to accumulate funds for making future purchases. Setting a savings target requires recognition that prices change over time. The rule of 72 suggests that with 4 percent inflation prices double in about 18 years. Thus, even with average inflation a long-term savings plan improperly accounting for inflation introduces serious errors.

Figure 4.1 illustrates that inflation and interest rates generally but not always move together. Chapter 11 explains that this positive correlation occurs because savers expecting high inflation tend to demand high interest. The actual interest rate observable in the marketplace is known as the *nominal interest rate*. The financial media often subtract the inflation rate from the nominal interest rate and report the result as the approximate *real interest rate*. The approximate real rate in figure 4.1 is shown as the dashed line. Throughout the previous 50 years the real rate averages about 3½ percent. Several times during the 1970s the real rate was negative. Probably high inflation caught savers by surprise and they erred by not demanding high interest (on the chart it looks like savers made up for the error in the early 1980s when inflation fell more than interest rates).

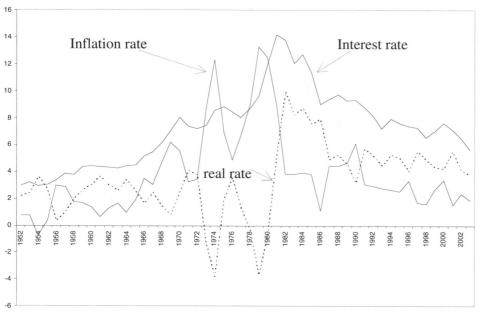

FIGURE 4.1
Interest and inflation rates, 1952-2003

Notes: The *Interest rate* is the annual average of monthly Moody's Seasoned AAA Corporate Bond Yield and the *Inflation rate* is the annual percentage change in Consumer Price Index for All Urban Consumers: All Items. The dashed line is the approximate real rate computed as *Interest rate* minus *Inflation rate*. Source data are from Federal Reserve Bank of St. Louis, http://research.stlouisfed.org/fred2/. Interest rate series Aaa is copyright by Moody's Investors Service; inflation series CPIAUCNS compiled by U.S. Department of Labor: Bureau of Labor Statistics.

Actual prices or cash flows at different times for the same good or service are called *current dollar prices* or *cash flows*. Adjust current dollar cash flows for inflation and obtain *constant dollar prices* or *cash flows*. Suppose, for example, that in 1991 an individual is comfortable earning income of $50,000. Say that over the subsequent 14 years the inflation rate is 3 percent per year. The current dollar income in 2005 providing the same standard of living equals $75,629 (= $50,000 x 1.03^{14}). The incomes of $50,000 in 1991 and $75,629 are current dollar cash flows – the numbers look different but after adjusting for inflation they represent equivalent purchasing power. Suppose that the person's actual current dollar income in 2005 (their paycheck!) is $70,000. The 2005 constant dollar income (measured in 1991 dollars) equals $46,278 (= $50,000 ÷ 1.03^{14}). Constant dollar income declines to $46,278 in 2005 from $50,000 in 1991, implying decline in purchasing power. This decline occurs even though current dollar income increases to $70,000 from $50,000.

Applying time value formulas in accordance with this rule properly accounts for effects of inflation.

> **RULE 4.3 How to integrate inflation into time value computation**
>
> Two procedures properly account for effects of inflation in the time value relation. They both lead to the same inferences. Use the one that is easiest to implement.
> *Rule 4.3A:* Specify all present and future cash flows in current dollars and apply the nominal discount rate.
> *Rule 4.3B:* Specify all present and future cash flows in constant dollars and apply the precise real discount rate, where
>
> $$(1 + \textit{real discount rate}) = \frac{1 + \textit{nominal discount rate}}{1 + \textit{inflation rate}}$$
>
> As an aside notice that the preceding formula precisely computes the *real rate* whereas a quick approximation formula is *real rate = nominal rate − inflation rate*.

First notice that the information requirements for applying rules 4.3 A and B differ. When one knows the discount rate and all future cash flows then apply 4.3A. When on the other hand one is more certain about constant dollar cash flows and the real rate then apply 4.3B. Notice second that computing the real rate as the nominal rate minus the inflation rate is not precisely correct for application in the time value framework; the former is a very close and easy-to-obtain approximation that's good for most (but not all) purposes.

The example below applies the rule to lump-sum time value formula 4.6.

EXAMPLE 12   Find the deposit for purchasing a house in an inflationary setting
There is a house that today costs $100,000 and, for peculiar reasons, in exactly 8 years you want to buy the house. You expect that because of inflation the house price will increase 7.9% per year. How much must you deposit today into an account that earns 11.4% per year such that the future purchase is perfectly financed?

SOLUTION
Applying rule 4.3A requires finding that in eight years the current dollar price of the house will be $183,726 (= $100,000 × 1.079^8). Discount the future current dollar cash flow of $183,726 with the nominal rate of 11.4 percent to find that the present value equals $77,462 (= $183,726 ÷ 1.114^8). A deposit today of $77,462 earning 11.4% for 8 years grows to become $183,726 and perfectly finances the house purchase.

Find the identical answer by applying rule 4.3B. Set the constant dollar future cash flow equal to an amount in today's dollars that purchases the target house. Constant dollar FV equals $100,000. Discount the constant dollar cash flow with the real rate. Given that the nominal rate is 11.4% and inflation is 7.9% then find the precise real rate equals 3.24% [1 + *real rate* = (1.114 / 1.079)]. As an aside note that the approximate real rate of 3.5% (= 11.4% – 7.9%) is 26 basis points greater than the precise real rate. Use formula 4.6 and discount the constant dollar future value of $100,000 with the real rate of 3.24% to find that the present value equals $77,462 (= $100,000 ÷ 1.0324^8). A deposit today of $77,462 earning a real rate of 3.24% for 8 years grows to become $100,000 of today's constant dollars and perfectly finances the house purchase.

The preceding analysis explains two procedures for arriving at the same correct answer. There is one often-used incorrect procedure – ignore inflation! A person observes that today's interest rate is 11.4% and that today's target house costs $100,000. It is seductive to set $100,000 as the target accumulation, to discount with 11.4% for 8 years, and to infer that today's deposit is $42,161 (= $100,000 ÷ 1.114^8). While today's deposit of $42,161 earning 11.4% for 8 years certainly grows to become $100,000 there will be insufficient funds for purchasing the house 8 years from now. The shortfall of $83,726 means missing the real target.

EXERCISES 4.4

Concept quiz
1. When inflation is high the interest rate tends to be high. Explain whether this tendency accentuates or dampens valuation errors that occur by ignoring inflation in the time value relations.

Numerical quickies
2. There is a house that today costs $168,000 and, for peculiar reasons, in exactly three years you want to buy the house. You expect that because of inflation the house price will increase 5.5% per year. The interest rate is 9.4% per year (compounded annually).
2a. Find the precise real rate of interest that the account earns. ©LS25a
2b. Find the price of the house at the time of purchase. ©LS25b

2c. How much must you deposit today into an account such that the future purchase is perfectly financed? ©LS25c

Numerical challenger

3. There is a house that today costs $148,000 and, for peculiar reasons, in exactly three years you want to buy the house. You expect that because of inflation the house price will increase 1.7% per year. The amount that you intend to deposit today is $113,000 (compounded annually). This deposit should grow so that it perfectly finances the purchase.

3a. Find the annual nominal interest rate that the account earns. ©LS26a

3b. Find the precise real annual interest rate that the account earns. ©LS26b

5. THE GENERAL TIME VALUE FORMULA FOR CASH FLOW STREAMS

Financial situations often involve a series of cash flows. There may be one cash flow at the beginning, one at the end, and one or more in the middle. Perhaps, for example, you withdraw or deposit money several times into a savings account. These situations fit within the general time value formula:

FORMULA 4.11 The general time value relation for mixed cash flows

$$PV = \sum_{t=1}^{N} \frac{CF_t}{(1+r)^t} + \frac{FV}{(1+r)^N} \; .$$

Variable definitions are the same as before, with the addition of CF_t as the cash flow at time t. The beginning wealth is PV and the ending wealth N periods later is FV. For some scenarios some variables might equal zero. That's okay. The periodic interest rate is r, where r equals the annual percentage rate i divided by m, the number of compounding periods per year. The first expression represents the summation of N different cash flows. Each cash flow, however, is divided by one plus the periodic interest rate raised to the tth power. In the general time value formula each particular cash flow may have its own unique value; they don't all have to be the same number.

Properly accounting for the timing of cash flows is crucial. A time line easily illustrates the cash flows.

The first cash flow, CF_1, occurs exactly one period after PV. When finding a present value, therefore, the formula implicitly takes away from CF_1 exactly one period of interest. The second cash flow, CF_2, arrives at time 2. Dividing CF_2 by one plus the periodic rate squared finds its present value. The last cash flow, CF_N, occurs exactly N periods after PV. When finding the present value of CF_N, exactly N periods of compound interest are removed. For FV, too, the same proportion of interest is discounted away.

CF_N and FV occur at the same point on the time line. Cash flows occurring at the same time are directly comparable. Cash flows occurring at different times are not directly comparable. The discounting process properly accounts for time value differences so that cash flows from different times are comparable. It is a real necessity to discount cash flows from different time periods before comparing them.

Quite a few different variables appear in formula 4.11. The compounding frequency m, however, almost always is specified. Otherwise, variables that might represent the unknown answer include FV, PV, N, or any one of the CF_t . To find any single unknown variable requires assigning numerical values to all other variables.

5.A. Ending wealth, *FV*, as the unknown

Suppose you make a couple of deposits and want to know the ending balance. For this scenario, FV is the unknown variable. Rearrange the general time value formula to isolate FV on the left-hand-side:

FORMULA 4.12 The general time value formula, solve for *FV*

$$FV = PV(1+r)^N + \sum_{t=1}^{N} CF_t(1+r)^{N-t} \ .$$

Substitute values for all right-hand-side variables and find the answer for *FV*.

EXAMPLE 12 Find the ending wealth for a mixed deposit stream

Your account earns interest at a 6.25 percent APR compounded quarterly. Today the bank credits the account with its quarterly interest and the end-of-day account balance becomes $1,250. You plan to deposit $300 one quarter from today, $325 two quarters from today, and $250 three quarters from today. What is the account's balance immediately after the last deposit?

SOLUTION

Beginning wealth, *PV*, is $1,250. The unknown variable is the account balance exactly three quarters from now. The three cash flows include CF_1 at $300, CF_2 at $325, and CF_3 at $250. The timing of cash flows is as follows:

```
0              1              2              3
+--------------+--------------+--------------+
$1,250         $300           $325          S250
                                            FV = ?
```

The compounding frequency, *m*, is 4 and the annual percentage rate is 6.25 percent. The periodic interest rate *r* therefore equals 0.0625 ÷ 4. Substitution into formula 4.12 shows:

$$FV = \$1{,}250\left(1 + \frac{.0625}{4}\right)^3 + \$300\left(1 + \frac{.0625}{4}\right)^2 + \$325\left(1 + \frac{.0625}{4}\right)^1 + \$250$$

$$= \$1{,}250\,(1.015625)^3 + \$300\,(1.015625)^2 + \$325\,(1.015625)^1 + \$250$$

$$= \$2{,}199.04$$

The account balance rises to $2,199.04 from $1,250 today, an increase of $949.04. This graphic shows the source of the accumulation.

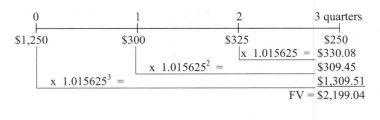

```
0              1              2            3 quarters
+--------------+--------------+--------------+
$1,250         $300           $325           $250
                                  x  1.015625 = $330.08
                      x 1.015625² =            $309.45
       x  1.015625³ =                        $1,309.51
                                        FV = $2,199.04
```

Knowing both the algebraic and time value approaches to solving this problem on the calculator are a good idea. Both approaches are discussed.

Time value computations are very sensitive to interest rate rounding. A rate of 6.25 percent generates very different answers than 6.30 percent. Typical credit card statements, for example, list the periodic interest rate to five or eight places to the right of the decimal point. It's real money so the bank pays attention to rounding errors.

Reduce rounding errors by storing values in the calculator's memories. The BAII Plus© memory stores eight significant digits, regardless of how many the display shows. That is, perhaps the display shows 0.0625 ÷ 4 equal 0.0156, but the actual value in memory is 0.01562500. The answer you get for your time value problems differs if you type in 0.0156 instead of 0.015625. The rounding error gets worse as N gets big.

Effective and efficient calculator usage stores values in memory instead of re-typing. The BAII Plus© has 10 memories, and their addresses equal the numbers 1, 2,…, 9, 0. Store the value on the display (with all eight of its significant digits) in memory by typing STO followed by the address of the desired memory. Recall the value in the memory at any time simply by typing RCL followed by the memory address.

For the algebraic solution to the preceding problem, compute and store in memory the value of 1+r, that is, one plus the periodic rate. Type

.0625 ÷ 4 + 1 = STO 1

Compute the ending wealth by typing

1250 × RCL 1 y^x 3 + 300 × RCL 1 x^2 + 325 × RCL 1 + 250 = .

The display shows $2,199.04.

To use time value functions for finding the ending wealth of mixed cash flow streams on the BAII Plus© involves two stages. The first stage enters the cash flow stream and finds its present value. To enter the cash flow stream, type CF. The calculator allows you to enter a column of numbers. To clear any unwanted numbers that already may be stored in this column, type 2nd CE/C . Enter this problem's cash flow stream as follows:

1250 ENTER ↓ 300 ENTER ↓ ↓ 325 ENTER ↓ ↓ 250 ENTER

Now find the present value of the stream given the rate is 6.25 percent compounded quarterly. Type:

NPV 6.25 ÷ 4 = ENTER ↓ CPT

The display shows $2,099. A deposit of $2,099 at time 0 compounds into exactly the same ending wealth as the problem's actual cash flow stream. That is, the ending wealth at time 3 is the same regardless of whether one deposits (1) $2,099 at time zero, or (2) $1,250 at time zero, plus $300 at time one, plus $325 at time two, plus $250 at time three. With $2,099 on the display, conclude the problem by typing:

PV 2nd I/Y 4 ENTER 2nd CPT 6.25 I/Y 3 N CPT FV

The answer of $2,199.04 appears on the display.

Total contributed principal is the sum of deposits, and equals $875. According to equation 4.8, therefore, the account earns total market interest during the next three quarters of $74.04. The graphic clearly shows the source of interest. The beginning balance of $1,250 grows to $1,309.51, implying that this term earns interest of $59.51. The time 1 deposit, $300, grows to $309.45, implying interest earnings of

$9.45. Finally, the $325 deposit grows to $330.08 implying interest earnings of $5.08. The last deposit earns no interest because the account balance is checked immediately after making the deposit.

Concept quiz
1. Generally speaking, should you make a small deposit today if it means that next period's deposit will be smaller? Or is it better to make no deposit today so that next period's deposit can be larger?

Numerical quickies
2. You invest $3,200 today. One year from today you invest $4,500. Finally, two years from today you invest $5,000. Your account earns 12.5% annual interest (compounded annually). How much is in the account immediately after the last deposit? How much is in the account three years from today? ©MC1a ©MC1b

3. You invest $900 today. One month from today you invest $500. Finally, five months from today you invest $750. Your account earns a 1.5% monthly periodic rate of return. How much is in the account immediately after the last deposit? ©MC2a

Numerical challenger
4. You deposit $1,000 today and exactly 9 months from today you deposit $1,200. Your account earns annual interest of 7.5% compounded monthly. How much is in the account one year from today? ©MC2b

5.B. Beginning wealth, *PV*, as the unknown

To solve for PV as the unknown variable, supply numerical values for all right-hand-side variables in the general time value formula 4.11:

$$PV = \sum_{t=1}^{N} \frac{CF_t}{(1+r)^t} + \frac{FV}{(1+r)^N} \, .$$

EXAMPLE 14 Find the present value of a mixed cash flow stream
An investment promises to return cash flow of $1,200 exactly six months from now, $3,000 exactly 18 months from now, and $4,500 exactly 24 months from today. An investor decides that the investment represents a fair deal if it can be bought at a price that provides a 15 percent annual rate of return, compounded semiannually. What is the fair price for the investment?

SOLUTION
The cash flows occur semiannually, and the time line shows:

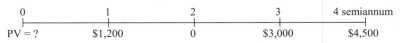

The unknown variable is *PV*. The right-hand side *r* equals 0.15 ÷ 2, or 0.075. The CF_t take values as shown on the time line (*N* is 4). *FV* equals zero for this scenario. *FV* takes on a non-zero value if there were some additional ending wealth, for example if revenue in addition to the $4,500 cash flow were generated. Substituting numbers into the present value formula shows:

$$PV = \frac{\$1,200}{\left(1+\frac{0.15}{2}\right)^1} + \frac{\$0}{\left(1+\frac{0.15}{2}\right)^2} + \frac{\$3,000}{\left(1+\frac{0.15}{2}\right)^3} + \frac{\$4,500}{\left(1+\frac{0.15}{2}\right)^4}$$

$$= \frac{\$1,200}{1.075^1} + \frac{\$0}{1.075^2} + \frac{\$3,000}{1.075^3} + \frac{\$4,500}{1.075^4}$$

$$= \$6,901$$

For the algebraic solution to the preceding problem, compute and store in memory the value of one plus the periodic rate. Type

.15 ÷ 2 + 1 = STO 1

Now compute the present value by typing

1200 ÷ RCL 1 + 3000 ÷ RCL 1 y^x 3 + 4500 ÷ RCL 1 y^x 4 =.
The display shows $6,901.

To use time value functions on the *BAII Plus©* type CF and clear unwanted numbers by typing 2nd CE/C. Now enter this problem's cash flow stream as follows:

↓ 1200 ENTER ↓ ↓ 0 ENTER ↓ ↓ 3000 ENTER ↓ ↓ 4500 ENTER

Now find the present value of the stream given the rate is 15 percent compounded semiannually. Type:

NPV 15 ÷ 2 = ENTER ↓ CPT

The display shows $6,901.

Whenever possible one should check whether the calculator solution seems reasonable. In this problem, the answer suggests that an investment today of $6,901 earns a fifteen percent rate of return if followed by returns of $1,200, $0, $3,000, and $4,500. The sum of returns equals $8,700. The cost of $6,901 seems "reasonably" less than $8,700 to support a fifteen percent rate of return.

The solution is correct, and the graphic below allows insight about discounting future wealth.

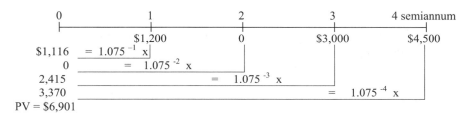

The above procedure divides each cash flow by one plus the periodic rate raised to some exponent. The division by a number larger than one yields an answer smaller than the cash flow. Effectively, the division removes market interest. The present value of a cash flow is the amount deposited today that grows and perfectly finances the cash flow.

For this example the investment returns $1,200 in six months, that is, in one semiannual period. The graphic shows that an $1,116 deposit today earning 7.5 percent semiannual interest grows to $1,200 after six months. The investor with a fifteen percent target annual rate of return, therefore, should pay $1,116 for this first return. After 18 months an additional cash flow of $3,000 occurs. The present value of this cash flow is $2,415. A deposit of $2,415 in a savings account that earns a 15 percent APR, compounded semiannually, accumulates market interest after 18 months equal to $585. The deposit, therefore, perfectly finances the withdrawal of $3,000. Finally, financing the final cash flow of $4,500 four semiannual periods from now requires a deposit today of $3,370. The $6,901 sum of deposits perfectly finances the planned withdrawals.

EXERCISES 4.5B
Numerical quickies
1. An investment promises to return $7,400 in one year and $9,000 in two years. What is the investment's cost today if it promises a 15 percent annual rate of return? ©MC4.

2. You forecast bills of $900 in one month, $500 in six months, and $750 in twelve months. You wish to make a deposit today that perfectly finances the bills. Your account earns a 7.5% annual return, compounded monthly. How much is today's deposit? ©MC3

Numerical challengers

3. Here are two future expenses that you want to save for today: $5,300 payable in 4 years, and $7,000 payable in 9 years. You make an investment today that perfectly finances the future expenses if the investment earns a target 10.8% average annual rate of return (compounded annually).
   3a. How much is your investment? ©MC5a
   3b. When it is time to pay the first expense, you make the expected withdrawal from the account. After the withdrawal what is the account balance? ©MC5b
   3c. The investment indeed grows sufficiently to finance your first expense. Unfortunately, for the entire investment horizon your actual annual rate of return falls short of the target by 90 basis points per year. When it is time to pay the second expense, how much money do you lack? ©MC5c

4. An investment promises two cash flows: $1,000 in exactly 9 months and $2,000 in 18 months. You purchase the investment at a price that promises a target annual rate of return of 14% compounded monthly. After the investment horizon concludes, however, the actual rate of return differs from the target because the second cash flow is smaller than promised (the first cash flow is on-target). If the actual annual rate of return is 12.5% compounded monthly, how much was the second cash flow? ©MC6a

5.C. The rate of return, *r*, as the unknown

The rate of return is the discount rate that equates the present value of cash flows to one other. The variable *r* in the general time value formula cannot be isolated alone on the left-hand-side because it appears in too many places with too many exponents. Financial calculators, however, use smart chips that easily find numerical values for *r*.

EXAMPLE 15 Find the target rate of return

Today you deposit $4,000 into an account with your broker. Your intention is to withdraw $2,000 in one year, $1,500 in two years, $1,000 in three years, and $500 in four years. Annual interest is credited to your account immediately before each withdrawal, and after the last withdrawal the account balance is zero. What annual percentage rate must the account earn?

SOLUTION

Sketch the cash flows onto the time line:

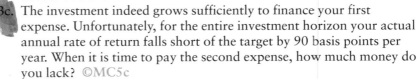

The sign of the time 0 cash flow is opposite the sign of cash flows 1 through 4 because the initial cash flow goes in the opposite direction than the others. For example, at time 0 money flows into the account. At all other times, money flows out of the account.

Substitute the numbers above into general time value formula 4.11:

$$\$4,000 = \frac{\$2,000}{(1+r)^1} + \frac{\$1,500}{(1+r)^2} + \frac{\$1,000}{(1+r)^3} + \frac{\$500}{(i+r)^4}$$

Without a financial calculator the only way to solve the above equation is by trial-and-error with different values for r. The financial calculator, however, easily finds that r equals 12.16 percent.

The table below shows more detail about the scenario.

The account begins at the end of period 0 with a deposit of $4,000. During the subsequent year the account accrues interest at a rate of 12.16 percent, the solution found above. Multiplying the rate times the beginning of period balance shows the account earns interest during the first year of $486.54. The account balance rises to reflect the interest, and immediately before the first withdrawal the balance is $4,486.54. The withdrawal of $2,000 occurs at the end of the first year, thereby bringing the balance down to $2,486.54.

The process repeats each year. Interest earnings equals 12.16 percent times the beginning of year balance. The interest is credited to the account and immediately the subsequent withdrawal occurs. Notice during the fourth year the beginning of year balance equals $445.78. The annual interest of $54.22 brings the account balance up to $500, exactly the amount of the last withdrawal. After the withdrawal, the account balance is zero.

The rate of return found by the general time value equation is the only meaningful rate at which the beginning wealth earns interest that perfectly finances the planned withdrawals. If the rate exceeds 12.16 percent then after the final withdrawal money still would remain in the account. Conversely, the last deposit would be underfunded with a rate smaller than 12.16 percent.

EXAMPLE 16 Find present value and the subsequent rate of return

An adventurous capitalist finds an investment that offers returns of $2,400 in three months, $3,500 in six months, and $8,200 in one year. The adventurist makes an offer to purchase the investment. At that price the rate of return equals the target 14 percent, compounded quarterly. The seller rejects the offer price. Instead, the seller counteroffers a price that is $400 greater than the offer. If the adventurous capitalist purchases the investment at the counteroffer price, what is the rate of return?

Table 4.6

Common components in the general time value relationship

	t = 0	t = 1	t = 2	t = 3	t = 4
beginning of period balance	$0.00	$4,000.00	$2,486.54	$1,288.99	$445.78
periodic interest earned	$0.00	$486.54	$302.45	$156.79	$54.22
new balance before cash flow	$0.00	$4,486.54	$2,788.89	$1,445.78	$500.00
end of period cash flow	$4,000.00	$–2,000.00	$–1,500.00	$–1,000.00	$–500.00
end of period balance	$4,000.00	$2,486.54	$1,288.99	$445.78	$0.00

SOLUTION

The time line describes the scenario:

```
   0            1            2            3          4 months
   |------------|------------|------------|------------|
 PV = ?       $2,400       $3,500         0          $8,200
```

The immediate computation finds the offer price. Use the general time value formula to remove a 14 percent rate of return (compounded quarterly) from the cash flows:

$$PV = \frac{\$2,400}{\left(1+\dfrac{0.14}{4}\right)^1} + \frac{\$3,500}{\left(1+\dfrac{0.14}{4}\right)^2} + \frac{\$0}{\left(1+\dfrac{0.14}{4}\right)^3} + \frac{\$8,200}{\left(1+\dfrac{0.14}{4}\right)^4}$$

$$= \frac{\$2,400}{1.035^1} + \frac{\$3,500}{1.035^2} + \frac{\$0}{1.035^3} + \frac{\$8,200}{1.035^4}$$

$$= \$12,732$$

The offer to purchase the investment is $12,732. The seller wants $400 more; that is, the counteroffer price is $13,132. In the above equation, set PV equal to $13,132 and let r adjust to satisfy the time value equation:

$$\$13,132 = \frac{\$2,400}{(1+r)^1} + \frac{\$3,500}{(1+r)^2} + \frac{\$0}{(1+r)^3} + \frac{\$8,200}{(1+r)^4}$$

Use the financial calculator to find that the periodic rate, r, equals 2.42 percent per quarter. The annual percentage rate therefore equals 9.68 percent (9.68 = 4 x 2.42).

CALCULATOR CLUE

You must use the advanced calculator functions to solve this problem because it does not have an algebraic solution. On the *BAII Plus*© type `CF` and clear unwanted numbers by typing `2nd` `CE/C`. Now enter this problem's cash flow stream as follows:

`↓` 2400 `ENTER` `↓` `↓` 3500 `ENTER` `↓` `↓` 0 `ENTER` `↓` `↓` 8200 `ENTER`

Now find the present value of the stream given the rate is 14 percent compounded quarterly. Type:

`NPV` 14 `÷` 4 `=` `ENTER` `↓` `CPT`

The display shows $12,732. You can't buy at that price, however, and must pay $400 more. With $12,732 still on the display, type:

`+` 400 `=` `+/−` `STO` 1

Now plug that higher price into the cash flow stream and compute the periodic rate of return, which must be multiplied by 4 to obtain the annual return:

`CF` `RCL` 1 `ENTER` `IRR` `CPT` `X` 4 `=`.

The display shows 9.68 percent.

At a price of $12,732 the cash flow stream provides a rate of return equal to the 14 percent target. At the higher a price of $13,132, however, the rate of return is 9.68 percent. The higher price reduces the rate of return to the adventurous capitalist by 432 basis points per year (432 basis points = 0.1400 − 0.0968).

EXERCISES 4.5C
Numerical quickies
   1. An investment that costs $12,000 promises to return $7,400 in one year
      and $9,000 in two years. What is the average annual rate of return? ©MC7.

2. A potential investment promises returns of $900 in one month, $1,000 in two months, and $3,200 in three months. You make an offer to purchase the investment for $4,000.

    2a. What is the annual percentage rate of return, compounded monthly, if you buy at the offer price and receive the promised returns? ©MC8a

    2b. The seller rejects your offer price, and counteroffers at $4,500. If you buy at the higher counteroffer price and receive the promised returns, by how many basis points does the annual percentage rate of return decline? ©MC8b

Numerical challengers

3. You forecast expenses of $5,800 payable in 4 months and $3,800 payable in 8 months. You make a deposit today of $8,350 that should perfectly finance the future expenditures. What annual percentage rate of return (compounded monthly) does the account earn? ©MC9

4. You forecast bills of $8,200 in one month, $5,100 in six months, and $4,750 in twelve months. You make a deposit today of $17,000 that should perfectly finance the bills. What annual percentage rate, compounded monthly, does the account earn? ©MC10

5. Here are two future expenses that you want to save for today: $2,700 payable in 4 years, and $6,100 payable in 9 years. You make an investment today that would perfectly finance the future expenses if the investment were to earn a target 7.5% average annual rate of return (compounded annually). Instead, however, the investment earns so much that after the last expense is made, your account still has $1,500 remaining. What was the actual annual percentage rate? ©MC11

ANSWERS TO CHAPTER 4 EXERCISES

EXERCISES 4.1

1. The percentage increase during the first period is larger than the percentage decline during the second. For example, if the stock price doubles to $20 from $10 during the first period, it is up 100%. But when it falls during the second period from $20 to $10 it is down only 50%. The arithmetic average will be positive, and larger than the geometric average rate of return of zero.

2. The statement is true. A column of, say, five prices makes a unique column of four rates of return. A column of four rates of return, however, can make an infinite number of columns of five prices. In this regard, prices carry more information than rates of return.

3. The geometric ROR is $(60 \div 40)^{0.5} - 1$, or 22.5%. The arithmetic ROR is $\{(19-40)/40 + (60-19)/19\} \div 2$, or 81.6%.

4. The answer is $20(1-.15)(1+.65) = 28.05

5. The geometric average rate of return obviously is negative because you lost money. Hence, the broker must be correctly quoting the arithmetic average. The sum of two periodic rates of return, divided by two, equals 20 percent. Let P_1 represent the portfolio value one year ago. Then using the definition for the arithmetic ROR shows
$\{[(P_1 - 10,000)/10,000] + [(9,150 - P_1)/P_1]\} \div 2 = 0.20$
Rearrange the above to obtain the following quadratic equation
$P_1{}^2 - 24,000\,P_1 + 91,500,000 = 0$
The two roots are $P_1 = $4,754$ or $P_1 = $19,245$. Both work and are legitimate answers.

EXERCISES 4.2A

1. Play with your calculator. Begin with PV = $1,000 and N = 10 years and r = 0.10. For this baseline case, FV equals $2,594. Double PV and FV doubles to $5,187 (a 100% increase). Double N to 20 and FV rises to

$6,727 (a 159% increase). Double r to 20% and FV rises to $6,192 (a 139% increase). For typical settings, doubling the investment horizon has the biggest impact. [N.B. Doubling N has a larger impact as long as the initial $N > \log(1 + 2r) \div \log(1 + r)$].

2. Find FV as $24(1.0625)^{375}$, or 179,293,000,000 . That is, $179 billion.
3. Find FV as $1,000(1.055)^5$, or $1,307. Total interest is $307.
4. Interest-on-principal is $5,000(0.12) per year, or $600. Over 18 years the interest-on-principal sums to 18($600), or $10,800. The total accumulation after 18 years is $5,000(1.12)^{18}$, or $38,449. Of the total accumulation, $5,000 is initial principal and $10,800 is interest-on-principal. The rest, $22,649, is interest-on-interest.
5. The balance at the beginning of the current year is the balance on which this year's interest is based. The balance after 3 years is $3,500(1.0875)^3$, or $4,501. This year's interest is $4,501(0.0875), or $394.
6. Because $2,500 = (0.0675)(beginning-of-year balance), the beginning-of-year balance is $2,500/(0.0675), or $37,037. The end of year balance therefore is $37,037 plus $2,500, which is $39,537.
7. The sum of monthly returns divided by 12 yields the arithmetic average monthly rate of return of 43.75 percent. First use this number as r in the time value relation. The beginning wealth, PV, is $12,500. The ending wealth after twelve months with r at 0.4375 is $12,500(1.4375)^{12}$, or $973,205. Now find the geometric average monthly rate of return as the product of the twelve "one plus monthly ROR" raised to the one-twelfth, minus one, which is −1.41 percent. Use this as r and find FV is $12,500(1 − 0.0141)^{12}$, or $10,542. There is a big-time difference between $10,542 and $973,205! The answer based on the geometric average is correct. Shareholders in Saf T Lok had quite a ride in 1997, and they ended up losing money.

EXERCISES 4.2B

1. When r > 0 then always PV < FV. Yet if rate of return r is negative then beginning wealth PV is less than ending wealth FV. Investments realize negative rates of return all too often.
2. Find that PV equals $19,500 ÷ $(1.16)^4$, which is $10,770.
3. Find PV as $3,500 ÷ $(1.0125)^8$, which is $3,169.
4. Find the amount of the deposit as $6,200 ÷ $(1.0125)^{14}$, which is $5,210. That deposit compounds at 1.05 percent per month for 14 months. The ending balance is $5,210(1.0105)^{14}$, which is $6,031. You lack $169.
5. Find the beginning of this year's balance as $2,200 ÷ 0.0625, which is $35,200. To obtain an accumulation of $35,200 over 17 years at 6.25% per year means the initial deposit was $35,200 ÷ $(1.0625)^{17}$, which is $12,559.

EXERCISES 4.2C

1. Find the N that satisfies the equation $6,000 = $2,400 $(1.14)^N$, which is N equals 7 years.
2. Find the N that satisfies the equation $100,000 = $2,660 $(1.12)^N$, which is N equals 32 years.
3. The beginning of year balance is $1,100 ÷ 0.0725, which is $15,172. Find the N that satisfies the equation $15,172 = $7,000 $(1.0725)^N$, which is N equals 11 years. Because it is eleven years from the time of the deposit until one year ago, the initial deposit occurred 12 years ago.
4. The account balance today is $14,095. Find the N that satisfies the following equality: $7,000(1.0725)^N$ = $14,095 or N is 10 years.
5. The key factor is the length of time until the pay-off occurs. As long as the loan's principal plus accrued interest is less than $29,800 then the deal is profitable. Find the N that satisfies the equation $29,800 = $15,300 $(1.0870)^N$, which is N equals 8. As long as the payoff occurs in less than 8 years the deal is profitable.

1. Find the r that satisfies $1,350(1 + r)^5 = $2,750$, which is r equals 15.29%.
2. Find the r that satisfies $900(1 + r)^8 = $2,700$, which is r equals 14.72%.
3. Find the r that satisfies $1(1 + r)^{24} = 2, which is r equals 2.93%.
4. The beginning of year balance was $8,200. For $8,200 to earn interest of $800 implies an annual interest rate of 9.76% (that is, $800/$8,200).
5. Find that the deposit equals $5,300 \div (1.0125)^{18}$, which is $4,238. Then find the rate r that satisfies $4,328(1 + r)^{18} = $5,080$, or r equals 1.01%.
6. The decision depends on A's price. Find that the rate of return on B satisfies $6,800(1 + r)^7 = $10,000$ or r is 5.66%. For A to return 5.66% suggests it's price is $8,000 \div 1.0566^{11}$, or $4,364. The decision rule is that if A costs less than $4,364 then choose A for its higher rate of return. If A costs more than $4,364 then choose B for its higher rate of return.

1. At 12% doubling occurs every 6 years. A $10,000 deposit grows to $20,000 after 6 years, $40,000 after 12 years, etc. An investor at age 55 has a 15 year savings horizon. The will finance about two and a half doubling periods by the time age 70 is reached. So the ending wealth is approximately halfway between $40,000 and $80,000 or $60,000. An investor at age 25 has a 45 year investment horizon, encompassing about 7 ½ doubling periods at 12 percent. The ending wealth for this investor is about $1.7 million. Complete the other 4 table cells with similar logic. Obtain a table that approximately appears as below.

age at time of investment	8% ROR	12% ROR	Horizon length to age 70
25 years old	$320,000	$1,700,000	45 years
40 years old	$80,000	$320,000	30 years
55 years old	$35,000	$60,000	15 years
	9 years	6 years	Length of doubling period

Note that an exact table is easily found with a financial calculator. Nonetheless, simple in-the-head approximations perhaps forcefully convey a key insight. Investment horizon and rate of return are both extremely important. The market, not the investor, largely determines rates of return. The investor controls the length of the investment horizon. Save young, make wise investments, and wealth accumulates.

1. Find FV as $1,200(1 + .055/12)^{60}$, or $1,579. Total interest is $379.
2. Find PV as $15,000 \div (1 + .0625/2)^{20}$, or $8,106.
3. Find PV as $4,200 \div (1 + .125/12)^{48}$, or $2,554.
4. The target accumulation is $5,650. Find N from $3,100 (1 + .09/4)^N = $5,650$, or N equals 27 quarters (6 3/4 years).
5. Find the amount you borrow as $6,200 \div (1 + .0825/12)^{14}$, or $5,633. This loan of $5,633 incurs interest such that the future sum is $5,633 (1 + .1075/12)^{14}$, or $6,382. You lack $182.
6. Find the beginning of this quarter's balance as $350 \div (0.055 / 4)$, which is $25,455. To obtain an accumulation of $25,455 over 14 years at a 5.5% annual rate compounded quarterly means the initial deposit was $25,455 \div (1 + .055/4)^{4(14)}$, which is $11,848.
7. The deposit equals $5,300 \div (1 + .0725/12)^{18}$, or $4,755. Next find the monthly periodic rate from $4,755 (1 + r)^{18} = $5,080$, or r is 0.37%. Multiply the monthly rate by twelve to get the annual percentage rate of 4.41%
8. The balance at the beginning of the current month is the balance on which this month's interest is based. The balance after 41 months is

$1,200(1+ .0775/12)^{41}$, or $1,562. This month's interest is $1,562 x 0.0775/12, or $10.09.

9. This quarter's interest of $620 equals $(0.0525/4)x$(B.O.P. Balance), so the beginning of period balance is $47,238. Add this quarter's interest to the beginning balance to get the end of period balance of $47,858.

10. This period's interest of $608 equals $(0.075/2)x$(B.O.P. Balance), so the beginning of period balance is $16,220. The end of period current balance therefore equals $16,828. Find N from the following: $16,828 = $9,000(1+ .075/2)^{N}$, or N is 17 semiannum (8½ years).

11. The account balance equals the initial principal plus total lifetime interest, or $4,521. Find N from the following: $4,521 = $3,200(1+ .065/12)^{N}$, or N is 64 months (5 years, 4 months).

12. Find the present value of costs. For example, with supplier X at a 4.4% discount payable on day 30 the present value of cost is $2,081 = $2,200(1 − .044)(1+ .128/365)^{-30}$. For supplier X at full price payable on day 140 the present value of cost is $2,095 = $2,200(1+ .128/365)^{-140}$. Similar computations for supplier Z shows that the present values of the discounted and full prices equal $1,965 and $1,979. The overall lowest cost is purchase at the discounted price from supplier Z.

EXERCISES 4.3B

1. Savers want to receive as much interest as often as possible. Savers benefit from increased compounding frequency. Borrowers want to pay as little interest as infrequently as possible. Borrowers benefit from diminished compounding frequency.

2. The EAR equals $(1 + 0.1570/12)^{12} – 1$, or 16.88%.

3. The best investment has the highest EAR. For the monthly deal the EAR is $(1 + 0.0934/12)^{12} – 1$, or 9.75%. For the daily deal the EAR is $(1 + 0.0924/365)^{365} – 1$, or 9.79%. The daily deal pays the most interest per annum.

4. Find the r that satisfies $3,250 (1 + r)^{32} = $3,860, which is r equals 0.54% per month. The APR is twelve times that, or 6.47%. The EAR is $(1 + 0.0054)^{12} – 1$, or 6.66%.

EXERCISES 4.4

1. The positive correlation between inflation and interest accentuates valuation errors that result from ignoring inflation. To see this accentuation examine two scenarios for accumulating $100 of real income over 10 years during which time the approximate real interest rate equals 4 percent. For scenario 1 suppose inflation and interest equal 2 percent and 6 percent, respectively. The ignorant saver discounts $100 for 10 years at 6 percent and believes that a deposit today of $55.84 (= $100 ÷ 1.06^{10}) perfectly finances the purchase. Over 10 years, however, the purchase prices grows to become $121.90 (= $100 x 1.02^{10}). For the low inflation environment there is a shortfall of $21.90 (since only $100 accumulates). For scenario 2 suppose inflation and interest equal 12 percent and 16 percent, respectively. The ignorant saver deposits today $22.67 (= $100 ÷ 1.16^{10}) and over 10 years the purchase prices grows to become $310.58 (= $100 x 1.12^{10}). For the high inflation environment there is a shortfall of $210.58. As percent of actual purchase price the shortfall equals 18% (=$21.90/$121.90) for the low inflation environment and 68% (=$210.58/$310.58) for the high inflation environment. Potential valuation errors accentuate with inflation because savers may incorrectly perceive more rapid wealth accumulation and therefore save less when, in fact, high inflation means future wealth simply won't buy as much!

2a. The precise real rate is $(1+.094) ÷ (1+.055) – 1$, or 3.70%.

2b. The actual house price is $168,000x(1+.055)^3$, or $192,273.

2c. The deposit is $192,273 \div (1+.094)^3$, or $150,666. This answer is identical to $168,000 \div (1+.037)^3$.

3a. Find that the actual house price is $148,000x(1+.017)^3$, or $155,677. Next use the lump-sum relation that $113,000x(1+r)^3 = $155,677$ and therefore r equals 11.3%.

3b. With r = 11.3% and inflation at 1.7%, find the actual real rate as 1.113 $\div$ 1.017 or 9.4%.

EXERCISES 4.5A

1. Precise answers require numbers, of course. When shifting the same dollar amounts, however, it always is better to make the deposits as soon as possible. For example, ending wealth is greater with a strategy that invests $25 this period and $75 next period, instead of a strategy that invests nothing this period and $100 next period. In general, though, deferring deposits is better when the size of the subsequent deposit increases faster than the discount rate.

2. Consider first the ending wealth immediately after the last deposit. Today's deposit contributes two years of interest to the ending wealth. Next year's deposit contributes one year of interest. The third deposit contributes no interest. The ending wealth therefore equals $3,200(1 + 0.125)^2 + $4,500(1 + 0.125)^1 + $5,000$. The account balance two years from today is $14,112. Consider now the account balance one additional year later. The simplest procedure multiplies the balance at the beginning of this last year, $14,112 by (1 + 0.125), which is $15,877. This is identical to $3,200(1.125)^3 + $4,500(1.125)^2 + $5,000(1.125)^1$.

3. Find the ending wealth immediately after the last deposit, which is five months from today. Today's deposit contributes five months of interest to the ending wealth. Next month's deposit contributes four months of interest. The last deposit contributes no interest. The ending wealth therefore equals $900(1 + 0.015)^5 + $500(1 + 0.015)^4 + 750, or $2,250.

4. Today's deposit contributes twelve months of interest to the ending wealth. The subsequent deposit contributes three months of interest. The ending wealth therefore equals $1,000(1 + 0.075/12)^{12} + $1,200(1 + 0.075/12)^3$, or $2,300.27.

EXERCISES 4.5B

1. Simply find the present value as $7,400/(1.15)^1 + $9,000/(1.15)^2$, which is $13,240.

2. The deposit equals the present value of $900/(1 + 0.075/12)^1 + $500/(1 + 0.075/12)^6 + $750/(1 + 0.075/12)^{12}$. The deposit is $2,072.

3a. The investment equals the present value of $5,300/(1.108)^4 + $7,000/(1.108)^9$. The investment is $6,298.

3b. The investment of $6,298 accumulates 10.8% interest for four years. The balance immediately before the first payment therefore is $6,298(1.108)^4$, or $9,492. The first expense of $5,300 is paid, thereby reducing the balance to $4,192.

3c. The investment of $6,298 accumulates 9.9% interest throughout the entire horizon (10.8% minus 90 basis points is 9.9%). The balance immediately before the first payment therefore is $6,298(1.099)^4$, or $9,187. The first expense of $5,300 is paid, thereby reducing the balance to $3,887. This balance grows for five more years to reach $3,887(1.099)^5$, or $6,232. Because your expense is $7,000 there is a shortfall of $768.

4. The cost of the investment is $1,000/(1 + 0.14/12)^9 + $2,000(1 + 0.14/12)^{18}$, or $2,524 . Find CF_2 by relating the cost to the discounted cash flows given the 12.5 percent actual rate of return:
$2,524 = $1,000 / (1+ 0.125/12)^9 + CF_2 / (1+ 0.125/12)^{18}$,
or CF_2 is $1,944.

EXERCISES 4.5C

1. Find the r that satisfies $12,000 = $7,400/(1+r)^1 + $9,000/(1+r)^2$, which is 22.8%.

2a. Find the r that satisfies the equality: $4,000 = $900/(1 + r)^1 + $1,000/(1 + r)^2 + $3,200/(1 + r)^3$. The monthly periodic rate, r, is 10.6%. The APR is twelve times that, or 126%.

2b. Find the r that satisfies the equality: $4,500 = $900/(1 + r)^1 + $1,000/(1 + r)^2 + $3,200/(1 + r)^3$. The monthly periodic rate, r, is 5.3%. The APR is twelve times that, or 63%. The higher price causes the APR to decline to 63% from the promised 126%, a decline of over 60 percent (that is, the decline exceeds 6,000 basis points).

3. Find the r that satisfies the equality: $8,350 = $5,800/(1 + r)^4 + $3,800/(1 + r)^8$. The monthly periodic rate, r, is 2.6%. The APR is twelve times that, or 30.6%.

4. Find the r that satisfies the equality: $17,000 = $8,200/(1 + r)^1 + $5,100/(1 + r)^6 + $4,750/(1 + r)^{12}$. The monthly periodic rate, r, is 1.16%. The APR is twelve times that, or 13.9%.

5. Find the amount of the investment as $2,700/(1.075)^4 + $6,100/(1.075)^9$, or $5,203. Now find the r that satisfies the equality: $5,203 = $2,700/(1 + r)^4 + ($6,100+$1,500)/(1 + r)^9$. The annual percentage rate, r, is 9.6%.

CHAPTER 5

Future and Present Values of Annuities

CHAPTER CONTENTS

Combining cash flows at different points in time requires accounting for differences in time value. The general time value formula for mixed cash flows from the previous chapter (formula 4.11) properly handles all situations. That approach, however, is very general because it accommodates situations where the cash flow each period is possibly a different amount. For some financial situations the cash flow each period is exactly the same amount. Consumer and mortgage loans, for example, generally have a fixed payment that is exactly the same every month. Many investment or savings plans, too, stipulate a constant periodic cash flow. Procedures simplify when the cash flows are all the same amount. In this chapter we examine cash flow streams in which the cash flow each period is exactly the same.

1. THE TIME VALUE FORMULA FOR CONSTANT ANNUITIES

Recall the previous chapter's general time value formula for mixed cash flow streams from formula 4.11:

$$PV = \sum_{t=1}^{N} \frac{CF_t}{(1+r)^t} + \frac{FV}{(1+r)^N} \; .$$

The preceding equation still is true. When $CF_1 = CF_2 = \ldots = CF_N$, however, the following simplification occurs:

FORMULA 5.1 Constant annuity time value formula

$$PV = \frac{CF}{(1+r)^1} + \frac{CF}{(1+r)^2} + \ldots + \frac{CF}{(1+r)^N} + \frac{FV}{(1+r)^N}$$

$$= (CF) \left\{ \frac{1-(1+r)^{-N}}{r} \right\} + FV(1+r)^{-N}$$

Equation 5.1 is the constant annuity time value formula. Variable definitions and cash flow timing are the same as before. *CF* is the periodic cash flow that occurs at times 1 through *N*. Each period *CF* is the same amount. There are *N* unique cash flows of amount *CF*. *PV* equals the beginning wealth one period before the first periodic cash flow. The ending wealth *N* periods later is *FV*. The last *CF* occurs at the same time as *FV*. The periodic interest rate *r* equals *i/m*, where *i* is the annual percentage rate and *m* is the number of compounding periods per year. The time line below illustrates the essential timing of cash flows.

Some textbooks refer to cash flows consistent with the preceding time line as *ordinary annuities*. That perspective maintains that cash flows occur at the end-of-periods. An alternative scenario pertains to *annuities due* in which case the cash flows are said to occur at the beginning-of-periods. The time line below illustrates essential timing for *annuities due*:

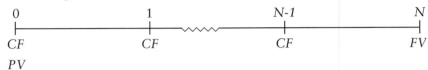

With an *annuity due* the first *CF* is concurrent with *PV*, the last *CF* occurs one period before *FV*, and still there are *N* occurrences of *CF*. Most calculators allow setting whether cash flows occur at end or beginning-of-periods. Practically speaking, however, as far as a time line goes the end of one period is the beginning of the next and so this distinction is a little arbitrary and potentially confusing. The important fact is occurrence of the first and last *CF!* All lessons in this book avoid potential confusion by eliminating labels *ordinary annuities* and *annuities due*. Instead, the lessons explicitly specify timing of cash flows—all *Calculator Clues* assume that you keep your calculator set to end-of-period!

The most significant simplification inherent with formula 5.1 is elimination of the summation expression. For example, suppose a cash flow stream contains 360 monthly cash flows (*N*=360) and all are exactly the same amount. Usage of the general time value formula in equation 4.11 involves summation of 360 different terms. The constant annuity time value formula in Equation 5.1 does not involve that summation. Instead, an exponent in one of the terms takes on the value 360.

Five variables appear in formula 5.1: *FV, PV, N, CF,* and *r*. When any four of the variables are set to numerical values, the fifth becomes an unknown that takes on a value satisfying the equation. Almost always the signs on *N* and *r* are positive and easy to interpret. The signs for *FV, PV,* and *CF,* however, may sometimes be positive and other times negative. Interpreting the signs on these variables is very important and sometimes complicated. The issue complicates further because different calculators sometimes adopt different rules regarding signage.

Here are three short lessons about variable signs for *FV, PV,* and *CF* in formula 5.1 (or any of its rearrangements shown in this chapter).

1. Signage is simple to interpret when one of the three variables is zero. For example, if *PV* equals zero because there is no beginning wealth but simply there are deposits *CF* and ending wealth *FV* then signage is simple. Likewise in the lump-sum relation when *CF* is zero then the signs on *FV* and *PV* are easy to interpret.

2. When *FV, PV,* and *CF* are <u>all</u> non-zero then remember the baseline scenario that formula 5.1 exemplifies. Beginning wealth *PV* flows into an account, periodic *CF* flow <u>out</u> of the account (like withdrawals), and ending wealth *FV* is the balance immediately after the last *CF*. For the preceding scenario all variables are <u>positive</u>. For scenarios that reverse the flow then reverse the sign. For example, when periodic deposits *CF* flow <u>into</u> the account assign in formula 5.1 a <u>negative</u> sign to *CF*.

3. Usually there are two approaches for signing <u>all</u> variables. Whatever is positive in approach 1 is negative in approach 2, and vice versa. Both approaches lead to the same correct numerical answer. For example, the previous paragraph states that when *PV* and *FV* are positive then periodic deposits have negative signs. An alternative approach reverses signs: when *PV* and *FV* are both negative then assign a positive sign to periodic deposits. The choice of signs in a problem is a relative issue.

The preceding paragraphs apply to formula 5.1 or any of its rearrangements shown throughout this chapter. Calculators adopt their own unique rules. On the *BAII Plus*© financial calculator variable signs are easier to interpret by taking the perspective of one of the problem participants. Assign a positive sign to money flowing into your pocket such as withdrawals or stock dividends. Deposits, however, flow out of your pocket and into the asset account. They are leaving your pocket so give them a negative sign.

The sections below discuss scenarios that rely on the constant annuity time value formula.

Concept quiz
1. Explain how inflation integrates into the constant annuity time value formula.

2. FUTURE VALUES OF ANNUITIES

Suppose you make a series of identical deposits and want to know the ending balance. For this scenario, *FV* is the unknown variable. Rearrange and isolate *FV* on the left-hand-side:

> **FORMULA 5.2 Future value of a constant annuity stream**
>
> $$FV = PV(1+r)^N - CF\left\{\frac{(1+r)^N - 1}{r}\right\}$$
>
> $$= PV(1+r)^N - CF\left\{FVIFA_{rate = r, \ periods = N}\right\}$$

Solving for *FV* requires assigning numerical values for *PV, N, CF*, and *r*.

The expression in curly brackets is the "future value interest factor for an annuity", abbreviated *FVIFA*. The expression depends only on *r* and *N*. The intuitive meaning of *FVIFA* is simply stated.

> **DEFINITION 5.1 Future value interest factor of annuities (FVIFA)**
>
> *FVIFA* is the future value of one dollar deposits made for N consecutive periods that earn the periodic discount rate *r*: $FVIFA_{r,N} = \frac{(1+r)^N - 1}{r}$

Bankers in an earlier era owned "time value books" containing FVIFA tables. The tables, similar to the one in Panel A of Table 1, Appendix 1, list a different N for each row and a different periodic rate for each column. The tables simply compute the value of the expression in curly brackets. Looking at the FVIFA table with a periodic rate equal to 15 percent and N equal to 10, for example, shows a table entry equal to 20.3037.

$$FVIFA_{rate = 15\%, \ N=10} = \left\{\frac{(1+.15)^{10} - 1}{.15}\right\}$$

$$= 20.3037$$

This means that if one dollar per year is deposited for ten years, and interest of 15 percent per year accrues, the account balance equals $20.30 immediately after the last deposit. Because contributed principal equals $15, the total market interest equals $5.30.

FVIFA tables enable easy computation of future sums even though the deposit is different than one dollar. With a $500 deposit, and the same rate of 15 percent for 10 years, the future value equals $500 x 20.3037, or $10,152. The tables are easy, but financial calculators and spreadsheets pretty much make the tables obsolete.

The variable signs in equation 5.2 deserve discussion. Begin with an example in which 10 percent interest compounds annually in a savings account for 2 years. With a beginning wealth *PV* of $100, and *CF* of $0, the ending *FV* wealth two periods later is $121 (that is, $121 = $100x1.10^2). This lump-sum scenario is shown in the time line below:

Now extend the example. Suppose that $20 is withdrawn from the account at times 1 and 2; that is, *CF* = $20. This annuity scenario is shown in this time line:

Recall that formula 5.1 (and its rearrangement in 5.2) assumes that when *PV*, *CF*, and *FV* are all positive that *CF* represents a withdrawal, or return of cash flow. This problem fits that description. On the right-hand-side of formula 5.2 subtract the positive *CF* from the positive $PV(1+r)^N$. How much now is the ending balance at time 2? Substitute into equation 5.2 to find that:

$$FV = \$100(1.10)^2 - \$20\left\{\frac{(1.10)^2 - 1}{0.10}\right\}$$

$$= \$121 - \$42$$

$$= \$79$$

The $42 subtracted-out equals the future value of the withdrawal stream. The withdrawals naturally diminish the ending balance below $121; it falls to $79.

CALCULATOR CLUE

The figure above also is computable with the time value functions. On the BAII Plus© type `2nd` `FV` to clear the time value memories. Type `2nd` `I/Y` 1 `ENTER` `2nd` `CPT` to enforce annual compounding. Then solve the preceding problem as follows:

100 `PV` 20 `+/−` `PMT` 2 `N` 10 `I/Y` `CPT` `FV`

The display shows $−79. The sign on the $100 initial deposit, `PV`, is positive because cash flows into the account to establish the balance. The sign on the two $20 withdrawals, `PMT`, is negative because cash flows out of the account. The sign on the ending wealth, `FV`, is negative because funds are available to flow out of the account.

2.A. Ending wealth, *FV*, as the unknown variable

Regular savings plans typically involve a series of deposits, a known interest rate, and the unknown variable is ending wealth. Consider the example below.

EXAMPLE 1 Find savings plan accumulation.
You wish to save for the holiday season by starting a regular savings plan at the local bank. Deposits will be made every week, with the first one today. In 40 weeks, at the time you make the final deposit, you will withdraw all accumulated funds. If your deposits are $75 weekly, and the annual interest rate of 6.25 percent compounds weekly, how much will be available for the withdrawal?

SOLUTION

First get the time line right. Deposits commence right now, time zero, and conclude exactly 40 weeks from today.

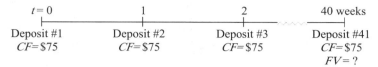

Count the number of deposits. The first deposit occurs at time 0, the second deposit at time 1, etc., and finally the forty-first deposit occurs at time 40. Because N is the number of cash flows, N equals 41. This highlights that N is properly thought of as the number of cash flows, not as a time subscript.

Other variable settings include r at $0.0625 \div 52$ (the APR, i, is 0.0625 and m is 52). CF definitely is $75, but is it positive or negative? Either approach is correct. Because the deposit flows out of your pocket, set CF to $\${-75}$. The beginning wealth, PV, equals zero because there is no account balance preceding the first cash flow. Notice that if a beginning balance were relevant for this problem, the timing requires the beginning wealth exactly one period before the first deposit.

Substitution of all settings into equation 5.2 shows:

$$ FV = \$0 - (\$\text{-}75)\left\{ \frac{\left(1+\frac{0.0625}{52}\right)^{41} - 1}{\frac{0.0625}{52}} \right\}. $$

$$ = \$3,150 $$

The account accumulates $3,150. The total contributed principal equals $3,075 (that is, $3,075 = 41 \times \$75$). The remainder of the accumulation, $75, is total market interest.

CALCULATOR CLUE

For the algebraic solution to the preceding problem, compute and store in memory the value of the periodic rate. See the discussion in the previous chapter that storing variables in the calculator's memory reduces rounding error. Type .0625 ÷ 52 = STO 1. Now compute the present value by typing RCL 1 + 1 = y^x 41 − 1 = ÷ RCL 1 × 75 =. The display shows $3,150.

The remainder of this chapter uses time value functions for solving problems. Solve the preceding problem by typing 2nd FV to clear the time value memories, and 2nd I/Y 52 ENTER 2nd CPT to enforce weekly compounding. Then type: 75 +/− PMT 41 N 6.25 I/Y CPT FV.

The display shows $3,150.

The signs are consistent with the earlier discussion. CF is negative because deposits represent monies flowing out of your pocket. FV takes on an opposite and positive sign, implying that at the end of the investment horizon monies are available to flow into your pocket. Notice, however, that all signs could have been reversed. If CF were positive then FV would be negative, but exactly the same answer obtains.

Beware! Your calculator gives you wrong answers as well as right ones. It has no conscience! Therefore there is a definite advantage for scenarios when easy approximation of an answer is possible. When the approximation is relatively close to the precise number from your time value calculation then likely the precise answer is correct. Conversely, when the approximation and precise answer are miles apart then this signals a need to double-check. The Rule of 72 from the previous chapter provides approximations within the lump-sum time value framework. The rule modifies for approximating the future value of a constant annuity stream. The modified rule requires some multiplication and is prone to larger approximation errors yet, still, the modified rule may sometimes be useful.

RULE 5.1 The modified rule of 72 for constant annuities

The Rule of 72 for lump-sums states that the approximate number of years in which a sum of money doubles, D, equals 72 divided by the annual rate of return. The modified rule approximates total future value, FV, as

$$FV = N \times CF \times (1 + \tfrac{1}{2}N/D),$$

where N is the number of years in the savings plan and CF is the constant <u>annual</u> deposit.

Intuition underlying the modified rule is that N/D is the savings plan as a proportion of the doubling period. Thus, $CF \times (1 + \tfrac{1}{2}N/D)$ represents the approximate average accumulation per year, which multiplied by number of years, equals total accumulation FV.

Suppose, for example, that you wish to approximate the future value of a stream of $1,200 annual deposits earning 6%. CF equals $1,200. Divide 72 by 6 and find that the doubling period D equals 12. All that remains is N, the number of years in the savings plan. Say that you save for 12 years, implying that N/D is 100%; you save for an entire doubling period. This is the approximation:

$$FV = 12 \times \$1{,}200 \times (1.5).$$

Average accumulation per year is about $1,800 (= $1,200 $\times$ 1.5); the first year's deposit doubles to become worth $2,400 and the last year contributes $1,200. The approximate answer is that FV equals $21,600 (= 12 $\times$ $1,800). The precise answer from the financial calculator is $20,244 (= $1,200 $\times$ $FVIFA_{r=6\%,\,N=12}$). The approximation overstates the precise value by about 7%. Bank on the precise number!

By saving for 6 years (implying N/D is 50%) then you have this approximation:

$$FV = 6 \times \$1{,}200 \times (1.25),$$

which is $9,000. The precise answer is $8,370 (= $1,200 $\times$ $FVIFA_{r=6\%,\,N=6}$). The overstatement is about 7½%.

The modified rule provides a method for checking the ball-park reasonableness of an answer even though its approximations tend to have more error than lump-sum approximations with the Rule of 72. Suppose, for example, that a savings plan deposits $200 monthly for 6 years (first deposit one month from now; last in exactly 6 years) at 12% compounded monthly. Approximate the answer with the *Modified Rule of 72*. The doubling period D is 6 years (= 72 ÷ 12), the annual cash flow CF is $2,400:

$$FV = 6 \times \$2{,}400 \times (1.5),$$

The approximate answer equals $21,600. Use the financial calculator to find that the precise answer is $20,942 (=$200 $\times$ $FVIFA_{r=12\% \div 12,\,N=72}$). That's pretty close!

EXERCISES 5.2A

Numerical quickies

1. Family friends of yours got a tax refund of $2,600 today. Instead of spending the money, they plan to deposit it into an account that earns 9.90% compounded annually. They expect to receive 10 same-sized annual tax refunds and to immediately deposit them into this account. Otherwise, they'll leave the account alone.

1a. Find the account balance after their last deposit. ©FV10am
1b. Find the amount of total interest that the account will earn. ©FV10bm
2. Your parents contribute $50 monthly to a college savings plan for you that earns 9.80% compounded monthly. The first deposit was exactly 9 years ago. Find the account balance after today's monthly deposit and crediting of monthly interest. ©FV7
3. Your company contributes $1,250 each quarter to your college for setting up a scholarship fund. The account earns 6.50% compounded quarterly. The first deposit was exactly 15 years ago and no funds have thus far been withdrawn. Find the account balance and total amount of accumulated interest after today's quarterly deposit and crediting of quarterly interest. ©FV8

Numerical challenger

4. An account is today credited with its annual interest thereby bringing the account balance to $12,490. The interest rate is 5.70% compounded annually. You plan to make annual withdrawals of $1,450 each. The first withdrawal is in exactly one year and the last in exactly 9 years. Find the account balance immediately after the last withdrawal. ©FV5
5. An account is today credited with its monthly interest thereby bringing the account balance to $8,290. The interest rate is 6.40% compounded monthly. You plan to make monthly withdrawals of $70 each. The first withdrawal is in exactly one month and the last in exactly 12 years. Find the account balance immediately after the last withdrawal. ©FV9

2.B. Using the annuity and lump-sum formulas together

The example below illustrates that some financial scenarios require usage of both lump-sum and annuity time value formulas.

EXAMPLE 2 Save an annuity and subsequently compound as a lump-sum.
With wages from a summer job you make a total of 4 deposits at $480 per month into a savings account earning 5.50% compounded monthly. At the time of the last deposit, you close the savings account and invest all the money in stocks with the intention of leaving the stocks alone for the subsequent 25 years (dividends automatically are reinvested). The stocks are expected to provide an average annual geometric return of 16% compounded monthly. When you finally sell the stocks, how much do you get?

SOLUTION
Examine the time line to ascertain clear understanding of the question.

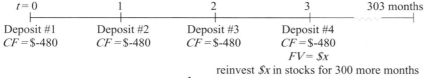

The problem has two stages. The first stage requires finding the accumulation in stocks at the time of the last deposit (the time line shows this unknown amount as x). This computation uses the annuity formula wherein N equals 4 (the number of deposits is 4), CF is $–480, and r is $0.0550 \div 12$. There is no beginning balance before the first cash flow, so PV is zero. Substitute into formula 5.2 and solve for FV.

$$FV = (\$480) \left\{ \frac{\left(1 + \frac{0.0550}{12}\right)^4 - 1}{\frac{0.0550}{12}} \right\}$$

$$= \$1,933$$

Four deposits plus total market interest accumulate $1,933. At the time of the last deposit, move all money out of the savings account and into the stock market. This occurs on the time line at $t=3$. Leave the money alone for 25 more years (300 months). The account accumulates market interest at a 16 percent annual percentage rate (compounded monthly). To find the ending wealth use the lump-sum time value formula, 4.8, and set N to 300; r to $0.16 \div 12$ and PV to $1,933. Solve for FV.

$$FV = \$1,933 \left(1 + \frac{0.16}{12} \right)^{300}$$

$$= \$102,798$$

Your summer job allows you to make four deposits totaling $1,920 (that is, $1,920 = 4 x $480). Your patience over the next 25 years allows the sum to grow to more than $100,000! Time, given a fair chance, can create a lot of wealth.

The preceding example applies the annuity formula to find an account balance at the conclusion of a savings annuity. Then the lump-sum formula compounds that balance into a future sum. The opposite timing pattern also occurs. That is, a lump-sum of money compounds into the future after which point the account is either increased or decreased by annuity activity. The example below illustrates this scenario.

EXAMPLE 3 Compound as a lump-sum and subsequently withdraw an annuity
Today you inherit an account with a balance of $4,400. For a while you don't do anything with the account but it continues to accrue interest at a rate of 8.50% compounded monthly. Exactly 10 months from today you start withdrawing $200 monthly from the account. You make a total of 24 consecutive monthly withdrawals. Find the account balance immediately after the last withdrawal.

SOLUTION
Examine the time line to ascertain clear understanding of the question.

```
  t = 0              9              10               33
  ├───∿∿∿───────────┼──────────────┼──────∿∿∿───────┤
 PV = $4,400      FV = $x       Withdrawal #1    Withdrawal #24
                Reset PV = $x     CF = $200         CF = $200
                                                    FV = ?
```

The problem has two stages. The first stage applies the lump-sum formula to find the balance FV <u>one period before</u> the first withdrawal:

$$FV = \$4,400 \left(1 + \frac{0.085}{12}\right)^9,$$
$$= \$4,689$$

At conclusion of stage one FV equals $\$4,689$. This represents $\$x$ on the graphic. The second stage uses the annuity formula wherein N equals 24 (the number of withdrawals), CF is $\$200$, and r is $0.085 \div 12$. Notice that the 1st withdrawal occurs 10 months from today, the 2nd in 11 months, ..., and 24th in 33 months. PV represents the account balance one period before the first cash flow and equals $\$4,689$. Substitute into formula 5.2 and solve for FV.

$$FV = \$4,689 \left(1 + \frac{0.085}{12}\right)^{24} - (\$200) \left\{ \frac{\left(1 + \frac{0.085}{12}\right)^{24} - 1}{\frac{0.09}{12}} \right\},$$
$$= \$342$$

You inherited $\$4,400$ and withdrew a total of $\$4,800$. Immediately after the last withdrawal the account still had a balance of $\$342$. Ain't *time value* wonderful!

CALCULATOR CLUE

Solve the preceding problem by typing `2nd` `FV` to clear the time value memories, and `2nd` `I/Y` 12 `ENTER` `2nd` `CPT` to enforce monthly compounding. Then type:

4400 `PV` 9 `N` 8.5 `I/Y` `CPT` `FV`.

The display shows $\$-4,689$ and represents the accumulation one period before the annuity activity. While this sum still shows on the display reset PV and add the annuity variables by typing:

`PV` 24 `N` 200 `PMT` `CPT` `FV`.

The display shows $\$342$. Notice that the PMT enter as positive numbers and are cash inflows for you. FV also displays as a positive number and is available for you.

EXERCISES 5.2B

Numerical quickies

1. With wages from a summer job you make a total of 5 deposits at $\$430$ per month into a savings account earning 5.10% compounded monthly. At the time of the last deposit, you close the savings account and invest all the money in stocks with the intention of leaving the stocks alone for the subsequent 21 years (dividends automatically are reinvested). The stocks are expected to provide an average annual geometric return of 12.00% compounded monthly. When you finally sell the stocks, how much do you get? ©FV3

Numerical challengers

2. Today you inherit an account with a balance of $\$2,600$. For a while you don't do anything with the account but it continues to accrue interest at a rate of 9.90% compounded monthly. Exactly 10 months from today you start an ambitious savings plan and deposit $\$230$ monthly into the account. You make a total of 16 consecutive monthly deposits. Find the account balance immediately after the last deposit. ©FV11
3. Today you inherit an account with a balance of $\$2,200$. For a while you don't do anything with the account but it continues to accrue interest at a

rate of 10.00% compounded monthly. Exactly 10 months from today you start withdrawing $150 monthly from the account. You make a total of 16 consecutive monthly withdrawals. Find the account balance immediately after the last withdrawal. ©FV12

4. Today you inherit an account with a balance of $5,800. For a while you don't do anything with the account but it continues to accrue interest. Exactly 17 months from today you start an ambitious savings plan and deposit $220 into the account. You plan to deposit that much each month. Exactly 36 months from today you reconsider your plan, make your last deposit, and make no additional deposits. You nonetheless leave the account alone and it continues to accrue interest at a rate of 6.6% compounded monthly. You finally close the account exactly 7 years from today. How much is the total accumulation? ©FV6

3. PRESENT VALUES OF ANNUITIES

Present value represents the initial worth of a cash flow stream. Many decisions require finding the present worth of future expected returns. Finding present value also requires specifying the target rate of return, or market interest, that is subtracted from future returns. The general time value formula for constant annuities is equation 5.1, restated below:

$$PV = (CF)\left\{\frac{1-(1+r)^{-N}}{r}\right\} + FV\,(1+r)^{-N}$$

$$= CF\,\{PVIFA_{rate\,=\,r,\,periods\,=\,N}\} + FV\,(1+r)^{-N}$$

Solving for PV requires assigning numerical values for FV, N, CF, and r.

The expression in curly brackets is the "present value interest factor for an annuity", abbreviated $PVIFA$. The expression depends only on r and N. The intuitive meaning of $PVIFA$ is simply stated.

> **DEFINITION 5.2 Present value interest factor of annuities (PVIFA)**
> $PVIFA$ is the initial deposit earning interest at the periodic rate r that perfectly finances a series of N consecutive one dollar withdrawals:
> $$PVIFA_{r,N} = \frac{1-(1+r)^{-N}}{r}$$

The bankers' time value books also contain $PVIFA$ tables. The tables, similar to the one in Panel B of Appendix 1, list a different N for each row and a different periodic rate for each column. The tables simply compute the value of the expression in curly brackets. Looking at the $PVIFA$ table with a periodic rate equal to 15 percent and N equal to 10, for example, shows a table entry equal to 5.0188.

$$PVIFA_{rate=15\%,\,N=10} = \left\{\frac{1-(1+.15)^{-10}}{.15}\right\}$$
$$= 5.0188$$

This means a deposit of $5.02 earning interest of 15 percent per year finances a withdrawal of one dollar per year for 10 years. The total withdrawals equal $10, implying total market interest equals $4.98 (that is, $4.98 = $10.00 − $5.02).

$PVIFA$ tables enable easy computation of present values even though withdrawals differ from one dollar. With a $500 withdrawal, and the same rate of 15 percent for 10 years, the present value equals 500 x 5.0188, or $2,509. Basically, the twenty-five hundred dollar deposit supports over the next ten years withdrawals totaling five thousand dollars. The tables are pretty obsolete, of course, because financial calculators are better.

3.A. Beginning wealth, *PV,* as the unknown variable

The following example specifies the cash flow stream and the target rate of return, and finds as the unknown variable the initial wealth supporting the stream.

EXAMPLE 4 What is the proper price for an annuity?
You might invest in an asset that will return cash flow to you of $2,100 per month for 72 months. Your target annual rate of return on the investment is 15 percent, compounded monthly. How much should you pay for the investment?

SOLUTION
The time line illustrates the timing implicit in the problem:

```
     0              1              2          72 months
     |--------------|--------------|~~~~~~~~~~|
  PV = ?       CF=$2,100      CF=$2,100      CF=$2,100
```

Substitute settings into equation 5.1 that *CF* equals $2,100 and N equals 72. There is no ending balance because the account is drawn to zero, so *FV* equals $0. The monthly periodic rate *r* equals 0.15 ÷ 12, or 0.0125.

CALCULATOR CLUE

Solve the preceding problem by typing `2nd` `FV` to clear the time value memories, and `2nd` `I/Y` 12 `ENTER` `2nd` `CPT` to enforce monthly compounding. Then type:

2100 `PMT` 72 `N` 15 `I/Y` `CPT` `PV`.
The display shows $99,314.

$$PV = (\$2,100)\left\{\frac{1-(1.0125)^{-72}}{.0125}\right\}$$

$$= \$99,314$$

You get a 15 percent annual rate of return when you pay $99,314 for an investment and get back 72 monthly returns of $2,100 each.

Formula 5.1 allows finding beginning wealth (*PV*) when there is an annuity cash flow history as well as an ending balance (*FV*). The annuity cash flows *CF* may be either deposits or withdrawals. The direction of the cash flows matter. When money flows out of the account (withdrawals) then in formula 5.1 *FV* and *CF* have the same sign. Conversely, for deposits the signs of *FV* and *CF* in formula 5.1 are opposites. The example below illustrates proper procedure for handling this type scenario.

EXAMPLE 5 Find PV given an ending balance plus a withdrawal history
A friend received an inheritance 4 years ago and put all funds into an account earning 10.00% compounded quarterly. Exactly one quarter after establishing the account the friend started withdrawing $950 per quarter. Today quarterly interest will be credited to the account and she'll make another quarterly withdrawal and then the balance will be $13,104. How much was the friend's inheritance?

SOLUTION
With an APR of 10.0% and quarterly compounding the periodic rate *r* equals 2.5% (=10.0% ÷4). The annuity cash flow *CF* equals $950 and N, the number of withdrawals, is 16. Notice that *CF* flows out of the account and into your friend's pocket so assign it a positive sign. *FV* is the balance immediately after the last withdrawal and equals $13,104. *FV* represent funds available to your friend as an inflow. *CF*

and FV have the same signs because they both flow out of the account and into your friend's pocket. Alternatively, if CF were a deposit (instead of a withdrawal) then its sign would be opposite the sign of FV. Always ascertain that cash flow timing considerations are consistent with formula 5.1: (a) PV occurs one period before the first CF; (b) FV occurs immediately after the last CF; and (c) there are N cash flows. Formula 5.1 is perfectly appropriate for this example. Substitute settings:

$$PV = (\$950)\left\{\frac{1-(1.025)^{-16}}{.025}\right\} + \$13,104(1.025^{-16})$$

$$= \$21,229$$

State the solution another way. Deposit $21,229 into an account earning 10% compounded quarterly, then beginning one quarter later withdraw $950 and make withdrawals for 16 quarters, then immediately after making the last withdrawal the account balance is $13,104.

CALCULATOR CLUE

Solve the preceding problem by typing `2nd` `FV` to clear the time value memories, and `2nd` `I/Y` `4` `ENTER` `2nd` `CPT` to enforce quarterly compounding. Then type:

`950` `PMT` `16` `N` `10` `I/Y` `13104` `FV` `CPT` `PV`.

The display shows $-21,229. That's the answer. The negative sign means that, unlike the withdrawals and ending balance that flow out of the account and into your friend's pocket, the beginning wealth PV flows into the account.

The time value relation is extremely flexible. Formula 5.1 includes five variables (PV, CF, FV, r and N). Supply numerical settings for any 4 and the 5th takes on a unique value called "the answer." Previous examples solve for PV and FV. Seldom does a situation call for finding N as unknown variable. Often, however, you may need to find the periodic rate of return r, as the two examples below illustrate.

EXAMPLE 6 Find PV for an annuity stream and then the actual ROR on counteroffer

You might invest in an asset that will return after-tax cash flow to you of $2,200 per month for 30 months (first cash flow one month from now), and after receiving the last cash flow you'll immediately receive after-tax net proceeds from liquidation equal to $15,000. You make an offer to buy the asset so that you'll get your "target" annual rate of return of 15.7% (compounded monthly). Instead, however, the seller makes a counteroffer that is $3,500 higher than your offer. Find your annual rate of return if you buy at the counteroffer price and receive the expected cash flows.

SOLUTION

With an APR of 15.7% and monthly compounding the periodic rate r equals 1.31% (= 15.7% ÷ 12). The 30 (= N) periodic cash flows CF of $2,200 are inflows for you, much like they are withdrawals from an asset account. Likewise, the liquidation proceeds of $15,000 (= FV) also is an inflow. In formula 5.1 assign CF and FV positive signs. Note that the cash flow timing considerations are consistent with formula 5.1. Substitute settings and solve for the offer price, PV:

$$PV = (\$2,200)\left\{\frac{1-(1.0131)^{-30}}{.0131}\right\} + \$15,000(1.0131^{-30}),$$

$$= \$64,455$$

You make an offer to buy the asset at \$64,455 but the seller counteroffers at \$67,955 (= \$64,455 + \$3,500). Now assign \$67,955 to PV and solve for the monthly rate of return r from formula 5.1:

$$\$64,455 = (2,200)\left\{\frac{1-(1+r)^{-30}}{r}\right\} + \$15,000(1+r)^{-30}.$$

The formula does not have a "closed-form solution," meaning that you cannot isolate r by itself on the left. Your financial calculator, however, is pretty smart and, as the accompanying *Calculator Clue* explains, finds that the APR for the actual rate of return is 11.95% (or 0.99% per month). The extra cost of \$3,500 reduces your annual rate of return by 375 BP (= 15.70% − 11.95%).

CALCULATOR CLUE

Solve the preceding problem by typing `2nd` `FV` to clear the time value memories, and `2nd` `I/Y` 12 `ENTER` `2nd` `CPT` to enforce monthly compounding. Then type:

2200 `PMT` 30 `N` 15.7 `I/Y` 15000 `FV` `CPT` `PV`.

The display shows \$−64,455. That's the offer price. The negative sign means that, unlike the periodic cash flows and liquidation proceeds that flow into your pocket and are positive, the beginning wealth PV flows out of your pocket. While the display still shows \$−64,455 perform these steps to get the counteroffer price and solve for the annual rate of return:

`+/−` `+` 3500 `=` `+/−` `PV` `CPT` `I/Y`.

The display shows that the actual annual rate of return is 11.95%

EXAMPLE 7 Find *PV* for an annuity stream and then the actual ROR on counteroffer
You might pursue an investment that incurs a large up-front cost today. Furthermore, it requires payments of \$7,500 per month for 24 months (first payment one month from now). Immediately after making the last payment, however, you will receive after-tax net proceeds of \$310,000. You make an offer to buy the asset so that you'll get your "target" annual rate of return of 14.2% (compounded monthly). Instead, however, the seller makes a counteroffer that is \$5,000 higher than your offer. Find your annual rate of return if you buy at the counteroffer price and receive the expected cash flows.

SOLUTION
This is similar to the previous example except for the signage. The 24 (= N) periodic cash flows CF of \$7,500 are outflows for you, sort of like deposits into an asset account, so assign a negative sign. But FV of \$310,000 is an inflow for you so in formula 5.1 make it positive. With a monthly periodic rate r equal to 1.18% (= 14.2% ÷ 12) solve for the offer price:

$$PV = (\$-7,500)\left\{\frac{1-(1.0118)^{-24}}{.0118}\right\} + \$310,000(1.0118)^{-24},$$

$$= \$77,846$$

Assign the counteroffer price of \$82,846 (= \$77,846 + \$5,000) to PV and solve for the monthly rate of return r from formula 5.1:

$$\$82,846 = (\$-7,500)\left\{\frac{1-(1+r)^{-24}}{r}\right\} + \$310,000(1+r)^{-24}.$$

The financial calculator finds that the APR for the actual rate of return is 12.61%, or 159 BP less than your target (= 14.20% – 12.61%).

CALCULATOR CLUE

Solve the preceding problem by typing `2nd` `FV` to clear the time value memories, and `2nd` `I/Y` 12 `ENTER` `2nd` `CPT` to enforce monthly compounding. Then type:

7500 `+/−` `PMT` 24 `N` 14.2 `I/Y` 310000 `FV` `CPT` `PV` `+/−` `+` 5000 `=` `+/−` `PV` `CPT` `I/Y`.

The display shows that the actual annual rate of return is 12.61%.

EXERCISES 5.3A

Numerical quickies

1. You might invest in an asset that will return after-tax cash flow to you of $1,200 per year for 8 years (first cash flow one year from now), after that the asset probably will be worthless. You make an offer to buy the asset so that you'll get a 8.80% rate of return (compounded annually). Find the offer price. ©PV8

2. You're quite fortunate because this afternoon, just like this date in each of the past 10 years, you shall withdraw $1,600 from an account that your guardian angel established for you exactly 11 years ago. After the withdrawal the balance will equal zero. The account earns 6.30% per year (compounded annually, interest is being credited this morning). Except for your 10 withdrawals the account has been untouched. Find the initial deposit that your guardian angel used to establish the account. ©PV5

3. You might invest in a security that will return after-tax cash flow to you of $1,600 per year for 9 years (first cash flow one year from now), after which the security likely can be sold for $7,700. You make an offer to buy the security so that you'll get a 8.50% rate of return (compounded annually). Find the offer price. ©PV9

Numerical challengers

4. A friend received an inheritance 6 years ago and put all funds into an account earning 8.50% compounded quarterly. Exactly one quarter after establishing the account the friend started a savings plan that deposits $650 per quarter. Today the quarterly deposit is due and quarterly interest will be credited to the account, thereby bringing the balance to $49,924. How much was the friend's inheritance? ©PV6

5. A friend received an inheritance 3 years ago and put all funds into an account earning 9.50% compounded quarterly. Exactly one quarter after establishing the account the friend started withdrawing $1,350 per quarter. Today quarterly interest will be credited to the account and she'll make another quarterly withdrawal and then the balance will be $11,403. How much was the friend's inheritance? ©PV7

6. You might invest in an asset that will return after-tax cash flow to you of $2,700 per month for 15 months (first cash flow one month from now), and after receiving the last cash flow you'll immediately receive after-tax net proceeds from liquidation equal to $95,600. You make an offer to buy the asset so that you'll get your "target" annual rate of return of 18.20% (compounded monthly).

6a. What is your offer price? ©PV10am

6b. Instead, however, the seller makes a counteroffer that is $9,600 higher than your offer. Find your annual rate of return if you buy at the counteroffer price and receive the expected cash flows. ©PV10bm

7. You might purchase an investment that incurs a large up-front cost today. Furthermore, it requires payments of $2,400 per month for 15 months (first payment one month from now). Immediately after making the last payment, however, you will receive after-tax net proceeds of $78,900. You make an offer to purchase the asset so that you'll get your "target" annual rate of return of 20.30% (compounded monthly).

7a. Find the up-front purchase price that you offer to pay today. ©PV11am

7b. The seller makes a counteroffer that is $6,000 higher than your offered purchase price. Find your annual rate of return if you buy at the counteroffer price and receive the expected cash flows. ©PV11bm

3.B. The special case of perpetuities

Suppose an account with $1 million earns 10 percent interest compounded annually. Each year the account earns $100,000 of interest (that is, $100,000 = 0.10 x $1,000,000). Each year, too, suppose you withdraw $100,000 from the account. Now ask the question, when will the account balance draw down to zero? The answer is: *never*. The account balance never goes to zero. The preceding scenario describes a perpetuity.

DEFINITION 5.3 PERPETUITY

A *perpetuity* is an account that maintains a specified principal balance perpetually even in the absence of subsequent deposits.

The balance never diminishes because all withdrawals consist exclusively of interest, not principal. For example, in the preceding illustration the balance begins at $1 million. Exactly one year later, immediately before the first withdrawal, the account earns periodic interest of $100,000 and the balance rises to $1,100,000. Then the $100,000 withdrawal occurs, the balance falls back to $1 million. The cycle repeats perpetually.

The perpetuity is a special case of the constant annuity time value relation shown in formula 5.1. Mathematically speaking, with a perpetuity N goes to infinity. As N gets larger and larger, the expression $(1+r)^N$ gets larger and larger, too (as long as $r > 0$, actually). Dividing this ever larger number into a future sum causes the present value of that sum to vanish. Cash flows way out yonder have virtually zero effect on present value—it's convergent!

The perpetuity formula relates beginning wealth, periodic cash flow, and rate of return as follows:

FORMULA 5.3 Present value of a perpetual and constant stream

$$PV = \frac{CF}{r}.$$

Variable definitions are the same as always. PV is the beginning balance, CF is the periodic cash flow. The periodic interest rate r equals the annual percentage rate i divided by m, the number of compounding periods per year.

The perpetuity relation has many useful applications. Endowment funds for non-profit foundations are perpetuities. The Ford Foundation, Annenberg Foundation, and many others, have huge balances that each year spin-off market interest. The foundations never consume their principal. Instead, the periodic market interest is the source of financing for grants that the foundation sponsors. These foundations will live forever. As the example below shows, too, universities rely on perpetuities to finance many important functions.

EXAMPLE 8 What size deposit sets up the memorial fund?

You wish to establish a fund at your alma mater that finances a $5,000 scholarship twice each year. The account earns a 12 percent average annual rate of return, compounded semiannually. How much do you need to deposit to establish the endowment fund?

SOLUTION

For this scenario, *CF* equals $5,000 and *i/m* equals 0.12 ÷ 2, or 0.06. Substitution into the perpetuity formula shows:

$$PV = \frac{\$5,000}{0.06}$$

$$= \$83,333$$

Make a deposit of $83,000 and forevermore your monies will spin-off $5,000 scholarships twice each year.

EXERCISES 5.3B

Numerical quickies

1. Your unrealistic dream is to win the lottery, deposit the money into an account earning 7.5% interest compounded annually, and forevermore draw out $1 million per year. Find the amount you need to win. ©PV13
2. An alumni group wants to establish an endowment fund for paying expenses associated with hiring a distinguished professor of business. The annual expenses should run about $140,000 (payable in 12 monthly installments). Find the size of the requisite endowment if the account earns 8.8% compounded monthly. ©PV12.
3. Your college has a fixed and constant endowment fund of $35 million that each year generates interest income for paying scholarships and faculty salaries. The interest rate has fallen from 10% a few years ago to 4% today (compounded annually). Find the decline in annual income that the college unfortunately faces. ©PV14

4. CASH FLOWS CONNECTING BEGINNING AND ENDING WEALTH

Many financial situations require finding the amount of each periodic cash flow that satisfies the constant annuity time value relation. Because the cash flows are all the same amount, equation 5.1 easily rearranges to get *CF* alone on the left-hand side. There are two equivalent rearrangements of the formula. The first rearrangement relies on the future value interest factor for an annuity found in *FVIVA* tables.

FORMULA 5.4 Cash flow as a function of FVIFA

$$CF = \left(PV(1+r)^N - FV\right) \Big/ \left\{\frac{(1+r)^N - 1}{r}\right\}$$

$$= \left(PV(1+r)^N - FV\right) \Big/ FVIFA_{rate = r, \ periods = N}$$

The second rearrangement relies on the present value interest factor for an annuity found in *PVIVA* tables.

$$CF = \left(PV - FV(1+r)^{-N}\right) \Big/ \left\{ \frac{1 - (1+r)^{-N}}{r} \right\}$$

$$= \left(PV - FV(1+r)^{-N}\right) \Big/ PVIFA_{rate = r,\ periods = N}$$

Equations 5.4 and 5.5 are identical in every significant way. Using one instead of the other is arbitrary since they give the same answer and require the same information. For a given problem setup, however, one might be easier to use.

4.A. Cash flow, CF, as the unknown variable

The examples below require finding the periodic cash flow that satisfies the time value formula. The first example specifies a future value and finds the unknown deposit. The second example specifies both present and future values.

EXAMPLE 9 Find the required deposit

Four years from today you expect to place a downpayment on your first house. You forecast the required downpayment at $18,000. The savings account earns 8.25 percent annual interest, compounded monthly. Your savings account balance today is $4,250 and you intend to make additional deposits each month. The first deposit is one month from today and the last is four years from today, immediately before you withdraw the entire accumulation of $18,000. How much is each monthly deposit?

SOLUTION

Use the time line to verify the timing of cash flows.

$t = 0$	1	2	48 months
begin with $4,250	Deposit #1	Deposit #2	Deposit #48
$PV = \$4,250$	$CF = ?$	$CF = ?$	$CF = ?$
			$FV = \$18,000$

Use equation 5.2 to solve for CF. The annual percentage rate i equals 8.25 percent and compounding occurs monthly, so m equals 12. The periodic interest rate r is 0.006875 (that is, $0.006875 = .0825 \div 12$).

$$CF = \left(\$4,250(1.006875)^{48} - \$18,000\right) \Big/ \left\{ \frac{(1.006875)^{48} - 1}{0.006875} \right\}$$

$$= \$-213.54$$

CALCULATOR CLUE

Solve the preceding problem by typing **2nd** **FV** to clear the time value memories, and **2nd** **I/Y** 12 **ENTER** **2nd** **CPT** to enforce monthly compounding. Then type:

4250 **PV** 18000 **+/−** **FV** 48 **N** 8.25 **I/Y** **CPT** **PMT**.

The display shows $213.54. Make 48 monthly deposits of $213.54 each and you'll accumulate the downpayment required to buy the house.

EXAMPLE 10 Find effect of ROR on monthly income

You are investing $65,000 today. You expect to receive monthly returns for 72 months with the first one exactly one month from today. At the time of the last monthly return you also expect to sell the investment for $82,000. You can either invest in a savings account earning 6 percent per annum or in a stock fund earning 18 percent per annum (compounded monthly). How much difference in monthly cash flow do the alternative investments provide?

SOLUTION

Inspect the time line for this problem.

The unknown variable is *CF*, the constant monthly cash flow. Known variables, however, include the beginning wealth, *PV*, at $65,000 and the ending wealth, *FV*, at $82,000. The number of cash flows, *N*, equals 72. The periodic rate differs according to the investment; *r* equals 0.06 ÷ 12 (that is, 0.005) for the savings account and 0.18 ÷ 12 (that is, 0.015) for the stock fund. In either case, substitute the known variables into equation 5.4 and solve for *CF*. For the savings account, substitution shows:

$$CF = \left(\$65,000(1.005)^{72} - \$82,000\right) \Big/ \left\{\frac{(1.005)^{72} - 1}{0.005}\right\}$$

$$= \$128$$

From the savings account the cash flowing into your pocket each month is $128.

The stock fund uses the higher periodic interest rate of 1.5 percent per month:

$$CF = \left(\$65,000(1.015)^{72} - \$82,000\right) \Big/ \left\{\frac{(1.015)^{72} - 1}{0.015}\right\}$$

$$= \$842$$

CALCULATOR CLUE

To solve this problem with the time value functions on the *BAII Plus*© type `2nd` `FV` to clear the time value memories. Type `2nd` `I/Y` 12 `ENTER` `2nd` `CPT` to enforce monthly compounding. Solve for the cash flow from the 6 percent savings account by typing:

65000 `PV` 82000 `+/−` `FV` 72 `N` 6 `I/Y` `CPT` `PMT`

The display shows that periodic cash flow equals $−128.

Obtain the cash flow for the 18 percent stock fund by entering only `I/Y`; the other variables may remain the same. While the display still shows $−128, type 18 `I/Y` `CPT` `PMT`

The display shows that periodic cash flow equals $−842.

The rate of return is three times larger on the stock fund than on the savings account (that is, 18% ÷ 6% = 3). The periodic cash flow from the stock fund, however, is more than six times larger than from the savings account (that is, $842 ÷ $128 = 6.6). The effect of compounding makes time value computations very sensitive to the rate of return.

EXERCISES 5.4A

Numerical quickies
 1. You wish to accumulate $10,000 for a special purpose. You today open an account that earns 7.0% compounded monthly by making the first of

many deposits, all the same size. Your last monthly deposit is in exactly 4 years. After that last deposit and crediting of monthly interest your target balance is reached. Find the amount of each deposit. ©FV16

2. Exactly 5 years ago you made a deposit that opened an account earning 13.0% compounded monthly. Every month since that time you have made a deposit of exactly the same amount. After today's deposit and crediting of monthly interest the account balance is $12,000. Find the amount of each deposit. ©FV14

3. You inherit an account with $14,000 that earns 8.0% compounded quarterly. One quarter later you make the first of 20 quarterly withdrawals, all the same size, and draw down the account to zero. Find the amount much of each withdrawal. ©FV13

Numerical challengers

4. Exactly 5 years ago you inherited an account with balance of $16,000 that earns 10.30% compounded quarterly. One quarter later you made the first of many quarterly deposits, all the same size. After today's deposit and crediting of quarterly interest the account balance is $68,200. Find the amount of each deposit. ©FV15

5. You are investing $12,000 today. You expect to receive monthly returns for 216 months with the first one exactly one month from today. At the time of the last monthly return you also expect to sell the investment for $10,000. You can either invest in a savings account earning 5.30% percent per annum or a stock fund earning 15.00% percent per annum (compounded monthly). How much difference in monthly cash flow do the alternative investments provide? ©FV18

6. Today you open an account with a $16,000 deposit that earns 11.20% compounded annually. You've set a target for the account so that in exactly 5 years its balance will be $30,000. To reach the target you'll adjust the balance annually; each year's adjustment will be exactly the same amount and the first adjustment occurs exactly one year from now. After the last annual adjustment in exactly 5 years, and crediting of that year's interest, the account balance exactly equals the target. Describe the annual adjustment that you make each year. ©FV17

4.B. Other two-stage problems

Many finance situations involve saving over time in order to finance withdrawals over time. Solving these problems often requires doing several sequential time value computations. Consider the examples below.

EXAMPLE 11 How big is the endowment's scholarships

You wish to establish an endowment fund that will provide student financial aid awards every semiannum, perpetually. You will make deposits semiannually equal to $4,000 each, with the first one today and the final one in 6 years. The first award is to be granted one semiannum after the last deposit. The savings rate always is 8.9% compounded semiannually. How much is each award?

SOLUTION

Examine the time line to ascertain a clear understanding of the words.

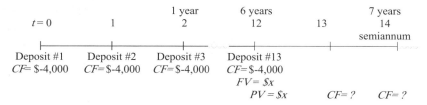

This problem has two stages: a deposit stage during which savings accumulate, and a withdrawal stage during which scholarships are withdrawn. The first deposit is today, time 0, and the final one occurs in six years. There are in total 13 deposits. A sum of money, say x, will have accumulated by the time of the last deposit. That sum represents for the second stage of the problem a beginning wealth that finances perpetual withdrawals. The question asks, how much is each withdrawal?

The first stage involves finding the future value of thirteen $4,000 semiannual deposits that earn interest at an annual rate of 8.9% (that is, 4.45% compounded semiannually). Use the constant annuity time value formula that solves for FV (equation 5.2):

$$FV = (\$4,000)\left\{\frac{(1.0445)^{13} - 1}{0.0445}\right\}.$$
$$= \$68,423$$

CALCULATOR CLUE

To solve this problem with the time value functions on the *BAII Plus©* type 2nd FV to clear the time value memories. Type 2nd I/Y 2 ENTER 2nd CPT to enforce semiannual compounding. Then solve for the accumulation at the conclusion of the savings stage by typing:

4000 +/- PMT 13 N 8.9 I/Y CPT FV.

The display shows the account balance equals $68,423 immediately after the last deposit. Now use the arithmetic keys and multiply the value on the display by the periodic rate of 0.0445 to obtain the periodic interest of $3,045.

The account balance immediately after the final deposit equals $68,423. This represents x on the timeline.

The scholarship exactly equals the interest that $68,423 earns per semiannum. With a semiannual rate of 4.45 percent, the cash flow financing the scholarship is

$$CF = (0.0445)(\$68,423)$$
$$= \$3,045.$$

The savings deposits finance scholarships of $3,045 per semiannum perpetually. By donating thirteen deposits totaling $52,000 (that is, $52,000 = 13\times\$4,000$) you endow an endless stream of students with resources for pursuing collegiate studies.

EXAMPLE 12 Saving young versus saving later
Your two twin sisters, Prudence and Candy, are pursuing two different financial strategies for early retirement. Both sisters intend to retire exactly 30 years from today. Candy does not want to start saving until exactly 10 years from today, at which time she'll make her first monthly deposit of $250. She'll continue making monthly deposits for 20 years, so that Candy's final deposit occurs exactly 30 years from today when she retires. The other sister, Prudence, plans to deposit $250 per month for 10 years with the first deposit today and the last one exactly 10 years from today. Prudence will not deposit anything beyond that, but she will let interest continue to accrue. The annual savings rate always is 12% compounded monthly. Both sisters intend to draw down the savings accounts to zero by making monthly withdrawals during retirement for 25 years. The first withdrawal is one month after retirement commences. How much monthly income should each sister expect in retirement?

SOLUTION
First examine the time line for late-starter Candy. Her first deposit is exactly 10 years, or 120 months, from today. Her last deposit is exactly 30 years, or 360 months, from today. Then in month 361, Candy commences withdrawing money from the account (the time line abbreviates withdrawal as "Wdw").

		10 years		30 years		55 years
$t=0$	1	120	121	360	361	660 months
		Dep #1	Dep #2	Dep #241	Wdw #1	Wdw #300
$CF=\$0$	$CF=\$0$	$CF=\$-250$	$CF=\$-250$	$CF=\$-250$		
				$FV=\$x$		
				$PV=\$x$	$CF=?$	$CF=?$

Throughout twenty years Candy makes 241 deposits at $250 each. Find the future value of this accumulation with the following settings: the account begins at $0 so PV is zero, N equals the number of deposits and is 241, CF is $–250, and the monthly periodic interest rate r is 0.01. Use equation 5.2 to solve for FV.

$$FV = (\$250)\left\{\frac{1.01^{241}-1}{0.01}\right\}.$$

$$= \$250{,}037$$

Candy has about one-quarter million dollars in her account immediately after making her final deposit. This future value is shown on the time line as $x. At that time Candy retires. For this retirement stage, the $250,037 represents a beginning wealth that finances a series of monthly withdrawals over 25 years (300 months). To find the amount of each withdrawal, use the constant annuity formula (equation 5.5) and set N to 300 and the monthly periodic rate to 0.01. Set PV to $250,037. Notice that this number was the answer for FV from the savings stage. Now this same number is PV for the retirement stage. Because the account is drawn down to zero, FV equals $0. Solve for CF.

$$CF = \$250{,}037 \Bigg/ \left\{\frac{1-1.01^{-300}}{.01}\right\}$$

$$= \$2{,}633$$

Candy makes wise investments, saving $250 per month for twenty years enabling her to retire on monthly income of $2,633 for twenty-five years. The power of compound interest is amazing!

Consider the case for Prudence. She saves immediately, as shown in the time line below.

		10 years		30 years		55 years
$t=0$	1	120	121	360	361	660 months
Dep #1	Dep #2	Dep #121			Wdw #1	Wdw #300
$CF=\$-250$	$CF=\$-250$	$CF=\$-250$				
	$FV=\$y$					
	$PV=\$y$			$FV=\$z$		
				$PV=\$z$	$CF=?$	$CF=?$

Prudence makes 121 monthly deposits of $250 each. Find the future value immediately upon making the last deposit: N is 121, PV is zero, CF is $–250, and the periodic interest rate is 0.01:

$$FV = (\$250)\left\{\frac{1.01^{121}-1}{0.01}\right\}$$

$$= \$58{,}335$$

After making the last deposit the account balance is $58,335. This future value is shown on the time line as $y. Prudence doesn't save anymore, but she lets the interest accrue for 20 years. During this time, her sister Candy is saving every month. Not Prudence, she is letting her money earn money. To find the balance in

Prudence's account after 20 years, use the lump-sum time value formula. Set N to 240 and the monthly periodic interest rate to 0.01. Set PV, the beginning wealth, to $58,335. Notice that this number was the answer for FV from the savings stage. Now this same number is PV for the retirement stage. There are no cash flows in the middle for Prudence:

$$FV = \$58,335(1.01^{240})$$

$$= \$635,415.$$

Prudence has almost two-thirds a million dollars when she retires. The time line shows this number as z. The $635,415 represents a beginning wealth that finances a series of monthly withdrawals over 25 years (300 months). To find the amount of each withdrawal, use the constant annuity formula (equation 5.5) and set N to 300, the monthly periodic interest rate to 0.01, and PV to $635,415. Because the account is drawn down to zero, FV equals $0. Solve for CF.

$$CF = \$635,415 \left/ \left\{ \frac{1 - 1.01^{-300}}{.01} \right\} \right.$$

$$= \$6.692$$

Prudence makes wise investments, saving $250 per month for ten years enabling her to retire on monthly income of $6,692 for twenty-five years.

CALCULATOR CLUE

To solve this problem with the time value functions on the *BAII Plus*© type `2nd` `FV` to clear the time value memories. Type `2nd` `I/Y` 12 `ENTER` `2nd` `CPT` to enforce monthly compounding. Solve for the accumulation for Candy upon retirement by typing:

250 `+/−` `PMT` 241 `N` 12 `I/Y` `CPT` `FV`.

The display shows the account balance equals $250,037 when Candy retires. Obtain the cash flow financed by this accumulation over the subsequent 300 months. While the display still shows $250,037 type

`PV` 0 `FV` 300 `N` `CPT` `PMT`.

The display shows Candy receives $2,633 per month during retirement.

Find the accumulation for Prudence at the conclusion of her savings stage by typing

250 `+/−` `PMT` 121 `N` 0 `PV` `CPT` `FV`.

The display shows Prudence accumulates $58,335. Compound this sum for 240 months. While the display still shows $58,335 type

`PV` 0 `PMT` 240 `N` `CPT` `FV`.

The display shows the account balance equals $635,415 when Prudence retires.

Obtain the cash flow financed by this accumulation over the subsequent 300 months. While the display still shows $635,415 type

`PV` 0 `FV` 300 `N` `CPT` `PMT`.

The display shows Prudence receives $6,692 per month during retirement.

Prudence saves half as much principal as her sister Candy. Nonetheless, Prudence retires on two-and-a-half times as much income. Total contributed principal equals $30,250 for Prudence and $60,250 for Candy (that is, total contributed principal equals $250 x #deposits, Prudence makes 121 deposits and Candy makes 241). Total withdrawals sum to about $2 million for Prudence and $0.8 million for

Candy (that is, the sum of withdrawals equals 300 x monthly income; Prudence gets $6,692 per month and Candy gets $2,633). Total accumulated interest, and not principal, represents almost all the money on which these retirees will live. The money made by their labor is less than the money made by their money! They needed to work and save, though, to earn the seed money for investing.

The preceding example vividly illustrates the big reward for saving early. The rule of 72 allows insight about why saving early is so important. At a 12 percent annual rate, the rule of 72 says that money doubles about every 6 years. Suppose a beginning sum is $30,000. The approximate value per doubling period is shown in the table below:

doubling period	number of years	wealth at end of doubling period
0	0	$ 30,000
1	6	$ 60,000
2	12	$120,000
3	18	$240,000
4	24	$480,000
5	30	$960,000

Wealth creation is not the same in every six-year period. The increase in wealth is $30,000 during the first six-year period and $480,000 during the last six year period. Roughly speaking, an individual may work and save for their entire career. And after 24 years perhaps their accumulation equals, say, $480,000. The wealth created, though, in one additional doubling period may easily exceed an entire lifetime of pension contributions. Finding an extra doubling period at the end of a career often is impossible. Saving early creates a huge difference in ending wealth. Through the magic of compound interest, your money can earn more money than your labor ever will. But you have got to give it time. Time itself has value.

EXERCISES 5.4B

Numerical challengers
1. Your first monthly deposit of $170 is made today and the last one is 2 years from today. You then increase the amount of each deposit. From 2 years and one month from today until exactly 9 years from today, you deposit $280 monthly. Upon making the last deposit you close the account. The savings rate always is 5.10% compounded monthly.
1a. When you close the account, how much is the total accumulation? ©FV1am
1b. When you close the account, you withdraw the entire accumulation. How much total interest did you earn? ©FV1bm
2. You are considering two different strategies for a savings account that you intend to close when you retire exactly 26 years from today. For Strategy 1, deposit $270 per month for 5 years (first deposit today; last one exactly 5 years from today); no new deposits will be made after the end of the deposit period, but interest continues to accrue until the account is closed. For Strategy 2, you'll make your first monthly deposit exactly 5 years from today, each monthly deposit also equals $270, and you'll continue making monthly deposits for 21 years, so that you make the final deposit exactly 26 years from today when you close the account. The savings rate always is 4.60% compounded monthly. Compare the accumulations at time of retirement from the two alternative strategies. ©FV4am
3. You wish to establish an endowment fund that will provide students with a $1,900 scholarship every semiannum, perpetually. To finance the scholarships you will make a series of equal deposits into a savings account. The deposits will be made semiannually, with the first one

today and the final one in 4 years. The first scholarship is to be awarded one semiannum after the last deposit. The savings rate is 7.90% compounded semiannually. How much is each deposit? ©TS1am

4. You wish to establish an endowment fund that will provide student financial aid awards every month, perpetually. To finance the scholarships you will make a series of equal deposits into a savings account. The monthly deposits will equal $2,800 each, with the first one today and the final one in 8 years. The first award is to be granted one month after the last deposit. The savings rate is 7.10% compounded monthly. How much is each award? ©TS1bm

5. Suppose an employee saves $235.17 per month for 34 years (each year there are 12 monthly deposits). The savings rate is 4.50% compounded monthly. The worker wishes to withdraw $2,090 per month, commencing exactly one month after making the last savings deposit. For how many months can they make withdrawals? ©TS2a

6. Suppose an employee saves $108.91 per month for 32 years (each year there are 12 monthly deposits). The savings rate is 6.00% compounded monthly. The worker wishes to withdraw the same amount each month for a total of 136 months, with the first withdrawal exactly one month after the last savings deposit. How much is each monthly withdrawal? ©TS2b

5. AMORTIZATION MECHANICS

Amortization means "spreading over time." Studying the nature of loans and repayment schedules involves investigating amortization mechanics. Loans represent perhaps the most useful application of time value principles. Most consumer loans and many business loans stipulate a payment that is the same each period. Each payment includes interest due that period, plus some repayment of principal. The loan payment remains constant throughout the entire life of the loan, and eventually the loan is repaid in full. The constant annuity formula in equation 5.1 governs loan mechanics. Restatement of that equation shows:

$$PV = (CF)\left\{\frac{1-(1+r)^{-N}}{r}\right\} + FV(1+r)^{-N}$$

> **FORMULA 5.6 Fixed payment amortized loans**
>
> $$\begin{pmatrix} Principle \\ outstanding \end{pmatrix} = \begin{pmatrix} periodic \\ loan \\ payment \end{pmatrix}\left\{\frac{1-(1+r)^{-N}}{r}\right\} + \begin{pmatrix} Balloon \\ payment \end{pmatrix}(1+r)^{-N}.$$

Variable definitions are the same as before. *PV* represents the principal that remains to be repaid with the *N* remaining payments. When a loan is new then *N* represents the number of payments over the complete loan term. *CF* represents the periodic loan payment and always is the same amount with a "fixed payment amortized loan." *FV* represents a balloon payment, that is, an extra surcharge due at the time of the last payment. The loan's periodic interest rate *r* equals the annual percentage rate *i* divided by *m*, the compounding and payment frequency.

5.A. Partitioning the payment into principal and interest

A loan to you by the bank is a lot like the savings account story told in the previous sections. The bank, however, makes a deposit in you. And every payment by you to the bank is just like the bank withdrawing money from its account. A loan is an asset for the lender. The asset requires an up-front cost, but generates a stream of future returns. A loan is a liability for the borrower. Nonetheless, the cash flows and balances satisfy the time value relations discussed previously.

Consider first a simplistic story in which a loan of $1,000 carries an 8 percent annual interest rate, and is repaid over three years with constant payments. The timeline below illustrates cash flows for this scenario.

```
        0           1           2           3
        |           |           |           |
   PV= $1,000    CF= ?       CF= ?        CF= ?
                                          FV= $0
```

The bank effectively makes a deposit in the borrower. The borrower pays 8 percent interest per year on the deposit. After one year, the loan balance of $1,000 plus accrued periodic interest of $80 (that is, $80 = 0.08 x $1,000) sums to $1,080. This sum equals the "payoff amount," also called "P&I" for principal and interest. The borrower might choose to completely cancel the loan by paying the bank $1,080. Most consumer loans provide borrowers the right to cancel loans by giving the bank the payoff amount. Thirty-year home mortgages, for example, are quite often paid off before thirty years because the homeowner-borrower sells the house, relocates, and repays the loan early. Some business loans allow early repayment without penalty, but some do not.

For our simplistic story, however, the loan is not repaid early. Instead, the borrower sends the bank a loan payment. The payment certainly includes the periodic interest of $80. But how much principal is repaid? The constant annuity formula provides an answer to this question. The payment, CF, is found by setting r to 0.08, N to 3, and PV to $1,000.

$$\$1,000 = (CF)\left\{\frac{1-(1.08)^{-3}}{0.08}\right\}$$

$$CF = \$1,000 / 2.5771$$

$$= \$388.03$$

A payment of $388.03 exactly repays the loan in three years.

CALCULATOR CLUE

To find the loan payment with the time value functions on the *BAII Plus*© type 2nd FV to clear the time value memories. Type 2nd I/Y 1 ENTER 2nd CPT to enforce annual compounding. Then solve for the loan payment by typing:

1000 PV 3 N 8 I/Y CPT PMT

The display shows that periodic cash flow for the loan payment is $–388.03.

The table below shows more detail about the scenario.

	t = 0	t = 1	t = 2	t = 3
beginning of period balance	$0.00	$1,000.00	$691.97	$359.30
periodic interest expense	$0.00	$80.00	$55.36	$28.73
new balance, "payoff amount"	$1,000.00	$1,080.00	$747.33	$388.03
end of period cash flow	$0.00	$–388.03	$–388.03	$–388.03
end of period balance	$1,000.00	$691.97	$359.30	$0.00

The payoff amount at the end of the first year is $1,080. The payment of $388.03 reduces the balance to $691.97 (that is, $691.97 = $1,080.00 – $388.03).

The bank partitions the loan payment into two parts. First, part of the payment pays the periodic interest expense. This part of the payment goes on the bank's financial statements as income. The remainder of the payment, as shown in the graphic below, repays principal.

1st payment
$388.03

$80.00 $308.03
interest   principal

The principal repaid with the first payment equals $308.03. The outstanding principal immediately before the first payment is $1,000. The first payment reduces outstanding principal to $691.97 (that is, $691.97 = $1,000.00 – $308.03).

Periodic interest during the second year equals the beginning of year balance ($691.97) times the 0.08 interest rate, or $55.36. The payment still equals the same $388.03, and is allocated as follows:

2nd payment
$388.03

$55.36 $332.67
interest   principal

The periodic interest expense in the second payment naturally is less than in the first payment because with each passing period the outstanding principal declines. Conversely, the proportion of a payment allocated to repaying principal increases throughout loan life.

The beginning of the third year finds the outstanding principal at $359.30. Interest of $28.73 accrues so that at the end of the third year the P&I equals $388.03. The final payment perfectly repays the loan.

3rd payment
$388.03

$28.73 $359.30
interest   principal

Notice that payments over the life of the loan sum to $1,164.09 (that is, $1,164.09 = 3 x $388.03). The amount borrowed equals $1,000 so total lifetime interest equals $164.09.

Very few loans actually have one payment per year. Most consumer loans stipulate monthly payments with monthly compounding of interest. A large number of corporate loans stipulate semiannual payments and semiannual compounding. The example below figures the payoff amount within a loan period.

EXAMPLE 13 Find the loan's payoff amount midway through the first billing cycle
You borrow $15,000 at 10.30% over 4 years (monthly payments) to finance your dream pre-owned car. Exactly 20 days after taking out the loan, you want to pay it off in-full because a better financing deal appears. There is no pre-payment penalty and 31 days are in the first monthly billing cycle. Find the payoff amount (principal plus interest).

SOLUTION
Since you have not yet made any payments then the outstanding principal equals $15,000, the original amount borrowed. The monthly periodic interest rate is 0.86% (= 10.30% ÷ 12). Thus, the total interest for the entire first month equals $128.75 (= $15,000 x 10.30% ÷ 12). You only owe interest for 20 days, however,

not the entire month. The bank computes intraperiod accrued interest by multiplying total monthly interest times the proportion of the month for which the loan is outstanding; in this case that proportion is 20/31st. Thus, the payoff amount is found as follows:

$$\binom{payoff}{amount} = \$15,000 + \$15,000 \left[\frac{0.1030}{12}\right]\left[\frac{20}{31}\right]$$

$$= \$15,083.06$$

Pay the bank $15,083.06 on the twentieth day after getting the loan and the obligation is repaid in-full.

Everyday of the loan-life interest accrues. The example below shows that for many typical situations the amount of lifetime interest may actually exceed the amount borrowed.

EXAMPLE 14 Find the loan's lifetime interest
Your uncle borrows $185,000 at 10.5% to be repaid monthly over 20 years. How much total interest is paid over the life of the loan?

SOLUTION
Total interest equals the difference between amount repaid and amount borrowed. To find the total amount repaid, first compute the payment with formula 5.6 by setting N to 240 (that is, 240 months = 20 years x 12 months/year), PV to $185,000, and the monthly periodic interest rate r to 0.105 ÷ 12, or 0.0088. FV is zero because the last payment repays the loan in full.

$$\$185,000 = (CF)\left\{\frac{1-(1.0088)^{-240}}{0.0088}\right\}$$

$$CF = \frac{\$185,000}{100.1623}$$

$$= \$1,847$$

The sum of 240 payments at $1,847 is $443,280 (that is, $443,280 = 240 x $1,847). Thus, the amount repaid equals $443,280 and the amount borrowed equals $185,000. The difference is interest:

$$total\ lifetime\ interest = \$443,280 - \$185,000$$

$$= \$258,280.$$

CALCULATOR CLUE

To solve this problem with the time value functions on the *BAII Plus*© type `2nd` `FV` to clear the time value memories. Type `2nd` `I/Y` 12 `ENTER` `2nd` `CPT` to enforce monthly compounding. Solve for the loan payment by typing:

185000 `PV` 240 `N` 10.5 `I/Y` `CPT` `PMT`. The display shows the loan payment is $–1,847.

Find the total payments by multiplying the figure on the display by 240, and subsequently subtract the principal. While $–1,847 is still on the display, type

`X` `RCL` `N` `=` `+/–` `RCL` `PV` `=`.

The display shows total lifetime interest is $258,280.

On many mortgages the lifetime interest may be larger than the amount borrowed. Still, however, most individuals feel very fortunate to live in an economy where borrowing is possible. In undeveloped economies it may be impossible to borrow for purchasing a large asset, such as a house. Financial markets create possibilities.

EXAMPLE 15 What is this payment's allocation to P&I

This morning you mailed your 18th monthly payment on your car loan. The original loan was for $12,500 at 9.5% for 48 months. Here are three questions. (i) How much of this morning's payment is interest? (ii) What is the outstanding balance after this morning's payment is credited to the loan? (iii) How much interest to-date has been paid?

SOLUTION

Again the first step is to find the payment. N equals 48, the monthly rate r is 0.095 ÷ 12 or 0.0079, PV is $12,500 and FV is zero.

$$\$12,500 = (CF)\left\{\frac{1-(1.0079)^{-48}}{0.0079}\right\}$$

$$CF = \frac{\$12,500}{39.8039}$$

$$= \$314.04$$

The timeline below shows the lifetime cash flows for the loan.

$t=0$	1	2	18	48 months
	Payment #1	Payment #2	Payment #18	Payment #48
PV = $12,500	CF = $314.04	CF = $314.04	CF = $314.04	CF = $314.04

To determine how much of the eighteenth payment is interest requires multiplying the monthly interest rate times the beginning of month balance. In other words, the first step is to find the loan balance at the beginning of the eighteenth month. One ridiculous procedure for determining the outstanding principal is to work through the amortization table for 17 months. This approach works because each of the 17 payments is partitioned into principal and interest. Each month the outstanding principal is marked down by the amount of repaid principal. This backward-looking approach, though, is not the best way.

A forward-looking approach posits that the beginning of the eighteenth month occurs immediately after the seventeenth payment is made. At this point in time, 31 payments remain (that is, 31 = 48 – 17). Discounting these 31 remaining payments removes the interest component, and the present value equals the outstanding balance. Find the outstanding principal when 31 payments remain by using equation 5.6 wherein CF equals $314.04, N equals 31, and r equals 0.095 ÷ 12, or 0.0079. Compute PV.

$$PV = (\$314.04)\left\{\frac{1-(1.0079)^{-31}}{0.0079}\right\}$$

$$= \$8,602.63$$

The outstanding principal equals just over eighty-six hundred dollars immediately after the seventeenth payment is made, that is, when there remain 31 payments. The periodic interest accruing during the subsequent month is $68.10 (that is, $68.10 = $8,602.63 x 0.095 ÷ 12). Partitioning of the eighteenth payment looks as follows:

18th payment
$314.04

/ \

$68.10 $245.94
interest   principal

The second question asks for the outstanding balance after the eighteenth payment. The $8,602.63 beginning of month balance goes down by $245.94 to equal $8,356.69 at the end of the month. The forward-looking approach that obtains the same answer finds the present value of the 30 remaining payments (that is, 30 = 48 – 18):

$$PV = (\$314.04)\left\{\frac{1-(1.0079)^{-30}}{0.0079}\right\}$$

$$= \$8,356.69$$

The third question asks how much interest to-date has been paid. Recognize that the original loan balance is $12,500 and after eighteen payments the balance is $8,356.69. The total principal repaid therefore equals $4,143.31 (that is, $4,143.31 = $12,500 – $8,356.69). Eighteen payments sum to $5,652.71 (that is, $5,652.72 = 18 x $314.04). The interest to-date is the difference between total payments and principal repaid, or $1,509.41 (that is, $1,509.41 = $5,652.71 – $4,143.31).

5.B. Re-pricing loans: book versus market value

The loan's outstanding principal is its book value. The book value may be computed by either of two procedures discussed previously. Procedure one relies on amortization mechanics to partition each payment into periodic interest and principal repayment. This procedure then steps through each payment and writes-down the outstanding balance by the amount of principal repaid. This first procedure is backward-looking and inefficient. The second procedure relies on the constant annuity time value formula to discount remaining payments. The discounting process, that is division by one plus the rate raised to an exponent, takes out the interest from all remaining cash flows. With this forward-looking procedure the sum of discounted cash flows equals the outstanding principal.

Loans are assets, and in today's sophisticated financial markets selling loans is commonplace. Banks and other mortgage originators lend money to prospective homeowners. The homeowner signs a legal document describing the rights and obligations of each party. The homeowner gets the money and buys the house. The lender gets the legal loan document. The loan document entitles the loan's owner to collect payments of an agreed upon amount for the next fifteen or thirty years.

The lender often holds on to the loan and receives payments for the next few decades. More commonly, however, the lender sells the loan document. Sometimes the loan sells at its book value. Sometimes it doesn't. Competitive forces determine the loan's market price. The constant annuity time value formula describes the relation between the market price and expected cash flows. Consider the following example.

EXAMPLE 16 Loan's book and market value

This morning your bank received the 26th monthly payment on a $250,000 thirty-year 9 percent mortgage. Your bank may continue to receive payments for the next 28 years or so. The bank, however, has an immediate need to raise cash because demand for local construction loans is booming. They thus choose to sell the loan in order to raise cash. Investors in the national market that buy similar mortgages are willing to accept a 7.75 percent annual rate of return. What are the loan's book value and market value?

SOLUTION

First we need to specify the loan's payment stream. At the original conditions N equals 360 (that is, 360 months = 30 years x 12 months/year), the monthly rate r is $0.09 \div 12$ or 0.0075, PV is $250,000 and FV is zero.

$$\$250,000 = (CF)\left\{\frac{1-(1.0075)^{-360}}{0.0075}\right\}$$

$$CF = \frac{\$250,000}{124.2819}$$

$$= \$2,011.56$$

The initial conditions stipulate that 360 payments of $2,011.50 completely repay the 9 percent $250,000 loan.

To find the outstanding principal immediately after receipt of the 26th payment, find the present value of the remaining payments. Set N to 334 (that is, 334 = 360 – 26) and solve formula 5.1 for PV when r is 0.0075 and CF is $2,011.56:

$$PV = (\$2,011.56)\left\{\frac{1-(1.0075)^{-334}}{0.0075}\right\}$$

$$= \$246,095.81$$

Note in passing that the borrower has repaid a little less than $4,000 even though the bank has received payments totaling more than $52,000 (that is, 26 x $2,011 > $52,000). That's a lot of interest!

The book value of the loan is its outstanding principal and equals $246,095.81. The market value is found by discounting the cash flow stream with the rate of return that investors are willing to accept. Today's investors are willing to accept 7.75 percent on this loan. This suggests that interest rates today are lower than 26 months ago when they were 9 percent. As everyone knows, interest rates rise and fall over time.

Find the present value by slightly modifying the preceding equation. Keep N at 334 and CF at $2,011.56. Change the rate, however, so that r equals $0.0775 \div 12$, or 0.0065:

$$PV = (\$2,011.56)\left\{\frac{1-(1.0065)^{-334}}{0.0065}\right\}$$

$$= \$275,191.22$$

CALCULATOR CLUE

To solve this problem with the time value functions on the *BAII Plus*© type `2nd` `FV` to clear the time value memories. Type `2nd` `I/Y` 12 `ENTER` `2nd` `CPT` to enforce monthly compounding. Solve for the payment by typing:

250000 `PV` 360 `N` 9 `I/Y` `CPT` `PMT` .

The display shows the loan payment is $–2,011.56. While $–2,011.56 is still on the display, find the principal outstanding after 26 payments are made by typing

`RCL` `N` `−` 26 = `N` `CPT` `PV` .

The display shows the loan's book value is $246,096 . Find the loan's market value with an annual market discount rate of 7.75 percent by typing

7.75 `I/Y` `CPT` `PV`

The display shows the loan's market value is $275,191.

The investor is willing to purchase the loan from the bank for more than $275 thousand dollars. The investor is not necessarily crazy, either, to pay this much for a loan that was originally $250,000. Purchasing the loan, after all, entitles the loan's owner to receive 334 payments of $2,011.56; the sum of payments is $671,859 (that is, $671,859 = 334 x $2,011.56). If a 7.75 percent rate of return represents a good deal in the current economic setting, then maybe the investment makes a lot of sense. The mortgage investor should exercise caution, however, because the borrower might come in the door tomorrow and payoff the loan's outstanding principal of $246,095.81 in which case the investor suffers an immediate loss.

EXERCISES 5.5

Concept quiz
1. Is it generally better for a household to borrow with a short-term or with a long-term loan (assume that fees, interest rates, and all else are equal)?
2. A homeowner borrowing $185,000 at 10.5% repayable monthly over 20 years pays lifetime interest of $258,280. Is this situation so ridiculous that the government should enact legislation limiting to something reasonable the amount of interest that households pay?

Numerical quickies
3. How much is the monthly interest on a 10.30% (compounded monthly) loan with beginning of month outstanding balance equal to $9,900?
   ©AM1
4. How much is the payment for a loan of $139,000 with an annual interest rate of 8.10% (compounded annually) repayable over 30 years with payments due annually? ©AM2
5. You borrow $20,000 at 9.60% over 3 years (monthly payments) to finance your dream pre-owned car. Exactly 15 days after taking out the loan, you want to pay it off in-full because a better financing deal appears. There is no pre-payment penalty and 31 days are in the monthly billing cycle. Find the payoff amount (principal plus interest). ©AM10a

6. Your search for a new car surely depends on the monthly payment that you can afford. The absolute maximum income that you can allocate to your car payment is $325 per month. If the loan's annual percentage rate is 8.10%, find the most that you can afford to borrow. ©AM6

7. You have just bought a house by borrowing $260,000 at a 7.90% annual interest rate (compounded monthly) repayable with fixed payments over 35 years. When finally in the far-off future you make your last payment, how much of that last payment will be principal and how much will be interest? ©AM9c

8. Your friend is taking out a mortgage for $153,000 at 9.80% repayable with monthly payments over 25 years. She respects your financial expertise and asks "how many payments will I have to make before I reduce the principal balance by half its original amount." You pull out your calculator, and tell her the number of payments she'll make to reduce the balance by half is: ©AM5a

Numerical challengers

9. You borrow $30,000 at 7.50% over 4 years (monthly payments) to finance your dream pre-owned car. Exactly 25 days after making payment number 3, you want to pay it off in-full because a better financing deal appears. There is no pre-payment penalty and 31 days are in the monthly billing cycle. Find the payoff amount (principal plus interest). ©AM10c

10. Suppose to purchase a car you borrow $20,000 repayable monthly over 4 years at an annual percentage interest rate of 9.80%. Contrast the interest paid during the first and second halves of the loan life. ©AM8

11. The Company borrowed $170,000 at 9.60% to be repaid monthly over 15 years. They just remitted payment number 78.

11a. How much interest-to date has been paid? ©AM3dm

11b. How much total interest is scheduled to be paid over the life of the loan? ©AM3cm

11c. How much of the next monthly payment is principal repayment? ©AM3im

ANSWERS TO CHAPTER 5 EXERCISES

EXERCISES 5.1

1. Rule 4.3 from the previous chapter applies to all time value formulas. When the cash flows are in current dollars then the proper discount rate is the nominal rate. When the cash flows are in constant dollars then the proper discount rate is the precise real rate. Consider what this means when each cash flow is exactly the same number.

   The numbers represent current dollars when each period exactly the same amount is paid (or received). This occurs, for example, when someone deposits $125 monthly into a savings account, or when a loan requires a $400 monthly payment, etc. Because these are current dollars the proper discount rate is the nominal rate. Any computations of *PV* or *FV* represent current dollar answers.

   The numbers represent constant dollars when each period the purchasing power of the cash flows is exactly the same. This occurs, for example, in a long-run plan when someone expects that deposits may rise over time due to effects of inflation and a rising salary. Maybe deposits begin at $125 monthly but next year, assuming 4 percent inflation and salary-hike, deposits will be 4 percent higher. Current dollar deposits rise but constant dollar deposits are constant. When entering these constant dollar deposits as *CF* then the proper discount rate is the precise real rate. Any computations of *PV* or *FV* represent constant dollar answers. To convert a constant dollar answer into a current dollar answer requires inflating the number by the inflation rate, exactly like inflating a current price to find the future price.

EXERCISES 5.2A

1a. Apply formula 5.2 and find $FV = \$2,600 \times (1.0990^{10} - 1) \div 0.0990$, which equals \$41,239.

1b. *Total contributed principal* equals \$26,000 (= 10 × \$2,600) so therefore *Total interest* equals \$15,239 (= \$41,239 - \$26,000).

2. If the first deposit were exactly one year ago and last one today there would have been 13 deposits (first deposit 12 months ago, 2nd 11 months ago, ..., 12th one month ago, 13th today). With first deposit 9 years ago there have been 109 total deposits (= 12 × 9 + 1). The monthly periodic rate is 0.82% (= 9.80% ÷ 12). Apply formula 5.2 and find $FV = \$50 \times (1.0082^{109} - 1) \div 0.0082$, which equals \$8,735 (reduce rounding errors on your calculator by storing settings or using the time value memories).

3. With first deposit 15 years ago there have been 61 total deposits (= 4 × 15 + 1). The quarterly periodic rate is 1.625% (= 6.50% ÷ 4). Apply formula 5.2 and find $FV = \$1,250 \times (1.01625^{61} - 1) \div 0.01625$, which equals \$128,709. The total contributed principal is \$76,250 (= 61 × \$1,250), which means that total interest equals \$52,459 (= \$128,709 − \$76,250).

4. This problem is just like the one from the opening paragraph of Section 2 (preceding subsection 2A). Apply formula 5.2 where *PV* is \$12,490 and *CF* is \$1,450 and *r* is 0.0570 and *N* is 9. Find $FV = \{\$12,490 \times 1.0570^{9}\} - \{\$1,450 \times (1.0570^{9} - 1) \div 0.0570\}$; which is \$4,113. Read the *Calculator Clue* preceding subsection 2A to learn more about signage for this problem.

5. The monthly periodic rate is 0.53% (= 6.40% ÷ 12). There are 144 withdrawals (= 12 × 12). Apply formula 5.2 to find $FV = \{\$8,290 \times 1.0053^{144}\} - \{\$70 \times (1.0053^{144} - 1) \div 0.0053\}$; which is \$2,725.

EXERCISES 5.2B

1. The monthly periodic rate *r* is 0.425% (= 5.1% ÷ 12). *PV* equals \$0 because there is no on-going balance prior to the first deposit. There are 5 deposits, *CF*, equal to \$430. Apply formula 5.2 to find the account balance immediately after the last deposit: $FV = \$430 \times (1.00425^{5} - 1) \div 0.00425$; which is \$2,168. Now leave that sum alone while it compounds for 252 months (= 12 × 21) at 1% per month (= 12% ÷ 12). Use the lump-sum formula: $FV = \$2,168 \times 1.00^{252}$ which is \$26,614.

2. The monthly periodic rate *r* is 0.825% (= 9.90% ÷ 12). *PV* initially equals \$2,600. There are 16 deposits, *CF*, equal to \$230 and the 1st one occurs 10 months from today, the 2nd one in 11 months, 3rd one in 12 months, ..., and 16th in 25 months. Note that *PV* compounds for 9 months to become \$2,800 (=\$2,600 × 1.00825^{9}) exactly one period before the first annuity cash flow. Apply formula 5.2 to find $FV = \{\$2,800 \times 1.00825^{16}\} - \{\$-230 \times (1.00825^{16} - 1) \div 0.00825\}$; which is \$3,193 + \$3,917; which is \$7,110. Note that both *PV* and *CF* increase *FV*.

3. The monthly periodic rate *r* is 0.833% (= 10% ÷ 12). *PV* initially equals \$2,200. There are 16 withdrawals, *CF*, equal to \$150 and the 1st one

occurs 10 months from today, the 2nd one in 11 months, 3rd one in 12 months, ..., and 16th in 25 months. Note that PV compounds for 9 months to become $2,371 (=$2,200 × 1.00833^9) exactly one period before the first annuity cash flow. Apply formula 5.2 to find FV = {$2,371 ×1.00833^{16}} – {$150 ×(1.00833^{16} – 1) ÷ 0.00833}; which is $2,707 – $2,556; which is $151. Note that both PV and CF are positive. PV, however, increases FV whereas CF is subtracted away and decreases FV.

4. The monthly periodic rate r is 0.55% (= 6.6% ÷ 12). PV initially equals $5,800. The 1st deposit occurs 17 months from today. the 2nd in 18 months, 3rd in 19 months, ..., and in 36 months the 20th deposit occurs (=36 – 17 + 1). Note that PV compounds for 16 months to become $6,332 (=$5,800 ×1.0055^{16}) exactly one period before the first annuity cash flow. Apply formula 5.2 to find that FV, the balance immediately after the last deposit is $11,704 (={$6,332 ×1.0055^{20}} – {$–230 ×(1.0055^{20} – 1) ÷ 0.0055}). Note that PV and CF have opposite sign yet both increase FV. Apply the lump-sum relation to the balance for another 48 months (= 84 – 36) and find that in 7 years FV equals $15,229 (={$11,704 ×1.0055^{48}).

EXERCISES 5.3A

1. Apply formula 5.1 in which CF equals $1,200 and N is 8. The periodic rate r is 8.8%. FV is the value of the asset immediately after delivering the last cash flow and equals zero. Solve and find that PV equals $6,691 (= $1,200 ×(1 – 1.088^{-8}) ÷ 0.088).

2. Apply formula 5.1 in which CF equals $1,600 and N, the number of cash flows, is 10. The periodic rate r is 6.3%. FV is the balance after the last cash flow and equals zero. Notice that PV occurs one period before the first cash flow and therefore formula 5.1 is perfectly appropriate. Solve and find that PV equals $11,611 (= $1,600 ×(1 – 1.063^{-10}) ÷ .063).

3. Apply formula 5.1 in which CF equals $1,600 and N is 9. The periodic rate r is 8.5%. FV is the value of the asset immediately after delivering the last cash flow and equals $7,700. Solve and find that PV equals $13,486 (= [$1,600 ×(1 – 1.085^{-9}) ÷ 0.085] + [$7,700 ×1.085^{-9}]).

4. Apply formula 5.1 in which the periodic rate r is 2.125% (=8.5% ÷ 4). CF flows out of your friend's pocket and into the account and equals $–650. The number of deposits N is 24. FV is the balance after the last deposit and equals $49,924. FV represent funds available to your friend as an inflow; CF and FV have opposite signs. Note also that PV occurs one period before the first cash flow and therefore formula 5.1 is perfectly appropriate. Solve and find that PV equals $18,018 {$PV$ = [$–650 ×(1 – 1.02125^{-24}) ÷ .02125] + ($49,924 ×1.02125^{-24})}. Find on the financial calculator with CF=$-650 and FV=$+49,925 that PV = $–18,018. On the financial calculator CF and PV are both positive because both flow into the account whereas FV flows out and its sign is negative.

5. Apply formula 5.1 in which the periodic rate r is 2.375% (=9.5% ÷ 4). CF equals $1,350 and N, the number of withdrawals, is 12. FV is the balance after the last withdrawal and equals $11,403. FV represent funds available to your friend as an inflow; CF and FV have the same signs. Note also that PV occurs one period before the first cash flow and therefore formula 5.1 is perfectly appropriate. Solve and find that PV equals $22,557 {= [$1,350 ×(1 – 1.02375^{-12}) ÷ .02375] + ($11,403 ×1.02375^{-12})}. Find on the financial calculator with CF=$650 and FV=$+11,403 that PV = $–22,557. Sign of PV is opposite CF and FV.

6a. Apply formula 5.1 in which the periodic rate r is 1.52% (=18.2% ÷ 12). CF equals $2,700 (assign it a positive sign) and the number of cash flows N is 15. FV, also positive, is $95,600. Solve with formula 5.1 and find that PV equals $112,259 (= [$2,700 \times (1 - 1.0152^{-15}) \div .0152] + ($95,600 \times 1.0152^{-15})\})$.

6b. The counteroffer equals $121,859 (= $112,259 + $9,600). Solve with your financial calculator this equation, $121,859 = [$2,700 \times (1 - (1+r)^{-15}) \div r] + ($95,600 \times (1+r)^{-15})\}$, and find that the annual rate of return equals 10.37%.

7a. Apply formula 5.1 in which the periodic rate r is 1.69% (=20.3% $\div$ 12). CF equals $2,400 (assign it a negative sign) and the number of cash flows N is 15. FV, assign it a positive sign, is $78,900. Solve with formula 5.1 and find that PV equals $29,786 (= [$-2,400 \times (1 - 1.0169^{-15}) \div .0152] + ($78,900 \times 1.0169^{-15})\})$.

7b. The counteroffer equals $35,786 (= $29,786 + $6,000). Solve with your financial calculator this equation, $35,786 = [$-2,400 \times (1 - (1+r)^{-15}) \div r] + ($78,900 \times (1+r)^{-15})\}$, and find that the annual rate of return equals 10.26%.

EXERCISES 5.3B

1. Apply formula 5.3 to find that PV, the amount of the deposit one period before the first withdrawal, equals $13.33 million (= $1 million $\div$ 0.075).

2. The periodic monthly cash flow CF equals $11,667 (= $140,000 $\div$ 12) and the periodic interest rate is 0.7333% (= 8.8% $\div$ 12). Apply formula 5.3 to find that PV, the amount of the requisite endowment, equals $1.59 million (= $11,667 $\div$ 0.0073).

3. With PV equal to $35 million and r at 10% the annual interest CF was $3.5 million ($CF = r \times PV$). It has fallen to $1.4 million (= .04 $\times$ $35 million), a decline of $2.1 million. Falling interest rates are not good for everybody.

EXERCISES 5.4A

1. Apply formula 5.4 in which the periodic rate r is 1.08% (=7.0% $\div$ 12). The number of deposits N is 49 (= 4 $\times$ 12 + 1). Beginning wealth PV is zero. FV occurs immediately after the last cash flow and therefore formula 5.4 (or 5.5) is perfectly appropriate. FV equals $10,000. Solve and find that CF equals $-177 {= [$0 - $10,000] $\div$ [(1.0058^{61} - 1) \div$ 0.0058]}. Recall that in formula 5.1, as in 5.4 which is simply a rearrangement, when PV and FV are positive then a positive CF signals a withdrawal whereas a negative CF signals a deposit.

2. Apply formula 5.4 in which the periodic rate r is 1.08% (=13.0% $\div$ 12). The number of deposits N is 61 (= 5 $\times$ 12 + 1). Beginning wealth PV is zero. FV occurs immediately after the last cash flow and therefore formula 5.4 (or 5.5) is perfectly appropriate. FV equals $12,000. Solve and find that CF equals $-140 {= [$0 - $12,000] $\div$ [(1.0108^{61} - 1) \div$ 0.0108]}.

3. Apply formula 5.4 in which the periodic rate r is 2.0% (=8.0% $\div$ 4). The number of withdrawals N is 20. Notice that beginning wealth PV occurs one period before the first cash flow, that FV is the balance after the last withdrawal and equals $0, and therefore formula 5.4 (or 5.5) is perfectly appropriate. Solve and find that CF equals $856 {= $14,000 $\times 1.02^{20} \div$ [(1.02^{20} - 1) \div 0.02]}.

4. Apply formula 5.4 in which the periodic rate r is 2.58% (=10.3% $\div$ 4). The number of withdrawals N is 21 (= 5 $\times$ 4 + 1). Notice that beginning wealth PV occurs one period before the first cash flow, that FV occurs immediately after the last cash flow, and therefore formula 5.4 (or 5.5) is perfectly appropriate. PV equals $16,000. FV is ending wealth and equals $68,200. Solve and find that CF equals $-1,493 {= [$16,000 $\times 1.0258^{21} - $68,200] \div$ [(1.0258^{21} - 1) \div 0.0258]}. The negative CF (given PV and FV are positive) means that CF are deposits. On the financial calculator assign PV a positive sign since that money flows into

the account, assign FV a negative sign since this is available to flow out of the account, and compute that PMT is positive – it too flows into the account.

5. Apply formula 5.4 in which the periodic rate r is 0.44% (=5.3% ÷ 12) for the savings account and 1.25% (=15.0% ÷ 12) for the stock fund. The number of withdrawals N is 216. Notice that beginning wealth PV occurs one period before the first cash flow, that FV occurs immediately after the last cash flow, and therefore formula 5.4 (or 5.5) is perfectly appropriate. PV equals $12,000. FV is ending wealth and equals $10,000. Solve and find that CF for the savings account equals $59 {= [$12,000 × 1.0125^{216} – $10,000] ÷ [($1.0125^{216}$ – 1) ÷ 0.0125]} and for the stock fund is $152 {= [$12,000 × 1.0125^{216} – $10,000] ÷ [($1.0125^{216}$ – 1) ÷ 0.0125]}. The positive CF (given PV and FV are positive) means that CF are withdrawals. On the financial calculator assign PV a positive sign since that money flows into the account, assign FV a negative sign since this is available to flow out of the account, and compute that PMT is negative – it too flows out of the account.

6. Apply formula 5.4 in which the periodic rate r is 11.20%. The number of withdrawals N is 5. Notice that beginning wealth PV of $16,000 occurs one period before the first cash flow, that FV of $30,000 occurs immediately after the last cash flow, and therefore formula 5.4 (or 5.5) is perfectly appropriate. Solve and find that CF equals $-447 {= [$16,000 ×1.1120^{5} – $30,000] ÷ [($1.1120^{5}$ – 1) ÷ 0.1120]}. The negative CF (given PV and FV are positive) means that CF are deposits. On the financial calculator assign PV a positive sign since that money flows into the account, assign FV a negative sign since this is available to flow out of the account, and compute that PMT is positive – it too flows into the account.

EXERCISES 5.4B

1a. The periodic rate r always is 0.42% (= 5.10% ÷ 12). The first stage is the annuity deposit stream of $170. The number of deposits N is 25 (= 2 × 12 + 1). PV at this point is zero, and CF is $-170; recall that for the formulas when PV and FV are positive then deposits are negative. Apply formula 5.2 to find the accumulation at time of last deposit for the first stage. Find that FV equals $4,474 {= $0 – $-170 ×[$1.0042^{25}$ – 1] ÷ 0.0042]}. That sum becomes the beginning balance one period before commencement of the second annuity deposit stream of $280. The number of deposits N in the second stage is 84 (= 12 × (9 – 2)). PV at this point is $4,474 and CF is $–280. Solve with formula 5.2 and find that FV equals $34,583 {= $4,474($1.0042^{84}$) – $–280 × [$1.0042^{84}$ – 1] ÷ 0.0042]}.

1b. You contributed principal of $4,250 (= 25 × $170) in the first stage and $23,520 (= 84 × $280) in the second stage. The bank added interest to your account of $6,813 (= $34,583 – $4,250 – $23,520).

2. The periodic rate r always is 0.38% (= 4.60% ÷ 12). For the first stage of Strategy 1 is the number of deposits N is 61 (= 5 × 12 + 1). PV at this point is zero, and CF is $–270; recall that for the formulas when PV and FV are positive then deposits are negative. Apply formula 5.2 to find the accumulation at time of last deposit for the first stage of Strategy 1. Find that FV equals $18,515 {= $0 – $–270 × [$1.0038^{61}$ – 1] ÷ 0.0038]}. Now apply the lump-sum relation to find the accumulation after 21 additional years (252 months): FV =$18,515 × 1.0038^{252} ; = $48,557. Strategy 2 has only one stage. The number of deposits N is 253 (= 21 × 12 + 1) and CF is $–270. Solve with formula 5.2 and find that FV equals $114,993 {= $0 – $–270 × [$1.0038^{253}$ – 1] ÷ 0.0038]}. After 26 years Strategy 1 accumulates $48,557 and Strategy 2 accumulates $114,993. Strategy 2 accumulates $66,436 more than Strategy 1.

3. The periodic rate r always is 3.95% (= 7.90% ÷ 2). Use perpetuity formula 5.3 to find the necessary account balance one period before the first scholarship. CF equals $1,900 so PV equals $48,101 (= $1,900 ÷ 0.0395). Now apply formula 5.4 to find the deposit history that accumulates an ending wealth FV of $48,101. PV at this point is zero and the number of deposits N is 9 (= 4 × 2 + 1). Find that CF equals $-4,555 {= ($0 − $48,101) ÷ [(1.0395^9 − 1) ÷ 0.0395]}. The negative sign signals that these are deposits.

4. The periodic rate r always is 0.59% (= 7.10% ÷ 12). Apply formula 5.2 to find the accumulation FV that results from 97 monthly deposits N (= 8 × 12 + 1) when CF equals $-2,800. PV equals $0. Find that FV equals $365,439 {= $0 − $-2,800 × [(1.0059^{97} − 1) ÷ 0.0059]}. Use perpetuity formula 5.3 to find the amount of monthly interest that this accumulation spins off. CF equals $2,162 (= $365,439 × 0.0059). The endowment fund will provide student financial aid awards of $2,162 every month forevermore.

5. The periodic rate r always is 0.38% (= 4.50% ÷ 12). Apply formula 5.2 to find the accumulation FV that results from 408 monthly deposits N (= 34 × 12) when CF equals $-235.17. PV equals $0. Find that FV equals $226,076 {= $0 − $-235.17 × [(1.0038^{408} − 1) ÷ 0.0038]}. Now apply formula 5.1 in which PV equals $226,076 and ending wealth FV equals $0 and CF equals $2,090. Substitution shows:
$$\$226,076 = (\$2,090) \times [(1 − 1.0038^{-N}) ÷ 0.0038]\}.$$
Use the financial calculator (or take logarithms) to find the N equals 139. The savings plan supports 139 monthly withdrawals of $2,090; that's about 12 1/2 years – hopefully the employee planned for inflation!

6. The periodic rate r always is 0.50% (= 6.0% ÷ 12). Apply formula 5.2 to find the accumulation FV that results from 384 monthly deposits N (= 32 × 12) when CF equals $-108.91. PV equals $0. Find that FV equals $126,083 {= $0 − $-108.91 × [(1.0050^{384} − 1) ÷ 0.0050]}. Now apply formula 5.4 to find the amount CF that a beginning wealth PV of $126,083 supports when N is 136 and FV equals $0. Find that CF equals $1,280 {= ($126,083 − $0) ÷ [(1.0050^{136} − 1) ÷ 0.0050]}. The positive sign signals that these are withdrawals.

EXERCISES 5.5

1. In general, whether a short-term loan is better than a long-term loan depends on the specific situation. One thing is absolutely certain: you pay more interest with a long-term loan than with a short-term loan (all else equal). But sometimes, paying the extra interest might be better.

   Collapse the story to these essentials: Say that you borrow $100 at 10%. Is it better (a) to repay $110 after one period or (b) to repay $121 after two periods? Definitely total lifetime interest is $10 with the 1-period loan and $21 with the 2-period loan. In both cases the geometric average periodic rate of return is 10%. But whether the 1-period loan is better than the 2-period loan largely depends on whether the marginal utility of money is constant. Marginal utility of money depends on what you do with the money.

   The marginal utility of money is very high when income is insufficient for covering needs. The pauper on the street has very high marginal utility for money because $1 may represent the difference between life (food & shelter) and death (starvation & exposure). Millionaires generally have relatively low marginal utility for money. For most households, however, life cycle factors (see table 9.4) affect marginal utility for money. Generally, marginal utility of money is highest during early and mid-career stages. Deferring loan payments into the remote future is worth the cost of interest when in the near term it means being able to afford baby food, furniture, and gas money to get to work.

Marginal utility of money generally is lower during late-career stage, however, because income is highest and expenses are declining with downsizing households. Using a longer-term loan to defer loan payments until the remote future may indeed be an intelligent strategy even though lifetime interest is higher.

Determining for on-going well-established complex companies whether a short-term loan is better than a long-term loan is even more complicated because of interaction between risk and rates of return. We need more lessons about the structure of finance before considering that issue.

2. The short answer is NO. Interest rates are determined by competitive forces of supply and demand in financial markets between borrowers and lenders. Households may avoid paying any interest at all by paying cash for everything. In many lesser developed countries the financial markets are so incomplete that loans for buying houses and cars just don't exist. These cash-only societies really dampen wealth accumulation. Financial markets allow households to capitalize future income; get the house now by borrowing in financial markets and repay the loan with salary that you'll earn later. Borrowing and investing and paying interest are a lot better than the alternative.

3. The monthly interest is $84.97 (= $9,900 × 0.1030 ÷ 12).

4. Use formula 5.6 and find $139,000 = PMT \times [(1 - 1.0810^{-30}) \div 0.0810]$; or PMT equals $12,464.

5. The accrued interest for 15 days is $77.42 {= $20,000 × (0.0960 ÷ 12) × (15 ÷ 31)}. The payoff amount therefore equals $20,077.42 (= $20,000 + $77.42).

6. The periodic payment declines as the loan term increases (all else equal). Compute the payment for different terms, say 3 years, 4 years, and 5 years. Use formula 5.6 with a monthly periodic rate r of 0.67% (= 8.10% ÷ 12) and 36 payments (N for 3 years) and find: $PV = \$325 \times [(1 - 1.0067^{-36}) \div 0.0067]$; or PV = $10,356. For 48 months you can afford to borrow $13,287 {= $325 × [(1 - 1.0067^{-48}) ÷ 0.0067]}. For 60 months you can afford to borrow $15,991 {= $325 × [(1 - 1.0067^{-60}) ÷ 0.0067]}.

7. The monthly periodic rate r is 0.66% (= 7.9% ÷ 12) and the number of payments N is 420 (= 35 × 12). First find the payment by using formula 5.6: $260,000 = PMT \times [(1 - 1.0066^{-420}) \div 0.0066]$; or PMT equals $1,827.82. Second find the principal outstanding when only 1 payment remains: $PV = \$1,827.82 \times [(1 - 1.0066^{-1}) \div 0.0066]$; or PV equals $1,815.87. The principal repaid with the last payment is $1,815.87. The interest during the last month is $11.95 (= $1,827.82 – $1,815.87), which also may have been computed as $1,815.87 × 7.9% ÷ 12.

8. The monthly periodic rate r is 0.82% (= 9.8% ÷ 12) and the number of payments N is 300 (= 25 × 12). First find the payment by using formula 5.6: $153,000 = PMT \times [(1 - 1.0082^{-300}) \div 0.0082]$; or PMT equals $1,368.80. Second, use the formula to find N when outstanding principal equals $76,500 (= $153,000 ÷ 2): $76,500 = 1,368.80 \times [(1 - 1.0082^{-N}) \div 0.0082]$; or N equals 75 (use the financial calculator to solve for N, or take logarithms). When 75 payments remain the principal is at half its original amount. That point in time occurs after making 225 payments (= 300 – 75).

9. The monthly periodic rate r is 0.63% (= 7.5% ÷ 12) and the number of payments N is 48 (= 4 × 12). First find the payment by using formula 5.6: $30,000 = PMT \times [(1 - 1.0063^{-48}) \div 0.0063]$; or PMT equals $725.37. Second find the principal outstanding at beginning of the fourth month, that is after three payments were made and 45 remain: $PV = \$725.37 \times [(1 - 1.0063^{-45}) \div 0.0063]$; or PV equals $28,376. Third find that the accrued interest for 25 days is $143 {= $28,376 × 0.0063 × (25 ÷ 31)}. The payoff amount therefore equals $28,519 (= $28,376 + $143).

10. The monthly periodic rate r is 0.82% (= 9.8% ÷ 12) and the number of payments N is 48 (= 4 × 12). First find the payment by using formula 5.6: $20,000 = PMT × [(1 – 1.0082^{-48}) ÷ 0.0082]$; or PMT equals $505.33. Now find the principal outstanding when 24 payments remain: $PV = $505.33 × [(1 – 1.0082^{-24}) ÷ 0.0082]$; or PV equals $10,973. The principal repaid during the first half of the loan life is $9,027 (= $20,000 – $10,973) and during the second half is $10,973. The total payments during either half sum to $12,128 (= $505.33 × 12). Total interest equals $3,101 (= $12,128 – $9,027) during the first half of the loan life and $1,155 (= $12,128 – $10,973) during the second half.

11a. The monthly periodic rate r is 0.80% (= 9.6% ÷ 12) and the number of payments N is 180 (= 15 × 12). First find the payment by using formula 5.6: $170,000 = PMT × [(1 – 1.0080^{-180}) ÷ 0.0080]$; or PMT equals $1,785.45. Now find the principal outstanding after 78 payments have been made, that is, when 102 payments remain: $PV = $1,785.45 × [(1 – 1.0080^{-102}) ÷ 0.0080]$; or PV equals $124,171. The principal repaid to-date equals $45,829 ($170,000 – $124,171). The sum of all payments remitted to-date equals $139,265 (= 78 × $1,785.45). The interest to-date equals $93,436 ($139,265 – $45,829).

11b. The sum of lifetime payments equals $321,382 (= 180 × $1,785.45). The lifetime interest equals $151,382 ($321,382 – $170,000).

11c. Since already we know that the principal outstanding after the 78th payment is $124,171 the problem is straightforward. Next month's periodic interest equals $993.46 ($124,171 × 0.096 ÷ 12). Notice therefore that next month's principal repayment is $792.09 ($1,785.45 – $993.46).

CHAPTER 6

Time Value Application 1, Capital Budgeting

Principles for computing present values have direct and important applications. Companies and individuals, for example, might compute present values to decide whether planned expenditures are advisable. Real estate investors might compute present values to identify profitable units. Securities investors might compare present values and costs in order to identify courses of action that create wealth. Selection of the discount rate for computing present values is an important step in these analyses and lessons in later chapters focus on determination of equilibrium discount rates. Chapter 6 takes financing rates as given and focuses on application of present value techniques to capital budgeting analyses.

1. ALTERNATIVE ASSESSMENT MEASURES AND RULES

The decision of whether or not a company should buy a new machine, a new building, develop and launch a new product, or perhaps even buy a new subsidiary, is always difficult. The decision-makers must decide which type of information they want to collect. Then they might collect the information by making phone calls, conducting surveys, reading reports, and doing a lot of legwork (or hiring MBAs to do it!). Ultimately, though, they must process the information and rely on keen intuition to interpret the signals.

The importance of intuition for capital budgeting decisions cannot be overstated. Two different individuals can look at the same scenario and reasonably come up with two different and opposite assessments. Some people obviously are gifted with special intuition. A lot of intuition, however, comes from experiential learning. Learning techniques for processing information, and using those techniques in situation after situation, develops keen intuition. Nonetheless, given a cash flow stream and the relevant discount rate then capital budgeting decisions often rely on 4 common assessment measures:

- average accounting rate of return
- payback period
- internal rate of return
- net present value

The average accounting rate of return suffers from several well-known biases and problems. Consequently, an in-depth discussion is not offered. In a nutshell, however, the average accounting rate of return relates a project's expected contribution to net income and its historical cost. The measure is okay over a short investment horizon when net income approximates cash flow. As the length of the project's time period increases, and as project's cash flow deviates from its contribution to net income, there is a decline in the information content of the average accounting rate of return. Discussions below offer insights about the other assessment measures.

1.A. Payback period

The strength of this measure is computational ease.

> **DEFINITION 6.1 Payback period**
> The payback period is the length of time required to recover an investment's cost.

EXAMPLE 1 Simplest payback period problem

A project costs $3,000 and returns after-tax cash flow of $1,000 per year for 5 years. What is the project's payback period?

SOLUTION

The payback period is 3 years because this is the length of time it takes to recover the cost.

The preceding example illustrates the simplicity of computing the payback period. The example below enables a little more insight about the measure.

EXAMPLE 2 Payback period for uneven cash flow stream

A capital investment costs $46,000. Your data suggests the investment generates after-tax cash flow of $2,500 per month throughout the first year, $1,500 per month throughout the second year, and $500 per month throughout the third year. What is the project's payback period?

SOLUTION

The payback period is the number of months required to recover the $46,000 cost. Examine the table below

month	monthly after-tax cash flow	cumulative cash flow
1	$2,500	$2,500
2	$2,500	$5,000
. . .		
11	$2,500	$27,500
12	$2,500	$30,000
13	$1,500	$31,500
. . .		
22	$1,500	$45,000
23	$1,500	$46,500

After 22 months the cash flows sum to $45,000. The cost almost, but not quite, has been recovered. By the end of the 23rd month, the cost is fully recovered.

The precise numerical value for the payback period depends on some information not given. There are two possibilities. (1) If the monthly cash flow occurs as a lump sum at the end of the month, then the payback period is 23 months. (2) If the cash flows accumulate uniformly throughout the month then the payback period is greater than 22 but less than 23 months. To compute the fractional month:

fractional period = cost not yet recovered ÷ periodic cash flow

$$= (46,000 - 45,000) / \$1,500$$

$$= 0.67.$$

The payback period would be 22.67 months.

The preceding example highlights some weaknesses of the payback period assessment measure. Decision-makers feed their intuition with the knowledge that if they spend $46,000 they will recover the cost within 23 months. But is this good or bad?

One problem with the payback period is that it doesn't render a "good vs. bad" decision. It is true, however, that *a short payback period is better than a long payback period (all else equal)*. As the length of the payback period increases there probably is an increase in the likelihood that something won't go as planned. An investment recovering its cost within 23 months almost surely is less risky than one recovering its cost in 10 years (all else equal).

Another problem with the payback period is that it ignores the time value of money. This shortcoming is easily corrected by computing and accumulating discounted values. This alternative measure is called the "discounted payback period."

EXAMPLE 3 Discounted payback period

For the data in example 2 above, what is the discounted payback period if the financing rate is 9.50% compounded monthly?

SOLUTION

Add a column to the table that computes the discounted value of each monthly cash flow.

month	monthly cash flow	discounted monthly cash flow	cumulative discounted cash flow
1	$2,500	$2,480	$2,480
2	$2,500	2,460	$4,540
. . .			
24	$1,500	1,242	44,074
25	$500	411	44,485
. . .			
28	$500	401	45,697
29	$500	398	46,095

The present value of $2,500 received in one month when discounted by a monthly periodic rate of $.095/12^{ths}$ is $2,480 (= $2,500 \div 1.00792$). The present values for all other monthly cash flows are found analogously. Subsequently, add together all discounted cash flows to find the cumulative sum each month. The discounted payback period is about 29 months (if the cash flow accumulates daily then the discounted payback is 28.76 months ($0.76 = (46,000 - 45,697) \div 398$).

The difference between discounted and regular payback periods for short horizons, such as 1 or 2 years, is qualitatively trivial. The difference becomes more significant as the time horizon increases.

Perhaps the biggest problem with the payback period, discounted or not, is that it ignores anything that happens beyond the payback period. For example, what would happen to the payback period for the above example if the cash flow did not terminate with conclusion of the third year. Suppose, for example, the investment were also to deliver $500,000 per month during months 37 through 48. How does this change in the cash flow stream affect the computation of the payback period? The answer: absolutely not at all! The payback period still would be about 23 months because that is how long it takes to recover the cost of $46,000. A big shortcoming of the payback period, especially when cash flows are not always the same size, is that its computation is independent of all on cash flows occurring after the payback point is reached. Significant cash flows might occur after the payback period elapses, however, and a good analysis should account for them.

Because the payback period is easy to apply, many rules-of-thumb are based on it. Some companies allow workgroups to make purchasing decisions, for example, when payback periods are less than one year. Payback periods longer than a year, however, might require approval from management higher-up. Regardless, more sophisticated assessment measures often are needed.

1.B. Internal rate of return ("IRR")

The *IRR* is the most popular capital budgeting assessment measure in use. It has a strong intuitive foundation and relies on a solid theoretical framework. This measure was originally introduced by legendary John Maynard Keynes in his best seller *The General Theory of Employment, Interest, and Money* (1936). Although Keynes called this measure the "marginal efficiency of capital", we know it today as the *IRR*. The measure is so widely used that most financial calculators name a button after it!

The *IRR* is the discount rate at which the present value of cash inflows equals the present value of cash outflows. The formula used for computing the *IRR* is

FORMULA 6.1 Internal rate of return, expanded version

$$\sum_{t=0}^{N} \frac{CF_t^{outflows}}{(1 + IRR)^t} = \sum_{t=0}^{N} \frac{CF_t^{inflows}}{(1 + IRR)^t}$$

Typically, the cash flow streams are known numbers, and the *IRR* is the only unknown variable in the equation. Quite often all the outflows occur at the beginning of a project *(t=0)* and simply equal the investment's cost, in which case the *IRR* definition is

FORMULA 6.2 Internal rate of return, concise version

$$cost = \sum_{t=0}^{N} \frac{CF_t^{inflows}}{(1 + IRR)^t}$$

The *IRR* usually cannot be isolated by itself on the left-hand-side. Instead, calculator or spreadsheet programs use a trial-and-error algorithm to find a value for the *IRR* satisfying the equality. While calculators and computers efficiently solve for the *IRR*, solving by-hand is often impractical.

The following decision rule guides usage of the *IRR*.

RULE 6.1 When the IRR says good deal!
A project is profitable when its *IRR* exceeds the financing rate.

Projects with a high *IRR* can be financed profitably at normal rates. At low financing rates, of course, they make even more money.

EXAMPLE 4 Simplest *IRR*

Reconsider the project that costs $3,000 and returns after-tax cash flow of $1,000 per year for 5 years. What is the project's *IRR*?

SOLUTION

The *IRR* is the number that satisfies the following equality.

$$\$3,000 = \frac{\$1,000}{(1+IRR)^1} + \frac{\$1,000}{(1+IRR)^2} + \frac{\$1,000}{(1+IRR)^3} + \frac{\$1,000}{(1+IRR)^4} + \frac{\$1,000}{(1+IRR)^5}.$$

The solution for the *IRR* is tedious to obtain by hand. A financial calculator, however, easily finds the *IRR* is 19.86%. The project is profitable as long as it can be financed at a rate less than 19.86%.

CALCULATOR CLUE

The *BAII Plus* calculator solves Example 4 with the CF function. Hit **CF** and **2nd** **CLR WORK** to clear any numbers previously stored in the cash flow memories. Now enter the cash flow stream for the problem. Type 3000 **+/−** **ENTER** to set the initial cash flow, CF0, equal to $−3,000. Now hit ⬇ , the down-arrow. This moves you to the subsequent cash flow. Hit 1000 **ENTER** to set CF1, cash flow one, at $1,000. Again hit ⬇ . Because you will receive $1,000 for five months, hit 5 **ENTER** to set the frequency for the first cash flow at five periods. The display shows F01=5. To compute the internal rate of return for the cash flow stream stored in the CF memories, hit **IRR** **CPT**. The answer of 19.86% appears on the display.

Because the cash flow each period is always the same number the problem also can be solved with the time value functions. Type **2nd** **FV** to clear the time value memories, and **2nd** **I/Y** 1 **ENTER** **2nd** **CPT** to set for annual compounding. Solve the preceding problem by typing:

3000 **+/−** **PV** 1000 **PMT** 5 **N** **CPT** **I/Y**

The answer of 19.86% appears on the display.

EXAMPLE 5 *IRR* for an uneven cash flow stream

Reconsider the investment that costs $46,000 and generates after-tax cash flow of $2,500 per month throughout the first year, $1,500 per month throughout the second year, and $500 per month throughout the third year. What is the project's *IRR*?

SOLUTION

The *IRR* is the number that satisfies the following equality

$$\$46,000 = \frac{\$2,500}{(1+IRR)^1} + \frac{\$2,500}{(1+IRR)^2} + ... + \frac{\$2,500}{(1+IRR)^{12}} + \frac{\$1,500}{(1+IRR)^{13}} + ... + \frac{\$1,500}{(1+IRR)^{24}}$$

$$\frac{\$500}{(1+IRR)^{25}} + ... + \frac{\$500}{(1+IRR)^{36}}$$

A financial calculator quickly solves the above equation and finds that the monthly IRR equals 1.27%. On an annual basis, this is equivalent to 15.24% annual percentage rate (multiply by 12). The project is profitable as long as the financing rate is less than a stated rate of 15.24% (compounded monthly).

The IRR results in a definite yes or no decision about whether the project is profitable. The measure properly reflects the time value of money. Also, it reflects the entire cash flow stream, not simply the front-end. These tremendous strengths of the measure undoubtedly contribute to its popularity.

The *IRR* has subtle shortcomings. First, a cash flow stream might have more than one *IRR*. This occurs especially when the cash flows switch signs several times; for example, outflows followed by inflows, followed by outflows, followed by inflows, etc. With multiple *IRR*, it is not clear which one is "right". Second, the *IRR* does not reveal how much wealth an investment creates. For example, an investment whose *IRR* is 20% for a company whose financing rate is 12% certainly creates wealth. It is entirely possible, though, that an alternative project whose *IRR* is 15% creates more wealth than the one with the 20% *IRR*. In other words, the *IRR* correlates imperfectly with wealth creation. Undoubtedly, the best investments are the ones that create the most wealth. A more sophisticated assessment measure is needed.

1.C. Net present value ("NPV")

NPV equals the amount of capitalized economic profit that an investment creates. Positive *NPV* investments should be pursued because they create wealth in excess of economic costs of production. Negative *NPV* investments should be avoided because they incur economic losses. Compute *NPV* as the present value of cash inflows minus the present value of outflows:

FORMULA 6.3 Net present value, expanded version

$$NPV = \sum_{t=0}^{N} \frac{CF_t^{inflows} - CF_t^{outflows}}{(1+r)^t} .$$

Quite often all the outflows occur at the beginning of a project *(t=0)* and simply equal the investment's cost. For this typical scenario,

FORMULA 6.4 Net present value, concise version

$$NPV = \sum_{t=0}^{N} \frac{CF_t^{inflows}}{(1+r)^t} - cost$$

EXAMPLE 6 Simplest *NPV*

Reconsider the project that costs $3,000 and returns after-tax cash flow of $1,000 per year for 5 years. What is the project's *NPV* if the financing rate is 9.5% compounded annually?

SOLUTION

The following equation depicts the *NPV* computation

$$NPV = \frac{\$1,000}{(1+.095)^1} + \frac{\$1,000}{(1+.095)^2} + \frac{\$1,000}{(1+.095)^3} + \frac{\$1,000}{(1+.095)^4} + \frac{\$1,000}{(1+.095)^5} - \$3,000$$

$$= \$3,839.71 - \$3000$$

$$= \$839.71$$

The *NPV* is a positive number. Thus, this project creates economic profit and is a feasible choice for the company.

EXAMPLE 7 *NPV* for uneven cash flow stream

Reconsider the investment that costs $46,000 and generates after-tax cash flow of $2,500 per month throughout the first year, $1,500 per month throughout the second year, and $500 per month throughout the third year. What is the project's *NPV* if the financing rate is 9.5% compounded monthly?

SOLUTION

The following equation specifies the project's *NPV*.

$$NPV = \frac{\$2,500}{(1+.095/12)^1} + \frac{\$2,500}{(1+.095/12)^2} + ... + \frac{\$2,500}{(1+.095/12)^{12}} + \frac{\$1,500}{(1+.095/12)^{13}}$$

$$+ ... + \frac{\$1,500}{(1+.095/12)^{24}} + \frac{\$500}{(1+.095/12)^{25}} + ... + \frac{\$500}{(1+.095/12)^{36}} - \$46,000$$

$$= \$48,793.20 - \$46,000$$

$$= \$2,793.20$$

A financial calculator quickly solves the above equation for the *NPV*. This project creates economic profit and is a feasible choice for the company.

CALCULATOR CLUE

To clear any numbers previously stored in the cash flow memories type CF 2nd CLR WORK. Now enter the cash flow stream for the problem:

46000 +/− ENTER ↓ 2500 ENTER ↓ 12 ENTER ↓ 1500 ENTER ↓ 12 ENTER ↓ 500 ENTER ↓ 12 ENTER.

To compute the net present value for the cash flow stream stored in the CF memories, hit NPV. The calculator prompts for the periodic financing rate. Enter the monthly rate by typing 9.5 ÷ 12 = ENTER . The display shows 0.7917, the monthly periodic financing rate. Now hit ↓ CPT. The display shows the net present value is $2,793.20. To compute NPV at any other rate, say 18 percent compounded monthly for example, type ↓ 18 ÷ 12 = ENTER ↓ CPT. The display shows NPV is $−1,231.75. The project is not profitable with an 18 percent annual financing rate.

Concept quiz

1. Methods for assessing the profitability of a cash flow stream seem so straightforward that capital budgeting decisions seem mechanical. Explain possible reasons, then, that "the importance of intuition for making capital budgeting decisions cannot be overstated."

Numerical quickies

2. A company pursues a cost-cutting initiative that costs $20,000 to implement. Thereafter, however, the initiative reduces after-tax costs by $5,500 per year perpetually. How long, in years, is the payback period? ©CB15

3. A company pursues a cost-cutting initiative that costs $23,000 to implement. Thereafter, however, the initiative reduces after-tax costs by $6,000 per year perpetually. The project financing rate is 14.7% compounded annually. How long, in years, is the discounted payback period? ©CB16a

4. The Company pays $22,000 for an asset that is expected to generate after-tax cash flows at a rate of $900 per month for the first year, $800 per month for the second year, and $700 per month for the third year. How long, in months, is the investment's payback period? ©CB1

5. A company pursues a cost-cutting initiative that costs $20,000 to implement. Thereafter, however, the initiative reduces after-tax costs by $3,500 per year perpetually. The project financing rate is 14.7% compounded annually. Find the project's net present value and internal rate of return. ©CB17a

6. The company buys an asset that costs $16,800 and returns net cash flow of $1,900 per year for 4 years, followed by $2,200 per year for 8 additional years. Find the asset's internal rate of return. ©CB11

7. The company buys an asset that costs $14,300 and returns net cash flow of $1,800 per year for 5 years, followed by $2,700 per year for 5 additional years. The company financing rate is 7.4% compounded annually. Find the asset's net present value. ©CB17a

8. The company considers investing in an asset that costs $11,900 and returns after-tax net cash flow of $170 per month for 3 years, followed by $280 per month for an additional 3 years. The company financing rate is 10.0%. According to the decision rule for the "internal rate of return", is this project a wise investment for the company? ©CB12

9. The company buys an asset that costs $11,200 and returns net cash flow of $160 per month for 3 years, followed by $270 per month for 3 additional years. The company financing rate is 10.9% compounded monthly. Find the asset's internal rate of return and net present value. ©CB19b

Numerical challengers

10. The bank issues a $168,000 mortgage for 25 years (monthly payments) at an annual rate of 10.40%. How long for the bank is the payback period? ©CB7

11. The Company pays $28,000 for an asset that is expected to generate after-tax cash flows at a rate of $1,100 per month for the first year, $1,300 per month for the second year, and $1,000 per month for the third year. The project financing rate is 15.3% compounded monthly. How long, in months, is the investment's <u>discounted</u> payback period? ©CB14

12. The bank issued a $148,000 15-year mortgage (monthly payments) with an annual interest rate of 10.40%. They just received payment number 74 and have decided to sell the loan. The buyer of the loan expects to receive an annual rate of return equal to 11.50%. For the original bank that issued the loan, what was the internal rate of return? ©CB8

2. SIGNIFICANCE OF NPV

Wealth creation is an incredibly important objective. Individuals, companies, and governments, all pursue this objective. Recall the discussion from early in the book about the corporate cash flow cycle. Financial market transactions capitalize economic profit when capitalists provide financing for entrepreneurs pursuing positive *NPV* investments. Positive *NPV* investments, especially ones representing expenditures for *PP&E*, exist when there is relatively strong demand for the goods and services the assets produce. Economic sectors where positive *NPV* investments exist are like "hot spots" and they attract financing. Entrepreneurs flock to the opportunity for wealth creation. In short, the wants and needs of society create the **potential** for wealth creation—the financial markets allow entrepreneurs to capture it.

NPV is an important concept that merits more discussion.

2.A. NPV represents economic profit

The following illustrates wealth creation by a positive *NPV* investment. Recall the example above when an investment costs $3,000 and returns after-tax cash flow of $1,000 per year for 5 years. With a financing rate of 9.5% the *NPV* is $839.71. Suppose the entrepreneur finances the entire $3,000 cost of the project, and also borrows an additional $839.71. The total loan amount, that is the source of financing, therefore equals $3,839.71. The entrepreneur uses the funds as follows:

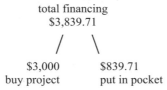

The entrepreneur pays $3,000 to the vendor in order to purchase the investment. The remainder of the money is "pocketed." Perhaps the money is held in a company cash account, perhaps it is paid-out as a dividend to shareholders or as a Christmas bonus to employees, etc. The important point is that the company has this extra money to use as it sees fit. The extra money equals NPV and represents economic profit.

Suppose the lender agrees to accept loan payments equal to the amount of the project cash flows. On all outstanding principal, however, the entrepreneur must pay 9.5 percent interest. The table below illustrates amortization mechanics for this loan.

year	beginning-of-year outstanding principal	end-of-year principal & accumulated interest	end-of-year project cash flow & loan payment	outstanding principal
1	$3,839.71	$4,204.48	$1,000	$3,204.48
2	$3,204.48	$3,508.91	$1,000	$2,508.91
3	$2,508.91	$2,747.25	$1,000	$1,747.25
4	$1,747.25	$1,913.24	$1,000	$913.24
5	$913.24	$1,000.00	$1,000	$0.00

At the end of the first year, the principal plus accumulated interest equals $4,204.48 (=1.095x$3,839.71). The company receives project cash flows of $1,000 and applies it all to the loan. The outstanding principal therefore drops to $3,204.48 (=$4,204.48 – $1,000). Each year additional interest accumulates, and the company uses the $1,000 project cash flow to pay down the loan. At the beginning of the fifth year, the outstanding balance of $913.24 incurs interest expense of $86.76 (=.095x$913.25), so that principal and accumulated interest is $1,000. The company receives the final project cash flow and completely repays the loan.

The project cash flows completely repay the loan. The loan is larger than the project cost, however. The economic profit equals the difference between the loan amount ($3,839.71) and the project cost ($3,000). The investment's net present value of $839.71 is the economic profit. For the scenario illustrated above, the company receives the new wealth up-front by borrowing more than the investment cost. The company is said to "capitalize" the economic profit. Alternatively, if the company borrows a lesser amount, say just enough (or less) to pay for the investment, then project cash flows would exceed the loan payments. The economic profit accrues in the future and the company is said to "amortize" the wealth. Regardless of whether the company amortizes or capitalizes the wealth, undertaking positive *NPV* investments creates wealth.

2.B. Relation between NPV and IRR

The *IRR* relates quite simply to *NPV*.

> **RULE 6.2 Identity between NPV and IRR**
> The IRR for a project is the financing rate at which the project's NPV is zero.

No economic profit is created when a project is financed at a rate equal to its *IRR*. Still, however, zero NPV investments are worthwhile because they allow the company to capture transformation value by combining factors of production and receiving revenues equal to economic production costs. If the financing rate were lower, the project would create economic profit for the company because *NPV* is positive when the financing rate is less than the *IRR*. Conversely, *NPV* is negative and economic losses accrue when the financing rate exceeds the *IRR*.

In most situations the *NPV* and *IRR* assessment measures lead to identical qualitative decisions about profitability. Perhaps more decision-makers use the *IRR* instead of *NPV* because individuals easily compare rates of return. The *IRR* is a percentage rate measure whereas *NPV* is a dollar measure. Both assessment tools require specification of the cash flow stream, too. They both use the financing rate, although in different order. Computing *NPV* requires up-front knowledge about the financing rate. The *IRR* procedure, conversely, computes the *IRR* number without up-front knowledge of the financing rate. Yet determining whether the computed *IRR* is good or bad requires comparison to the financing rate. Thus, information requirements of the two approaches are identical. The discussion below explains, however, that the *NPV* measure quite often is more useful than *IRR*. *NPV* is therefore the most sophisticated assessment measure of profitability.

B1. The NPV profile

The "NPV Profile" is a graph showing the relation between financing rate and *NPV*. The horizontal axis spans the domain of possible financing rates. The vertical axis measures *NPV*.

Each dot on the line represents the net present value for a given financing rate. The maximum wealth that the project could possibly create would occur if the financing rate were zero. This, of course, is extremely unlikely. Nonetheless, the coordinates at the vertical intercept include a financing rate of zero and an *NPV* of $2,000. Notice that computing *NPV* for a zero financing rate is easy. Simply add together the cash inflows and subtract the cost:

$$NPV = \frac{\$1,000}{(1+0.0)^1} + \frac{\$1,000}{(1+0.0)^2} + \frac{\$1,000}{(1+0.0)^3} + \frac{\$1,000}{(1+0.0)^4} + \frac{\$1,000}{(1+0.0)^5} - \$3,000$$

$$= \$1,000 + \$1,000 + \$1,000 + \$1,000 + \$1,000 - \$3000$$

$$= \$2,000$$

The *NPV* declines as the financing rate increases. This occurs because rising financing rates consume the cash flows, thereby leaving less residual wealth for the company. As the chart shows, the *NPV* is $839.71 with the 9.5% financing rate.

The point where the line crosses the horizontal axis is special. The coordinates at the horizontal intercept include an *NPV* of $0 and a financing rate of 19.86%. Because the IRR equals the financing rate when *NPV* is zero, the following rule is always true.

> **RULE 6.3 Significance of the horizontal intercept in the NPV profile**
> The rate at which the *NPV* profile crosses the horizontal axis is the *IRR*.

For all financing rates less than the *IRR*, that is to the left of the horizontal intercept, *NPV* is a positive number. Conversely, *NPV* is negative for all financing rates greater than the *IRR*.

B2. Ranking competing investments

The *IRR* formula links all cash flows within a time value framework. One problem with the *IRR*, however, occurs when comparing *IRR* for alternative projects. The ranking of *IRR* does not necessarily correspond to the ranking of *NPV*. Always the project with the biggest *NPV* creates the most wealth. But the project with the biggest *IRR* does not necessarily create the most wealth. Sometimes it does, sometimes it doesn't. The *IRR* correlate imperfectly with wealth creation. Plotting two *NPV* profiles on the same graph easily illustrates why *IRR* ranking does not correlate with *NPV* ranking.

Compare these two projects. Project Smooth costs $3,000 and returns $1,000 per year for five years. The previous section illustrates the *NPV* profile for Project Smooth. Project Latebloom offers the following cash flow stream:

Use the financial calculator to compute coordinates for Latebloom's *NPV* profile, and overlay it onto the one already obtained for Project Smooth.

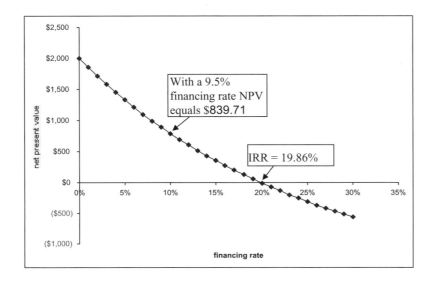

FIGURE 6.1
NPV profile for a capital budgeting project

The IRR is bigger for Project Steady than for Project Latebloom. Ranking project profitability by IRR is wrong, however. Always Project Steady has the biggest IRR. But only sometimes does it create the most wealth.

Inspect the *NPV* profile and observe that at a 5 percent financing rate the *NPV* is bigger for Project Latebloom than for Project Steady. Latebloom's line at 5 percent is above Steady's line. For a given financing rate, the project whose line is on top creates the most wealth. The lines cross so the one on top changes. At low financing rates Latebloom is on top and Latebloom's *NPV* exceeds Steady's. At high financing rates, say 15%, Steady's line is on top and Steady creates more wealth.

NPV is the amount of economic profit and *NPV* depends on the financing rate. The sensitivity of a cash flow stream to a change in financing rate varies among projects. In the *NPV* profile above, for example, moving rightward along the graph shows a decline in *NPV* for both Latebloom and Steady. This decline is natural because a rising rate reduces the discounted value of future cash inflows. But Latebloom's *NPV* declines more than Steady's. Latebloom's cash flow stream is more sensitive than Steady's to the financing rate.

Differential sensitivity of cash flow streams to financing rates creates an intriguing economic situation that runs counterintuitive to first impression. People tend to think that because one cash inflow stream is better than the other in a 15 percent interest rate environment, it should be better in a 5 percent environment, too. After all, the inflows are not changing, only the financing rate is changing. Yet the preceding *NPV* profile clearly shows project profitability, and project ranking, depend explicitly on the financing rate. An entrepreneur with access to low-cost financing might conclude Project Latebloom is better than Project Steady. Another entrepreneur with access only to high-cost financing might conclude Project Steady is best. And they both are right, even though they reach opposite conclusions!

Cross-over rates Draw two lines on a graph and they intersect unless they are parallel. *NPV* profiles for two different projects never will be parallel except in the special case where one is a linear transformation of the other. For example, the profiles are parallel when one's cash flows always equals twice the other's. That rarely happens. So two *NPV* profiles almost surely cross-over. When *NPV* profiles cross-over there is a reversal in profitability rank.

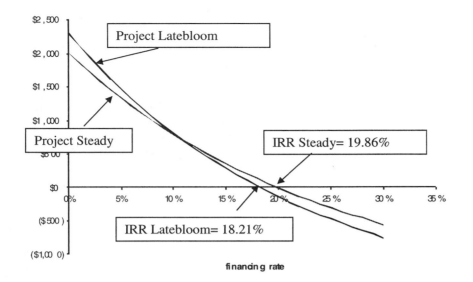

Figure 6.2
NPV profiles for two projects

Figure 6.3 shows three possible cross-over scenarios. In all scenarios the horizontal axis measures the financing rate and vertical axis measures the *NPV* of a project at that financing rate.

In the left-most figure the cross-over point occurs to the left of the vertical axis. The financing rate in that quadrant is negative. Financing rates cannot be negative. For all reasonable financing rates, therefore, the *NPV* is bigger for project B than *A*. B is more profitable than A for every plausible financing rate.

The center figure shows the scenario illustrated by the example about projects Steady and Latebloom. The cross-over point occurs at a rate for which the *NPV* is positive for both projects *C* and *D*. The most profitable project is *C* at relatively low financing rates. Project *D* is most profitable at rates somewhat higher than the cross-over point. Once financing rates get too high, however, both projects *D* and *C* have negative *NPV*.

In the right-most figure the cross-over point occurs at a relatively high financing rate. During the range in which *NPV* is positive, however, one fact is clear. If either project is profitable, then *F* is more profitable than *E*.

The cross-over point occurs when the *NPV* of the two projects are equal. The financing rate at the cross-over point is called the cross-over rate "*COR*". Use formula 6.4 to set the *NPV* of two projects, call them *A* and *B*, equal to each other. Then rearrange to obtain the following formula for finding the *COR*.

FORMULA 6.5 The cross-over financing rate "COR"

$$cost^A - cost^B = \sum_{t=0}^{N} \frac{CF_t^{inflows\,for\,A} - CF_t^{inflows\,for\,B}}{(1+COR)^t} \; .$$

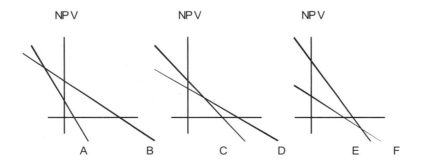

FIGURE 6.3
Potential configurations for cross-over rates

In a typical problem all the cash flows and costs are known numbers. Finding the *COR* requires a trial and error algorithm identical to the one for finding the *IRR*. The following example shows that financial calculators easily find the cross-over rate.

EXAMPLE 8 Find *COR* for projects Steady and Latebloom

The table below summarizes cash flow streams for the two projects illustrated in the *NPV* profiles previously. Exactly what is the cross-over financing rate?

t =	0	1	2	3	4	5
Steady	$-3,000	1,000	1,000	1,000	1,000	1,000
Latebloom	$-2,700	200	600	1,000	1,400	1,800

SOLUTION

Substitute cash flows into formula 6.5 to obtain the following equation.

$$\$3,000 - \$2,700 = \frac{1,000-200}{(1+COR)^1} + \frac{1,000-600}{(1+COR)^2} + \frac{1,000-1,000}{(1+COR)^3} + \frac{1,000-1,400}{(1+COR)^4} + \frac{1,000-1,800}{(1+COR)^5}$$

$$-\$300 = \frac{800}{(1+COR)^1} + \frac{400}{(1+COR)^2} + \frac{0}{(1+COR)^3} + \frac{-400}{(1+COR)^4} + \frac{-800}{(1+COR)^5}$$

The solution for *COR* is found on a financial calculator as 10.62%.

At a financing rate of 10.62% Projects Steady and Latebloom create exactly the same amount of wealth. The amount of *NPV* is found by taking the present value of either project's cash flow stream. Computations show *NPV* at the cross-over point is $731.38. A summary of profitability assessments at different financing rates yields the following table.

for this financing rate	obtain this profitability assessment
financing rate < 10.62%	both projects create wealth Latebloom creates more wealth than Steady
10.62% < financing rate < 18.21%	both projects create wealth Steady creates more wealth than Latebloom
18.21% < financing rate < 19.86%	Steady creates wealth Latebloom destroys wealth
19.86% < financing rate	both projects destroy wealth Latebloom destroys more wealth than Steady

CALCULATOR CLUE

To solve Example 8 clear any numbers previously stored in the cash flow memories. Type `CF` `2nd` `CLR WORK`. Now enter the cash flow stream from the preceding equation:

300 `+/-` `ENTER` `↓` 800 `ENTER` `↓` `↓` 400 `ENTER` `↓` `↓` 0 `ENTER` `↓` `↓` 400 `+/-` `ENTER` `↓` `↓` 800 `+/-` `ENTER` .

These cash flows constitute the incremental cash flow stream associated with switching from Project Latebloom to Project Steady. That is, suppose you already were to own Project Latebloom. Now figure the effects of switching to Project Steady. At time zero pay an extra $300 to buy Project Steady ($CF_0 = -300$). Because of the switch you receive an extra 800 at time 1 ($CF_1 = 800$), an extra 400 at time 2 ($CF_2 = 400$), nothing extra at time 3 ($CF_3 = 0$), at time 4 receive 400 less ($CF_4 = -400$), and at time 5 receive 800 less ($CF_5 = -800$). To compute the internal rate of return for the cash flow stream stored in the CF memories, hit `IRR` `CPT`. The display shows 10.62 percent. This is *COR*, the financing rate at the cross-over point.

Concept quiz

1. True or false: A company should pursue Project L costing $100 that returns $110 in one period and is financed at 10% instead of pursuing Project H that costs $100, returns $115, and is financed at 15%.

2. Discuss how net present value from a capital budgeting project relates to wealth creation and the economic profit shown as the droplet in the cash flow cycle in chapter 1 (figure 1.3).

Numerical quickies

3. Should a company pursue Project L costing $100 that returns $110 in one period and is financed at 10% or Project H that costs $100, returns $116, and is financed at 15%. ©CB20

4. Your company is looking at an investment that today costs $4,600 and returns after-tax cash flow exactly one year, two years, and three years from today, respectively, equal to $2,000; $2,500; and $2,900. The company intends to finance the investment at a rate of 14.2% and to repay the loan (principal and interest) with the investment cash flows as they occur. How much wealth will the investment create? ©CB4

5. The company must invest in either project X or Y. The company knows that X and Y would have identical net present values if the financing rate were 7.5%. The internal rate of return is 14.6% for project X and 20.2% for project Y. What is the likely relation between the company financing rate and ranking of project NPV. ©CB6

Numerical challengers

6. Consider the following cash flows for two mutually exclusive investments:

	t=0	t=1	t=2	t=3
A	($660)	$472	$281	$112
B	($780)	$88	$250	$738

Your boss claims that projects A and B represent exactly the same net present value for your company. You politely point out that, because of differences in cash flow timing, the only way these projects have the same net present value is if your company's actual financing rate equals one specific number. Find that rate. ©CB2b

7. Consider the following cash flows for two mutually exclusive investments:

	t=0	t=1	t=2	t=3
A	($670)	$498	$309	$128
B	($890)	$104	$303	$919

Discuss the project ranking for various financing rates. ©CB2a

8. Consider the following cash flows for two mutually exclusive investments:

	t=0	t=1	t=2	t=3
A	($620)	$457	$280	$115
B	($760)	$88	$255	$768

Under very special circumstances, the two projects offer exactly the same net present value. How much is that net present value? ©CB2c

3. INCREMENTAL CASH FLOW STREAMS

Quite often sound financial decisions require comparison of alternative outcomes. A company trying to decide whether a new machine should replace an old machine, for example, must compare two different cash flow streams: the status quo stream if they do nothing versus the new stream if they pursue replacement. The incremental cash flow equals the change in cash flow resulting from a financial decision.

FORMULA 6.6 Incremental cash flows, general version

$$\Delta CF_t = \text{change in cash flow resulting from a decision}$$
$$= CF_t^{\,new\ situation} - CF_t^{\,old\ situation}$$

Profitability assessments of incremental cash flow streams rely on tools discussed in the previous sections.

EXAMPLE 9 Assess the profitability of refinancing a mortgage

Awhile ago you took out a 30-year mortgage (monthly payments) for $130,000 at 9.25% and payment number 45 was paid this morning. You are deciding whether this afternoon you should refinance the outstanding principal by borrowing at today's lower rate of 6.75% an amount that just pays off the old loan. The new loan is for 30 years as of today. The total fees for getting the new loan equal 3% of the borrowed principal, and you will pay the fees today with funds from your savings account. Find the payback period, the *IRR*, and the *NPV* of the incremental cash flow stream resulting from refinancing the mortgage.

SOLUTION

First find the cash flow stream for the original loan from today forward. Compute the amount of each payment with the original loan from formula 5.6:

$$\$130,000 = (CF)\left\{\frac{1-\left(1+\frac{0.0925}{12}\right)^{-360}}{\frac{0.0925}{12}}\right\}$$

$$CF = \$1,069.48$$

The 45th payment is due this morning. This means that 315 payments remain. The cash flow stream for the status quo, that is if you do *not* refinance, appears like this:

$t=0$	1	2		315
$0	$1,069.48	$1,069.48		$1,069.48

Notice that the payment made this morning is an irrelevant sunk cost and is not on the time line.

Now specify the cash flow stream resulting from refinancing. The amount of the new loan equals the outstanding principal for the old loan. Find the principal outstanding when 315 payments remain from the following formula.

$$PV = \$1,069.48\left\{\frac{1-\left(1+\frac{0.0925}{12}\right)^{-315}}{\frac{0.0925}{12}}\right\}$$

$$= \$126,391.20$$

The fees equal 3% of the outstanding balance, or $3,791.74.

For this problem you choose to pay the fees with funds from your savings account. Some problems in Exercises 6.3 pay the fees by borrowing with the new loan enough to pay off the old loan plus pay the fees. That situation incurs no up-front out-of-pocket costs and doesn't require money in the savings account. That common strategy *amortizes* the fees over the life of the loan. In practice, homeowners also often *capitalize* home equity that may have accrued from inflating house prices by borrowing even more than the original loan's initial balance. They use the money for renovations, vacations, reducing credit card balances, etc.

Compute the payment for the new 30-year loan at 6.75% as follows.

$$\$126,391.20 = (CF) \left\{ \frac{1 - \left(1 + 0.0675 \middle/ 12\right)^{-360}}{0.0675 \middle/ 12} \right\}$$

$$CF = \$819.77$$

The monthly payments for the new loan, $819.77, represent a significant reduction in the monthly mortgage payment. This motivates refinancing. The cash flow stream attached to the new loan includes the fees paid today and 360 monthly payments.

Incremental cash flows are relevant to profitability assessments. Use formula 6.6 to compute incremental cash flows.

for t = 0: $\quad\quad\quad\quad\Delta CF_0 = \$-3,791.74 - 0;$ $\quad\quad\quad = \$-3,791.74$

for t = 1 to 315: $\quad\Delta CF_t = \$-819.77 - (\$-1,069.48);$ $\quad = \$249.71$

for t = 316 to 360: $\quad\Delta CF_t = \$-819.77 - 0;$ $\quad\quad\quad = \$-819.77$

This time line summarizes the incremental cash flow stream for the refinancing decision.

The result of refinancing is an immediate cost of $3,791.74, followed by 315 monthly savings of $249.71, followed by an additional 45 monthly payments of $819.77. Notice that without refinancing there would be no payments in months 316 through 360. Refinancing extends the length of time payments must be made.

The traditional payback period is the length of time required to recover the up-front fees. Divide $3,791.74 by $249.71 to compute the payback period as 15.2 months. The cost is fully recovered when the 16th payment is made. A traditional rule of thumb proclaims that mortgage refinancing is a good idea if the payback period is less than 24 months. According to that rule, refinancing makes sense.

The annual *IRR* for the refinancing decision satisfies this equation:

$$\$3,791.74 = \frac{\$249.71}{(1 + IRR/12)} + \frac{\$249.71}{(1 + IRR/12)^2} + ... + \frac{\$249.71}{(1 + IRR/12)^{315}} + \frac{\$-819.77}{(1 + IRR/12)^{316}}$$

$$+ ... + \frac{\$-819.77}{(1 + IRR/12)^{360}}$$

The *IRR* equals -5.79%. It conveys no meaning, thereby highlighting one of the subtle problems inherent with the *IRR*.

This is a fairly typical and realistic problem. The incremental cash flow stream, however, contains several sign reversals. The initial cash flow is negative, then 315 positive cash flows follow, and 45 negative cash flows conclude the stream. This atypical pattern throws a wrench into the mathematical process and renders the *IRR* rather useless. For this reason *NPV* is always considered a more reliable assessment tool.

Assess the NPV of the preceding incremental cash flow stream with this equation.

$$NPV = \frac{\$249.71}{(1+\frac{APR}{12})^1} + \frac{\$249.71}{(1+\frac{APR}{12})^2} + \ldots + \frac{\$249.71}{(1+\frac{APR}{12})^{315}} + \frac{\$-819.77}{(1+\frac{APR}{12})^{316}}$$

$$+ \ldots + \frac{\$-819.77}{(1+\frac{APR}{12})^{360}} - \$3,791.74$$

The *APR* is the annual percentage rate for computing the present value. The financial calculator easily computes that with *APR* = 6.75% the *NPV* is $27,461 and with *APR* = 9.25% the *NPV* is $22,953. *NPV* is positive for any reasonable discount rate. This refinancing creates substantial personal wealth.

CALCULATOR CLUE

To solve Example 9 on the *BAII Plus©* type `2nd` `FV` to clear the time value memories. Type `2nd` `I/Y` 12 `ENTER` `2nd` `CPT` to enforce monthly compounding. Solve for the payment for the original loan by typing:

130000 `PV` 360 `N` 9.25 `I/Y` `CPT` `PMT`.

The display shows the loan payment is $−1,069.48. While $−1,069.48 is still on the display, hit `STO` `1` to store the original loan payment in memory 1.

Find the principal outstanding when 315 payments remain by typing 315 `N` `CPT` `PV`. The display shows the loan's book value is $126,391.20 . While this number is on the display, compute the fees by typing `x` .03 `=`. The display shows fees equal $3,791.74. Hit `STO` `2` to store the fees in memory 2.

Find the loan payment for the new loan by typing 360 `N` 6.75 `I/Y` `CPT` `PMT`.

The display shows the new loan payment is $−819.77. While $−819.77 is still on the display, hit `STO` `3` to store the new loan payment in memory 3.

Compute the amount of the monthly savings by typing `RCL` `3` `−` `RCL` `1` `=`

The display shows the monthly savings is $249.71. While $249.71 is still on the display, hit `STO` `4` to store the monthly savings in memory 4.

Compute the payback period by typing `RCL` `2` `÷` `RCL` `4` `=`

The display shows the payback period is 15.2 months.

Now enter the incremental cash flow stream in order to find *IRR* and *NPV*. To clear any numbers previously stored in the cash flow memories type `CF` `2nd` `CLR WORK`. Now type:

`RCL` `2` `+/−` `ENTER` `↓` `RCL` `4` `ENTER` `↓` 315 `ENTER` `↓` `RCL` `3` `ENTER` `↓` 45 `ENTER` `IRR` `CPT`

The display shows the monthly *IRR* is a nonsensical −0.45 percent.

Find *NPV* at a 6.75% financing rate by typing

`NPV` 6.75 `÷` 12 `=` `ENTER` `↓` `CPT`.

The display shows the *NPV* is $27,461.

3.A. Choosing the proper stream to analyze

Most business capital budgeting decisions involve standard financial statement analyses. Correct analyses assess profitability by focusing on cash flow instead of net income. Recall discussions from the cash flow section of chapter 3. There are as many different cash flow streams as there are accounts for money to flow into: $CF^{to\ shareholders}$, $CF^{to\ creditors}$, $CF^{from\ assets}$, $CF^{from\ operations}$, and *Cash surplus*. Suppose that for a proposed project a business correctly forecasts all the various cash flow streams. On which stream does the company base profitability assessments? This rule summarizes the answer.

> **RULE 6.4 The relevant cash flow stream for profitability assessments**
>
> Capital budgeting analyses assess the profitability of incremental cash flows from assets.

Cash flow from assets identically equals the cash flow to capitalists (see formula 3.8). Consequently the proper discount rate for computing the present value of $CF^{from\ assets}$ *for a project* the average financing rate that the company is required to pay all capitalists, creditors <u>and</u> shareholders alike. The company *cost of capital* is the discount rate for finding net present value of company investment opportunities and is the focus of lessons in chapter 11. For now, however, manipulate formula 3.10 specifying cash flow from assets and obtain the following formula for incremental cash flow.

> **FORMULA 6.7 Incremental cash flow from assets, precise version**
>
> $\Delta CF^{from\ assets} = (\Delta EBITDA)x(1 - tax\ rate) + (tax\ rate)x(\Delta Depreciation\ deduction)$,
>
> where *EBITDA* equals "earnings before interest, taxes, depreciation and amortization" (that is, sales minus variable costs, which is the same as sales minus cost-of-goods sold minus selling, general, and administrative expenses; see the discussion following formula 3.9.)

Formula 6.7 measures periodic incremental cash flow from assets, $\Delta CF^{from\ assets}$, that results from undertaking a project. First right-hand-side term, $\Delta EBITDA$, represents change before taxes and financing costs of cash revenues minus cash costs. Multiplication of $\Delta EBITDA$ by *(1 – tax rate)* implies that every dollar of *EBITDA* incurs taxes equal to the tax rate. In reality, however, the company claims tax deductions. Every dollar of tax deduction reduces *Taxes due* by an amount equal to the tax rate. For example, consider a simplistic scenario in which $\Delta EBITDA$ is $100, the tax rate is 30%, and depreciation deductions are $25. Substitute into formula 6.7:

$\Delta CF^{from\ assets} = \$100(1 - 0.30) + 0.30(\$25)$,

$= \$100 - \$30 + \$7.50$,

$= \$77.50$.

EBITDA of $100 incurs proportional taxes of $30. In reality, though, the company does not pay $30 in taxes because they claim deductions of $25. The depreciation tax shield reduces the tax bill by $7.50; *Taxes due* equal $22.50 (= $30 – $7.50). Hence, the incremental cash flow for the company is actually $77.50 (= $100 – $22.50). Obtain the same answer of $77.50 by an alternate route, namely subtract *Depreciation* from *EBITDA* to get *EBIT* and then subtract *Taxes due* and add back in the non-cash *Depreciation* deduction (this alternate also appears in formula 3.10):

$\Delta CF\ from\ assets = \Delta EBITx(1-\ tax\ rate) + \Delta Depreciation$

$= (\$100 - \$25)(1 - 0.30) + \$25$,

$= \$77.50$.

The alternative is equivalent to formula 6.7.

Depreciation deductions reduce taxable income and consequently are an important tax shield. Another important tax shield is *Interest expense*. Companies deduct *Interest expense* in order to compute *Taxable income* (see Table 2.4, for example). Right now, however, the lesson properly focuses on the role of depreciation deductions in determining incremental cash flow from assets and ignores the interest tax shield. The NPV profitability assessment procedure removes financing costs by discounting, and division by $(1 + r)^t$ is tantamount to subtraction of financing costs. The NPV procedure accounts for the interest tax shield through the company discount rate, or cost of capital, as chapter 11 discusses.

Recall that the company uses funds on *Capital expenditures* yet the IRS disallows immediate deduction of the entire expenditure for computing that year's *Taxable income*. A million dollars spent on wages is immediately subtracted from *Sales* for computing *Taxable income*, but a million dollars spent on *PP&E* is not. Instead, the government requires that companies spread the deductions over time. After all, the asset provides returns over many time periods. When U.S. corporate income taxes were first collected in 1913 the government required that businesses allocate deductions from *Capital expenditures* along a straight-line pattern over a tax life roughly equal to the asset service life. In 1945 the government completed a major assessment of how long things last: tax lives were set for typewriters, tractors, tools and dies and thousands of other assets based on engineering studies and surveys. In 1954 the government introduced alternatives to straight-line patterns, namely sum-of-years digits and declining-balance schedules. In 1981 a significant simplification to tax depreciation policy occurred when the government severed the direct link between a specific asset-type and its unique tax-life. Instead, a half-dozen "classes" were created, each with its own tax life, and each class encompasses many different types of assets.

Persistent and on-going tinkering of tax depreciation policies by Congress attests to importance of this tax shield to politicians in Washington and to companies everywhere. Actual tax depreciation laws are more complex today than in 1981 because there are more asset classes and more exceptions. Furthermore, sometimes Congress enacts "temporary" policies and therefore tax depreciation schedules may vary from year to year. For purposes of our lessons all problems suppose that tax depreciation deductions compute either from straight-line schedules or from the *Modified Accelerated Cost Recovery System* ("MACRS") in Table 6.1.

Obtain the periodic tax depreciation deduction by multiplying the "basis" times the percentage weight from Table 6.1 (or a straight-line weight of $1/L$, where L is the tax life). The basis represents the amount being depreciated over time. Compute the basis as the asset cost, that is the *Capital expenditure*, plus amounts paid for items such as sales tax, freight charges, and installation and testing fees. The basis does not depend on whether the asset is bought with cash from a checking account or with funds borrowed from debt or equity. The basis, in other words, reflects the use of funds not the source. The example below computes and discounts tax depreciation deductions.

EXAMPLE 10 Contrast MACRS and straight-line discounted tax depreciation deductions

The company is buying, shipping, and installing a lot of computer equipment this year. The company may choose to depreciate the basis along either the 5-year MACRS schedule or with a 5-year straight line schedule (each deduction is 1/5 the basis). Which choice is most advantageous for the company?

SOLUTION

The answer for this problem is very general irrespective of whether the cost is $100 or $100,000 and irrespective of whether the financing rate is 5% or 15% and irrespective of whether the tax rate is 28% or 34%. The most advantageous choice

Examples of asset types in the Recovery class	
3-year	Tractor units for over-the-road use.
5-year	Automobiles, taxis, buses, and trucks. Computers and peripheral equipment. Office machinery such as typewriters, calculators and copiers. Any property used in research and experimentation. Breeding cattle and dairy cattle. Appliances, carpets, furniture, etc., used in a residential real estate rental activity
7-year	Office furniture and fixtures. Agricultural machinery and equipment. Any property that does not have a class life and has not been designated by law as being in any other class.
10-year	Vessels, barges, and tugs. Any single purpose agricultural or horticultural structure Any tree or vine bearing fruits or nuts.
15-year	Certain improvements made directly to land or added to it such as shrubbery, fences, roads, and bridges.
20-year	Farm buildings (other than single purpose agricultural or horticultural structures).
27 1/2-year	Residential rental property.
39-year	Non-residential rental property.

Tax depreciation deduction (%weight) for the Recovery class

year of use	3-year	5-year	7-year	10-year	15-year	20-year
1	33.33	20.00	14.29	10.00	5.00	3.750
2	44.45	32.00	24.49	18.00	9.50	7.219
3	14.81	19.20	17.49	14.40	8.55	6.677
4	7.41	11.52	12.49	11.52	7.70	6.177
5		11.52	8.93	9.22	6.93	5.713
6		5.76	8.92	7.37	6.23	5.285
7			8.93	6.55	5.90	4.888
8			4.46	6.55	5.90	4.522
9				6.56	5.91	4.462
10				6.55	5.90	4.461
11				3.28	5.91	4.462
12					5.90	4.461
13					5.91	4.462
14					5.90	4.461
15					5.91	4.462
16					2.95	4.461
17						4.462
18						4.461
19						4.462
20						4.461
21						2.231

TABLE 6.1
Tax depreciation schedules for the Modified Accelerated Cost Recovery System (MACRS).

Source: Publication 946, U.S. Internal Revenue Service.

offers the highest present value of tax savings; and that is the one with the highest present value of tax depreciation deductions.

Say for simplicity that the basis is $100 and the financing rate is 15%. With the straight-line schedule the deduction equals $20 per year for 5 years (= $100 x 1/5). Find the present value of the straight-line tax depreciation deductions with the constant annuity formula:

$$PV = \$20 \times \left\{ \frac{1 - 1.15^{-5}}{0.15} \right\}$$

$$= \$67.04.$$

The basis of $100 depreciated with a 5-year straight-line schedule provides discounted tax depreciation deductions of $67.04 (that is, 67 cents per dollar of basis). With a 34 percent tax rate the depreciation tax shield provides discounted tax savings of $22.79 (= 0.34 x $67.04; that is, 22.8 cents per dollar of basis).

Compute the 5-year MACRS discounted deductions by using the weights from Table 6.1. The weight during the first year of use is 20% so the deduction is $20. During second year of use the weight is 32% so the deduction is $32; etc. Find the present value of the 5-year MACRS tax depreciation deductions given the 15% discount rate:

$$PV = (\$20 \times 1.15^{-1}) + (\$32 \times 1.15^{-2}) + (\$19.20 \times 1.15^{-3}) + (\$11.52 \times 1.15^{-4}) + (\$11.52 \times 1.15^{-5}) + (\$5.76 \times 1.15^{-6}),$$

$$= \$69.02.$$

The basis of $100 depreciated with a 5-year MACRS class provides discounted tax depreciation deductions of $69.02 (that is, 69 cents per dollar of basis). With a 34 percent tax rate the depreciation tax shield provides discounted tax savings of $23.47 (= 0.34 x $69.02; that is, 23.5 cents per dollar of basis).

Preceding computations show that the 5-year MACRS schedule provides more discounted tax savings than the 5-year straight-line schedule. There is an important *caveat* about this. Actual tax law generally stipulates a "half-year convention" for the first year of use because, on average, usage probably begins halfway through the year. Thus, the depreciation deduction for the first year by straight-line actually is $10 (= $100 x 1/5 x 1/2). Deductions in years 2 through 5 equal $20 each. Then during the sixth year of use the remaining $10 deduction is taken. This diminishes discounted tax savings by straight-line (to $62.67) and makes the *MACRS* choice even better. For simplicity, problems herein ignore the half-life convention when applying straight-line tax depreciation schedules. Table 6.1, of course, already reflects the half-year convention for *MACRS* and weights apply as listed.

Incremental cash flows include exclusively the change induced by this project. Quite often the changes are very complex and often hard to perfectly predict. The next section considers complications. For now, however, consider examples showing a simple scenario in which an asset has one up-front cost, delivers a stream of cash flows shielded from taxes by depreciation deductions, and the asset has zero salvage value at the end of the project life.

EXAMPLE 11 Assess profitability of an expansion project with straight-line, no salvage value

A proposed two-year project has expected sales that begin at $28,000 during the first year and rise 8% during the second year. Start-up costs are $18,000 and variable costs equal 60% of sales. The start-up costs are depreciated to zero by straight-line over a two-year tax life. No salvageable assets remain beyond the project life. The company's tax rate is 39%, and the project's average financing rate is 14%. What are the *IRR* and *NPV* of the project's incremental cash flow stream?

SOLUTION

We are told that $CF_0 = -18,000$. Use formula 6.7 to find the change in cash flows caused by the project during the first and second years. For this story, the cash flows if the project is not undertaken equal zero. Thus, $\Delta CF^{from\ assets}$ simply equals the cash flow that the project generates.

$$\Delta CF_1^{from\ assets} = 28,000 \times (1 - .6) \times (1 - .39) + (.39)(18,000/2) = 10,342$$

$$\Delta CF_2^{from\ assets} = 28,000 \times (1.08) \times (1 - .6) \times (1 - .39) + (.39)(18,000/2) = 10,889$$

Solve for the *IRR* from the following equation:

$$\$18,000 = \$10,342/(1+IRR)^1 + \$10,889/(1+IRR)^2$$

Compute that the IRR is 11.64%. Therefore, the investment is profitable as long as the firm's financing rate is less than 11.64%.

Solve for NPV from the following equation:

$$NPV = \$10,342/(1+.14)^1 + \$10,889/(1+.14)^2 - \$18,000$$

The NPV of the inflows is $\$-550$, confirming that the project destroys wealth at a 14 percent financing rate.

EXAMPLE 12 Assess profitability of cost reductions with $MACRS$, no salvage value

A proposed project is expected to reduce pretax operating costs by \$75,000 per year for 4 years. The project requires incremental expenses of \$200,000. The company is eligible to depreciate the entire expense within the 3-year $MACRS$ class. No salvageable assets remain beyond the project life. The company's tax rate is 34%, and the project's average financing rate is 12%. Find the IRR and NPV of the project's incremental cash flow stream.

SOLUTION

We are told that $CF_0 = \$-200,000$. Use formula 6.7 to find the change in cash flows caused by the project during years 1-to-5. Notice that $\Delta EBITDA$ equals \$75,000 per year and that the MACRS weights are from table 6.1.

$$\Delta CF_1^{from\ assets} = \$75,000 \times (1-.34) + (.34) \times (\$200,000 \times 0.3333)$$

$$= \$49,500 + \$22,664$$

$$= \$72,164.$$

$$\Delta CF_2^{from\ assets} = \$49,500 + (.34) \times (\$200,000 \times 0.4445); = \$79,726$$

$$\Delta CF_3^{from\ assets} = \$49,500 + (.34) \times (\$200,000 \times 0.1481); = \$59,571$$

$$\Delta CF_4^{from\ assets} = \$49,500 + (.34) \times (\$200,000 \times 0.0741); = \$54,539.$$

Solve for the IRR from the following equation:

$$\$200,000 = \$72,164/(1+IRR)^1 + \$79,726/(1+IRR)^2 + \$59,571/(1+IRR)^3$$
$$+ \$54,539/(1+IRR)^4$$

Compute that the IRR is 13.26%. The investment is therefore profitable as long as the firm's financing rate is less than 13.26%.

The problem states that the financing rate is 12%. Solve for NPV:

$$NPV = \$72,164/1.12^1 + \$79,726/1.12^2 + \$59,571/1.12^3 + \$54,539/1.12^4$$
$$- \$200,000$$

The NPV is \$5,051 confirming that the project creates economic profit with a 12 percent financing rate.

3.B. Complications to initial and terminal cash flows

Typically formula 6.7 properly specifies incremental cash flow from assets during the middle periods of the project. Complications often arise, however, during beginning and ending periods.

initial cash flow: CF_0 definitely includes the capital expenditure. Quite often, too, installation and shipping costs associate with the project. Include these additional costs in CF_0. These additional costs also increase the depreciable base on which deductions are computed. Another cost to include in CF_0 is requisite increases in *Net working capital*. Perhaps, for example, a project may require that a company increase the amount of standing inventory, receivables, or payables. Include this one time increase of NWC in CF_0. This cost is not included in the depreciable basis, however.

terminal cash flow: CF_N includes the incremental cash flow from assets that formula 6.7 specifies. Additionally, however, this cash flow in the last period includes the after-tax liquidation value of any assets. Also include funds released due to declines in *Net working capital* occurring at the conclusion of the project.
The following example uses the preceding principles.

EXAMPLE 13 Assess profitability of an expansion project with salvage value and working capital requirements

The Company is considering a short-term expansion into a new product line making commemorative plates for the Olympics which are scheduled to occur 4-years henceforward. The following factors weigh in the decision:

a. the plate presser costs $32,000 and may be depreciated for tax purposes along a 7-year MACRS class (weights equal 14.29%, 24.49%, 17.49%, 12.49%, 8.93%, 8.92%, 8.93%, and 4.46%)
b. installation and shipping cost $4,000
c. the project requires an increase in *Net working capital* of $3,000
d. product development and market study fees of $6,000 were spent developing the plan
e. commemorative plates sell for $30 each and variable costs are $16 per plate
f. projected sales over the next 4 years are 500 plates, 800 plates, 1000 plates, and 2000 plates (thereafter sales would be zero).
g. the plate presser loses half its market value for each year of use; it will be sold after the 4th year
h. the financing rate is 14% and the tax rate is 34%

What are the *IRR* and *NPV* of the project's incremental cash flow stream?

SOLUTION

Initial cash flow for this project equals the capital expenditure plus installation and shipping costs plus the increase in *Net working capital*. Notice the market study fees are an irrelevant sunk cost and do not contribute to the initial cash flow.

$$CF_0 = -(\$32,000 + 4,000 + 3,000) ; = \$-39,000$$

Computing cash flow from assets during subsequent periods requires specification of depreciation deductions. The depreciation deduction equals the MACRS weight times the depreciable basis. The weights are given in the problem set-up. The depreciable basis is given below.

depreciable basis = capital expenditure + shipping and installation costs

$$= \$32,000 + 4,000$$

$$= \$36,000$$

The table summarizes components of the cash flow from assets

period	MACRS weight	depreciation deduction	sales – variable costs
1	0.1429	$5,143	$7,000
2	0.2449	8,816	11,200
3	0.1749	6,297	14,000
4	0.1249	4,498	28,000

Application of formula 6.7 to the preceding numbers yields the following.

$$\Delta CF_1^{from\ assets} = 7,000 \times (1 - .34) + (.34)(5,143) = \$6,369$$

$$\Delta CF_2^{from\ assets} = 11,200 \times (1 - .34) + (.34)(8,816) = \$10,389$$

$$\Delta CF_3^{from\ assets} = 14,000 \times (1 - .34) + (.34)(6,297) = \$11,381$$

$$\Delta CF_4^{from\ assets} = 28,000 \times (1 - .34) + (.34)(4,498) = \$20,009$$

Adjust the cash flow during year 4 to reflect the release of *Net working capital* ($3,000) and the after-tax proceeds from selling the plate press. To find the latter, compute first the selling price of the asset. Because its market value declines by half each year,

$$selling\ price = (1/2)*(\$32,000)*(1/2)*(1/2)*(1/2)$$

$$= \$2,000$$

The net proceeds to the company of the asset sale take into account tax effects that occur when an asset is sold:

net proceeds from sale = selling price – recapture taxes

Recapture taxes are computed as:

recapture taxes = tax rate × (selling price – Remaining Book Value),

where

Remaining Book Value = original basis – accumulated deductions

Notice that if the selling price equals the Remaining Book Value then recapture taxes equal zero. Alternatively, the company must pay extra taxes if the asset is sold for more than its book value. The company receives tax relief if the asset is sold for less than its book value. Compute the asset's remaining book value after the 4th deduction has been taken as follows:

Remaining Book Value = $36,000 – ($5,143 + $8,816 + $6,297 + $4,498)

$$= \$11,246$$

(NOTE: The *BAII Plus* automatically computes Remaining Book Value. After finding the 4th depreciation deduction as described in the preceding Calculator Clue, hit the down arrow to see the value for RBV is $11,246). Compute recapture taxes as:

$$recapture\ taxes = 0.34 \times (\$2,000 - \$11,246),$$

$$= \$-3,143$$

This represents tax relief. The company sells the asset for less than its book value, and this capital loss saves them $3,143 in taxes. Finally, find the net proceeds from the sale:

$$net\ proceeds\ from\ sale = \$2,000 - (\$-3,143)$$

$$= \$5,143$$

Compute the terminal cash flow during the fourth year as follows.

$$\Delta CF_4 = \$20,009 + \$3,000 + \$5,143$$

$$= \$28,152$$

The three terms represent the cash flow from assets, the release of net working capital, and the net proceeds from the sale of the asset.

The following time line summarizes the project's incremental cash flow stream.

0	1	2	3	4
-39,000	+6,369	+10,389	+11,381	+28,152

The *IRR* for the preceding stream equals 12.9 percent and satisfies this equation.

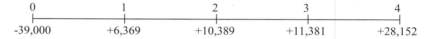

$$\$39,000 = \frac{\$6,369}{(1+IRR)^1} + \frac{\$10,389}{(1+IRR)^2} + \frac{\$11,381}{(1+IRR)^3} + \frac{\$28,152}{(1+IRR)^4}.$$

Compute from this equation that *NPV* with a 14 percent financing rate equals $-1,069.

$$NPV = \frac{\$6,369}{(1.14)^1} + \frac{\$10,389}{(1.14)^{2\ 3}} + \frac{\$11,381}{(1.14)} + \frac{\$28,152}{(1.14)^4} - \$39,000.$$

EXERCISES 6.3

Concept quiz

1. Suppose a company plans to make a zero net present value investment in a real capital asset. Unexpectedly the federal government announces adoption of a new tax policy that, instead of spreading depreciation deductions over a lengthy tax life, instead allows an immediate deduction for the entire capital expenditure. Discuss likely effects of the policy change on the optimal company plan for capital expenditures.

Numerical quickies

2. The company has *Capital expenditure* of $40,000 that is being depreciated along the 3-year MACRS class (weights = 33.33%, 44.45%, and 14.81%, and 7.41%). They face a 30% tax rate and 9.5% financing rate. Compute the present value of tax savings resulting from the depreciation deductions for this *Capital expenditure*. ©CB23

3. Companies X and Y both spend $100,000 on heavy equipment. They each face a 35% tax rate and 12% financing rate. Company X elects to take straight-line tax depreciation deductions over the next 4 years. Company Y elects to use the 3-year MACRS class for tax taking depreciation deductions (weights = 33.33%, 44.45%, and 14.81%, and 7.41%). Compute for each company the present value of tax savings resulting from the deductions. ©CB21

4. Two years ago the company had *Capital expenditure* of $32,000 that it is depreciating along the 3-year MACRS class (weights = 33.33%, 44.45%, and 14.81%, and 7.41%). The company has just taken their second annual deduction. They today are selling the asset for $5,300. Find the net proceeds from the sale given that they face a 35% tax rate and otherwise have substantial taxable income. ©CB24

Numerical challengers

5. The company invests $70,000 in an asset that should increase pre-tax revenue by $15,400 per year perpetually. The asset is depreciated for tax purposes by straight-line over 5 years. If the company faces a 30% tax rate and 13.9% financing rate, what is the investment's Net Present Value? ©CB13

6. Your company is analyzing purchase of a machine costing $4,000 today. The investment promises to add $10,000 to sales one year from today, $12,500 two years from today, and $14,500 three years from today. Incremental cash costs should consume 80% of the incremental sales. The tax rate is 30% and the company's financing rate is 12.9%. The investment cost is depreciated to zero over a 3-year straight-line schedule. Find the project's net present value and internal rate of return. ©CB10a

7. A proposed project is expected to reduce pretax operating costs by $63,000 per year for 4 years. The project requires incremental expenses of $137,900. The company is eligible to depreciate the entire expense within the 3-year *MACRS* class (weights = 33.33%, 44.45%, and 14.81%, and 7.41%). No salvageable assets remain beyond the project life. The company's tax rate is 35%, and the project's average financing rate is 9.7%. Find the *IRR* and *NPV* of the project's incremental cash flow stream. ©CB25b

8. The Company is considering a short-term expansion into a new product line making commemorative plates for the Olympics which are scheduled to occur 4-years henceforward. From the following factors that may weigh in the decision, find the net present value and internal rate of return for the project. ©CB22a
   a. the plate presser costs $140,600 and may be depreciated for tax purposes along a 7-year MACRS class (weights equal 14.29%, 24.49%, 17.49%, 12.49%, 8.93%, 8.92%, 8.93%, and 4.46%)
   b. installation and shipping costs equal $3,800
   c. the project requires an increase in *Net working capital* of $5,600
   d. product development and market study fees of $4,100 already have been spent developing the plan
   e. commemorative plates sell for $20.40 each and variable costs are $16.50 per plate
   f. projected sales over the next 4 years are 6,000 plates, 9,000 plates, 13,000 plates, and 18,000 plates (thereafter sales would be zero).
   g. the plate presser loses half its market value for each year of use; it will be sold after the 4th year
   h. the financing rate is 14.4% and the tax rate is 30%

9. You took out a 30-year mortgage (monthly payments) for $275,000 at 8.0% and payment number 77 is due today. You are deciding whether you should refinance the outstanding principal by borrowing at today's lower rate of 6.25% an amount that just pays off the old loan. The new loan is for 20 years as of today. The total fees for getting the new loan equal 2.8% of the borrowed principal, and you will pay the fees with money in your savings account.

9a. What is the payback period for recovering the cost of the fees? ©CB3em

9b. How much would you save in interest expense over the life of the loan? ©CB3dm

9c. What is the net present value of the refinancing venture if your "personal discount rate" is 9%. ©CB3cm

9d. Find the internal rate of return for the financing venture.

10. You took out a 20-year mortgage (monthly payments) for $125,000 at 7.25% and payment number 55 is due today. You are deciding whether you should refinance the outstanding principal by borrowing at today's lower rate of 5.75% an amount that pays off the old loan. The new loan is for 20 years as of today. The total fees for getting the new loan equal 2.3% of the borrowed principal, and you will amortize the fees over the life of the new loan.

10a. What is the payback period for recovering the cost of the fees?

10b. How much would you save in interest expense over the life of the loan? ©CB3bm

10c. What is the net present value of the refinancing venture if your "personal discount rate" is 12%. ©CB3am

10d. Find the internal rate of return for the financing venture.

ANSWERS TO CHAPTER 6 EXERCISES

EXERCISES 6.1

1. First understand exactly what constitutes a capital budgeting decision: find the best real asset-increasing use for money. There is a rich academic literature attesting to the complexity of the theory of capital investment. Several factors that complicate capital budgeting decisions are discussed below.

(1) Cash flow estimates usually are imprecise. Later lessons in this book teach that when a range of possible outcomes exist then statistical ideas of risk and uncertainty become relevant. Imagine, for example, a situation in which a capital investment most likely returns net cash flow in one year of $10,000 but, of course, there is no guarantee. Other possible outcomes may be that it loses $1,000 or gains $15,000. Assessment measures of profitability that this section introduces do not fully accommodate a range of uncertain outcomes. That's one place where intuition of the decision-maker may make a difference.

(2) The relevant financing rate often is difficult to identify. Later lessons in this book teach that financing rates are dynamic. That is, a financing rate generally depends on the use to which the money is put. Maybe a company or household can borrow at 6% for one purpose, but for other purposes the rate may differ. Obviously this complicates application of the IRR and NPV decision rules because they require knowledge of the relevant financing rate. Decision-maker intuition once again may make a difference.

(3) Changing circumstances require flexibility, yet making a capital budgeting commitment in one direction may inhibit subsequent flexibility. For example, a later lesson in this chapter explains that refinancing a mortgage from a high interest rate, say 10%, down to a lower rate, say 7%, saves the borrower money. Yet refinancing is costly. Surely dropping a rate from 10% to 7% is worth the cost. But once the move to 7% has been made then the advantage of subsequent moves diminishes. That is, if one refinances at 7% and rates subsequently bottom at 6% then it's unlikely refinancing from 7% to 6% is profitable. It may have been better for the decision-maker to not refinance at 7% but rather to wait until 6% (but that was an uncertain outcome). Making a capital budgeting decision today typically opens some subsequent real options while closing others. Later lessons in this book teach that options are valuable. Once again, intuition of the decision-maker potentially makes a difference!

2. The payback period equals the length of time required to recover $20,000. That is 3.6 years (= $20,000 ÷ $5,500).

3. Discounted revenue for the first year is $5,231 (= $6,000 × 1.147^{-1}). The second year contributes discounted cash flow of $4,561 (= $6,000 × 1.147^{-2}) and brings the cumulative total to $9,792 (= $5,231 + $4,561). Continue and find that discounted cash flows for the first six years sums to $22,891. The discounted payback period is a tad longer than 6 years. An easy way to find this answer is with the time value functions on the financial calculator. Set $PV = -23000$; $PMT = 6000$; $I/Y = 14.7$ ($P/Y = 1$), and compute that $N = 6.02$.

4. The first 12 months pay back $10,800 (= $900 × 12) of the $22,000 cost, implying payback period exceeds one year. The cost remaining to be recovered beyond one year is $11,200 (= $22,000 – $10,800). The second year contributes $9,600 (= $800 × 12), meaning that cost of $1,600 (= $11,200 – $9,600) still remains to be recovered. The number of months in the third year required for recovering $1,600 is 2.3 months (= $1,600 ÷ $700). The payback period is 26.3 months (= 2 × 12 + 2.3), or 27 months if cash flow occurs as an end-of-month lump-sum.

5. Use perpetuity formula 5.3 to find the present value of $4,500 per year forever: $PV = \$3,500 \div 0.147$; or PV equals $23,810. Likewise, use the perpetuity formula to solve for the discount rate that equates discounted cash flows to cost: $r = \$3,500 \div \$20,000$; or r equals 17.5%. Note that *NPV>0* and *IRR>financing rate* so the rules say that this project creates wealth.

6. The annual IRR satisfies formula 6.2:
$$\$16,800 = \$1,900 \times \{(1+IRR)^{-1} + \ldots + (1+IRR)^{-4}\} + \$2,200 \times \{(1+IRR)^{-5} + \ldots + (1+IRR)^{-12}\}$$
Use the financial calculator to find that the IRR is 6.63%.

7. The NPV is found with formula 6.4:
$$NPV = \$1,800 \times \{1.074^{-1} + \ldots + 1.074^{-5}\} + \$2,700 \times \{1.074^{-6} + \ldots + 1.074^{-9}\} - \$14,300.$$
The NPV equals $-656. It's not economically profitable.

8. The IRR is found with formula 6.2:
$$\$11,900 = \$170 \times \{(1+IRR/12)^{-1} + \ldots + (1+IRR/12)^{-36}\} + \$280 \times \{(1+IRR/12)^{-37} + \ldots + (1+IRR/12)^{-72}\}$$
Use the financial calculator to find that the monthly periodic rate is 0.79%. The periodic rate equals *IRR/12*. Therefore, the annual IRR is 9.47% (= 0.79% × 12). The IRR decision rule says that when the IRR is less than the financing rate (9.47% < 10% for this problem) then the project incurs economic losses – this is a bad deal!

9. The monthly periodic rate r is 0.91% (= 10.9% ÷ 12). The NPV is found with formula 6.4:
$$NPV = \$160 \times \{1.0091^{-1} + \ldots + 1.0091^{-36}\} + \$270 \times \{1.0091^{-37} + \ldots + 1.0091^{-84}\} - \$11,200.$$
The NPV equals $1,253. It creates wealth. The IRR is found with formula 6.2:
$$\$11,200 = \$160 \times \{(1+IRR/12)^{-1} + \ldots + (1+IRR/12)^{-36}\} + \$270 \times \{(1+IRR/12)^{-37} + \ldots + (1+IRR/12)^{-84}\}$$
Use the financial calculator to find that the annual IRR is 14.0% (= 1.16% × 12).

10. The monthly periodic rate r is 0.87% (= 10.4% ÷ 12) and the number of payments N is 300 (= 25 × 12). First find the payment by using formula 5.6: $168,000 = PMT \times [(1 - 1.0087^{-300}) \div 0.0087]$; or PMT equals $1,574.24. Now find that the number of months required for the bank to collect $168,000 is 106.7 months (= $168,000 ÷ $1,574.24). The payback period equals 107 months (about 9 years).

11. Use the *CF* worksheet on the financial calculator to solve this problem. Set *CF0* = 0 and *CF01* = 1100 and *F01* = 12. Hit *NPV* and set $I = 1.275\%$

(=15.3 ÷ 12). Compute that *NPV* equals $12,168. Total discounted cash flow for the first year sums to $12,168 and has not yet recovered the cost. Hit *CF* (don't clear existing entries) and scroll down to set *CF02* = 1300 and *F02* = 12. Hit *NPV* (keep *I* = 1.275%) and compute that *NPV* equals $24,520. The discounted payback period is longer than 2 years. The discounted cost that remains to be recovered during the third year is $3,480 (= $28,000 – $24,520). Find the number of months into the third year required for recovering this amount as follows. An easy way to find the remaining months is with the time value functions on the financial calculator. Set *PV* = -3480; *PMT* = 1000; *I/Y* = 15.3 (*P/Y* = 1), and compute that *N* = 5.4. The discounted payback period equals 29.4 months (= 24 + 5.4).

12. The monthly periodic rate *r* is 0.87% (= 10.4% ÷ 12) and the number of payments *N* is 180 (= 15 × 12). First find the payment by using formula 5.6: $148,000 = *PMT* × [(1 – 1.0087^{-180}) ÷ 0.0087]; or *PMT* equals $1,627. Now find the present value of the outstanding payments when discounted with a monthly periodic rate of 0.96% (= 11.5% ÷ 12) and 106 payments remain (= 180 – 74): *PV* = $1,627 × [(1 – 1.0096^{-106}) ÷ 0.0096]; or *PV* equals $107,989. Now find the annual *IRR* for a project that costs $148,000 and returns $1,627 for 74 months and, upon receiving the last monthly cash flow, also returns a balloon payment of $107,989. Use formula 6.2:

$$148{,}000 = \$1{,}627 \times \{(1+IRR/12)^{-1} + \ldots + (1+IRR/12)^{-74}\} + \$107{,}989 \times (1+IRR/12)^{-74}\}$$

Find with the financial calculator that the annual *IRR* equals 10.0% (or 0.83% monthly).

EXERCISES 6.2

1. The net present values of L (= $110/1.10^1 – $100) and H (= $115/1.15^1 – $100) are equal at zero. Hence, the capitalized values of economic profit equal zero for both projects. Rule 1.1 states that the goal of the company is to pursue policies that maximize capitalized value of wealth creation so projects L and H are equivalent, neither is better, and the statement is false. There are, however, two important underlying issues that merit mention.
(1) Later lessons teach that market equilibrium drives net present values to zero in both real asset and financial markets. Hence, for projects L and H to attract different financing rates yet still offer zero NPV means that something else about these projects differ. That difference, as later lessons explain, is risk. In an equilibrium setting the problem setup implies that high-returning project H has higher risk than low-returning project Z.
(2) The future values of incremental wealth differ. Project H returns $15 to capitalists whereas L returns only $10. In an equilibrium setting they both offer zero NPV to the company; they both offer zero NPV to capitalists providing financing. One project is not better than the other and company as well as capitalist are indifferent between L and H. Still, however, future values differ because more wealth accumulates for capitalists at 15% than at 10%; and capitalists include shareholders as well as creditors.

2. Net present value is identical to economic profit. The existence of positive net present value attracts entrepreneurial activity. At equilibrium economic profit and net present value equal zero. Occurrence of zero net present value does not mean that wealth creation equals zero. Companies capture transformation value even though economic profits may equal zero. Thus, economic equilibrium does not imply absence of wealth creation. To the contrary, consider a case in which the monetary inflation rate is zero, the nominal financing rate is 4%, and a company

makes a zero net present value investment. The project generates sufficient revenues that pay for economic costs of production. The company pays the capitalist a 4% real rate, thereby increasing the capitalist's real wealth. A zero net present value investment creates transformation value that in actuality is shared by all stakeholders and all capitalists in accordance with their respective bargaining position under shadow of principal-agent relations.

3. The net present values of L (= $110/1.10^1 - 100) and H (= $116/1.15^1 - 100) are $0, and $1, respectively. Hence, the capitalized value of created wealth is greater for Project H. Rule 1.1 states that the goal of the company is to pursue policies that maximize capitalized value of wealth creation so project H is better.

4. NPV is found with formula 6.4:
$$NPV = \$2{,}000 \times 1.142^{-1} + \$2{,}500 \times 1.142^{-2} + \$2{,}900 \times 1.142^{-3} - \$4{,}600.$$
The NPV equals $1,015. The project creates wealth. The company could capitalize the wealth by borrowing $5,615 (= $4,600 + $1,015). Instead, however, the problem states the company only borrows $4,600 and pays as it goes. The future value of the wealth remaining for the company after the third cash flow and financing payment equals the future value of NPV. Use the lump-sum relation to find that the future value of $1,015 at 14.2% for 3 years is $1,512 (= $1,015 \times 1.142^3$).

5. The problem states that the cross-over rate equals 7.5% and that $IRR_Y > IRR_X$. Sketch this onto an NPV Profile and see that $NPV_Y > NPV_X$ when the financing rate exceeds 7.5%. Most likely for a financing rate less than 7.5% then $NPV_Y < NPV_X$.

6. Apply formula 6.5 and subtract cash flows A from B. Then use the financial calculator to solve for the COR from:
$$\$120 = \${-}384 \times (1+COR)^{-1} + \${-}31 \times (1+COR)^{-2} + \$626 \times (1+COR)^{-3}.$$
The cross-over rate is 7.49%. At that rate the NPVs are equal.

7. Sketch the NPV profile for each project by finding the two intercepts for each project. That is, use the financial calculator to solve for the IRR from:
$$\$670 = \$498 \times (1+IRR)^{-1} + \$309 \times (1+IRR)^{-2} + \$128 \times (1+IRR)^{-3}.$$
The IRR for A is 24.0%. That's the horizontal intercept for project A. Its vertical intercept equals its NPV given a discount rate of zero. That NPV is:
$$NPV_{@r=0\%} = \$498 + \$309 + \$128 - \$670; = \$265.$$
Do analogous computations for B and find that its IRR equals 16.7% and its NPV at 0% financing rate is $436. The profiles cross. Use formula 6.5 to find the cross-over rate:
$$\$220 = \${-}394 \times (1+COR)^{-1} + \${-}6 \times (1+COR)^{-2} + \$791 \times (1+COR)^{-3}.$$
The cross-over rate is 10.9%. Answer the question as follows:
$NPV_A < NPV_B$ when r < 10.9%.
$NPV_A > NPV_B$ when r > 10.9%.
Note that NPV_B goes negative when r exceeds 16.7% and NPV_A goes negative when r exceeds 24.0%.

8. Apply formula 6.5 and subtract cash flows A from B. Then use the financial calculator to solve for the COR from:
$$\$140 = \${-}339 \times (1+COR)^{-1} + \${-}25 \times (1+COR)^{-2} + \$653 \times (1+COR)^{-3}.$$
The cross-over rate is 9.45%. At that rate the NPVs are equal. Find the NPV of either project with formula 6.4 at 9.45%:
$$NPV = \$457 \times 1.0945^{-1} + \$280 \times 1.0945^{-2} + \$115 \times 1.0945^{-3} - \$620.$$
The NPV equals $119.

EXERCISES 6.3

1. Before the policy change the investment had zero net present value. Say it cost a million dollars. Before the policy change the company was splitting the million dollars of tax depreciation deductions across several years in accordance with the asset's tax depreciation schedule. Then the government declared that the company could take the entire one million dollar

deduction immediately. The present value of the deductions to the company definitely increases; discounted tax savings increase, too. This fiscal stimulus by the government (at least in the short-run) transforms the zero NPV project into a positive NPV project (and probably some projects that were negative NPV now become positive NPV). The policy change creates economic profit, a so-called windfall, and probably stimulates capital investment. In the absence of any response by capitalists and stakeholders then surely the windfall accrues to equity. The capital goods supplier, however, sees the droplet forming (see figure 1.3) and competes for his share, too, perhaps by raising the price of the capital asset.

2. The deductions equal the weight times the *Capital expenditure*. The tax savings equals the tax rate times the deduction. Find the present value of tax savings resulting from the depreciation deductions from this:
$$PV = 0.30 \times \$40,000 \times \{0.3333 \times 1.095^{-1} + 0.4445 \times 1.095^{-2} + 0.1481 \times 1.095^{-3} + 0.0741 \times 1.095^{-4}\},$$
which equals $10,073.

3. Each dollar of tax deductions reduces taxable income by $1 and saves the company 35 cents of taxes (the tax rate times $1). For company X the deduction is $25,000 per year for 4 years. The discounted tax savings equal
$$PV = 0.35 \times \$25,000 \times \{1.12^{-1} + 1.12^{-2} + 1.12^{-3} + 1.12^{-4}\},$$
which is $26,577. For company Y the deduction equals $100,000 times the MACRS weight.
The discounted tax savings equal
$$PV = 0.35 \times \$100,000 \times \{0.3333 \times 1.12^{-1} + 0.4445 \times 1.12^{-2} + 0.1481 \times 1.12^{-3} + 0.0741 \times 1.12^{-4}\},$$
which is $28,155. The discounted tax savings are bigger for company Y so they are better off than company X. Whenever a company *accelerates* tax depreciation deductions by taking them sooner rather than later, the company is better off.

4. The net proceeds from the sale equal the sale price of $5,300 adjusted for any recapture taxes or credits associating with the sale. Computing recapture taxes requires finding the remaining book value for the asset, which in turn equals the deductions that have not yet been taken:
remaining book value $= \$32,000 \times (0.1481 + 0.0741); = \$7,114.$
They sell the asset for less than its book value so effectively the company may claim a capital loss. Every dollar of loss saves 35 cents of taxes. The net proceeds from the sale equal:
net proceeds from the sale $= \$5,300 + 0.35 \times (7,114 - \$5,300); = \$5,935.$

5. The deduction each year for 5 years is $14,000 (= $70,000 ÷ 5). The depreciation tax savings therefore equals $4,200 each year (= $14,000 × 0.34). The incremental cash flow for the first 5 years is the same as in year 1:
$$\Delta CF_1 = [\$15,400 \times (1 - 0.30)] + [0.30 \times \$70,000 \div 5],$$
$$= [\$10,780] + [\$4,200]$$
$$= \$22,008.$$
From year 6 and thereafter the incremental cash flow each year is $10,780 because the depreciation tax shield will have expired. Find the NPV with a 13.9% financing rate as:
$$NPV = \$14,980 \times \{1.139^{-1} + \ldots + 1.139^{-5}\} + \{\$10,780 \times 1.139^{-5} \div 0.139\} - \$70,000.$$
NPV is $22,008. Note the same answer is found by finding the perpetuity value of $10,780 and then adding back in the annuity value of the depreciation tax savings:
$$NPV = \$10,780 \div 0.139 + \$4,200 \times \{1.139^{-1} + \ldots + 1.139^{-5}\} - \$70,000$$
$$= \$22,008.$$

6. The implication is that in one year *Sales* of $10,000 minus cash costs of $8,000 equals *EBITDA* of $2,000. The company would pay 30%, or $600, in proportional taxes except that a depreciation deduction of $1,333 (= $4,000 ÷ 3) provides tax savings of $400 (= $1,333 × 0.30).

The company therefore actually pays taxes of only $200. Subtracting $200 from *Sales* minus cash costs leaves the company with incremental cash flow of $1,800. Quickly get the same number by applying formula 6.7:

$$\Delta CF_1 = [\$10,000 \times (1 - 0.80) \times (1 - 0.30)] + [0.30 \times \$4,000 \div 3],$$
$$= [\$10,000 \times 0.14] + [\$400]$$
$$= \$1,800.$$

Note that for cash flows 2 and 3 you can quickly compute:

$$\Delta CF_2 = [\$12,500 \times 0.14] + [\$400]$$
$$= \$2,150$$
$$\text{and} \ \ \Delta CF_3 = [\$14,500 \times 0.14] + [\$400]$$
$$= \$2,430$$

The annual IRR satisfies formula 6.2:

$$\$4,000 = \$1,800 \times (1+IRR)^{-1} + \$2,150 \times (1+IRR)^{-2} + \$2,430 \times (1+IRR)^{-3}$$

Use the financial calculator to find that the IRR is 26.0%. The NPV is found with formula 6.4 and a financing rate of 12.9%:

$$NPV = \$1,800 \times 1.129^{-1} + \$2,150 \times 1.129^{-2} + \$2,430 \times 1.129^{-3} - \$4,000.$$

The NPV equals $970. It's economically profitable.

7. Initial cash flow at time 0 equals the asset cost of $137,900. Find $CF^{from\ assets}$ for years 1 through 4 as follows:

$$CF_1 = \$63,000 \times (1 - 0.35) + 0.35 \times \$137,900 \times 0.3333;$$
$$= \$40,950 + \$48,265 \times 0.3333;$$
$$= \$57,037.$$
$$CF_2 = \$40,950 + \$48,265 \times 0.4445; = \$62,404.$$
$$CF_3 = \$40,950 + \$48,265 \times 0.1481; = \$48,098.$$
$$CF_4 = \$40,950 + \$48,265 \times 0.0741; = \$44,526.$$

The IRR satisfies:

$$\$137,900 = \$57,037 \times (1+IRR)^{-1} + \$62,404 \times (1+IRR)^{-2} + \$48,098 \times (1+IRR)^{-3} + \$44,526 \times (1+IRR)^{-4},$$

The *IRR* of 20.0% exceeds the 9.7% average financing rate. Find NPV as:

$$NPV = \$57,037 \times 1.097^{-1} + \$62,404 \times 1.097^{-2} + \$48,098 \times 1.097^{-3} + \$44,526 \times 1.097^{-4} - \$137,900;$$

or *NPV* equals $33,129. The project creates economic profit and is good.

8. Initial cash flow at time 0 equals the asset cost of $140,600 plus installation and shipping costs of $3,800 plus *Net working capital* of $5,600. That sum of $150,000 is a cash outflow. Note that the basis for tax depreciation deductions of $144,400 equals the asset cost of $140,600 plus installation and shipping costs of $3,800. Each plate generates *EBITDA* of $3.90 (= $20.40 − $16.50). Total *EBITDA* equals $3.90 times number of plates sold. Apply formula 6.7 for cash flows 1 to 3:

$$CF_1 = \$3.90 \times 6,000 \times (1 - 0.30) + 0.30 \times 0.1429 \times \$144,400; = \$22,570.$$
$$CF_2 = \$3.90 \times 9,000 \times (1 - 0.30) + 0.30 \times 0.2449 \times \$144,400; = \$35,179.$$
$$CF_3 = \$3.90 \times 13,000 \times (1 - 0.30) + 0.30 \times 0.1749 \times \$144,400; = \$43,067.$$

Cash flow 4 adjusts for release of *Net working capital* and *Net proceeds from sale*:

$$CF_4 = \$3.90 \times 18,000 \times (1 - 0.30) + 0.30 \times 0.1249 \times \$144,400 + \$5,600 + Net\ proceeds\ from\ sale;$$
$$= \$60,151 + Net\ proceeds\ from\ sale.$$

The *Net proceeds from sale* equal the sale price of $17,575 (=$140,600 × 1/2 × 1/2 × 1/2) adjusted for recapture taxes or credits associating with the sale. Computing recapture taxes requires finding the remaining book value for the asset, which in turn equals the deductions that have not yet been taken:

Remaining book value = $144,400 × (0.0893 + 0.0892 + 0.0893 + 0.0445); = $45,111.

They sell the asset for less than its book value so the company pays recapture taxes on the capital gain. Thus:

Net proceeds from the sale = $17,575 + 0.30 × (45,111 − $17,575);
= $25,836.

and

$CF_4 = \$60{,}151 + \$25{,}836; = \$85{,}986.$

Now find NPV:

$NPV = \$22{,}570 \times 1.144^{-1} + \$35{,}179 \times 1.144^{-2} + \$43{,}067 \times 1.144^{-3} + \$85{,}986 \times 1.144^{-4} - \$150{,}000.$

NPV equals $-24,423 and indicates this project is NOT profitable.
The IRR is:

$\$150{,}000 = \$22{,}570 \times (1+IRR)^{-1} + \$35{,}179 \times (1+IRR)^{-2} + \$43{,}067 \times (1+IRR)^{-3} + \$85{,}986 \times (1+IRR)^{-4},$

or IRR equals 7.6% and is less than the financing rate.

9a. First find the payment on the original loan given the monthly periodic rate of 0.67% (= 8% ÷ 12) and term of 360 months:

$\$275{,}000 = PMT \times \{ [1 - (1.0067)^{-360}] \div 0.0067 \}.$

Find that PMT = $2,018. If you sent in 77 payments then there remain 283 payments (= 360 – 77). Solve for principal outstanding PV in this equation.

$PV = \$2{,}018 \times \{ [1 - (1.0067)^{-283}] \div 0.0067 \}.$

Find that PV= $256,511. That's the original loan's outstanding principal. The fees for the new loan equal $7,182 (= $256,511 × 0.028) and are paid from your savings account. The new loan exactly pays off the original loan and, with a term of 240 months (= 20 × 12) and monthly periodic rate of 0.52% (= 6.25% ÷ 12), satisfies this:

$\$256{,}511 = PMT \times \{ [1 - (1.0052)^{-240}] \div 0.0052 \}.$

or PMT = $1,875. The monthly payment declines to $1,875 from $2,018 and represents monthly savings of $143. It takes 51 months to recover the fees (= $7,182 ÷ $143), that's the payback period (about 4 1/4 years).

9b. Use results from the preceding part and find that the original loan's outstanding principal equals $256,511 and the payment is $2,018. If you send in an additional 283 payments of $2,018 each that represents total expenditure of $571,052 (= 283 × $2,018) and total interest of $314,541 (=$571,052 - $256,511).

For the new loan the original principal equals $256,511 and the payment is $1,875. Submitting 240 payments of $1,875 each represents total expenditure of $449,979 (=240 × $1,875) and total interest of $193,467 (=$449,979 - $256,511).

The refinancing saves you $121,074 of interest over the life of the loan (= $314,541 - $193,467). That's a lot, but comparing dollars across different time periods requires accounting for time value effects. You really should be evaluating with NPV!

9c. Use results from the preceding parts and find that the incremental cash flow equals $7,182 at time 0 because you pay fees up front from your savings account. Then for 240 months the incremental cash flow for you is $143 (= $-1,875 – $-2,018) because your payments are lower if you refinance. Then for the 43 months (= 283 – 240) after that your incremental cash flow equals $2,018 because you'll be making zero payments for the new loan but would still be paying off the old loan; you are saving money during these months if you refinance. The NPV for you with a periodic rate of 0.75% (= 9% ÷ 12) satisfies this formula:

$NPV = \$143 \times \{ [1 - (1.0075)^{-240}] \div 0.0075 \} + \$2{,}018 \times (1.0075)^{-240} \times \{ [1 - (1.0075)^{-43}] \div 0.0075 \} - \$7{,}182$

which is $21,008. This creates wealth for you. Note that using the monthly market interest rate of 0.52% (= 6.25% ÷ 12) for discounting shows NPV is $34,667. Wealth creation either way is substantial.

9d. The annual IRR for you satisfies this formula:

$\$7{,}182 = \$143 \times \{(1+IRR/12)^{-1} + \ldots + (1+IRR/12)^{-240}\} + \$2{,}018 \times \{(1+IRR/12)^{-241} + \ldots + (1+IRR/12)^{-283}\}$

The monthly periodic rate found by the financial calculator is 2.09%, or about 25% per annum. If you apply the IRR rule it too says refinance.

10a. First find the payment on the original loan given the monthly periodic rate of 0.60% (= 7.25% ÷ 12) and term of 240 months:

$125,000 = PMT × { [1 − (1.0060)$^{-240}$] ÷ 0.0060 }.

Find that PMT = $988. If you sent in 55 payments, then there remain 185 payments (= 240 − 55). Solve for principal outstanding PV in this equation.

PV = $988 × { [1 − (1.0060)$^{-185}$] ÷ 0.0060 }.

Find that PV= $109,868. That's the original loan's outstanding principal. The fees for the new loan equal $2,527 (= $109,868 × 0.023) and are paid by increasing the amount of the loan to pay for the fees. The new loan equals $112,395 (= $109,868 × 1.023) with a term of 240 months and monthly periodic rate of 0.48% (= 5.75% ÷ 12), satisfies this:

$112,395 = PMT × { [1 − (1.0048)$^{-240}$] ÷ 0.0048 },

or PMT = $789. The monthly payment declines to $789 from $988 and represents monthly savings of $199. It takes 13 months to recover the fees (= $2,527 ÷ $199); that's the payback period.

10b. Use results from the preceding part and find that the loan's outstanding principal equals $109,868 and the payment is $988. If you send in an additional 185 payments of $988 each that represents total expenditure of $182,774 (= 185 × $988) and total interest of $72,906 (=$182,774 − $109,868).

For the new loan the original principal equals $112,395 and the payment is $789. If you send in 240 payments of $789 each that represents total expenditure of $189,386 (=240 × $789), and total interest of $76,991 (=$189,386 − $112,395).

The refinancing actually costs you an extra $4,085 over the life of the loan (= $72,906 − $76,991), which is why you really should be evaluating with NPV!

10c. Use results from the preceding parts and find that the incremental cash flow equals $0 at time 0 (because you amortize the fees then you don't pay anything up front). Then for 185 months the incremental cash flow for you is $199 (= $-789 − $-988) because your payments are lower if you refinance. Then for the 55 months after that your incremental cash flow equals $-789 because you'll be making payments for the new loan but would not have paid anything these months with the old loan. The NPV for you with a periodic rate of 1% (= 12% ÷ 12) satisfies this formula:

NPV = $199 × {1.01^{-1} + ... + 1.01^{-185}} + $-789 × {1.01^{-186} + ... + 1.01^{-240}}

which is $11,465. This creates wealth for you. Note that using the monthly market interest rate of 0.48% (= 5.75% ÷ 12) for discounting shows NPV is $8,657. Wealth creation either way is substantial.

10d. The annual IRR for you satisfies this formula:

0 = $199 × {(1+IRR/12)$^{-1}$ + ... + (1+IRR/12)$^{-185}$} + $-789 × {(1+IRR/12)$^{-186}$ + ... + (1+IRR/12)$^{-240}$}

The monthly periodic rate found by the financial calculator is 0.14%, or about 1.6% per annum. This number is hogwash because if you apply the IRR rule it says <u>don't</u> refinance. That's wrong! This problem exemplifies a scenario in which the IRR is not trustworthy because the cash flows switch signs from positive to negative. NPV always is reliable.

CHAPTER 7

Time Value Application 2, Bond Valuation

CHAPTER CONTENTS

A bond is an "IOU" that a company or government issues in order to borrow money. The bond represents a legal contract that defines specific obligations to which the issuer agrees. The most significant obligation is the schedule of cash flows that the issuer promises to pay the lender. In essence, when the lender gives money to the issuer, and in return the issuer gives the lender the bond, the lender is purchasing the bond; the lender is a bond investor. The investor probably buys the bond because they want the cash flows that the bond promises.

Analysis of bond cash flows relies on time value techniques. Bond analyses offer excellent opportunity for practicing and developing intuition about present value procedures. The analysis of bonds also is relevant because almost every individual at some point owns bonds, even if only indirectly through pension savings.

Chapter 9 presents details about different types of financial securities in the bond and other credit markets. For now, however, lessons focus on important time value characteristics of bonds.

1. BOND BASICS: NOTATION, QUOTATION, AND CASH FLOW

The bond market is much larger than the stock market. Companies issue both bonds and stocks. While corporate issuers certainly are important participants in the bond market, the largest issuers are governments—state, local and federal governments and their sponsored agencies issue a lot of bonds.

Table 7.1 offers perspective on relative size of trading activity in U.S. bond markets. Column 1 shows that trading in U.S. Treasury securities during 2004 averages more than $500 billion per day. Column 5 shows for comparative purposes that stock trading on the New York Stock Exchange during 2004 averages $46 billion per day, less than 1/10th the trading in Treasuries. Media attention on stocks in the popular press is huge. Media attention on bonds is subdued perhaps because the volatility and variety of stories underlying company stocks are more exciting than the staid but rich bond markets. Around the globe the bond markets always are much larger than stock markets – primarily because governments don't issue stock but apparently love to borrow with bonds.

The table also lists daily trading in U.S. Agency securities issued by organizations such as the Federal Home Loan Bank Board; municipal securities issued by hospitals, airports, transportation authorities, and a slew of other public enterprises; and column 4 lists average daily trading volume for long-term corporate bonds. Even though, as chapter 9 discusses, these different securities have unique institutional characteristics their time value characteristics are nearly identical.

TABLE 7.1

Average daily trading volume of selected financial securities

	Average Daily Trading Volume ($ billions)				
	U.S. Treasury Securities - 1 -	U.S. Agency Securities - 2 -	Long-Term Municipal Securities - 3 -	Corporate Securities - 4 -	NYSE Stocks - 5 -
1991	$128	$6	not available	not available	$6
1992	152	6			7
1993	174	9			9
1994	191	16			10
1995	193	24			12
1996	204	31			16
1997	212	40			23
1998	227	48			29
1999	187	55			35
2000	207	73			43
2001	298	90	9		41
2002	366	82	9	19	40
2003	434	82	11	21	36
2004	501	77	12	21	46

Notes: Data for 2004 include trading in U.S.A. through June 30 for columns 1-4 and through November 30 for column 5. Columns 1-4 reflect primary dealer activity; column 3 includes both dealer-to-dealer and customer-to-dealer transactions; column 4 is for securities with maturities of more than one year. Source: Federal Reserve Bank of New York and compiled by www.bondmarkets.com.

Some corporate bonds trade on the New York Stock Exchange. On the NYSE, however, bond transactions are modest relative to stock transactions. Most bonds do not trade on an exchange. They trade in private markets set-up among institutions like brokerage houses, banks, pension funds, investment bankers, etc. Participants in the private market communicate through sophisticated telecommunication and computer links. The Bloomberg Financial Network and bondmarkets.com are among the most widely used computer networks for the private bond market.

Private market transactions are not subject to the same scrutiny as, say, transactions occurring on an organized exchange like the NYSE. Trades on organized exchanges are guaranteed by the exchange's "clearinghouse." For example, suppose an investor bids and pays $1 million for bonds. If the trade were on the NYSE then the investor is assured they will take delivery of the bonds. If the other party were to "take the money and run", the NYSE would step in, deliver the bonds, and pursue the fleeing party. In the private market, however, buyer beware—there is substantial "counter-party risk". The exchange clearinghouse guarantees that investors execute the transaction faithfully, but the clearinghouse does *not* guarantee that the bond issuer will make the promised payments. The bond owner bears the risk that the issuer might go bankrupt.

A few companies, such as Moody's or Standard & Poor's, rate the "quality" of bonds by analyzing the financial health of the issuer. Moody's and Standard & Poor's make money by selling the ratings information to traders or anyone else that might want it. By looking at the bond rating, the potential investor gets an idea about the likelihood that the bond issuer can pay the scheduled cash flows. Ratings such as "AAA" suggest the issuer is strong and reliable; "AA" is still strong, but less so. Bonds in the "BBB" to "B" category carry a little more risk than A-rated bonds. The riskiest rating of all is in the "C" category. These bonds often are referred to as junk bonds.

Most bond trades occur between one investor and another. Recall that only once in a primary market transaction is the issuer involved in selling a bond. Thereafter, however, the bond may change hands from one investor to another in secondary market transactions. The trades might happen for many reasons; perhaps investors have different expectations about future interest rates, or maybe they have different cash requirements. Regardless, the bond issuer promises to pay the bond owner, whoever it may be, a specified schedule of cash flows.

Cash flows from corporate and government bonds generally differ from the cash flows that attach to consumer loans. Car loans and home mortgages, for example, consist of periodic payments that include both interest and principal; recall that these are called "fixed payment loans". Corporate and goverment bonds, however, generally are "balloon loans". Payments consist only of interest, until the last payment (the "balloon"), at which time one huge payment repays the principal in-full.

Glean insight about bond cash flows and terminology by examining the table below showing standard price quotes.

BOND QUOTES

Issuer	Current Yield	Volume	Close	Net Change
AMR 8.10s18	7.9	3	102 3/8	−5/8
ATT 4 1/2 s16	4.8	55	98 1/2	. . .
ATT 8 5/8s 31	8.1	82	111 1/2	+1/2
Motrla zr23	. . .	30	73 3/4	−1
Unisys 8s15	cv	73	97 7/8	−3/8

The table shows quotations for 5 bonds. For all bonds some traits are always the same. All bonds, for example, promise to pay their annual interest in two semi-annual installments. Also, the face value for each bond, that is outstanding principal, is $1,000.

The first entry on each row is the bond issuer. Issuer for the first bond is the AMR company, the owner of American Airlines. AMR borrowed $1,000 at some-time in the past, we can't tell how long ago simply by looking at this quote. Regardless, this bond promises interest payments at a rate of 8.10% per year. This is the bond's *coupon rate;* the coupon rate determines the periodic interest payment that the bond owner receives. The interest payment is referred to as the "coupon" because long ago the bonds were issued with detachable coupons that the owner mailed to the company in order to request their interest payment. The coupon equals the face value times the coupon rate divided by two.

FORMULA 7.1 Semiannual coupon

The interest payment for a bond is paid semiannually and is called a coupon. The semiannual coupon is computed as

$$coupon = face\ value \times annual\ coupon\ rate \div 2$$

The AMR bond pays total interest per year of $81 (= $1,000 x 0.081), payable in two semiannual payments of $40.50 each

The two digits following the coupon rate, 18, represent the year that the bond matures and repays its principal. AMR promises to pay the owner of this bond $1,000 in 2018. We can't tell the exact day of the year that the bond matures simply by looking at this quote. Regardless, the bond investor has a good idea about the bond cash flows because of the identifier "8.10s18". The letter "s" in the bond quote has no meaning; it simply separates the different numbers. When traders discuss this bond they refer to it as the "AMR eight-point-tens of eighteen"; pronounce the "s".

The column with label "Close", 102 3/8, implies that the last trade of the day was at one-hundred-two and three-eighths per cent of face value.

FORMULA 7.2 Bond price

Bond prices in the U.S.A. typically are quoted as a percent of par. The dollar price of the bond is computed as

$$bond\ price = face\ value \times quoted\ percentage\ price$$

For the AMR bond quoted at 102 3/8, the price is

AMR bond price = $1,000 x 102.375%

$$= \$1,023.75$$

The investor purchasing the bond pays $1,023.75 in order to receive a coupon of $41.50 every six months, and upon receiving the final coupon in 2018, the owner receives an additional balloon payment of $1,000. Beyond 2018, the AMR company has no obligations because this loan is paid-in-full.

The column with label "Current yield" shows that for the AMR eight-point-tens of ninety-eight, the current yield is 7.9%. *Current yield* equals the annual interest payment divided by the current price.

FORMULA 7.3 Current yield

current yield = face value x annual coupon rate ÷ bond price

The current yield for the AMR 8.10s18 equals the $81 annual coupon divided by the price of $1,023.75, which equals 7.9%.

Many investors compare the current yield from bonds to the interest rate paid on a savings account. For example, an investor pays $1,023.75 for this bond and receives $81 interest per year, representing an effective interest rate of 7.9%. Suppose the bank savings account rate is 5 percent. The bond's current yield obviously is higher than the savings rate at the bank, but then again, this bond is a little riskier than a savings account! Investors decide whether the extra 290 basis points of return from the bond is worth the extra risk.

Several other types of bonds also are quoted in the table. Rows 2 and 3 list two bonds issued by AT&T. One of the bonds matures in the near future, so it probably was issued a long time ago. The other bond matures in the remote future and so probably was issued in the recent past. It is very common for large companies to have many different bond issues outstanding at the same time.

The Motorola bond in row 4 is different from the preceding ones because the Motorola's coupon rate is zero percent; the "zr" in the bond quote means "zero". This bond *never* pays interest at all! A natural question is why any investor would be willing to purchase a bond that doesn't pay interest. The answer is that investors buy it for a low price. Notice that to receive the $1,000 face value Motorola promises to pay in the year 2023, an investor need pay only $737.50 to purchase the bond. The price for the Motorola bond is substantially less than the other bond's prices. Investors for a zero coupon bond earn their rate of return by paying a small price.

The last row shows that the Unisys issue is a "convertible bond" (cv). This bond provides its owner, under certain circumstances, the right to convert the bond into stock. The convertible bond price tends to be affected by factors affecting both bond and stock markets.

2. RELATION BETWEEN PRICE AND YIELD-TO-MATURITY

The yield-to-maturity ("YTM") is the discount rate that equates the present value of promised cash flows to the bond price, as shown in formula 7.4.

FORMULA 7.4 Yield-to-maturity and bond cash flows

$$bond\ price = \frac{coupon_1}{\left(1+YTM/_2\right)^1} + \frac{coupon_2}{\left(1+YTM/_2\right)^2} + \ldots + \frac{coupon_N}{\left(1+YTM/_2\right)^N} + \frac{face\ value}{\left(1+YTM/_2\right)^N}$$

$$= coupon \left\{ \frac{1 - \left(1+YTM/_2\right)^{-N}}{YTM/_2} \right\}$$

N is the number of expected coupons. The right-hand-side sums $N + 1$ terms. The first N terms equal the present value of N expected coupons. They sum to the coupon multiplied by $\text{PVIFA}_{\text{YTM, N}}$. The last term is the present value of the principal repayment (i.e., the face value). The investor receives the face value at the same time that the final coupon is paid so the two last terms on the right-hand-side are both discounted N periods. The yield-to-maturity is an annual percentage rate. The formula divides the yield-to-maturity by two because interest compounds semiannually.

Formula 7.4 is analogous to the constant annuity time value equation from formula 5.1. Only the names have been changed. Bond price on the left-hand-side represents the present value of expected cash flows. The yield-to-maturity represents the internal rate of return for the bond investment. The *YTM* is the discount rate that equates the bond price to the present value of the cash flow stream. The *YTM* and *IRR* are conceptually equivalent. The *YTM* nomenclature exclusively applies to bond cash flows, whereas the *IRR* nomenclature appears in discussions about almost any type of investment.

For most applications, known variables for the preceding equation include the *coupon, face value*, and *N*. Of the remaining two variables, *YTM* and bond price, either one might be the known variable which means the other is the unknown. Sometimes a trader might be given the price and want to know the implied yield-to-maturity, whereas in other cases the trader might know the desired yield-to-maturity and wants to know the implied price. A financial calculator easily solves for any variable, as long as there only is one unknown.

EXAMPLE 1 Find YTM and counteroffer price

Suppose that for the "AT&T eight-and-five-eighths of 31" listed in row 3 there remain 39 semiannual coupons before the bond is retired in year 2031. (a) Find the yield-to-maturity at the quoted price of 111½. (b) You wish to make a bid on this bond so that your yield-to-maturity equals 7.72%. How much should you bid?

SOLUTION

The coupon rate of 8 5/8 implies that the annual interest payment for the bond equals $86.25. Each semiannual coupon therefore equals $43.125 (the payments actually alternate between $43.12 one time and $43.13 the next time, but ignore this technicality.) Substitute in formula 7.4 that *coupon* = $43.125, N = 39, *face value* = $1,000, and set the initial bond price at $1,115. Solve for the unknown *YTM* from this setup.

$$\$1,115 = \frac{\$43.125}{\left(1 + {YTM}/_2\right)^1} + \frac{\$43.125}{\left(1 + {YTM}/_2\right)^2} + ... + \frac{\$43.125}{\left(1 + {YTM}/_2\right)^{39}} + \frac{\$1,000}{\left(1 + {YTM}/_2\right)^{39}}$$

$$\$1,115 = \$43.125 \left\{ \frac{1 - \left(1 + {YTM}/_2\right)^{-39}}{{YTM}/_2} \right\} + \frac{\$1,000}{\left(1 + {YTM}/_2\right)^{39}}$$

$$YTM = 7.49\%$$

The accompanying *Calculator Clue* describes steps for finding that the yield-to-maturity at the quoted price equals 7.49%. Consider now the second part of the question. You wish to make a bid to buy the bond such that the yield-to-maturity is 7.72%. The time line illustrates the scenario.

today @ t=0	coupon #1	coupon #2	coupon #39
PV = ?	$43.125	$43.125	$43.125
			FV = $1,000

YTM = 7.72%. The unknown *bond price* represents the present value at which the known cash flows provide the known target rate of return.

$$bond\ price = \frac{43.125}{\left(1+\frac{.0772}{2}\right)^1} + \frac{43.125}{\left(1+\frac{.0772}{2}\right)^2} + ...+ \frac{43.125}{\left(1+\frac{.0772}{2}\right)^{39}} + \frac{1,000}{\left(1+\frac{.0772}{2}\right)^{39}}$$

$$= \$1,090.46$$

The annual rate of return is 7.72% if you pay $1,090.46 and receive 39 semiannual coupons of $43.125 each, along with $1,000 at the same time the last coupon is received.

The preceding example shows that if you buy the AT&T eight-and-five-eighths of 31 for $1,090.46 and receive the stipulated cash flows through the maturity date in 2031 that you'll get your 7.72% target rate of return. Suppose, however, that you buy the bond today and in six months receive the first coupon of $43.125 and sell the bond? What is the <u>annual</u> rate of return from that venture?

The answer requires the bond price six months from now. Preceding discussion states that bond price implies yield-to-maturity, and vice versa. That is, knowing one means knowing the other. For this question suppose that the yield-to-maturity remains constant. Six months from now the bond price equals the discounted sum of all remaining cash flows. Only difference is that one coupon will have been received and so only 38 coupons remain. Substitute settings into formula 7.4 just as in Example 1 and re-compute the bond price prevailing six months from now when N = 38.

$$bond\ price = \frac{\$43.125}{\left(1+\frac{.0772}{2}\right)^1} + \frac{\$43.125}{\left(1+\frac{.0772}{2}\right)^2} +...+ \frac{\$43.125}{\left(1+\frac{.0772}{2}\right)^{38}} + \frac{\$1,000}{\left(1+\frac{.0772}{2}\right)^{38}}$$

$$= \$1,089.43$$

The bond price declines to $1,089.43 in six months from $1,090.46 today. That's a capital loss of $1.03. Find the annual rate of return *ROR* for the scenario shown in this time line

$$
\begin{array}{ccc}
t{=}0 & & 1 \\
\vdash & \! & \dashv \\
PV = \$1,090.46 & & PMT = \$43.125 \\
& & FV = \$1,089.43
\end{array}
$$

and that satisfies the general time value formula 5.1

$$\overbrace{\$1,090.46}^{PV} = \overbrace{\frac{\$43.125}{\left(1+\frac{ROR}{2}\right)^1}}^{CF_1} + \overbrace{\frac{\$1,089.43}{\left(1+\frac{ROR}{2}\right)^1}}^{FV}$$

$$\left(1 + ROR/_2\right) = \frac{\$1,132.56}{\$1,090.46}$$

$$ROR = 7.72\%.$$

The annual rate of return for this deal, even though there is a capital loss, equals the yield-to-maturity of 7.72%. Rule 7.1 summarizes this lesson.

> **RULE 7.1 Actual *ROR* equals *YTM* whenever interest rates remain constant**
> The actual rate of return for a bond investment equals the yield-to-maturity irrespective of the investment horizon whenever the yield-to-maturity remains constant.

The yield-to-maturity also is called the *promised yield*. Buy the bond, receive the coupons, and if you sell the bond at anytime then, as long as the yield-to-maturity remains constant, the investment's actual internal rate of return equals the promised yield-to-maturity. The nearby *Calculator Clue* validates this rule when you buy the bond in the second row of the quote table: the AT&T four-and-one-halfs of 16; assume that initially 18 coupons remain; assume you receive a dozen coupons and sell the bond and yield-to-maturity remains constant.

> **CALCULATOR CLUE**
>
> These are the steps to find the actual annual rate of return for the AT&T four-and-one-halfs of 16 at ninety-eight and one-half after receiving a dozen coupons (initially 18 coupons remain; *YTM* remains constant). Set-up the calculator by typing `2nd` `FV` to clear the time value memories and `2nd` `I/Y` 2 `ENTER` `2nd` `CPT` to enforce semiannual compounding.
>
> Set the initial coupon and find the yield-to-maturity.
>
> 45 `÷` 2 `=` `PMT` 1000 `FV` 18 `N` 985 `+/−` `PV` `STO` 1 `CPT` `I/Y` .
>
> The display shows the YTM is 4.71%. Notice the keystrokes store the initial price of $985 in memory 1 because the number is used again later. Now use these steps find the price after receiving a dozen coupons.
>
> `RCL` `N` `−` 12 `=` `N` `CPT` `PV` .
>
> The display shows the price of the bond is $994.29 when 6 coupons remain and the *YTM* equals 4.71%. Now use these steps to compute the actual rate of return when the cost is $985, the cash inflows equal $22.50 every six months for six years, and immediately after the twelfth periodic cash flow there is an additional inflow of $994.29:
>
> `+/−` `FV` `RCL` 1 `PV` 12 `N` `CPT` `I/Y` .
>
> The display shows that the actual rate of return equals 4.71%, just as expected.

Preceding discussions show that *YTM*, the promised yield, properly measures the total rate of return even though returns accrue two different ways. Some return comes from coupons and other return comes from capital gains (or losses). This formula shows that the *YTM* partitions total return into these two sources.

> **FORMULA 7.5 Components for bonds of the promised yield-to-maturity**
>
> $$yield\text{–}to\text{–}maturity = \frac{coupon}{bond\ price} + \%\Delta(bond\ price)$$
>
> $$= \left(\begin{array}{c} current \\ yield \end{array}\right) + \left(\begin{array}{c} capital \\ gains \\ yield \end{array}\right)$$

The total return from a bond investment has two sources. A current income component provides immediate cash flow in the form of coupons while a changing price component causes capital gains or losses. Table 7.2 contrasts characteristics for these two components.

TABLE 7.2
Component characteristics for the total rate of return

Current yield (coupon / price)	Capital gains yield (% Δ price)
• realized cash flow	• accrued cash flow
• immediately taxable	• taxes are deferred
• relatively predictable & more certain	• very unpredictable & more uncertain
• relatively large and usually the main reason for buying the bond	• relatively small and not a significant decision variable (except for zero coupon bonds)

The table shows the coupon is a realized and taxable cash flow that is fairly predictable. Bond investors usually purchase the bond for the primary purpose of receiving the coupons. The expected capital gain (or loss), conversely, is an accrual that is usually relatively small and is not taxable until the security is sold. Two alternative bonds may provide the same expected total rate of return. They may not be equally appealing, however, if the partitioning of their total returns into coupons and capital gains varies.

Zero coupon bonds are an exception to the preceding discussion. Their current yield equals zero because they pay no coupons. The entire total return for a zero coupon bond therefore occurs as capital gains. The Internal Revenue Service has special laws requiring bondholders of zero coupon bonds to pay taxes on capital gains as they accrue. Can't escape the IRS!

EXERCISES 7.2

Concept quiz

1. A company intends to issue $1 million of bonds with coupon rate of 6.25% for financing *Capital expenditures*. They must choose between 5-year or 20-year bonds. Otherwise, the bonds are identical. Discuss possible considerations that might influence the decision.

Numerical quickies

2. The company today issues a 10-year $1,000 bond that carries a 6.5 percent coupon rate. Find the total interest that the company expects to pay over the lifetime of the bond. ©BD9
3. Today is a day in December 2525 and a zero coupon bond that matures in June 2538 has an annual yield-to-maturity of 7.00% (semiannual compounding). Find the bond price. ©BD10a
4. Today is a day in June 2525 and a zero coupon bond that matures in December 2539 has a quoted price of 26.00 percent of par (semiannual compounding). Find the annual yield-to-maturity. ©BD10b
5. A 10-year bond with a 4.40% coupon rate was issued with a 5.37% yield to maturity. Find the bond price at time of issue. ©BD7a
6. A 20-year bond with a 7.80% coupon rate was issued at a price of $1,130. Find the bond yield to maturity at time of issue. ©BD7b
7. Today is a day in June 2525 and a bond with annual coupon rate of 12.40% just yesterday paid a coupon. The bond matures in June 2545 and its annual yield-to-maturity equals 8.80% (semiannual compounding). Find the bond price. ©BD11a
8. Today is a day in June 2525 and a bond with annual coupon rate of 2.90% just yesterday paid a coupon. The bond matures in June 2540 and its quoted bond price is 71.21 percent of par (semiannual compounding). Find the annual yield-to-maturity. ©BD11b

9. Today is a day in March 2525 and a bond with annual coupon rate of 3.80% just yesterday paid a coupon. The bond matures in September 2536 and its quoted bond price is 74.47 percent of par (semiannual compounding). Find the current yield and capital gains yield. ©BD12a

10. Today is a day in November 2525 and a bond with annual coupon rate of 5.40% just yesterday paid a coupon. The bond matures in May 2537 and its quoted bond price is 74.53 percent of par (semiannual compounding). You wish to make a bid such that your promised rate of return is 30 basis points greater than the quoted annual yield-to-maturity. Find the price as percent of par that you offer for the bond. ©BD13a

11. A bond with a coupon rate of 7.30% has a price that today equals $868.92 . The $1,000 bond pays coupons every 6 months, 30 coupons remain, and a coupon was paid yesterday. Suppose you buy this bond at today's price and hold it so that you receive 20 coupons. You sell the bond upon receiving that last coupon. Find the selling price if the bond's yield-to-maturity remains constant. ©BD14

3. BOND PRICE MOVEMENTS

Bond prices, like stock prices, change with time. The time value principles previously presented govern the relationships, however. Inspection of bond prices in the preceding quote table shows a range from 73 3/4 to 111 1/2 percent of par. Rearrangement and experimentation of formula 7.4 reveals that the relation between coupon rate and yield to maturity determines the level of the bond price.

> **RULE 7.2 Relation between yield-to-maturity, coupon rate, and bond price**
>
> $$Bond\ price \begin{Bmatrix} > \\ = \\ < \end{Bmatrix} \$1,000\ when\ coupon\ rate \begin{Bmatrix} > \\ = \\ < \end{Bmatrix} YTM.$$
>
> The bond price exceeds face value and the bond is said to sell at a *premium* when coupon rate > yield-to-maturity. Conversely, bond price is less than face value and the bond is said to sell at a *discount* when the coupon rate < YTM. When coupon rate and yield to maturity are equal the bond price equals face value and the bond is said to sell at *par*.

Borrowers usually set coupon rates so that the bonds sell in the primary market at a price near face value. The coupon rate is printed on the bond and is unchanging. The overall level of interest rates, on the other hand, rises and falls with economic factors such as inflation. Yield-to-maturity for any particular bond correlates highly with the overall level of rates. Thus, a bond "born" in a 10% interest rate environment probably has a 10% coupon rate and sells at par. If interest rates subsequently drop to 7% then its likely price rises. New bonds of that era tend to have 7% coupon rates and sell at par. The old bond with 10% coupon rate generates higher coupons than the new 7% bonds and, hence, the price of the old 10% bond rises to reflect its advantageous cash flow.

A 10% bond in a 7% world sells for more than $1,000! The bond sells at a premium. Conversely, a 10% bond in a 13% world sells for less than $1,000. This bond sells at a discount to face value. The preceding discussion exemplifies Rule 7.3:

$$\text{Existing bond prices} \left\{ \begin{array}{c} \textit{rise} \\ \textit{fall} \end{array} \right\} \text{when subsequent interest rates} \left\{ \begin{array}{c} \textit{fall} \\ \textit{rise} \end{array} \right\}.$$

Rule 7.3 is strictly true for exclusively the relation between a particular bond's price and yield-to-maturity. Because a particular *YTM* generally rises or falls with the overall level of interest rates, though, the rule is generally true. A violation may occur if, for example, a particular bond suddenly becomes riskier due to financial distress of the issuing company. For that scenario the particular bond price falls and yield-to-maturity rises irrespective of whether overall interest rates are rising or falling. Still, rule 7.3 is a useful generalization.

3.A. Constant interest rates and scientific amortization

Suppose interest rates remain constant. What happens to the bond price over time? The clear answer is that over time the bond price converges to face value (as long as the bond does not default). Imagine that a bond maturing tomorrow delivers cash flow of $1,000. The market value of the bond today is a smidgeon away from $1,000 irrespective of whether the coupon rate is 1% or 20%. Figure 7.1 illustrates this phenomenon.

FIGURE 7.1
Evolution of bond price over time given constant yield-to-maturity

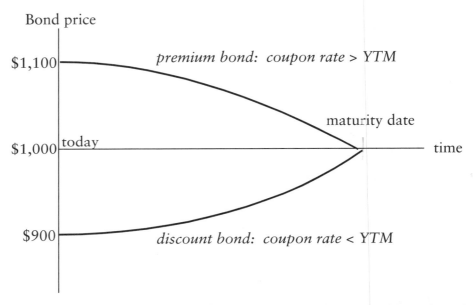

Notes The premium bond with $1,100 price today converges by the maturity date to its face value of $1,000. The discount bond with price of $900 also converges to face value.

Scientific amortization refers to the evolutionary path of bond price from its current price toward face value given yield-to-maturity remains constant. The path is predictable and depends exclusively on diminishing *N*, number of coupons, in formula 7.4. Beneath the horizontal axis in Figure 7.1 is the evolution of price for a discount bond with current price about $900. The price certainly rises by the maturity date to $1,000. Suppose that the maturity date is 20 years from today. If the price were to rise by straight-line from $900 up to $1,000 then in 10 years the price would equal $950. Notice, however, there is slight curvature in the scientific amortization time-path. The price on the curve halfway between today and the maturity date is below $950.

Likewise, the curve above the axis illustrates motion for a premium bond as its price declines from today's $1,100 to the $1,000 maturity price. The price for the premium bond at a point in time halfway between today and the maturity date is somewhat above $1,050.

Even though both bonds possibly provide the same total rate of return there is a huge difference in relative importance of current yield versus capital gains yield. The discount bond generates a total capital gain of $100; the premium bond a capital loss of $100. Still, as the example below shows, the promised rate of return can be identical.

EXAMPLE 2 Find coupon rates at which a premium and discount bond have equal YTM

Two bonds have identical 10% yield-to-maturity and 20 years (40 coupons) remain until maturity. One is a discount bond with price of $900. The other is a premium bond with price of $1,100. (a) Compare their coupon rates. (b) Compare according to scientific amortization their current yields expected in 12 years.

SOLUTION

Use formula 7.4 in which *Face value* = $1,000, N = 40, and yield-to-maturity is 10%. Set the bond price and find the unknown periodic coupon. For the discount bond solve this formula.

$$\$900 = coupon \left\{ \frac{1 - \left(1 + 0.10\big/_2\right)^{-40}}{0.10\big/_2} \right\} + \frac{\$1,000}{\left(1 + 0.10\big/_2\right)^{40}}$$

$$coupon = \$44.17$$

The discount bond pays $88.34 interest per year [= $44.17 × 2] implying an annual coupon rate of 8.83% [= $88.34 ÷ *Face value*] and current yield of 9.82% [= $88.34 ÷ $900]. Because total rate of return equals 10 percent, by the way, the annual capital gains yield today for the discount bond equals 18 basis points [= 10% − 9.82%].

Similar computations for the premium bond with price of $1,100 show that its semiannual coupon equals $55.83; annual coupon rate equals 11.16%; current yield is 10.15%, and annual capital gains yield is -15 basis points.

Summary of the solution for part (a) is that in an economic environment when yield-to-maturities equal 10% then a 20-year bond with coupon rate of 8.83% has price of $900. A 20-year bond with coupon rate of 11.16% has price of $1,100. They both provide the same total rate of return of 10% even though the discount bond provides relatively small coupons plus capital gains whereas the premium bond provides relatively large coupons plus capital losses.

Scientific amortization presumes that the coupon rate and yield-to-maturity remain constant. Changing with time, however, are number of remaining coupons, price, and partitioning of *YTM* into current yield and capital gains yield.

For part (b) find the price prevailing when 8 years remain to maturity (N = 16). For the discount bond find the price from this formula:

$$bond\ price = \$44.17 \left\{ \frac{1 - \left(1 + 0.10\big/_2\right)^{-16}}{0.10\big/_2} \right\} + \frac{\$1,000}{\left(1 + 0.10\big/_2\right)^{16}}$$

$$= \$936.84$$

The annual interest of $88.34 remains constant, of course, but the price rises to $936.84 in twelve years from $900 today. The current yield therefore declines to 9.43% in twelve years [= $88.34 ÷ $936.84] from 9.82% today. The current yield is declining and capital gains yield is increasing. In figure 7.1 the capital gains yield relates to the slope of the curve showing the bond price. For the discount bond on the curve beneath the horizontal axis the line is getting steeper as time to maturity approaches. The slope becomes a bigger positive number and capital gains become an increasingly larger proportion of total return (but the capital gain still remains much smaller than the coupon.)

Twelve years from today the price of the premium bond equals $1,063 and current yield increases to 10.50% from 10.15% today. Notice that the curve for the premium bond turns steeply downward as maturity nears. The capital gains yield is negative, implying capital losses, and over time becomes even more negative. The relatively large coupon and current yield, however, assure the total rate of return equals the 10% yield-to-maturity, just as promised. Scientific amortization shows that even with constant yield-to-maturity the current yield over time rises for premium bonds and falls for discount bonds.

CALCULATOR CLUE

Solve example 2 with these steps. Set-up the calculator by typing `2nd` `FV` to clear the time value memories and `2nd` `I/Y` 2 `ENTER` `2nd` `CPT` to enforce semiannual compounding.

Find coupon rate and current yield for the 20-year discount bond with price of $900 and 10% yield-to-maturity:

1000 `FV` 40 `N` 900 `+/−` `PV` 10 `I/Y` `CPT` `PMT` .

The display shows the semiannual coupon equals $44.17. Find the annual interest

`×` 2 `=` ,

equals $88.34, thereby implying the 8.834% annual coupon rate. Find today's current yield:

`÷` `RCL` `PV` `+/−` `=` .

The display shows that the annual current yield today equals 9.82%. Now use these steps to find the price and current yield twelve years from today:

`RCL` `N` `−` 24 `=` `N` `CPT` `PV` `RCL` `PMT` `×` 2 `=` `÷` `RCL` `PV` `+/−` `=`.

The display shows the current yield equals 9.43% when 16 coupons remain. Easily perform the same steps for the premium bond.

3.B. Horizon analysis and changes in interest rate

Analysts devote substantial resources trying to predict whether future interest rates, like stock prices, will rise or fall. Changing interest rates affect bond prices as shown in rule 7.3. Time value relations perfectly specify how the total rate of return for a bond investment relates to interest rate predictions. *Horizon analysis* for bonds finds the total rate of return resulting from a predicted change in interest rates. The example below illustrates horizon analysis.

EXAMPLE 3 Horizon analysis for a 6-month holding period

Today is a day in February 2525 and a bond with annual coupon rate of 7.50% and price of $950 just yesterday paid a coupon. The bond matures in August 2534 (semiannual compounding). Suppose you buy the bond at today's price, hold it

6 months, receive a coupon, and sell the bond. Contrast the annual rate of return from the investment if the bond yield-to-maturity 6 months from now (a) is lower by 125 basis points, or (b) is higher by 125 basis points.

SOLUTION

Find first the promised yield-to-maturity with formula 7.4. To find N count the number of semiannual periods between February 2525 and August 2534. There are 8 complete years from 2526 to 2533 inclusively (2533 − 2526 + 1) with two coupons each, that's 16, plus two coupons in 2534 and one remaining in 2525 bringing the total to 19. With *Face value* of $1,000 and price of $950 and coupon of $37.50 solve this formula:

$$\$950 = \$37.50 \left\{ \frac{1-\left(1+^{YTM}\!/_2\right)^{-19}}{^{YTM}\!/_2} \right\} + \frac{\$1,000}{\left(1+^{YTM}\!/_2\right)^{19}}$$

or $YTM = 8.27\%$.

The promised yield of 8.27% equals the actual rate of return <u>if</u> the YTM were to remain constant, but it doesn't. For scenario (a) the YTM falls by 125 basis points to become 7.02%. Solve for the price existing 6-months from today given that N diminishes to 18 and YTM equals 7.02%

$$bond\ price = \$37.50 \left\{ \frac{1-\left(1+^{0.0702}\!/_2\right)^{-18}}{^{0.0702}\!/_2} \right\} + \frac{\$1,000}{\left(1+^{0.0702}\!/_2\right)^{18}}$$

$$= \$1,031.62$$

Cash flows for this deal include purchase of a bond today for $950 and receipt in 6 months of a $37.50 coupon plus $1,031.62 selling price. Total ending wealth over the six month horizon equals $1,069.12 [= $37.50 + $1,031.62]. Find the annual rate of return ROR as:

$$ROR = \left(\frac{\$1,069.12 - \$950}{\$950}\right) \times 2$$

$$= 25.08\%.$$

Cast these cash flows within a "savings account scenario:" deposit $950 into the account and six months later withdraw $1,069.12 and, given interest compounds semiannually and the account balance after the withdrawal is zero, the account pays interest at a 25.08% annual percentage rate.

The return is much larger than the promised yield of 8.27% because by end of the investment horizon the interest rate falls. According to rule 7.3 a falling interest rate causes bond prices to rise. The bondholder benefits.

Scenario (b) with a rising interest rate is not so favorable for the investor because YTM rises and bond price falls. With new YTM of 9.52% [= 8.27% + 1.25%] the bond price in 6 months when $N = 18$ is $879.68. The ROR equals -6.91%. Existing bondholders lose money when interest rates rise.

EXAMPLE 4 Horizon analysis for an *N*-year holding period

A bond with annual coupon rate of 8.40% and price of $1,075 just yesterday paid a coupon. A total of 24 coupons remain to be paid. Suppose you buy the bond at today's price, hold it 2½ years, receive 5 coupons, and then sell the bond. Find the annual rate of return throughout the investment horizon if at the time you sell the bond its yield-to-maturity has fallen a total of 200 basis points.

SOLUTION

This is very similar to example 3 except that the horizon is 5 periods (instead of 1). With *N* = 24 and *Face value* = $1,000 and *bond price* = $1,075 and *Coupon* = $42 compute that the promised yield-to-maturity equals 7.44%. After 5 coupons have been received there remain 18. With *N* = 19 and the yield-to-maturity of 5.44% [= 7.44% - 2%] the new price equals $1,217. The annual rate of return pertains to this timeline:

today @ t=0	coupon #1	coupon #2	coupon #5
PV = $1,075	$42	$42	$42
			FV = $1,217

and satisfies constant annuity formula 5.1:

$$\$1,075 = \$42 \left\{ \frac{1 - \left(1 + ROR/_2\right)^{-5}}{ROR/_2} \right\} + \frac{\$1,217}{\left(1 + ROR/_2\right)^5}$$

or   *ROR = 12.5%.*

The falling interest rate pushes the actual *ROR* above the promised yield.

EXERCISES 7.3B

Concept quiz

1. The IRS requires that an investor in a zero coupon bond declare as taxable income the price change occurring along a standard amortization path. Discuss whether an investor generally may prefer to compute the price change with a straight-line path or with a scientific amortization path.

Numerical quickies

2. Bond X has annual coupon rate of 6.8%, 20 coupons remain until maturity, and its price is $920. Premium bond Z with price of $1,060 also has 20 coupons remaining. Under what condition is the yield-to-maturity larger for bond Z than for bond X? ©BD18

3. Today is a day in August 2525 and a bond with annual yield-to-maturity of 7.00% just yesterday paid a coupon. The bond matures in February 2530 and its quoted bond price is 83.64 percent of par (semiannual compounding). Find the annual coupon rate and today's current yield. ©BD16b

Numerical challengers

4. A bond with yield-to-maturity of 7.40% and 17 coupons remaining until maturity has a price today of $1,170. Find the coupon rate, today's current yield, and current yield expected after 11 coupons have been received (assume scientific amortization and constant *YTM*). ©BD15

5. Today is a day in June 2525 and a bond with annual yield-to-maturity of 11.20% just yesterday paid a coupon. The bond matures in June 2540 and its quoted bond price today is 77.72 percent of par (semiannual compounding). Contrast the annual capital gains yield today with the annual capital gains yield for the six months that conclude with June 2540 (assume scientific amortization and constant *YTM*). ©BD17b

6. A bond with annual coupon rate of 5.10% and price of $1,090 just yesterday paid a coupon. A total of 23 coupons remain to be paid. Suppose you buy the bond at today's price, hold it and receive 8 coupons, and then sell the bond. If at the time you sell the bond its yield-to-maturity has decreased a total of 50 basis points find bond selling price and the annual rate of return throughout the investment horizon. ©BD19b

— Exam 3

3.C. Riding the yield curve

Will future interest rates rise or fall? Interest rate movements often affect economic activity. The question is therefore important for main street consumers deciding about house and car purchases, for Wall Street investors deciding about bond portfolios, and for Washington policymakers deciding on national growth and employment objectives. Besides the issue of rising or falling, however, there is another subtlety: short-term and long-term interest rates likely differ!

The *yield curve* is a snap-shot of yield-to-maturities on a sample of bonds identical in every way except for term to maturity. Figure 7.2 illustrates a *normal* yield curve.

FIGURE 7.2
Normal yield curve

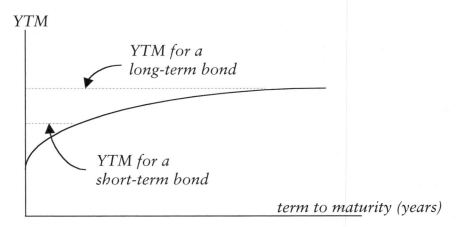

Notes Each dot on the curve represents a bond identical to all others in the figure except for difference in term to maturity. The yield-to-maturity is normally lower for short-term rates and higher for long-term rates. The yield curve shape changes, however, rising, falling, flattening, and sometimes inverting so that short-term rates are biggest. The normal yield curve is the normal shape, however.

Lessons in chapter 11 explain factors shaping the yield curve. For now, however, focus on time value relationships inherent with bonds. Already Rule 3 instructs that bond price moves inversely with yield-to-maturity. Inspection of figure 7.2 shows that *YTM* normally falls as maturity nears. Surely if one holds a long-term bond until maturity then the actual *ROR* equals promised *YTM*. But if the bond is sold early then perhaps the investor benefits from a strategy known as *riding the yield curve*. The example below illustrates the strategy.

EXAMPLE 5 Riding the yield curve

You expect that, for a given term, interest rates will remain unchanged. As is normal, the yield curve is sloped upward and yield increases with the term of the bond. The yield-to-maturity for a 2-year zero-coupon bond is 8.25%. For a 4-year zero-coupon bond, the yield to maturity is 8.45%. You enhance your returns for a 2-year investment horizon by following a strategy called "riding the yield curve". You buy the long-term bond and sell it after its yield has fallen to the short term rate. What is your rate of return from riding the yield curve?

SOLUTION

The price of the 2 year zero-coupon bond is:

$$PV = \$1,000 / (1 + {}^{.0825}\!/_2)^4$$

$$= \$850.71.$$

If you buy the bond now and it matures at $1000 two years (4 half-years) from now, your *ROR* is 8.25%.

Instead of buying the 2-year bond and holding it to maturity, however, you buy the 4-year bond and hold it two years. The price of the 4 year bond today is determined from the following present value relation:

$$PV = \$1,000 \,/\, (1 + {}^{.0845}\!/_2)^8$$

$$= \$718.17.$$

Two years from now its yield-to-maturity will fall to 8.25% because the yield curve remains unchanged. Thus, its price will be

$$PV = \$1,000 \,/\, (1 + {}^{.0825}\!/_2)^4$$

$$= \$850.71.$$

In other words, today's 4-year bond in 2 years will have the same price as today's 2-year bond! If you buy the 4-year bond and hold it for two years, your annual ROR (compounded semiannually) is determined from the following relation:

$$\$718.17 = \$850.71 \,/\, (1 + {}^{ROR}\!/_2)^4$$

Use algebra or your calculator to find that *ROR* equals 8.65% . This strategy increases your return by 40BP above the 2 year bond rate!

CALCULATOR CLUE

Solve example 5 with these steps. Set-up the calculator by typing `2nd` `FV` to clear the time value memories and `2nd` `I/Y` 2 `ENTER` `2nd` `CPT` to enforce semiannual compounding.

Find and store in memory the prices for the 2-year bond:

1000 `+/−` `FV` 4 `N` 8.25 `I/Y` `CPT` `PV` `STO` `1`

and for the 4-year bond

8 `N` 8.45 `I/Y` `CPT` `PV` `STO` `2`

Now find the annual *ROR* throughout the 4-period investment horizon:

`RCL` `1` `+/−` `FV` `RCL` `2` `PV` 4 `N` `CPT` `I/Y` .

The display shows that the annual *ROR* equals 8.65%. This is 40 basis points bigger than the 2-year *YTM*.

EXERCISES 7.3C

Numerical quickies

1. The yield-to-maturity for a zero coupon bond is 10.30% for a 1-year bond and 11.36% for a 2-year bond. You wish to make a 1-year investment and obviously can buy the 1-year bond and hold it to maturity. Suppose, however, that you think the yield curve will remain the same throughout the future. You can pursue an alternative strategy of buying a 2-year bond, holding it for 1 year, and selling it when it has 1 year remaining to maturity. How does this alternative strategy enhance your average annual rate of return? (Assume, if necessary, that you can buy fractions of bonds.) ©BD5b

2. The yield-to-maturity for a zero coupon bond is 11.80% for a 1-year bond, 12.70% for a 2-year bond, and 13.26% for a 3-year bond. You wish to make a 2-year investment and obviously can buy the 2-year bond and hold it to maturity. Suppose, however, that you think the yield curve will remain the same throughout the future. You can pursue an alternative strategy of buying a 3-year bond, holding it for 2 years, and selling it when it has one year remaining to maturity. Relative to the 2-year yield-to-maturity, by how many basis points does this alternative strategy enhance your average annual rate of return? (Assume, if necessary, that you can buy fractions of bonds.) ©BD5a

3. The yield-to-maturity for a zero coupon bond is 11.20% for a 1-year bond, 11.97% for a 2-year bond, and 12.31% for a 3-year bond. You think the yield curve will remain the same throughout the future. You wish to make a 1-year investment, that is, buy a bond today and sell it in one year. You can pursue three alternative strategies, call them S1, S2, and S3. For strategy S1, you buy the 1-year bond and hold it to maturity, in which case your annual rate of return obviously is 11.20%. For S2, buy a 2-year bond today and sell it when it has 1 year remaining to maturity. For S3, buy a 3-year bond today and sell it when it has 2 years remaining to maturity. What are your average annual rates of return for strategies S2 and S3? (Assume, if necessary, that you can buy fractions of bonds.) ©BD5c

ANSWERS TO CHAPTER 7 EXERCISES

EXERCISES 7.2

1. Rule 1.1 states that the goal of the company is to pursue policies that maximize capitalized value of wealth creation. Just like most households are "price-takers" in their consumer goods marketplace, so too most companies are "rate-takers" in the financing sources marketplace. This means that most companies cannot capture incremental economic profit from their financing source. Instead, they capitalize incremental wealth by transforming factors of production from stakeholder markets into goods and services that customers want. To the extent that competitive financing sources are willing to lend the company $1 million at 6.25%, irrespective of whether the term is 5-years or 20-years, suggests they both offer zero NPV to the company; they both offer zero NPV to capitalists providing financing. In such a case one loan-term is not better than the other and company as well as capitalist are indifferent between the two. There are, however, important underlying issues that merit mention. Also, re-read answers for conceptual questions #1 in Sections 5.5 and 6.2 because they too relate to this question.

(a) Later lessons teach that equilibrium interest rates typically depend on loan-term. Usually 5-year interest rates are less than 20-year rates. Hence, interest *per year* usually is less for a 5-year than a 20-year loan. Cash flow differences typically translate into risk differences. Regardless of rate difference, however, the 20-year loan may be riskier for the company due to its lengthier obligation period and this may translate into higher financing rates *for equity*. Later lessons consider interaction between risk and equilibrium financing rates.

(b) Often companies and households match the term of financing sources with the length of the expected service stream from underlying real capital assets. In other words, finance short-term assets with short-term liabilities and long-term assets with long-term liabilities. Introducing a *gap* between implied maturities of assets and liabilities generally increases overall risk for equity.

(c) Future growth opportunities for the company affect its marginal utility of money. The marginal utility of money is very high when the company has unusually large short-term cash-needs (as in the land-rich cash-poor balance sheet scenario). Deferring repayment of principal into the remote future may be worth the cost of interest when in the near term it means being able to pay unusually large research and development costs thereby allowing the company to survive. And if the company expects to invent and launch a blockbuster product sometime down the road then long-term financing may indeed be an intelligent strategy even though lifetime interest is higher.

2. The company pays $65 interest per year (two equal semiannual installments of $32.50) for 10 years for a total of $650 interest.

3. Biggest difficulty with this problem is counting the number of semiannual periods between December 2525 and June 2538. There are 12 complete years from 2526 to 2537 inclusively (2537 − 2526 + 1) with two coupons each, that's 24, plus 1 in 2538 and none remaining in 2525, bringing the total to 25. Use formula 7.4 wherein N= 25, coupon = $0, YTM = 7.00%, face value = $1,000 and solve for the unknown bond price.

   bond price = $1,000 × $(1+0.07/2)^{-25}$; or *bond price* = $423.

4. Count the number of semiannual periods between June 2525 and December 2539. There are 13 complete years from 2526 to 2538 inclusively (2538 − 2526 + 1) with two coupons each, that's 26, plus two in 2539 plus one remaining in 2525 bringing the total to 29. Use formula 7.4 wherein N= 29, coupon = $0, bond price = $260, face value = $1,000 and solve for the unknown YTM.

   $260 = $1,000 × $(1+YTM/2)^{-29}$; or YTM = 9.51%.

5. Bond cash flows equal 20 coupons of $22 each plus the $1,000 repayment of principal. Find the bond price with formula 7.4 when the annual yield-to-maturity equals 5.37%:

   bond price = $22 × $\{1 − (1+ 0.0537/2)^{-20}\} ÷ 0.0537/2$ + $1,000 × $(1+0.0537/2)^{-20}$

   The bond price at time of issue was $926. This means that the issuing company in a primary market transaction received $926 and promised to pay the bond investor the cash flows listed above.

6. Bond cash flows equal 40 coupons of $39 each plus the $1,000 repayment of principal. Find the annual yield-to-maturity with formula 7.4 when the bond price equals $1,130:

   $1,130 = $39 × $\{1 − (1 + YTM/2)^{-40}\} ÷ YTM/2$ + $1,000 × $(1 + YTM/2)^{-40}$

   Use a financial calculator to find that the yield-to-maturity at time of issue was $6.62%.

7. Count the number of semiannual periods between June 2525 and June 2545. There are 19 complete years from 2526 to 2544 inclusively (2544 − 2526 + 1) with two coupons each, that's 38, plus one in 2545 plus one remaining in 2525 bringing the total to 40. Use formula 7.4 wherein N= 40, coupon = $62, YTM = 8.80%, face value = $1,000 and solve for the unknown bond price.

   bond price = $62 × $\{1 − (1 + 0.0880/2)^{-40}\} ÷ 0.0880/2$ + $1,000 × $(1 + 0.0880/2)^{-40}$

   or bond price equals $1,336.

8. Count the number of semiannual periods between June 2525 and June 2540. There are 14 complete years from 2526 to 2539 inclusively (2539 − 2526 + 1) with two coupons each, that's 28, plus one in 2540 plus one remaining in 2525 bringing the total to 30. Use formula 7.4 wherein N= 30, coupon = $14.50, bond price = $712.10, face value = $1,000 and solve for the unknown YTM.

   $712.10 = $14.50 × $\{1 − (1+YTM/2)^{-30}\} ÷ YTM/2$ + $1,000 × $(1 + YTM/2)^{-30}$

   or YTM equals 5.8%.

9. Count the number of semiannual periods between March 2525 and September 2536. There are 10 complete years from 2526 to 2535 inclusively (2535 − 2526 + 1) with two coupons each, that's 20, plus two in 2536 plus one remaining in 2525 bringing the total to 23. Use formula 7.4 wherein N= 23, coupon = $19.00, bond price = $744.70, face value = $1,000 and solve for the unknown YTM.

   $744.70 = $19.00 × $\{1 − (1+YTM/2)^{-23}\} ÷ YTM/2$ + $1,000 × $(1 + YTM/2)^{-23}$

   or YTM equals 7.08%.

Formula 7.5 shows that the yield-to-maturity equals the current yield plus capital gains yield. Annual current yield equals 5.10% [= \$38/\$744.70] and capital gains yield therefore must equal 1.98% [= 7.08% - 5.10%].

10. Count the number of semiannual periods between November 2525 and May 2537. There are 11 complete years from 2526 to 2536 inclusively (2536 – 2526 + 1) with two coupons each, that's 22, plus one in 2537 and none remaining in 2525 bringing the total to 23. Use formula 7.4 wherein N= 23, coupon = \$27.00, bond price = \$745.30, face value = \$1,000 and solve for the unknown YTM.

$744.70 = \$27.00 \times \{1 - (1+YTM/2)^{-23}\} \div YTM/2 + \$1,000 \times (1+YTM/2)^{-23}$

or YTM equals 9.00%.

You wish to get a 9.30% return [= 9.00% + 0.30]. Get the counteroffer price:

$price = \$27.00 \times \{1 - (1+0.0930/2)^{-23}\} \div 0.0930/2 + \$1,000 \times (1 + 0.0930/2)^{-23}$

or price equals \$728.03. Your offer is 72.8 percent of par.

11. Use formula 7.4 wherein N= 30, coupon = \$36.50, bond price = \$868.92, face value = \$1,000 and solve for the unknown YTM.

$868.92 = \$36.50 \times \{1 - (1 + YTM/2)^{-30}\} \div YTM/2 + \$1,000 \times (1+YTM/2)^{-30}$

or YTM equals 8.90%.

After 20 coupons are received there remain 10. Find the new price:

$price = \$36.50 \times \{1 - (1 + 00890/2)^{-10}\} \div 00890/2 + \$1,000 \times (1+00890/2)^{-10}$

or price equals \$936.54.

EXERCISES 7.3B

1. The financial incentive of a tax payer is of course following the law. Beyond that, however, it's generally better to pay less than more and to pay later than sooner. The total price change over the life of the bond, and hence total taxes, is the same irrespective of the amortization path. The path affects the timing of the tax payments; the timing affects the present value of tax liabilities. Investors prefer to reduce present value of tax liabilities.

   Inspection of figure 7.1 reveals that the scientific amortization path for a discount bond lays beneath the straight-line connecting "today's price" with "\$1,000 maturity face value." The straight-line path accelerates the price change and increases the present value of taxes. The scientific amortization path delays price change and reduces present value of taxes.

2. Quick computation with the financial calculator shows that bond X has a 7.98% yield-to-maturity. Z has YTM of 7.98% when its semiannual coupon equals \$44.29. That equals an annual coupon rate of 8.86%. When the coupon rate for Z exceeds 8.86% then Z's yield-to-maturity exceeds X's.

3. Count the number of semiannual periods between August 2525 and February 2530. There are 4 complete years from 2526 to 2529 inclusively (2529 – 2526 + 1) with two coupons each, that's 8, plus one in 2530 and none remaining in 2525 bringing the total to 9. Use formula 7.4 wherein N= 9, YTM= 7%, bond price = \$836.40, face value = \$1,000 and solve for the unknown coupon.

$836.40 = coupon \times \{1 - (1 + 0.07/2)^{-9}\} \div 0.07/2 + \$1,000 \times (1 + 0.07/2)^{-9}$

or coupon equals \$13.50. Double that to get the interest per year equal \$27.00, implying a coupon rate of 2.70%. Divide annual interest by price to obtain today's current yield of 3.23%.

4. Use formula 7.4 wherein $N = 17$, $YTM = 7.4$, bond price = $1,170, face value = $1,000 and solve for the unknown coupon.

$1,170 = coupon $\times \{1 - (1 + 0.074/2)^{-17}\} \div 0.074/2 + \$1,000 \times (1 + 0.074/2)^{-17}$

or coupon $50.65. Double that to get the interest per year equal $101.30, implying a coupon rate of 10.13%. Divide annual interest by price to obtain today's current yield of 8.66%.

Find the price after receiving 11 coupons by setting $N = 6$ and compute that price is $1,072. The current yield at that time is 9.45%.

5. Count the number of semiannual periods between June 2525 and June 2540. There are 14 complete years from 2526 to 2539 inclusively (2539 − 2526 + 1) with two coupons each, that's 28, plus one in 2540 and one remaining in 2525 bringing the total to 30. Use formula 7.4 wherein $N = 30$, $YTM = 11.20\%$, bond price = $777.20, face value = $1,000 and solve for the unknown coupon.

$777.20 = coupon $\times \{1 - (1 + 0.112/2)^{-30}\} \div 0.112/2 + \$1,000 \times (1 + 0.112/2)^{-30}$

or coupon equals $40.50. Double that to get the interest per year equals $81.00, implying a coupon rate of 8.10%. Divide annual interest by price to obtain today's current yield of 10.42%. Subtract from YTM to get today's annual capital gains yield of 0.78%.

For the last semiannual period find the bond price as

price = ($1,000 + $40.50) $\div$ (1 + 0.112/2); = $985.32.

The bond price during that period rises to $1,000. The annual capital gains yield is $2 \times (\$1,000 - \$985.32) \div \$985.32$ which is 2.98%. Note also that the annual current yield during that semiannum equals 8.22% [= $81 ÷ $985.32]. Capital gains yield plus current yield equals YTM.

6. Use formula 7.4 wherein $N = 23$, coupon = $25.50, bond price = $1,090, face value = $1,000 and solve for the original and unknown YTM.

$1,090 = \$25.50 \times \{1 - (1 + YTM/2)^{-23}\} \div YTM/2 + \$1,000 \times (1 + YTM/2)^{-23}$

The original YTM equals 4.11%. It decreased to become 3.61% and N decreases to become 15. Solve for the selling bond price:

price = $25.50 $\times \{1 - (1 + 0.0361/2)^{-15}\} \div 0.0361/2 + \$1,000 \times (1 + 0.0361/2)^{-15}$

The selling price of the bond is $1,097. Solve for the annual ROR throughout the 8 period investment horizon:

$1,090 = \$25.50 \times \{1 - (1 + ROR/2)^{-8}\} \div ROR/2 + \$1,097 \times (1 + ROR/2)^{-8}$

The annual ROR equals 4.75%.

EXERCISES 7.3C

1. Find the prices today for the bonds:

$P_1 = \$1,000 \div (1 + .103/2)^2$; = $904.44;
$P_2 = \$1,000 \div (1 + .1136/2)^4$; = $801.73.

The bond that today has 2 half-years remaining to maturity and promising a 10.3% yield has price of $904.44. The bond with 4 half-years to maturity and promising an 11.36% yield has price of $801.73. Buy the 2-year bond today for $801.73 and sell it next year (after two semiannual periods) when it has 1 year remaining to maturity and forecast price of $904.44. That ROR is found with the lump-sum time value formula 4.6:

$904.44 = \$801.73 (1 + ROR/2)^2$;

or ROR for that 2-semiannum investment equals 12.43%. Buy a 1-year bond and get 10.30% or buy a 2-year bond and hold it one year and, given constant yield curve, make 12.43%. The difference is 213 basis points.

2. Find the prices today for the bonds:
$P_1 = \$1,000 \div (1 + .1180/2)^2; = \$891.68;$
$P_2 = \$1,000 \div (1 + .1270/2)^4; = \$781.72.$
$P_3 = \$1,000 \div (1 + .1326/2)^6; = \$680.34.$
Buy the 3-year bond today for $680.34 and sell it in two year (after four semiannual periods elapse) when it has 1 year remaining to maturity and forecast price of $891.68. That *ROR* is found with the lump-sum time value formula 4.6:
$\$891.68 = \$680.34 (1 + ROR/2)^4;$
or *ROR* for that 4-semiannum investment equals 13.99%. Buy a 2-year bond and get 12.70% or buy a 3-year bond and hold it two years and, given constant yield curve, make 13.99%. The difference is 129 basis points.

3. Find the prices today for the bonds:
$P_1 = \$1,000 \div (1 + .1120/2)^2; = \$896.75;$
$P_2 = \$1,000 \div (1 + .1197/2)^4; = \$792.54.$
$P_3 = \$1,000 \div (1 + .1231/2)^6; = \$698.81.$

For S2 find the *ROR* from buying a 2-year bond today for $792.54 and selling it in one year (after two semiannual periods elapse) when it has 1 year remaining to maturity and forecast price of *$896.75*. That *ROR* is found with the lump-sum time value formula 4.6:
$\$896.75 = \$792.54 (1 + ROR/2)^2;$
or *ROR* for that 2-semiannum investment equals 12.74%.

For S3 find the *ROR* from buying a 3-year bond today for $698.81 and selling it in one year (after two semiannual periods elapse) when it has 2 years remaining to maturity and forecast price of $792.54. That *ROR* is found with the lump-sum time value formula 4.6:
$\$792.54 = \$698.81 (1 + ROR/2)^2;$
or *ROR* for that 2-semiannum investment equals 12.99%.
S1 promises 11.20%. S2 promises 12.74%. And S3 promises 12.99%. A plot of these points is known as the *rolling yield curve for a 1-year horizon*.

CHAPTER 8

Time Value Application 3, Stock Valuation

CHAPTER CONTENTS

The financial media focus on stock markets. When stock prices plummet, headlines tout all types of causes. When an election is forthcoming, prognosticators proclaim likely effects on stock prices. When financial gurus advertise self-help revivals and hawk newsletters, *prima facie* evidence is superior stock picking performance. Predicting stock price movements sometimes seems in our society to be the mother of all mysteries.

Even though access to information and stock market statistics today are better than ever, the basic notion about forces that drive stock prices is about the same as three-quarters a century ago. Famous books from the 1930s, *Security Analysis* by Benjamin Graham and David Dodd, *The Theory of Investment Value* by John Burr Williams, and *The General Theory of Employment, Interest, and Money* by John Maynard Keynes, recognize two factors determining stock prices.

- The speculative factor relates stock price movements to market psychology and investor trading behavior.
- The entrepreneurial factor relates stock price movements to consensus expectations about the discounted value of company cash flows.

Both factors are important determinants of stock prices and merit discussion. This chapter proceeds in section 1 to contrast the speculative and entrepreneurial factors. Section 2 discusses stock valuation by discounting expected dividends. Section 3 investigates the most commonly used approach for analyzing stocks: price multiples.

1. TECHNICAL VERSUS FUNDAMENTAL ANALYSIS

The most significant difference between speculative and entrepreneurial factors pertains to timing. Stock prices in the long-run require support from sales, profit, and cash flow. The entrepreneurial factor explains the long-run sustenance of stock prices. Fundamental analyses relate stock prices to entrepreneurial factors. Stock prices in the short-run appear sometimes to vibrate randomly, as if driven by animal spirits. The speculative factor explains short-term price movements. Technical analyses relate stock prices to speculative factors.

Specific sectors or stocks somehow become market favorites and investors flock to them like a herd. Potential profits or losses are huge when the herd is on the move. Technical analyses decipher market psychology by using where the stock price has been in order to predict where the price is going.

The oldest and most common technical analysis trading strategy employs a moving average stock price. A simple N-period moving average stock price equals the sum of N consecutive prices divided by N

TABLE 8.1
Computing moving average stock prices

day -1-	closing price -2-	long—run moving average (5-day) -3-	short-run moving average (signal) (1-day) -4-	short-run moving average (signal) (2-day) -5-
1	$40.00	...		
2	$41.50	...		
3	$42.25	...		
4	$40.75	...		
5	$42.50	$41.40	$42.50 (buy)	$41.63 (buy)
6	$41.00	$41.60	$41.00 (sell)	$41.75 (buy)
7	$40.25	$41.35	$40.25 (sell)	$40.63 (sell)
8	$39.85	$40.87	$39.85 (sell)	$40.05 (sell)
9	$41.50	$41.02	$41.50 (buy)	$40.68 (sell)
10	$40.25	$40.57	$40.25 (sell)	$40.88 (buy)

FORMULA 8.1 Simple moving average stock price

$$(N- period\ moving\ average\ stock\ price)_v = \frac{\sum_{t=0}^{N-1} price_{v-t}}{N}$$

Consider the daily stock prices in Table 8.1.

The company stock price for the last trade of the first day is $40.00. The financial media report this number as the closing stock price. The table does not present the highest price of the day, the lowest price of the day, nor the beginning price of the day. Those prices exist and often are available. Many technical analysts may use these additional numbers to personalize trading strategies. For our purposes, however, let's say we are interested in computing the 5-day simple moving average closing stock price. The computation requires five daily prices. At the end of day 5 the stock closes at a price of $42.50 and finally enough data exists to compute the 5-day moving average from formula 8.1:

$$(5-day\ moving\ average\ stock\ price)_5 = \frac{\sum_{t=0}^{4} price_{5-t}}{5}$$

$$= \frac{\$40.00 + 41.50 + 42.25 + 40.75 + 42.50}{5}$$

$$= \$41.40$$

The 5-day moving average stock price on day 5 equals $41.40.

This technical trading strategy computes and compares two moving averages of different length. The comparison generates a buy or sell signal according to the following rule:

RULE 8.1 The moving average trading strategy
A buy signal results when the short-run moving average becomes bigger than the long-run moving average. Conversely, a sell signal results when the short-run moving average becomes smaller than the long-run moving average.

An important academic study in the prestigious *Journal of Finance* (William Brock, Josef Lakonishok, and Blake LeBaron, 1992) reports that the most popular lengths are 200 days for the long-run moving average and 1 day for the short-run moving average. The study concludes that throughout the past century this technical trading strategy significantly outperforms overall market returns.

The data in table 8.1 enable a simple illustration for implementing the strategy. Consider first the case where the long-run average depends on five daily prices, and the short-run average uses one day. On day five the short-run 1-day average equals the closing price of $42.50 (an average computed from one number simply equals that number!). The long-run 5-day average for this day equals $41.40. The signal is "buy" because the short-run 1-day average surpasses the long-run 5-day moving average. The trading strategy suggests that if you don't own the stock then buy it; if you already own it then hold it.

On day 6 the closing price is $41.00 . Calculations show that the 5-day moving average becomes $41.60:

$$(5-day\ moving\ average\ stock\ price)_6 = \frac{\sum_{t=0}^{4} price_{6-t}}{5}$$

$$= \frac{41.50 + 42.25 + 40.75 + 42.50 + 41.00}{5}$$

$$= \$41.60$$

On day 6 the signal is "sell" because the short-run 1-day average of $41.00 is smaller than the long-run 5-day moving average of $41.60. The trading strategy suggests that if you own the stock then sell it; if you don't own it then don't buy it (A more aggressive strategy involves short-selling the stock. A later chapter discusses short-sales).

Scan down column 4 of Table 8.1 and observe that the signal from the 1-day moving average remains "sell" until day 9. At that time, the signal switches to buy because the closing stock price of $41.50 surpasses the 5-day moving average of $40.57. This signal reverses the next day, however, indicating a rather quick in-and-out position on the stock.

Figure 8.1 charts the data for the previous example. Notice that a signal reversal occurs whenever the short-run moving average crosses the long-run moving average. At the far left the short-run moving average is above the long-run moving average. It crosses from above, heading down, and causes a sell signal. Later toward the right, the short-run moving average crosses from below (heading up) causing a buy signal, only to reverse itself immediately.

The short-run moving average is not restricted to equal one day. Column 5 of Table 8.1 lists the 2-day moving average. On day 6, for example, the 2-day moving average equals the sum of the two prices, $41.00 and $42.50, divided by two. Comparison of the 2-day and 5-day moving averages generates a buy signal: the 2-day

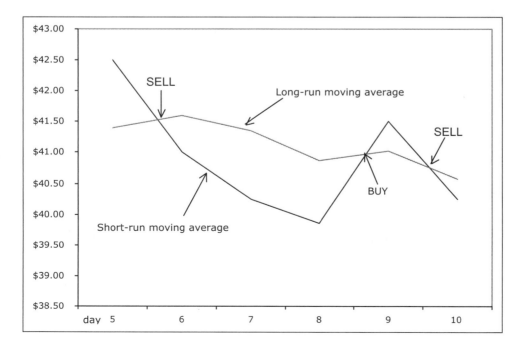

FIGURE 8.1
Moving average trading strategy based on data in table 8.1

moving average ($41.75) exceeds the 5-day moving average ($41.60). The signal on day 6 depends on which short-run moving average is used. Comparison of the long-run average with a 1-day moving average generates a sell signal, but comparison with a 2-day average generates a buy signal. Additional contradictions may arise if instead of 5 days the long-run moving average were 50 days, 100 days, or 200 days. Ambiguities abound with technical trading rules. Comparison of columns 4 and 5 shows several instances when signals conflict. Nonetheless, the study by Brock, Lakonishok, and LeBaron (*op cit.*) finds that the moving average rule, irrespective of length, performs pretty good.

The signal reverses from buy-to-sell, or vice versa, whenever the short-run moving average crosses the long-run moving average. The cross-over price for a signal reversal is found from the following formula:

FORMULA 8.2 Cross-over price for a signal reversal, general version

$$\left(\begin{array}{c} cross-over\ price \\ for\ a\ signal\ reversal \end{array} \right)_v = \frac{S\left(L \times MA^L_{v-1} - price_{v-L}\right) - L\left(S \times MA^S_{v-1} - price_{v-S}\right)}{L - S}$$

where L and S equals the number of periods in the long-run and short-run moving averages, respectively, MA equals the respective moving average at the end of the prior period, and $price_{-t}$ equals the stock price t periods previously.

The example below illustrates the usefulness of the preceding formula.

EXAMPLE 1 Find the cross-over price for a 5-day v. 30-day moving average strategy

At the market close yesterday the 30-day moving average share price for the company stock was $22.50 and the 5-day moving average was $21.75. The share prices 30 and 5 days ago were $18.75 and $23.25, respectively. According to a trading rule that generates a signal when the 5-day and 30-day moving averages cross, what would be today's closing stock price that generates a signal reversal?

SOLUTION

Realize that at the close of market yesterday a "sell" signal prevails because the short-run average of $21.75 is less than the long-run average of $22.50. The investor following this trading rule consequently does not own this stock. The point is to find the price that the stock would have to climb to today so that the signal becomes "buy." Substitute the numbers for this problem into formula 8.2 and compute:

$$\left(\begin{array}{c} cross-over\ price \\ for\ a\ signal\ reversal \end{array} \right) = \frac{5(30 \times \$22.50 - \$18.75) - 30(5 \times \$21.75 - \$23.25)}{30 - 5}$$

$$= \frac{\$716.25}{25}$$

$$= \$28.65$$

For this stock to get on the buy-list today its price would have to rise to $28.65.

Formula 8.2 simplifies when the length of the short-run moving average is one day. The simplification occurs because yesterday's one-day moving average is yesterday's price, and the second term in the numerator disappears:

FORMULA 8.3 Cross-over price for a signal reversal when the short-run is 1-day

$$\left(\begin{array}{c} cross-over\ price \\ for\ a\ signal\ reversal \end{array} \right)_v = \frac{L \times MA^L_{v-1} - price_{v-L}}{L - 1}$$

The preceding formula enables computation of a cross-over price which, when compared to the most recent stock price, provides a percentage change required for a signal reversal.

EXAMPLE 2 Use the 1-day v. 60-day moving average to find required percentage price change

At the market close for company stock yesterday the 60-day moving average and closing share prices were $38.50 and $43.75, respectively. The share price 60 days ago was $35.25. The trader uses a rule that generates a signal when the current closing price crosses the 60-day moving average. How much would today's price have to change relative to yesterday's close for this stock to get on the sell-list?

SOLUTION

Yesterday's closing price exceeds the 60-day moving average, which explains why the trader already owns the stock. Find the cross-over price by substitution into formula 8.3:

$$\left(\begin{array}{c} cross-over\ price \\ for\ a\ signal\ reversal \end{array} \right) = \frac{60 \times \$38.50 - \$35.25}{60 - 1}$$

$$= \$38.56$$

The stock goes on the sell-list if the price falls to $38.56. This represents a decline of 11.9% relative to yesterday's close of $43.75; that is, −11.9% = ($38.56 − $43.75) ÷ $43.75.

The moving average trading rule modifies easily to accommodate the style and beliefs of any investor. The proper length of moving averages, as discussed above, is debatable. Furthermore, one investor might insist that a signal reversal be confirmed for 3 subsequent periods before executing a trade. Another investor might insist that the short-run average surpass the cross-over price by 3 percent before executing a trade. Ambiguities abound with technical trading rules.

Financial science offers no insights about proper construction of technical trading rules. Bookstores nonetheless contain dozens of titles that technically analyze short-run price movements. The books often proclaim golden rules for deciphering market psychology. Yet human behavior and crowd psychology are difficult to predict. A later chapter discusses why technical trading rules should **not** consistently provide market-beating returns. Most knowledgeable investors and finance professors believe that the stock price history cannot predict where the price is going next. Predicting the effect of the speculative factor on stock prices seems as imprecise as predicting which fads or sayings will catch-on, or predicting the next turn in direction for a flock of flying birds.

> "For this reason, training in speculation, however intelligent and thorough, is likely to prove a misfortune to the individual, since it may lead him into market activities which, starting in most cases with small successes, almost invariably end in major disaster."
> Benjamin Graham and David Dodd. *Security Analysis,* 1934, page 12.

Fundamental analysis relates stock prices to entrepreneurial factors. Entrepreneurial factors shape company cash flows. Expectations about future cash flows support today's stock price. And time value principles fundamentally link present values to future cash flows.

EXERCISES 8.1

Numerical quickies

1. The 20-day moving average share price for the company stock at the close of market yesterday was $26.00. The share price 20 days ago was

$21.25. According to a trading rule that generates a signal when the share price crosses the 20-day moving average, what would be today's cross-over price that generates a signal reversal? ©TK1

2. At the close of market yesterday the 20-day and 2-day moving average share prices for the company stock were $25.25 and $23.00, respectively. The share prices 20 and 2 days ago were $20.50 and $23.50, respectively. According to a trading rule that generates a signal when the 2-day moving average crosses the 20-day moving average, what would be today's cross-over stock price that generates a signal reversal? ©TK3

3. At the close of market yesterday the 5-day and 2-day moving average share prices for the company stock were $39.75 and $36.25, respectively. The share prices 5 and 2 days ago were $32.25 and $37.00, respectively. According to a trading rule that generates a signal when the 2-day moving average crosses the 5-day moving average, what would be today's cross-over stock price that generates a signal reversal? ©TK4

2. INTRINSIC VALUE FOR STOCKS

Fundamental analysis generates a buy or sell signal by relating today's stock price to an estimate of the stock's current intrinsic value. In the 1930s Benjamin Graham and David Dodd forcefully explored analysis of security values from company fundamentals and J.B. Williams introduced intrinsic value for common stocks as present value of expected dividends. Intrinsic value is a subjective estimate of a stock's "true value" and equals the discounted sum of an investment's expected cash flows.

FORMULA 8.4 Intrinsic value, general version

$$\begin{pmatrix} stock \\ value \end{pmatrix}_0 = \sum_{t=1}^{\infty} \frac{CF_t}{(1+r)^t}$$

The intrinsic value relation contains three components: a cash flow stream, a discount rate, and the stock value. Given any two components, the third is pre-determined. The stock value represents intrinsic value when the known variables are the cash flow stream and discount rate. The stock value represents the actual stock price when either the discount rate or cash flow stream is the unknown variable.

Intrinsic value is a subjective assessment because typically the analyst estimates either the cash flow stream or discount rate. Rarely are these variables known with 100 percent confidence. Different analysts likely use different numbers. Computations of intrinsic value consequently differ between analysts. Intrinsic value, like beauty, often is in the eye of the beholder.

Comparison of intrinsic value with the actual trading price enables insight about whether the stock is under or overvalued. Rule 8.2 summarizes the investment strategy.

RULE 8.2 The intrinsic value trading strategy
The signal a fundamental analysis generates is that:

$$if \begin{pmatrix} intrinsic \\ value \end{pmatrix}_t \begin{Bmatrix} > \\ < \end{Bmatrix} \begin{pmatrix} actual \\ price \end{pmatrix}_t \quad then \begin{Bmatrix} buy \\ sell \end{Bmatrix}.$$

When intrinsic value exceeds the actual price the asset is undervalued. The asset is worth more than it costs. Always buy undervalued assets. When intrinsic value is less than the actual price then the asset is overvalued.

The example on the following page reinforces the notion that basic fundamental analysis is an application of time value principles.

EXAMPLE 3 Find intrinsic value given specific future cash flows

Your best assessment is that a particular share will pay dividends of $1.40 one year from now, $1.75 in 2 years, and $2.00 in 3 years. You believe that the share could be sold in 3 years for $30. You won't undertake the investment for an expected rate of return less than 16%. What to you is the share's intrinsic value today?

SOLUTION

Use formula 8.4. The cash flow stream and discount rate are known. Stock value is the unknown variable and represents intrinsic value:

$$\binom{intrinsic}{value} = \sum_{t=1}^{\infty} \frac{CF_t}{(1 + r)^t}$$

$$= \frac{\$1.40}{1.16} + \frac{\$1.75}{(1.16)^2} + \frac{\$2.00 + \$30.00}{(1.16)^3}$$

$$= \$23.00$$

The stock's intrinsic value according to your convictions is $23. If the actual price is $23 or less then put the stock on your buy-list. State the implication differently. If $23 is deposited in a savings account and one year later $1.40 is withdrawn, two years later $1.75 is withdrawn, three years later $32 is withdrawn, and after the last withdrawal the account balance is zero, then the account pays an interest rate of 16 percent. At a price of $23 the stock satisfies your criterion of a 16 percent rate of return.

The preceding example demonstrates that intrinsic value identically equals the present value of a discounted cash flow stream. The next example shows that formula 8.4 usefully finds the rate of return, too.

EXAMPLE 4 Find the rate of return on a counter-offer

You offer $23 for the share that you expect to return dividends of $1.40 one year from now, $1.75 in 2 years, $2.00 in 3 years, and also in 3 years you believe the share could be sold for $30. Your offer is rejected and instead a counter-offer of $24 is accepted. What is the rate of return if you buy at the counter-offer price and receive the expected cash flows?

SOLUTION

Use formula 8.4 and set stock value equal to the actual stock price. Solve for r:

$$\$24.00 = \frac{\$1.40}{(1 + r)^1} + \frac{\$1.75}{(1 + r)^2} + \frac{\$2.00 + \$30.00}{(1 + r)^3}$$

Use the calculator to find that r, the geometric average annual rate of return, equals 14.29%.

CALCULATOR CLUE

You must use the advanced calculator functions to solve this problem because it does not have an algebraic solution. On the *BAII Plus©* type CF and clear unwanted numbers by typing 2nd CE/C. Now enter this problem's cash flow stream as follows:

24 +/- ENTER ↓ 1.40 ENTER ↓ ↓ 1.75 ENTER ↓ ↓ 32 ENTER

Now find the periodic rate of return that satisfies this time value formula.

Hit: IRR CPT

The display shows 14.29 percent.

Before continuing lessons on stock valuation, learn a little about distribution and acquisition of equities in the U.S.A.

STREET–BITE Distribution and acquisition of U.S. equities

Who owns stocks and how do they get them? A survey of U.S. households in 2002 by the Investment Company Institute (see www.ici.org) and the Securities Industry Association (see www.sia.com) estimates that 1-out-of-2 U.S. households own equity securities (52.7 million households or 49.5% of total). This is substantially higher than the 1-out-of-5 households owning stocks in 1983. Stock ownership in the U.S. definitely is spreading from Wall Street toward Main Street. Table 8.2 tabulates some survey results.

TABLE 8.2 Number of U.S. households owning equities, 2002

	Millions of households (% of total)		
	Total	Inside employer retirement plans	Outside employer retirement plans
Own any type of equity	52.7 (49.5%)	36.2 (34.0%)	35.9 (33.7%)
Type: stock mutual funds	47.0 (44.2%)	33.2 (31.2%)	28.7 (27.0%)
individual stock	25.4 (23.9%)	8.8 (8.3%)	21.0 (19.7%)

Source: *Equity Ownership in America*, © 2002 by the Investment Company Institute and the Securities Industry Association. Notes: Ownership inside employer-sponsored retirement plans includes 401k, 403b, federal, state, or local plans, SEP-IRAs, SAR-SEP-IRAs, and SIMPLE IRAs. Roth IRAs and traditional IRAs are not employer-sponsored plans. Excludes stock options.

There are two types of equity securities that households may own: stock mutual funds or individual stocks. Chapter 9 explains that mutual funds collect money from many investors and pool the funds together to buy diversified portfolios of individual stocks. The middle row of the first column shows that 47 million households (44.2%) own stock mutual funds. The bottom row of column 1 shows that ownership of individual stocks is much lower (23.9%). Some households, of course, own both types.

There are two settings within which households acquire equity securities: inside an employer-sponsored retirement plan or independently. Chapter 9 explains that retirement pension plans, especially 401k defined contribution plans, have grown phenomenally over the past two decades. Comparison of row 1, columns 2 and 3, shows that ownership of any equity is about the same inside or outside of pension plans. Row 2 affirms that similarity. Row 3, however, shows that of the 25.4 million households owning individual stocks fully 21.0 million own stocks outside pension plans. 8.8 million households own individual stocks inside employer-sponsored retirement plans and nearly three-quarters of those (6.0 million) own employer stock.

The bottom-right cell containing 21.0 million households represents individual stock investors – about 1-out-of-5 households in 2002. Among these hardcore investors, however, less than half (46%) conducted a stock transaction during the preceding year.

The survey also reports that equity investors generally have equity portfolios of moderate value. Of 52.7 million households owning any equity nearly half have securities (mutual funds and individual stocks) totaling less than $50,000; only 7 percent exceed $500,000. Among households owning any equity the median number of equity investments is 4 unique securities or mutual funds. This is a modest number.

Once an investor decides to buy or sell a stock then trade execution generally occurs in any one of these different market settings.

New York Stock Exchange (NYSE) is the focus of a chapter 3 *Street-bite* and many facts about the NYSE appear there. The NYSE lists stocks for about 2,750 large capitalization companies. Total NYSE market cap is about $11 trillion in 2004 with average daily trading volume near 1,500 million shares worth $46 billion. It is the *big board*.

Nasdaq began as a public service initiative of the National Association of Securities Dealers (NASD). The Securities Act of 1933 established NASD in response to public outcry over the stock market crash of 1929 and the ensuing Great American Depression. Today all brokers or companies working with securities and the public must join NASD, obtain NASD licenses, and follow NASD regulations (see www.nasd.com). This self-regulatory organization in 1971 began collecting and distributing hard-to-get stock price quotations for many equities that were not listed on a stock exchange. The NASD Automated Quotation system (Nasdaq) allowed for market-makers to carry inventory of stocks and post bid prices for buying or ask prices for selling stocks. Nasdaq does not have a physical trading floor but instead is a telecommunications network with thousands of market-makers trading stocks for about 3,300 companies. Nasdaq is technically not a stock exchange but rather is a network of market-makers. Total market cap for Nasdaq stocks in 2004 is $2.7 trillion and daily trading volume averages 1,300 million shares worth $27 billion. In 1998 Nasdaq acquired the American Stock Exchange. In January 2000 NASD announced intentions to separate from Nasdaq. That separation was complete by mid-2002 and today Nasdaq is a publicly traded profit-making stock exchange (see www.nasdaq.com). That is, investors can buy stock with the Nasdaq name on it and receive profits that the company earns from fees and services provided to stock traders. In the meantime, the Nasdaq spin-off enables NASD to concentrate on their self-regulatory, Congressionally mandated mission of bringing integrity to the markets and confidence to investors (and also to operate their subsidiary company, the AMEX).

National Stock Exchange (NSX) is the third largest stock market in the U.S.A. NSX was founded in 1885 as the Cincinnati Stock Exchange. In 1995 they moved to Chicago and in 2003 changed name to the *National Stock Exchange* (see www.cincinnatistock.com). In 1980 NSX replaced their physical trading floor and became the first all-electronic stock exchange in the country. NSX daily trading volume averages about 500 million shares in 2004. Majority of trades are for stocks that also trade on Nasdaq. About one-third of all trades involving Nasdaq-listed stocks occur at the NSX instead of through Nasdaq market-makers. Similarly, about 15% of Amex-listed stock trades occur at NSX. The NSX also trades about 20 million shares per day of NYSE-listed stocks.

Pacific Stock Exchange (PCX) in San Francisco was founded in 1862. In 1999 PCX became the first U.S. stock exchange to demutualize, meaning switch from a member-owned organization like the NYSE and instead operate as a for-profit publicly traded company. In 2002 the Pacific Exchange closed its equities floors and migrated stock trading to the Archipelago Exchange *(ArcaEx)*, an *electronic communications network* ("ECN"). ArcaEx trades Nasdaq-listed equity securities and exchange listed equity securities, including those traded on the New York Stock Exchange and American Stock Exchange. ArcaEx and other ECNs offer corporate issuers and investors the advantages of meeting directly, without intermediaries, within a fully electronic and totally transparent environment. ArcaEx began trading operations in March 2002. More than 500 million equity shares change hands each day on ArcaEx. Another huge ECN is Instinet (see www.instinet.com and www.inet.com). Daily volume of U.S. equities for these Reuters subsidiaries averages 800 million shares. They also trade foreign company stocks.

American Stock Exchange (AMEX) organized at beginning of the 20th century in New York City and primarily traded stocks for companies too small to satisfy listing requirements on the NYSE. The AMEX in the early 1990s introduced *exchange traded funds* that today have total market cap of about $200 billion. AMEX lists equities for about 800 companies. Acquired by NASDAQ in 1998 the AMEX today operates as a subsidiary of NASD.

Three regional exchanges: The Philadelphia Stock Exchange (PHLX) was founded in 1790 and is the nation's oldest. In 2004 the PHLX demutualized and is now a publicly traded for-profit company. Daily volume for stocks traded at PHLX in January 2005 averages about 9 million shares, down about 50% from the preceding January. The PHLX has a stronger market position trading 1,600 equity options, 19 sectors index options, and currency options and futures. The *Boston Stock Exchange (BSE)* was founded in 1834 and average daily volume today is about 50 million shares worth about $1.4 billion. The *Chicago Stock Exchange (CHX)* was founded in 1882. In 1949 CHX merges with the exchanges of St. Louis, Cleveland and Minneapolis/St. Paul to form the Midwest Stock Exchange and in 1959 they absorbed the New Orleans Stock Exchange. In 1993 they changed their name back to the Chicago Stock Exchange. In 2005 daily trading volume averages about 65 million shares worth about $1.8 billion. *Over-the-counter stocks (OTC)* in nearly 10,000 small and new companies are not traded on any of the preceding markets. Instead, they are bought and sold over the telephone or by computer. Many OTC stocks are called *penny stocks* because they cost less than a dollar. When you pay a dime for a stock it doesn't take much to double your money, but then again *buyer beware!* Two quotation services provide online real-time price quotes for OTC stocks. The *Pink sheets* were founded in 1904 by the National Quotation Bureau (see www.pinksheets.com). Today the company name is Pink Sheets LLC, a privately owned company headquartered in New York. The pink sheets quote stock prices for companies that do not register with the SEC and are not required to file financial statements with the government. The Penny Stock Reform Act of 1990 mandated that the SEC establish an alternate quotation system for OTC stocks in accordance with the Securities Exchange Act of 1934. In June 1990 the *OTC Bulletin Board (OTCBB,* see www.otcbb.com) began operation to provide transparency in the OTC equities market. The OTCBB provides price quotes for approximately 3,300 OTC stocks for companies that register and file financial statements with the SEC. OTCBB securities are traded by a community of market-makers that enter quotes through a highly sophisticated, closed computer network that is a subpart of the Nasdaq system. Daily trading volume of domestic equities on the OTCBB in 2005 averages 2,400 million shares worth $240 million for an average price of ten cents a share.

Preceding discussion highlights two tendencies about the U.S. equity market. First, the market is very competitive with many layers and alternative routes for trade execution. Second, the equity market is rapidly growing and changing.

EXERCISES 8.2

Numerical quickies

1. The stock for a start-up company probably will pay no dividends until exactly 8 years from today. At that time it will pay $6.80 per year forever. You assess the intrinsic value of the stock with a 10.3% discount rate. Find the stock's intrinsic value today. ©ST20

2. A company you are interested in just declared their annual dividend of $2.20. You expect the annual dividend next year will be larger by 4.4%, at which time you expect the stock could sell for $24. What is the intrinsic value today that would provide you with a 12.2% annual rate of return from investing in the stock? ©ST6

3. The company stock paid a dividend this morning of $3.00 and its current stock price is $84. You think that a year from now the dividend will be $3.60 and the stock price will be $89. Find the rate of return if you buy the stock now at the current price, and in one year you receive the expected dividend and then sell the stock at the expected price. ©ST11

4. A stock you are buying today promises no dividends for a long time. In exactly 10 years you expect the stock will pay its first annual dividend of $3.70. At that time, you also believe that the stock could be sold for $34.00. If today you can buy the stock for $13.64, what is the expected annual rate of return on the stock investment? ©ST12

Numerical challenger

5. A stock you are buying today promises no dividends for a long time. In exactly 5 years you expect the stock will pay its first annual dividend of $5.60 which you expect will be paid annually forever. If today you can buy the stock for $40.43, what is the expected annual rate of return on the stock investment? ©ST21

2.A. Preferred stocks with constant dividends

Preferred stock has characteristics of both bonds and common stocks. Preferred stock, like a bond, stipulates the amount of cash flow that the investor receives. The periodic cash flow for preferred stock is called a dividend. Companies promise to pay preferred dividends, like common dividends, every calendar quarter when financial circumstances permit. If the company cannot pay a dividend, however, the investor has no legal recourse to force payment or bankruptcy. Most preferred stocks have covenants stipulating that when a company misses a preferred dividend they cannot pay any common dividends until preferred shareholders get all missed dividends. Preferred stocks, like common stocks, never mature. The company promises to pay dividends forever.

Preferred stocks trade on exchanges by the same procedures as common stocks. The preferred dividend for a particular stock is constant. The preferred stock for AMR (American Airlines) in the table above, for example, promises to pay $6.40 per annum forever. What do you think would happen to the price of AMR preferred stock if American Airlines suddenly won major flight contracts with every government in Europe and South America? The answer: probably nothing! Maybe the price of the common stock would skyrocket as investors suddenly realize future profits will be larger than previously expected. The preferred dividend, however, is fixed at $6.40 per year forever. The price of preferred consequently responds more to discount rate changes than to the good fortunes of the company. Because the dividend is constant, the formula for value relation simplifies to the perpetuity formula:

FORMULA 8.5 Intrinsic value, stocks with constant dividends

$$\left(\frac{stock}{value}\right)_0 = \sum_{t=1}^{\infty} \frac{dividend}{(1 + r)^t}$$

$$= \frac{dividend}{r}$$

As before, when stock value is the unknown variable it represents intrinsic value. When stock value is the actual stock price then the unknown variable is probably r. Even though dividends actually are paid quarterly (the AMR pays $1.60 four times a year), computations in this book assume dividend payments occur annually. This is strictly for convenience.

The following example gleans insight about pricing preferred stocks.

EXAMPLE 5 Find the preferred stock's intrinsic value
A share of AMR preferred stock paid a $6.40 annual dividend yesterday. You would buy the preferred stock if its return is 275 basis points more than the bank interest rate on 36-month Certificates of Deposit ("CD"). The 36-month CD rate today is 5.25 percent, and the preferred stock price is $74.50. What to you is the stock's intrinsic value, and should you buy it?

SOLUTION

There are two ways to view this problem. Both lead to the same qualitative answer, both use formula 8.5, and each is valid by itself. First find the stock's intrinsic value:

$$\left(\begin{array}{c}intrinsic\\value\end{array}\right) = \frac{\$6.40}{(0.0525 + 0.0275)}$$

$$= \$80.00$$

Comparison shows that the intrinsic value of $80 exceeds the stock price of $74.50 and a buy signal exists.

The second way to reach the same conclusion uses formula 8.5 with the price and dividend as known values. Solve for the rate of return the preferred stock promises:

$$\$74.50 = \frac{\$6.40}{r}$$

$$r = 8.59\%$$

The preferred stock promises 334 basis points more than the CD ($= 0.0859 - 0.0525$). The investment satisfies the criterion for a buy signal.

Solid blue-chip companies with little default risk typically issue preferred stocks. Investors in preferred stocks typically compare the preferred stock's rate of return with alternative investments, such as bank CDs. The example below shows that preferred stocks, even in the absence of significant default risk, still are riskier than CDs.

EXAMPLE 6 Find the rate of return upon conclusion of a preferred stock
investment

You buy today for $74.50 a share of AMR preferred stock that yesterday paid a $6.40 annual dividend. The preferred stock promises a risk premium of 334 basis points relative to the 5.25 percent 36-month CD rate. You own the stock and collect the subsequent two annual dividends. You sell the preferred stock upon receipt of the second dividend. The CD rate at the time of the sell is 3 percent higher than today, while the risk premium on the preferred stock is constant. What is the average annual rate of return for the investment?

SOLUTION

The time line below shows the investment cash flows.

0	1	2
CF= $-74.50	CF= $6.40	CF= $6.40
		sell price = ?

Use formula 8.5 with r equal to 6.34 percent to find the price at time of sell:

$$\left(\begin{array}{c}stock\\value\end{array}\right)_2 = \frac{\$6.40}{(0.0525 + 0.0334 + 0.0300)}$$

$$= \$55.22$$

The $6.40 dividend plus the $55.22 sell price brings CF_2 to $61.62. The rate of return from the investment satisfies the following equation:

$$\$74.50 = \frac{\$6.40}{(1 + r)^1} + \frac{\$61.62}{(1 + r)^2}$$

Solve on the calculator and find that r, the geometric average annual rate of return, equals –4.66%. The preferred stock investment performs miserably. The CD may promise a lower rate of return but preferred stock carries the risk of a falling share price in response to rising interest rates.

CALCULATOR CLUE

You may solve example 6 on the *BAII Plus*© with either the `CF` menu or the time value keys. Use time value keys by typing `2nd` `FV` and `2nd` `I/Y` 1 `ENTER` `CE/C` to clear memories and enforce annual compounding. Now enter the dividend and compute selling price as follows:

74.5 `+/−` `PV` 6.40 `PMT` `÷` `(` .0525 `+` .0334 `+` .03 `)` `=` `FV` 2 `N` `CPT` `I/Y`.

The display shows –4.66%.

EXERCISES 8.2A

Numerical quickies

1. You notice that the local electric company pays a $6 annual dividend on its preferred stock. The current price of the stock is $78. Find the promised rate of return for the preferred stock. ©ST23

2. The company preferred stock pays a $3.75 annual dividend. The local bank pays 4.5% interest on 5-year CDs. You consider the preferred stock an attractive investment if its *ROR* is 175 basis points more than the CD rate. Find your assessment of the preferred stock intrinsic value. ©ST22

3. The company preferred stock yesterday paid $6.25 annual dividend and today's stock price is $101.50. The local bank pays 4.65% interest on CDs. You consider the preferred stock an attractive investment if its *ROR* is 200 basis points more than the CD rate. Find the actual risk premium and is this stock a *buy* or a *sell*? ©ST24

Numerical challenger

4. The company preferred stock just yesterday paid its annual dividend of $5.00 per share. Today's share price is $58.10. You believe the dividend yield is abnormally high but that, over the next two years, it will revert to its normal value of 6.50%. Your strategy is to buy the stock today and receive annual dividends for two years. Upon receiving the last dividend you expect the dividend yield will be normal, and your strategy is to sell the stock at that time. Compute the expected annual rate of return for the strategy. ©ST7

5. The company preferred stock just yesterday paid its annual dividend of $6.00 per share. Today's share price is $52.25. You believe the dividend yield is abnormally high but that it will revert to its normal value of 7.0%. Your strategy is to buy the stock today and receive annual dividends for 4 years. Upon receiving the last dividend you expect the dividend yield will be normal. Your strategy is to sell the stock at that time. Compute the expected annual rate of return for the strategy. ©ST25

Exam 3

2.B. Common stocks with growing dividends

The intrinsic value relation in formula 8.4 broadly applies to almost any investment decision. Finding an asset's true worth, however, requires specific assumptions about future cash flows. With common stocks the situation is amazingly complex because, unlike preferred stocks, future cash flows are totally unspecified. Some analysts compute common stock intrinsic value by discounting operating cash flow. Other analysts discount dividends. Some analysts forecast cash flows growing rapidly in nearby years and more slowly in remote years. Other analysts specify smooth growth at a constant geometric rate. Fundamental analysis, like technical analysis, abounds with ambiguities. Fundamental analysis, however, rests on strong logical and theoretical foundations: present values relate to the discounted sum of expected cash flows.

Investors receive common stock cash flows from two sources. First, the investor receives dividend distributions from the company. Second, the investor receives a cash inflow upon selling the stock. Example 3 computes intrinsic value as the discounted sum of dividends and expected sale proceeds. But the sale proceeds represent a transfer of wealth from the buyer to the seller. And what cash flow does the subsequent investor expect to receive from purchasing the stock? Dividends and sale proceeds. Stretching into infinity the only cash flow the stock ever will generate is dividends and sale proceeds. Specifying that investors possess rational expectations about future dividends leads to the conclusion that sale proceeds wash-out and are irrelevant to valuation. Today's common stock intrinsic value equals the discounted sum of the infinite dividend stream:

> **FORMULA 8.6 Intrinsic value is the discounted sum of the infinite dividend stream**

$$\left(\frac{stock}{value}\right)_0 = \sum_{t=1}^{\infty} \frac{dividend_t}{(1+r)^t}$$

B1. The dividend growth rate

Computing intrinsic value with formula 8.6 requires numbers for the discount rate and each and every one of the infinite dividends. It's pretty hard to come up with so many numbers. The problem is made tractable by restricting the shape of the dividend stream. Interesting insights, for example, occur in the special case when dividends grow at a constant rate. Smooth dividend growth at rate g satisfies the following equality:

> **FORMULA 8.7 Constant growth rate for dividends**

$$dividend_s = dividend_{s-t}(1+g)^t$$

Smooth dividend growth occurs when one period's dividend *always* is g percent bigger than the previous period's dividend.

EXAMPLE 7 Find the dividend growth rate from two observations
A share of company stock paid a dividend today of $4.60. Five years ago the dividend was $2.90. Suppose the dividend grows smoothly at a constant rate. Find (i) the dividend growth rate, and (ii) next year's dividend.

SOLUTION
Use formula 8.7 to find (i) the dividend growth rate:

$$\$4.60 = \$2.90(1+g)^5$$

$$g = \left(\frac{\$4.60}{\$2.90}\right)^{1/5} - 1$$

$$g = 9.67\%$$

A dividend that today is $4.60 and five year ago was $2.90 grows at a geometric average annual rate of 9.67 percent. Find (ii) the dividend next year that is 9.67 percent larger than this year's dividend:

$$dividend_1 = dividend_0 \, (1 + g)^1$$

$$= \$4.60 \, (1.0967)$$

$$= \$5.04$$

Inspection of company reports shows that dividends seldom grow smoothly. Table 8.3 shows a typical history of annual dividends.

Each year's percentage change varies from as high as 44 percent to as low as –15 percent. Dividends definitely do not change by exactly the same amount each year. Dividend growth definitely is not smooth.

Suppose the company just paid the $3.30 annual dividend at time 7 and you wish to estimate from the dividend history the growth rate with formula 8.7. Choosing the proper beginning year is problematic. The geometric average annual percentage change from year 6 to 7 equals 3.12 percent. From year 5 through year 7, however, the estimate of g equals 10.55 percent (column 4, row 5; $(3.30/2.70)^{1/2} - 1$). From year three's dividend of $2.60 until year seven's dividend of $3.30 the g is 6.14 percent (that is, $0.0614 = (3.30/2.60)^{1/4} - 1$). Forecasting future dividends depends a lot on estimating g, and estimates of g from the dividend history are ambiguous.

Statistical procedures come to the rescue. We can estimate g from the data in table 8.3 by assuming that formula 8.7 is generally true but that random white noise causes vibration in observable growth rates. Rewrite formula 8.4 as

$$\log(dividend_t) = \log(dividend_0(1 + g)^t)$$

Apply simple math rules and add the white noise and find

$$\log(dividend_t) = \log(dividend_0) + t\log(1 + g) + noise_t$$

The important point about the preceding formula is that *our calculator* uses the formula to estimate the growth rate g! This example offers a lesson about that handy tool.

EXAMPLE 8 Find the best estimate of the dividend growth rate from Table 8.3
Yesterday the company paid its annual dividend of $3.30 as shown in row 7 of Table 8.3. Assume that dividends grow smoothly in accordance with constant growth formula 8.7. Each year, however, there may be random white noise errors. Compute the best estimate of the dividend growth rate and plot the function that shows dividends growing smoothly. Also, find the best estimate for next year's dividend ($t = 8$).

year$_t$ -1-	annual dividend$_t$ -2-	% change from year $t - 1$ -3-	g from time t to time 7 -4-
1	$1.80	. . .	10.63%
2	$1.80	0.00%	12.89%
3	$2.60	44.44%	6.14%
4	$2.20	–15.38%	14.47%
5	$2.70	22.73%	10.55%
6	$3.20	18.52%	3.12%
7	$3.30	3.12%	. . .

TABLE 8.3
A typical dividend history

SOLUTION

Follow the steps in this *Calculator Clue* to perform the statistical analysis.

CALCULATOR CLUE

The *BAII Plus©* calculator contains a spreadsheet that enables easy estimation of *g* for example 8 that best fits formula 8.7. On the *BAII Plus©* type `2nd` `DATA` (the data key is the same as the 7 key). The calculator opens a worksheet that contains two columns for holding data. The calculator refers to the two columns of data as column X and column Y. For this problem column X contains the period number and column Y contains the dividend amount. Clear unwanted numbers already stored in the data worksheet by typing `2nd` `CE/C`. Enter this problem's data by typing

1 `ENTER` ↓ 1.80 `ENTER`

↓ 2 `ENTER` ↓ 1.80 `ENTER`

↓ 3 `ENTER` ↓ 2.60 `ENTER`

↓ 4 `ENTER` ↓ 2.20 `ENTER`

↓ 5 `ENTER` ↓ 2.70 `ENTER`

↓ 6 `ENTER` ↓ 3.20 `ENTER`

↓ 7 `ENTER` ↓ 3.30 `ENTER`

The preceding keystrokes set $X_1 = 1$ and $Y_1 = 1.80$, . . . , $X_7 = 7$ and $Y_7 = 3.30$. Note that the X column also could contain 1995, 1996, . . . , 2001 and exactly the same estimate of *g* would result. Find the statistical estimate of the growth rate from the data in memory by typing `2nd` `STAT`. Now hit `2nd` `SET` repeatedly until the display says "EXP". With this setting the calculator finds the exponential growth rate that best fits the Y and X columns. The statistics course calls this procedure an ordinary least squares estimate of the log(Y) on a trendline X.

To find the growth rate estimate hit ↓ repeatedly (probably 9 times) until the display shows "b = 1.1134" . The number equals one plus the growth rate. For the data in table 8.4, the best estimate of the dividend growth rate equals 11.34 percent. This growth rate is an important input for fundamental analyses of common stock intrinsic value.

Next find the dividend expected at time 8. Hit ↓ two more times until the display shows "X' = ". Type

8 `ENTER` ↓ `CPT` .

The display shows that Y'_8 , the dividend expected at time 8, equals $3.76.

Figure 8.2 portrays findings for Example 8. Dots labeled div_t represent the actual dividend history from table 8.3. The solid line represents the path of expected dividends implied by the statistical analysis. Each triangular marked point on the line represents an expected dividend. Plug into your calculator that "X' = 7" and compute that expected $div_7 = \$3.38$. Actual div_7 of $3.30 was less than expected by 8 cents. The white noise this period, $noise_7$, was minus 8 cents. The figure illustrates the noise at a given point in time as the distance between the actual dividend (the dot) minus the expected dividend (the triangle).

Project the line to time 8 and find that expected div_8 equals $3.76. In reality the actual dividend probably won't exactly equal $3.76 because some noise will occur. Still, the expected value of the noise according to the statistical model is zero. As far as we can trust that formula 8.7 is correct and that noise is white then the best estimate of next period's dividend is $3.76.

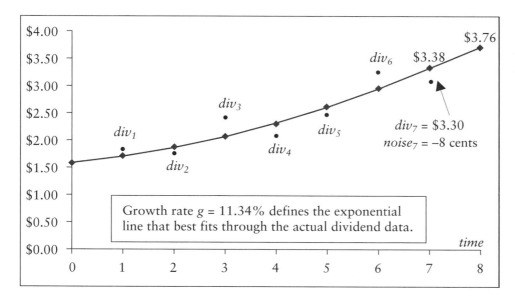

Growth rate $g = 11.34\%$ defines the exponential line that best fits through the actual dividend data.

B2. The constant growth dividend valuation model

Restricting the dividend cash flow stream to change through time at a constant rate g allows simplification of the intrinsic value relation. Stock value relates to the discounted sum of the perpetual and smoothly growing dividend stream as follows:

$$\left(\frac{stock}{value}\right)_0 = \frac{dividend_1}{(1+r)^1} + \frac{dividend_2}{(1+r)^2} + \frac{dividend_3}{(1+r)^3} + ... \text{ to } \infty$$

$$= \frac{dividend_1}{(1+r)^1} + \frac{dividend_1(1+g)^1}{(1+r)^2} + \frac{dividend_1(1+g)^2}{(1+r)^3} + ... \text{ to } \infty$$

The left-hand-side of the above formula equals either of two metrics. "Stock value" represents intrinsic value when all right-hand-side values are specified. Alternatively, "stock value" represents the observed stock price when one of the right-hand-side variables is the unknown.

The right-hand-side represents the discounted sum of the infinite dividend stream. Summing all terms could be rather time consuming because there always is at least one more number to add. For the realistic case when $g < r$ the sum is convergent. That is, the numerator rises slower than the denominator. One-plus-r raised to the fiftieth power is much larger than one-plus-g to the fiftieth. The terms far to the right vanish. Stated differently, the contribution to present value of a dividend received 50-years from now is nil.

Formula 8.8 shows the discounted sum of the infinite dividend stream when $g < r$

> **FORMULA 8.8 Intrinsic value, constant growth dividend valuation model**
>
> $$\left(\frac{stock}{value}\right)_0 = \frac{dividend_1}{r-g}$$
>
> $$= \frac{dividend_0(1+g)}{r-g}$$

The two lines in formula 8.8 present algebraically equivalent representations of the constant growth dividend valuation model (also known as the Gordon dividend growth model). The cash flow timing implicit with formula 8.8 is that the stock valuation occurs at time 0. The seller just received $dividend_0$ whereas the buyer expects to receive $dividend_1$ in exactly one period. The last line of formula 8.8 recognizes that with constant growth $dividend_1$ equals $dividend_0$ times $(1+g)$.

EXAMPLE 9 Constant growth dividend valuation, simplest example

A share of company stock paid its annual dividend of $1.16 exactly 4 years ago. You expect that next year's dividend will equal $1.60. You believe the stock represents a fair investment if it were to offer a risk premium of 750 basis points relative to the current Treasury yield of 4.90 percent. The stock's current price is $20. According to the constant growth dividend valuation model: (i) sketch the expected dividend stream; (ii) compute the stock's current intrinsic value; and (iii) should you buy the stock?

SOLUTION

There are 5 years between "4 years ago" and "next year". Use formula 8.7 to find the dividend growth rate:

$$\$1.60 = \$1.16(1 + g)^5$$

$$g = 6.64\%$$

Each year's dividend is 6.64 percent larger than the previous year's. Sketch (i) the dividend stream as follows

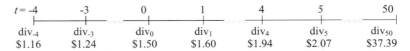

$t = -4$	-3	0	1	4	5	50
div_{-4}	div_{-3}	div_0	div_1	div_4	div_5	div_{50}
$1.16	$1.24	$1.50	$1.60	$1.94	$2.07	$37.39

The time line assumes that four years ago occurs at time −4, that right now is time 0, and that next year is time 1.

Find (ii) the stock's current intrinsic value. The discount rate, r, equals the 4.90 percent risk free rate plus the 7.5 percent risk premium; $r = 12.4$ percent. You could compute intrinsic value as

$$\left(\frac{stock}{value}\right)_0 = \frac{\$1.60}{(1 + .124)^1} + ... + \frac{\$1.94}{(1 + .124)^4} + \frac{\$2.07}{(1 + .124)^5} + ... + \frac{\$37.39}{(1 + .124)^{50}} \text{ to } \infty$$

Formula 8.8 enables a simpler and more efficient calculation that obtains exactly the same answer as summing the infinite terms above:

$$\left(\frac{stock}{value}\right)_0 = \frac{\$1.60}{0.1240 - 0.0664}$$

$$= \$27.78$$

Finally (iii), invoke the decision rule. The stock's intrinsic value of $27.78 exceeds the actual stock price of $20. The stock is worth more than it costs, so put it on the buy list! If the actual share price instantly moved up to the intrinsic value, the investor would realize a 38.9% rate of return (that is, $0.3890 = 27.78/20 - 1$).

Investment professionals often use intrinsic value estimates to rank stocks from most promising to least promising. Stocks that appear significantly undervalued are most promising. Professionals do not expect the share price to move instantly up to intrinsic value. Instead, the expectation is that over a longer horizon, say one year, the share price converges to intrinsic value.

Next year's intrinsic value, however, differs from today's intrinsic value. Glean insight about the relation between next year's and today's intrinsic values by constructing a ratio with formula 8.8.

$$\left(\frac{intrinsic}{value}\right)_1 \bigg/ \left(\frac{intrinsic}{value}\right)_0 = \frac{dividend_1(1 + g)}{r - g} \bigg/ \frac{dividend_1}{r - g}$$

$$= (1 + g)$$

Next year's intrinsic value is *g* percent bigger than this year's. The constant growth dividend valuation model implicitly assumes that intrinsic value, just like the dividend, grows smoothly at rate *g*. The example below uses this insight.

EXAMPLE 10 Find ROR when today's price converges to next year's intrinsic value
The company just paid its annual dividend of $3.30 per share. You believe that the dividend grows smoothly at a 9.8 percent annual rate. Today's price-to-earnings ratio is 12.5, and the company's payout ratio always is 80%. You assess the stock's intrinsic value by discounting future dividends with a 16 percent annual rate. You buy the stock at today's price with the expectation that the price next year converges to next year's intrinsic value. What is the expected annual rate of return on this stock investment?

SOLUTION
The periodic rate of return, according to formula 4.2, equals the percentage change in wealth. Beginning wealth equals today's stock price because this is the amount you pay for the investment. Ending wealth equals next year's stock price plus the dividend. Thus, the shareholders' rate of return is:

$$ROR_t = \frac{price_t + dividend_t - price_{t-1}}{price_{t-1}}$$

Find the rate of return throughout the next year (ROR_1) by substituting values for the three right-hand-side variables.

Next year's dividend equals today's dividend times *(1 + g):*

$$dividend_1 = \$3.30\,(1 + .098)$$

$$= \$3.62$$

You expect to receive a dividend next year of $3.62, at which time you might sell the stock.

Today's price stems from the definition for the price to earnings ratio:

$$price\text{-}to\text{-}earnings\ ratio = \frac{price}{earnings}$$

$$= 12.5$$

Earnings times the payout ratio equals dividends. Because today's payout ratio and dividend equal 0.80 and $3.30, respectively, find today's share price as:

$$12.5 = \frac{price_0}{\$3.30/0.80}$$

$$price_0 = \$51.56$$

The investment today costs $51.56.

Finding next year's price requires finding next year's intrinsic value. First, however, use formula 8.8 to find this year's intrinsic value:

$$\left(\frac{stock}{value}\right)_0 = \frac{\$3.30\,(1 + .0980)}{0.16 - 0.0980}$$

$$= \$58.44$$

Next year's intrinsic value simply equals this year's intrinsic value times $(1 + g)$. Thus, next year's price is $64.17 (that is, $64.17 = $58.55(1.098)$).

Substitute and find

$$ROR_1 = \frac{\$64.17 + 3.62 - 51.56}{51.56}$$

$$= 31.48\%$$

The stock investment promises a hefty return!

EXERCISES 8.2B

Numerical quickies

1. Exactly 8 years ago the company paid a 32 cent annual dividend. Today's annual dividend is $1.22. Find the average annual dividend growth rate throughout the past 8 years. ©ST5

2. Yesterday (year-end 2525) the company paid its annual dividend of $1.45. The annual dividend history is:

year	dividend
2521	$0.87
2522	$1.07
2523	$1.16
2524	$1.20

Assume that dividends grow smoothly in accordance with the constant exponential growth model, even though each year there may be random errors that on average equal zero. Compute the best estimate of the dividend growth rate and find the expected values for dividends in years 2524 and 2525. ©ST18

3. Yesterday (year-end 2525) the company paid its annual dividend of $1.60. You believe that the stock merits a buy recommendation if it returns 16% per year. Your estimate of intrinsic value assumes that dividends grow smoothly in accordance with the constant exponential growth model. The annual dividend history is:

year	dividend
2521	$0.99
2522	$1.28
2523	$1.26
2524	$1.63

Find the best estimate of the dividend growth rate and intrinsic value. ©ST13

4. The Company dividend appears to grow smoothly at a constant exponential rate of 5.5%. Analysts forecast that next year's dividend should equal $3.80. For you to receive a 14% average annual rate of return, how much should you offer for the stock? ©ST19

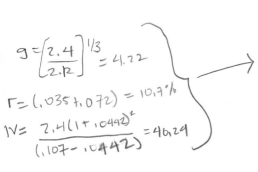

5. The Company is expected to announce their annual dividend tomorrow. One year ago they paid a dividend of $2.40, and 4 years ago they paid $2.12. You believe that future dividends will grow by the same rate as past ones. You are aware that riskless government securities are yielding 3.5%, and you make an offer to purchase the stock so that you earn 7.2% above the risk-free rate. How much is your offer price? ©ST2am

6. The company yesterday paid their annual dividend of $2.00 and the share price was $35.10. The company growth rate is 8.6%. Suppose the stock is always priced in accordance with the constant growth dividend valuation model. Find the stock's annual total rate of return. ©ST9

Numerical challengers

7. The Company is expected to announce their annual dividend tomorrow. One year ago they paid a dividend of $1.60 and 8 years ago they paid

$1.00. You believe that future dividends will grow by the same rate as past ones. You are aware that riskless government securities are yielding 3.7%, and you make an offer to purchase the stock so that you earn 10.3% above the riskless rate. Due to market conditions, you must purchase the stock for $7.50 above your offer price. Find your expected total rate of return at this higher purchase price. ©ST2bm

8. The company just paid its annual dividend of $4.25. You believe the dividend will grow perpetually at 7.8% per annum. Today's price-to-earnings ratio is 10.9 and the payout ratio always equals 65%. You assess intrinsic value with a 16.6% discount rate. Find the one-year rate of return from buying the stock today and holding it one year, given that next year's share price converges to next year's intrinsic value. ©ST8

2.C. Total return partitions into dividend and capital gain yields

Stocks compensate investors two ways. Stockholders receive dividends when the company pays them. Stockholders receive capital gains when market forces push the share price higher. Both are important components of the total rate of return.

Discussion in the time value chapters establishes that the discount rate, r, represents the total rate of return. Rearrange formula 8.8 for a specification of r from the constant growth dividend valuation model:

FORMULA 8.9 Components for stocks of the total rate of return

$$r = \frac{dividend_1}{\left(\begin{array}{c} stock \\ value \end{array}\right)_0} + g$$

$$= \left(\begin{array}{c} expected \\ dividend \\ yield \end{array}\right) + \left(\begin{array}{c} capital \\ gains \\ yield \end{array}\right)$$

The total return from a stock investment has two sources. A current income component provides immediate cash flow in the form of dividends, a changing price component causes capital gains or losses. Table 8.4 contrasts characteristics for these two components.

The table shows the dividend is a realized and taxable cash flow that is fairly predictable and relatively small. The expected capital gains, conversely, is an accrual that is not taxable until the security is sold. Predicting capital gains is relatively difficult, but they comprise the largest component of total stock returns. These characteristics are important when selecting stocks. Two alternative stocks, for example, may provide the same expected total rate of return. The stocks may not be equally appealing, however, if the partitioning of their total returns into dividends and capital gains varies.

The actual share price set through market trading arguably equals the best estimate of a stock's true value. Linking the actual stock price to a good estimate of the

Expected dividend yield ($dividend_1 / price_0$)	Capital gains yield (g)
realized cash flow	accrued cash flow
immediately taxable	taxes are deferred
relatively predictable & more certain	very unpredictable & more uncertain
relatively small, averaging 1 to 4%	relatively large, averaging 8 to 12%

TABLE 8.4
Component characteristics for the total rate of return

growth rate enables insight about the promised total rate of return. The example below relies on formula 8.9 to answer a powerful question.

EXAMPLE 11 Find the total rate of return

The company just increased its annual dividend by 32 cents relative to last year, so that today's dividend per share is $4.06. Dividends for this company grow smoothly at a constant rate. The payout ratio is constant at 65 percent. The stock's price-to-earnings ratio today equals 17.3, and you believe the market properly values the stock. What is the expected total rate of return that the constant growth dividend valuation model implies?

SOLUTION

The percentage change in dividend equals the growth rate:

$$g = \frac{dividend_0 - dividend_{-1}}{dividend_{-1}}$$

$$= \frac{\$0.32}{\$4.06 - \$0.32}$$

$$= 8.56\%$$

Use the definition for the price-to-earnings ratio to find the current price (recall that earnings equals dividend ÷ payout ratio):

$$17.3 = \frac{price_0}{\$4.06/0.65}$$

$$price_0 = \$108.06$$

Formula 8.9 specifies the total rate of return:

$$r = \frac{\$4.06\,(1+.0856)}{\$108.06} + 0.0856$$

$$= 4.07\% + 8.56\%$$

$$= 12.63\%$$

The bottom line inference is as simple as 1-2-3: *If* (1) you are confident about the growth rate; (2) persistent and smooth growth is reasonably accurate; and (3) the actual stock price is the best guess about true value, *then* the expected rate of return from a stock investment equals, as formula 8.9 shows, the sum of the expected dividend yield plus the growth rate.

Dividend yields historically are an important component of the total rate of return. Dividends in the preceding example are the source of about one-third of the total rate of return. That historically is a realistic partition for the total rate of return.

During the 1990s dividends declined in relative importance. Dividend yields for S&P 500 companies averaged less than 2 percent, even though total returns averaged about 15 percent. Growth gained glamour with investors. Perhaps, however, this is only cyclical crowd behavior. After a sustained flat-to-falling stock market maybe investors will flock back toward fundamentally strong dividend yields. It's hard to predict the direction they'll turn next!

EXERCISES 8.2

Numerical quickies

1. A share of company stock just paid its annual dividend of $1.45. Exactly 4 years ago the dividend was $0.90. Your analyst tells you the stock's

expected dividend yield is 5%. You believe the constant growth dividend valuation model applies perfectly to this properly valued stock. Find (i) the expected total rate of return and (ii) the stock's current intrinsic value. ©ST16

2. You pick up the *Wall Street Journal* and see that riskless government securities are offering 6.35%. You read that the Company just increased their annual dividend by $0.12 cents so that today it is paying a $1.94 dividend per share. You also read that its share price is $36.20 . You believe the constant growth dividend valuation model applies perfectly to this properly valued stock. What is the implied risk premium that is earned from owning the stock; that is, by how much does the expected return on the stock exceed the riskless interest rate? ©ST17

Numerical Challengers

3. The company just increased its annual dividend by $0.71 relative to last year, so that today's dividend per share is $8.02. Dividends for this company grow smoothly at a constant rate. The payout ratio is constant at 25%. The stock's price-to-earnings ratio today equals 15.0, and you believe the market properly values the stock. Partition the expected total rate of return that the constant growth dividend valuation model implies into the leading dividend yield and capital gains yield. ©ST14b

4. You believe that if today you buy a share of Company stock and sell it in one year for $33.72 your total rate of return should equal 17.1%. You expect share price movements will reflect a capital gains yield of 10.9%. Just yesterday the company paid its annual dividend. According to the constant dividend growth model, what dividend should you expect next year? ©ST4a

3. THE FUNDAMENTAL SEARCH FOR TRUE INTRINSIC VALUE

Assessing a stock's intrinsic value provides important information for investment decision-making. Finding an asset's true intrinsic value and subsequently investing only in undervalued stocks does not, however, guarantee superior investment performance. Imagine that you discover a stock selling for $70 really is worth $100. Imagine, too, that you are absolutely right. Are you certain that if you buy the stock you will realize the $30 capital gain? Absolutely not! You only make the excess return if the market pushes the price up to its proper level. If the market pushes the price even lower then you lose. Perhaps the market is wrong and you are right. But we are all price-takers in financial markets and the best we can do is make educated investment decisions and trust our forecast of expected outcomes.

Stock prices in the long run and on-average must nonetheless follow intrinsic values. Serious investors search for true intrinsic values. The two subsections below investigate important elements of fundamental analysis. The first subsection examines in more detail the role of growth. The second subsection investigates multiplier analysis.

3.A. Intrinsic value and the sustainable growth rate

Growth is an extremely important component of total return. Growing sales, net income, dividends, and cash flow support rising stock prices. Yet how much growth can a company sustain? For this answer, recall the lessons from financial accounting about sustainable growth. A company growing at the sustainable growth rate maintains steady asset turnover, net profit margin, payout policy, and debt ratio. Formula 8.10 reprints the sustainable growth rate equation presented previously as formula 3.4. These three formulations are algebraically equivalent:

$$g^{sustainable} = \frac{R_t(1+D_t/SE_t)}{A_t - R_t(1+D_t/SE_t)}$$

$$= \frac{(retention\,ratio)(ROE)}{1-(retention\,ratio)(ROE)} \qquad when\ ROE = \frac{Net\ income_t}{Stockholders\ equity_t}$$

$$= (retention\,ratio)(ROE) \qquad when\ ROE = \frac{Net\ income_t}{Stockholders\ equity_{t-1}}$$

The variables *R, A, D,* and *SE* denote *New retained earnings, Total assets, Total debt,* and *Stockholders' equity,* respectively.

The top line (formula 8.10a) uses from the income statement *New retained earnings* (R_t) and from the contemporaneous balance sheet *Total assets* (A_t), *Total debt* (D_t), and *Stockholders equity* (SE_t). The middle and bottom lines (8.10b and 8.10c, respectively) use the retention ratio (that is, *1 – dividends/Net income*) and return-on-equity (*ROE*). The *ROE* is the ambiguous ratio of a flow and a balance with different definitions in-use. The two *ROE* definitions above differ because *Net income* is divided by *Stockholders equity* at either the end or beginning of period.

The sustainable growth rate is an important consideration when assessing the likelihood of sustainable support for today's stock price.

EXAMPLE 12 Sustainable growth and the one-year ROR
The company just paid a dividend of $1.60 per share. The company has a 14 percent return on equity (= *net income_t* ÷ stockholders equity_t), a 30 percent payout ratio (= *dividends ÷ net income*), and today's price-to-earnings ratio is 18.1. You believe the company operates at their sustainable growth rate. Find (i) the implied total rate of return if the stock is properly valued; (ii) today's intrinsic value when assessed with a 16 percent discount rate; and (iii) the annual rate of return from purchasing the stock at today's price and selling it next year after the price has converged to next year's intrinsic value.

SOLUTION
Computing the implied total rate of return with formula 8.9 requires finding numbers for *g* and *dividend*, and using the actual share price as *stock value*. Compute $g^{sustainable}$ with formula 8.10b since this *ROE* definition corresponds to the problem set-up. The *retention ratio* equals (1 – *payout ratio*). Thus:

$$g^{sustainable} = \frac{(1 - 0.30)(0.14)}{1 - (1 - 0.30)(0.14)}$$

$$= 10.86\%$$

Find today's share price from the price-to-earnings ratio definition:

$$18.1 = \frac{price_0}{\$1.60/0.30}$$

$$price_0 = \$96.53$$

Substitute into formula 8.9 and find (i) the implied total rate of return:

$$r = \frac{\$1.60\,(1+.1086)}{\$96.53} + 0.1086$$

$$= 12.70\%$$

Notice that the 12.7 percent implied total rate of return is less than the 16 percent discount rate with which you intend to assess intrinsic value.

Find (ii) intrinsic value with formula 8.8:

$$\left(\frac{stock}{value}\right)_0 = \frac{\$1.60\ (1+.1086)}{0.16 - 0.1086}$$

$$= \$34.54$$

The intrinsic value of $34.54 is significantly less than the actual stock price of $96.53 and suggests rather extreme overvaluation.

Finding (iii) the one year ROR from purchasing the stock at today's price requires numbers for next year's dividend and intrinsic value. The dividend and intrinsic value grow at $g^{sustainable}$. Thus:

$$ROR_1 = \frac{price_1 + dividend_1 - price_0}{price_0}$$

$$= \frac{\$34.54(1.1086) + \$1.60(1.1086) - \$96.53}{\$96.53}$$

$$= -58.49\%$$

The investment likely represents a losing proposition. Sustainable growth does not seem able to sustain the current stock price. Either the lofty price results from speculative factors or, alternatively, an error in the fundamental analysis wrongly depresses the intrinsic value estimate.

EXERCISES 8.3A

Numerical quickies

1. The Company just paid a dividend of $2.30 per share. The Company offers a 17.10% return on equity (= *Net income$_t$* ÷ *Stockholders equity$_t$*), a 60% payout ratio (= dividends ÷ net income), and equity investors assess intrinsic value with a 8.8% rate of return. The Company always operates at their sustainable growth rate and successfully holds constant all relevant financial ratios. Find the share's intrinsic value. ©SV2a

2. The Company's total assets at year-end 2525 equal $6,200 and are financed by debt of $2,500 and stockholder's equity of $3,700 (160 shares outstanding). Their sales for year 2525 were $6,820 and yielded a net profit margin (= net income ÷ sales) of 2.70%; the payout ratio (= dividends ÷ net income) always is 60%. The price-to-earnings ratio at year-end 2525 is 6.28. For the foreseeable future the company intends to operate at their sustainable growth rate. Assess the share's intrinsic value by using a 10.9% discount rate. Contrast intrinsic value with share price. ©SV1a

Numerical challengers

3. The Company just announced earnings per share of $3.50, which means that their price to earnings ratio is 16.79. The Company has an asset turnover ratio (= *Sales$_t$* ÷ *Total assets$_t$*) of 2.09, a net profit margin (= *Net income ÷ Sales*) of 4.6%, a debt ratio (= *Total debt* ÷ *Total assets*) of 40%, and a payout ratio (= *Dividends ÷ Net income*) of 45%. The Company always operates at their sustainable growth rate and successfully holds constant all relevant financial ratios. You would like to invest in the stock such that you'll get a 13.8% total rate of return. Contrast intrinsic value with share price. ©SV3a

4. Company *Total assets* at year-end 2525 equal $3,900 and are financed by *Total debt* of $1,300 and *Stockholders' equity* of $2,600 (200 shares outstanding). Their *Sales* for year 2525 equal $8,190 and yielded a net profit margin *(= Net income ÷ Sales)* of 1.70%; the payout ratio *(= Dividends ÷ Net income)* always is 55%. The price-to-earnings ratio at year-end 2525 is 7.5. For the foreseeable future, the company intends to operate at their sustainable growth rate. You assess the share's intrinsic value by using a 11.7% discount rate. Suppose you buy the share today at its market price of 12/31/2525. You hold the stock until 12/31/2526 at which time you receive next year's dividend. Also, suppose the market share price has converged to its intrinsic value of 12/31/2526. What is the one-year rate-of-return from investing in the share? ©SV4dm

3.B. Price multiples and fundamental analysis

The most common fundamental analysis does not explicitly discount expected cash flow streams. Instead the analysis compares fundamental ratios for a prospective investment with those from a peer group. Typical fundamental ratios include the price-to-earnings, price-to-book, price-to-cash flow, and price-to-sales. Other ratios are possible but all contain stock price in the numerator. The variable in the denominator always is per share, too. Each fundamental ratio measures the market value per dollar of the variable in the denominator.

The data in table 8.5 illustrates a multiplier analysis for six dominant companies in the air courier industry. Suppose the prospective investment is FedEx. The recent share price of FedEx on the New York Stock Exchange is $44.29. Column 1 clearly shows that among this peer group the share price for FedEx is highest. The relevant question, however, is whether the price undervalues the share's intrinsic value.

Multiplier analyses glean valuation insights by relating the share price to a key measure of entrepreneurial activity. The most popular fundamental ratio in the financial press is the P/E, that is price divided by earnings per share. For FedEx the P/E is 17.8. This indicates that the market assigns a value of $17.80 to every dollar of FedEx earnings. For AirNet Systems the market values a dollar of earnings at only $7.10. A common but often incorrect conclusion is that the likelihood of overvaluation increases as the fundamental ratio gets higher. Naive signals from the P/E ratio suggest that FedEx is overvalued relative to AirNet. But Airborne and TNT appear even more overvalued!

Multiplier analyses make implicit assumptions about future cash flow streams. The P/E analysis, for example, assumes that the present value of future earnings per dollar of current earnings is identical for all members of the peer group. The assumption quite often is wrong.

TABLE 8.5
Multiples for a peer group of air courier companies.

Company (ticker)	stock price -1-	price-to-earnings -2-	price-to-book -3-	price-to-cash flow -3-	price-to-sales -5-
Air T, Inc. (AIRT)	$ 4.00	10.0	1.18	5.5	0.17
Airborne, Inc. (ABF)	12.65	45.2	0.69	2.5	0.19
AirNet Systems, Inc. (ANS)	4.25	7.1	0.60	2.3	0.34
Atlas Air, Inc. (CGO)	35.47	15.6	2.60	7.4	1.71
FedEx Corporation (FDX)	44.29	17.8	2.45	6.7	0.66
TNT Post Group N.V. (TP)	25.94	51.9	5.78	17.3	1.42

Source: American Association of Individual Investors, February 2001.

The constant growth dividend valuation model allows important insights about multiplier analyses. Formula 8.8 expresses intrinsic value as the discounted sum of expected dividends. With a constant payout ratio, however, substitution and rearrangement shows:

$$\left(\frac{stock}{value}\right)_0 = \frac{dividend_1}{r - g}$$

$$= \frac{payout \times earnings_1}{r - g}$$

Divide both sides by $earnings_1$ to obtain:

$$\left(\frac{stock}{value}\right)_0 \Big/ earnings_1 = \frac{payout}{r - g}$$

When numbers are given for all variables except *stock value*, then *stock value* represents intrinsic value. The right-hand-side of the formula computes the "intrinsic P/E ratio." Alternatively, when *stock value* and *earnings* are set to the actual numbers then the ratio is the actual price-to-leading-earnings ratio (the earnings next period are known as "leading earnings").

Intrinsic value of earnings equals present value of earnings. In the constant growth special case the intrinsic value equals the payout ratio divided by $(r - g)$. Differences among companies in r, g, and payout policies justify differences in P/E ratios. Fundamental ratios should differ when present values of expected cash flow streams differ.

Consider the effect on the intrinsic P/E ratio if companies have different growth rates. Inspect formula 8.11 and notice that as *g* gets bigger the intrinsic P/E ratio gets larger. We expect, all else equal, that ever-larger growth rates correspond with ever-larger P/E ratios. For the five years ending with table 8.6, in fact, annual average growth in operating cash flow is 1.4 percent for AirNet Systems and 9.0 percent for FedEx. It is even higher for Airborne. Perhaps the P/E ratio is larger for FedEx than for AirNet due to differences in growth, and valuation effects have nothing to do with it.

Differences in discount rates also impact the intrinsic P/E ratio. Inspect formula 8.11 and notice that as *r* gets bigger the intrinsic P/E ratio gets smaller. Larger *r* correspond to higher risk premia. That is, two identical cash flow streams have different present values if their risks differ. We expect, all else equal, that riskier companies associate with small P/E ratios irrespective of valuation effects. The market capitalization of AirNet Systems is $46 million and its stock price is extremely volatile. FedEx market capitalization exceeds $12 billion and its stock price is less volatile. Perhaps the P/E ratio is larger for FedEx than for AirNet due to differences in risk, and valuation effects have nothing to do with it.

Consider finally the effect on the intrinsic P/E ratio if companies have different payout policies. This consideration requires recognition that the payout ratio has offsetting effects. A direct effect is that higher payout ratios associate with ever-larger P/E ratios because the dividend stream is a larger proportion of earnings. This effect appears in the numerator of formula 8.11. An indirect effect appears in the denominator. Higher payout ratios associate with smaller growth rates (see formula 8.10c). Smaller growth rates in turn associate with ever-smaller P/E ratios. The effect of the payout policy on the intrinsic P/E ratio is ambiguous due to offsetting effects.

Additional insight about the effect of payout policy on intrinsic value results by generalizing formula 8.11. Formula 8.10c shows:

$$g = (1 - payout) \times ROE$$

Represent the *ROE* as the total rate of return *r* multiplied by a constant:

$$ROE = \alpha r$$

The number α simply equals a constant of proportionality that depends on a company's investment and financing opportunities. ROE measures the book rate of return that the company earns on its investments. Discount rate *r* measures the rate of return that shareholders earn from capital. Substitution into the intrinsic P/E formula and rearrangement shows:

FORMULA 8.12 The intrinsic P/E ratio, general version

$$\left.\left(\frac{stock}{value}\right)_0 \middle/ earnings_1 = \frac{1}{r}\left[\frac{payout}{1 - \alpha(1 - payout)}\right]\right.$$

The intrinsic P/E ratio equals the reciprocal of the discount rate multiplied by the term in square brackets. The term in square brackets captures the effect of payout policy on intrinsic value. The effect of the payout policy depends on the value of α.

The constant α equals 1 when *ROE* equals *r*. For this special case the intrinsic P/E ratio simplifies as follows:

$$\left.\left(\frac{stock}{value}\right)_0 \middle/ earnings_1 = \frac{1}{r}\right.$$

When the rate of return investors receive on their stock (*r*) exactly equals the rate of return the company earns from its investments (*ROE*), company payout policy is irrelevant and the intrinsic P/E ratio equals the reciprocal of the discount rate. This special case typifies mature competitive industries in which economic profit equals zero.

The constant α exceeds 1 when *ROE* exceeds *r*. For this special case an ever-larger payout ratio makes an ever-smaller intrinsic P/E ratio. The stock market penalizes high payout policies when company investment opportunities surpass rates of return that shareholders earn from financial investments. Because company opportunities are exceptional, shareholders prefer that the company retain earnings and grow.

Alternatively, the constant α is less than 1 when *ROE* is smaller than *r*. For this special case an ever-larger payout ratio makes an ever-larger intrinsic P/E ratio. The stock market rewards high payout policies because company investment opportunities are subpar. Shareholders prefer that the company payout earnings thereby allowing shareholders the opportunity to reinvest the money in alternative uses.

The upshot of multiplier analysis is that many factors cause variation in fundamental ratios besides valuation errors. Using a fundamental ratio to infer misvaluation requires extreme care constructing the peer group. Undeniably if one company is a clone of the other in every imaginable way, that everything about the two is identical except the share prices, then a valuation inference is valid. As differences arise between company characteristics, however, the inference weakens. And every company, like every household, is unique. Fundamental differences in entrepreneurial factors cause differences in intrinsic values.

EXERCISES 8.3B

Conceptual
1. Suppose the company stock price is $56, earnings per share is $1.56, operating cash flow per share is $3.19, and book value per share is $24.78. For a carefully constructed peer group you find the following average multiples: the price-to-earnings ratio is 30, the price-to-cash flow ratio is 15; the price-to-book is 3. Compare the company and peer group multiples and, assuming the peers are virtual clones of the company, make inferences about the company share price. ©ST10

ANSWERS TO CHAPTER 8 EXERCISES

EXERCISES 8.1

1. The short-run is 1 day and long-run is 20 days. Use formula 8.3 and compute the cross-over price = (20 x $26 – $21.25) / (20 – 1), which is $26.25.
2. The short-run is 2 days and long-run is 20 days. Use formula 8.2 and compute the cross-over price = { 2 x (20 x $25.25 – $20.50) – 20 x (2 x $23 – $23.50) } / (20 – 2), which is $28.83.
3. The short-run is 2 days and long-run is 5 days. Use formula 8.2 and compute the cross-over price = { 2 x (5 x $39.75 – $32.25) – 5 x (2 x $36.25 – $37.00) } / (5 – 2), which is $51.83.

EXERCISES 8.2

1. The present value of the perpetual stream is $6.80 / 0.103, which is $66.01. That present value exists one period before the first dividend, that is 7 years from now. Discount $66.01 / 1.103^7 and find the intrinsic value today equals $33.24.
2. You don't get yesterday's dividend, but in one year will receive $2.30 (= 1.044 x $2.20). Sell the stock for $24 and get a total of $26.30. Discount with 12.2% and find the intrinsic value is $23.44 (= $26.30 / 1.122).
3. This solution relies on standard time value relationships. In one year you receive a total of $92.60 (= $89 + $3.60). Present value today is $84. Use the lump-sum formula to find the ROR is 10.2% (= ($92.60 / $84)^1 – 1).
4. In ten years receive a total of $37.70 (= $34 + $3.70). Present value today is $13.64. Use the lump-sum formula to find the ROR is 10.7% (= ($37.70 / $13.64)$^{1/10}$ – 1).
5. The present value at time 4 of the perpetuity is $5.60 / ROR. Discount it back 4 periods and use formula 8.4 and find the ROR:
   $$\$40.43 = \$0 \times PVIFA_{ROR, 4} + (1 + ROR)^{-4} \times (\$5.60 / ROR).$$
   Solve this on the financial calculator by setting CF_0 = $-40.43; CF_1 = 0 for 4 periods; CF_2 = $5.60 for 100 (the value of the perpetuity for the first 100 years is basically the same as for the first million years). Compute that IRR equals 9.56%.

EXERCISES 8.2A

1. Use formula 8.5 and find the ROR is 7.69% (= $6 / $78).
2. Add 175 BP to 4.5% and find that the target ROR for the preferred stock is 6.25% (= .0450 + .0175). Find the intrinsic value with formula 8.5:
   intrinsic value = $3.75 / 0.0625; = $60.00.
3. Find the actual ROR for the preferred stock with formula 8.5:
   $101.50 = $6.25 / ROR; or ROR = 6.16%.
   The actual risk premium that the preferred stock offers investors equals the difference between 6.16% and the CD rate of 4.65%. The risk premium is 141 basis points (= 0.0616 – 0.0465). Note that the risk premium is not big enough to satisfy your preferred risk premium of 6.65% (= .0465 + .0200). Find the intrinsic value with
   intrinsic value = $6.25 / 0.0665; = $93.98.
   The intrinsic value (= $93.98) is less than the actual price (= $101.50) and according to rule 8.2 this is a sell.
4. You pay $58.10 at time 0 and receive $5 at time 1. Then at time 2 you receive $5 plus the sell price. The sell price satisfies the perpetuity formula *price = PMT/r* , or *price* = $5 / .065, or *price* = $76.92.
   Total cash flow at time 2 is $81.92. The annual rate of return satisfies the equality
   $$\$58.10 = \$5/(1+r) + 81.92/(1+r)^2.$$
   Use the financial calculator and find that r = 23.1%

5. You pay $52.25 at time 0 and receive $6 at times 1-3. Then at time 4 you receive $6 plus the sell price. The sell price satisfies the perpetuity formula *price = PMT/r*, or *price* = $6 / 0.07, or *price* = $85.71. The annual rate of return equals 22.9% and satisfies constant annuity formula 5.1 wherein *CF* = $6, *FV* = $85.71, *PV* = $52.25, and *N* = 4:

$$\$52.25 = [\$6 \times (1 - (1+r)^{-4}) \div r] + (\$85.71 \times (1+r)^{-4})\}$$

EXERCISES 8.2B

1. $g = (\$1.22 / \$0.32)^{1/8} - 1$; or $g = 18.2\%$.
2. This problem involves execution of the *Calculator clue* in Example 8 for the 5 data points in this problem. Enter the data, set the calculator to EXPonential, solve that $b = 1.1203$ which implies that $g = 12.03\%$. Enter that X' = 4 and find that the expected $div_{2524} = \$1.27$. Likewise, $div_{2525} = \$1.42$.
3. Execute calculator clue from Example 8 and solve that $b = 1.1277$ which implies that $g = 12.77\%$. Enter that X' = 6 and find that the expected $div_{2526} = \$1.91$. Use formula 8.8 to find that intrinsic value equals $59.06 (= \$1.91 / (0.16 - 0.1277)$. The stock is a buy if the actual price is less than $59.
4. Use formula 8.8 to find that intrinsic value equals $44.71 (= \$3.80 / (0.14 - 0.055)$. The stock is a buy if actual price is less than $44.71.
5. Find that $g = 4.22\%$ [$=(\$2.40 / \$2.12)^{1/3} - 1$. Then find that $r = 10.7\%$ (= 0.035 + 0.072). Then use formula 8.8 to find that intrinsic value equals $40.24 [= \$2.40(1 + 0.0422)^2 / (0.1070 - 0.0422); = \$2.61 / 0.0648]$. *[handwritten: STZam]*
6. Use formula 8.8 to find unknown variable *r* equals 14.8%:

   $35.10 = \$2.00 / (r - 0.086)$; or $r = \$2.00 / \$35.10 + 0.086$.
7. Find that $g = 6.94\%$ [$=(\$1.60 / \$1.00)^{1/7} - 1$]. Then find that $r = 14.0\%$ (= 0.037 + 0.103). Then use formula 8.8 to find that intrinsic value equals $25.94 [= \$2.40(1 + 0.0694)^2 / (0.1400 - 0.0694); = \$1.83 / 0.0706]$. You offer to purchase for $25.94 and seller counteroffers at $33.44.

   Again use formula 8.8 but this time find that unknown variable *r* equals 12.4%: $33.44 = \$1.83 / (r - 0.0694)$; or $r = \$1.83 / \$33.44 + 0.0694$.
8. First find today's price by using the P/E ratio and dividend:

   $P_0 / E_0 = 10.9$; $E_0 \times payout = div_0$; $E_0 = \$4.25 / 0.65$; $P_0 = 10.9 \times (\$4.25 / 0.65)$; or $P_0 = \$71.27$.

   Now use formula 8.8 to find intrinsic value equals $52.06 [V_0 = \$4.25 (1 + 0.078) / (0.1660 - 0.0780); = \$4.58 / 0.0880]$. Note that next year's intrinsic value is $56.12 [= \$52.06 \times (1 + 0.078)]$.

   Buy the stock today for $71.27 and in one year receive a dividend of $4.58 and sell the stock for $56.12. Find that the *ROR* equals -14.8% [= (\$56.12 + \$4.58 - \$71.27) / \$71.27].

EXERCISES 8.2c

1. Find the dividend growth rate as $g = (\$1.45 \div \$0.90)^{1/4}$; $g = 12.66\%$. The total rate of return equals, according to formula 8.9, the sum of the growth rate (12.66%) and the expected dividend yield (5%). Thus, *r* equals 17.66 percent. All numbers required by formula 8.8 to find intrinsic value are known:

   $V_0 = div_0(1+g)/(r-g)$; $= \$1.45(1.1266) / (.1766 - .1266)$; $V_0 = \$32.67$.
2. First observe that $g = (div_1 - div_0)/div_0$; $g = .12/(1.94 - .12)$; $g = 6.59\%$. Now use formula 8.9 to find that $r = div_1/V_0 + g$; $r = \$1.94(1.0659)/\$36.20 + 6.59\%$; or $r = 12.31\%$. The share offers a risk premium relative to the government security equal to 5.96% (= 12.31% - 6.35%).
3. Find *g* by dividing the dividend increase by last period's dividend:

   $g = \$0.71 / (\$8.02 - \$0.71)$; or $g = 9.71\%$.

Find today's price by using the P/E ratio and dividend:
$P_0 / E_0 = 15$; $E_0 \times payout = div_0$; $E_0 = \$8.02 / 0.25$; $P_0 = 15 \times (\$8.02 / 0.25)$; or $P_0 = \$481.20$.

Now use formula 8.8 (or 8.9) wherein intrinsic value equals \$481.20 and solve for the unknown total rate of return r:
$\$481.20 = \$8.02(1 + 0.0971) / (r - 0.0971)$; or $r = \$8.80 / \$481.20 + 0.0971$; or $r = 1.83\% + 9.71\%$; $= 11.54\%$.

The 11.54% total rate of return includes a 1.83% leading dividend yield plus a 9.71% capital gains yield.

4. The total rate of return r of 17.1% equals the capital gains yield of 10.9% plus the leading dividend yield, implying the dividend yield is 6.2% (= 0.171 − 0.109). Today's price is 10.9% smaller than next period's price; today's price is \$30.41 (= \$33.72 / 1.109). Thus, 6.2% = $div_1 / \$30.41$, or $div_1 = \$1.89$.

EXERCISES 8.3A

1. The *Retention ratio* is 0.40 (= 1 − 0.60). Use formula 8.10b to find the sustainable growth rate is 7.34% [= 0.40 × 0.1710 / (1 − (0.40 × 0.1710))]. Use formula 8.8 to find intrinsic value is \$169.36 [= \$2.30(1.0734) / (0.0880 − 0.0734)].

2. Compute that *New Retained earnings*$_{2525}$ equals \$73.66 (= \$6,820 × 0.0270 × (1 − 0.60)]. Use formula 8.10a to find the sustainable growth rate is 2.03% [= \$73.66 (1 + \$2,500/\$3,700) / (\$6,200 − {\$73.66 (1 + \$2,500/\$3,700)})]. Compute that div_{2525} equals \$0.69 (= \$6,820 × 0.0270 × 0.60 / 160) and div_{2526} is \$0.70 (= \$0.69 × 1.027). Use formula 8.8 to find that intrinsic value equals \$7.94 per share [= \$0.70 / (0.109 − 0.0203)].

   Find price P_{2525} by using the P/E ratio and dividend:
   $P_{2525} / E_{2525} = 6.28$; $E_{2525} = \$0.69 / 0.60$; $P_{2525} = 6.28 \times (\$0.69 / 0.60)$; or $P_{2525} = \$7.23$. The stock is undervalued by 9.9% [= (\$7.94 − \$7.23) / \$7.23].

3. Use the DuPont decomposition of *ROE* from formula 2.8 to compute that *ROE* equals 16.02% [= 0.046 × 2.09 × (1 − 0.40)$^{-1}$]. Use formula 8.10b with retention ratio of 55% (= 1 − 0.45) to find the sustainable growth rate is 9.66% [= 0.55 × 0.1602 / (1 − (0.55 × 0.1602))]. Use formula 8.8 to find intrinsic value is \$92.81 [= \$3.50 (1.0966) / (0.1380 − 0.0966)].

   Find price P_{2525} by using the P/E ratio and dividend:
   $P_{2525} / E_{2525} = 16.79$; $E_{2525} = \$3.50 / 0.45$; $P_{2525} = 16.79 \times (\$3.50 / 0.45)$; or $P_{2525} = \$130.59$. The stock is overvalued by 28.9% [= (\$92.81 − \$130.59) / \$130.59].

4. Compute that *New Retained earnings*$_{2525}$ equals \$62.65 (= \$8,190 × 0.0170 × (1 − 0.55)]. Use formula 8.10a to find the sustainable growth rate is 2.47% [= \$62.65 (1 + \$1,300/\$2,600) / (\$3,900 − {\$62.65 (1 + \$1,300/\$2,600)})]. Compute that div_{2525} equals \$0.38 (= \$8,190 × 0.0170 × 0.55 / 200) and div_{2526} is \$0.39 (= 0.38 × 1.0247). Use formula 8.8 to find that intrinsic value V_{2525} equals \$4.25 per share [= \$0.39 / (0.117 − 0.0247)]. Intrinsic value V_{2526} equals \$4.36 (= \$4.25 × 1.0247).

   Find price P_{2525} by using the P/E ratio and dividend:
   $P_{2525} / E_{2525} = 7.5$; $E_{2525} = \$0.38 / 0.55$; $P_{2525} = 7.5 \times (\$0.38 / 0.55)$; or $P_{2525} = \$5.22$. The stock is overvalued by 18.6% [= (\$4.25 − \$5.22) / \$5.22].

   Buy the stock at \$5.22 and one year later receive a dividend of \$0.39 and sell the stock for \$4.36. The *ROR* is -9.0%.

1. Tabulate the price multiples.

	Industry	Company	Inference about company
P / E	30	35.9 (= $56 / $1.56)	overvalued
P / CF	15	17.6 (= $56 / $3.19)	overvalued
P / B	3	2.3 (= $56 / $24.78)	undervalued

The multiples give mixed signals. This happens often. Statistical studies suggest that the price-to-book ratio contains significant information about subsequent stock returns. Those studies find that P/E and P/CF are unrelated to stock returns. The analysis suggests, albeit unconvincingly, that the company stock may be undervalued. Almost certainly, however, differences in multiples suggest that the stock market does not believe the company and peer group are clones.

Till now, the book's focus has been how flows and balances within different settings pertain to fundamental time value relationships. Now, however, we turn a corner and shift focus to a more complex issue. Instead of time value, the focus becomes transformation value and the importance of diversification benefits.

Transformation value is the value-added by combining different inputs to produce a unique output. A special case of transformation value is the diversification benefit from combining security cash flow streams.

Assigning value to diversification benefits requires intense study of the risk-return relation. From this study we learn about forces that drive financial market rates of return. Realize that all previous lessons employ the discount rate, that is the periodic rate of return, as though it were an *exogenous* number pulled out of the air; like "suppose the discount rate is 5%," or "what is the rate of return if you invest $100 and get back $110?" Lessons of the next few chapters, however, seek insights about the question "what is the financial rate of return consistent with market equilibrium?" Our objective is to *endogenously* determine discount rates. Part 2 of *Lessons about the Structure of Finance* teaches how market forces determine equilibrium financial rates of return.

CHAPTER 9

Buy-Side Demand, Sell-Side Supply, and Rationale for Financial Market Equilibrium

CHAPTER CONTENTS

Lessons about financial market equilibrium include some of the most important concepts in finance. The first lesson occurs in Section 1 with an overview on forces of supply and demand that drive security prices. Section 2 examines significant market participants that demand financial securities. Then Section 3 switches sides and examines security supply. Lessons from Section 4 about the "Efficient market hypothesis (EMH)" provide the rationale for determining how forces in financial markets establish equilibrium rates of return.

1. SUPPLY AND DEMAND IN THE FINANCIAL MARKETS

Financial security prices, just like other prices, respond to the forces of supply and demand. An increase in the demand for securities leads to a price increase, all else equal. Likewise, an increase in supply causes security prices to fall. Security price movements translate into rates of return. The supply and demand for financial securities is an important and often overlooked determinant of equilibrium rates of return.

A loose definition in the financial markets for the supply-side is the "sell-side." Companies want to sell stocks and bonds because they seek financing sources. People that work in the "sell-side" help companies, and governments too, issue securities and raise cash. Other people work on the demand-side, known loosely as the "buy-side." Institutional investors demand securities to put into huge portfolios, or brokers drum-up business by looking for individuals that want to buy stocks. Table 9.1 presents a sampling for the distribution of workers on both sides of the street. About 50,000 people that work with financial securities are members of the "Association for Investment Management and Research" *(www.aimr.com)*. The table shows that the largest numbers of members are on the buy-side. The sell-side is much smaller, at least-by number of employee-members. It is as though securities issued by business and government funnel into the financial markets through a small opening, after which many, many buyers use the securities to pursue many diverse objectives.

TABLE 9.1

Distribution by employment of 50,000 members of the Association for Investment Management and Research *Source: www.aimr.com, 2003.*

Buy-side total employment: 67%

45% Institutional investors These AIMR members typically are in-house analysts or investment managers who research, select and manage investments for their own institutions (mutual or pension funds, banks, etc.)
    24% Investment companies and mutual funds
    13% Banks
     5% Insurance companies
     3% Pension funds
16% Investment advisors and counselors These AIMR members serve either institutional investors or high net-worth individuals or both. They analyze and recommend appropriate investments and manage client portfolios.
6% Investment consultants These AIMR members help clients identify investment goals and find the right advisors or counselors to manage their investments.

Sell-side total employment: 18%

These AIMR members typically are analysts that research and rate financial securities. They mostly work at investment banks and brokerage firms. Investment banks advise companies and underwrite stock and bond issues. Broker-dealers act as intermediaries between buyers and sellers.

Other: 15%

These AIMR members typically work with government regulatory agencies, or in academics, or in specialty finance areas.

Supply and demand for financial securities determine equilibrium rates of return. Figure 9.1 illustrates supply and demand schedules for financial securities in the primary market. The downward sloping demand schedule D_0 depicts normal buy-side demand for securities. When security prices are high the quantity demanded is low and vice versa. The equilibrium price for financial securities, p_0, occurs where the demand and supply schedules intersect.

The supply schedule for primary market securities is extremely elastic. This means it is very flat, maybe even horizontal. A small change in equilibrium price associates with an extreme change in quantity of securities supplied. Consider, for example, an upward shift in the demand schedule. The demand schedule shifts whenever there is a change in the behavioral characteristics, expectations, or incentives of major buy-side players. For example, perhaps changing household demographics increase security demand, or perhaps Congress enacts legislation increasing intermediary security demand, or perhaps the latest news reports hearten consensus expectations and investor optimism. If the supply schedule were inelastic, that is, if the supply curve were vertical through the point (q_0, p_0), then the demand shift from D_0 to D_1 would push the equilibrium price to p_n. With elastic security supply, however, the equilibrium quantity and price become (q_1, p_1). Quantity supplied in the primary market changes significantly in response to demand shifts, but equilibrium prices (all else equal) are quite robust.

The elastic supply of securities is a consequence of opportunistic company behavior. The company cash flow cycle from chapter 1 depicts a company issuing securities in financial markets in order to transform real goods and services from stakeholder markets into products that customers want. When companies perceive

FIGURE 9.1

Supply and demand schedules for primary market financial securities

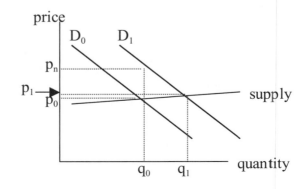

an economically profitable opportunity to make a product, the company finds the financing required for pursuing the project. A lesson from the capital budgeting chapter is that companies pursue positive net present value projects. The quantity of securities supplied rises whenever entrepreneurs perceive the existence of positive NPV opportunities. Conversely, the supply of primary market securities dries up when opportunities evaporate.

2. MAJOR PLAYERS FOR THE BUY-SIDE

Table 9.2 lists the financial assets owned by major players on the buy-side. The top left cell shows that Households directly own $10.2 *trillion* of financial assets. This makes households the largest investor group on the buy-side. All the other major players are "institutional buyers." Collectively, the institutions are bigger than the households. Remember, however, that the financing source for most of these institutions is households. The institutions are financial intermediaries. The intermediaries collect funds from households for the primary purpose of buying securities in financial markets (except for nonprofit institutions which largely are on-going self-financing companies that pursue private missions). Households invest money in financial markets two ways: directly (column 1) and indirectly through intermediaries (columns 2,3,4,6). Find below a brief discussion about the effect that each of the major players has on the buy-side demand for financial securities.

2.A. Households

The single largest type of financial security owned by households is "corporate equities". Households, as table 9.2 shows, directly own $5.2 trillion of stocks. Households also collect interest through direct ownership of $2.1 trillion of credit market instruments. The category "mutual fund shares" ($2.5 trillion) represents indirect ownership of equities and credit market instruments.

Household demand for financial securities depends on many factors. Clearly, household demand for stocks and other financial securities depends to a large extent on household income. Several factors correlate with household income, and consequently these factors affect buy-side demand for financial securities.

Educational accomplishment correlates with income (thank goodness!). Table 9.3 lists average earnings of U.S. workers by highest level of educational attainment and age. Scanning down any column shows that income generally increases with age. Scanning along any row shows that income increases with education. The value of a degree, irrespective of age, is significant. Education increases income potential—and income potential raises the buy-side demand for financial assets!

	Households -1-	Pension & retirement funds 2-2	Mutual funds -3-	Insurance companies -4-	Nonprofit institutions -5-	Bank sector -6-
total financial assets	$10,171	$6,352	$6,376	$4,088	$1,958	$8,636
credit market instruments	$2,074	$1,510	$2,761	$2,593	$ 474	$2,922
corporate equities	$5,247	$3,148	$2,836	$1,029	$ 769	$ 37
mutual fund shares	$2,540	$ 652	...	$ 44	$ 43	$ 25
other financial assets	$ 310	$1,042	$ 779	$ 466	$ 672	$5,680

TABLE 9.2
Financial assets for the buy-side, by type of investor and asset type. All dollars in billions, end-of-year balances, 2001.

Notes: Data are from the Board of Governors of the Federal Reserve System, "Flow of Funds Accounts for the United States". (1) Household total financial assets are from table L100 and exclude "deposits, equity in noncorporate business, investment in bank personal trusts, security credit, life insurance reserves, pension fund reserves." Each entry in column 1 subsequently is net of nonprofit assets (approximation) by adjusting with data from table L100a Nonprofit Organizations. (2) Column 2 includes data for private and government employee retirement funds from tables L119 and L120. (3) Column 3 includes data for mutual funds and money market funds from tables L121 and L122. (4) Column 4 is from table L117. (5) Column 5 is for end-of-year 1999 from table L100a. (6) Column 6 includes data for commercial banking, savings institutions, & credit unions from tables L109, L114, and L115. For column 6, credit market instruments include government and municipal securities plus corporate and foreign bonds.

TABLE 9.3

Average earnings in the U.S.A. by highest degree earned, 1998. Dollars in thousands.

Age in 1998	High school diploma	Some college, no degree	Associate degree	Bachelor's degree	Master's degree	Professional degree	Doctorate
	-1-	-2-	-3-	-4-	-5-	-6-	-7-
All persons	24.6	27.0	32.2	45.7	55.6	101.0	86.8
25 to 34	24.0	26.9	28.1	39.8	46.8	58.0	60.9
35 to 44	27.4	34.2	35.4	50.2	56.8	100.2	94.9
45 to 54	28.9	36.9	37.5	54.9	62.2	116.3	87.7
55 to 64	27.6	34.2	35.7	50.1	57.6	132.3	97.2
>=65	18.7	19.1	17.6	30.6	35.6	104.1	78.3

Source: U.S. Census Bureau, Statistical Abstract of the United States: 2001, table no. 218.

The demand for financial securities by households probably responds to changes in underlying societal factors. Some authors argue, for example, that changing population demographics exert forces on security prices. The argument is that as a huge mass of aging "baby-boomers" moves through mid-life when careers and income reach their maximum, the demand for securities is a little higher than it might otherwise have been. Conversely, when a proportionately large number of households eventually downsize and draw-down retirement savings there may be a relative decline in security demand. The statistical evidence that demographic movements drive security prices is inconclusive. Undeniably, however, prices respond to the forces of supply and demand so therefore the arguments merit attention.

Household attitudes toward risk also merit discussion. Sometimes societal events, such as fear of war or recession, may cause households to reduce the overall financial risk of assets owned. Usually risk-exposure is less from owning credit market instruments than equities. Conceivably, then, widespread shifts in risk attitudes may drive buy-side demand and cause one type of asset to be substituted for another. Equally important is that household risk attitudes generally depend on the individual's life-cycle stage. Table 9.4 describes how household attitudes toward risk and return generally change with age.

A common generalization is that the adult life cycle comprises 5 stages. The early career stage typically begins at commencement from secondary or tertiary or vocational education. The individual finds a job (and usually several job-changes), locates a mate, and refines professional interests. The mid-career stage typically involves home ownership, children, community volunteerism, and career/income advancement. Late career stage probably attains maximum income and, with children going to college, also attains maximum expenditures. Early and late retirement generally are varying stages of asset deccumulation and changing interests.

Table 9.4 shows that the typical household in the early career stage of the life cycle seeks high growth, high risk securities for long-term investments. As time passes, the household shifts toward low risk credit market instruments of shorter investment horizon. Surely the buy-side demand by an individual household changes as the life cycle evolves. Also interesting to consider is the extent to which large-scale demographic changes in the population interact with life cycle profiles to affect aggregate demand for financial securities. Household behavior drives the political economy.

2.B. Pension funds

Pension funds are among the largest institutional investors in the U.S.A. and, consequently, their behavior is important for understanding equilibrium rates of return. Each pay period workers contribute wages to retirement accounts. The managers of the account buy financial securities so that the account accumulates wealth and, eventually, provides financial security for workers after they retire. The companies that manage the retirement accounts are called "pension funds."

TABLE 9.4

Considerations relevant to households for buy-side decision-making. Adapted from "Investment decisions and your personal investment profile", Maria Crawford Scott, *American Association of Individual Investors Journal*, 1993.

	Explanation	Range	Security Groups With These Characteristics	Household life-cycle profile
Risk Tolerance	How much of a loss can you stomach over a one-year period without abandoning your investment plan?	Low: 0% to 5% loss Moderate: 6% to 15% loss High: 16% to 25% loss	Low: Money market funds, certificates of deposit ("CDs") Moderate: Intermediate and long-term bonds, conservative high dividend-paying stocks High: Growth stocks	*Life cycle stage and risk tolerance* Early career: high Mid-career: high Late-career: moderate Early retirement: moderate Late retirement: low
Return Needs	What form of portfolio return do you need to emphasize: income, growth or both?	Income: Steady source of annual income Growth/Income: Some steady annual income, but some growth is also needed Growth: Growth to assure real (after inflation) increase in portfolio value	Income: Bonds Growth/Income: Dividend-paying stocks Growth: Growth Stocks	*Life cycle stage and return needs* Early career: growth Mid-career: growth Late-career: growth Early retirement: growth/income Late retirement: income
Time Horizon	How soon do you need to take the money out of your investment portfolio?	Short horizon: 1 to 5 years Long horizon: Over 5 years	Short: Money market funds, CDs, short-term bonds; intermediate-term bonds (less than 5 years) Long: Growth stocks, aggressive growth stocks	*Life cycle stage and time horizon* Early career: long Mid-career: long Late-career: long Early retirement: short/long Late retirement: short/long
Tax Exposure	Based on your annual income, at what tax bracket will additional income from portfolio earnings and gains be taxed?	Lower tax exposure: Annual income is such that marginal tax bracket is among lower rates Higher tax exposure: Annual income is such that marginal tax bracket is among higher rates	Higher tax exposure securities (stressed by lower tax-exposure investors): Fixed income securities, high dividend paying stocks Lower tax exposure securities (stressed by high tax-exposure investors): Municipal bonds, non-dividend paying growth stocks	*Life cycle stage and tax exposure* Early career: lower Mid-career: higher Late-career: higher Early retirement: lower Late retirement: lower

Table 9.5 shows phenomenal growth during the past two decades in retirement assets. Households embrace pension funds as a primary savings vehicle. There are obviously many fewer pension fund companies than households. This huge concentration of wealth means that pension fund managers exert more influence than any other investor group on buy-side demand for financial assets.

There are two primary types of pension plans that an employer may offer employees: a *defined benefit plan* or a *defined contribution plan*. The plans differ by the type of promise that the employer makes to employees.

B1. Defined benefit retirement plans

A defined benefit plan is the traditional type of pension plan. Many of the oldest and largest companies, such as IBM and ATT, as well as most government employers (city, county, state, and federal agencies), enroll workers in defined benefit plans. Each pay period the worker makes contributions (often mandatory) to the plan, and perhaps the employer matches the contribution. The defined benefit plan promises to pay specific sums of money to the workers when they retire. Once an employee is eligible for retirement (eligibility often occurs when age plus years-of-service equals a specific number), then a formula similar to this determines the retirement benefit:

monthly pension = 2.0125% x (years of service) x (highest annual salary) ÷12

All plans use their own formula. With the preceding formula, for example, a worker retiring after 30 years of service and an annual salary of $50,000 receives a monthly pension of $2,516. The benefit continues for life. Typically, however, pension plans allow for participants to cash-out upon quitting or retiring as long as the worker satisfies vesting requirements. For example, consider a schoolteacher that contributes to a defined benefit plan with a 10-year vesting period. Once employment passes the 10-year mark, the schoolteacher qualifies for the pension benefit, even though he/she may quit the job long before retirement. Upon quitting, the individual may elect to immediately receive a one-time lump sum payment, thereby cashing-out the plan, or he/she may leave the money in the pension fund and eventually receive a monthly pension throughout retirement. Some retirees may receive pensions from several different plans, depending on their work history.

Traditional defined benefit plans have become less common during the past few decades. The largest difficulty is the liability that the company incurs because of its legally binding promise to deliver future retirement benefits. It is costly for the company to maintain and accumulate the assets necessary for delivering its pension promises. Even keeping track of vesting records for ex-employees that quit long ago is a distraction unrelated to the employer's main line of business. And accounting policies for monitoring the present value of accumulated benefit obligations are complex, even affecting the company's earnings per share. Another difficulty with defined benefit plans is that the ownership of the assets accumulating for payment of retirement benefits is unclear. Do the pension assets belong to the employer on whose balance sheet the assets (and liability) appear? Or do the pension assets belong to the employee that sacrificed wages? And what happens in event of merger or bankruptcy? Court judgments about these questions are all over the place.

TABLE 9.5
Assets of Private and Public Pension Funds, 1980—2000.

	1980 -1-	1985 -2-	1990 -3-	1995 -4-	2000 -5-
Total assets, all pension funds	$882	$1,885	$3,089	$5,269	$9,043
credit market instruments	298	581	912	1,162	1,582
corporate equities	276	636	877	2,080	3,936
mutual fund shares	7	11	40	327	838
other assets	301	657	1,260	1,700	2,687

Notes: Dollars in billions. Includes assets held at life insurance companies.

Source: U.S. Census Bureau, Statistical Abstract of the United States: 2001, table no. 1218.

Defined benefit plans largely mimic ideas enacted with the Social Security Act of 1935 as part of Franklin Roosevelt's "New Deal." Defined benefit plans were a grand idea, but they are disappearing - they are too costly for businesses to maintain. Someday, they may be too costly for government, too.

B2. Defined contribution retirement plans

Defined contribution plans make absolutely no promises about retirement benefits. Instead, defined contribution plans promise the amount that the employer contributes each pay period to the employee's pension fund. Typically, the employee contributes a portion of wages to the pension plan. The employer matches all or part of the contribution. With a one-to-one match, for example, the employee may contribute 5% and the employer contributes 5%. This represents an instantaneous doubling of employee wealth—a 100% rate of return without any risk! Employees definitely should contribute up to the limit that the employer matches.

Among the several types of defined contribution plans, the 401(k) plan is most popular. Table 9.6 shows the rapid increase in number of qualified plans that employers sponsor. The 401(k) plan, like all defined contribution plans, shifts responsibility of financial security away from the employer and toward the employee. The retirement benefits that the employee receives depend on the performance of the investments. With good investments it will be a plentiful retirement, but if things go badly the pension may be inadequate. The employer makes no promises and bears no burden about the size of retirement benefits with a defined contribution plan.

In most cases, the employer hires an external company to manage the defined contribution plan. The management company, that is the pension fund, communicates directly with the employee about investing the contributions. Many pension funds provide employees with several investment choices. The largest pension fund managing retirement accounts for most professors in the U.S.A., for example, is the TIAA-CREF Company. This pension fund allows professors to allocate contributions into many different asset classes: a diversified stock fund, a global equities fund, a growth stock fund, an equity index fund, a bond fund, a real estate fund, a money market fund, etc.

In some pension plans the employer severely restricts employer choices. Sometimes, as with the infamous debacle of the Enron bankruptcy in 2001, the employer forces the employee to hold company stock. This episode caused the U.S. Congress to amend laws that limit employer abuses of 401(k) plans. Despite the few bad instances, defined contribution plans are growing quickly. Evidence suggests that they may encourage higher savings rates, and certainly they empower employees for taking charge of retirement dreams.

2.C. Mutual funds

Mutual funds also are among the largest institutional buyers of financial securities in the U.S.A. Mutual funds collect money from many investors. The fund managers carefully analyze possibilities and use the money to buy assets. Quite often the man-

TABLE 9.6
Summary of 401(k) defined contribution plans.

	1985 -1-	1990 -2-	1995 -3-	2000 -4-
Number of 401(k) plans	29,869	97,614	200,813	320,000
active participants (thousands) in 401(k) plans	10,339	19,548	28,061	42,000
assets (billions) in 401(k) plans	$144	$385	$864	$1,800
assets (billions) in all private defined contribution plans	$424	$713	$1,329	$2,511

Source: U.S. Census Bureau, Statistical Abstract of the United States: 2001, table no. 535., except column 4 which is adapted from information at the Employees Benefit Research Institute website (www.ebri.org)

agers select assets subject to guidelines that the mutual fund *prospectus* describes. The prospectus is an official document describing the mutual fund to prospective investors. The Securities Exchange Commission requires that the prospectus contains specific information such as mutual fund objectives and policies, risks that the fund faces, fees that investors pay, and investor services that the fund offers. The mutual fund balance sheet in table 9.7 provides insight on how a mutual fund operates.

Notice that "shares" appear on both sides of the above balance sheet. On the right-hand-side, the mutual fund issues its own shares to investors (mostly households) in order to raise money. The money probably flows most immediately into the checking account. The fund managers then analyze prospective uses of the cash and, eventually, may purchase common stocks for companies such as IBM. Paper-on-the-left and paper-on-the-right—such is a financial intermediary!

The financial securities that mutual funds purchase almost always may be bought directly by households. Relative to direct ownership, however, households realize several advantages by owning mutual funds.

(a) Diversification benefits accrue from ownership of mutual funds because each fund typically own dozens or more different security issues. Owning one share of a mutual fund represents indirect ownership of many different securities.

(b) Investing in a mutual fund typically is easier and involves fewer transaction costs or commissions than investing directly in stocks and bonds.

(c) Mutual funds hire talented professional investment managers. Most individual households cannot allocate as much time as a full-time fund manager collecting information and monitoring securities.

(d) The astounding variety of mutual funds presents investors with access to a convenient mechanism for pursuing personal investment objectives. Even though two funds may hold exactly the same set of securities, fund characteristics may differ dramatically when each fund allocates among component stocks differently. The analogy is that there are many different ways to combine flour, sugar, and eggs—each combination tastes really different, too.

There are about 8,000 mutual funds in the U.S.A. pursuing many different investment objectives. Table 9.8 describes several common categories for mutual funds. The categories are not mutually exclusive and perhaps one fund may qualify for several different categories.

The incredible variety of objectives illustrates how mutual fund managers exert buy-side demand pressure in many sectors of financial markets. Mutual funds also

TABLE 9.7
Balance sheet for CREF Growth Mutual fund, 12/31/2002

Assets	($millions)	Liabilities
2.4 million shares American Express	84.9	223.2 Debt & misc.
3.9 million shares Amgen, Inc.	187.2	7,743.2 Mutual fund shares
0.6 million shares Anheuser-Busch	31.3	(176.3 million)
1.6 million shares Avon Products	84.9	
0.1 million shares Black & Decker	5.9	
15.9 million shares Cisco Systems	208.9	
0.1 million shares Electronic Arts, Inc.	3.1	
3.1 million shares Fannie Mae	199.5	
0.1 million shares Genentech	3.8	
14.8 million shares General Electric	360.1	
15.0 million shares Intel	233.7	
2.4 million shares IBM	184.2	
5.4 million shares Johnson & Johnson	291.6	
8.4 million shares Microsoft	435.9	
4.4 million shares PepsiCo, Inc.	186.8	
11.2 million shares Pfizer	343.2	
0.7 million shares Starbucks Corp.	14.2	
0.7 million shares United Parcel Serv.	44.3	
other equities & misc. assets	5,062.9	
Total assets	$7,966.4	$7,966.4

Source: Teachers Insurance and Annuity Association—College Retirement Equities Fund (TIAA-CREF), New York.

TABLE 9.8
Summary of mutual fund categories.

Notable risk and return characteristics -1-	Types of financial securities that the mutual fund owns -2-
1. Money market mutual funds Risk of losing principal is nil. Rates of return are relatively low and follow movements in short-term interest rates.	These funds own short-term credit market securities issued by U.S. corporations and federal, state and local governments and their agencies. The interest income that the fund receives generally is taxable income to investors.
2. Bond mutual funds Risk of losing principal depends on two separate traits: quality and term. The lowest quality are junk bond funds which may have high risk. High quality bond funds have lower risk. Long-term bond funds have higher risk of sharp price declines; short-term bonds funds have less price risk. Bond fund rates of return: (1) have a long-run average that is larger than money market but smaller than equity funds; (2) move inversely with interest rates. Falling interest rates push up the returns for existing bond fund investors, especially long-term bonds.	*2a. Taxable bond funds* These funds own short or long-term credit market securities issued by U.S. corporations and federal, state and local governments and their agencies. The interest income that the fund receives generally is taxable income to investors. *2b. Tax-exempt bond funds* These funds own credit market securities called "municipal bonds." Investors do not pay federal taxes on interest from municipal bonds (state tax liability depends on details). The tax-exempt interest rate, all else equal, is less than the taxable interest rate. Municipal bonds presumably finance public goods such as schools, hospitals, and transportation projects. There are two types of municipal bonds. Repayment of "revenue bonds" depends on cash flows that the project generates. Repayment of "general obligation bonds" depends on the creditworthiness of the government organization that sponsors the issue.
3. Equity mutual funds	*3a. Index funds* The objective of equity index mutual funds is to closely match the movement in an underlying stock index, such as the S&P500, or Dow Jones Industrial Average, etc. The funds do not promise to pick great stocks, they simply promise to track the target index. *3b. Growth funds* The objective for managers of equity growth funds is identification of companies with strong sales, asset, and/or profit growth.
Risks generally are higher for equity mutual funds than for bond mutual funds. Equity mutual fund risk reflects component security risks although the fund realizes diversification benefits. Foreign equity investment introduces additional risks. Long-run average rates of return are higher for equity mutual funds than any other category.	*3c. Value funds* The objective for managers of equity value funds is identification of stocks that appear undervalued relative to peers. *3d. Income funds* The objective for managers of equity income funds is identification of companies that pay relatively large dividends. *3e. Sector funds* The prospectus sometimes restricts an equity mutual fund to buy stocks for companies satisfying a criterion. The criterion usually describes a specific market sector. Common criteria include (1) line of business, for example, biomedical mutual fund versus telecommunications fund; (2) company size, for example, small versus large market capitalization company;

Notable risk and return characteristics -1-	Types of financial securities that the mutual fund owns -2-
3. Equity mutual funds (cont.)	(3) geographical, for example, U.S.A. companies versus European companies versus Latin American companies; (4) economic backdrop, for example "emerging economies" versus "developed nation status".
4. Balanced mutual funds Risk of loss usually is less for a balanced fund than for a pure equity fund. Returns tend to be less volatile, too.	A balanced mutual fund diversifies broadly across many types of both bonds and equities.
5. Real estate mutual funds Risk of loss usually is less for a real estate fund than for a pure equity fund. Returns tend to be less volatile, too.	The objective for managers of real estate mutual funds is identification of prime commercial properties that promise relatively high rental incomes and opportunities for price appreciation. These "real estate investment trusts (REITs)" are subject to different regulations because the asset side of the balance sheet contains bricks-and-mortar as well as financial securities.

are important players on the sell-side. Later in this section appears discussion about mutual fund sell-side characteristics.

2.D. Insurance companies

Table 9.2 shows the value of financial assets owned by insurance companies equals $4.1 trillion at year-end 2001. Insurance companies accumulate funds by selling products that promise customers financial benefits when specific events occur. Quite often (but not always) the events are catastrophic: car insurance pays benefits when accidents happen, fire insurance pays benefits when buildings burn, life insurance pays benefits when, well, you get the idea. The availability of insurance products dates to ancient times when marine insurance provided coverage for ships transporting goods across treacherous seas. Then as now, customers buy insurance and usually hope they never file a claim. But when the catastrophic event occurs the insurance allows the customer to rebuild and carry-on. Insurance companies survive through the centuries because customers face risks—insurance helps customers manage risk.

The price that customers pay for an insurance policy is the "premium." Insurance companies exert buy-side demand for financial securities because accumulated annual premiums usually exceed annual benefits paid to claimants. The insurance company invests the excess in order to accumulate the wealth required for paying future claims. Table 9.9 presents information about the size of different insurance markets.

TABLE 9.9
Annual insurance premiums by line ($billions)

	1990 -1-	1995 -2-	1999 -3-
Life insurance premiums	$ 77	$103	$120
Annuity premiums	129	158	270
Health insurance premiums	58	90	100
Automobile insurance premiums	95	119	137
Other property and casualty premiums	123	141	150

Source: U.S. Census Bureau, Statistical Abstract of the United States: 2001, table nos. 1222 and 1226. "Other property and casualty" includes premiums for homeowners and commercial multiple peril, fire insurance, and all other lines.

Automobile premiums grow over time in response to inflation and demographic effects, but this not a high growth segment. Other property and casualty insurers face severe challenges due to dramatic changes in the American landscape. Prior to 1992 many insurers placed the probability of a $10 billion catastrophe near zero percent. Premiums were priced on that assumption. Hurricane Andrew blew through the southeast in 1992 and insurance claims totaled $15.5 billion. California's Northridge earthquake of 1994 caused claims of $12.5 billion. During year 2000 the homeowners insurance industry paid benefits totaling $36 billion; they paid-out $1.11 for every one-dollar received in premiums. The payments arose from huge unexpected claims due to mold, wildfires, and storms. And the World Trade Center catastrophe of 9/11/2001 will cause insurance companies to pay claims of perhaps $50 billion. When the insurance industry must pay tens of billions of dollars in claims, they must sell securities that already they own. Arguably security prices respond to such shifts in supply and demand.

The fastest growing segment of the insurance market is for annuities. Life insurance annuities represent savings vehicles. These financial products include "fixed annuities" and the more popular "variable annuities." The customer pays premiums and receives a policy that promises to pay benefits once a specific age or condition is met. The benefit is either a fixed amount, in which case the annuity is analogous to a defined benefit retirement plan. Or the benefit is variable and depends on performance of underlying financial assets; the variable annuity is analogous to a defined contribution retirement plan. The annuity represents the fastest growing insurance product even though, ironically, it is a product for which a benefit is not triggered by a catastrophic event.

The McCarran-Ferguson Act of 1945 stipulates that insurance commissions in each state regulate insurance companies operating in that state. Insurance companies, however, are lobbying for removal of barriers to interstate commerce. Just as insurance companies found profits by offering traditional retirement products, so too they seek profits by integrating interstate insurance products. Policy-makers must decide whether the increasing mobilization of households and businesses and integration of financial markets justifies changing the realm of insurance regulation. The effects on buy-side demand for financial assets by insurance companies likely would change, too.

2.E. Nonprofit institutions

Henry Ford and his son Edsel established the Ford Foundation in 1936. Total assets for the Ford Foundation in 2002 are $9 billion. Mostly these are financial assets. Andrew Carnegie in 1911 founded the Carnegie Foundation and today their financial assets total $2 billion. Harvard University, established in 1636, owns an endowment fund with financial assets worth $17 billion in 2002. The Bill and Melinda Gates Foundation, established in January 2002, has financial assets surpassing $25 billion. The financial assets owned by these and other nonprofit institutions provide financing that enable the institutions to pursue their missions. The mission of the Ford and Carnegie foundations is betterment of the human existence; the mission of the Harvard endowment is to foster learning by students and faculty. Table 9.2 lists financial assets for nonprofit institutions in the U.S.A. at a fairly hefty $2.0 trillion. Foundation and endowment funds exert buy-side demand for financial assets because they invest in securities.

Endowments and foundations accumulate wealth in order to award grants or spend money in pursuit of their mission. University endowments, for example, own credit market securities that provide interest income. The endowment uses the income to pay for student scholarships or faculty salaries. Endowments and foundations also hire investment managers that analyze equity securities with the intention of "buying-low, selling-high" and providing profit for the institutional mission. Table 9.10 lists the largest university endowment funds in the U.S.A.

TABLE 9.10

The largest university endowment funds, 2002.

Institution	Value in 2002 ($billions)
private universities	
Harvard University	$17.2
Yale University	10.5
Princeton University	8.3
Stanford University	7.6
Massachusetts Institute of Technology	5.4
Emory University	4.6
Columbia University	4.2
Washington University	3.5
University of Pennsylvania	3.4
University of Chicago	3.3
public universities	
University of Texas System	8.6
University of California	4.2
The Texas A&M University System	3.7
University of Michigan	3.4
University of Virginia	1.7
University of Minnesota	1.3
University of Pittsburgh	1.2
University of Washington	1.1
Purdue University	1.1
UNC at Chapel Hill and foundations	1.1

Source: National Association of College and University Business Officers (*www.nacubo.org*), reprinted in Chronicle of Higher Education.

2.F. Commercial banking, savings institutions, and credit unions

Commercial banks, savings institutions, and credit unions together own more financial assets than all other institutions. The influence of the bank sector on buy-side demand for financial securities, however, has been limited by government regulations. Glean insight about these institutions through inspection of selected line items from the balance sheet for the commercial banking sector:

Notice that for banks a large liability is deposits. A customer or business that deposits money at the bank is a source of financing for the bank. The bank receives the deposit and the increasing liability represents a source of funds. Probably next

TABLE 9.11

Financial assets and selected liabilities for U.S. commercial banks, year-end 2001, dollars in billions.

Financial Assets			Selected Liabilities
Vault Cash	47	627	Checkable deposits
Receivables at Federal Reserve	15	2,478	Small time and savings deposits
U.S. government securities	940	918	Large time deposits
Municipal securities	120	562	Credit market instruments
Corporate and foreign bonds	376		
Mortgages	1,790		
Consumer credit	558		
Other loans	1,596		
Corporate equities	9		
Mutual fund shares	21		
Other financial assets	1,359		
Total financial assets	$6,831		

Source: Flow of Funds Accounts of the United States

the bank puts the money into the vault and the increasing asset represents a use of funds. The bank eventually puts the money to other uses in order to generate profit. The biggest use of funds is lending for mortgages and other loans. Borrowers repay loans with interest and, for the bank, interest is income. Loans are the banking sector's largest income-producing asset.

Buy-side demand by banks for marketable financial securities largely is limited to U.S. government securities, corporate bonds, and municipal securities. Banks due to historical reasons do not (yet) own many equities.

History of the banking system is fascinating. The importance of banks since the middle ages discourages politicians from taking a hands-off approach. Businesses must borrow money to make money, banks choose which businesses (and households) receive loans, and politicians enable legislation directing banks to lend toward objectives satisfying the common good.

Congress chartered "The First Bank of the United States" in 1791 to engage in general commercial banking and perform treasury functions for the federal government. The bank was privately owned and rife with controversy. It was disbanded in 1811 and replaced by the "Second Bank of the United States." President Andrew Jackson in 1836 closed that one. Between 1838 and World War 1 thousands of banks in the U.S.A. issued their own bank notes. The private bank notes were commonly accepted as a medium of exchange. Hence, they were currencies. The first truly national currency issued by the federal government was in 1863, but private bank notes persisted. Throughout the 1800s many different currencies were commonplace in the U.S.A. (8,000 different currencies in 1860!). Travelers going from Philadelphia to Chicago might exchange currency issued by a Pennsylvania bank into currency issued by an Illinois bank. Exchange rates among bank notes varied in much the same way that international exchange rates vary today. Bank notes during "panics" often became worthless because issuing banks went bankrupt.

Enabling of the Federal Reserve System in 1913 assured movement toward a pervasive national currency valid for all debts, public and private. By that time, however, a dual banking system was in place that continues through today. Banks today organize with either "state" or "national" charters. The type of charter historically meant different regulatory requirements. Today, however, differences largely have vanished except that the government chartering the bank empowers a regulatory agency monitoring the bank.

Widespread losses by banks from securities investments during the Great Depression of 1929-1934 and subsequent bank failures caused Congress to pass laws tightly restricting commercial bank activities. The laws effectively placed "firewalls" between companies that differed by line of business or even by geography. Interstate banking was prohibited, banks could not dally with securities, insurers could not dally with banking, etc. Congress also established the Federal Deposit Insurance Corporation (FDIC) for the purpose of guaranteeing deposits, thereby eliminating bank panics. Today the FDIC insures each account for up to $100,000.

Commercial banks tended to focus on business lending so Congress passed laws facilitating mortgage lending by Savings Institutions and Credit Unions. Millions of households realized the dream of homeownership due to these beneficial policies. Continued economic growth and increasing integration of financial markets gave rise, however, to an environment in which micro-managing regulations caused more harm than good. Finally, in 1999 Congress passed the Financial Services Modernization Act (Gramm-Leach-Bliley Act). This law allows banks, securities firms, and insurance companies, to affiliate under a parent financial holding company. The law also stipulates regulation that depends on the company's functional activities: the Federal Reserve regulates banking activities, The Securities and Exchange Commission regulates companies dealing with securities, and state insurance commissions regulate insurance activities within that state. The Financial Services Modernization Act uninstalls dysfunctional firewalls installed during the 1930s.

Table 9.12 summarizes information about different institutions in the bank sector of the U.S.A.

TABLE 9.12
Institutions in the bank sector.

	Commercial banking -1-	Savings Institutions -2-	Credit Unions -3-
Thousands of banks / branches			
1990	12.4 / 50.3	2.8 / 18.8	12.9
2000	8.3 / 64.7	1.6 / 12.9	10.3
Total assets ($billions)			
1990	$3,389	$1,259	$198
2000	$6,239	$1,223	$438

Source: U.S. Census Bureau, Statistical Abstract of the United States: 2001, table nos. 1173, 1175, 1183, and 1184.

The bank sector is consolidating and the number of companies is diminishing (but branches and assets are increasing). Still, however, there are over 8,000 commercial banks in the U.S.A. Realize that in most other developed nations the numbers of banks are in the low hundreds, not thousands. The large number in the U.S.A. is a historical artifact of the segmentation enforced by Congressional firewalls. Meanwhile, the overall asset base for the bank sector is increasing. Credit unions are benefiting from rules relaxing the common-bond requirement for membership. Commercial banks (and presumably households and businesses, too) are benefiting from the 1999 law that removes restrictions on financial activities. The effect of consolidation on the buy-side demand for financial securities is uncertain yet extremely important.

3. CHARACTERISTICS ON THE SELL-SIDE

The "sell-side" of financial markets loosely refers to security suppliers. Where do financial securities come from, what are they like, how are they made? The lessons below examine these types of questions.

Table 9.13 lists financial securities on the sell-side by type of instrument. The table lists the balance of credit market securities at year-end 2001 as $29.5 *trillion* dollars. The market value of all equities was about half that, at $15.2 trillion. Finally, mutual funds participate on both buy and sell sides because their balance sheets list shares as both assets and liabilities. The $6.6 trillion of mutual fund assets is mostly already counted in the credit and equity market totals. The remainder of this section discusses characteristics for the sell-side supply of financial securities.

3.A. Credit market securities

The common characteristic for credit market securities is that the cash flow stream is relatively well specified. The issuer promises to repay principal plus interest to the lender and, in the event of default, the lender often has claims on the issuer's assets that are senior to any equity claimants. Still, many other characteristics of credit market securities vary widely, as the discussion below reveals.

A1. Open market paper
All "open market" securities mature in less than 270 days, and most mature in less than 60 days. Recall that according to one of the categorization schemes for financial markets in chapter 1 (table 1.2), the "money market" contains all securities with original maturity of 1-year or less. Securities with longer maturities are in the "capital markets." All open market paper is in the money market. Open market paper ($1,446 billion) includes two general security classes: commercial paper ($1,441 billion) and bankers' acceptances ($5 billion). Bankers acceptances represent contracts in which the bank acts as an intermediary between two companies. The bank issues an "acceptance" to one company in exchange for cash. The acceptance stipulates that another company receives the cash after satisfying some condition, such as delivery of goods or services to the first company. The relatively small

Type of Instrument	$ billions 12/31/2001
Total credit market debt	*$29,471*
Open market paper	$1,446
U.S. government securities	$8,324
Municipal securities	$1,685
Corporate and foreign bonds	$5,692
Mortgages	$7,592
Consumer credit	$1,703
Other credit market debt	$3,030
Total corporate equities	*$15,245*
Basic Materials (551 companies)	$447
Capital Goods (513 companies)	$292
Conglomerates (36 companies)	$608
Consumer Cyclical (474 companies)	$573
Consumer Non-Cyclical (331 companies)	$755
Energy (364 companies)	$1,045
Financial (1,538 companies)	$2,738
Health Care (942 companies)	$1,627
Services (2,194 companies)	$3,185
Technology (2,295 companies)	$3,332
Transportation (170 companies)	$180
Utilities (166 companies)	$463
Mutual funds & exchange traded funds	*$6,597*
Money market mutual funds	$2,241
Open-end long-term mutual funds	$4,135
Closed-end funds	$138
Exchange traded funds	$83

Notes: All dollars in billions. The credit market total and its components are from the Board of Governors of the Federal Reserve System, "Flow of Funds Accounts for the United States", table L4. Equity market total also is from table L4. Equity components are from the American Association of Individual Investors, February 2001, and include 9,574 public corporations. Sector totals from AAII ($22.7 trillion) are scaled to fit the FRB total. Mutual fund data are from FRB tables L121, L122, and L123.

size of bankers' acceptances means that "open market paper" and "commercial paper" are nearly synonyms.

Companies that issue open market securities realize an increase in a liability on the balance sheet. For issuing companies, open market securities are a financing source. The companies borrow cash for this very short-term because their intended use of the cash also is short-term. Generally speaking, companies obtain short-term financing for short-term uses, long-term financing for long-term uses. Figure 9.2 shows the types of companies that issue open market paper.

Nonfinancial corporate businesses in the U.S.A. ("NFC") had $190 billion of commercial paper outstanding at year-end 2001—that represents 13% of total open market securities. Mostly the companies borrow this money to provide customers with credit. The NFC consolidated balance sheet shows, to some extent, *Receivables* on the asset side that are financed by commercial paper on the liability side.

Many companies do not issue their own commercial paper. Instead, they outsource customer financing. "Finance & funding companies", for example, raise money by issuing commercial paper in financial markets (24% of the total open market paper according to figure 9.2). The companies subsequently use the money to offer short-term consumer loans for purchases of durable goods such as refrigerators, furniture, automobiles, etc. The loan may be offered directly to consumers

FIGURE 9.2
Issuers of outstanding open market securities, 12/31/2001.

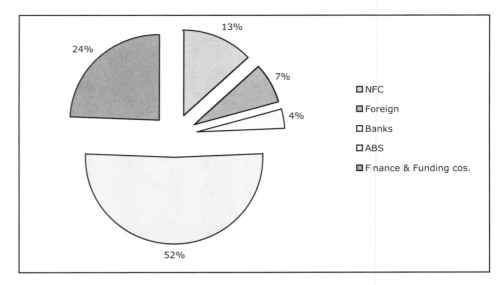

Notes: "NFC" is nonfinancial corporate U.S. companies. "Foreign" represents non-U.S. issuers. "Banks" represents commercial bank issuers. "ABS" are asset-backed commercial paper. Data are from the Board of Governors of the Federal Reserve System, "Flow of Funds Accounts for the United States", table L208.

and subsequently the consumer finds the right retailer. Alternatively, a retailer may contract directly for a finance company to offer its customers credit. For example, perhaps a retailer makes a credit sale (meaning there is no immediate cash revenue) thereby causing a decrease in *Inventory*. Instead of increasing *Receivables*, however, the retailer contracts with a finance company for immediate revenue (perhaps at a discounted sale price). The finance company subsequently receives payment from the customer (with interest, of course). The source of money that the finance company uses to pay the retailer is from issuance of commercial paper.

"ABS" in figure 9.2 stands for short-term asset-backed securities and at year-end 2001 they represent 52% ($745 billion) of all commercial paper outstanding in the U.S.A. The balance sheet for the company creating the ABS provides key insight about this important security. The company issues (that is, sells) the asset backed security, the sale represents a source of financing, and there is an increase on the liability side for the line item "ABS". Investors purchasing the ABS includes institutional players on the buy-side (pension funds, etc.). Companies creating open market ABS use the money to purchase *Receivables* from hundreds of different companies. The balance sheet's asset side lists all the different *Receivables* on which the ABS have a claim. Ownership of an asset-backed security represents indirect ownership of revenues from a large pool of financial assets.

Commercial banks issue about 4% of all outstanding open market paper. Mostly, these are certificates of deposit ("CD's"). CD's represent a liability to the bank. The bank sells the CD to an investor. Investors purchasing the CD include major players on the buy-side (household, pension funds, etc.) The bank stipulates a specific rate of interest that the investment earns. The investor commits the funds for a specific time period. CD's vary in size: relatively small ones appeal primarily to households; large ones over $1 million appeal primarily to institutional investors. The large ones include "negotiable certificates of deposits" (NCD's) for which a rather active secondary market exists. NCD investors may hold the security until the bank repays the principal, thereby retiring the security. Or they may find another investor that wants to buy it.

Repurchase agreements ("repos") are another common type of short-term credit market security. There is, in fact, a very active market for overnight repos. The bank (or any other company) issuing a repo receives cash and delivers to the buyer a portfolio of securities, usually U.S. government securities (or less common is delivery of only the repo security itself). The issuer promises to buy-back the securities (or repo) at a later date for a somewhat higher price. Why do banks go to so much trouble to invest money for, say, only 1 day. Consider this: a bank with $10 million of idle cash prefers to put the money to use even if only for a day—a day's interest on $10 million at a 5% annual interest rate is $1,370. And there are a lot of days in the year.

A2. U.S. government securities

The U.S. government is the largest sell-side supplier of credit market securities in the world. The government sells securities in order to pay for the infrastructure, national defense, and social programs that are vital components of the U.S. political economy. The outstanding balance of U.S. government securities at year-end 2001, $8.3 *trillion*, includes three primary security classes: Treasury securities (41%), government sponsored enterprise securities (25%), and federally related mortgage pools (34%).

Treasury securities   The U.S. Treasury sells securities to finance the national debt. The full faith and credit of the U.S. government guarantees the timely payment of principal and interest on Treasury securities. The interest income from Treasury securities generally is taxable at the federal level but exempt from state and local income taxes. About 5% of Treasury securities outstanding are traditional U.S. Savings Bonds. These non-marketable securities appeal to households and are sold today in denominations ranging from $50 to $10,000. Throughout history different types of savings bonds have been called "liberty bonds", "patriot bonds", etc. Most savings bonds that the Treasury sells today are classified as either Series EE, Series HH, or Series I. Series EE and I savings bonds accrue interest monthly at a variable rate and the interest is compounded semiannually. The Series I interest rate tracks the inflation rate, the Series EE interest rate tracks a 5-year interest rate. Investors receive all income when they redeem the savings bond. Series HH savings bonds have a fixed interest rate, interest is paid-out semiannually and, upon redemption, the investor receives the face value. All owners of U.S. Savings Bonds register with the Treasury. In event of loss, the bonds are replaceable. The savings bonds earn interest for up to 30 years, they may be redeemed early, but they may not be sold. Households may buy U.S. Savings Bonds at over 40,000 financial institutions nationwide, or online with a credit card at *www.savingsbonds.gov*

About 95% of U.S. Treasury securities are marketable, and active secondary markets make these the most widely traded securities in the world. About one-third of all Treasury security owners are outside the U.S.A. Figure 9.3 shows the four classes of marketable Treasury securities.

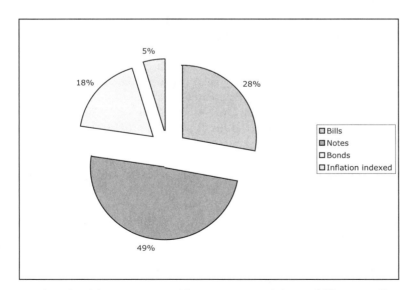

FIGURE 9.3
Types of marketable Treasury securities.

Notes: Total marketable Treasury securities at 12/31/2002 is $3,380 billion according to the Board of Governors of the Federal Reserve System, "Flow of Funds Accounts for the United States", table L209. Percentage composition by instrument face value is from The Bureau of the Public Debt, "Monthly statement of the public debt, 2/28/2003" (*www.publicdebt.treas.gov*)

Perhaps U.S. Treasury bills are the world's most risk-free security. T-bills have maturity of one-year or less (and the majority are less than 26 weeks), meaning that they trade in the money market. This also means that T-bill prices are less sensitive to interest rate changes than are the longer-term notes and bonds. T-bills do not pay interest, but instead sell at auction for a price that is less than face value. When redeemed at maturity for face value, the price appreciation represents the investor's profit. T-bill price and return mechanics certainly abide by time value principles. An historical formula, however, relates quoted price and T-bill rate:

$$\begin{pmatrix} T-bill \\ price \\ per\ \$1,000 \end{pmatrix} = \$1,000 \left(1 - \frac{(days\text{-}to\text{-}maturity)(T\text{-}bill\ rate)}{360} \right)$$

Look at a recent *Wall Street Journal* and you may see, for example, a listing for a T-bill with 113 days-to-maturity and rate of 1.05%. Substitute these values into the formula to compute the T-bill price of $996.70. The investor pays $996.70 for the T-bill and 113 days later receives $1,000. The profit, that is the "interest", is a modest $3.30. Low risk T-bills certainly provide low returns!

Treasury notes comprise 49% of all Treasury securities. T-notes have original maturities between one and ten years, but today's most common issues are for 2-years, 5-years, and 10-years. Treasury bonds have original maturities between 10 and 30 years. No 30-year T-bonds have been issued since mid-2002. T-notes and T-bonds pay interest semiannually. Prices are determined at auction.

During the 1990s the Treasury began selling notes and bonds that provide a return indexed to the inflation rate. The coupon rate is constant, but the principal value adjusts by the percentage change in consumer price index since date of issue. The amount of each semiannual interest payment equals the semiannual coupon rate times the inflation-adjusted principal value. These securities comprise only 5% of Treasury issues outstanding. The importance of inflation-indexed Treasury's on future sell-side security supply probably will increase when inflation accelerates.

Government sponsored enterprise securities The U.S. Congress responds to political economic pressure and establishes enterprises that provide financing in pursuit of a public objective. Government sponsored enterprises ("GSE's") are not included in the Federal budget because they are private companies. Several GSE's issue equity that trades on stock exchanges just as if they were a regular corporation. Debt that a GSE issues is not backed by the full faith and credit of the U.S. government. GSE debt sometimes is referred to as "agency debt." The default risk for agency debt is somewhat greater than Treasury securities but less than corporate bond risk. Many buy-side investors believe that the U.S. government never would allow a GSE to fail. Table 9.14 lists the main GSE's.

The Sallie Mae story is particularly relevant to students, and particularly illustrative of GSE history. Sallie Mae was created as a shareholder-owned government sponsored enterprise by the Education Amendments of 1972. The public policy objective of this GSE is to expand the funds available for student loans. Sallie Mae pursues this objective by purchasing student loans from eligible financial institutions (they also generally support student credit needs by making loans directly to students). For example, a student may have loans from several different commercial banks or credit unions. The student may fill out a form (available at *http://www.salliemae.com/*) that authorizes Sallie Mae to purchase the loans from all the different institutions. The source of funds for Sallie Mae to buy the loans is by issuance of agency securities (institutional investors purchase the securities). Sallie Mae offers the student an advantageous plan that consolidates all loans, that perhaps schedules payments that are relatively small at first and gradually rise each year. In the 1990s Sallie Mae was criticized because of mismanagement and high student default rates. Congress responded in 1996 with a law requiring immediate and whole privatization of Sallie Mae, and liquidation by September 30, 2008. The political consensus

TABLE 9.14

Government sponsored enterprises

Enterprise & objective	Outstanding debt issued to finance direct loans ($ billions) fiscal year 2001
Student Loan Marketing Association "Sallie Mae" is a for-profit financial corporation chartered to increase the availability of student loans.	$47
Federal National Mortgage Association and *Federal Home Loan Mortgage Corporation* "Fannie Mae" and "Freddie Mac" provide liquidity to the market for residential mortgages and help increase the availability of mortgage credit to low- and moderate-income families and in underserved areas.	$1,258
Farm Credit System Institutions of the FCS provide privately financed credit to agricultural and rural communities.	$83
Federal Home Loan Bank Board The "FHLB" assists banks, insurance companies, savings institutions, and credit unions in providing financing for housing and community development.	$612

Notes: All dollars in billions. GSE total credit market instruments outstanding at year-end 2001 equal $2,114 billion (Board of Governors of the Federal Reserve System, "Flow of Funds Accounts for the United States", table L124). Table entries are from "The Budget for Fiscal Year 2004", pp. 1123–1131, *http://www.whitehouse.gov/omb/budget/fy2004/pdf/appendix/GOV.pdf.*

was that this GSE was hurting the public policy objective more than it was helping, that the private sector could do a better job, and that the government should cease involvement. Sallie Mae will cease to exist—many argue that it simply is a matter of time until the government backs away from all GSE's.

4. RATIONALE FOR FINANCIAL MARKET EQUILIBRIUM

Security supply in the primary financial market directly mirrors opportunities in real asset markets. Real asset markets, and hence the elastic supply of securities, are more stable than ever-changing buy-side security demand. Relatively frequent shifts in normal demand provide more information than relatively infrequent shifts in elastic supply about equilibrium prices. Inferences on financial market equilibrium focus primarily on investor behavior.

4.A. Expected returns equilibrate with required returns

An investor's expected rate of return from a stock investment equates security price to discounted returns.

> **DEFINITION 9.1 Expected rate of return ($ROR^{expected}$)**
> The "expected rate of return" is the discount rate that equates the actual security price to the discounted sum of expected cash flows. $ROR^{expected}$ is the internal rate of return for that cash flow stream.

Company profitability, sales trends, market share, growth opportunities, price multiples, these and other information sources shape expected rates of return.

A trading rule from the stock valuation chapter is that an unconstrained investor buys a stock when the security's intrinsic value exceeds its price. The investor implicitly figures expected cash flows from the stock. Maybe they are dividends growing at a smooth constant rate. Maybe they are not. Regardless, the investor implicitly establishes the minimal acceptable rate of return at which the stock would be considered a "buy." Define the "required rate of return" as follows.

> **DEFINITION 9.2 Required rate of return ($ROR^{required}$)**
> The "required rate of return" is the minimum discount rate that an investor willingly accepts for computing intrinsic value.

The investor implicitly uses $ROR^{required}$ to discount expected cash flows and arrives at the stock's intrinsic value. If the stock price is less than intrinsic value then the investor perceives the stock as a buy. Restatement of this rule follows:

> **RULE 9.1 Restatement of the intrinsic value trading strategy**
> The signal a fundamental analysis generates is that:
>
> $$if\ ROR_t^{expected} \begin{Bmatrix} > \\ < \end{Bmatrix} ROR_t^{required}\ then\ \begin{pmatrix} intrinsic \\ value \end{pmatrix}_t \begin{Bmatrix} > \\ < \end{Bmatrix} \begin{pmatrix} actual \\ price \end{pmatrix}_t so \begin{Bmatrix} buy \\ sell \end{Bmatrix}$$

When $ROR^{expected}$ exceeds $ROR^{required}$ the asset is undervalued and the asset returns more than the investor requires. Always buy undervalued assets. When $ROR^{expected}$ is less than $ROR^{required}$ the asset is overvalued. Financial market equilibrium occurs when expected and required rates of return are equal.

> **FORMULA 9.1 Financial market equilibrium condition**
> The financial market for a specific security, say security A, is at equilibrium when that security's expected and required rates of return are equal:
>
> $$ROR_A^{expected} = ROR_A^{required}$$

The section below presents a lesson on long-run relations between risk and return.

4.B. Historical record of financial market rates of return

Historical data provide insight about long-run risk and rates of return. Figure 9.4 illustrates movement in financial rates of return by showing the value at year-end 2001 of a $1 investment made at year-end 1925. A one-dollar investment in Treasury bills would have grown to become worth $17 (all figures assume automatic reinvestment of the total return). The 1,600% cumulative rate of return from T-bills is pretty big because the 76-year sample period is pretty long. Investment in long-term government bonds results in ending wealth of $51, about thrice the accumulation from T-bills. Long-term corporate bonds grow even more, to $72, and a $1 investment in large company stocks grows to an incredible $2,279. Finally, the average small company stock investment of $1 from 1925 attains an ending wealth in 2001 of $7,860.

Table 9.15 summarizes statistics about annual rates of return that underlie the preceding figures. Columns 1 and 2 list average annual ROR computed by the arithmetic and geometric approaches, respectfully. The general discussion about these measurements (see chapter 4, formulas 4.3 and 4.4) establishes that the geometric average annual ROR properly links beginning and ending wealth in accordance with the lump-sum time value relation (formula 4.6). The sensitivity of wealth accumulation over long horizons to the rate of return is apparent through comparison of $ROR^{geometric}$ in the bottom two rows. The annual average is about 180 basis points bigger for small company stocks than for large company stocks (12.5 versus 10.7 percent), yet the total accumulations differ by more than three-fold ($7,860 versus $2,279). Relevant to the current topic, however, is the tendency for all numbers to get bigger as one scans down the table.

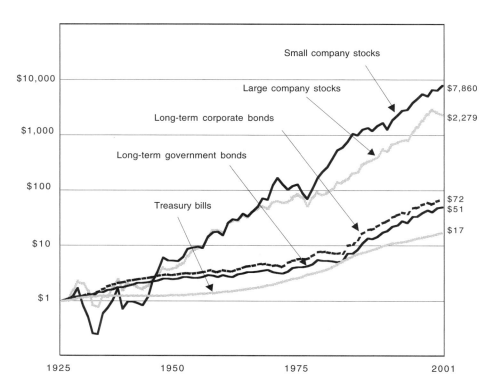

FIGURE 9.4

Growth of a $1 investment at year-end 1925 in different asset classes

Source: "Stocks, bonds, bills, and inflation: 2001 yearbook." Ibbotson Associates, Chicago IL, page 26.

Column 3 lists standard deviations of annual rates of return for each asset class. The standard deviation ("σ") measures dispersion or volatility. Much discussion appears later about σ but, for now, suffice to say that σ relates directly to risk. Column 4 illustrates the frequency distribution of annual rates of return. The distribution for Treasury bills clusters tightly toward the middle. The dispersion of T-bill returns is low—its σ is relatively low, too. Scanning down the table shows increasing dispersion and increasing σ. Table 9.15 reveals an almost perfect alignment: average rates of return rise with risk!

Table 9.16 reveals insight about risk that always is important to remember. Columns 1 and 2 of panel A list the minimum and maximum annual rates of return for each asset class, and column 3 lists the number of times the annual ROR is positive. The sample period from 1926 until 2001 contains 76 annual ROR. The minimum and maximum for T-bills equal –0.02% and 14.7%, whereas for small company stocks the extrema equal –58.0% and 142.9%, respectively. High risk investments naturally have a higher likelihood of extreme outcomes.

Panel B cumulates five consecutive annual returns together and recomputes statistics for the entire five-year horizon. The sample period from 1926 until 2001 contains 72 overlapping 5-year windows. In all 72 five-year windows T-bills provide

	Arithmetic mean	Geometric mean	Standard deviation	Frequency distribution
	-1-	-2-	-3-	-4-
U.S. Treasury bills	3.9%	3.8%	3.2%	
Long-term government bonds	5.7	5.3	9.4	
Long-term corporate bonds	6.1	5.8	8.6	
Large company stocks	12.7	10.7	20.2	
Small company stocks	17.3	12.5	33.2	
				- 0% +

TABLE 9.15

Summary statistics for annual rates of return

Source: "Stocks, bonds, bills, and inflation: 2001 yearbook." Ibbotson Associates, Chicago IL, page 31.

TABLE 9.16

Maximum and minimum values of returns for 1-, 5-, 10-, 15-, and 20-year holding periods (compound annual rates of return in percent)

	Minimum value (year)	Maximum value (year)	# windows with ROR > 0
	-1-	-2-	-3-
Panel A: 1-year investment horizon (76 non-overlapping 1-year windows)			
U.S. Treasury bills	−0.02 (1938)	14.7 (1981)	75
Long-term government bonds	−9.2 (1967)	40.4 (1982)	55
Long-term corporate bonds	−8.1 (1969)	42.6 (1982)	59
Large company stocks	−43.3 (1931)	54.0 (1933)	54
Small company stocks	−58.0 (1937)	142.9 (1933)	53
Panel B: 5-year investment horizons (72 overlapping 5-year windows)			
U.S. Treasury bills	0.1 (1938-42)	11.1 (1979-83)	72
Long-term government bonds	−2.14 (1965-69)	21.6 (1982-86)	66
Long-term corporate bonds	−2.2 (1965-69)	22.5 (1982-86)	69
Large company stocks	−12.5 (1928-32)	28.6 (1995-99)	65
Small company stocks	−27.5 (1928-32)	45.9 (1941-45)	63
Panel C: 10-year investment horizons (67 overlapping 10-year windows)			
U.S. Treasury bills	0.1 (1933-42)	9.2 (1978-87)	67
Long-term government bonds	−0.1 (1950-59)	15.6 (1982-91)	66
Long-term corporate bonds	1.0 (1947-56)	16.3 (1982-91)	67
Large company stocks	−0.9 (1929-38)	20.1 (1949-58)	65
Small company stocks	−5.7 (1929-38)	30.4 (1975-84)	65
Panel D: 15-year investment horizons (62 overlapping 15-year windows)			
U.S. Treasury bills	0.2 (1933-47)	8.3 (1977-91)	62
Long-term government bonds	0.4 (1955-69)	13.5 (1981-95)	62
Long-term corporate bonds	1.0 (1955-69)	13.7 (1982-96)	62
Large company stocks	0.6 (1929-43)	18.9 (1985-99)	62
Small company stocks	−1.3 (1927-41)	23.3 (1975-89)	59
Panel E: 20-year investment horizons (57 overlapping 20-year windows)			
U.S. Treasury bills	0.4 (1931-50)	7.7 (1972-91)	57
Long-term government bonds	0.7 (1950-69)	12.1 (1982-01)	57
Long-term corporate bonds	1.3 (1950-69)	12.1 (1982-01)	57
Large company stocks	3.1 (1929-48)	17.9 (1980-99)	57
Small company stocks	5.7 (1929-48)	21.1 (1942-61)	57

Source: "Stocks, bonds, bills, and inflation: 2001 yearbook." Ibbotson Associates, Chicago IL, page 41.

positive cumulative returns. Small company stocks have positive cumulative returns for 63 of 72 overlapping 5-year windows. Small company stocks lose money during nine 5-year windows (that is, the odds of losing with a 5-year investment horizon was one-out-of-eight). Indeed, $100 invested in small company stocks at year-end 1927 was worth only $77.50 by year-end 1932.

Panel D cumulates fifteen consecutive annual returns together and recomputes statistics for the entire fifteen-year horizon. The sample period from 1926 until 2001 contains 62 overlapping fifteen-year windows. Large company stocks provide positive cumulative returns in all 62 windows (although from 1929-1943 the cumulative return is less than 1 percent!). For small company stocks, however, there are three 15-year windows for which cumulative returns are negative. In those cases high risk did not get high return. For the long 20-year investment horizon that panel E tabulates, small company stocks provide positive returns for 57-out-of-57 overlapping 20-year windows.

An important insight is that high risk investments do not always earn high returns. Quite often, even for decades-long investment horizons, high risk investments may receive paltry or negative returns. Yet in efficient financial markets logic dictates a positive relation between risk and equilibrium rates of return. Formula 9.2 summarizes this dictum:

The required rate of return for security A, denoted $ROR_A^{required}$, compensates investors for bearing risk by offering, in the long-run and on-average, a positive risk premium:

$$ROR_A^{required} = ROR^{risk\text{-}free} + (security\ risk\ premium)_A,$$

where $ROR^{risk\text{-}free}$ denotes the nominal risk-free interest rate.

Investors that completely forgo risk may invest in T-bills, for example, and earn the risk-free rate $ROR^{risk\text{-}free}$. Yet to pursue a higher risk investment, investors require the promise of higher returns. Investors require a risk premium.

Without the promise of a positive risk premium investors shy away from risky investments. High risk earns high return in the long-run but, always remember, one never can be sure exactly how long is the long run.

4.C. The efficient markets hypothesis implies expected returns vibrate around required returns

Analysts and serious investors spend time and money gathering information and developing forecasts for expected rates of return. One of the most important hypotheses in financial science explores the importance of information for forecasting equilibrium rates of return. Ideas inherent with the "efficient market hypothesis" were formalized by Eugene Fama (University of Chicago) and popularized by Burton Malkiel (Princeton University) during the early 1970s. This definition contains the crux of the hypothesis:

DEFINITION 9.3 Efficient market hypothesis ("EMH")

A market is efficient with respect to an information event if it is impossible to devise a trading strategy that uses the information to consistently earn economic profit.

In an informationally efficient market satisfying the preceding definition all security prices quickly adjust to new information. This means that by the time the marginal investor learns information that may move a stock's price, other market participants already acted on it, the stock price already moved to its new and fair position, and already the stock price reflects consensus expectations about the future. The information has no marginal value to the marginal investor because the stock price embodies all available information.

A simplistic analogy for the EMH is this: there are no five-dollar-bills lying on the sidewalk of the busiest street in town. This analogous hypothesis obviously is true (at least 99.99999999% of the time!). If there were a five-dollar-bill on the sidewalk, someone else already would have picked it up. You cannot walk down a busy street and find five-dollar bills just like you cannot listen to the news and use what you hear to consistently earn economic profit.

An important implication of the EMH is that equilibrium rates of return, in the long run and on average, are not driven by information about company profitability, sales trends, market share, growth opportunities, price-multiples, or any of the other information events that possibly shape expected rates of return. Unanticipated information events cause price adjustments after the fact. Before the fact, however, investors anticipate information thereby causing convergence of $ROR^{expected}$ with $ROR^{required}$. Ex ante equilibrium rates of return vibrate around required returns. Before continuing our investigation of the relation between risk and return, consider important nuances of the efficient market hypothesis.

C1. Nuances of the efficient market hypothesis

This subsection examines the EMH and overviews tests of market efficiency. The hypothesis pertains to all well-developed financial markets. Typically, however, the stock market is the stage on which most discussions of the EMH center (including the discussion below). First, consider components of EMH definition 9.3 that are notable.

1. The financial market may be efficient with respect to one information event but not others. The question "is the stock market efficient?" is underspecified and does not have a definite answer. Instead, a definite information event must be specified for which a definite yes/no answer exists. For example, a valid question is this: "is the stock market efficient with respect to announcement of a stock split?"

2. The EMH argues that stock prices quickly respond to new information. The price adjustment process, however, takes (some) time. The length of time varies from seconds, to minutes, and maybe longer for surprising information that is difficult to assess. Lengthy adjustment periods may reflect information complexity rather than market inefficiency. Sometimes, for example, new information about a single event reaches the market in bits and pieces. Consequently, the price response may diffuse across time. The important issue is whether security prices adjust to unanticipated changes in consensus expectations.

3. There is no violation of the EMH simply because a trading strategy uses information and (once) earns economic profit. Instead, the EMH argues that a trading strategy cannot *consistently* earn economic profit.

4. If the EMH is true then all security prices are "fair." This means that consensus expectations push prices to the point that none are undervalued nor overvalued. Security investment earns a return that depends exclusively on risk and unanticipated changes in consensus expectations.

5. The EMH uses economic profit as its benchmark for comparison. Perhaps a trading strategy consistently earns positive accounting profit, but this does not violate the EMH. Instead, the EMH argues that a trading strategy cannot consistently earn returns that exceed fair compensation for risk exposure.

Figure 9.5 shows possible price adjustments to an information event. Perhaps the event is announcement of a stock split, or a merger, corporate name change, labor strike, or even announcement of federal legislation changing the regulatory environment. Time is on the horizontal axis. For convenience, the three panels break the entire time horizon into three subperiods. The middle panel illustrates the subperiod with the information event. The top and bottom panels are the pre-event and post-event time-windows, respectively.

The vertical axis always shows the *cumulative abnormal return* ("CAR"). The CAR equals the cumulative economic profit that the stock earns. Compute the CAR in two steps. The first step computes each period's abnormal return. The periodic abnormal return equals the stock's actual ROR minus the ROR earned by a security (or securities) of equivalent risk that is unaffected by the event. This latter ROR is the "control sample ROR" and its subtraction from the actual ROR adjusts for fair returns that normally accrue. The periodic abnormal return represents the economic profit the security earns per period and its frequency may be daily or monthly. The second step sums the periodic abnormal returns for all periods within a time-window. The sum equals the CAR and represents total economic profit throughout the window.

Panel A illustrates how the CAR moves during the pre-event window. The CAR vibrates around zero before anticipation of the event begins. Securities at equilibrium earn zero economic profit, thereby implying a CAR of zero. At some point the market starts anticipating the event. Perhaps rumors trigger the anticipation, or perhaps the company begins fitting the profile of companies that tend to experience the event. Regardless, consensus expectations about the company change and, according to the EMH, the stock price responds by reflecting the expected event. If the market anticipates that the event will be good news (such as higher company profitability), the price rises abnormally and the CAR gets bigger. Anticipation of bad news pushes the CAR negative. Figure 9.5 illustrates that total economic profit

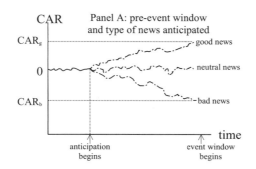

FIGURE 9.5

Price adjustment process to an information event

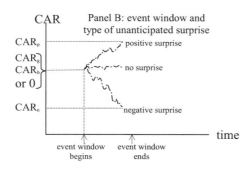

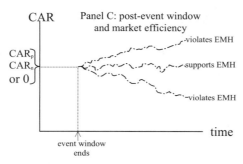

throughout the pre-event window sums to CAR_g and CAR_b in anticipation of good news and bad news, respectively. With anticipation of neutral news, or if the market never anticipates the event, the CAR continues vibration around zero.

Panel B illustrates how the CAR moves during the event window. An event window begins when finally the anticipation is over and facts arrive. The CAR when the event window begins has whatever value is attained in Panel A (either CAR_g or CAR_b or 0). Movement of the CAR during the event window depends on the accuracy of the anticipation. When actual information is better than expected the CAR moves up toward CAR_p. The positive surprise drives up the stock price as the market digests the new information. Conversely, for negative surprises the stock price moves down and the CAR drops to CAR_n. With accurate anticipation the CAR does not move because there is no surprise.

Sometimes it may seem puzzling when a company's stock price hardly responds to an announcement of significant news. The explanation is that the market accurately anticipated the news. Likewise, sometimes a company announces bad news but the stock price rises. Why? The answer is that the market anticipated worse news. When finally the company announces that things are bad, but the market perceives it's not as bad as expected, the positive surprise sends the stock price upwards.

The event window ends when consensus expectations fully digest effects of the event on company cash flows. The length of the event window may be seconds, minutes, days, or more. Regardless, once the flow of new information ceases then the event window closes.

Panel C illustrates how the CAR moves during the post-event window. The EMH claims that the stock price quickly reflects all available information. As long as the post-event window is absent of new information then, according to the EMH, actual stock returns contain zero economic profits. The CAR should vibrate around whatever value is attained in Panel B (either CAR_p or CAR_n or 0). The EMH claims that during the post-event window the CAR drifts sideways, neither rising nor falling significantly. Significant drift, up or down, violates the EMH.

Hundreds of tests on market efficiency examine many different types of information events. Information events belong to either of three traditional categories. "Weak" information events pertain exclusively to stock market data such as historical prices, trading volume, price multiples, calendar effects, etc. "Semi-strong" information events pertain to all publicly available data such as economic or political announcements, corporate news, etc. "Strong" information events pertain to all data, public and private, such as insider or managerial insights. Irrespective of category, an efficient market exists when a trading strategy cannot use an information event to consistently earn economic profit. The super-majority of studies on financial market efficiency find tendencies that figure 9.5 illustrates as supportive of the EMH.

A handful of studies find tendencies violating the EMH. Important reasons why a CAR may show significant non-zero drift during the post-event window include:

(1) The information flow is wrongly identified. Perhaps the post-event window contains new information that drives the CAR. Perhaps even the event window is mis-specified. Occurrence of this type of error means that the EMH may be rejected even though it really is true.

(2) The control sample ROR may be computed wrongly. The control sample ROR purports to measure the stock's rate of return that would have occurred if the information event did not exist. But in actuality the event exists and divining what might have happened if it didn't exist is difficult. Reliance on CARs necessarily results in a joint test of two hypotheses: (a) market efficiency is true and (b) control sample design is correct. It is impossible to know which reason causes the significant drift in CARs. Medical studies face an analogous problem asking what happens to patients if they take a medicine versus what happens if they don't—in actuality some patients take it and the control sample pretends to mimic those same patients as if they hadn't. Stock market studies, like medical ones, generate controversial findings.

(3) The EMH is false for this particular type of information event. This implies existence of a trading strategy that consistently earns economic profit. As large numbers of investors utilize the strategy its effectiveness probably would disappear.

With efficient markets no trading strategy consistently earns positive economic profits because no investor consistently finds new information offering an advantage for predicting $ROR^{expected}$. The implication is that expected rates of return vibrate around required rates of return like a rubber band conforms to a deck of playing cards. New information may momentarily stretch $ROR^{expected}$ away from $ROR^{required}$, but very quickly it snaps back into place. Rule 9.2 summarizes this lesson.

> **RULE 9.2 Risk determines $ROR^{equilibrium}$**
> Equilibrium rates of return track required returns in efficient financial markets. Required returns depend exclusively on risk. Risk, and risk alone, determines the level of equilibrium rates of return.

Equilibrium rates of return track required returns in efficient financial markets, and required returns depend exclusively on risk.

CHAPTER 10
Measuring Risk, Return, and Diversification Benefits

Lessons from the previous chapter explain that expected rates of return depend on time value principles that Part 1 of this book discusses. Investors digest information and perceive a cash flow stream, they observe the actual security price, and $ROR^{expected}$ is the discount rate that links price with present value of expected cash flows.

Required rates of return depend on fundamentally different principles. Investor perceptions of tradeoffs and opportunity costs drive determination of $ROR^{required}$. The required rate of return, restated below, largely depends on risk:

> **FORMULA 10.1   Required rate of return ($ROR^{required}$)**
>
> The "required rate of return" is the minimum discount rate that an investor willingly accepts for computing intrinsic value. The required rate of return for security A equals the nominal riskfree interest rate ($ROR^{risk\text{-}free}$) plus that security's risk premium:
>
> $$ROR_A^{required} = ROR^{risk\text{-}free} + (security\ risk\ premium)_A.$$

Investors may purchase riskless government securities and earn rate $ROR^{risk\text{-}free}$. For bearing risk, however, investors must perceive and receive, in the long-run and on-average, a positive risk premium. The risk premium induces investors to bear risk – stated differently, the risk premium compensates investors for bearing risk.

The previous chapter also explains that in efficient financial markets $ROR^{expected}$ vibrate around $ROR^{required}$. Equilibrium occurs when expected and required returns are equal. Consequently, equilibrium rates of return track required returns. Explanations of market equilibrium focus on explanations of the relation between risk and return. This chapter presents several lessons on risk and return. Section 1 explains how risk and return relate to the dominance concept. Section 2 examines primary risk sources. Sections 3 & 4 introduce measures for risk, return, and diversification benefits.

1. OVERVIEW OF RISK, RETURN, AND THE DOMINANCE CONCEPT

Financial science generally assumes that investors prefer more return instead of less return, and less risk instead of more risk. The dominance concept helps us understand implications of investor risk preferences.

One strategy dominates the alternative if in every dimension the strategy is at least as good or better than the alternative.

Every comparison of two alternatives shows either the existence of dominance or a trade-off. When dominance exists, investors prefer the dominant strategy. When a trade-off exists, one strategy is better than the alternative in some ways, worse in other ways, and the one that is best depends on other factors.

For investment applications, a dominant strategy is one whose expected return equals or exceeds the alternative's, while the strategy's risk is less than the alternative's. The absence of dominance implies the existence of a trade-off. Figure 10.1 illustrates for financial investments the concept of dominance versus trade-off. The vertical axis measures expected rate of return and horizontal axis measures risk. Suppose an investor contemplates buying either security A or security B. Consider the risk-return characteristics at point A. Now consider how characteristics change by moving to point B. The top panel illustrates that with movement from point A toward B the return increases—and that is good. Risk decreases—that is good, too. It's a win-win move. Security B dominates A. To the extent that investors only care about risk and return, and that our graph properly portrays them, B is preferable to A in every dimension. When an investor faces a constraint that only one security may be bought, A or B, then the decision is a no-brainer. Investors prefer dominant strategies, B dominates A, so buy B.

Now consider comparison of securities B and C shown in the lower panel. Security C has more risk—that is bad. But security C also has more return—and that is good. Securities B and C coexist as trade-offs. The one that is best does not depend on the security characteristics. Instead, the one that is best depends on risk preferences of the investor. To some investors the extra return may be worth the extra risk, whereas to other investors the trade-off may not be worthy. We cannot say whether C is a better choice than B by looking simply at the security risk-return

FIGURE 10.1
Risk, return, and dominance

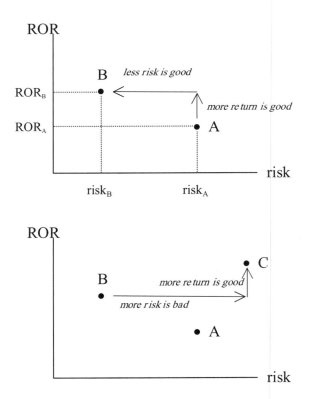

characteristics. Information about the investor risk preferences is crucial. Similar analysis shows no dominance between A and C either. A and C coexist as trade-offs.

When one security dominates the alternative, the security risk-return characteristics determine which is best. When there is not dominance, that is they coexist as trade-offs, then the securities do not determine which is best—investor risk preferences do. For this reason many advertisements in the financial press advocate the importance of tailoring investment decisions to the investor's personal situation. Individuals in early life-cycle stages (see table 9.4) generally have longer investment horizons and tolerate high risk strategies. Retirees, conversely, generally have shorter horizons and possess low risk tolerances.

Investments expose investors to risk that emanates from many sources. At the most basic level, however, all sources of risk belong to one of two classes: idiosyncratic risk or systematic risk.

> **DEFINITION 10.2 Two primal risk classes: idiosyncratic and systematic**
> *Idiosyncratic risk* is unique to a specific security and may be reduced or eliminated through prudent diversification strategies.
> *Systematic risk* is unaffected by diversification strategies and is common to all securities although security sensitivities to systematic risk may vary.

The definitions emphasize the importance of diversification attributes for classifying risk. Financial theory shows that diversification eliminates risk when the distribution of risk across securities and markets has certain properties. In reality, however, there are many sources of risk with varying and "in-between" properties. Pigeonholing risk sources into one class or the other is difficult. The classification scheme, nonetheless, is useful. There exist, at the limit, two types of risk: risk that can be managed or eliminated (idiosyncratic) and risk that can't (systematic).

EXERCISES 10.1

Conceptual
1. Your analysis of common stocks for companies X and Y lead you to believe their expected rates of return and standard deviation of returns are as listed below. Is there dominance or a tradeoff? ©ER6

	E(ROR)	σ
security X	15.9%	15.7%
security Y	16.4%	13.0%

2. Suppose that you are able to perfectly measure risk and expected return, and the bigger the number the bigger the risk or return. Measurements of (*risk, return*) for three possible asset investments, call them X, Y, and Z, are as follows: X: (20,9); Y: (4,6); Z: (11,7). Compare the three with regards to dominance or tradeoff. ©ER11

3. Suppose that you are able to perfectly measure expected return. Also, suppose that there exist two different kinds of risk that you can measure, call them $Risk_1$ and $Risk_2$. The amount of $Risk_1$ an investment possesses is totally unrelated to the amount of $Risk_2$ that it possesses. Three possible asset investments, call them A, B, and C, have measurements for ($Risk_1$, $Risk_2$, *return*) as follows: A: (10,40,8); B: (10,20,9); C: (15,50,10). Compare the three with regards to dominance or tradeoff. ©ER10

2. SOURCES OF IDIOSYNCRATIC RISK

When a company issues a credit market security they promise to repay principal plus interest to the investor. But there is no guarantee. When a company issues a common stock the hopeful investor expects to collect future dividends or capital gains. But there is no guarantee. These securities have risk, yet where does it come from? What are the sources of risk?

Traditional sources of idiosyncratic security risk have been known for a long time. Subsections below discuss several prominent risk sources. The sources are not mutually exclusive and, perhaps, not every security exposes its investor to each type of risk.

Liquidity risk

The lesson on liquidity ratios in chapter 2 (section 3.A) teaches that a *liquid* asset is one that easily and quickly converts to cash at a fair value. Not all financial securities convert to cash with the same liquidity. Some securities trade so frequently that changes in market value are observable second-by-second. They are very liquid. Other securities may not trade for months at a time (or even longer!); these are illiquid. Imagine an investor comparing two securities. Suppose the two promise identical cash flow streams but one is frequently traded whereas the other is not. The investor knows that the liquid security is easier to buy or sell at the prevailing market value. Trading the illiquid security is riskier because willing traders aren't as prevalent. All else equal, demand and equilibrium price are greater for a liquid security than for an illiquid one. In other words, liquidity is a source of idiosyncratic risk:

> **DEFINITION 10.3 Liquidity risk premuim**
>
> *Liquidity risk* refers to the likelihood that a security easily and quickly converts to cash at the prevailing market value. The *liquidity risk premium*, nil for very liquid securities, gets bigger as liquidity diminishes:
>
> $$\text{When security liquidity} \begin{Bmatrix} increases \\ decreases \end{Bmatrix} \text{then the liquidity risk premium} \begin{Bmatrix} decreases \\ increases \end{Bmatrix}.$$

Common stocks trade with different frequencies, thereby suggesting differing liquidities. Table 10.1 tabulates facts about equity liquidity for the New York Stock Exchange and for NASDAQ.

TABLE 10.1

Quintile breakpoints on equity liquidity variables.

% of stocks with less than number at right	Average value of trades per day ($1,000s) - 1 -	Average number of shares traded per day (1,000s) - 2 -	Share turnover period (days) - 3 -
NYSE (2,555 stocks)			
100% (maximum)	$534,188	36,632	193,000
80%	$13,038	561	810
60%	$3,186	173	423
40%	$791	62	273
20%	$200	18	170
0% (minimum)	$0.18	0.01 shares	0.8 days
NASDAQ (3,650 stocks)			
100% (maximum)	$1,539,746	56,884	infinite
80%	$1,514	194	1327
60%	$254	52	640
40%	$65	16	326
20%	$16	4	145
0% (minimum)	$0.00	0.00 shares	0.6 days

Data are from the Center for Research in Security Prices monthly prices dataset (CRSP). All entries based on volume and prices for December 2002 (22 trading days). The "share turnover period" equals total common shares outstanding ÷ (monthly share volume/22).

Column 1 of the upper panel shows that among 2,555 stocks on the NYSE the average value of trades per day ranges from a maximum of $535,188,000 (that's half-billion dollars per day!) to a minimum of $180. This suggests a huge difference in liquidity! Stock for the company at the upper percentile (IBM) is more liquid than stock for the company at the lowest percentile (Companhia de Bebidas das

Americas). Inspection of this column shows that daily dollar volume for 20% of all companies on the NYSE averages less than $200,000.

The lower panel lists analogous facts for 3,650 NASDAQ stocks. The most traded NASDAQ stock (Microsoft) averages daily volume of $1.54 billion (that's almost 3 times more than for IBM). Generally, however, dollar volume is less for stocks on NASDAQ than NYSE. Sixty percent of NASDAQ stocks, for example, average dollar volume less than $254,000 – this would put them at or below the 21st percentile on the NYSE.

Columns 2 and 3 examine other measures of equity liquidity. Column 2 lists number of shares instead of dollar value. The maximum number of shares traded per day is 36.6 million (for Lucent Technologies) on the NYSE and 56.9 million (for Cisco Systems) on NASDAQ. Twenty percent of stocks on the NYSE trade fewer than 18,000 shares per day; on NASDAQ twenty percent trade fewer than 4,000 shares.

Column 3 offers another comparison of equity liquidity by examining the "share turnover period." The share turnover period is number of days that, at average daily share volume, the entire balance of outstanding company stock would be traded. With IBM, for example, there are 1,690 million shares outstanding and average daily volume (throughout December 2002) is 6.89 million shares. At this rate it takes 245 days to completely turnover all IBM shares (245 = 1,690,088,000 ÷ 6,892,745). The IBM share turnover period, 245 days, is at the 34th percentile of all NYSE stocks. The table shows that 60% of all NYSE stocks have turnover periods less than 423 days. The 54th percentile is 365 days, implying that it takes longer than one year for 46% of NYSE stocks to completely turnover all outstanding shares.

Column 3 for NASDAQ presents a similar picture. A turnover ratio of 365 days is at the 41st percentile and indicates it takes longer than one year for 59% of NASDAQ stocks to completely turnover all outstanding shares. Even though columns 1 and 2 suggest NYSE stocks are more liquid than NASDAQ stocks, column 3 shows lesser differences among share turnover periods.

Table 10.2 shows other similarities between NYSE and NASDAQ equity liquidity. Column 1 for the NYSE ranks in descending order the 2,555 stocks by average value of trades per day. The top 20% (511 stocks) account for 86.7% of all total daily trading volume (by dollars). The bottom 60% (1,533 stocks) account for only 3.4% of all trading. There is a huge concentration of trading activity. This is reminiscent of tables from chapter 1 that show a huge concentration of business activity in the upper crust of large companies.

Column 2 for the NYSE ranks in descending order the 2,555 stocks by average daily share volume. The top 20% (511 stocks) account for 83.1% of total shares traded. Columns 1 and 2 convey similar stories. NASDAQ trading concentrates even more.

The median shareprices in parentheses of columns 2 and 3 convey insights about the relation between stock price and liquidity. The most liquid stocks are in the "biggest quintile" when sorted by average daily share volume. Conversely, when sorted by the share turnover period the most liquid stocks are in the "smallest quintile." Observe that for NYSE stocks the most liquid stocks have high stock prices. As liquidity diminishes so too does the shareprice. The relation is different for the NYSE than for NASDAQ. For NASDAQ stocks there is a significant quadratic relation between liquidity and shareprice. A stock with a relatively high price is likely to be extreme – it's either extremely liquid or extremely illiquid. Medium liquidity NASDAQ stocks tend to have relatively low stock prices.

TABLE 10.2

Percentage of total trading volume (and median stock price) in each quintile according to various liquidity measures.

	Percentage of total dollar volume for all stocks in quintile (and median stock price) when sorted by "Average value of trades per day" - 1 -	Percentage of total shares traded for all stocks in quintile (and median stock price) when sorted by "Average daily share volume" - 2 -	Percentage of total shares traded for all stocks in quintile (and median stock price) when sorted by "Share turnover period" - 3 -
NYSE 2,555 stocks 1.43 billion average daily volume (shares) $34.5 billion average daily volume (dollars) $16.44 median share price			
biggest quintile	86.7%	83.1% ($23.81)	1.0% ($13.64)
upper middle	10.0%	11.4% ($22.47)	9.1% ($13.40)
middle	2.6%	3.9% ($16.24)	19.8% ($19.93)
lower middle	0.7%	1.3% ($13.91)	27.6% ($21.51)
smallest quintile	0.1%	0.3% ($13.43)	42.4% ($20.45)
NASDAQ 3,650 stocks 1.35 billion average daily volume (shares) $19.4 billion average daily volume (dollars) $6.51 median share price			
biggest quintile	96.8%	91.9% ($10.24)	0.2% ($8.00)
upper middle	2.5%	5.9% ($5.31)	0.9% ($4.91)
middle	0.5%	1.7% ($4.05)	2.7% ($3.94)
lower middle	0.1%	0.5% ($5.48)	11.3% ($5.72)
smallest quintile	0.0%	0.1% ($9.47)	84.8% ($11.55)

Liquidity risk also is pertinent to credit market securities. The common consensus is that liquidity risk is greater for credit market securities than for equities, with the notable exception of U.S. Treasury securities which are the most liquid of all. Certainly the market for corporate notes and bonds is less complete than the market for equities. This occurs even though, as table 9.13 shows, the value of credit market securities in the U.S. exceeds the value of equities. Perhaps greater liquidity risk for credit market securities is attributable to two facts. First, there is relatively less company information available for many issuers of credit market securities. Many credit market issuers do not issue publicly traded stock and are not subject to the same disclosure requirements as public companies. Investor interest wanes and liquidity may lessen when information about the issuer becomes scant. Second, a large publicly traded company may have more than a dozen different credit market securities outstanding but only one common stock! The number of securities in the credit market, in other words, is orders of magnitude larger than the number of equity securities and this may translate into greater liquidity risk premia for credit market securities.

Term risk

Term is the time period for which a financial contract is valid. Chapter 7 illustrates that market financing rates normally are lower for short-term securities. *Term risk* is a catchall for phenomena that cause two securities with different term to have different required returns even though they are alike in every other way (e.g., identical liquidity, default risk, etc.). *Term* is a source of idiosyncratic risk.

DEFINITION 10.4 Term risk premuim

Term risk relates to the timing of cash flows that a security implicitly or explicitly promises. The *term risk premium*, nil for very short-term securities, normally gets bigger as term increases:

When the timing of security cash flows tilt toward the $\left\{ \begin{array}{l} \textit{near-term} \\ \textit{remote future} \end{array} \right\}$.

then normally the term risk premuim $\left\{ \begin{array}{l} \textit{decreases} \\ \textit{increases} \end{array} \right\}$.

Term risk is a dynamic concept that reflects complex phenomena occurring as cash flows distribute across time. Term risk affects all types of investments. Credit market securities have differing maturities – the term risk premium increases with maturity (all else equal). Real estate and other capital budgeting projects have different payback periods – the term risk premium increases with payback period (all else equal). Equities trade for many different kinds of companies – startups sometimes don't return dividends for decades.

Financial research establishes that when two securities are alike in every way except term then the following factors may influence the term risk premium.

1. *Price risk:* Discounted values of long-term cash flow streams are more sensitive than short-term cash flow streams to changes in the discount rate (see chapter 7). Consequently, near-term price movement is relatively volatile for a long-term security. The price in the near-term becomes very relevant if liquidation becomes necessary. Perhaps investors respond to greater uncertainty about near-term prices for long-term securities by increasing the term risk premium.

2. *Inflation and expectations risk:* Required rates of return compensate investors for opportunity costs such as: decline in purchasing power of money caused by inflation; interest rates on alternative investments. People develop expectations that sometimes suggest levels of near-term inflation and interest rates may not persist. For example, they may think that rates may be steadily rising for awhile and then falling, or vice versa. Term risk premia for short and long-term securities differ (all else equal) due to embodiment of expectations over the relevant horizon. Find the approximate inflation component of the term risk premium as:

$$\left(\begin{array}{c} \textit{inflation premium} \\ \textit{for N} - \textit{period} \\ \textit{horizon} \end{array} \right) = \sum_{t=1}^{N} \frac{(\textit{inflation rate})_t}{N}$$

Suppose, for example, that over the next one year expected inflation is 0% but that during the second year expected inflation is 10%, during the third year 20% and during the 4th year 0%. The inflation premium equals 0% on a one-year bond, 5% on a 2-year bond, 10% on a 3-year bond, and 7 1/2% on a 4-year bond.

3. *Reinvestment option:* A short-term security returns invested capital to the investor who then has an option for reinvesting. At that time the investor has an option to reinvest the capital in another security, or use the money to party, etc. A longer term security does not provide that option because cash flow tilts toward the remote future. Perhaps the reinvestment option is valuable and investors require more return <u>per year</u> as compensation for its sacrifice.

4. *Nonlinear risk:* Investors normally respond to an increasing term by demanding more return <u>per year</u>. This revealed behavior suggests that perhaps risk is nonlinear. Research with stochastic financial models suggests that investors may behave as though two years of risk "compounds" and requires more than twice the compensation of one year's risk. That is, while getting 10% for one year may be adequate, the addition to term of an extra year requires more than an additional year of 10% returns.

The timing of cash flows differs across securities. Some securities promise returns in the near-term. Others offer returns in the remote-term. Investors overwhelmingly reveal a preference for near-term returns. To the extent that equilibrium rates of return rise with risk, the implication is that risk normally rises with term. Timing and duration of the expected cash flow stream determine the term risk premium.

Default risk

Default occurs when a borrower is unable to make payments promised to creditors. When default occurs then bankruptcy or reorganization become possibilities. When a borrower defaults on one loan then all the securities they have issued become at-risk. The likelihood of default is a source of idiosyncratic risk.

DEFINITION 10.5 Default risk premium

Default risk refers to the likelihood that an issuer may be unable to fulfill financial obligations. The *default risk premium*, nil for short-term U.S. government credit market securities, gets bigger as the likelihood of default increases:

When the likelihood of default by the issuer $\begin{Bmatrix} increases \\ decreases \end{Bmatrix}$.

then the default risk premuim $\begin{Bmatrix} increases \\ decreases \end{Bmatrix}$.

Issuers of financial securities hire rating agencies to assess security default risk. The agencies assign ratings to many different types of securities issued by many different types of organizations. With corporate bonds, for example, the ratings range from triple-A for highest quality bonds (lowest default risk) to C-grade for lowest quality (highest default risk). Default risk, however, also affects equities because shareholders lose when the company defaults on its bonds.

Company default risk depends on many factors. Glean important lessons about default risk by re-examining the stylized income statement from chapter 2 (section 3c, Breakeven ratios):

Sales revenue	$p\,Q$
- *Total fixed costs*	F
- <u>*Total variable costs*</u>	<u>$v\,Q$</u>
= *Earnings before interest & taxes*	*EBIT*
- *Interest*	I
- *Taxes*	T
- <u>*Preferred dividends*</u>	<u>PD</u>
= *Earnings available for common*	*EAC*

The variable Q represents the quantity of product that the company sells, p is the unit sales price of the product (p times Q equals total *Sales revenue*), and v is the variable cost per unit. Default risk relates to the inability of the company to fulfill financial obligations. Recall that the cash flow diagram from chapter 1 (figure 1.3) illustrates the company transferring wealth to two groups of economic entities: stakeholders in real asset markets and capitalists in financial markets. Discussions below refer to the preceding stylized income statement to explain how financial obligations to stakeholders and capitalists relate to default risk.

Operating leverage Senior financial obligations include operating expenses that the company owes employees and other stakeholders in real asset markets. The preceding income statement categorizes operating costs as either "fixed" or "variable." The "operating breakeven point" occurs when company *Sales revenue* equals fixed plus variable operating costs. That is, when *EBIT* equals zero the company is at the operating breakeven point (see formula 2.9). Companies prefer to operate as far beyond breakeven as possible because, as everybody knows, sales fluctuate through time. Fluctuations in sales and costs influence the default risk premium. The degree of operating leverage measures the sensitivity of operating income to sales fluctuations:

FORMULA 10.2 Degree of operating leverage (*DOL*)

The "degree of operating leverage" measures the percentage change in *EBIT* that results from a 1% sales increase:

$$\begin{pmatrix} degree\ of \\ operating \\ leverage \end{pmatrix} = \frac{\%\Delta\ EBIT}{\%\Delta\ Sales\ revenue}$$

$$= \frac{(p - v)Q}{(p - v)Q - F}$$

$$= \frac{Sales\ revenue - total\ variable\ costs}{EBIT}$$

where *p* is the unit price of the product, *v* is the variable cost per unit, *F* is *Total fixed costs*, and *Q* represents the quantity of product that the company sells. This model assumes the ratio of *Total variable costs* to *Sales revenue* is constant.

The numerator of the *DOL* formula usually is bigger than the denominator. Consequently, the *DOL* usually is bigger than one. The *DOL* is huge when *Sales revenue* barely surpasses *Total variable* plus *fixed costs*. As *Sales* grow far beyond *fixed costs* the *DOL* diminishes toward unity.

EXAMPLE 1 Find and interpret the degree of operating leverage
The most recent annual report lists company *Sales revenue* at $175,000. Cost analysis suggests that annual *Total fixed costs* and *Total variable costs* equal $42,000 and $108,000, respectively. Find and interpret the company's degree of operating leverage.

SOLUTION
For this problem plug the numbers into formula 10.2:

$$\begin{pmatrix} degree\ of \\ operating \\ leverage \end{pmatrix}_{@Sales=\$175,000} = \frac{175,000 - 108,000}{175,000 - 42,000 - 108,000}$$

$$= 2.68$$

The DOL of 2.68 means *EBIT* increases (or decreases) about 2 2/3% for every 1% increase (or decrease) in *Sales revenue*.

The most recent annual report shows that sales of $175,000 generate *Earnings before interest and taxes* of $25,000 (= $175,000 - $42,000 - $108,000). Suppose, for example, that sales were up 1%, that is, $1,750. The additional sales incur additional variable costs of $1,080 (variable costs equal 61.71% of sales; $1,080 = 0.6171 x $1,750). The additional *EBIT* equals $670 (=$1,750 - $1,080), which is 2.68% of $25,000. Conversely, if sales were down 1% then *EBIT* falls 2.68%. The *DOL* allows quick approximation of the sensitivity of *EBIT* to sales fluctuations. If sales were to rise (or decline) 8%, for example, *EBIT* rises (or falls) approximately 21% (≈ 2.68 x 8%).

DOL formulas depend on the amount of sales. As an alternative scenario for the preceding example consider if company sales were $150,000. Then the *DOL* equals 3.72 {= [$150,000 - (0.6171 x $150,000)] ÷ [$150,000 - $42,000 – (0.6171 x $150,000)] }. When company *Sales revenue* nears the operating breakeven point then the relatively large *DOL* means a 1% fluctuation in sales has a huge effect on *EBIT*. Conversely, if company sales were $200,000 then the *DOL* equals 2.21 {= [$200,000 - (0.6171 x $200,000)] ÷ [$200,000 - $42,000 – (0.6171 x $200,000)] }.

The degree of operating leverage directly measures the robustness of operating income to sales fluctuations. Companies operating near breakeven have high operating leverage and face relatively high default risk. Companies fortunate to operate well-beyond breakeven have a relatively small degree of operating leverage and, all else equal, face relatively low default risk.

Financial leverage The bottom-half of the income statement documents cash flows from company to capitalists in financial markets. The company sends interest to creditors and dividends to shareholders. Payments to creditors are financial obligations that relate directly to default risk. Shareholders are residual claimants on company cash flows and cannot force default. Shareholders nonetheless have a financial stake that depends on whether the company defaults.

The lesson on debt management ratios in chapter 2 (section 3.A) teaches that a company's excess borrowing capacity relates to its ability to obtain further credit. It's bad news, as hopefully you know, when one borrows up to the credit limit because default and bankruptcy may be one misfortune away. Analysis of the preceding stylized income statement allows further insights on how default risk depends on debt.

The *Earnings available for common (EAC)* equals *EBIT*, minus *Interest expense (IE)*, minus *Taxes*, minus *Preferred dividends (PD)*. When *Taxes* are proportional to taxable income we may write:

$$EAC = (EBIT - IE)(1 - tax\ rate) - PD.$$

Manipulation of the preceding equation yields the following formula.

FORMULA 10.3 Degree of financial leverage (*DFL*)

The "degree of financial leverage" measures the percentage change in *Earnings available for common* that results from a 1% increase in *Earnings before interest and taxes*:

$$\left(\begin{array}{c} degree\ of \\ financial \\ leverage \end{array}\right) = \frac{\%\Delta\ Earnings\ available\ for\ common}{\%\Delta\ EBIT}$$

$$= \frac{EBIT}{EBIT - IE - PD/(1\text{-}tax\ rate)}$$

where *IE* and *PD* represent *Interest expense* and *Preferred dividends*, respectively.

The numerator of the *DFL* formula usually is bigger than the denominator. Consequently, the *DFL* usually is bigger than one. The *DFL* grows huge as *Interest* consumes more and more of *EBIT*. Glean insight on the *DFL* with the following example.

EXAMPLE 2 Find and interpret the degree of financial leverage
Analysis of the most recent annual report reveals the following entries:

Sales revenue	$175,000
- Total fixed costs	42,000
- Total variable costs	108,000
= Earnings before interest & taxes	25,000
- Interest	8,500
- Taxes (@30% tax rate)	4,950
- Preferred dividends	2,000
= Earnings available for common	$ 9,550

Find and interpret the company's degree of financial leverage.

SOLUTION
Plug relevant numbers into the *DFL* formula:

$$\begin{pmatrix} degree\ of \\ financial \\ leverage \end{pmatrix}_{@EBIT=\$25,000} = \frac{25,000}{25,000 - 8,500 - {2,000}/{(1-0.30)}}$$

$$= 1.83$$

The DFL of 1.83 means *EAC* increases (or decreases) 1.83% for every 1% increase (or decrease) in *EBIT*. Suppose, for example, that *EBIT* were up 1%, that is, $250. The additional taxable income incurs additional taxes of $75 (= 0.30 x $250). The *Interest* and *Preferred dividends* remain constant yet the *Earnings available for common* increases $175 (= $250 - $75). This represents an increase in *EAC* of 1.83% (=$175 ÷ $9,550). Analogously, if *EBIT* were to fall 8% then *EAC*, all else equal, would fall almost 15% (≈ 8% x 1.83).

A key insight is that the *DFL* increases as the company increases reliance on debt financing. Examine formula 10.3 and notice that the *DFL* gets bigger as *Interest* consumes a larger share of *EBIT*. Rising reliance on debt incurs higher interest expenses and rising default risk. A relatively huge *DFL* is an indicator of relatively large default risk.

Consider, for example, that interest were $15,000 instead of the $8,500 shown in the annual report. The *DFL* for this alternative scenario is 3.50 {= $25,000 ÷ [$25,000 - $15,000 – ($2,000/0.70)] }. The sensitivity of *EAC* to fluctuations in *EBIT* almost doubles. And as the previous subsection explains, fluctuations in *Sales* cause fluctuations in *EBIT* - a company with relatively large debt payments has relatively high default risk and volatile earnings for common.

The final insight from the stylized income statement combines the *DFL* and *DOL* to infer effects of sales fluctuations on *Earnings available for common*.

The "degree of total leverage" measures the percentage change in *Earnings available for common (EAC)* that results from a 1% increase in *Sales revenue*:

$$\left(\begin{array}{c}degree\ of\\ total\\ leverage\end{array}\right) = \frac{\%\Delta\ Earnings\ available\ for\ common}{\%\Delta\ Sales\ revenue}$$

$$= \left(\begin{array}{c}degree\ of\\ operating\\ leverage\end{array}\right)\left(\begin{array}{c}degree\ of\\ financial\\ leverage\end{array}\right)$$

$$= \frac{Sales\ revenue - Total\ variable\ costs}{EBIT - IE - {PD}/{(1\text{-}tax\ rate)}}$$

For the income statement from preceding examples the *DOL* equals 2.68 and the *DFL* equals 1.83. Multiply the two and find, according to the middle version of formula 10.4, that the degree of total leverage equals 4.91 (= 2.68 x 1.38). This means that *Earnings available for common* moves 4.91% in response to a 1% fluctuation in *Sales revenue*. Increase sales by $1,750 and, for example, *EAC* increases by about $469 {that is, $469 = .0491 x $9,550; or equivalently, $469 = [$1,750 – (0.6171 x $1,750)] x (1 – 0.30)}. The identical *DTL* of 4.91 computes from the lower version of formula 10.4:

$$\left(\begin{array}{c}degree\ of\\ total\\ leverage\end{array}\right)_{@Sales=\$175,000} = \frac{175,000 - 108,000}{25,000 - 8,500 - {2,000}/{(1 - 0.30)}}$$

$$= 4.91$$

The *DTL* depends on the level of sales. When *Sales revenue* barely surpasses the total breakeven point (see formula 2.10) the *DTL* gets huge. If sales, for example, were $150,000 then the *DTL* equals 14.11 {that is, 14.11 = [$150,000 – (0.6171 x $150,000)] ÷ [($150,000 - $42,000 -(0.6171 x $150,000) - $8,500 - $2,000/(1 – 0.30)}. With a *DTL* of 14.11 a one percent sales decline translates into a 14% decline in *Earnings available for common*. That's a lot!

The leverage concept is universally important and has wide application. Consider a household with one wage earner making an after-tax annual salary of $60,000 and paying annual fixed expenses of $40,000. This wage earner contributes $20,000 of discretionary income to the household. Now suppose a second member of the household considers a job that clears $30,000. While at first glance one may perceive the salary of the second wage earner ($30,000) is half-as-important as the first wage earner ($60,000 salary), the leverage concept comes into play. Due to the second wage earner household discretionary income more than doubles, rising to $50,000 from $20,000! Leverage amplifies outcomes (in finance and physics, too). Analysis of the stylized income statement reveals that companies with relatively large operating and financial leverage probably have volatile earnings and substantial default risk.

Other common sources of idiosyncratic risk

The nearly infinite variety of financial securities implies that there are nearly infinite sources of idiosyncratic risk. Here are a few notable sources.

Repayment risk: Sometimes an issuer may repay the liability early, thereby yanking the security out of the investor's hands. Repayment may occur through several different mechanisms. For example, investors in asset-backed securities ("ABS", see chapter 9, section 3A) may receive loan payments that homeowners make on mortgages. Perhaps ABS investors expect to receive cash flows for twenty years. But when an unusually high percentage of homeowners refinance then the asset-back security gets repaid early. The investor does not lose money but, on the other hand, the cash flows do not occur as expected. An analogous situation occurs when companies unexpectedly repay bonds early. Evidence indicates that equilibrium rates of return increase with the likelihood of early yet unexpected repayment.

Exchange rate risk: Some securities trade across international boundaries. These securities therefore expose investors to risk that currency exchange rates may unexpectedly change. An investor, for example, may send U.S. dollars to a New York mutual fund that converts dollars into yen in order to purchase Japanese stocks. Even though the stock price may rise over time on the Tokyo Stock Exchange, generating a gain in yen, adverse exchange rate movement can completely offset the gain when funds reconvert into U.S. dollars. Investors likely demand a risk premium for bearing exchange rate risk.

Political risk: Other securities depend on government-legislated guarantees for repayment of principal and interest. These securities therefore expose investors to risk that political considerations may unexpectedly change the legislation guaranteeing security cash flows.

Catastrophes: There even exist securities that provide cash flows dependent on catastrophes such as earthquakes or hurricanes. Hence, one can rightly say that earthquakes and weather are sources of idiosyncratic risk. Each and every security has unique risks that are security-specific. Financial theory shows that the independence of risk sources across securities is assurance that prudent diversification strategies may manage or eliminate idiosyncratic risks.

EXERCISES 10.2

Conceptual
1. What is the extent of the range for the leverage measures, and explain the economic significance of extreme values.

3. STATISTICAL MEASUREMENTS OF RISK AND RETURN

Explaining equilibrium in financial markets requires explaining how returns relate to risk. Fortunately, a rather sterile statistical setting offers excellent opportunity for learning fundamental characteristics about risk and return. For this imaginary laboratory setting suppose that all possible outcomes from a financial investment are known, as well as their likelihoods. Formulas below reliably measure the risk and rate of return for the investment.

3.A. Measures for individual securitites

When all possible outcomes from a financial investment are known, and furthermore the probabilities for each outcome are known, too, the expected value for the rate of return is given by this formula:

FORMULA 10.5 *E(ROR)* given probabilities and outcomes

$$\begin{pmatrix} \text{expected} \\ \text{value of} \\ \text{the ROR for} \\ \text{security } j \end{pmatrix} \equiv E(ROR_j)$$

$$E(ROR_j) = \sum_{i=1}^{N} probability_i \times ROR_{i,j}$$

Three right-hand-side variables include: the probability that the ith outcome occurs is $probability_i$, the rate of return occurring for asset j when outcome i actually happens is ROR_i, and the total number of outcomes is N.

Formula 10.5 coins the phrase "expected" rate of return for $E(ROR)$. This nomenclature is consistent with standard statistical practices and all finance books follow this tradition. An important realization, however, is that $E(ROR)$ is <u>not</u> the same concept as $ROR^{expected}$. The expected rate of return for a financial investment, $ROR^{expected}$, represents the internal rate of return that equates, either implicitly or explicitly, the observable price to a cash flow stream consistent with the investor's information and expectations. Time value formulas and relationships determine $ROR^{expected}$. $E(ROR)$ represents a simple summary statistic spit out by a simple statistical formula.

This lesson's objective is teaching how the "required" rate of return, $ROR^{required}$, relates to risk. For this purpose we rely on examining the statistical relation between $E(ROR)$ and risk. Ironically by studying $E(ROR)$ we learn more about $ROR^{required}$ than about $ROR^{expected}$. At equilibrium, of course, expected and required rates of return are equal.

The example below uses formula 10.5 in a very simple setting.

EXAMPLE 3 Either win-big or lose it all

An investment costs $1,200. There is a 75 percent chance it returns $1,800. Otherwise, it loses everything. Find the expected value for the rate of return.

SOLUTION

For this problem the first step is finding the rates of return for the two different outcomes. For outcome one the investment returns $1,800 and the rate of return is:

$$ROR_1 = (\$1,800 - \$1,200) / \$1,200$$

$$= 50\%$$

Outcome two loses everything and ROR_2 is −100%. Now apply formula 10.5 and multiply the probability times the ROR:

$$E(ROR) = (0.75 \times 0.50) + (0.25 \times (-1.0))$$

$$= 12.5\%$$

The expected value for the rate of return is 12.5 percent.

The preceding simplistic example illustrates several attributes of $E(ROR)$.

1. The sum of probabilities over all outcomes equals 100 percent.
2. In formula 10.5 probabilities must be entered as decimal equivalents (for example, the probability of 75 percent is 0.75). ROR may be entered either way, as decimal equivalents or percent (for example, 50 percent on the calculator may be 0.50 or 50), but proper interpretation of the answer must be internally consistent. For example, the above ROR of 0.50 and −1.0 yield the answer 0.125 and the interpretation is 12.5 percent. All lessons in this book use decimal equivalents for all computations.
3. $E(ROR)$ is a number that may not itself be one of the outcomes. Possible outcomes in the previous example are 75 percent and −100 percent whereas $E(ROR)$ is 12.5 percent. The number represents the mean of the probability distribution function and conveys intuitive content. Knowing, for example, that the mean number of children per U.S.A. household is 2.3 conveys information even though we may be quite certain that no household has exactly 2.3 children.

Measuring risk for a financial investment is complex and fraught with difficulty. Still, the standard deviation of rates of return emerges as the most widely used measurement. The formula for σ in our sterile laboratory setting is this:

FORMULA 10.6 σ given probabilities and outcomes
The standard deviation of returns for asset j equals the square root of the probability weighted sum of squared deviations from $E(ROR)$. That is,

$$\begin{pmatrix} standard \\ deviation \end{pmatrix} \equiv \sigma_j$$

$$\sigma_j = \left[\sum_{i=1}^{N} probability_i \times (ROR_{i,j} - E(ROR_j))^2 \right]^{1/2}$$

Several characteristics of the standard deviation merit mention.

1. σ treats upside and downside returns identically. That is, σ gets bigger as the dispersion of outcomes increases irrespective of whether the dispersion occurs on the downside (a loss) or upside (a gain). Most investors interpret risk as the chance of loss, not as the chance of gain, σ is an imperfect risk measure because it treats losses and gains the same.

2. σ is the square root of σ^2, the variance. A ranking of investments by standard deviation, smallest to largest or vice versa, is identical to a ranking by variance. The two measures differ in that σ measures "percent" whereas σ^2 measures "percent-squared." Because many people lack intuition about "percent-squareds", and also because E(ROR) also measures "percent", discussions about risk usually focus on σ.

3. σ conveys information about the size of confidence intervals. Statistical tables show that about 95 percent of all normally distributed outcomes lie within two standard deviations of the mean. Suppose, for example, that the small company stock returns underlying table 9.15 were normally distributed. A mean of 12.5% and standard deviation of 33.2% implies with 95% confidence that next year's stock return lies approximately between –54% and +79% (that is, the mean plus and minus 2σ.)

The following example is a final reminder that the expected rate of return links the current stock price to future cash flows.

EXAMPLE 4 Find *E(ROR)* given future stock prices
Your analysis of a small company convinces you that future movements in their stock price depend on how many automakers adopt the company's product innovations. The current price for this non-dividend paying stock is $20. The table below summarizes your belief about future outcomes.

#automakers adopting product	probability	resultant intrinsic value for stock price
1	30%	$35
2	20%	$45
3	10%	$65

If no automakers adopt the product then the company goes bankrupt and the stock is worthless. Contrast this small company's risk and return with the long-run averages in table 9.15.

SOLUTION
For this problem the first step is finding the rates of return for the four different outcomes. Assume that the stock price moves to the "resultant intrinsic value" from its beginning amount of $20. The table below summarizes resultant rates of return.

#automakers adopting product	ROR computation	resultant ROR
0	(0—20) / 20	–100%
1	(35—20) / 20	75%
2	(45—20) / 20	125%
3	(65—20) / 20	225%

The probability for bankruptcy is 60%. Apply formula 10.5 to find *E(ROR)*.

$$E(ROR) = (0.30 \times 0.75) + (0.20 \times 1.25) + (0.10 \times 2.25) + (0.60 \times (-1.0))$$

$$= 10.0\%$$

Apply formula 10.6 to find σ.

$$\sigma = \left\{ \begin{array}{l} 0.30\,(0.75-0.10)^2 \\ +\ 0.20\,(1.25-0.10)^2 \\ +\ 0.10\,(2.25-0.10)^2 \\ +\ 0.60\,(-1.0-0.10)^2 \end{array} \right\}^{1/2}$$

$$=\ 125\%$$

Table 9.15 shows that the long run average rate of return for small company stocks is 12.5% with a standard deviation of 33.2%. This particular company has smaller return (10%) and bigger risk (125%) than the average small company stock. This particular company is dominated by the average investment in small company stock.

Company profitability, sales trends, market share, growth opportunities, price multiples, these and other information sources shape expected rates of return. Required rates of return, conversely, depend exclusively on risk. In order to narrow focus on the relation between risk and return our lessons become a little more statistical.

EXAMPLE 5 Compute and compare stock risk and return to find dominance or trade off

The business cycle obviously affects total rates of return on equities. Business economists predict the following outcomes for the economy and associated rates of return on equities for the Alpha Company and the Zed Company.

	expanding economy	stagnant economy	recession
probability	30%	50%	20%
ROR Alpha	28%	–3%	24%
ROR Zed	0%	12%	10%

a. You might invest in one of these company stocks. You cannot invest in both companies but rather must select only one. Explain your choice.

b. Your friend tells you that a security they own, Lambda Corp, has expected return of 10% and standard deviation of returns equal to 16%. How does this one stock compare to the other two?

SOLUTION

a. For this problem,

$$E(ROR_{Alpha}) = .30(.28) + .50(-.03) + .20(.24)$$

$$= 11.70\%$$

and $\quad \sigma_{Alpha} = \{\,.30(.28 - .1170)^2 + .50(-.03 - .1170)^2 + .20(.24 - .1170)^2\,\}^{1/2}$

$$= 14.77\%$$

Similar computations for Zed show:

$$E(ROR_{Zed}) = 8.00\%$$

and $\quad \sigma_{Zed} = 5.29\%$

Determining whether Zed or Alpha is best uses the "dominance" concept. For those companies, there is *not* a case of dominance. That is, there exists a trade-off. Notice that for Zed the expected return is lower, which is bad, but its risk is lower too, which is good. Because there is a trade-off, one stock is not necessarily better than the other. The decision about which is best depends on the risk preferences of the individual investor. If you are a high risk investor (wealthy or long investment horizon) choose Alpha whereas if you prefer low risk (cash poor or short investment horizon) choose Zed.

b. Figure 10.2 summarizes risk-return characteristics of the 3 securities.

Between Alpha and Zed there is a trade-off, as stated previously, so one security is not necessarily better than the other. Alpha compares to Lambda differently, however. If one were to own Lambda and switch to Alpha, the expected return increases (which is good) and risk decreases (which also is good). There is not a trade-off between Lambda and Alpha. Instead, there is a case of dominance. Alpha dominates Lambda because Alpha has higher return and less risk. When one stock dominates the other, the choice about which is best does not depend

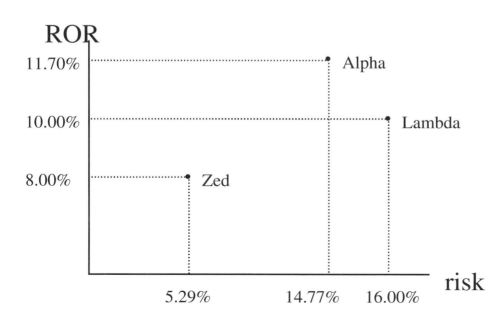

FIGURE 10.2
Risk and return for Example 5

on the risk preferences of the investor. Instead, one stock is better than the other one for all rational investors. Alpha is better than Lambda (as long as the investor believes these numbers, that is.) Similar logic shows that between Lambda and Zed there is a trade-off.

A summary of the preceding analysis is that an investor restricted to own only one of these stocks (and not two or three) should never choose Lambda. Feasible choices include only Alpha and Zed. The choice about which of these two is best depends on investor risk preferences. Is the extra but uncertain 3.70% return from Alpha worth the extra 9.48% risk? At this point we say only the investor knows for sure.

Obtaining probabilities for many different outcomes is usually impractical. Instead, insights about security risk often rely on the rule that past performance is a good predictor of the future. Many believe that, like a leopard can't change its spots, high risk securities of the past tend to be high risk securities in the future. Formulas really simplify when historical outcomes are equally likely to repeat. The formula for E(ROR) is simply the arithmetic average:

FORMULA 10.7 *E(ROR)* with equally likely outcomes

$$E(ROR_j) = \frac{\sum_{i=1}^{N} ROR_{i,j}}{N}$$

The formula for the standard deviation with equally likely outcomes also simplifies.

FORMULA 10.8 σ equally likely outcomes

$$\sigma_j = \left[\frac{\sum_{i=1}^{N} (ROR_{i,j})^2}{N} - E(ROR)^2 \right]^{1/2}$$

The biggest simplification of all, however, is that with equally likely outcomes all statistics compute automatically with calculators such as the Texas Instruments BAII Plus. Consider this example below:

EXAMPLE 6 With equally likely outcomes find dominance or trade-off

Two securities, X and Y, have exhibited the following returns over the past 5 years:

	1	2	3	4	5
X:	15.15%	3.45%	−0.05%	−1.15%	14.85%
Y:	6.25%	8.45%	6.35%	10.45%	3.85%

You believe that past performance is a perfect predictor of future performance. Contrast the expected returns and risk for each security if owned in isolation.

SOLUTION

For security X:

$$E(ROR_X) = (.1515 + .0345 - .0005 - .0115 + .1485) / 5$$

$$= 6.45\%$$

and $\sigma_X = \{(.1515^2 + .0345^2 + .0005^2 + .0115^2 + .1485^2)/5 - .0645^2\}^{1/2}$

$$= 7.15\%.$$

Similar computations for Y show that its expected return is 7.07% and standard deviation is 2.23%.

Summarize these findings as follows:

security	E(ROR)	σ
X	6.45%	7.15%
Y	7.07	2.23

Security Y dominates security X; Y is better on all counts because it has higher return and less risk. Nobody that owns only one of these securities should own X.

CALCULATOR CLUE

The *BAII Plus*© calculator contains a spreadsheet that enables easy estimation of statistics when all outcomes are equally likely. On the *BAII Plus*© type **2ⁿᵈ DATA** (the data key is the same as the 7 key). The calculator opens a worksheet that contains two columns for holding data. The calculator refers to the two columns of data as column X and column Y. For this problem columns X and Y contain the rates of return for securities X and Y, respectively. Clear unwanted numbers already stored in the data worksheet by typing **2ⁿᵈ CE/C**. Enter this problem's data by typing

1515 ENTER	↓.0625 ENTER
↓.0345 ENTER	↓.0845 ENTER
↓.0005 =/− ENTER	↓.0635 ENTER
↓.0115 =/− ENTER	↓.1045 ENTER
↓.1485 ENTER	↓.0385 ENTER

The preceding keystrokes set $X_1 = 15.15\%$ and $Y_1 = 6.25\%$, ... , $X_5 = 14.85\%$ and $Y_5 = 3.85\%$. Find the statistical estimates of the mean and standard deviation for the data in memory by typing **2ⁿᵈ STAT**. Make sure the display shows "LIN". Hit ↓ 2 times and the display shows "X-bar = .0645". This is $E(ROR_X)$. *Hit ↓ 2 more times and the display shows "σ_X = .0715",* the standard deviation of X. Hit ↓ once and the display shows "Y-bar = .0707", and hit ↓ 2 more times to see "σ_Y = .0223". Note that the calculator also shows an alternative computation for the standard deviation, "S_X" and "S_Y". The difference between σ and S is that the former divides by N, whereas the latter divides by N−1. Our assumption for problems in this book is that the data represent the population of future outcomes so therefore reliance on σ is appropriate.

EXERCISES 10.3A

Numerical quickies

1. You invest $900. The odds are 50% you will get back $1,300. Otherwise, you lose everything. What is the expected rate of return on this brilliant financial investment? ©ER4

2. Your analysis of a small company convinces you that future movements in their stock price depend on how many big companies adopt the small company's product innovations. Today's price for this non-dividend-paying small company stock is $6. The table below summarizes your beliefs about future outcomes.

#big companies adopting product	probability	resultant intrinsic value for stock price
1	40%	$11
2	20%	$17

If no big companies adopt the product then the small company goes bankrupt and the stock is worthless. Compute this small company stock's measurements for risk [= σ] and return [= E(ROR)]. ©ER16

3. Your analysis of common stocks for companies X and Y lead you to believe rates of return depend as follows on the future strength of the economy. Compare X and Y with regards to dominance or tradeoff. ©ER5

	weak	moderate	strong
probability	25%	40%	35%
%return X	4.0%	6.1%	25.7%
%return Y	7.3%	22.1%	10.7%

4. Each pair of rates of return for securities X and Y listed below is equally likely. Find the standard deviation and expected rates of return for securities X and Y, and also compare the two regarding dominance or tradeoff. ©ER12

| X: | -3.2% | 11.5% | 22.3% | 12.1% |
| Y: | 18.7% | 27.1% | 14.2% | 7.5% |

3.B. Measures for portfolios of securities

A portfolio is a collection of many different types of assets. Investors sometimes hold a portfolio with stocks from many companies. Mutual funds may hold a portfolio with bonds from many different issuers. Businesses may hold a portfolio with many different types of real capital goods. Different assets in a portfolio potentially provide different rates of return. Lessons below focus on how portfolio risk and return characteristics relate to component assets.

Time value lessons from chapter 4 show that for a time series of periodic security returns the geometric average rate of return properly measures the percentage change in wealth. The example below demonstrates that measuring a portfolio's periodic rate of return from component asset periodic returns is somewhat different.

This example demonstrates that portfolio behavior sometimes differs from preconceptions.

EXAMPLE 7 Find the periodic ROR for a portfolio of stocks A, B, and C
At the beginning (t=0), you invest $1000 equally among three different shares (A, B, and C). The prices for each of the three shares changes so that now, at t=1, your holdings are worth:

	A	B	C
p(0)=	$333.33	$333.33	$333.33
p(1)=	$191.00	$633.00	$200.00

Find each share's periodic rate of return and then compute the average return (arithmetic and geometric).

SOLUTION

	A	B	C	wealth
p(0)=	$333.33	$333.33	$333.33	$1,000
p(1)=	$191.00	$633.00	$200.00	$1,024
ROR=	–42.70%	89.90%	–40.00%	%ΔWealth = 2.40%

Compute periodic security returns as follows (formula 4.2):

ROR = (end-of-period wealth ÷ beginning-of-period wealth) –1

For example, security A's rate of return is –42.7% [= (191 ÷ 333.33) –1], security B's is 89.90%, etc. Next, recall formula 4.3 for an arithmetic average return:

arithmetic average rate of return = Σ ROR_t ÷ N .

$$= (-.4270 +.8990 -.40) ÷ 3$$

$$= 2.40\%$$

Compute the geometric average with formula 4.4 as

$$geometric\ average$$
$$rate\ of\ return = \{(1+ROR_1) \times (1+ROR_2) \times \ldots \times (1+ROR_N)\}^{1/N} \div 1$$
$$= [(1+(-.427))(1+.8990)(1-.40)]^{1/3} - 1$$
$$= -13.25\%$$

Add together the values of all shares; this is the total portfolio wealth. Notice it begins at $1000 and rises to $1,024. Its percentage change is 2.40% (=$1,024 ÷ 1,000 −1). The arithmetic and geometric average rates of return computed above equal 2.40% and -13.25%, respectively. The arithmetic average *ROR* across all securities is a proper measurement for the portfolio's periodic rate of return.

For a portfolio the arithmetic average of component periodic *ROR* corresponds to the actual change in wealth. Formula 10.9 summarizes this finding.

FORMULA 10.9 E(ROR_portfolio)

The periodic rate of return for a portfolio is a weighted average of component returns:

$$E(ROR_{portfolio}) = \sum_{j=1}^{M} w_j\, E(ROR_j),$$

where w_j is the proportion of portfolio wealth allocated to asset j and M is how many assets the portfolio contains. $E(ROR_j)$ is the expected value of the rate of return from formula 10.5.

In the preceding example securities A, B, and C provide periodic rates of return equal to -42.70%, 89.90%, and -40.00%, respectively, and 1/3 of funds are invested in each. Applying formula 10.9 to find the portfolio periodic rate of return shows:

$$E(ROR_{portfolio}) = 1/3(-.4270) + 1/3(.8990) + 1/3(-.40)$$
$$= -2.40\%.$$

This is the same answer that example 7 obtains. Now apply formula 10.9 to example 5 from the previous section.

EXAMPLE 8   Find portfolio E(ROR) and σ for Alpha and Zed

The business cycle obviously affects total rates of return on equities. Business economists predict the following outcomes for the economy and associated rates of return on equities for the Alpha Company and the Zed Company.

	expanding economy	stagnant economy	recession
probability	30%	50%	20%
ROR Alpha	28%	-3%	24%
ROR Zed	0%	12%	10%

Suppose you invest 25% of your funds in Alpha and the remainder in Zed. Find the portfolio's *E(ROR)* and σ.

SOLUTION

Example 5 applies formulas 10.5 and 10.6 to find the following summary statistics for Alpha and Zed:

	E(ROR)	σ
Alpha	11.70%	14.77%
Zed	8.00%	5.29%

Now apply formula 10.9 and compute the portfolio return as the weighted average of component returns:

$$E(ROR_{1/4Alpha + 3/4Zed}) = .25(.1170) + .75(.0800)$$

$$= 8.93\%$$

The portfolio return, 8.93%, is an average of Alpha's 11.7% and Zed's 8.0%. The portfolio return is nearer the asset with the most weight; $E(ROR_{1/4Alpha + 3/4Zed})$ is three-quarters closer to Zed.

One approach for finding portfolio risk specifies the portfolio ROR for each outcome – then compute σ with formula 10.6. With an expanding economy every $1 invested in Alpha returns 28 cents profit. A quarter-dollar investment returns only 7 cents. Zed returns 0 in an expanding economy. The portfolio returns 7 cents of profit in an expanding economy when the allocation is 25% Alpha, 75% Zed. Use similar logic to prepare the below listing portfolio rates of return for the three different outcomes.

	expanding economy	stagnant economy	recession
probability	30%	50%	20%
1/4Alpha + 3/4Zed	1/4(.28) + 3/4(0) = 7.00%	1/4(-.03) + 3/4(.12) = 8.25%	1/4(.24) + 3/4(.10) = 13.50%

Apply formula 10.6 to the entries in the bottom row:

$$\sigma_{1/4Alpha + 3/4Zed} = \{.30(.0700-.0893)^2 + .50(.0825-.0893)^2 + .20(.1350-.0893)^2\}^{1/2}$$

$$= 2.35\%$$

The portfolio risk, $\sigma_{1/4Alpha + 3/4Zed}$, is not an average of component risks. It in fact is less than any individual security suggesting that some risk, almost magically, simply vanishes. The portfolio offers *diversification benefits*.

CALCULATOR CLUE

Example 5 includes a *Calculator Clue* that computes and stores the mean and standard deviation for Alpha in memories 1 and 2 and analogous numbers for Zed in memories 4 and 5. Compute the average return for the portfolio that allocates 25% Alpha and 75% Zed with these keystrokes:

RCL 1 x .25 + RCL 4 x .75 = STO 7 .

The display shows the portfolio return equals 7.66%. Now obtain portfolio returns for the three different states. Store the 3 returns in memories 3, 6, and 9 for later use:

.25 x .28 + .75 x 0 = STO 3 .

.25 x .03 +/– + .75 x .12 = STO 6 .

.25 x .24 + .75 x .10 = STO 9 .

Now get the portfolio standard deviation:

.3 x ((RCL 3 – RCL 7)) x² + .5 x ((RCL 6 – RCL 7)) x² + .2 x
((RCL 9 – RCL 7)) x² = √ STO 8 .

Memories 7 and 8 contain the mean and standard deviation for a portfolio that allocates 25% Alpha, 75% Zed.

Numerical quickies

1. At the beginning of last month about 40% of your $6,250 portfolio was in stock X; stock Y accounted for 30% and stock Z for the rest. Monthly rates of return equaled -12% for stock X, 20% for Y, and -24% for Z. Find last month's percentage change in total portfolio wealth. ©ER13

2. The expected rate of return on common stock for company X equals 5.9%. For Company Y, the expected rate of return is 23.5%. You wish to form a portfolio by allocating some of your funds in Company X and the remainder in Company Y. In order to form a portfolio whose expected return equals 15.2%, what proportion of funds should be invested in Company X? ©ER3

Challengers

3. You form a portfolio that invests 30% of total funds in stock X and 70% in stock Z. Two possible outcomes exist. The probability is 30% that the first outcome occurs, in which case the rates of return equal 10% for X and 38% for Z. The probability is 70% that the second outcome occurs, in which case the rates of return equal 45% for X and 8% for Z. Find the expected return and standard deviation of portfolio returns. ©ER9a, ©ER9b

4. Your analysis of outcomes for sales and the associated rate of return on common stocks for companies X and Y are shown below. You intend to form a portfolio by allocating 35% of your funds in Company X, and the remainder in Company Y. Find the expected return and standard deviation of portfolio returns. ©ER13

	declining	flat	rising
probability	35%	30%	35%
%return X	-1.9%	5.4%	17.7%
%return Y	-6.5%	15.4%	2.1%

5. Each pair of rates of return for securities X and Y listed below is equally likely. You wish to form a portfolio by allocating 25% of funds in Company X and the remainder in Company Y. Find the standard deviation and expected rate of return for the portfolio. ©ER14

X:	-3.9%	4.6%	21.9%	17.6%
Y:	13.4%	13.4%	12.5%	6.7%

4. BENEFITS FROM DIVERSIFICATION

Creating portfolios possibly creates diversification benefits. The previous example computes that the "risk" of securities Alpha and Zed, that is σ_{Alpha} and σ_{Zed} respectively, equal 14.77% and 5.29%. Allocating 25% of funds in Alpha and 75% in Zed creates a portfolio with a risk of 2.35% - less than either individual security. For this situation the portfolio offers diversification benefits. Figure 10.3 illustrates risk-return characteristics for these securities.

First consider return characteristics. Figure 10.3 illustrates return on the vertical axis. Zed is a relatively low return asset (8.00%) whereas Alpha is a relatively high return asset (11.70%). Adjacent to the vertical axis is a little "step ladder." It begins at 8.00% $(=E(ROR_{Zed}))$ and steps up by quarters toward 11.70%. A portfolio with 1/4Alpha+3/4Zed is on the first step; it is one-fourth the distance toward $E(ROR_{Alpha})$. If the allocation were half-and-half the resultant portfolio ROR

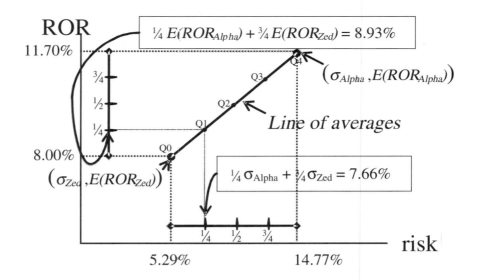

would be on the second step, halfway between 8.00% and 11.70%. The return smoothly steps from the low return toward the high return as the allocation in Alpha steadily increases. $E(ROR)$ for the portfolio is a weighted average of component returns.

The average risk of components in a portfolio is given by this formula:

> **FORMULA 10.10 Portfolio average risk, $\sigma_{average}$**
> The portfolio's average risk is a weighted average of component risks:
>
> $$\sigma_{average} = \sum_{j=1}^{M} w_j\, \sigma_j \,,$$
>
> where w_j is the proportion of portfolio wealth allocated to asset j and M is how many assets the portfolio contains. σ_j is the standard deviation of returns for asset j.

Figure 10.3 illustrates risk on the horizontal axis. Zed is a relatively low risk asset (5.29%) whereas Alpha is a relatively high risk asset (14.77%). With one-quarter allocation to Alpha, three-quarters to Zed, compute average risk like this

$$
\begin{aligned}
\sigma_{average} &= 1/4\sigma_{Alpha} + 3/4\sigma_{Zed} \\
&= .25(.1477) + .75(.0529) \\
&= 7.66\%
\end{aligned}
$$

Adjacent to the horizontal axis is a little "step ladder." It begins at 5.29% ($=\sigma_{Zed}$) and steps out by quarters toward 14.77%. A portfolio with 1/4Alpha+3/4Zed is out one step, one-fourth the distance toward σ_{Alpha} with $\sigma_{average}$ equal to 7.66%. If the allocation were half-and-half the resultant $\sigma_{average}$ for the portfolio would be out two steps, halfway between 5.29% and 14.77%.

The solid line with points Q_0, Q_1, ..., Q_4 shows combinations of $\sigma_{average}$ and $E(ROR_{portfolio})$ for different allocations and is the line of averages for securities Alpha and Zed. Every point on the line measures average risk and return for a unique portfolio allocation. Point Q_0 represents 100% allocation in Zed ($w_{Zed}=1.0$, $w_{Alpha}=0$). Q_1, represents return and average risk for the portfolio with 1/4Alpha+3/4Zed. Its coordinates are one-quarter the distance between Alpha and Zed. Q_2 represents the fifty-fifty portfolio. Its return and average risk is midway between Alpha and Zed. Q_4 at the other end of the line of averages is the all-Alpha allocation ($w_{Zed}=0$, $w_{Alpha}=1$). Allocation to Alpha increases from 0 to 100% with movement from Q_0 toward Q_4.

The portfolio with 1/4Alpha+3/4Zed has average risk of 7.66% but actual risk of 2.35%. The benefit from diversification is a reduction in risk of 5.31%.

DEFINITION 10.6 Portfolio diversification benefit ("DB")

The diversification benefit ("DB") from forming a portfolio equals the difference between the average component risk and actual portfolio risk:

$$\begin{pmatrix} Diversification \\ benefit \end{pmatrix} = \sigma_{average} - \sigma_{portfolio}.$$

Lessons earlier in this chapter explain that investors prefer less risk. Hence, diversification benefits are valuable because, all else equal, investors prefer risk reduction.

CALCULATOR CLUE

After completion of the *Calculator Clue* for Example 8 the mean and standard deviation for Alpha are in memories 1 and 2, analogous numbers for Zed are in memories 4 and 5, and analogous numbers for the portfolio that allocates 25% Alpha and 75% Zed are in memories 7 and 8. Compute the average risk of the portfolio with these keystrokes:

RCL 2 x .25 + RCL 5 x .75 = STO 0.

The display shows the average risk is 7.66%. Now obtain the diversification benefits:

RCL 0 - RCL 8 =

The display shows the diversification benefits equal 531 basis points.

4.A. Relation between diversification benefits and correlation

The preceding example computes portfolio risk by figuring the standard deviation of returns for each different outcome (e.g., stagnant economy, etc.). Formula 10.11 allows direct computation of portfolio risk:

FORMULA 10.11 Actual risk for a 2-security portfolio ("$\sigma_{portfolio}$")

$$\sigma_{portfolio} = \{w_x^2\, \sigma_x^2 + w_y^2\, \sigma_y^2 + 2w_x\, \sigma_x\, w_y\, \sigma_y\, \rho_{x,y}\}^{1/2},$$

where w_x and w_y denote the proportion of portfolio wealth allocated to asset X and Y, respectively, and $\rho_{X,Y}$ is the correlation coefficient.

The correlation coefficient is a number between -1 and +1 and measures the extent to which two variables move together.

The diversification benefit that a portfolio creates depends on the amount of correlation between component assets. Formula 10.11 shows $\sigma_{portfolio}$ relates directly with ρ. That is, relatively large ρ implies relatively large $\sigma_{portfolio}$ and small ρ implies relatively small $\sigma_{portfolio}$. Examine this graphic.

Huge DB	*Moderate to large DB*	*None to few DB*
$\rho = -1.0$	$\rho = 0.0$	$\rho = +1.0$
Perfect negative correlation (opposites)	*Uncorrelated*	*Perfect positive correlation (similars)*

With perfect positive correlation ($\rho = 1.0$) the returns for two assets always move together. When one is up the other is up. When one is down the other is down. They always follow each other. Because they always follow each other there exist few diversification benefits from combining these assets into a portfolio.

With perfect negative correlation ($\rho = -1.0$) the returns for two assets always move oppositely. When one is up the other is down. When one is down the other is up. Because they always move oppositely a lot of offsetting occurs, thereby smoothing outcomes and reducing risk. There exist huge diversification benefits from combining these assets into a portfolio.

A correlation coefficient near zero means that returns between two assets are uncorrelated. There is no reliable relation between the two. When one is up the other sometimes is down, but sometimes it's up. They are completely unrelated. Combining these assets into a portfolio creates moderate to large diversification benefits.

The formula for computing ρ when all outcomes for assets X and Y are equally likely is this:

FORMULA 10.12 Correlation coefficient (ρ) with equally likely outcomes

$$\rho_{x,y} = \left\{ \frac{\sum_{i=1}^{N}(ROR_{i,x} \times ROR_{i,y})}{N} - (E(ROR_x) \times E(ROR_y)) \right\} \div \sigma_x \sigma_y$$

The expression in curly brackets is the *covariance*. The correlation coefficient and covariance always have the same sign. Always $-1 \leq \rho \leq +1$ whereas covariance is unbounded.

The previous section explains that when all outcomes are equally likely computations simplify, largely because calculators such as the Texas Instruments BAII Plus compute statistics automatically – these calculators also compute ρ! Consider this example.

EXAMPLE 9 With equally likely outcomes find portfolio diversification benefits
Two securities, X and Y, exhibit the following returns over the past 5 years:

	1	2	3	4	5
X:	15.15%	3.45%	-0.05%	-1.15%	14.85%
Y:	6.25%	8.45%	6.35%	10.45%	3.85%

You believe that past performance is a perfect predictor of future performance. Find the diversification benefits for the portfolio that allocates 40% to X and 60% to Y.

SOLUTION
Follow example 6 in the previous section that uses formula 10.6 and 10.7 to compute that $\sigma_X = 7.15\%$ and $\sigma_Y = 2.23\%$. Then formula 10.10 finds:

$$\sigma_{average} = 0.40(.0715) + 0.60(.0223)$$
$$= 4.20\% .$$

Computing the actual portfolio risk requires the correlation coefficient from formula 10.12:

$$\rho_{x,y} = \left\{ \frac{.1515(.0625) + .0345(.0845) + (-.0005)(.0635) + (-.0115)(.1045) + (.1485)(.0385)}{5} \right.$$
$$\left. - (.0645)(.0707) \right\} \div (.0715)(.0223)$$
$$= -0.7444$$

The large negative coefficient suggests huge diversification benefits. Substitute into formula 10.11 to find the risk for the portfolio with 40%X + 60%Y.

$$\sigma_{40\%X + 60\%Y} = \left\{ .40^2(.0715^2) + .60^2(.0223^2) + 2(.40)(.0715)(.60)(.0223)(-.7444) \right\}^{1/2}$$

$$= 2.07\%$$

Diversification benefits equal the difference between average and actual risks:

$$DB = 4.20\% - 2.07\%$$

$$= 2.13\%, \text{ that is, 213 basis points.}$$

CALCULATOR CLUE

Follow example 6 and enter the data for X and Y into the BAII Plus© DATA worksheet. Then find and store the statistical estimates of the standard deviations and correlation coefficient. It's a good idea to rely on stored numbers for calculations instead of re-typing. Hit 2nd STAT and make sure the display shows "LIN". Hit ↓ 4 times and the display shows "σ_X = .0715" so hit STO 4. Hit ↓ 3 more times to see "σ_Y = .0223" so hit STO 5. Hit ↓ 3 more times to see "$r = -.7444$". This is the correlation coefficient so hit STO 3. Now obtain average risk with these keystrokes:

.4 x RCL 4 + .6 x RCL 5 = .

The display shows 4.20% so hit STO 9. Obtain actual risk like this:

.4 x² x RCL 4 x² + .6 x² x RCL 5 x² + 2 x .4 x RCL 4 x .6 x RCL 5 x RCL 3 = √

The display shows 2.07% so hit STO 0. Compute DB as

RCL 9 - RCL 0 =

The display shows the final answer of 213 basis points.

EXERCISES 10.4A

Conceptual

1. Listed below are rates of return for securities X, Y, and Z for 5 different periods. Without performing any computations, comment on the correlation between the different securities.

	period 1	2	3	4	5
X:	-3.9%	4.6%	21.9%	17.6%	14.1%
Y:	13.4%	13.1%	12.5%	12.7%	12.9%
Z:	4.3%	15.2%	3.2%	-3.7%	1.4%

Numerical quickies

2. The standard deviation of expected returns for investments X and Y equal 14.5% and 9.5% , respectively. The correlation between returns for X and Y is 0.30. If you allocate 80% of your funds to X, and the remainder to Y, what is the portfolio's standard deviation of expected returns?
©MR3am

3. Investment risk, as measured by the standard deviation of returns, equals 21.0% for stock X and 12.1% for stock Y. The correlation between the securities is zero. You form a portfolio allocated 40% in X and 60% in Y. Find the diversification benefit, measured as percent reduction in risk, for the portfolio. ©ER8b

4. Each pair of rates of return for securities X and Y listed below is equally likely. You wish to form a portfolio by allocating 30% of funds in Company X and the remainder in Company Y. Find the diversification benefit, measured as the standard deviation reduction in basis points (BP), that the portfolio provides. ©ER15

| X: | -3.2% | 4.9% | 22.3% | 15.8% |
| Y: | 20.9% | 13.0% | 8.2% | 6.0% |

Challengers

5. You form a portfolio that invests 60% of total funds in stock X and 40% in stock Z. Two possible outcomes exist. The probability is 15% that the first outcome occurs, in which case the rates of return equal 10% for X and 37% for Z. The probability is 85% that the second outcome occurs, in which case the rates of return equal 30% for X and 12% for Z. Find the diversification benefit, measured as the standard deviation reduction in basis points (BP), that the portfolio provides. ©ER9c

6. The standard deviation of returns equals 10.5% for stock X and 21.5% for stock Z. The correlation between the two stocks equals -0.20. You make a portfolio that allocates 75% of funds to stock X. The remainder is put in stock Z. Find the diversification benefit, measured as the standard deviation reduction in basis points (BP), that the portfolio provides. ©ER7

4.B. The minimum risk portfolio and investment advice

Several preceding examples return a familiar finding: *the portfolio risk sometimes is less than the risk of every individual component security!* This raises a very interesting question: *What allocation scheme provides the least risky portfolio and why does it matter?* This subsection looks at that lesson.

The question's quantitative solution is surprisingly simple. Formula 10.13 gives the allocation in a 2-security portfolio that provides the least risky portfolio.

FORMULA 10.13 Allocation at minimum risk portfolio ("$w^{min\ \sigma}$")
The proportional allocation to security X that generates the minimum risk portfolio for all possible combinations of securities X and Y is this:

$$w_X^{minimum\ risk} = \frac{\sigma_Y^2 - covariance_{X,Y}}{\sigma_X^2 + \sigma_Y^2 - (2x\ covariance_{X,Y})}$$

Use formula 10.13 to find the weight for one security. Subtract from 100% the weight found above to find the weight for the other security.

Formula 10.13 implies $w_X^{min\ \sigma}$ increases as σ_Y increases. That is, as Y gets riskier then put more into X in order to form the minimum risk portfolio. Also notice that formula 10.13 depends on covariance between securities. Covariance is intuitively analogous to correlation, as the discussion for formula 10.12 suggests, except that the correlation coefficient is restricted to range between plus and minus one whereas covariance is unrestricted.

EXAMPLE 10 With equally likely outcomes find minimum risk portfolio and *DB*
Two securities, *X* and *Y*, exhibit the following returns over the past 5 years:

	1	2	3	4	5
X:	15.15%	3.45%	-0.05%	-1.15%	14.85%
Y:	6.25%	8.45%	6.35%	10.45%	3.85%

You believe that past performance is a perfect predictor of future performance. Find the risk, return and diversification benefits for the minimum risk portfolio containing securities *X* and *Y*.

SOLUTION
Follow example 9 and find that $\sigma_X = 7.15\%$, $\sigma_Y = 2.23\%$, and $\rho_{X,Y} = -0.7444$. Then use formula 10.13 to compute:

$$w_x^{min\ \sigma} = \frac{.0233^2 - (.0223)(.0715)(-.7444)}{.0715^2 + .0223^2 - 2(.0223)(.0715)(-.7444)}$$

$$= 21.12\%$$

The minimum risk portfolio that combines stocks *X* and *Y* invests 21.12% in *X*. The amount to invest in Y is 100% minus 21.12%, or $w_Y^{min\ \sigma} = 78.88\%$.

For the minimum risk portfolio obtain the average return and average risk,

$$E(ROR_{21.12\%X + 78.88\%Y}) = .2112\ (.0645)\ +\ .7888\ (.0707)$$

$$= 6.94\%\ ,$$

$$\sigma_{average} = 0.2112(.0715)\ +\ 0.7888(.0223)$$

$$= 3.27\%\ .$$

Find the actual risk for this portfolio:

$$\sigma_{21.12\%X + 78.88\%Y} = \left\{ \begin{array}{l} .2112^2\ (.0715)\ +\ .7888^2(.0223^2) \\ +\ 2(.2112)(.0715)(.7888)(.0223^2)(-.7444) \end{array} \right\}^{1/2}$$

$$= 1.19\%$$

Because of negative correlation between component securities the minimum risk portfolio offers huge diversification benefits.

$$DB = 3.27\%\ -\ 1.19\%$$

$$= 2.08\%$$

Among all possible portfolios containing securities *X* and *Y* the one with least possible risk has *E(ROR)* of 6.94%, σ of 1.19%, and the portfolio creates diversification benefits of 208 basis points.

The qualitative answer to the question "why does the minimum risk portfolio matter" is straightforward, too. Discover its significance by comparing these three investment strategies: Strategy 1 ("S1") invests 100% of funds in security X; Strategy 2 ("S2") invests 100% of funds in Y; Strategy 3 ("S3") invests in the minimum risk portfolio comprising securities X and Y.

Here is a summary of risk-return characteristics for these 3 strategies:

allocation	E(ROR)	σ
S1: 100% X	6.45%	7.15%
S2: 100% Y	7.07%	2.23%
S3: 21.12%X + 78.88%Y	6.94%	1.19%

Figure 10.4 illustrates the three strategies.

First compare S1, the all-X allocation, with S2, the all-Y allocation. Security Y dominates security X because Y has higher return and less risk. Nobody that owns only one of these securities should own X. The choice between S1 and S2 is a no-brainer: choose S2 and go with Y.

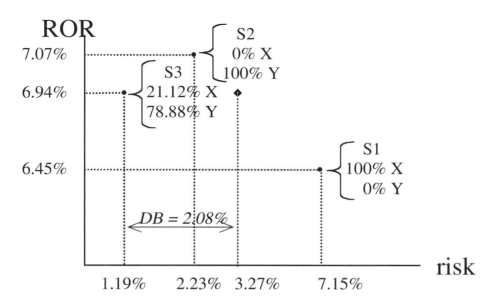

FIGURE 10.4
X, Y, and the minimum
risk portfolio

Thus far it may appear that X is a loser with little redeeming value. But hold on! Strategy S3 shows that mixing a little X with a lot of Y allows a unique opportunity. S3 and S2 coexist as tradeoffs. This means both are feasible investments that appeal to investors with differing attitudes toward the risk-return tradeoff. S2 is for high-risk, high-return preferences whereas S3 is for low-risk, low-return preferences. Asset X, even though dominated, has purpose, a *raison d'être*. X is a loser by itself but when placed in a portfolio X offers something unique – a mechanism for trading off risk and return.

Implications of this lesson are profound and far-reaching. Imagine an aging relative that owns all-Y because at their point in the financial life cycle (see table 9.4) they gladly tradeoff risk for lower return. Pretend that X and Y are the only available investments and that you both believe the numbers in figure 10.4. You both know that X, with its high risk and low return, is a dominated dog. But you have financial training and offer this loved one the following observation: *Sell 21% of your holding in low risk Y and use the money to buy high risk X and the overall portfolio risk will fall!* And you are right!

Perhaps it seems counterintuitive that you may reduce portfolio risk by selling a low risk asset and buying a high risk asset. The key, however, is that creating portfolios possibly creates diversification benefits. These benefits are valuable; they are a special type of transformation value. From this lesson emerges a stronger intuition - *putting all your eggs in one basket is a risky strategy.*

The minimum risk portfolio is not necessarily the "best" allocation. But it is not dominated. It coexists with many other allocation schemes as part of the *feasible allocation set*:

RULE 10.1 Feasible allocation set ("FAS") for 2-security portfolios
The feasible allocation set for a portfolio comprising two securities includes all allocations that are not dominated. All portfolios in the *FAS* coexist as tradeoffs. The *FAS* includes all portfolios with allocation for the highest returning asset greater than or equal to its allocation in the minimum risk portfolio.

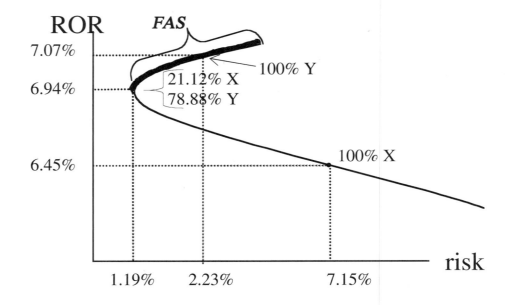

FIGURE 10.5
Risk-return profile for securities X and Y

The minimum risk portfolio represents, as figure 10.5 illustrates, the beginning of the *FAS*. This figure shows the "Risk-return profile for securities X and Y," a graph of all portfolios formed by combining securities X and Y in every possible allocation.

The risk-return profile is the parabola that passes through three labeled points: the 100%X allocation toward the lower right, the minimum risk portfolio at the left tip of the parabola, and the 100%Y allocation toward the upper middle. Each unique point on the parabola represents a different portfolio with a unique allocation of funds between X and Y. Movement along the lower portion of the parabola from the all-X allocation toward the minimum risk portfolio occurs smoothly as w_x diminishes from 100% to 21.12%. Movement along the upper portion of the parabola from the minimum risk portfolio toward the all-Y allocation occurs smoothly as w_x diminishes from 21.12% to 0%.

The feasible allocation set in figure 10.5 is the bold portion of the parabola that begins at the minimum risk portfolio and extends <u>above</u> and to the right. The *FAS* includes the 100% allocation in security Y. For all portfolios in the *FAS* the allocation to Y exceeds 78.88% of funds. All these are good investment choices and the one that is best depends on the risk preferences of the investor.

Dominated portfolios are <u>below</u> and to the right of the minimum risk portfolio. These include the 100%X allocation. For all dominated portfolios the allocation to X exceeds 21.12%. These are bad investment choices for every investor, irrespective of risk preferences.

Inspection of the risk-return profile for securities X and Y leads to this advice for investors that consider creating a portfolio containing either or both of these securities. These two equivalent statements are consistent with rule 10.1:

Always allocate more than 78.88% of funds in security Y.
Always allocate less than 21.12% of funds in security X.

An important step in determining investment advice is finding the feasible allocation set; finding the minimum risk portfolio makes that simple.

EXERCISES 10.4B

Conceptual

1. Is the objective "minimizing portfolio risk" the same as "maximizing diversification benefit"?

2. Formula 10.13 computes the allocation in each of two securities that yields least risky portfolio possible. Definition 10.6 defines *Diversification benefit* as the difference between actual and average portfolio risk. Simplify the formulas and find *DB* at the minimum risk for the following special case $\rho = +1$.

Numerical quickies

3. Throughout the past, the return for Large Cap Stocks has averaged 11.2% and the standard deviation has been 32.8%. For International Stocks, the return has averaged 15.0% and the standard deviation 37.1%. The correlation between the returns for these two assets has been -0.10. What is the percentage allocation of funds in Large Cap Stocks that results in a portfolio with the lowest possible risk; the remaining funds are to be invested in the other asset. ©MR2am

Challengers

4. The standard deviation of expected returns for investments X and Y equal 14.0% and 22.0%, respectively. The correlation between returns for X and Y is -0.50. How much risk reduction, that is diversification benefit in basis points, does the minimum risk portfolio provide? ©MR4am

5. Your analysis suggests that each pair of outcomes is equally likely:

| %return Alpha | 0.0% | 5.2% | 22.2% | 13.8% |
| %return Zed | 23.7% | 23.8% | 9.2% | -4.8% |

   a. Find the combination of Alpha and Zed that yield the minimum risk portfolio. ©MR1am
   b. Find σ and *E(ROR)* of the minimum risk portfolio. ©MR1dm
   c. How much diversification benefit, that is risk reduction in basis points, does the minimum risk portfolio provide? ©MR1fm

4.C. The risk-return profile for 2-security portfolios

The risk-return profile shows risk and return measurements for all possible portfolios comprised of two securities. The following rule about risk-return profiles always is true.

> **RULE 10.2 Shape of 2-security risk-return profiles**
> The risk-return profile is a parabola that opens to the right and is symmetric around a horizontal ray passing through the minimum risk portfolio. Correlation between component securities determines the extent of inflection in the parabola.

Figure 10.6 on the following page shows plausible risk-return profiles for two generic securities, call them *A* and *B*. This discussion is true irrespective of whether the securities coexist as tradeoffs or one is dominant. The all-*A* portfolio (w_A=100%, w_B=0%) as well as the all-*B* portfolio (w_A=0%, w_B=100%) always lie somewhere on the parabola.

When the correlation coefficient between returns for securities *A* and *B* is relatively large then there is not much bow or inflection in the parabola. The diversification benefit from creating a portfolio with *A* and *B* consequently is small. The limiting case occurs with perfect positive correlation when $\rho = +1$. For this special case the parabola actually is coincident with the line of averages connecting securities *A* and *B* – the *DB* equals zero.

When component securities are moderately correlated, uncorrelated, or even negatively correlated then the parabola has a lot of flex, like an archery bow pulled tightly. Diversification benefits consequently are moderate to large. The limiting

FIGURE 10.6
**Risk-return profiles
depend on correlation**

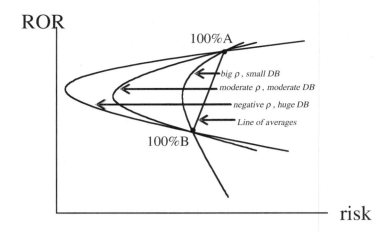

case occurs with perfect negative correlation. For this special case the parabola actually kisses the vertical axis – the minimum risk portfolio has $\sigma = 0$ when $\rho = -1$. The *DB* is huge when component securities offset each other's extreme outcomes.

A second rule for risk-return profiles pertains to the allocation at the minimum risk portfolio. Before presenting the new rule learn some lessons about the risk-return parabola. Realize that just as two points determine the location of a line, three points determine the location of a parabola. Each point on the parabola represents a unique portfolio. It's simplest and most useful to find the risk-return coordinates for these three portfolios:

> (i) the all-*A* portfolio;
> (ii) the all-*B* portfolio;
> (iii) the minimum risk portfolio.

Previous examples show how to obtain measures of *E(ROR)* and σ for securities *A* and *B*, and formula 10.13 allows computation of those measures for the minimum risk portfolio.

Sometimes the answer from formula 10.13 is a negative number. When the proportional allocation for security *A* is a negative number, that is $w_A^{min\ \sigma}<0$, the minimum risk portfolio takes a *short* position in security *A*. Whereas a long position in an asset ($w>0$) means the asset is owned, a short position ($w>0$) means the asset is owed – it is a liability! Suppose, for example, an investor forms a $1,000 portfolio with securities *A* and *B* where $w_B=1.25$ and $w_A=-0.25$. Notice that the sum of weights equals 100% as required. The weight in *A* is -25%. The investor takes a short position by borrowing and selling $250 worth of security *A*. Next the investor allocates 125% of portfolio wealth ($1,250) and buys security *B*. The financing source for the purchase is $1,000 of initial endowment plus $250 from the short sale. The short sale increases the investor's liabilities - an increase in a liability is a source of financing.

The objective of most financial investments is making profit. One way to profit is *buy low now and sell high later*. Buy the stock today for $50, for example, and sell later for $70. In developed financial markets, however, short sales are fairly common. Short sales reverse the timing to *sell high now and buy low later*. A short sale occurs, for example, when you borrow a share from your broker and sell the stock today for $50. The broker sells stock from inventory and credits your account with the proceeds. You are obligated to eventually cover your short position. Motivation for covering the short sale may include: (1) the stock price later drops, say to $30, and you order the broker to buy it so you can take your profit. You sold high, bought low, and profited. Motivation also may occur because: (2) the stock price later rises, say to $70, and you wish to cut your losses. For this case you sold high but unfortunately bought higher. A third motivation may be: (3) the broker for whatever reason wants the stock back and has the right to force you at any time to cover the short position.

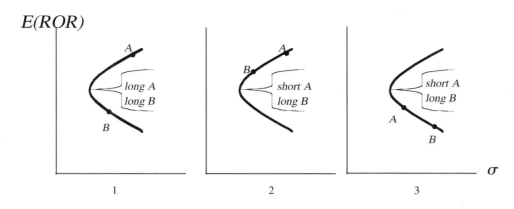

$E(ROR)$

long A
long B

short A
long B

short A
long B

σ

1   2   3

Figure 10.7 illustrates several possible allocations at the minimum risk portfolio. Graph 1 on the left is the standard that occurs when the minimum risk portfolio includes a long position for both securities. In this case both weights w_A and w_B range between 0 and 100%. This case usually occurs when correlation among component securities is moderate, low, or negative.

The situation that graph 2 depicts usually occurs when highly correlated securities coexist as tradeoffs. For the all-A portfolio, that is at point A, w_A equals 100%. As one moves down the parabola w_A declines. For the all-B portfolio w_A equals 0. Beneath point B the weight w_A is negative. The minimum risk portfolio involves a short position in A ($w_A<0$) and a long position in B ($w_B>100\%$).

The situation that graph 3 depicts usually occurs when two securities strongly correlate and one is dominant. The minimum risk portfolio involves a long position in A ($w_A>100\%$) and a short position in B ($w_B<0$).

Rule 10.3 pertains to all risk return profiles and summarizes the preceding tendencies.

> **RULE 10.3 Long or short positions and the minimum risk portfolio**
> When the weight from formula 10.13 is between 0 and 100% then the minimum risk portfolio lies between component securities and involves a long position in both. When the weight is negative or bigger than 100% the minimum risk portfolio takes a short position on one security, long on the other.

Sometimes investment policies disallow short positions. Short positions, after all, are riskier than long positions because short positions expose investors to unlimited losses. Perhaps an institutional investor declares in their prospectus that the company does not use short sales. Alternatively, perhaps an individual investor abides a "just say no" philosophy for short sales. For those situations the finding of a negative weight simply means the asset is avoided, its weight in the portfolio is zero, and the other asset's weight becomes 100%.

Interpreting risk-return profiles provides fairly strong answers to important questions. The information requirement for making the risk-return profile includes $E(ROR)$ and σ for each security as well as the correlation coefficient.

EXAMPLE 11 Find investment advice given summary statistics for large and small caps

Table 9.15 shows that since 1925 the annual rate of return for large capitalization stocks ("LC") averages 12.7% and the standard deviation is 20.2%. The return for small cap stocks ("SC") averages 17.3% and the standard deviation 33.2%. The correlation coefficient between returns for these two assets is 0.429. You believe these long-run historical statistics likely persist into the long-run future. What portfolios containing these two asset classes are in the feasible allocation set?

SOLUTION

The weight for large cap stocks at the minimum risk portfolio is found with formula 10.13

$$w_{LC}^{min\ \sigma} = \frac{.332^2 - (.332)(.202)(.429)}{.202^2 + .332^2 - 2(.332)(.202)(.429)}$$

$$= 87.1\%$$

The minimum risk portfolio from combining asset classes LC and SC invests 87.1% in LC and, consequently, 12.9% in SC (12.9% = 100% - 87.1%). Because $E(ROR_{SC}) > E(ROR_{LC})$ rule 10.1 stipulates that the FAS includes all portfolios allocating 12.9% or more to SC. Restate the findings like this:

Always allocate more than 12.9% of funds in small cap stocks.
Always allocate less than 87.1% of funds in large cap stocks.

Figure 10.8 qualitatively depicts the scenario.

Figure 10.8 offers pretty strong investment advice that is based on 75 years of history. Incredibly, too, the advice relies on <u>one</u> computation (formula 10.13) and a few rules! To assign numbers on the axis, or to compute diversification benefits, etc., requires more effort. Yet the qualitative advice flows fairly simply.

The fundamental structure underlying these lessons is well known in the investments industry. Predicting future outcomes by relying on historical statistics is a widespread practice. Formula 10.13 uses three summary statistics as inputs: σ for one security, σ for the other, and ρ. Statisticians call these "higher order" statistics; maybe you remember from your Stats class that the mean is the first moment and variance is the second moment. Studies show that higher order statistics are relatively stationary. This means that stocks with high standard deviation of returns for the last few years continue in the future to have high standard deviation, stocks that tended to strongly correlate during the last few years continue in the future to strongly correlate, etc. This suggests that computations of formula 10.13 for weights at the minimum risk portfolio are relatively reliable.

Unfortunately, knowing composition of the minimum risk portfolio is insufficient for formulating investment advice. Rule 10.1 clearly states that the FAS includes portfolios with increasing allocation to the highest returning asset. Well here is the problem – nothing predicts the highest returning asset very well. The first moment, that is $E(ROR)$, is very unstable (chapter 2 states the best among many terrible predictors of return is the equity price-to-book ratio; chapter 9 explains this instability of returns with the efficient market hypothesis)! Sometimes stocks are up,

FIGURE 10.8
Risk-return profile for large (LC) and small cap (SC) stocks

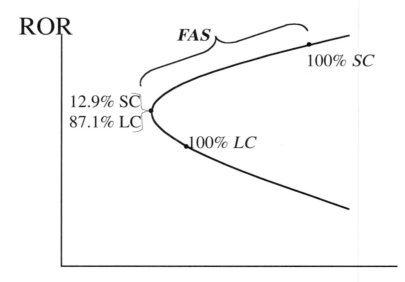

sometimes they're down, sometimes last year's winners are next year's winners, and sometimes they're losers. Predicting future stock performance is the mother of all mysteries! This example drives home the seriousness of this shortcoming for modern portfolio theory.

EXAMPLE 12 Find investment advice given σ and ρ for 2 mutual funds

You are forming a portfolio with two mutual funds. The standard deviation of returns for the HealthSciences fund ("HS") is 28.6%. For the Global Equities fund ("GE") the standard deviation is 34.4%. The correlation coefficient between returns for these two assets has been 0.157. Formulate appropriate investment advice.

SOLUTION

The weight for HS stocks at the minimum risk portfolio is found with formula 10.13

$$w_{HS}^{min \ \sigma} = \frac{.344^2 - (.344)(.286)(.107)}{.286^2 + .344^2 - 2(.344)(.286)(.107)}$$

$$= 60.2\%$$

The minimum risk portfolio combining mutual funds HS and GE invests 60.2% in HS and, consequently, 39.8% in GE (39.8% = 100% - 60.2%). It involves a long position in each fund. The minimum risk portfolio is not "best", but it certainly is not dominated.

The setup provides no information about $E(ROR_{HS})$ or $E(ROR_{GE})$. There are only two possibilities, however. Either $E(ROR_{HS})$ is bigger or $E(ROR_{GE})$ is bigger. Figure 10.9 shows the alternative scenarios.

Both scenarios have the same ranking of standard deviations $(\sigma_{GE} > \sigma_{HS})$ and allocation at the minimum risk portfolio. The scenarios differ only because of which return is bigger.

For the scenario on the left $E(ROR_{GE})$ is bigger. The feasible allocation set includes all portfolios that allocate more than 39.8% in GE. The all-GE portfolio is in the FAS. The minimum risk portfolio dominates the all-HS portfolio.

For the scenario on the right $E(ROR_{HS})$ is bigger. The feasible allocation set includes all portfolios that allocate more than 60.2% in HS. The all-HS portfolio is in the FAS. The minimum risk portfolio dominates the all-GE portfolio.

The two scenarios generate exactly opposite investment advice! The only point in common is the minimum risk portfolio – it's not dominated and is a member of the feasible allocation set irrespective of expectations about returns.

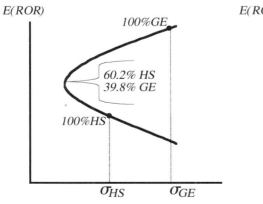

$E(ROR_{GE})$ is bigger

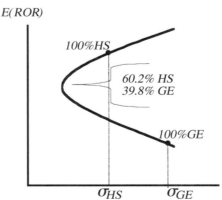

$E(ROR_{HS})$ is bigger

FIGURE 10.9
Two scenarios for investment advice

Famed investor (and second richest man in the U.S.A.) Warren Buffet once said he doesn't understand why people invest in their second, third, or even tenth best choice. He says they should just pick the winner. Consider Mr. Buffet's statement within the context of example 12 and figure 10.9.

When an investor is clueless about which asset will provide the highest return then there exists danger from putting all eggs in one basket. The danger is that *after the fact* the basket is a loser. Diversification offers protection against losers. Inclusion of the minimum risk portfolio in the feasible allocation set, irrespective of outcome, offers a convincing lesson that diversified investing assures a reasonable outcome. Extreme outcomes of component securities in diversified portfolios smooth overall portfolio returns. You may be certain, but don't be disappointed, that investment in a diversified portfolio returns less *after the fact* than if one had simply invested in winners. The problem for most investors (except apparently for Mr. Buffet!) is knowing winners *before the fact*. Hence, diversify!

Lessons in chapter 9 explain that $ROR^{expected}$ is the internal rate of return linking observed asset prices with anticipations and information. Sterile statistical studies cannot predict expected rates of return – modern portfolio theory has limitations providing investment advice. The studies convincingly establish, however, that diversification creates valuable benefits! The importance of modern portfolio theory is <u>not</u> for predicting $ROR^{expected}$, but rather for showing how $ROR^{required}$ relate to diversification benefits. Determination of a security's equilibrium return depends on the diversification benefit that the security contributes to a well-diversified portfolio.

EXERCISES 10.4C

Conceptual

1. You are pretty sure that security X will be a winner whereas Y will be a loser. You intend to buy one or both of these (but no others). What does the story about "feasible allocation set" imply about investment advice for you?
2. Suppose that you are interested in two securities, call them X and Y. You have no idea about their expected returns or correlation. You are confident, however, that their risks are identical. You want to make a portfolio from either or both securities. Your only criterion is to create a portfolio that is not dominated, that is, choose a portfolio in the feasible allocation set. Describe what you should do.
3. According to formula 10.13, under what conditions does the minimum risk portfolio involve a short position in one security?

Numerical quickies

4. Throughout the past the return for type X stocks has averaged 11.9% and the standard deviation has been 27.6%. For type Y stocks the return has averaged 16.2% and the standard deviation 34.8%. The correlation between the returns for these two assets has been 0.13. You expect these tendencies to persist into the future. What is the most comprehensive allocation rule that correctly describes all portfolios in the feasible allocation set? ©MR5
5. The standard deviation of expected returns for investments X and Y equal 18.0% and 11.0%, respectively. The correlation between returns for X and Y is 0.40 . Find the combination of X and Y that yield the minimum risk portfolio. If your objective is to form a portfolio with these two securities that is not dominated by any other combination, what should you do? ©MR3cm

Challengers

6. Each pair of outcomes listed below is equally likely.

%return Alpha	4.0%	10.0%	24.2%	14.5%
%return Zed	22.4%	26.2%	13.1%	-7.4%

Describe the portfolios that are in the feasible allocation set. ©MR1em

EXERCISES 10.1

1. Y is better with regards to $E(ROR)$ because it's bigger. Y is better with regards to σ because it's smaller. Y dominates X because it's better in every dimension.

2. For these three securities there are 3 possible pairs of securities to compare. Compare X to Y. X's risk of 20 is worse than Y's risk of 4 (for convenience use "worse" to denote "less preferable"; "better" denotes "more preferable"). X's return of 9 is better than Y's return of 6. X is better in some ways whereas Y is better in other ways. X and Y coexist as tradeoffs.
   Compare X to Z. X's risk of 20 is worse than Z's risk of 11. X's return of 9 is better than Z's return of 7. X is better in some ways whereas Z is better in other ways. X and Z coexist as tradeoffs.
   Compare Y to Z. Y's risk of 4 is better than Z's risk of 11. Y's return of 6 is worse than Z's return of 7. Y is better in some ways whereas Z is better in other ways. Y and Z coexist as tradeoffs.
   The three comparisons show that each coexists with the other as a tradeoff. That's the bottom line inference. A more thoughtful analysis doesn't change the answer, but it adds a qualification. Movement from X to Z involves a decline in risk of 9 units and a decline in return of 2 units. That implies a 4.50 tradeoff in risk per unit of return (4.50 = 9/2). Movement from Z to Y implies a 7 unit decline in risk and 1 unit decline in return, or 7.00 tradeoff of risk per unit of return. An investor at X that prefers to reduce risk finds that movement to Z reduces risk quite a bit, but that further movement to Y provides a lot of risk reduction with very little additional reduction in return. In other words, X is the best high risk, high return choice. As far as the low risk, low return choice goes, Y and Z coexist as tradeoffs, but Y is likely (but not definitely) a better choice than Z.

3. For this problem there are two kinds of risk and each is bad. Rank the three choices from best to worst for the two risk and 1 return measures (for convenience use "better" to denote "more preferable"; "worse" denotes "less preferable").

	Risk$_1$	Risk$_2$	Return
best	A & B	B	C
middle		A	B
worst	C	C	A

Now compare the 3 possible pairs of securities:
Compare A to C. In some ways A is better but in other ways C is better. A and C coexist as tradeoffs.
Compare B to C. In some ways B is better but in other ways C is better. B and C coexist as tradeoffs.
Compare A to B. With regards to Risk1 there is a tie between A and B. B is better than A with regards to $Risk_2$ and B is better with regards to $Return$. Thus, B is as at least as good or better than A in every way. B dominates A.

EXERCISES 10.2

1. DOL, DFL, and DTL are similar formulas because each is a ratio such as $x/(x-y)$. The variable x equals $(p-v)Q$ for the DOL, $EBIT$ for the DFL, etc. The variable y equals Total fixed costs for the DOL, $Interest$ for the DFL, etc. There seems to be an economic restriction that $y \geq 0$. For example, fixed costs or interest cannot be negative. This means that as the x variable gets larger the ratio converges to 1.0. That is, eventually the x

gets so big that y gets swamped. At the upper limit, then, for companies operating well beyond breakeven the effect of a 1% increase in *Sales revenue* is a 1% increase in *EBIT* and a 1% increase in *EAC*.

Consider what happens to the formulas when y consumes more and more of x. For example, as *Total fixed costs* approaches *(Sales revenue – Total variable costs)* then the denominator of the *DOL* formula approaches zero. The *DOL* approaches infinity. But the economic significance of a *DOL* equal to 10.0 probably is the same as for a *DOL* equal to 10 million. Both are relatively large. Furthermore, when x equals y the *DOL* is mathematically undefined. That means it's economically undefined, too, except to say that it's relatively big!

Another noteworthy property of these formulas occurs when the ratio is negative. For example, a company with *Sales revenue* less than operating costs may have a negative *DOL*. A negative *DOL* suggests that a 1% increase in sales leads to a decrease in *EBIT* - but that is false when p>v. The upshot is that the *DOL*, *DFL*, and *DTL* formulas may have no economic meaning when they result in negative numbers.

Despite these impracticalities, the stylized income statement yields some pretty valuable insights for assessing idiosyncratic company risk!

EXERCISES 10.3A

1. $ROR_{win} = \$1,300/\$900 - 1; = 44.44\%$. $ROR_{lose} = -100\%$. Now find the weighted average: $E(ROR) = 0.50(44.44\%) + 0.50(-100\%); = -27.78\%$

2. First find the rates of return based on number of adoptees. $ROR_0 = -100\%$. $ROR_1 = \$11/\$6 - 1; = 83.33\%$. $ROR_2 = \$17/\$6 - 1; = 183.33\%$. Now find the weighted average: $E(ROR) = 0.40(-100\%) + 0.40(83.33\%) + 0.20(183.33\%); = 30.0\%$. Now find $\sigma = [\ 0.4(-1.0 - 0.30)^2 + 0.4(0.8333 - 0.30)^2 + .2(1.8333 - 0.30)^2\ ]^{0.5}; = 112\%$.

3. This problem is analogous to example 5. Use formulas 10.5 and 10.6 to compute $(\sigma, E(ROR))$ for company X:(9.77,12.44); and Y:(6.41,14.41). There is a tradeoff.

4. This problem is analogous to example 6. Use formulas 10.7 and 10.8 or, preferably, allow the BAII Plus calculator to perform the calculations. Find that (Risk, return) equals (9.09%,10.68%) for X and (7.12%,16.88%) for Y; also Y dominates X

EXERCISES 10.3B

1. Use formula 10.9 to compute the weighted average (notice that the allocation for stock Z equals 30%): $E(ROR_{portfolio}) = 40\%(-12\%) + 30\%(20\%) + 30\%(-24\%); = -6.0\%$

2. Use formula 10.9 and solve for the weight in X. Notice that the weight for Y equals $(1 - w_x)$.
$$E(ROR_{portfolio}) = w_x(ROR_x) + (1 - w_x)(ROR_Y)$$
$$0.152 = w_x(0.059) + (1 - w_x)(0.235)$$
$$-0.0830 = -0.176 w_x$$
$$w_x = 47.16\%$$
The portfolio that allocates 47.16% in X and 52.84% in Y has expected return of 15.2%.

3. Find the portfolio *ROR* for the different outcomes given a 30% weight in X, 70% in Z. For outcome 1 the portfolio $ROR = .30(.10) + .70(.38); = 29.60\%$. For outcome 2 the portfolio $ROR = .30(.45) + .70(.08); = 19.10\%$. Now apply formulas 10.5 and 10.6 to the preceding portfolio *ROR* given that the probability of state 1 is 30% and state 2 is 70%. Compute that $E(ROR_{portfolio}) = 4.81\%$ and $\sigma_{portfolio} = 22.3\%$.

4. Find the portfolio *ROR* for the different outcomes given a 35% weight in X, 65% in Y. For outcome "declining" the portfolio $ROR = .35(-0.019) + .65(-0.065); = -4.89\%$. For outcome "flat" the portfolio $ROR = .35(0.054) + .65(0.154); = 11.90\%$. For outcome "rising" the portfolio

$ROR = .35(0.177) + .65(0.021); = 7.56\%$. Now use formulas 10.5 and 10.6 and apply the state probabilities of 35%, 30%, and 35%, respectively, to the preceding portfolio ROR. Compute that $E(ROR_{portfolio}) = 4.50\%$ and $\sigma_{portfolio} = 7.11\%$.

5. Find the portfolio ROR for the different outcomes given a 25% weight in X, 75% in Y. For outcomes in column 1 the portfolio $ROR = .25(-0.039) + .75(0.134); = 9.08\%$. For outcomes in column 2 the portfolio $ROR = .25(0.046) + .75(0.134); = 11.20\%$. For outcomes in column 3 the portfolio $ROR = .25(0.219) + .75(0.125); = 14.85\%$. For outcomes in column 4 the portfolio $ROR = .25(0.176) + .75(0.067); = 9.43\%$. Now use formulas 10.5 and 10.6 with probabilities of 1/4 for each of the preceding portfolio ROR. Compute that $E(ROR_{portfolio}) = 11.14\%$ and $\sigma_{portfolio} = 2.3\%$.

EXERCISES 10.4A

1. Find below arrows indicating whether the rates of return rise or fall relative to the preceding period. For example, the ROR for X is -3.9% in period 1, 4.6% in period 2 (this is ↑ from period 1) and 21.9% in period 3 (this is ↑ from period 2).

	period 1	2	3	4	5
X:		↑	↑	↓	↓
Y:		↓	↓	↑	↑
Z:		↑	↓	↓	↑

Comparison of X and Y shows that in 4-of-4 cases the arrows are in opposite directions. This demonstrates extreme negative correlation. Notice that negative correlation exists between X and Y even though the movement in Y is very slight. The standard deviation of Y is relatively tiny, but its correlation with X is a relatively huge negative number. Comparison of Y and Z shows that half the time the arrows are in the same direction, half the time they are different. This one is hard to call; computation shows correlation is moderately positive. Comparison of X and Z shows that in 3-4 cases the arrows are in opposite directions. This suggests moderate-to-strong negative correlation.

2. Just plug the numbers into formula 10.11 and find $\sigma_{portfolio} = \{.8^2(.145^2) + .2^2(.095^2) + 2(.8)(.145)(.2)(.095)(.3)\}^{1/2}; = 12.3\%$.

3. Just plug the numbers into formula 10.11 and find the actual risk, $\sigma_{portfolio} = \{.4^2(.21^2) + .6^2(.121^2) + 0\}^{1/2}; = 11.1\%$. Use formula 10.10 to find the average risk, $\sigma_{average} = .4(.21) + .6(.121); = 15.7\%$. The diversification benefit, measured as percent reduction in risk, equals 15.7% - 11.1%, or 4.6%.

4. Follow the "Calculator clue" following example 9 and let the calculator automatically compute that $\sigma_x = 9.81\%$; $\sigma_y = 5.72\%$; and $\rho = -0.9099$. Use formula 10.10 to find $\sigma_{average} = .3(.0981) + .7(.0572); = 6.94\%$. Use formula 10.11 to find $\sigma_{portfolio} = \{.3^2(.0981^2) + .7^2(.0572^2) + 2(.3)(.0981)(.7)(.0572)(-0.9099)\}^{1/2}$ 1.80%. The diversification benefit equals 6.94% - 1.80%, or 514 BP.

5. Apply formula 10.6 to the given ROR and find that $\sigma_X = 7.1\%$ and $\sigma_Z = 8.9\%$. Use formula 10.10 to find $\sigma_{average} = .6(.071) + .6(.089); = 7.85\%$. Now obtain the actual portfolio risk. First find the portfolio ROR for the different outcomes given a 60% weight in X, 40% in Z. For outcome 1 the portfolio $ROR = .60(.10) + .40(.37); = 20.80\%$. For outcome 2 the portfolio $ROR = .60(.30) + .40(.12); = 22.80\%$. Now apply formula 10.6 to the preceding portfolio ROR given that the probability of state 1 is 15% and state 2 is 85%. Compute that $\sigma_{portfolio} = 0.71\%$. The diversification benefit is almost total risk reduction, that is, $DB = 7.85\% - 0.71\%; = 714$ BP.

6. Just plug the numbers into formula 10.11 and find the actual risk, $\sigma_{portfolio} = \{.75^2(.105^2) + .25^2(.215^2) + 2(.75)(.105)(.25)(.215)(-0.20)\}^{1/2}$; = 8.60%. Use formula 10.10 to find the average risk, $\sigma_{average} = .75(.105) + .25(.215)$; = 13.25%. The diversification benefit, measured as percent reduction in risk, equals 13.25% - 8.60%, or 4.65%.

1. Examples 9 and 10 use the same data. Example 9 finds that with a 40:60% allocation in X:Y the diversification benefit equals 213 basis points. Example 10 finds that the minimum risk portfolio allocates 21.12% X, 78.88% Y and attains diversification benefit of 208 basis points. The objective "minimizing portfolio risk" is *NOT* the same as "maximizing diversification benefit". The minimum risk portfolio occurs at the leftmost tip of the parabola. The maximum diversification benefit occurs where the slope of the parabola exactly equals the slope of the $\sigma_{average}$ line that connects X and Y.

2. Simplify formula 10.11 with $\rho = 1$.
$$\sigma_{portfolio} = \{w_X^2\sigma_X^2 + w_Y^2\sigma_Y^2 + 2\,w_X\sigma_X\,w_Y\sigma_Y)\}^{1/2}$$
$$= \{\,(w_X\sigma_X + w_Y\sigma_Y)(w_X\sigma_X + w_Y\sigma_Y)\,\}^{1/2}$$
$$= w_X\sigma_X + w_Y\sigma_Y$$
Formula 10.10 is
$$\sigma_{average} = w_X\sigma_X + w_Y\sigma_Y$$
Definition 10.6 shows
$$DB = \sigma_{average} - \sigma_{portfolio}$$
$$= w_X\sigma_X + w_Y\sigma_Y - (w_X\sigma_X + w_Y\sigma_Y)$$
$$= 0$$
The diversification benefit from combining two perfectly correlated securities is zero.

3. Plug numbers into formula 10.13 for Large cap *("LC")* and International Stocks *("IS")*.
$$w_{LC}{}^{min\,\sigma} = \{0.371^2 - (0.328)(0.371)(-0.10)\} / \{0.328^2 + 0.371^2 - 2(0.328)(0.371)(-0.10)\};\ = 55.6\%$$
For these data the minimum risk portfolio allocates 55.6% in Large caps and 44.4% in International stocks.

4. Plug numbers into formula 10.13 for X and Y.
$$w_X{}^{min\,\sigma} = \{0.22^2 - (0.14)(0.22)(-0.10)\} / \{0.14^2 + 0.22^2 - 2(0.14)(0.22)(-0.50)\};\ = 64.6\%.$$
The minimum risk portfolio allocates 64.6% in X and 35.4% in Y. Now plug into formula 10.11 and find the actual risk, $\sigma_{portfolio} = \{.646^2(.14^2) + .354^2(.22^2) + 2(.646)(.14)(.354)(.22)(-0.50)\}^{1/2}$; = 8.50%. Use formula 10.10 to find the average risk, $\sigma_{average} = .646(.14) + .354(.22)$; = 16.85%. The diversification benefit, measured as percent reduction in risk, equals 16.85% - 8.50%, or 835 BP.

5a. Let your calculator automatically compute that $\sigma_{Alpha}= 8.46\%$; $\sigma_{Zed}= 11.86\%$; $\rho = -0.6803$. Plug numbers into formula 10.13 for Alpha and Zed.
$$w_{Alpha}{}^{min\,\sigma} = \{0.1186^2 - (0.0846)(0.1186)(-0.6803)\} / \{0.0846^2 + 0.1186^2 - 2(0.0846)(0.1186)(-0.6803)\};\ = 59.9\%.$$
The minimum risk portfolio allocates 59.9% in Alpha and 40.1% in Zed.

5b. Now plug into formula 10.9 and find the actual return, $E(ROR_{portfolio}) = .599(.1030) + .401(.1298)$; = 11.40%. Now plug into formula 10.11 and find the actual risk, $\sigma_{portfolio} = \{.599^2(.0846^2) + .401^2(.1186^2) + 2(.599)(.0846)(.401)(.1186)(-0.6803)\}^{1/2}$; = 3.90%.

5c. Use formula 10.10 to find the average risk, $\sigma_{average} = .599(.0846) + .401(.1186)$; = 9.82%. The diversification benefit, measured as percent reduction in risk, equals 9.82% - 3.90%, or 592 BP.

1. Financial science suggests that you dig deeper into the facts. The feasible allocation set includes portfolios that prudently tradeoff risk for return. The facts above state absolutely nothing about risk. Reconsider the possible outcomes. If you are 100% confident that X will be winner and Y a loser then definitely X is in the feasible allocation set. Go for it! But are you really 100% confident?

2. All that you know is $\sigma_X = \sigma_Y$, just call it σ. Solve formula 10.13

$$w_X^{min\ \sigma} = \{\sigma^2 - \sigma\ \sigma\ \rho\} / \{\sigma^2 + \sigma^2 - 2\sigma\ \sigma\ \rho\}$$
$$= \sigma^2\{1 - \rho\} / \{2\sigma^2\ (1 - \rho)\ \}$$
$$= 1/2$$

The minimum risk portfolio invests half all assets in X, half in Y. That strategy is the only one that for sure is not dominated. When you're uncertain how to invest then diversification is wise.

3. Solve formula 10.13 by setting $w_X^{min\ \sigma}$ equal to 1. This is a sort of breakeven point beyond which one security is *super*long and the other is *short*.

$$1.0 = \{\sigma_Y^2 - \sigma_X\ \sigma_Y\ \rho\} / \{\sigma_X^2 + \sigma_Y^2 - 2\sigma_X\ \sigma_Y\ \rho\}$$
$$\{\sigma_X^2 + \sigma_Y^2 - 2\sigma_X\ \sigma_Y\ \rho\} = \{\sigma_Y^2 - \sigma_X\ \sigma_Y\ \rho\}$$
$$\sigma_X^2 = \sigma_X\ \sigma_Y\ \rho$$
$$or\ \rho = \sigma_X \div \sigma_Y$$

When the correlation coefficient equals the ratio of standard deviations then the allocation at the minimum risk portfolio is 100% for one security, 0% for the other. When ρ exceeds the ratio of standard deviations then the minimum risk portfolio involves a short position in one security. For example, suppose $\sigma_X = 12\%$ and $\sigma_Y = 15\%$. The ratio of standard deviations is 12/15, or 0.80 (put the largest on bottom so that the ratio, like ρ, is less than one). If ρ were 0.80, solve for the allocation to X at the minimum risk portfolio.

$$w_X^{min\ \sigma} = \{.15^2 - (.12)(.15)(0.8)\} / \{(.12^2) + (.15^2) - 2(.12)(.15)(0.8)\}$$
$$= 100\%$$

The weight $w_Y^{min\ \sigma}$ is 0%. When ρ equals the ratio of standard deviations the minimum risk portfolio include only one security (the tip of the parabola is the point representing the smallest σ security). Suppose that with $\sigma_X = 12\%$ and $\sigma_Y = 15\%$ the ρ were 0.90. Solve for the allocation to X at the minimum risk portfolio.

$$w_X^{min\ \sigma} = \{.15^2 - (.12)(.15)(0.9)\} / \{(.12^2) + (.15^2) - 2(.12)(.15)(0.9)\}$$
$$= 140\%$$

The weight $w_Y^{min\ \sigma}$ is -40%; the negative sign means a short position. With a relatively large ρ the minimum risk portfolio involves a short position in one security.

4. Solve for the allocation to X at the minimum risk portfolio.

$$w_X^{min\ \sigma} = \{.348^2 - (.276)(.348)(0.14)\} / \{(.276^2) + (.348^2) -$$
$$2(.276)(.348)(0.13)\}$$
$$= 63.2\%$$

The weight $w_Y^{min\ \sigma}$ is 35.8%. Because the setup states $E(ROR_X) < E(ROR_Y)$ then always allocate 63.2% or less in X. Stating this same rule from the other perspective, always allocate 35.8% or more in Y.

5. Solve for the allocation to X at the minimum risk portfolio.

$$w_X^{min\ \sigma} = \{.11^2 - (.18)(.11)(0.4)\} / \{(.18^2) + (.11^2) - 2(.18)(.11)(0.4)\}$$
$$= 14.6\%$$

The weight $w_Y^{min\ \sigma}$ is 85.4%. The setup does not provide the expected returns. Definitely the allocation (w_X, w_Y) of (14.6%, 85.4%) is in the feasible allocation set. Otherwise, weighting one or the other security more heavily requires confidence. With confidence that $E(ROR_X) > E(ROR_Y)$ then always allocate 14.6% or more in X. Conversely, with confidence that $E(ROR_X) < E(ROR_Y)$ then always allocate 85.4% or more in Y. Moving away from the a well-diversified portfolio requires confidence in the ability to pick high return assets.

6. Let the calculator compute all statistics for you: $E(ROR_{Alpha}) = 13.18\%$; $\sigma_{Alpha} = 7.38\%$; $E(ROR_{Zed}) = 13.58\%$; $\sigma_{Zed} = 13.01\%$ and $\rho = -.4013\%$. Solve for the allocation to *Alpha* at the minimum risk portfolio.

$$w_{Alpha}^{min\ \sigma} = \{.1301^2 - (.0738)(.1301)(-.4013)\} / \{(.0738^2) + (.1301^2) - 2(.0738)(.1301)(-.4013)\}$$
$$= 69.1\%$$

The weight $w_{Zed}^{min\ \sigma}$ is 30.9%. Because $E(ROR_{Alpha}) > E(ROR_{Zed})$ then always allocate 69.1% or more in *Alpha*. Stating this same rule from the other perspective, always allocate 30.9% or less in *Zed*. Note in passing, however, that $E(ROR_{Alpha}) \approx E(ROR_{Zed})$ so, given these expectations, all portfolios containing these two securities have approximately the same return. For a given return investors generally should minimize risk.

CHAPTER 11

Determination of Equilibrium Returns

CHAPTER CONTENTS

Companies and households allocate resources toward many different types of capital investments. Companies may own a variety of brands, patents, factories, or even subsidiary companies. Mutual funds own many diverse securities. Households own human capital, housing, and an array of financial securities. For any company, regardless of definition, their set of capital investments represents a diversified portfolio. Diversification reduces or eliminates idiosyncratic risk. Diversification benefit DB equals difference between actual portfolio risk and average risk of components. DB is a measurement for risk reduction. Because companies and investors are risk averse then risk reduction is valuable. In competitive and perfect capital markets there exists an equilibrium price for risk reduction. This chapter investigates the relation between diversification benefits, equilibrium risk premia and determination of equilibrium financial rates of return.

1. THE EFFICIENT FRONTIER AND THE MARKET PRICE FOR RISK

Figure 11.1 shows in panel 1 the risk-return profile for a two security portfolio. The profile shows that between A and B there is no dominance. Instead, risk trades-off for return between relatively low risk B and high risk A. The *feasible allocation set* of non-dominated portfolios containing securities A and B is the upper surface of the parabola. The profile also shows that the 100% B portfolio is not in the feasible allocation set. Instead, the investor that prefers a low risk and return position, say because of life-cycle effects, is better off to create a diversified portfolio by selling a little bit of low risk B and buying high risk A. Overall portfolio risk actually declines while return increases.

There are a lot more than two securities available for investment. Panel 2 overlays the risk-return profile for securities C and D. That risk-return profile has its own feasible allocation set. Similarly, there exist risk-return profiles and feasible allocation sets for two-security portfolios containing exclusively A and C, or A and D, or B and C. Combine 3 securities, say A+B+C, and there exists yet another feasible allocation set that projects a parabola onto panel 2. There are more than 10,000 publicly traded equities in the U.S.A., plus thousands of different bonds, and literally untold capital investment opportunities. For all of them exist little parabolas that map the feasible allocation sets. Panel 3 figuratively shows all of them. Panel 3 also shows that despite their number there nonetheless exists a *top of tops*.

FIGURE 11.1
Risk-return profiles and the Efficient frontier

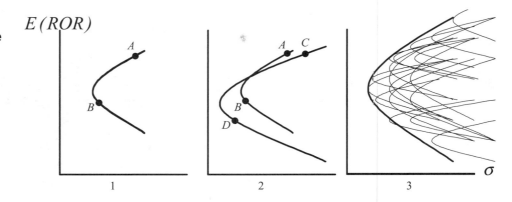

The set of points along the upper surface in panel 3 made from the highest reaches of all component feasible allocation sets is the *efficient frontier*.

> **DEFINITION 11.1 Efficient frontier**
> The *efficient frontier* is the set of portfolios that are not dominated and that are formed from all possible risky capital investments.

Discoverer of the efficient frontier concept is Harry Markowitz. For this work and subsequent development of *modern portfolio theory* Harry Markowitz received the 1990 Nobel Prize in Economic Science. Investment performance measurements often compare risk and return of specific investment strategies with the efficient frontier. A money manager is aware that obtaining a return and subjecting clients to an amount of risk that places his or her fund in the interior of the efficient frontier is not very good. Portfolios in the interior are dominated because their return is subpar compensation for their risk. Performance anywhere on the efficient frontier is excellent. Interpretation thus far suggests that all portfolios on the frontier coexist as trade-offs, none is better than the other, and the one that is best for any specific investor depends on personal risk-return preferences.

Next stop in development of modern portfolio theory is introduction of the risk-free asset. Figure 11.2 shows how this seemingly trivial technicality dramatically alters interpretations.

The risk-free rate of return $ROR^{risk\text{-}free}$ is a certain outcome that is uncorrelated with anything in the short-term. Chapter 9 reports that U.S. Treasury bills often are regarded as the world's most risk-free security. Purchase a T-bill and be assured of the rate of return irrespective of whether the stock market is up or down, or interest rates rise or fall, or economic activity swoons or booms. For the risk-free asset $\sigma_{rf} = 0$.

FIGURE 11.2
Efficient frontier and the Capital market line

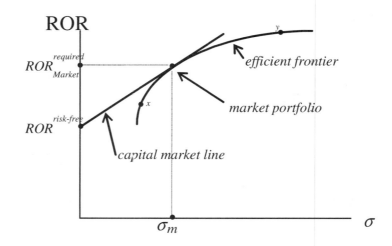

Consider an investment that forms a two-asset portfolio by combining the risk-free asset with portfolio X on the efficient frontier. Find shape of the resultant risk-return profile by applying formula 10.11 for actual portfolio risk:

$$\sigma_{portfolio} = \left\{ w^2_X \sigma^2_X + w^2_{rf} \quad \sigma^2_{rf} + 2w_X \sigma_X w_{rf} \quad \sigma_{rf} \rho_{X,rf} \right\}^{\frac{1}{2}}.$$

But the risk-free asset has σ_{rf} of zero and furthermore risk-free return is uncorrelated with anything so $\rho_{X,rf}$ equals zero, too. Simplify the preceding formula and find

$$\sigma_{portfolio} = w_X \sigma_X.$$

Allocate 20% of funds to X and 80% at $ROR^{risk-free}$. Actual portfolio risk equals 20% of σ_X. A 50% allocation gets 50% of X's risk; 90% in X gets 90% of X's risk. In other words, combining the risk-free asset with risky investment X yields a risk-return profile that is a straight line-of-averages connecting points $ROR^{risk-free}$ and X.

Notice the straight-line connecting points $ROR^{risk-free}$ and X (not shown) lies beneath the bold line coming out of $ROR^{risk-free}$ that is shown. Notice also that the straight-line connecting points $ROR^{risk-free}$ and Y (not shown) lies beneath the bold line. The bold line extending from $ROR^{risk-free}$ and *tangent* to the efficient frontier is special because it contains portfolios dominating all others on the diagram. This line is the *capital market line*.

> ### DEFINITION 11.2 Capital market line
> The *capital market line* is the set of portfolios that combine the risky portfolio at point of tangency on the efficient frontier with the risk-free asset. Portfolios on the capital market line are not dominated by any other capital investments.

Interpretation now suggests that one specific portfolio on the efficient frontier is better than all others. That specific portfolio at the point of tangency is the *market portfolio*. Market portfolio components include all possible risky capital assets where the weight in any one equals that asset's total market capitalization as a proportion of total global market cap. Nobody in the world really thinks that the *true* market portfolio actually exists in anybody's holdings. Investment constraints and a litany of causes suggest that mixing the market portfolio with the risk-free asset is an ideal but impractical outcome. Practically speaking, however, many financial professionals think of the market portfolio as a broad collection of securities like those in the SP500. Despite its impracticalities the capital market line concept enables important insights.

Let σ_m and $ROR^{required}_{Market}$ denote risk and required rate of return for the market portfolio. Slope of the capital market line is easily found as rise over run.

> ### FORMULA 11.1 Market price for risk
> The slope of the capital market line measures the equilibrium *price for risk*.
>
> $$\begin{pmatrix} Slope\ of\ the \\ capital\ market\ line \end{pmatrix} = \frac{ROR^{required}_{Market} - ROR^{risk-free}}{\sigma_m}$$
>
> $$= \frac{market\ risk\ premium}{\%total\ market\ risk}.$$

Recall formula 10.1 defining $ROR^{required}$ and realize that numerator of formula 11.1 measures required *risk premium* for the market portfolio. The denominator measures market portfolio risk. Slope of the capital market line measures required risk premium per unit of risk for the market portfolio and represents the equilibrium *price for risk*.

Suppose the risk-free rate on T-bills, for example, is 5% and the required return on the market portfolio is 12%. The market risk premium equals 7% (= 12% - 5%). Investors for this scenario choose between investing in risk-free T-bills offering 5% or investing in the risky market portfolio returning 12% (or some combination of both). The 7% risk premium is the consensus required compensation for bearing extra risk. Suppose also that σ_m = 21%. Slope of the capital market line equals $\frac{1}{3}$ (= 7% ÷ 21%). The market price for one percentage point of risk is 33 basis points (= $\frac{1}{3} \times 1\%$). Equilibrium trade-off on a $100 marginal investment for accepting an extra percentage point of risk is 33 cents of extra return (= $100 × 0.0033).

Risk-free rate of return $ROR^{risk-free}$ has a special place on the capital market line and plays a significant role for financial equilibrium. $ROR^{required}$ for any capital investment equals risk-free rate $ROR^{risk-free}$ plus a risk premium (see formula 10.1). Chapter 10 also reports that at the limit, two types of risk exist: risk that can be managed or eliminated (idiosyncratic) and risk that can't (systematic). Formula 11.2 restates $ROR^{required}$ as a function of idiosyncratic and systematic risk.

FORMULA 11.2 Required rate of return $ROR^{required}$ and component risk premia

The "required rate of return" is the minimum discount rate that an investor willingly accepts for computing intrinsic value. The required rate of return for any capital investment A denoted $ROR_A^{required}$ equals the risk-free rate plus that asset's risk premium:

$$ROR_A^{required} = ROR^{risk-free} + (security\ risk\ premium)_A$$

where $ROR^{risk-free}$ is the short-term risk-free rate and

$$\begin{pmatrix} security \\ risk \\ premium \end{pmatrix}_A = f \left\{ \begin{pmatrix} systematic \\ risk \\ premium \end{pmatrix}_A , \overbrace{\begin{pmatrix} liquidity \\ risk \\ premium \end{pmatrix}_A , \begin{pmatrix} term \\ risk \\ premium \end{pmatrix}_A , \begin{pmatrix} default \\ risk \\ premium \end{pmatrix}_A}^{sources\ of\ idiosyncratic\ risk} \right\}$$

The implicit function f{.} depends upon all possible sources of systematic and idiosyncratic risk in ways that are not fully understood. The function shows one source of systematic risk (but there may be more) and three sources of idiosyncratic risk (these are the main ones but there may be more of these, too). The systematic risk premium relates directly to the market price for risk from the *Capital market line*. Security investment occurs when $ROR^{required}$ is less than $ROR^{expected}$ (see rule 9.1).

Formula 11.2 expresses the risk premium as a function of different risk sources. The explicit mechanism by which risk premium depends on risk sources is unknown. Hence, the function is *implicit*. Many times finance practitioners adopt an *ad hoc* approach and simply add together premia for different factors that affect a specific security. For example, perhaps an analyst concludes that a specific small cap stock commands a 7% systematic risk premium and 1½% liquidity risk premium for a total risk premium of 850 basis points. Find $ROR^{required}$ by adding 8.5% to the risk-free rate and consider the investment a buy if $ROR^{expected} >$ $ROR^{required}$.

While much remains unknown about how different risk sources determine the security risk premium a lot nonetheless is known. Later lessons relate systematic risk premia to the market price of risk. First, however, consider determination of the benchmark risk-free rate of return.

1. Analysts tell you that the risk-free rate of return equals 5.0% and the market portfolio's required rate of return and risk (standard deviation) equal 11.0% and 24%, respectively. Compute according to the *Capital market line* the equilibrium price for risk. For an increase in personal portfolio risk of five percentage points (and no extra diversification benefit) how much is the increase in required risk premium. ©AP11b

2. The risk-free rate of return equals 3.0% and the market portfolio's required rate of return and risk (standard deviation) equal 12.5% and 14.0%, respectively. Suppose that the equilibrium price for risk computes according to the *Capital market line*. Your objective is to combine the risk-free asset with the market portfolio in order to create a portfolio with required return equal to 4.9%. Find the allocation that satisfies your objective. ©AP12

3. The risk-free rate of return equals 3.5% and the market portfolio's required rate of return and risk (standard deviation) equal 8.0% and 17.0%, respectively. Suppose that the equilibrium price for risk computes according to the *Capital market line*. Your objective is to combine the risk-free asset with the market portfolio in order to create a portfolio with standard deviation of returns equal to 12%. Find the allocation that satisfies your objective. ©AP13

4. The risk-free rate of return equals 4.0% and the market portfolio's required rate of return and risk (standard deviation) equal 8.5% and 16.5%, respectively. Suppose that the equilibrium price for risk computes according to the *Capital market line*. Your objective is to combine the risk-free asset with the market portfolio in order to create a portfolio that earns a risk premium of 3.9%. Find the allocation that satisfies your objective. ©AP14

2. EQUILIBRIUM RATES OF RETURN FOR CREDIT MARKET SECURITIES

Financial studies establish that over time market rates of return and risk premia change. Presumable causes relate to shifts in investor confidence, overall market liquidity, and any of myriad factors influencing buy-side demand or sell-side supply for financial securities. Preceding lessons establish that $ROR^{risk-free}$ is a core rate important for explaining financial equilibrium. Figure 11.3 shows supply and demand schedules driving determination of the short-term risk-free rate $ROR^{risk-free}$. The explanation below is adaptation of a theory described by Irving Fisher in 1930 and coined the *loanable funds theory of interest*.

Buy-side demand for securities is shown as demand schedule D_0. Buy-side demand emanates from institutional investors plus households. Participants on the buy-side for securities are investors, also known as savers. The buy-side for *securities* is another way of describing the supply-side for *loanable funds*.

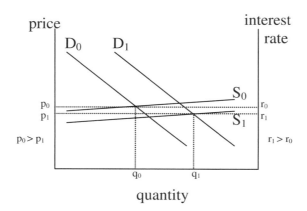

FIGURE 11.3
Supply and demand schedules for risk-free credit market securities

Sell-side supply for credit market *securities* generally includes the companies and government entities that issue securities for borrowing money. For exclusive consideration of risk-free securities, however, the only supplier is the U.S. Treasury. The Treasury competes with private sector companies for *loanable funds*. Supply schedule S_0 for risk-free securities represents demand for loanable funds. Slope of the supply schedule is important for quantitative insights but for most qualitative lessons below the steepness is irrelevant. It's drawn flat (elastic) to look similar to figure 9.1 in the discussion about buy-side demand and sell-side supply for financial securities.

With original supply and demand schedules S_0 and D_0 the equilibrium price and quantity of risk-free securities equal p_0 and q_0, respectively. Time value lessons teach that for a given cash flow stream there is a one-to-one relation between price and rate of return. Risk-free rate r_0 associates with price p_0. For example, with a risk-free security maturing in 1 year and equilibrium price p_0 of $950 (for principal of $1,000) equilibrium risk-free rate r_0 equals 5.26% (= $1,000 ÷ $950 − 1, see formula 4.5).

Over time stuff happens that shifts supply and/or demand schedules. For the moment suppose they shift to S_1 and D_1. The figure illustrates that the equilibrium price and quantity change to p_1 and q_1, respectively. For the way these curves are drawn (supply is pretty flat) there is a relatively large increase in equilibrium quantity. Equilibrium price, however, declines only slightly ($p_0 > p_1$). Suppose, for example, that price declines from p_0 of $950 to p_1 of $940. The new equilibrium risk-free rate r_1 equals 6.38% (= $1,000 ÷ $940 − 1). Price relates inversely with interest rates, $r_1 > r_0$, and numbers along the right "Interest rate" vertical axis get bigger toward the bottom.

Chapter 9 discusses buy-side participants and factors affecting them. A few buy-side considerations are mentioned here.

Credit market competition for loanable funds: During an economic expansion companies borrow money for purchasing plant and equipment and other factors of production from stakeholders. Households, too, borrow money for improvements and competition for loanable funds heats up. Private sector borrowing crowds out the government and the demand curve D_0 shifts left as private credit market securities substitute in portfolios for risk-free securities. For a given supply schedule S_0 the equilibrium security price declines and equilibrium $ROR^{risk-free}$ increases (irrespective of supply schedule slope). Conversely, during economic contractions there are not many private credit market securities, risk-free securities become the only game in town, demand curve shifts right toward D_1 and equilibrium $ROR^{risk-free}$ declines.

Confidence or nervousness: Political and economic world events sometimes trigger a flight to quality. Risk-free Treasury securities are the safest, highest quality possible investment. Nervousness causes the demand curve to shift right, say to D_1. For a given supply schedule S_0 the equilibrium price rises and short-term risk-free rate $ROR^{risk-free}$ declines (irrespective of supply schedule slope). Conversely, an increase in buy-side confidence for alternative investments shifts the demand curve for risk-free securities left, equilibrium price falls, and equilibrium $ROR^{risk-free}$ rises.

Now consider outcomes when there is a shift in sell-side supply of risk-free credit market securities.

Government surpluses and deficits: When tax revenues are insufficient for paying government expenditures then the Treasury issues securities and borrows loanable funds. This shifts the supply schedule for risk-free credit market securities rightward toward S_1. For a given demand schedule D_0 the equilibrium price declines and risk-free rate $ROR^{risk-free}$ rises (irrespective of supply schedule slope). Conversely, when the rare surplus occurs then the supply curve shifts left, equilibrium price rises, and equilibrium $ROR^{risk-free}$ falls.

Preceding explanations are simplifications of complex economic phenomena about which many complications exist. Especially confusing is when both supply and demand curves shift or when feedback effects exist. When both schedules shift then qualitative outcomes depend on relative steepness of the schedules. Consider complicating feedback effects from government deficits. Perhaps Congress cuts taxes and the deficit grows (S shifts right and $ROR^{risk-free}$ rises) but the tax cut stimulates private sector economic activity (D shifts left and $ROR^{risk-free}$ rises) and then eventually tax revenues rise (and S shifts left) thereby pushing $ROR^{risk-free}$ lower than it began. There are many stories that one can tell about complex economic phenomena, some more plausible than others. Seldom are outcomes definite and certain.

2.A. Risk-free rate of return and the term premium

By definition the rate $ROR^{risk-free}$ has zero risk premium. Satisfying the definition requires a very short-term security that is very liquid with absolutely no default risk. For most applications short-term Treasury bills satisfy the definition. Financial markets received a tiny jolt toward year-end 2004 when political deadlock in Congress led to inaction raising the government debt ceiling. That led to the remote possibility that the Treasury would lack authority to borrow additional money necessary for repaying principal coming due. Inability to repay principal means *default!* Financial mavens around the globe questioned whether U.S. Treasury securities should continue to be considered default free or whether instead investors should insist on a default risk premium. A rising default risk premium increases government borrowing costs. Congress quit bickering and raised the debt ceiling, the Treasury issued securities to satisfy current obligations, and the question receded to the back burner. Competitive markets, not the government, determine T-bill rates (the government decides how much to borrow). Perhaps buy-side demand for Treasury securities requires a tiny default premium but $ROR^{risk-free}$ does not.

Formula 11.2 shows that $ROR^{required}$ depends on systematic and idiosyncratic risk sources. For the risk-free rate the default and liquidity risk premia are nil and, for reasons discussed later, the systematic risk premium also is zero. There is, however, a term risk premium within $ROR^{risk-free}$. Figure 11.4 allows comparison of interest rates for 20-year Treasury bonds and 30-day bills with the inflation rate and

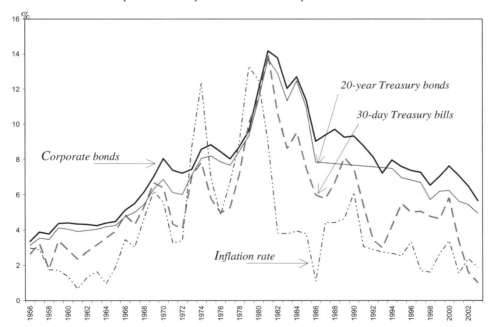

FIGURE 11.4
Inflation and interest rates for corporate bonds and U.S. government securities.

Notes: The *inflation rate* is the annual percentage change in Consumer Price Index for All Urban Consumers: All Items. *Corporate bond rate* is the annual average of monthly Moody's Seasoned Aaa Corporate Bond Yield. 20-year constant maturity Treasury bond data is not available 1987-1993. Source data are from Federal Reserve Bank of St. Louis. Interest rate series Aaa is copyright by Moody's Investors Service.

high-quality corporate bond rates. Rates on the 20-year Treasury bond average about 1.25% higher than the 30-day rate. The term premium, as chapter 9 explains, depends on many dynamic factors among which inflation and future expectations are most important. The 30-day T-bill rate is an annual rate and even though inflation over 30 days is not "huge" the inflation premium gets big when annualized. With double-digit inflation around 1980 annual rates on 30-day T-bills exceeded $14\frac{1}{2}\%$.

Risk-free rates exclude risk premia for all sources of systematic and idiosyncratic risk *except* term. The term risk premium relates to *time* and risk-free securities embody time so they cannot be *totally* risk-free. They are, however, free of default risk, liquidity risk, etc. Throughout the past half-century variation in short-term risk-free rates occurs largely because of the inflation component in the term premium. Formula 11.3 shows $ROR_N^{risk-free}$, the equilibrium risk-free rate for a highly liquid and default-free security that matures in N periods.

FORMULA 11.3 Nominal risk-free rate $ROR^{risk-free}$ and the *inflation premium*

The observable short-term, very liquid, default free interest rate is *nominal $ROR^{risk-free}$*. Relation between the rate for a risk-free security maturing in N periods ($N \geq 1$), denoted $ROR_N^{risk-free}$, and term risk premium approximates as follows:

$$ROR_N^{risk-free} = \begin{pmatrix} short-term \\ real\ risk-free \\ interest\ rate \end{pmatrix} + \begin{pmatrix} term\ risk\ premium \\ for\ N-period \\ horizon \end{pmatrix}$$

For the special case when the inflation premium is the only component in the term risk premium:

$$ROR_N^{risk-free} = \begin{pmatrix} short-term \\ real\ risk-free \\ interest\ rate \end{pmatrix} + \left(\sum_{t=1}^{N} \frac{(inflation\ rate)_t}{N} \right).$$

The *inflation premium* equals the arithmetic average periodic inflation rate expected throughout term N. Short-term nominal risk-free interest rate $ROR^{risk-free}$ is identical to $ROR_1^{risk-free}$.

Today a significant amount of complex financial research is investigating determinants of term risk. Future research undoubtedly will reveal many important and fundamental lessons about the term structure of risk premia. For current purposes, however, consider the special case when inflation is the only component in the term risk premium.

EXAMPLE 1 Find risk-free interest rates given the real rate and expected inflation rates

The short-term <u>real</u> risk-free interest rate averages 4%. Suppose that expected inflation is 3% over the next year, 6% during the second year, and 8% thereafter for 2 years after which it drops to 5% per year perpetually. Given that inflation is the only component of the term premium for risk-free securities find today's interest rates for risk-free securities with terms of 1 to 5 years. Also, what is the rate on a 20-year risk-free security?

SOLUTION

The risk-free rate $ROR_N^{risk-free}$ equals 4% plus the inflation premium over the next N years. That means $ROR^{risk-free}$ is 7% (that is, $ROR_1^{risk-free} = 4\% + 3\%$). Inflation premium on a two-year bond is 4.5% [= (3% + 6%)/2] so the two-year bond rate $ROR_2^{risk-free}$ is 8.5%. Inflation premium on a three-year bond is 5.7% [= (3% + 6% + 8%)/2] so the three-year bond rate $ROR_3^{risk-free}$ is 9.7%. Likewise, for 4 and

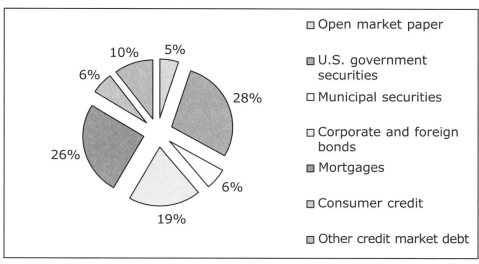

FIGURE 11.5
Components of U.S. credit market securities

Open market paper

U.S. government securities

Municipal securities

Corporate and foreign bonds

Mortgages

Consumer credit

Other credit market debt

Notes: The credit market total is $29,471 billion at 12/31/2001. Data are from the Board of Governors of the Federal Reserve System, "Flow of Funds Accounts for the United States", table L4.

5–year risk-free securities the rates equal 10.25% [= 4% + (3% + 6% + 8% + 8%)/4] and 10.0% [= 4% + (3% + 6% + 8% + 8% + 5%)/5], respectively. The 20-year risk-free rate $ROR_{20}^{risk\text{-}free}$ is 9.25% [= 4% + (3% + 6% + 8% + 8% + 16 × 5%)/20].

2.B. Other credit market securities

Chapter 9 discusses the many types of credit market securities and figure 11.5 shows their share of the U.S. credit market. Two types of securities sum to more than half the credit market: U.S. Treasury securities (28%) and mortgages (26%). Already the preceding subsection discusses required returns for risk-free Treasury securities. Financial analysts often compute required rates of return for credit market securities by adding risk premia to the risk-free return.

Two procedures exist for adding risk premia to the risk-free rate and they usually lead to different answers. One approach adds risk premia to short-term $ROR^{risk\text{-}free}$ per formula 11.2. The other approach adds risk premia to $ROR_N^{risk\text{-}free}$ where N is the term of the credit market security under analysis. The difference pertains exclusively to handling the term risk premium. Strict application of formula 11.2 requires measuring the term premium for the security under analysis. For example, the term premium for a 20-year mortgage equals the excess by which the 20-year mortgage rate exceeds the rate on an otherwise identical short-term mortgage security. On the other hand if the analyst believes that $ROR_{20}^{risk\text{-}free}$ properly embodies the term risk premium applicable to a 20-year mortgage then the analyst adds to the 20-year Treasury rate a default risk premium, liquidity risk premium, etc. The spread between long-term and short-term mortgages often correlates over time with the spread between long-term and short-term Treasury securities. But sometimes it doesn't. An internet search for "risk premium" finds hundreds of thousands of hits. The issue is extremely important to companies as well as to finance professors – much remains unknown about determination of risk premia.

EXERCISES 11.2

1. The short-term <u>real</u> risk-free interest rate averages 3.0%. Suppose that expected inflation is 5.6% over the next year, 5.9% during the second year, and 6.2% thereafter perpetually. Inflation is the only component of the term premium for risk-free securities. Find today's interest rates for risk-free securities with terms of 2 years, 4 years and 20-years. ©AP15

3. EQUILIBRIUM RATES OF RETURN FOR EQUITY MARKET SECURITIES

Formula 11.2 properly specifies the required rate of return and risk premium for any and all capital investments. For equity securities previous lessons on diversification benefits are very helpful. For the special limiting case when all sources of idiosyncratic risk distribute like white-noise across all securities then diversification completely eliminates idiosyncratic risk. Only systematic risk remains in the market portfolio. For that special limiting case formula 11.2 simplifies as shown below.

When all idiosyncratic risk vanishes through diversification then idiosyncratic risk is irrelevant for determining required rates of return. This does not mean that idiosyncratic risk does not exist. Rather, idiosyncratic risk merits zero compensation because it vanishes in well-diversified portfolios. Definition 10.2 states that systematic risk is unaffected by diversification strategies but that security sensitivities to systematic risk vary. Correlation coefficient $\rho_{A,Market}$ directly measures that sensitivity.

Risk for security A equals σ_A. Lessons from chapter 9 show that combining two assets creates diversification benefit DB. As correlation between assets diminishes then DB increases. Formula 11.4 shows that all of σ_A does not merit compensation because adding A to the market portfolio possibly creates DB and some of A's risk vanishes. Correlation coefficient $\rho_{A,Market}$ measures proportion of σ_A that receives the market price for risk.

FORMULA 11.4 Systematic risk premium and the market price for risk

The required rate of return for any capital investment A denoted $ROR_A^{required}$ equals short-term risk-free rate $ROR^{risk\text{-}free}$ plus that asset's risk premium. When idiosyncratic risk may be eliminated completely through diversification and only one source of systematic risk exists then:

$$ROR_A^{required} = ROR^{risk\text{-}free} + \rho_{A,Market}\, \sigma_A \overbrace{\left(\frac{ROR_{market}^{required} - ROR^{risk\text{-}free}}{\sigma_m} \right)}^{\text{systematic risk premium for security } A}$$

$$= ROR^{risk\text{-}free} + \rho_{A,Market}\, \sigma_A \left(\begin{array}{c} market\ price \\ for\ risk \end{array} \right).$$

Rates of return for security A carry risk σ_A. Correlation between rates of return for A and the market portfolio equals $\rho_{A,Market}$. The *market price for risk* equals slope of the *Capital market line* and represents required return per unit of risk. The correlation coefficient $\rho_{A,Market}$ measures the proportion of A's risk that requires the market price for risk.

EXAMPLE 2 Find required rate of return given the risk-free rate and summary statistics

Suppose the risk-free rate on T-bills is 5% and the required return on the market portfolio is 12%. Suppose also that $\sigma_m = 21\%$ and that risk for security X is $\sigma_x = 27\%$. Correlation $\rho_{X,Market}$ between X and the market portfolio is 0.40. Find the risk premium and required rate of return for security X.

SOLUTION

The market price for risk equals the market risk premium of 7% (= 12% − 5%) divided by market risk σ_m and equals $\frac{1}{3}$. Risk σ_x equals 27% and if each percentage point of risk received the equilibrium market price for risk then the risk premium for X would equal 9% (= 27% × 1/3). Because correlation $\rho_{X,Market}$ equals 0.40, however, the risk premium only equals 3.6% (= 9% × 0.40). Thus, $ROR_X^{required}$ is 8.6% (= 5% + 3.6%).

Formula 11.4 shows that the systematic risk premium for security A equals σ_A times $\rho_{A,Market}$ times market price for risk. When $\rho_{A,Market}$ equals zero then systematic risk premium equals zero. Solve formula 11.4 with $\rho_{A,Market} = 0$ and find that $ROR_A^{required}$ equals $ROR^{risk\text{-}free}$ irrespective of security risk. Similarly set $\rho_{A,Market} = 1$ and solve formula 11.4. Find that securities that correlate perfectly with the market portfolio receive the full market price of risk for every unit of risk σ_A.

Figure 11.6 illustrates rays for different correlation coefficients. The topmost line passing from $ROR^{risk\text{-}free}$ through $ROR_{market}^{required}$ is the capital market line. Its slope measures the market price for risk as in formula 11.1. The figure labels the market portfolio. The efficient frontier (not shown) is tangent to the capital market line at the market portfolio. All securities that correlate perfectly with the market portfolio lie on the ray coincident with the capital market line. No specific security lies on this ray further out than the market portfolio, however, because all specific capital investments lie on or inside the efficient frontier. No portfolio on the efficient frontier is dominated by any specific capital investment (panel 3 in figure 11.1 illustrates this principle).

Securities X and Y lie on the same ray because their correlation coefficients with the market portfolio are equal at 0.83. Eighty-three percent of their respective risks, σ_x and σ_y, command the market price for risk. Slope for this particular ray containing securities X and Y equals 83 percent of the capital market line slope. Along any ray of correlation for which ρ exceeds zero the required rate of return increases with security risk. But when $\rho \leq 0$ the situation changes. Security Z in figure 11.6 is uncorrelated with the market portfolio ($\rho_{Z,Market} = 0$) and hence the risk premium for Z is zero. The ray stretching horizontally from $ROR^{risk\text{-}free}$ contains all securities that are uncorrelated with the market portfolio. Some securities may have lower σ than others and vice versa. For all of them, however, the required rate of return equals the short-term risk-free rate. Securities with $\rho = 0$ contribute absolutely zero risk to a well-diversified market portfolio so zero percent of their risk merits a premium.

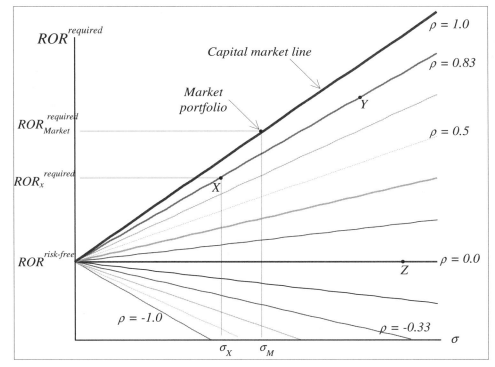

FIGURE 11.6
Capital market line and the rays of correlation

Notes: Coefficient ρ measures correlation between rates of return for the market portfolio and a specific security. All securities with the same ρ are pushed onto the respective ray of correlation. Correlation coefficients between the market portfolio and securities X and Y equal 0.83. Consequently, their required rates of return align onto the same ray. Eighty-three percent of their respective risks, σ_x and σ_y, require compensation at the market price for risk. Because $\sigma_x < \sigma_y$ then $ROR_x^{required} < ROR_y^{required}$. For security Z the risk σ_z is even higher but $ROR_Z^{required}$ equals $ROR^{risk\text{-}free}$ because Z is uncorrelated with the market portfolio and merits zero risk premium.

Many securities possess high risk σ while also having low required rates of return. Any security A for which $\sigma_A > \sigma_M$ and $ROR_A^{required} < ROR_{Market}^{required}$ is dominated by the market portfolio. The entire area southwest of the market portfolio represents bad stand-alone investments. Investors with a poorly diversified portfolio that hold high-risk securities with low market correlation subject themselves to sub-par compensation for amount of risk carried.

Securities that correlate negatively with the market portfolio would lie on rays that slope downward. Required rates of return for these securities would be less than the risk-free rate (systematic risk premia would be negative). But if such securities existed then this specific source of systematic risk could be eliminated by diversification. This specific systematic risk factor would become just another type of idiosyncratic risk that could be diversified away. By definition, however, systematic risk does not vanish through diversification. Perhaps today there are several sources of systematic risk, some affecting credit markets and others equity markets. Financial research that study different sources of systematic risk are *multifactor* risk models. As financial markets evolve and create new securities then arguably the number of systematic risk sources declines. Almost certainly there were many more types of systematic nondiversifiable risk factors a century ago than exist today. The many sources of idiosyncratic risk that exist today probably were systematic risk sources long ago – growth of financial markets creates diversification benefits.

EXAMPLE 3 Analyze two securities for by comparing $ROR^{required}$ with $ROR^{expected}$

You want to add one additional stock to your well-diversified portfolio and are considering two alternatives. Information about stock A leads you to believe that its expected rate of return is 10%, the standard deviation of expected returns is 38%, and that its correlation with the market portfolio is 0.35. For stock B those figures are $ROR^{expected} = 12\%$, $\sigma_B = 32\%$, and $\rho_{B,Market} = 0.90$. The risk-free rate is 5%, the required return for the market portfolio is 11%, and $\sigma_M = 22\%$. Determine which one of these securities, if either, should be added to your portfolio.

SOLUTION

Rule 9.1 provides the investment decision rule to invest when expected rate of return exceeds required rate of return. For this example notice that stock A has lower expected return than B and also $\sigma_A > \sigma_B$. Figure 11.7 shows this situation. Comparison of A directly with B suggests that B dominates A and that therefore B is a better choice for addition to the portfolio. That analysis is incomplete and wrong!

FIGURE 11.7
Expected return and σ for example 3

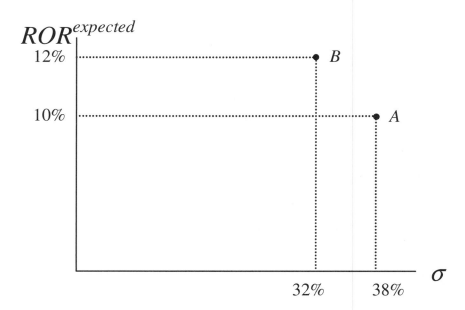

Lessons above establish that σ does not properly measure risk relevant for determining risk premia due to existence of diversification benefits. The illustration of dominance in figure 11.7 is misleading. The portion of σ that represents relevant risk is measured by the correlation coefficient with the market portfolio. Use formula 11.4 to find *required* rates of return and subsequently compare them to *expected* rates of return.

Compute that the market price for risk equals the market risk premium of 6% (= 11% − 5%) divided by market risk σ_m and equals 0.2727. Compute that $ROR_A^{required}$ equals 8.63% [= 5% + (0.35 × 38% × 0.2727]. Security A is a reasonable choice for addition to a well-diversified portfolio because $ROR_A^{expected}$ > $ROR_A^{required}$. Compute that $ROR_B^{required}$ equals 12.85% [= 5% + (0.90 × 32% × 0.2727]. The 12% expected rate of return for B does not fully compensate for its relevant risk; that is, $ROR_B^{expected}$ < $ROR_B^{required}$ so do not buy B. Add security A to your portfolio. The impression from figure 11.7 that B dominates A is a mirage.

3.A. Beta and the Capital asset pricing model

The maxim that high risk gets high return does not apply when using σ to measure risk. Correlation between security and market rates of return reduce risk and create diversification benefits. Rearrange formula 11.4 for $ROR^{required}$ and find an alternative risk measure: *beta (β)*.

FORMULA 11.5 Beta and the *Capital asset pricing model ("CAPM")*

The required risk premium for any capital investment A equals required rate of return $ROR_A^{required}$ minus short-term risk-free rate $ROR^{risk-free}$. When idiosyncratic risk may be eliminated completely through diversification and only one source of systematic risk exists then the ratio of security to market risk premia is

$$\beta_A = \frac{\text{systematic risk premium for security A}}{\text{risk premium for market portfolio}}$$

$$= \frac{covariance_{A,Market}}{\sigma^2_{market}}. \quad (11.5a)$$

Rearrange the top line and obtain a formula known as the *Capital asset pricing model*:

$$ROR_A^{required} = ROR^{risk-free} + \overbrace{\beta_A \left(ROR_{market}^{required} - ROR^{risk-free}\right)}^{\text{systematic risk premium for security A}}. \quad (11.5b)$$

β_A measures proportion of market risk premium applicable to security A.

Inspection of *CAPM* formula 11.5b shows that required returns increase with beta. When $\beta_A = 0$ then the security systematic risk premium is zero and $ROR_A^{required}$ = $ROR^{risk-free}$. When β is 1.0 then the security risk premium equals 100% the market portfolio risk premium. This linear relation between security required rate of return and beta is shown in figure 11.8 as the *Security market line*.

DEFINITION 11.3 *Security market line (SML)*

The *Security market line* is the graph showing the required rate of return as a linear function of the equity β. Slope of the SML equals the required risk premium for the market portfolio, $ROR_{Market}^{required} - ROR^{risk-free}$.

When idiosyncratic risk may be eliminated completely through diversification and only one source of systematic risk exists then the security risk premium rises

FIGURE 11.8
The Security market line

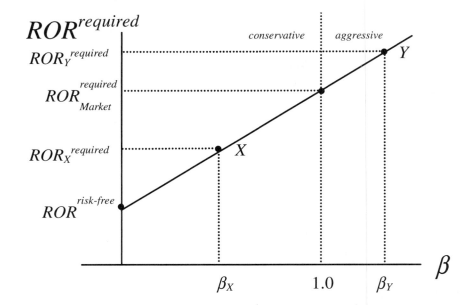

proportionately with β. The slope of the security market line equals the required risk premium for the market portfolio. Securities with $\beta < 1$, such as security X in figure 11.8, possess relatively low systematic risk. These securities are known as *conservative* securities and observations show that they tend to be less volatile than the overall market. Securities with $\beta > 1$, such as security Y in figure 11.8, possess relatively high systematic risk and require risk premium bigger than the market portfolio. These relatively high-risk securities are known as *aggressive* securities and they tend to be more volatile than market. Some conservative securities may have low σ and others have high σ – likewise for aggressive securities. Some conservative securities may have higher σ than aggressive securities! β not σ measures risk relevant for the systematic security risk premium.

EXAMPLE 4 Revisit example 3 that compares for two securities $ROR^{required}$ with $ROR^{expected}$

The previous example says that for stock A the expected rate of return is 10%, $\sigma_A = 38\%$, and $\rho_{A,Market} = 0.35$. For stock B those figures are $ROR^{expected} = 12\%$, $\sigma_B = 32\%$, and $\rho_{B,Market} = 0.90$. The risk-free rate is 5%, the required return for the market portfolio is 11%, and $\sigma_M = 22\%$. Find betas and required rates of return for these securities.

SOLUTION

Formula 11.5a computes β as the ratio of covariance between security and market returns divided by variance of market returns. Covariance between any two variables always has the same sign as their correlation coefficient (see discussion at formula 10.12). The difference is that ρ takes on values exclusively between -1 and +1 whereas covariance takes on a number about as big as the variable measurements squared. Formula 10.12 shows that $covariance_{x,y} = \rho_{x,y} \times \sigma_x \times \sigma_y$. Substitute this into formula 11.5a:

$$\beta_A = \frac{\overbrace{0.35 \times 0.38 \times 0.22}^{covariance_{A,Market}}}{0.22^2} = 0.6045.$$

Security A has a beta smaller than 1 and is therefore a conservative security. Investment in A requires a risk premium equal to 60.45% the market premium. That is,

$$ROR_A^{required} = 5\% + 0.6045\,(11\% - 5\%) = 8.63\%.$$

The expected rate of return for security A of 10% exceeds the required return so it's a buy. Perform analogous computations for security B.

$$\beta_B = \frac{\overbrace{0.90 \times 0.32 \times 0.22}^{covariance_{B,Market}}}{0.22^2} = 1.3091,$$

and

$$ROR_B{}^{required} = 5\% + 1.3091 \,(11\% - 5\%) = 12.85\%.$$

The 12% expected rate of return for B does not fully compensate for its relevant risk; that is, $ROR_B{}^{expected} < ROR_B{}^{required}$ so put B on the *sell* list.

Numbers obtained here support identical inferences as example 3. Add security A to your portfolio and avoid B. The illusion from figure 11.7 that B dominates A is a mirage that easily corrects by substituting measurement of risk by β instead of σ. See figure 11.9.

β measures systematic risk and so figure 11.9 is a risk-return graph. Definitely there is no dominance in figure 11.9 between securities A and B. Instead, the decision about which security is best depends on something that is not on the graph. It depends on the equilibrium price for risk and market risk premium. When we take those factors into consideration as formula 11.5b stipulates then a clear decision emerges: security A is worth adding to a well-diversified portfolio and B is not.

The required rate of return is the minimum discount rate an investor willingly accepts for computing intrinsic value. Once the investor obtains $ROR^{required}$ then information about expected cash flows may be collected and intrinsic value computed. This chapter presents many lessons about finding required rates of return for different situations. When the *CAPM* situation fits, namely idiosyncratic risk is perfectly diversifiable and only one source of systematic risk exists, then formula 11.5b provides a discount rate useful for finding intrinsic value. The example below combines the *CAPM* with the constant growth dividend valuation model from chapter 8.

EXAMPLE 5 Effect of company policy change on $ROR^{required}$ and intrinsic value
The company conducts a study that finds their digital products division is less volatile than their traditional magazine division. The study concludes that expan-

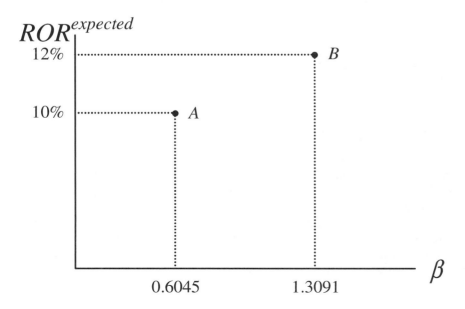

FIGURE 11.9
Expected return and β for examples 3 & 4

sion of the digital products division will diminish company beta to 0.80 from 1.20. The profit margin is lower for digital products, however, and the expansion will diminish dividend growth rate to 5% from 7%. Suppose that the required rate of return for the market portfolio is 14%, that the risk-free rate is 6%, and that a $2.00 dividend was just paid. Assume that the stock price equals the present value of dividends when discounted by the required rate of return from the CAPM. Find the effect of the policy change on the stock price.

SOLUTION
This solution relies on dividend valuation formula 8.8 for finding intrinsic value:

$$V_0 = div_0 (1 + g)/(r - g)$$

The solution strategy computes intrinsic value before and after the policy change. The setup directly states all variables for V_o except for the discount rate r which obtains from the CAPM formula. Before the policy change find the required rate of return:

$$ROR^{required} = 6\% + 1.20 (14\% - 6\%) = 15.6\%.$$

Find intrinsic value before the policy change

$$V_o^{before} = \$2.00(1 + 0.07) / (0.156 - 0.07) = \$24.88.$$

After the policy change the dividend growth rate drops to 5% and β falls to 0.80. Find the new required rate of return

$$ROR^{required} = 6\% + 0.80 (14\% - 6\%) = 12.4\%$$

and new intrinsic value

$$V_o^{after} = \$2.00(1 + 0.05) / (0.124 - 0.05) = \$28.38.$$

This policy change increases the price by 14.0% (= $28.38 ÷ $24.88 − 1).

Financial market equilibrium occurs when required and expected returns are equal. The required return includes the risk premium. The expected return is the internal rate of return that equates actual price with expected cash flows. The example below applies these fundamental lessons in a simple problem.

EXAMPLE 6 Compute $ROR^{expected}$ from information and $ROR^{required}$ from CAPM and buy or sell
The company beta is 1.25, its dividend growth rate is 6%, just yesterday it paid a dividend of $0.70, and today's share price is $12.50. Most likely today's share price equals today's intrinsic value. Furthermore, the share price moves in accordance with the dividend constant growth model. The economy wide risk free interest rate is 5% and the required risk premium for the market portfolio is 8%. The stock represents a good investment if the expected total rate of return implied by the dividend constant growth model exceeds the required rate of return implied by the capital asset pricing model. Determine whether the stock is a *buy* or *sell*.

SOLUTION

This solution relies on dividend valuation formula 8.8 and solves for the unknown discount rate r. That discount rate is the *expected* rate of return from the stock investment. Substitute numerical settings into the valuation formula:

$$V_0 = div_0(1 + g)/(r - g),$$

$$\$12.50 = \$0.70 \ (1 + 0.06) \ / \ (r + 0.06) \ or \ r = 11.94\%.$$

$ROR^{expected}$ is 6 basis points shy of 12%. Find $ROR^{required}$ with the *CAPM* formula:

$$ROR^{required} = 5\% + 1.25 \ (8\%) = 15.0\%.$$

When the stock is added to a well-diversified portfolio the required return is 15%. The expected return is about 12% and does not compensate for risk. That puts the stock on the *sell* list. Realize that the stock fares even worse in a poorly diversified portfolio.

A1. Estimating β and risk-adjusted returns

Common and well-tested approaches for estimating company beta rely on historical stock returns. Typically a broad index such as the SP500 proxies for return on the market portfolio. That market rate of return serves as explanatory variable and security stock returns serve as the dependent variable. Estimation procedures usually ignore data on $ROR^{risk-free}$ because T-bill rates move so little during any reasonable sample period that the data do not contribute accuracy to the estimation. A typical sample period for estimating β may include 30 monthly or 120 daily observations. Fortunately, the *BAII Plus*© calculator allows simple computation of β from a few observations and teaches procedural fundamentals.

Suppose that five periodic rates of return for security A and for the overall market portfolio are these:

	ROR1	ROR2	ROR3	ROR4	ROR5
Security A	18%	-4%	6%	21%	5%
Market	15%	-2%	7%	16%	5%

Use the accompanying *Calculator clue* and easily compute that $\beta_A = 1.36$. This particular application of the *CAPM* that regresses security returns on market returns is *the market model*.

The best estimate for β from the market model suggests that security *A* requires a systematic risk premium that is 136.36% as large as the required return for the market portfolio. Investment equilibrium prevails when required and expected returns are equal. Estimation of the market model assumes an equilibrium relation between security and market rates of return as in:

$$ROR_A^{equilibrium} = alpha + (beta \times ROR_{Market}^{actual}),$$

where *alpha* and *beta* are the best estimates of the intercept (= *alpha*) and slope (= *beta*) from the market model. Difference between actual and equilibrium security rates of return represents economic profit (or loss) and is the *risk-adjusted return*.

FORMULA 11.6 Risk-adjusted return is economic profit

The risk-adjusted rate of return for any capital investment *A*, denoted $ROR_A^{risk-adjusted}$ equals the actual rate of return minus the equilibrium rate of return $ROR_A^{equilibrium}$:

$$ROR_A^{risk-adjusted} = ROR_A^{actual} - ROR_A^{equilibrium}.$$

The risk-adjusted return equals economic profit or loss accruing during the period.

When idiosyncratic risk may be eliminated completely through diversification and only one source of systematic risk exists then, subject to standard statistical assumptions, the *CAPM* provides a procedure through the market model for estimating risk-adjusted returns.

Historical data for the on-going illustration with security *A* and the market portfolio suggest that β_A equals 1.3636. Suppose that for the most recent period the market was up 3% while security *A* was down 6%. Let's compute the periodic risk-adjusted return for security *A*. For the numbers already in the calculator *alpha* = −1.9811 and *beta* = 1.3636. Because the actual market return was 3% find best estimate of the equilibrium return:

$$ROR_A{}^{equilibrium} \;=\; -1.9811 + (\,1.3636 \times 3\%), \;=\; 2.11\%$$

The stock *should* have been up 2.11% when the market was up 3%. But the stock fell 6%. From formula 11.6 find the risk-adjusted return:

$$ROR_A{}^{risk\text{-}adjusted} \;=\; -6\% - 2.11\% \;=\; -8.11\%.$$

Shareholders bore the burden of an 8.11% economic loss.

CALCULATOR CLUE

Enter data for security *A* and the market portfolio into the *BAII Plus*© calculator as the previous *Calculator clue* describes. Next find the equilibrium return given a 3% market return. While in the STAT function hit ↓ until the display shows "X' = ". Type

3 ENTER   ↓   CPT .

The display shows that Y' is 2.1095%; this equals the security equilibrium return given the 3% market return. Now subtract the entry on the display from the actual security return of −6% with these keystrokes:

 +/−   − 6 = .

The display shows risk-adjusted return equals -8.1095%.

Risk-adjusted returns are useful for many purposes. Regulated utility companies such as Edison Electric often present risk-adjusted returns to public commissions when arguing for electric utility rates. Sometimes class-action shareholder suits against management present risk-adjusted returns to bolster argument of managerial malfeasance. Table 9.5 illustrates the efficient market hypothesis by relying on *cumulative abnormal returns*. The periodic abnormal return is identical to the risk-adjusted return. Literally thousands of studies by companies and professors in finance, accounting, and economics use the preceding methodology for computing effects of events on company economic profit. Shareholders, *ceteris paribus*, are recipients of unexpected windfall gains and losses. Risk-adjusted returns measure economic profit.

EXERCISES 11.3

1. The company's beta is 1.25 and the required risk premium for the market portfolio is 8.0%. What equilibrium risk premium for the company's stock is implied by the Capital Asset Pricing Model? ©AP7

2. The economy wide risk free interest rate is 5.0% and the required risk premium for the market portfolio is 7.5%. At the same time, the company's required risk premium according to the Capital Asset Pricing Model is 9.0%. What is the company's β? ©AP4a

3. You want to add an additional stock to your portfolio and will rely on the *Capital asset pricing model* to determine whether a security should be added to your portfolio. The risk-free rate is 4.6% and the required return on the market portfolio is 10.7%. For stock X the expected return is 10.70% and the beta is 0.94.

3a. Should stock X be added to your well-diversified portfolio? ©AP1a

3b. For stock Y the expected return is 12.60% and the beta is 0.61. Between X and Y determine which one of these securities should be added to your portfolio.

3c. For stock Z the expected return is 10.25% and the beta is 0.85. Between X and Z determine which one of these securities should be added to your portfolio.

4. The company beta is 1.50, its dividend growth rate is 11.2%, and just yesterday it paid a dividend of $1.30. The economy wide risk free interest rate is 5.0% and the expected risk premium for the market portfolio is 8.0%. Find the stock's intrinsic value using the dividend constant growth model and the equilibrium total rate of return implied by Capital Asset Pricing Model. ©AP6a

5. The company beta is 1.10, its dividend growth rate is 7.4%, just yesterday it paid a dividend of $1.60, and today's share price is $17. Most likely today's share price equals today's intrinsic value. Furthermore, the share price moves in accordance with the dividend constant growth model. The economy wide risk free interest rate is 4% and the required risk premium for the market portfolio is 7%. The stock represents a good investment if the expected total rate of return implied by the dividend constant growth model exceeds the required rate of return implied by the capital asset pricing model. Determine whether the stock is a *buy* or *sell*. ©AP5b

6. The economy wide <u>real</u> risk-free rate is 2.5%, the inflation premium is 1.5%, and the market risk premium is 7.5%. At the same time, the company beta is 0.90, its dividend growth rate is 5.5%, and it just paid a dividend of $0.75 per share. Due to sudden and unexpected political events, the market risk premium increases by 100 basis points. What is the likely resultant percentage change in the intrinsic value of the company's shares? ©AP8

7. The economy wide <u>real</u> risk free interest rate is 3.5%, the inflation premium is 2.5%, and the market risk premium is 10.0%. At the same time, the company beta is 0.85, its dividend growth rate is 7.0%, and it just paid a dividend of $1.10 per share. The company anticipates a change in production plan that should affect its beta and dividend growth rate. The new beta becomes 0.70 and the growth rate becomes 8.70%. What is the likely resultant percentage change in the intrinsic value of the company's shares? ©AP9

8. You have the following information about equity rates of returns for the past 5 periods.

	obs 1	obs 2	obs 3	obs 4	obs 5
company *ROR*	19%	15%	-2%	18%	8%
market *ROR*	15%	15%	-6%	20%	11%

8a. Based on the above observations, what is the company's β? ©AP2am

8b. The most recent information suggests that the current period market return is -7% and the security return is 5%. Use the market model to find the company risk-adjusted rate of return? ©AP2dm

4. THE COMPANY COST OF CAPITAL

Rule 6.4 states that companies assess profitability of investment opportunities by discounting incremental cash flow from assets. When net present value of asset cash flow is positive the project captures economic profit for the company. Management distributes the resultant economic profit to capitalists and stakeholders in accordance with relative strength of principal-agent relationships. Conversely, undertaking negative net present value investments destroys wealth and is to be avoided. The discount rate for finding present values obviously influences computations.

Selection of the proper discount rate relies on some of the most important concepts in finance.

> **DEFINITION 11.4 Company cost of capital**
> The company cost of capital is the discount rate for computing net present value of company investment opportunities.

Inspection of any balance sheet shows that a variety of debt and equity financing sources support company assets. For pursuit of entrepreneurial activities companies obtain financing from many sources. Some projects borrow from the bank or issue bonds to obtain financing. Other projects rely exclusively on cash already in the checking account. And every now and then the company issues equity to raise capital. For many companies, especially large on-going concerns, the process of raising capital does not uniformly match the process of making investments. There is a separation between investment and financing decisions. Irrespective of a particular project's financing method the company cost of capital for discounting asset cash flows is a weighted average of financing rates for all financing sources.

> **FORMULA 11.7 Weighted average cost of capital ROR^{wacc}**
> The discount rate appropriate for assessing net present value of investment opportunities for company A equals a weighted average of debt and equity financing rates. Compute that discount rate, denoted ROR_A^{wacc}, as follows:
>
> $$ROR_A^{wacc} = w_{debt}\, i_A \left(1 - \frac{tax}{rate} \right) + w_{equity}\, ROR_A^{required}.$$
>
> Weights w_{debt} and w_{equity} sum to 100% and measure the proportion of existing long-term financing provided by debt and equity. The pretax interest rate i_A is the yield-to-maturity on company long-term debt. ROR_A^{wacc} applies to any capital investment for company A irrespective of actual financing method for that specific project.

Formula 11.7 ignores many technical complications in order to focus on the fundamental lesson that the cost of capital is an average of all company financing costs. A short list of significant technicalities (among many, many that exist) includes the following.

Project specific risk: The most significant technicality is implicit assumption that risk of the investment opportunity approximately equals average risk of the company's existing assets. For opportunities with above average risk the cost of capital should include an additional risk premium and vice versa.

Capital structure weights: Irrespective of a particular project's financing method the company cost of capital for discounting asset cash flows is a weighted average of financing rates for all financing sources. Important technicalities pertain to measuring the weights. Liability side of the balance sheet lists historical financing sources. Arguably, however, there are many biases on balance sheets. Foremost, perhaps, is divergence between book values and market values for long-term liabilities. Weights may be based upon either; book values are handier but economic arguments suggest market values may be better. Another difficulty is whether weights should be based on actual measurements or on target measurements. For example, a company actively reducing their debt-ratio may prefer to use target instead of actual weights for computing the company cost of capital.

EXAMPLE 7 Find the weighted average cost of capital for a simple setting
The company is evaluating profitability of a long-term investment opportunity. Their balance sheet shows that 35% of long term financing relies on debt at a 7.25% pretax interest rate. The other 65% is *Stockholders equity*. The company marginal tax rate is 34%. Statistical estimates find that company β is 1.40. The

short-term risk-free rate currently is 4.5% and the company believes that the required risk premium for the market portfolio is 8%. Find the company's weighted average cost of capital appropriate for computing net present value of investment opportunities.

SOLUTION

The setup provides all numbers that formula 11.7 needs except for the cost of equity financing. Find this financing rate with *CAPM* formula 11.5b (naturally this is valid only when idiosyncratic risk is perfectly diversifiable and only one source of systematic risk exists):

$$ROR^{required} \quad = \quad 4.5\% + 1.40\,(8\%) \quad = \quad 15.70\%.$$

Now substitute all numbers into formula 11.7 and compute the *WACC*:

$$ROR^{wacc} = 0.35 \times 7.25\% \times (1 - 0.34) + 0.65 \times 15.70\% = 11.88\%.$$

If the company insists that all investment opportunities possess internal rates of return exceeding 11.88% then net present values will be positive. Often the company cost of capital is referred to as the *hurdle rate* for investment.

EXERCISES 11.4

1. The company is evaluating profitability of a long-term investment opportunity. Their balance sheet shows that 65% of long term financing relies on debt at a 8.5% pretax interest rate. The other 35% is *Stockholders equity*. The company marginal tax rate is 34%. Statistical estimates find that company β is 0.85. The short-term risk-free rate currently is 5% and the company believes that the required risk premium for the market portfolio is 7.5%. Find the company's weighted average cost of capital appropriate for computing net present value of investment opportunities. ©CC1

2. A company pursues a cost-cutting initiative that costs $27,000 to implement. Thereafter, however, the initiative reduces after-tax costs by $5,000 per year perpetually. The company relies on 29% debt financing at a 7.2% pretax interest rate. The company marginal tax rate is 37%. The company β is 1.39, short-term risk-free rate is 4.0%, and required risk premium for the market portfolio is 10.5%. Find the project's net present value. ©CC2

ANSWERS TO CHAPTER 11 EXERCISES

EXERCISES 11.1

1. The market risk premium equals 6% (= 11% - 5%). Also, σ_m = 24% so slope of the capital market line equals ¼ (= 6% ÷ 24%). The market price for one percentage point of risk is 25 basis points (= ¼ × 1%) and for extra risk of 5% the increase in required risk premium is 1.25% (= ¼ × 5%).

2. The risk-return profile for combinations of the risk-free asset and the market portfolio lies along the line of averages connecting those two points. Let w_{rf} and $(1 - w_{rf})$ equal the proportions invested in the risk-free asset and the market portfolio, respectively. The portfolio rate of return always is an average of component returns. Thus, in order to obtain a 4.9% rate of return write:

$$0.049 = w_{rf} \times 0.030 + (1 - w_{rf}) \times 0.125; \text{ or } w_{rf} = 0.80.$$

Investing 80% of capital in the risk-free asset and 20% in the market portfolio satisfies the objective.

3. Let w_{rf} and $(1 - w_{rf})$ equal the proportions invested in the risk-free asset and the market portfolio, respectively. The portfolio risk *when the correlation between components equals zero* is an average of component risks. Thus, in order to obtain a portfolio risk of 12% write:

   $0.12 = w_{rf} \times 0.0 + (1 - w_{rf}) \times 0.17$; or $w_{rf} = 0.2941$.

   Investing 29.4% of capital in the risk-free asset and 70.6% in the market portfolio satisfies the objective.

4. The risk-return profile for combinations of the risk-free asset and the market portfolio lies along the line of averages connecting those two points. Let w_{rf} and $(1 - w_{rf})$ equal the proportions invested in the risk-free asset and the market portfolio, respectively. To obtain a 3.9% risk premium requires a 7.9% portfolio rate of return. Write:

   $0.079 = w_{rf} \times 0.04 + (1 - w_{rf}) \times 0.085$; or $w_{rf} = 0.1333$.

   Investing 13.3% of capital in the risk-free asset and 86.7% in the market portfolio satisfies the objective.

EXERCISES 11.2

1. The risk-free rate $ROR_2^{risk\text{-}free}$ equals 3% plus the inflation premium of 5.75% [= (5.6% + 5.9%)/2] which is 8.75%. Inflation premium on a four-year bond is 5.7% [= (5.6% + 5.9% + 2 × 6.2%)/4] so $ROR_4^{risk\text{-}free}$ is 8.97%. The 20-year risk-free rate $ROR_{20}^{risk\text{-}free}$ is 9.15% [= 3% + (5.6% + 5.9% + 18 × 6.2%)/20].

EXERCISES 11.3

1. β equals the proportion of market risk premium that the security garners and is 10.0% (= 1.25 × 8%).

2. Ratio of security to market risk premium equals β and is 1.20 (= 9.0% ÷ 7.5%).

3a. Use *CAPM* formula 11.5b to find required return and consider the security a buy if $ROR^{required} < ROR^{expected}$. For security X required return is 10.33% [= 4.6% + 0.94 × (10.7% – 4.6%)] and its expected return is bigger so it's a buy.

3b. For security Y required return is 8.32% [= 4.6% + 0.61 × (10.7% – 4.6%)] and its expected return is bigger so it too is a buy. For X and Y expected returns exceed required returns so they are both buys. But which one is best? Notice that on a graph of $ROR^{expected}$ versus β like figure 11.9 that security Y dominates X so X is the one to add.

3c. For security Z required return is 9.78% [= 4.6% + 0.85 × (10.7% – 4.6%)] and its expected return is bigger so it too is a buy. For X and Y expected returns exceed required returns so they are both buys. But which one is best? Notice that on a graph of $ROR^{expected}$ versus β like figure 11.9 that there is a trade-off between relatively high risk/return X and low risk/return Z; there is no dominance. We could, however, apply the market price for risk from the *Capital market line* to determine whether the extra return for X compensates for its extra risk (that deduction also requires information about correlation coefficient ρ_{xy}, too). The problem does not give enough information to make that deduction, however. Bottom line is this: both X and Z are good but we can't tell which is best without additional information.

4. Use the *CAPM* to compute that $ROR^{required}$ equals 17% [= 5% + (1.50 × 8%)]. At equilibrium required and expected returns are equal. Hence, use 17% in the intrinsic valuation formula for constant growth dividends. Intrinsic value equals $24.92 [= $1.30 × (1 + 0.112) ÷ (0.17 – 0.112).

5. Solve for the unknown discount rate r from the intrinsic value formula with constant growth of dividends. Compute that this $ROR^{expected}$ equals 17.51% [= $1.60 × 1.074 ÷ $17) + 7.4%. Use the *CAPM* to

compute that $ROR^{required}$ equals 12.75% [= 4% + (1.10 × 7%)]. The expected return more than compensates for risk and places the stock on the *buy* list.

6. The <u>real</u> risk-free rate is 2.5% and the inflation premium is 1.5%. Use formula 11.3 to find that the <u>nominal</u> risk-free rate is 4.0% (= 2.5% + 1.5%). Now use the *CAPM* to compute that $ROR^{required}$ before the political crisis equals 10.75% [= 4.0% + (0.90 × 7.5%)]. At equilibrium required and expected returns are equal. Hence, use 10.75% in the formula for constant growth dividends to find that intrinsic value equals $15.07 [= $0.75 × (1 + 0.055) ÷ (0.1075 – 0.055)]. After the political crisis use the *CAPM* to compute that $ROR^{required}$ equals 11.65% [= 4.0% + (0.90 × 8.5%)]. The intrinsic value moves to $12.87 [= $0.75 × (1 + 0.055) ÷ (0.1165 – 0.055)], a decline of 14.6% (= $12.87 ÷ $15.07 – 1).

7. Use formula 11.3 to find that the <u>nominal</u> risk-free rate is 6.0% (= 3.5% + 2.5%). Now use the *CAPM* to compute that $ROR^{required}$ before change in production plan equals 14.5% [= 6.0% + (0.85 × 10%)]. Use 14.5% in the formula for constant growth dividends to find that intrinsic value equals $15.69 [= $1.10 × (1 + 0.07) ÷ (0.145 – 0.07)]. After the change compute that $ROR^{required}$ equals 13.0% [= 6.0% + (0.70 × 10%)]. The intrinsic value moves to $27.81 [= $1.10 × (1 + 0.087) ÷ (0.13 – 0.087)], an increase of 77.2% (= $27.81 ÷ $15.69 – 1).

8a. Use the DATA and STAT functions on the calculator to find that "b = 0.8259." The beta equals 0.8259. Notice as an aside that the calculator also displays σ_x = 8.97% (that equals market standard deviation σ_M), σ_y = 7.81% (that equals security standard deviation σ_A), and r = 0.95 (that is the correlation $\rho_{A,M}$). Use these numbers and verify that formula 11.5a also computes that β = 0.83. The number on the display for "a = 2.5154" is the intercept *(alpha)* for the regression and appears below.

8b. Easily compute this answer by following the *Calculator clue* in the text. Find from the calculator that alpha = 2.5154, beta = 0.8259, and compute that when the market return is –7% the security equilibrium return is –3.2% [= 2.5154 + (0.8259 × -7%)]. Compute with formula 11.6 that $ROR^{risk-adjusted}$ equals 8.27% [= 5% – (-3.27%)].

EXERCISES 11.4

1. Use formula 11.5b to find $ROR^{required}$ is 11.375% [= 5% + 0.85 (7.5%)]. Now substitute all numbers into formula 11.7 and compute the *WACC* is 7.63% [= 0.65 × 8.5% × (1 – 0.34) + 0.35 × 11.375%] .

2. Use formula 11.5b to find $ROR^{required}$ is 18.60% [= 4% + 1.39 (10.5%)]. Now substitute all numbers into formula 11.7 and compute the *WACC* is 14.52% [= 0.29 × 7.2% × (1 – 0.37) + 0.71 × 18.60%]. Now find the NPV of the perpetuity is $7,440 [= $5,000/0.145 – $27,000].

PART THREE

Increasing maturation of financial markets makes arbitrage opportunities possible. Recall this definition from the preface.

> *Arbitrage value* exists when prices or rates in different markets misalign, thereby providing a temporary opportunity for instantaneous profit.

The essence of arbitrage is that when different financial securities have cash flow streams that somehow interact then the interaction sometimes imposes restrictions on the security prices. For example, consider arbitrage possibilities when a share of Microsoft may be bought in one market for $25 and, at the same time, may be sold in another market for $27. The cash flow stream from one share of Microsoft promises to be identical with every other share's. These shares consequently should trade for the same price even though they are in different markets. Traders with access to both markets will capture value by taking advantage of this fleeting price discrepancy—buy at $25 and instantly sell at $27. Arbitrage pressures force these prices into narrow tolerance ranges. Part 3 of *Lessons about the Structure of Finance* examines financial arbitrage and shows usefulness of risk management applications.

CHAPTER 12

Financial Arbitrage

CHAPTER CONTENTS

In well-developed financial markets securities allow businesses to manage risk. Risk management strategies often involve two or more simultaneous positions in different markets. The ability to manage risk occurs because multiple positions potentially eliminate uncertainty. By eliminating uncertainty the outcomes no longer depend upon subsequent price movements.

The futures markets were the first risk management markets to develop. For millennia sea captains have plied the oceans transporting scarce commodities. The uncertainty facing merchants needing those commodities was rather substantial. What price would the sea captains charge? Was the ship even carrying the commodity, or had unimaginable storms or other calamity decimated crops in some distant land? The sea captains worried whether there was a ready market for the product in port. In the midst of this substantial uncertainty, a few entrepreneurs saw significant opportunity.

Middlemen began writing contracts guaranteeing the right to buy or sell the commodity in the future. Merchants were able to lock in the buy price long before the ship arrived. The sea captain no longer had to worry whether some other ship arrived a week earlier, thereby glutting the commodity market. The captain could lock in the sell price before arrival by signing a contract with the middlemen. The middlemen sometimes would guess right and make money. Other times they would lose money. But they were providing a valuable service. They were absorbing risk. Economic forces dictate that providing a valuable service merits fair compensation. The middlemen flourished. Futures markets moved society forward.

This chapter formally but simply introduces fundamental lessons about arbitrage. The arbitrage process is the third and final source of value in *Lessons about the Structure of Finance*. It is perhaps most powerful of all financial forces and merits study. Section 1 explains the arbitrage concept and provides brief examples. Sections 2 and 3 examine risk management strategies associating with futures and options markets, respectively. Section 4 focuses on very powerful international arbitrage relationships that bind global financial markets.

1. THE ARBITRAGE CONCEPT

An arbitrage opportunity exists when prices in several markets misalign thereby providing temporary potential for certain profit. Consider a simple example in which there exist two markets for gold: the spot market and the futures market. A spot market is a "cash and carry" market. Most consumer markets are spot markets. The grocery store is a spot market because the price on the shelf represents the price to take immediate possession of the commodity. The stock exchange is a spot market because when you pay the asked price you immediately get ownership in the stock. For gold the spot and futures markets are large, active, and competitive.

A futures contract locks in today the price to be paid in the future for buying or selling a commodity. The payment occurs at time of delivery and the contract is free to enter. Existence of complete and competitive markets means that prices in spot and futures markets align in accordance with the formula below.

> **FORMULA 12.1 No-arbitrage equilibrium, simplest scenario**
> When interim cash flows such as warehouse fees, adjustment costs, dividends, etc., equal zero then prices in spot and futures markets satisfy this condition.
>
> $$\begin{pmatrix} no-arbitrage \\ spot\ price \end{pmatrix} = \begin{pmatrix} no-arbitrage \\ futures\ price \end{pmatrix} \Big/ (1+r)^N$$

There are four variables in formula 12.1. Given values for any three, the fourth may be determined. Usually, however, length of futures contract N and discount rate are known and predetermined.

Competitive behavior of market participants determines spot and futures prices. The prices, however, align as formula 12.1 stipulates or else arbitrage profit exists.

> **DEFINITION 12.1 Arbitrage profit and the no-arbitrage equilibrium**
> Arbitrage profit is a certain return exceeding the risk-free return. Arbitrage profit is economic profit and represents a form of wealth creation. At equilibrium arbitrage profit equals zero because market forces drive certain returns to the risk-free return. Prices and rates force a *no-arbitrage* equilibrium in which arbitrage profits vibrate around zero.

No-arbitrage equilibrium formula 12.1 is analogous to lump-sum time value formula 4.6. Supply the actual value for the futures price in formula 12.1 (analogous to FV) and solve for the no-arbitrage spot price (analogous to PV). If the actual spot price differs from the no-arbitrage spot price then an opportunity exists to capture arbitrage profit. Present value of arbitrage profit equals difference between actual and no-arbitrage spot prices.

Likewise in formula 12.1 supply the actual value for the spot price and solve for the no-arbitrage futures price. If the actual futures price differs from the no-arbitrage futures price then an arbitrage opportunity exists. Future value of arbitrage profit equals difference between actual and no-arbitrage futures prices.

In reality an actual price may deviate very slightly from its underlying no-arbitrage price. Perhaps the difference is so slight that capturing the resultant arbitrage profit is not worth the time, trouble, or transaction cost. Once the arbitrage profit is large enough, however, competitive behavior is assurance that prices snap back into place as formula 12.1 stipulates. Arbitrage profit is like money lying on the sidewalk of the busiest street in town - someone picks it up. The example below illustrates the arbitrage process.

EXAMPLE 1 Futures Arbitrage

Your company is a middleman that buys, sells, and stores warehouses full of gold. Today's spot price for gold is $310 per ounce. Your company is able to invest and borrow at the risk-free interest rate of 9.9%. Furthermore, your company can store and safeguard, if necessary, additional gold for virtually free. Describe the arbitrage forces if today's futures price for delivery in one year is (a) $275, or (b) $350.

SOLUTION

Use formula 12.1 given that r equals 0.099 and N equals 1. For part a, take as given today's futures price of $275. This means that today the company can lock in the right to buy or sell gold in one year for a price of $275. Use the formula to find the corresponding no-arbitrage spot price.

$$no\text{-}arbitrage\ spot\ price = \$275\ /\ (1.099)$$

$$= \$250.23$$

The actual spot price of $310 differs from the no-arbitrage spot price of $250.23. This temporary mispricing by $59.77 (=$310–$250.23) represents present value of arbitrage profit. The following strategy captures the arbitrage profit.

Gold is overvalued in the spot market because its actual spot price of $310 is larger than its no-arbitrage price of $250.23. The no-arbitrage price is somewhat analogous to the gold's "intrinsic value." Always sell an overvalued asset and buy an undervalued one.

Sell gold in the spot market. That is, sell today an ounce of gold from your warehouse and collect $310. Subsequently invest the $310 for one year at 9.9%. Simultaneously take a position in the futures market whereby you agree to buy gold in one year at today's futures price of $275. These actions suggest you have taken a short position in the spot market and a long position in the futures market. When an asset is overvalued in the spot market then the asset is undervalued in the futures market, and vice versa.

One year from today the financial investment of $310 matures and returns $340.69 (= $310x1.099). Fulfill obligations for your long futures position by buying gold at $275 per ounce. You are left in one year with $65.69 (=$340.69–$275) and exactly the same amount of gold in the warehouse as today. That $65.69 equals future value of arbitrage profit. Its present value is $59.77 (=$65.69 ÷ 1.099). Arbitrage profit exactly equals the amount of the mispricing.

For the preceding strategy the future value of arbitrage profit equals $65.69 and accrues at end of the investment horizon. An alternative approach capitalizes arbitrage profit, collecting its present value at the beginning. Sell gold today in the spot market and collect $310. Go long in the futures market and obligate to buy an ounce for $275 in one year (thereby replacing the ounce you sell today). Instead of investing the full $310 at 9.9%, simply invest $250.23. Pocket the other $59.77 (= $310 - $250.23) and use it for whatever purpose you want. This pocket money is "free" arbitrage profit. In one year the investment grows and returns $275 (= $250.23 x 1.099) which is exactly the amount required for fulfilling the long futures obligation.

b. For this question today's futures price equals $350. This means that today the company can lock in the right to buy or sell gold in one year for a price of $350. Use formula 12.1 to find the corresponding no-arbitrage spot price.

$$no\text{-}arbitrage\ spot\ price = \$350 / (1.099)$$
$$= \$318.47$$

The actual spot price of $310 differs from the no-arbitrage spot price of $318.47. This temporary mispricing by $8.47 represents arbitrage profit. Use the following arbitrage strategy to capture the arbitrage profit.

Gold is undervalued in the spot market because its actual spot price of $310 is smaller than its no-arbitrage price of $318.47. Borrow $310 at 9.9 percent to buy gold in the spot market. Put the gold in your warehouse. Simultaneously take a position in the futures market whereby you agree to sell gold in one year at today's futures price of $350. These actions suggest you have taken a long position in the spot market and a short position in the futures market.

One year from today fulfill obligations for your short futures position by taking an ounce of gold out of the warehouse and selling it for $350 per ounce. Repay the loan's $340.69 principal and interest (=$310x1.099). You are left in one year with $9.31 (=$350-$340.69) and exactly the same amount of gold in the warehouse as today. That $9.31 equals the future value of the arbitrage profit. Its present value is $8.47 (=$9.31 ÷ 1.099). The arbitrage profit exactly equals the amount of the mispricing.

The example above illustrates that arbitrage profit exists when prices in the spot and futures markets improperly align. The example below reinforces the irrelevance of expectations on the no-arbitrage equilibrium.

EXAMPLE 2 Stock Index Arbitrage

The SP2 Stock Index equals the sum of stock prices for companies A and Z. These companies never pay dividends. Today's stock prices equal $37 and $78 for stocks A and Z, respectively. The interest rate at which you may borrow and invest is 9.4%. What is today's prudent futures price for a one year contract on the SP2 index if you expect stock prices (a) to rise 25%, or (b) to fall 25%?

SOLUTION

The SP2 today equals the sum of 37 and 78. The SP2 in the spot market is 115. Use formula 12.1 to find the no-arbitrage futures price.

No-arbitrage spot price = No-arbitrage futures price / (1 + r)

115 = No-arbitrage futures price / (1.094).

No-arbitrage futures price = 125.81 .

a. A portfolio containing one share of each stock today is worth $115. You expect the stock prices to rise 25 percent above their current level. Thus, in one year you expect the portfolio to be worth $143.75. Suppose that today you observe the futures price is 135. You view this as a keen opportunity to take a long position in the futures market because you would love next year to buy stocks for $135 that would be worth $143.75. You reason that next year you could buy at $135 and instantaneously sell at $143.75 in the stock market. This strategy sounds sensible but is inherent with risk.

The actual futures price of 135 overvalues no-arbitrage futures price is 125.81. Capture the arbitrage profit by today going short in the futures market and long in the spot market. Borrow $115 at 9.4 percent and immediately buy the stocks. Simultaneously go short in the futures market thereby guaranteeing sale of the stock in one year at $135.

One year from today fulfill obligations of the futures contract by selling the stocks for $135. Take the proceeds and repay the loan's $125.81 principal and interest (=$115x1.094). You are left in one year with $9.19 (=$135–$125.81). That sum equals the future value of the arbitrage profit. Its present value is $8.40 (=$9.19 ÷ 1.094). The arbitrage profit exactly equals the difference between the actual and the no-arbitrage spot prices (=135–125.81). You make the arbitrage profit without any risk and without any cost. Capitalize the arbitrage profit, if you wish, by immediately borrowing $123.40 and buying the stocks for $115 and pocketing $8.40.

Notice that to capture the arbitrage profit you take a short position in the futures market, even though today's futures price for next year is less than the spot price you expect to prevail next year.

b. A portfolio worth $115 today containing one share of each stock is expected to be worth $86.25 in one year (=115x(1–.25)). Suppose that today you observe the futures price is 100. First reaction might be taking a short position in the futures market because you would love next year to sell stocks for $100 that could be purchased at that instant for $86.25. This strategy is not taking advantage of the apparent arbitrage opportunity.

The actual futures price of 100 overvalues the no-arbitrage futures price of 125.81. Capture the arbitrage profit by today going long in the futures market and short in the spot market. Reinvest the proceeds from the $115 short sale at 9.4 percent.

One year from today the loan matures and returns $125.81. Fulfill obligations of the futures contract by buying the stocks for $100. You are left in one year with $25.81 (=$125.81–$100). That sum equals the future value of the arbitrage profit. Its present value is $23.59 (=$25.81 ÷ 1.094). Present value of arbitrage profit exactly equals the difference between actual and no-arbitrage spot prices (=$115–$100/1.094). You make the arbitrage profit without any risk and without any cost.

Expectations about spot prices in the future have little relation with today's futures prices. This uncoupling of subsequent price movements from financial outcomes provides internal structure for most risk management decisions.

EXERCISES 12.1

Numerical quickies

1. Your company buys, sells, and stores warehouses full of gold. Today, the futures price for gold with delivery in one year is $370 per ounce. The spot price is $390 per ounce. Your company is able to invest and borrow at the risk-free interest rate of 6.9%. Furthermore, your company can, if necessary, store and safeguard an additional 1000 ounces of gold for virtually free. Find the present value of arbitrage profits on 1000 ounces of gold and describe the strategy for capitalizing that profit. ©FT2b

2. The SP2 Index equals the sum of stock prices for companies Y and Z. Today's stock prices equal $48 and $40 for stocks Y and Z, respectively. Today's futures price for the SP2 with delivery in 1-year is $110.58. The interest rate at which you may borrow and invest is 11.2%. Find the present value of stock index arbitrage profits and describe the strategy for capitalizing that profit. ©TQ17

2. FUTURES CONTRACTS

By taking a position on a futures contract an investor agrees to either buy or sell an underlying commodity at a specified future date. The investor agreeing to sell is taking a "short" position. The investor agreeing to buy is taking a "long" position. Regardless, each party entering the contract agrees today upon a price to be paid in the future. Table 12.1 lists active U.S. futures exchanges and commodities that they trade. Recent establishment or reorganization of several exchanges attests to dramatic changes occurring in financial markets. The variety of commodities traded attests to usefulness of futures contracts for pursuing business objectives. These exchanges do not exist solely to serve as speculative dins of greed. Instead, they exist and thrive because they allow companies and investors to pursue diverse investment and business objectives.

TABLE 12.1

Active futures exchanges in the U.S.A.

Exchange	Major Commodities	Remarks
CBOE Futures Exchange, LLC (CFE)	Volatility Indexes	CFE is a subsidiary of the Chicago Board Options (CBOE). Exchange Established 2003.
Chicago Board of Trade (CBOT)	Grains, soybeans, US Treasury notes and bonds, other interest rates, and stock indexes.	Organized as a grain cash market in 1848, the CBOT is generally considered to be the oldest organized futures exchange. While experts disagree about the exact date when "true" futures trading began, CBOT cash contracts evolved into what are now considered futures contracts. Shortly before the civil war, traders at the CBOT began trading "to-arrive" or forward contracts in agricultural commodities including wheat, corn, and oats. In 1859, the CBOT was granted a charter by the Illinois legislature which, among other things, standardized grades and provided for inspectors of grain to be appointed by the CBOT, whose decisions were binding on members. In 1865, formal trading rules were instituted particularly concerning margin and delivery procedures. In 1877 the CBOT began publishing futures prices, and in 1883 the first clearing organization was established to clear CBOT contracts, initially on a voluntary basis.

Chicago Mercantile Exchange (CME)	Livestock, dairy products, stock indexes, Eurodollars and other interest rates, currencies	CME was originally known as the Chicago Butter and Egg Board, which was formed in 1898. It became the CME in 1919, trading futures on a variety of agricultural products.
Kansas City Board of Trade (KCBT)	Wheat, natural gas, and stock indexes	KCBT was established by local Kansas City merchants in 1869 as a means of trading grain. Futures trading in grains began in 1876.
Minneapolis Grain Exchange (MGE)	Spring wheat	MGE was established by the Minneapolis Chamber of Commerce in 1881 as an organization designed to promote trade in grains and to prevent abuses. In 1947, it became the MGE.
NQLX LLC Futures Exchange (NQLX)	Security futures products	NQLX originally established in 2001 as the Nasdaq LIFFE LLC Futures Exchange, and it operated as a joint venture of the Nasdaq Stock Market and the London International Financial Futures and Options Exchange (LIFFE). NQLX's relationship with Nasdaq ended on July 24, 2003, and it was renamed as NQLX.
New York Board of Trade (NYBOT)	Coffee, sugar, cocoa, cotton, frozen concentrated orange juice, currencies.	NYBOT was formed in 1998 when the Coffee, Sugar and Cocoa Exchange (CSCE) and the New York Cotton Exchange (NYCE) entered into a merger agreement, which was to occur in several stages. In June 2004 when the merger was completed, the CSCE's and NYCE's contract market designations were extinguished and transferred to NYBOT.
New York Mercantile Exchange (NYMEX)	Energy products	NYMEX was founded in 1872 as the Butter and Cheese Exchange of New York and became the New York Mercantile Exchange in 1882. COMEX was founded in 1933 from the merger of the National Metal Exchange, the Rubber Exchange of New York, the National Raw Silk Exchange, and the New York Hide Exchange (the oldest of these exchanges was founded in 1882). Since 1994, COMEX has operated as a subsidiary of NYMEX.
The COMEX Division (COMEX)	Metals	
Philadelphia Board of Trade (PBOT)	Currencies	The PBOT was established in 1985 as a subsidiary of the Philadelphia Stock Exchange.
U.S. Futures Exchange, LLC (Eurex US)	US Treasury Notes and Bonds	Eurex US formed in 2004 and is owned 80% by U.S. Exchange Holdings, Inc., a Delaware corporation that is a separately capitalized wholly-owned subsidiary of Eurex Frankfurt, AG, and 20% by Exchange Place Holdings, L.P., a Delaware limited partnership.

Source: Commodity Futures Trading Commission. http://www.cftc.gov/dea/deadcms_table.htm

Most futures exchanges actually adjust accounts for daily movements in futures prices. This process of "marking-to-market" adds complexity but does not affect overall relationships. Consequently, for all scenarios herein assume that cash flows only occur at inception and liquidation. The "contract value" is the total sum to be paid (long-side) or received (short-side) at time of delivery:

FORMULA 12.2 Contract value

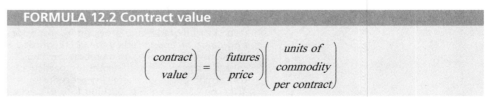

$$\left(\begin{array}{c} contract \\ value \end{array} \right) = \left(\begin{array}{c} futures \\ price \end{array} \right) \left(\begin{array}{c} units\ of \\ commodity \\ per\ contract \end{array} \right)$$

Contract value equals amount of money that the long side pays to take delivery of the commodity. Alternatively, this is the amount that the short side receives upon delivering the commodity.

There is no cost to purchase a futures contract—they are "free". There is a requirement, however, that each investor submit collateral to the futures exchange. The collateral is returned regardless of subsequent profitability. The collateral is called the "margin requirement." The formula for computing the margin requirement is:

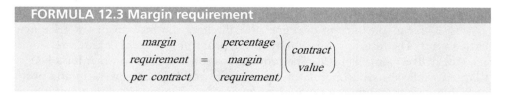

FORMULA 12.3 Margin requirement

$$\begin{pmatrix} margin \\ requirement \\ per\ contract \end{pmatrix} = \begin{pmatrix} percentage \\ margin \\ requirement \end{pmatrix} \begin{pmatrix} contract \\ value \end{pmatrix}$$

Each investor, long side as well as short, submits to the futures exchange the margin requirement.

Most futures contracts do not result in delivery. Instead, investors close their position with the futures exchange by settling in cash and they do **not** transact in the commodity. The act of closing a futures position also is called *covering, offsetting,* or *unwinding*. Upon closing a futures position the investor realizes either a profit or a loss that relates directly to change in futures price during the time that the position was open. The profit per contract is given by the formulas below:

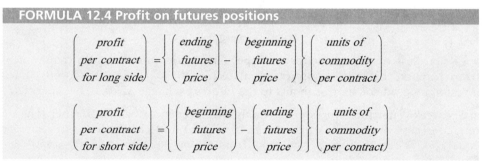

FORMULA 12.4 Profit on futures positions

$$\begin{pmatrix} profit \\ per\ contract \\ for\ long\ side \end{pmatrix} = \left\{ \begin{pmatrix} ending \\ futures \\ price \end{pmatrix} - \begin{pmatrix} beginning \\ futures \\ price \end{pmatrix} \right\} \begin{pmatrix} units\ of \\ commodity \\ per\ contract \end{pmatrix}$$

$$\begin{pmatrix} profit \\ per\ contract \\ for\ short\ side \end{pmatrix} = \left\{ \begin{pmatrix} beginning \\ futures \\ price \end{pmatrix} - \begin{pmatrix} ending \\ futures \\ price \end{pmatrix} \right\} \begin{pmatrix} units\ of \\ commodity \\ per\ contract \end{pmatrix}$$

When the futures price rises during the time the contract is open, the long side profits whereas the short side loses. Conversely, when the futures price falls the long side loses and the short side profits.

Close inspection of the preceding profit formulas shows that the long-side's profit is the negative of the short side's. In other words, this is a zero-sum venture because one side's profit exactly equals the other side's loss. The exchange neither makes nor loses money on the change in future's price, they simply act as a middle-man to facilitate the transaction.

The spot price is the price for immediate delivery; it is the "cash-and-carry" price. Imagine a futures contract with delivery 1 day from now. If the spot price today is, say, 80 cents per pound, it is likely that today's futures price for delivery tomorrow is not far away from 80 cents. Indeed, the futures and spot prices converge as delivery date approaches.

There are two reasons a trader might enter a position with a futures contract. First, a company may lock-in future prices in order to manage risk and narrow possible outcomes. This is the *hedging motive*. An alternative reason for entering the contract is the *speculative motive*. Table 12.2 contrasts hedgers and speculators.

	trader with a hedging motive	trader with a speculative motive
attachment to the underlying commodity	they expect or already have taken a position in the underlying commodity	the type of commodity covered by the contract is almost irrelevant
importance of the underlying commodity price	movements in the commodity price have modest effect on the overall outcome	movements in the commodity price almost totally determine the outcome
importance of the profit or loss on the futures contract	whether the futures contract turns a profit or a loss is largely irrelevant to the overall outcome	the outcome depends exclusively on whether the futures contract makes a profit or a loss

TABLE 12.2
Comparison of hedging and speculative motives

A hedger is, for example, a farmer growing cotton that uses the futures contract to lock-in the selling price of cotton. They certainly care to trade a cotton contract rather than, say, a contract on silver. To a speculator, however, there is not much difference between futures contracts on silver or cotton since they have no real interest in the underlying commodity. Likewise, once the hedger locks in the price with the futures contract there is some indifference about subsequent movements in the price (at least as far as the current deal goes; for the long-run movements in price may matter a lot). The futures position may turn a profit or loss that is of little relevance since the delivery price is fixed. The profit or loss on a futures contract for a hedger is largely irrelevant. To a speculator, however, favorable price movement and profit from the position motivates the trade. The example below considers a speculative position for a futures contract.

EXAMPLE 3 Speculator rate of return

The *Wall Street Journal* shows that silver futures for delivery in 4 months have a margin requirement of one percent. They are quoted as follows:

SILVER 5,000 oz., cents per oz; last = 540.60

You anticipate a rise in the price of silver and therefore enter long on one contract. What is your rate of return if six weeks later when you close the contract the futures price is (a) 547.20 cents per ounce, or (b) 531.30 cents per ounce?

SOLUTION

Regardless of motive, hedging or speculating, the initial margin requirement from formula 12.3 per contract equals $270.30(=0.01×$5,406×5,000). Each investor, long side or short, submits to the futures exchange $270.30 per contract.

a. Six weeks later the futures price equals 547.2 cents per oz. Thus, enter long on one contract when futures price is $540.6 cents and close when futures price equals 547.2 cents. Profit per contract from a long position is $330 (=($5.472 − $5.406) x 5,000).

When you close your position at the futures exchange you receive a check for $330, plus you get a refund of the $270.30 initial margin. Your rate of return is determined from the usual formula that

$$\text{rate-of-return} = (\text{ending wealth - beginning wealth}) \div \text{beginning wealth}$$

$$= \text{profit} \div \text{beginning wealth}$$

$$= \$330.00 \div \$270.30$$

$$= 122.09\%$$

The rate of return exceeds 100% implying that your money more than doubles. Notice that to take a position in the contract you had to ante $270.30. Although this money is not a cost, rather it is collateral, this sum nonetheless represents beginning wealth. Ending wealth equals return of collateral, $270.30, plus profit from the futures position, $330.00. Ending wealth of $600.30 is certainly double beginning wealth.

b. For this problem enter long on one contract when futures price is $540.6 cents and close your position when futures price equals 531.3 cents. Profit per contract from your long position is $-465 [= $5.313 – $5.406) x 5,000). When you close your position at the futures exchange you must send them a check for $465; you do get a refund of the $270.30 initial margin. Your rate of return is -172% (= $-465 ÷ 270.30).

The rate of return exceeds –100% implying that you lose more than you put up. Indeed this is true. You ante $270.30 as initial margin. Upon closing your position, send in another $465, which is partially offset by the refund of $270.30. Nonetheless, your net cash flow upon closing your position is $–194.70 (= $–465 + $270.30). This investment is so bad that you pay to get in and you pay to get out. With standard investments it typically is impossible to lose more than 100%. Speculative investments on futures are especially risky, though, because your potential losses often are unlimited—you can lose more than 100%.

EXAMPLE 4 Hedging with commodity futures contracts

The *Wall Street Journal* shows that cotton futures for delivery in 3 months have a margin requirement of 3/4s of one percent. They are quoted as follows:

COTTON 50,000 lbs., cents per lb; settle = 89.43

You are in the cotton-growing business and expect to deliver 100,000 lbs of cotton to the local gin in 3 months. You enter short on 2 contracts so that you can "guarantee" the price. Describe the cash flows for the following scenarios:

a. the spot price at the time of delivery is 80 cents per pound.
b. the spot price at the time of delivery is $1.00 per pound.
c. ALL your crops are destroyed by drought and the spot price at the time of delivery skyrockets to $2 per pound.

SOLUTION

a. The quote shows that each party agrees upon a futures price of 89.43 cents per pound. "Contract value" is from formula 12.2 and equals $44,715 (= $0.8943 x 50,000). The contract value represents the amount of money that in three months the long side pays to take delivery of the cotton. Alternatively, this is the amount that the short side receives upon making delivery. Formula 12.3 finds that the margin requirement equals $335.36 (= 0.0075 x $44,715). Each investor, long side as well as short, submits to the futures exchange $335.36 per contract. For two contracts, the margin requirement is $670.72.

At delivery, the futures and spot prices converge. For this problem, enter short on two contracts when the futures price is 89.43 cents and close when the futures price equals 80 cents. Profit per contract upon closing the short position is

$$profit\ per\ contract = (\$0.8943 - \$0.80)\ (50,000)$$

$$= \$4,715$$

The profit for two contracts is $9,430. Effectively, you make money from this position because you agree to sell cotton for 89.43 cents and then, three months later, the price of cotton falls to 80 cents. Your right-to-sell cotton at a high price is valuable and you profit from owning this right!

You receive $9,430 from the exchange upon closing your position. You also get back the margin requirement of $670.72 that you paid at the beginning, but the margin "washes out".

At the local gin deliver 100,000 pounds of cotton and receive the spot price of 80 cents per pound for a total of $80,000. The $9,430 profit from the futures position brings ending financial wealth (ignoring the irrelevant margin) to $89,430.

By relying on futures contracts you effectively "locked-in" the futures price of 89.43 cents prevalent three months before your harvest. By locking-in the price, you actually enhanced your position relative to what it would have been had you simply "floated" with the spot price.

b. For this problem futures and spot prices converge at delivery to $1 per pound. Enter short on two contracts when futures price is 89.43 cents and close when futures price equals 100 cents. Profit per contract upon closing the short position is

$$profit\ per\ contract = (\$0.8943 - \$1.00)\ (50,000)$$

$$= \$\text{-}5,285$$

Cover your position at the futures exchange by sending them a check for $5,285 per contract. For two contracts, the total loss is $10,570. Effectively, you lose money from this position because you agree to sell cotton for 89.43 cents and then, three months later, the price of cotton rises to 100 cents per pound. Your obligation-to-sell cotton at a relatively low price is costly!

You pay $10,570 to the futures exchange upon closing your position. You get back from the exchange the margin requirement of $670.72 that you paid at the beginning, but the margin "washes out".

At the local gin you deliver your 100,000 pounds of cotton and receive the spot price of 100 cents per pound for a total of $100,000. Subtract the $10,570 loss from the futures position and find that ending wealth (ignoring the irrelevant margin) equals $89,430.

Once again, the futures contract allows you to "lock-in" the futures price of 89.43 cents prevalent three months before your harvest. In this situation, however, you would have been better off had you "floated" with the spot price.

There is no way to be certain whether prices will be rising or falling. This uncertainty about future prices implies risk. Many businesses realize that by utilizing futures contracts they can effectively control the risk associated with price fluctuations. Futures contracts enhance entrepreneurial opportunities for locking-in outcomes.

c. Drought is devastating cotton crops, its price is skyrocketing, and this is really bad. Because you are short, the rising price means you are losing money in the futures market. Enter short on two contracts when the futures price is 89.43 cents, and close when the futures and spot prices converge at 200 cents. Profit per contract upon closing the short position is

$$profit\ per\ contract = (\$0.8943 - \$2.00)\ (50,000)$$

$$= \$\text{--}55,285$$

Cover your position at the futures exchange by sending them a check for $55,285 per contract. For two contracts, the total loss is $110,570. This outcome might be tolerable if you could sell your cotton at the local gin for $200,000; that is, 100,000 pounds at $2 per pound. But your crop was destroyed. Somehow you have to pay off the futures exchange, or they will send their lawyers after you and foreclose on the farm. Seldom is hedging totally risk-free.

2.A. Currency transactions

U.S. companies could insist on working with a foreign company only if the foreign company agrees to transact in U.S. dollars. That shortsighted approach doesn't work well in today's globally competitive marketplace. If the U.S. company wants the job, then they must do what it takes to obtain the job even if that means working with foreign currency.

More than a hundred currencies trade in the global market place. Table 12.3 lists countries, name of their currency, and currency prices measured in U.S. dollars. Some currencies are seldom heard about, such as the *dongo* of Vietnam. Other currency names, such as dollar, are very common. A very short list of countries, however, use the dollar with George Washington's picture (U.S.A. and its territories, Ecuador, Liberia, and Turk Islands). Otherwise, there is big difference in the value of a Canadian dollar versus a Singapore dollar - the currency name is simply a label.

Country or principality	Currency name	Currency price in USD	Country or principality	Currency name	Currency price in USD
Albania	Lek	$0.0103	Lesotho	Maloti	$0.1686
Algeria	Dinar	$0.0138	Liberia	US$	$1.0000
Angola	NewKwanza	$0.0115	Libya	Dinar	$0.7692
Antigua	EastCaribbean$	$0.3745	Liechtenstein	SwissFranc	$0.8432
Argentina	Peso	$0.3417	Lithuania	Lita	$0.3778
Armenia	Dram	$0.0021	Macau	Pataca	$0.1249
Aruba	Florin	$0.5587	Macedonia	Denar	$0.0212
Australia	Dollar	$0.7748	MadagascarDR	MalagasyAriary	$0.0005
Azerbaijan	Manat	$0.0002	Malawi	Kwacha	$0.0093
Bahamas	Dollar	$1.0000	Malaysia	Ringgite	$0.2632
Bahrain	Dinar	$2.6525	Maldives	Rufiya	$0.0778
Bangladesh	Taka	$0.0164	MaliRep	CFAFranc	$0.0020
Barbados	Dollar	$0.5025	Malta	Lira	$3.0257
Belarus	Ruble	$0.0005	Martinique	Franc	$0.1345
Belize	Dollar	$0.5076	Mauritania	Ouguiya	$0.0038
Benin	CFAFranc	$0.0020	Mauritius	Rupee	$0.0353
Bermuda	Dollar	$1.0101	Mexico	Peso	$0.0889
Bhutan	Ngultrum	$0.0229	Moldova	Leu	$0.0796
Bolivia	Bolivian	$0.1241	Mongolia	Tugrik	$0.0008
Bosnia&Herzeg	ConvertibleMark	$0.6720	Montserrat	EastCaribbean$	$0.3745
Botswana	Pula	$0.2246	Morocco	Dirham	$0.1175
BouvetIsland	Krone	$0.1581	Mozambique	Metical	$0.0001
Brazil	Real	$0.3781	Myanmar	Kyat	$0.1558
Brunei	Dollar	$0.6108	Namibia	Dollar	$0.1682
Bulgaria	Lev	$0.6670	NauruIsland	Australia$	$0.7745
BurkinaFaso	CFAFranc	$0.0020	Nepal	Rupee	$0.0139
Burundi	Franc	$0.0009	NetherlandsAntilles	Guilder	$0.5618
Cambodia	Riel	$0.0003	NewZealand	Dollar	$0.7119
Cameroon	CFAFranc	$0.0020	Nicaragua	CordobaOro	$0.0618
Canada	Dollar	$0.8059	Nigeria	Nairam	$0.0076
CapeVerdeIsl	Escudo	$0.0118	Norway	Krone	$0.1581
CaymanIslands	Dollar	$1.2195	Oman	SulRial	$2.5974
CentralAfricanRep	CFAFranc	$0.0020	Pakistan	Rupee	$0.0169
Chad	CFAFranc	$0.0020	Panama	Balboa	$1.0000
Chile	Peso	$0.0017	PapuaNewGuinea	Kina	$0.3260
China	Yuan	$0.1208	Paraguay	Guaranid	$0.0002
Colombia	Peso	$0.0004	Peru	NuevoSol	$0.3069
Comoros	Franc	$0.0026	Philippines	Peso	$0.0182
CongoDemRep	CFAFranc	$0.0020	PitcairnIsland	NZ$	$0.7118
Congo,PeopleRep	CFAFranc	$0.0020	Poland	Zloty	$0.3221
CostaRica	Colon	$0.0022	PuertoRico	US$	$1.0000
Croatia	Kuna	$0.1730	Qatar	Rial	$0.2748
Cuba	Peso	$1.0000	Reunion,Iledela	Franc	$0.1345
Cyprus	Pound	$2.2371	Romania	Leu	$0.0000
CzechRepublic	Koruna	$0.0432	Russia	Ruble (official)	$0.0356
Denmark	Krone	$0.1753	Rwanda	Franc	$0.0018
Djibouti	Franc	$0.0057	SaintChristopher	EastCaribbean$	$0.3745
Dominica	EastCaribbean$	$0.3745	SaintHelena	Pound	$1.8875
DominicanRep	Peso	$0.0365	SaintLucia	EastCaribbean$	$0.3745
Ecuador	US$	$1.0000	SaintPierre	Franc	$0.1345
Egypt	Pound	$0.1713	SaintVincent	EastCaribbean$	$0.3745
ElSalvador	Colon	$0.1143	Samoa,American	US$	$1.0000
EquatorialGuinea	CFAFranc	$0.0020	Samoa,Western	Tala	$0.3825
Estonia	Kroon	$0.0834	SaoTomeandPrincip	Dobra	$0.0001
Ethiopia	Birro	$0.1150	SaudiArabia	Riyal	$0.2667
EuropeanUnion	Euro	$1.3046	Senegal	CFAFranc	$0.0020
FaeroeIslands	DanishKrone	$0.1753	Seychelles	Rupee	$0.1846
FalklandIslands	Pound	$1.5952	SierraLeone	Leone	$0.0004
Fiji	Dollar	$0.6053	Singapore	Dollar	$0.6116
FrenchGuiana	Franc	$0.1345	Slovakia	Koruna	$0.0341
Gabon	CFAFranc	$0.0020	Slovenia	Tolar	$0.0054
Gambia	Dalasi	$0.0343	SolomonIslands	Dollar	$0.1375
Ghana	Cedi	$0.0001	Somalia	Shilling	$0.0003
Gibraltar	Pound	$1.8875	SouthAfrica	Rand	$0.1682
Greenland	DanishKrone	$0.1753	SriLanka	Rupee	$0.0101
Grenada	EastCaribbean$	$0.3745	Sudan	Dinar	$0.0039
Guadeloupe	Franc	$0.1345	SudanRep	Pound	$0.0004
Guam	US$	$1.0000	Suriname	Guilder	$0.0004
Guatemala	Quetzal	$0.1290	Swaziland	Lilangeni	$0.1685
GuineaBissau	CFAFranc	$0.0020	Sweden	Krona	$0.1433
GuineaRep	Franc	$0.0004	Switzerland	Franc	$0.8433
Guyana	Dollar	$0.0056	Syria	Pound	$0.0191
Haiti	Gourde	$0.0276	Taiwan	Dollar	$0.0315
HondurasRep	Lempira	$0.0535	Tanzania	Shilling	$0.0009
HongKong	Dollar	$0.1282	Thailand	Baht	$0.0260

TABLE 12.3

World currency prices measured in U.S. dollars

Country	Currency	Price	Country	Currency	Price
Hungary	Forint	$0.0053	Togo,Rep	CFAFranc	$0.0020
Iceland	Krona	$0.0161	TongaIslands	Pa'anga	$0.5245
India	Rupee	$0.0229	Trinidad&Tobago	Dollar	$0.1595
Indonesia	Rupia	$0.0001	Tunisia	Dinar	$0.8081
Iran	Rialo	$0.0001	Turkey	NewLira	$0.7479
Israel	Shekel	$0.2276	Turks&Caicos	US$	$1.0000
IvoryCoast	CFAFranc	$0.0020	Uganda	Shilling	$0.0006
Jamaica	Dollar	$0.0163	Ukraine	Hryvnia	$0.1882
Japan	Yen	$0.0097	UnitedArabEmir.	Dirham	$0.2723
Jordan	Dinar	$1.4104	UnitedKingdom	PoundSterling	$1.8879
Kazakhstan	Tenge	$0.0077	Uruguay	Peso	$0.0399
Kenya	Shilling	$0.0130	Vanuatu	Vatu	$0.0092
Kiribati	Australia$	$0.7745	Venezuela	Bolivar	$0.0005
Korea,North	Won	$0.4545	Vietnam	Dongo	$0.0001
Korea,South	Won	$0.0010	VirginIslands	US$	$1.0000
Kuwait	Dinar	$3.4247	Yemen	Riala	$0.0055
Laos,PeopleDR	Kip	$0.0001	Yugoslavia	NewDinar	$0.0162
Latvia	Lat	$1.8737	Zambia	Kwacha	$0.0002
Lebanon	Pound	$0.0007	Zimbabwe	Dollar	$0.0002

Notes: The table shows foreign-exchange quotations from Reuters for January 28, 2005.
Source: Wall Street Journal http://online.wsj.com/documents/mktindex.htm?worldval.htm.

Currency prices move as wildly as stock prices. Uncertainty about exchange rate movements introduces risk. Futures contracts on currencies provide a mechanism for business to manage exchange rate risk because they hedge against currency depreciation or appreciation. Currency depreciation or appreciation signifies that a currency's value is declining or increasing. The numeraire is the currency measuring the price of another currency. Most but not all transactions rely on U.S. dollar as numeraire. For this lesson suppose one unit of foreign currency named FC has a price measured by a numeraire currency named NC that equals *a*, as in:

$$1\ FC\ =\ a\ NC.$$

For example, in Table 12.3 the price in dollars of one Mexican peso is 8.89 cents and therefore

$$1\ Mexican\ peso\ =\ 0.0889\ U.S.\ dollars.$$

Rule 12.1 summarizes effect of currency appreciation and depreciation on currency price.

RULE 12.1 Currency appreciation and depreciation

Let *a* equal initial price measured in numeraire currency called *NC* for one foreign currency called *FC*. Let *x* equal the percentage appreciation (x > 0) or depreciation (x < 0) that occurs in the currency price. The price of one *FC* after the change is:

$$1\ FC =\ a\ (1 + x)\ NC.$$

When x is positive the new price of one *FC* is bigger than the old price; this signifies the FC has appreciated (or strengthened) and *NC* depreciated (or weakened). Conversely, a declining price for *FC* implies a depreciating *FC* and appreciating numeraire.

For example, if the Mexican peso appreciates 4 percent relative to the U.S. dollar then find the new price as follows:

$$1\ Mexican\ peso\ =\ 0.0889\ (1 + 0.04)\ U.S.\ dollars,$$

or $\quad 1\ Mexican\ peso\ =\ 0.0925\ U.S.\ dollars.$

The price for 1 peso after it appreciates is 9 1/4 U.S. cents. The peso strengthened and the dollar weakened. The example below applies rule 12.1 and shows how exchange rate risk possibly hurts company performance.

EXAMPLE 5 Currency exchange rate risk and the pretax rate of return

Williams Imagineering Co. of Huntsville is preparing a bid to deliver expert software to the Riccar Co. of Lucerne, Switzerland. Williams estimates that they can produce the software over the next 4 months at a pretax cost of 80,000 U.S. dollars ("USD").

   a. If Williams believes that Riccar were willing to pay for the software in US dollars, how much should Williams bid on the project such that they obtain a 20% pretax rate of return (= Pretax profit ÷ Sales revenue)?
   b. Williams anticipates they have a higher likelihood of winning the job if they accept payment from Riccar denominated in Swiss francs (CHF). Currently, the spot price is 1CHF = 0.8433 USD. What should the bid equal, in CHF, if Williams expects exchange rates to remain constant.
   c. Find affect on pretax rate of return if Williams makes the bid from part b and the exchange rate fluctuates so that in 4 months price of the CHF (i) depreciates or (ii) appreciates 15% relative to the dollar.

SOLUTION

   a. The pretax cost is $80,000 and Williams wants a 20% pretax rate of return. Thus,

   Pretax rate of return = (Sales Revenue – pretax costs) ÷ Sales revenue

   0.20 = (Sales Revenue – $80,000) ÷ Sales revenue

   Sales revenue = $100,000

   The bid should equal $100,000. Subtraction of the $80,000 pretax costs nets pretax profit of $20,000. The pretax rate of return then equals 20% (= $20,000 ÷ $100,000).

   b. The problem tells us that the current spot price is:

   1 CHF = 0.8433 USD

   Williams wants to receive $100,000 USD so its equivalent value in CHF is

   (100,000/0.7865) CHF = 100,000 USD

   or   *118,582 CHF = 100,000 USD*

   If Williams does the job for 118,582 CHF and exchange rates remain constant then Williams is able to convert their CHF into $100,000. This yields $20,000 pretax profit and a 20% pretax rate of return (= $20,000 ÷ $100,000).

c (i). For this problem price of the CHF depreciates 15% relative to the USD and the new currency price in four months for one franc becomes 71.68 US cents (= 0.8433 (1 – 0.15)). The company receives 118,582 CHF for doing the job and exchanges their francs as follows:

   118,582 CHF   =   118,582 (0.7168) USD

   =   85,000 USD

   The 118,582 CHF that Williams receives from Riccar exchanges into 85,000 USD. Actual *Sales revenue* is 15% less than the target of $100,000. Subtraction of $80,000 in pretax costs from actual *Sales revenue* of yields $5,000 of pretax profit and 5.88% pretax rate of return (= $5,000 ÷ $85,000). Effectively, Williams is hurt because the dollar strengthens and they are paid in a foreign currency worth less USD than expected.

c (ii). For this problem price of the CHF appreciates 15% relative to the USD and the new currency price becomes 96.98 US cents (= 0.8433 (1 + 0.15)). The company exchanges 118,582 francs into 115,000 USD (= 118,582 × 0.9698).

Actual *Sales revenue* is 15% larger than target. Subtraction of pretax costs from actual *Sales revenue* yields $35,000 of pretax profit and 30.4% pretax rate of return (= $35,000 ÷ $115,000). Williams is helped because the dollar weakens and they are being paid in a foreign currency that is worth more USD than expected.

Company management may make excellent plans for producing, marketing, and distributing products to clients. Because of factors beyond company control, however, exchange rate risk may sink the best laid plans. Currency prices change as wildly as stock prices and effects can be disastrous for companies conducting international commerce. Almost every large multinational company hedges currency exchange rate risk. The example below considers such a scenario.

EXAMPLE 6 Hedging currency exchange rate risk with a futures contract

The Company produces specialized equipment at a cost of $275,000. They wish to sell the equipment in June to a British client paying with sterling pounds ("GBP") so that the pretax rate of return (= *Pretax profit ÷ Sales revenue*) is 16%. Today's exchange rate quoted in USD per GBP is $1.8879 in the spot market and $1.9450 in the futures market for June delivery. The Company today hedges the revenue by taking an appropriate position on currency futures contracts (assume contracts exist for fractional quantities). By June the spot price of the pound has depreciated 8% relative to the USD; the June futures and spot prices converge. In June the company sells the GBP in the local spot market and closes its futures position with a cash settlement. Find the Company's net revenue associated with the sale. Is the hedge beneficial?

SOLUTION

The pretax cost is $275,000 and target pretax rate of return equals 16%. Thus,

$$0.16 = (Sales\ Revenue - \$275,000) ÷ Sales\ revenue$$

or *Sales revenue* = $327,381.

The company plans to sell the equipment for $327,381. The buyer, however, expects to pay in British pounds. The company uses a futures contract to lock-in the selling price of 1 GBP at $1.9450. The company takes a *short* position in the futures market. The company immediately knows that the selling price in GBP is:

1 GBP	=	*1.9450 USD,*
(327,381/1.945) GBP	=	*327,381 USD,*
168,319 GBP	=	*327,381 USD.*

The company immediately informs the British client that the selling price for the equipment is 168,319 pounds payable in June upon delivery.

The spot price for 1 GBP in June is $1.7369 (= $1.8879 × (1 - 0.08)) because the spot price of the pound depreciates 8%. The company exchanges pounds at the local bank for $292,348 (= $1.7369 × 168,319). They close their futures position on 168,319 GBP at a futures price of $1.7369 (futures price converges to spot price). Beginning futures price was $1.9450. Profit for the short futures position from formula 12.4 equals $35,033 (= 168,319 × ($1.9450 - $1.7369)). The currency exchange at the local bank plus profit on the futures contract totals $327,381. Subtract the pretax cost of $275,000 and find pretax rate of return equals the 16% target.

The futures market hedge is beneficial. Company receives payment in June in British pounds that are worth less USD than expected because the pound depreciated. The hedge let them avoid an unexpected loss.

Numerical quickies

1. Awhile ago futures contracts for crawdads (1250 lbs. per contract) traded at a futures price of $3.90 per lb. Today the futures price is $3.71. The margin on the contract is 2.25%. Find for a speculative investor that was long one contract during this period the profit (or loss) and rate of return. ©FT1b

2. The Company hopes to win a job for delivering its product to an overseas client. The Company must submit a bid to the client stating the cost of the job and the client decides whether or not to hire the Company. The Company estimates they can produce the product over the next few months at a pretax cost of $110,000. Their target pretax profit margin (= Pretax profit (Sales revenue) for this job is 12%. The Company is willing to accept payment from the client in foreign currency (krone). The spot exchange rate today is 1 USD = 1.35 krone.

2a. The company makes a bid such that if exchange rates remain constant the company gets the target pretax profit margin. How much in krone does the bid equal? ©FT4am

2b. The client agrees to pay the Company its requested bid, but by the time the Company receives the payment the price of the krone has appreciated by 10 percent relative to the dollar. Find the actual pretax profit margin. ©FT4cm

3. A futures contract provides the opportunity to lock-in the exchange rate at which you can buy or sell 100,000 pesos. The futures price quoted in U.S. cents per peso currently is 76.60. The margin requirement is 1.75%. You enter short on one contract. Thereafter, the price of the peso appreciates 6% relative to the USD. You then close your futures position. Find your profit (or loss) and rate of return. ©FT5a

4. This is January and the Company plans on harvesting 40,000 bushels of soybeans in October. Currently, soybeans cost $3.00 per bushel in the cash market and $3.10 in the futures market for November delivery. The Company today goes short on 4 contracts (10,000 bushels each). In October, the Company delivers 40,000 bushels in the local market for the cash price of $4.00. Also in October the Company closes its futures position on the November contracts at a futures price of $4.30. Find the Company's net revenue and the benefit of the hedging strategy. ©FT3a

5. This is January and the Company plans on receiving from its foreign subsidiary 120,000 sucre in June. Today's exchange rate quoted in U.S. cents per sucre is 74.20 in the local spot market and 74.50 in the futures market for July delivery. The Company today goes short on 5 contracts (24,000 sucre each). By June the price of the sucre has depreciated 4% relative to the USD; this percentage change is reflected in both the spot and futures exchange rates. So in June the Company sells in the local spot market and, also, the Company closes its futures position with a cash settlement. What is the Company's net revenue associated with these transactions? ©FT6a

3. OPTION CONTRACTS

Increasing sophistication of financial markets led to development within recent decades of another widely available financial security: the *option*.

> **DEFINITION 12.2 Long option position**
>
> A long option position is the right but not the obligation to buy (*call* option) or sell (*put* option) an underlying asset (the *underlier*) at a fixed price (the *strike* price) on or before an expiration date (*expiry*).

Options exist on many different types of underlying assets: stocks, currencies, indexes, commodities, interest rates, etc. Some options are private business-to-business contracts with substantial counterparty risk. Other options are issued by companies to key stakeholders or capitalists. Yet other options are standardized and marketable securities that trade on exchanges such as the American Stock Exchange (AMEX), Chicago Board Options Exchange (CBOE), or the International Securities Exchange (ISE). Lessons herein focus on marketable options.

Marketable stock options are especially popular. A call option contract on IBM with strike price of $50 and expiry next January, for example, provides the owner of the option the right to buy 100 shares of IBM for $50 per share anytime on or before expiration next January. The call option is especially valuable when IBM trades for a price bigger than $50. If IBM were trading at $80, for example, the call option provides its owner with a $30 advantage for purchasing a share. If on the other hand the price of IBM were below $50 at expiry then the owner of the call option throws away the option because it offers no advantage.

A long put option position provides the right to sell the underlier at the strike price on or before expiry. A Microsoft put option with strike of $40 is especially valuable when, for example, Microsoft trades for $25. Owner of the put option contract can sell 100 shares for $40 each, an advantage of $15 per share.

Option contracts are valuable tools. Getting into a long option position requires purchasing the option and paying the market price. The price of an option is called the premium. Losses on long option positions are limited because, unlike futures contracts which entail an obligation, a long option position always may be discarded. Table 12.4 compares characteristics of futures and options.

TABLE 12.4
Characteristics of futures and option contracts

	futures contract (long or short)	long option position (call or put)	short option position (call or put)
initial cash flow	free to enter but requires deposit of refundable collateral *(margin)*	requires payment of purchase price *(premium)* to the short-side	receives purchase price (premium) from the long-side
terminal cash flow	profit increases as underlier price rises (long-side) or falls (short-side); otherwise loss is unlimited	profit increases as underlier price rises (call) or falls (put); otherwise loss is limited to premium	when long-side discards option terminal CF= 0; otherwise loss is unlimited
obligation	either buy (long-side) or sell (short-side) underlier at fixed futures price or buyout contract	pay the purchase price and have right to exercise or discard the option	fulfill wish of long-side and sell (call) or buy (put) underlier at the strike price

Figure 12.1 illustrates number of option contracts traded on five major exchanges since 1973 when the CBOE began trading call options (the CBOE started trading put options in 1977). Total U.S. option contracts traded in year 2003 is 908 million (this includes stock options, index options, etc.). In 1993 the total is 232 million. This represents an average growth rate of 14.6% per year - that's a fairly big growth rate. Investors increasingly rely on options for attaining financial objectives.

Especially noteworthy is history of the International Securities Exchange (ISE) in New York. This exchange was founded in year 2000 as a fully electronic options exchange by Bill Porter, previous chairman of E*Trade, and several other entrepreneurs. The steep line for ISE in figure 12.1 shows how this new exchange has grown in 5 years to rival the decades old CBOE and surpass the centuries old AMEX. A visit to company website www.iseoptions.com is recommended.

Trades of all option contracts at the CBOE in 2003 represent about 31% of U.S. option trading (ISE is 27% in 2003). Daily dollar volume at the CBOE is nearly $600 million of which 56% are for call contracts and 44% for put contracts. The average premium per contract in 2003 at the CBOE is $522. The CBOE trades options for stocks (61%), indexes (39%), and interest rates (less than 1%). For CBOE stock options in 2003 the premium averages $200, that's $2 per share of stock.

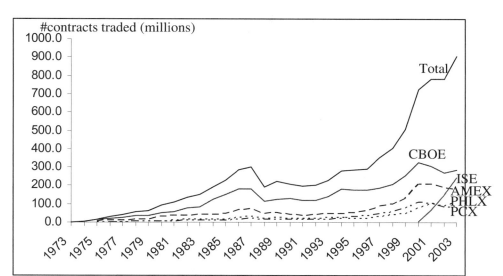

Notes: Total is the sum of contracts traded on these five exchanges: Chicago Board Options Exchange (CBOE), International Securities Exchange (ISE), American Stock Exchange (AMEX), Philadelphia Stock Exchange (PHLX), and Pacific Stock Exchange (PCX). Source: Chicago Board Options Exchange http://www.cboe.com/data/marketstats-2003.pdf

Trading volume at option exchanges over the past decade has been phenomenal. Lessons from previous chapters show that stock market trading has grown phenomenally, too. Dollar volume of options trading in 2003 approximately equals 5% of stock market volume. Some options trading surely is speculative in nature, but options nonetheless provide financial managers with opportunities for implementing risk management strategies. Sections below offer lessons on how companies and investors utilize options.

3.A. Call options

A call option provides the owner with the right to buy an underlying asset on or before expiry at a fixed strike price. Purchase of a call option requires paying its market price to the seller (the seller is the short-side for this trade). The option price, also known as the premium, rises and falls in response to market demand. The single most important factor driving the premium is the price of the underlier. A call option to buy IBM for a $50 strike price, for example, is more valuable when IBM trades at $80 than at $51. Option contracts, like futures, derive value based upon price of the underlying asset. Futures and options for this reason are known as derivative securities.

The payoff on a call option at expiry equals:

FORMULA 12.5 Call option payoff for a stock option

$$\begin{pmatrix} call\ option \\ payoff \\ at\ expiry \end{pmatrix} = maximum\left[0,\ \left(\begin{matrix} stock \\ price \end{matrix} - \begin{matrix} strike \\ price \end{matrix} \right) \right]$$

The option payoff is zero if the stock price at expiry is less than the strike price. Conversely, the payoff surpasses zero as the stock price rises above the strike price. Terminal payoff for a long call option position increases with price of the underlier.

The option investment yields a profit of $0, and hence a 0% rate of return, when the payoff just equals the initial cost of purchasing the option. The stock price at expiry that yields the 0% rate of return for the option is called the "break-even stock price." Solve for this break-even stock price from the following definition for a non-zero payoff:

payoff for an in-the-money call option = stock price – strike price.

Set the payoff equal to the initial cost of the option, and solve for the break-even stock price:

$$\left(\begin{array}{c} \text{initial} \\ \text{cost of} \\ \text{call option} \end{array}\right) = \left(\begin{array}{c} \text{break} - \text{even} \\ \text{stock price} \end{array} - \begin{array}{c} \text{strike} \\ \text{price} \end{array}\right)$$

$$\left(\begin{array}{c} \text{break} - \text{even} \\ \text{stock price} \end{array}\right) = \left(\begin{array}{c} \text{strike} \quad \text{initial} \\ \text{price} + \text{cost of} \\ \text{call option} \end{array}\right)$$

The break-even stock price equals the sum of strike price and initial cost of the option.

EXAMPLE 7 Call option rate of return

Common stock for Microsoft Co. is currently trading at $83.50. A call option on the stock with expiry in three months and strike of $90 is priced at $7 1/8. Explain whether the following statements are accurate?

    a. If the stock price at expiry is $87 then investment in the stock would have provided a lower rate of return than investment in the option.

    b. If the stock price at expiry is $94 then investment in the option would have provided a lower rate of return than investment in the stock.

    c. If the stock price at expiry is $100 then investment in the option would have provided a greater rate of return than investment in the stock.

SOLUTION

    a. Notice that the option's rate of return is –100% because the stock price, $87, is less than the strike, $90. The stock price ends slightly (+4.19%) higher than its beginning price of $83.50. Without making any computations whatsoever, we see the stock rate of return exceeds the option rate of return so the statement is false.

    b. For this problem, the strike is 90 and the original option cost is 7 1/8. The break-even stock price is:

$$\left(\begin{array}{c} \text{break} - \text{even} \\ \text{stock price} \end{array}\right) = 90 + 7.125$$

$$= \$97.125$$

When the stock price at expiry is $97 1/8 the payoff equals $7 1/8. This exactly equals the initial cost of the option, and implies the profit and rate of return from the option investment equals zero.

    The actual stock price at expiry, $94, is less than the break-even stock price of $97. Computations are unnecessary to realize that the rate of return on the option investment is negative. The stock rate of return, which obviously in positive, exceeds the option rate of return so the statement is true.

    c. This problem requires a few computations in order to determine whether the statement is true or false. The percentage change in the stock price is 19.76%; the stock begins at $83.50 and ends at $100.00. Compare this to the option rate of return. First, find the payoff when the stock price at expiry is $100:

$$\text{call option payoff} = \text{maximum} [\, 0\,,\, 100 - 90\,]$$

$$= \$10\,.$$

For the option investment, the payoff is $10 whereas the initial cost is $7 1/8. To find the rate of return. The rate of return is 40.3% (=($10 ÷ 7.725)-1) The option rate of return exceeds the stock rate of return so the statement is true.

EXAMPLE 8 Find stock price giving call option ROR

You buy 1 share of stock at $41 and also purchase one call option with strike of $40 at a price of $1.50 . What is the stock price at expiry such that your overall rate of return on the position is: (a) 0%; (b) 10%; (c) –10%?

SOLUTION

a. You buy 1 share for $41 and one call option for $1.50. Your total initial cost therefore equals $42.50. The rate of return on your investment in this position compares the beginning wealth of $42.50 with your ending wealth. To receive a zero percent rate of return, as in this problem, your ending wealth equals $42.50.

The ending wealth equals the sum of the stock price at expiry plus the payoff on the call option. The call option payoff is

call option payoff =   maximum [0 , stock price –40]

Setting the desired ending wealth to its components shows

ending wealth =   stock price + maximum [0 , stock price –40]

$42.50 =   stock price + maximum [0 , stock price –40]

To solve for the stock price we must check each of the two conditions in the payoff function. If the resultant stock price is logically consistent with the stipulated condition, then it is the answer.

To check the first condition in the payoff function, suppose the stock price is less than $40. The call option payoff subsequently equals zero. The equation for ending wealth given this condition is

$42.50 =   stock price + 0 ,

or   stock price = $42.50 .

The resultant stock price is *in*consistent with the stipulated condition. Therefore, this is **not** the answer.

To check the second condition in the payoff function, suppose the stock price exceeds $40. The call option payoff subsequently is positive. The equation for ending wealth given this condition is

$42.50 =   stock price + stock price – 40 ,

or   stock price = $41.25 .

The resultant stock price is consistent with the stipulated condition. Therefore, this **is** the answer.

When the stock price at expiry equals $41.25, the call option payoff is $1.25. The call option payoff, together with the share that you own, have a total value of $42.50—an amount exactly equal to your initial investment.

b. Because your rate of return is 10%, and your beginning wealth is $42.50, your ending wealth is $46.75 (=$42.50 × 1.10). As in the previous problem, equate the ending wealth to the sum of the stock price at expiry plus the call option payoff. Solve for the stock price for both conditions in the payoff function.

To check the first condition in the payoff function, suppose the stock price is less than $40. The call option payoff subsequently equals zero. The equation for ending wealth given this condition is

$46.75 =   stock price + 0 ,

or   stock price = $46.75 .

The resultant stock price is *in*consistent with the stipulated condition. Therefore, this is **not** the answer.

To check the second condition in the payoff function, suppose the stock price exceeds $40. The call option payoff subsequently is positive. The equation for ending wealth given this condition is

$$\$46.75 = \text{stock price} + \text{stock price} - 40 ,$$

or $\text{stock price} = \$43.375 .$

The resultant stock price is consistent with the stipulated condition. Therefore, this is the answer.

c. Solve for the ending wealth given an initial wealth of $42.50 and –10% rate of return.

$$-0.10 = (\text{ending wealth} \div \$42.50) - 1$$

$$\text{ending wealth} = \$38.25 .$$

Equate the ending wealth to the sum of the stock price at expiry plus the call option payoff, and check for both conditions.

To check the first condition in the payoff function, suppose the stock price is less than $40. The call option payoff subsequently equals zero. The equation for ending wealth given this condition is

$$\$38.25 = \text{stock price} + 0 , \quad \text{or} \quad \text{stock price} = \$38.25 .$$

The resultant stock price is consistent with the stipulated condition. Therefore, this is a correct answer. To be complete, check the second condition that the stock price exceeds $40. The call option payoff subsequently is positive. The equation for ending wealth given this condition is

$$\$38.25 = \text{stock price} + \text{stock price} - 40 , \quad \text{or} \quad \text{stock price} = \$39.125 .$$

The resultant stock price is *in*consistent with the stipulated condition. Therefore, this is not an answer.

EXAMPLE 9 Call option portfolio insurance

You pursue a 2-year investment strategy that is tied to the good fortunes of the General Electric company. Instead of buying shares in GE, however, you instead pursue a portfolio insurance strategy that invests 90% of your $10,000 in a safe money market account earning 7.8% compounded monthly. The remainder of your funds is allocated to long term call options ("LEAPS") on General Electric. The options expire 24 months from now, have a strike of 110, and cost $12.50. The GE shareprice is 103. Suppose you can buy fractional options.

    a. How much is invested in options and how much in the safe asset?
    b. What is the floor below which your wealth will not dip?
    c. If at expiry GE is up 30%, what is your position's rate of return?

SOLUTION

a. Ninety percent of your $10,000 is invested in the money market; this is $9,000. The remaining $1,000 is invested in call options that cost $12.50 each. You buy 80 call options.

b. You will not lose the $9,000 invested in the money market regardless of occurrences in the stock market. In fact, you also are certainly going to earn interest on your money market account, although there is uncertainty about exactly what the rate may equal. Given that the interest rate is 7.8% compounded monthly, and your money is invested for 24 months, then your ending balance for the money market account is determined as follows:

$$FV = 9000 \times (1 + .078/12)^{24}$$

$$= \$10,514 .$$

No matter what, you at least end with $10,514 after 24 months. Notice that in the worst case you lose the $1,000 invested in options. This worst case occurs if the GE shareprice in 2-years is less than the strike of $110. Still, however, your rate of return for this worst case scenario is 5.14%.

c. When GE rises 30%, it closes at $133.90. The payoff on each option is $23.90. For your 80 options, the total payoff is $1,912. Add this to the money market terminal value of $10,514 and the total position is worth $12,426. This is a 24.26% return. It is less than the 30% movement in shareprice, but then again this portfolio insurance strategy limits downside risk—your downside loss is a +5.14% gain, and your upside potential is unlimited.

3.B. Put options

The put option payoff is

FORMULA 12.6 Put option payoff

$$\begin{pmatrix} put\ option \\ payoff \\ at\ expiry \end{pmatrix} = maximum \left[0, \left(\begin{matrix} strike \\ price \end{matrix} - \begin{matrix} stock \\ price \end{matrix} \right) \right]$$

The option payoff is zero if the stock price at expiry exceeds the strike price. Conversely, the payoff surpasses zero as the stock price falls below the strike price—the put option gains as the stock price falls.

EXAMPLE 10 Put option portfolio insurance

You buy 100 shares of Pacific Dunlop at $43 per share and also purchase 100 put options with strike of $40 at a price of $ 3/8.

   a. If the stock price at expiry equals $46 then what is your overall rate of return?
   b. What is the stock price at expiry such that your overall rate of return is 0%?
   c. How does your portfolio perform if the share price falls below $40?

SOLUTION

a. You buy 100 shares for $4,300 and 100 put options for $37.50 . Your total initial cost therefore equals $4,337.50. The rate of return on your investment in this position compares the beginning wealth of $4,337.50 with your ending wealth.

   The ending wealth equals the sum of the stock price at expiry plus the payoff on the put option. For this problem, the stock price at expiry is $46. The put option payoff is zero because the actual stock price exceeds the strike. Consequently, the only asset of value at expiry is the 100 shares. The shares are worth a total of $4,600. The rate of return is therefore 6.04% [= ($4,600 / $4,337.50) −1].

b. A zero rate of return occurs when your ending wealth is $4337.50. Setting the desired ending wealth to the sum of its components shows that for all 100 shares:

$$ending\ wealth = 100 \times \{ stock\ price + maximum\ [\ 0\ ,\ 40 - stock\ price\ ]\ \}$$

$$\$4,337.50 = 100 \times \{ stock\ price + maximum\ [\ 0\ ,\ 40 - stock\ price\ ]\ \}$$

$$\$43.375 = stock\ price + maximum\ [\ 0\ ,\ 40 - stock\ price\ ]$$

To solve for the stock price we must check each of the two conditions in the payoff function. If the resultant stock price is logically consistent with the stipulated condition, then it is the answer.

   To check the first condition in the payoff function, suppose the stock price exceeds $40. The put option payoff subsequently equals zero. The equation for ending wealth given this condition is

$$\$43.375 = stock\ price + 0,$$

or $stock\ price = \$43.375.$

The resultant stock price is consistent with the stipulated condition. Therefore, this *is* an answer.

For completeness, check the second condition in the payoff function. Suppose the stock price is less than $40. The "put" option payoff subsequently is positive. The equation for ending wealth given this condition is

$$\$43.375 \;=\; stock\ price + 40 - stock\ price \;,$$

or $\qquad \$43.375 = 40$

This answer is *in*consistent. Therefore, this is **not** the answer.

When the stock price at expiry equals $43.375, the put option is worthless but the share that you own exactly equals your initial investment.

c. Below a shareprice of $40, the put offers a positive payoff equal to 40 – P, where P is the shareprice. Your share is worth P, and your option pays off 40 – P. Your ending wealth is the sum of these two:

$$ending\ wealth \;=\; 100 \times (\,P + 40 - P\,)$$
$$=\; \$4,000$$

No matter how low the shareprice falls, you always end up with $4,000. Your worst case rate of return therefore equals

$$rate\ of\ return \;=\; (\,ending\ wealth \div beginning\ wealth\,) - 1$$
$$=\; (\,\$4,000 \div \$4,337.50\,) - 1$$
$$=\; -7.79\%$$

EXAMPLE 11 Straddle

Due to political events you believe that the markets are unusually nervous. You also believe that the uncertainty will be resolved in the near future and that consequently stocks either will rise or fall, but they likely will not remain unchanged. You therefore enter long in a "straddle" on IBM stock options. In particular, you go long on one put option with strike of 60 and price of $0.13, and you go long on one call with strike of 60 and price of $1.25. The share currently is trading at $61.

    a. What is the maximum possible loss?
    b. Suppose the stock price at expiry is $65 . What is the rate of return for the straddle?
    c. What is the stock price at expiry such that the rate of return on the straddle is 0%?

SOLUTION

a. The initial investment is $0.13 for the put and $1.25 for the call, totaling $1.38. This is the most you can lose. The payoff equals zero for both the call and the put when the stock price at expiry equals the strike price. For both options, the strike price is $60. Thus, you'll lose everything if the shareprice at expiry is $60.

When the stock price at expiry is below $60, your put generates a payoff whereas the call is worthless. When the stock price at expiry exceeds $60 the call generates a payoff whereas the put is worthless. The worst case outcome is a $60 stock price.

b. When the stock price at expiry equals $65 the put is worthless whereas the call generates a $5 payoff per share. Your ending wealth therefore is $5. Your rate of return is 262% [= ($5.00 – $1.38) / $1.38].

c. The rate of return is zero when the total payoff equals the initial cost of $1.38. There are two possible scenarios. One possibility occurs when the put generates the $1.38 payoff while the call is worthless. The other possibility occurs when the call generates the $1.38 payoff while the put is worthless.

When the stock price at expiry is less than the $60 strike by $1.38, the put generates a payoff of $1.38. Thus, at a stock price of $58.62 (= $60 – $1.38) the rate of return on the straddle is zero. Any stock price less than $58.62 implies a positive rate of return for the straddle.

When the stock price at expiry exceeds the $60 strike by $1.38, the call generates a payoff of $1.38. Thus, at a stock price of $61.38 (= $60 + $1.38) the rate of return on the straddle is zero. Any stock price greater than $61.38 implies a positive rate of return for the straddle.

EXERCISES 12.3

Numerical quickies

1. A common stock has a current share price of $10.80. A call option on the stock with strike of $2.50 has an option price of $5.00. How much is the arbitrage profit? ©DS10

2. Company shares have a current market price of $69.00. A call option on the shares has a strike of $70 and a price of $1.00. Find the rate of return on the call option investment if at expiry the percentage change in shareprice is 21%. ©DS2a

3. Suppose a call option with strike of 60 costs $5.60.

3a. Find the underlying stock price at expiry such that the profit is zero. ©DS3a

3b. Find the underlying stock price at expiry such that the rate of return on the option investment is 160%. ©DS3b

4. You buy 1 share of stock at $20.35 and also purchase one put option with strike of $25.00 and option price of $7.75. Find the stock price at expiry such that your overall rate of return on the position is 21%. ©DS22

5. You buy 1 share of stock at $33.20 and also purchase one put option with strike of $35 and price of $4.00.

5a. Find the overall rate of return on your position for the worst-case outcome. ©DS4bm

5b. Suppose the percentage change in stock price at expiry is 8%. Find the overall rate of return from the position. ©DS4am

6. You buy a put option on 3,000 Euros with a strike of 1.10 USD for a price of 0.0560 USD per Euro. At expiry, the spot exchange rate is 1 Euro = 0.89 USD and you cash in the options at their payoff value (if any). Find the rate of return from this speculative transaction. ©DS5a

Numerical challengers

7. Your company purchases a call option on Corn in order to hedge its production costs. The quote for the option looks like this:

CORN 5,000 bushels; cents per bushel

strike	call last
208	14.10

The spot price of corn at expiry is $2.55 per bushel and the option price converged to its intrinsic value. How much money did this strategy save your company? ©DS24

8. You have $14,000 to invest in Company shares that currently trade at $25.20. You choose to invest 10% of your funds in long-term call options with a strike of 30 that currently are quoted at $0.70. The options expire in 10 months. The other funds will be placed into a money market earning 5.5% compounded monthly.

8a. Find the rate of return for the holding period in the worst-case outcome. ©DS6bm

8b. Find the rate of return for the holding period on the total investment position if the share price is up 28% at expiry. ©DS6am

9. The price of Company stock currently is $38.60. You have $10,000 available for investing in the good fortunes of the Company. Instead of buying the stock, however, you pursue a portfolio insurance strategy that invests in a money market account earning 7.20% compounded monthly. Also, you invest in call options on the Company stock with a strike of $47.50 and option price of $3.50 (assume you can buy fractions of options). Your allocation assures you that, even in a worst-case scenario, you will not lose more than $2,000 of your original principal. Suppose that at the conclusion of your 28 month investment horizon the Company stock has risen 30%. Find the ending wealth and rate of return for the investment strategy. ©DS17a

10. Many individual investors employ a "buy-and-write" investment strategy that involves a long stock position and short call position. You implement the strategy by buying a stock at price $40.65 and writing a call with strike of $50.00 and option price of $5.60. In one year you receive the stock's annual dividend of $2.85.

10a. Find the maximum annual rate of return that you can possibly earn from this buy-and-write strategy. ©DS23

10b. Suppose that in one year the stock price has increased 11%. Find the amount by which the rate of return for this buy-and-write strategy exceeds the rate of return for the stock-only strategy. ©DS19b

11. Today is Jan. 2, 2525 and the Company plans to exchange 4,000 Euros with its international subsidiary in 3 months. A put option on Euros with a strike of 1.12 USD and expiry in 3 months costs 0.043 USD per Euro. The Company buys put options on 4,000 Euros. In 3 months, just prior to expiration of the options, the spot exchange rate is 1 Euro = 0.92 USD. The Company cashes in the options at their intrinsic value and sells 4,000 Euros at the spot exchange rate. Find the net revenue in USD of exchanging the Euros. ©DS5b

12. The share price of Company stock currently is $54.00. Due to a pending court case there is a lot of uncertainty about the Company. You believe the share price might either rise a lot or fall a lot. You do not buy the share. Instead, you buy one call option that costs $9.80 and you buy one put option that costs $0.90. For both options, the strike is 45.

12a. Describe how possible rates of return depend on the stock price at expiry. ©DS8

12b. Describe the outcome(s) that generate a 30% overall rate of return from investment in the options. ©DS7c

12c. If at expiry the share price is $36.60 what is your overall rate of return? ©DS7b

13. You have accumulated 1,800 shares of company stock because of a generous employee stock ownership plan. Today's share price is $32.50. You use a collar to lock-in the value 8 months from now of today's stock holdings. The collar takes a long position on 1,800 put options with strike of 35 and per unit option price of $7.50. Also you take a short position on 1,800 call options with strike of 45 and per unit option price of $4.00. Compute the initial cash flow for the collar, the maximum ending wealth, and the minimum ending wealth. ©DS9

4. IMPORTANT INTERNATIONAL ARBITRAGE RELATIONSHIPS

International currency flows lubricate global business. Currencies are commodities. Like all other commodities they have prices. When a business wishes to exchange, say, $100 for British pounds the business effectively sells U.S. dollars and buys British pounds. The exchange rate represents the currency price. This currency exchange in every way is analogous to a trip to the grocery store to buy milk. You sell your dollars and buy the milk. The price of milk represents the exchange rate between milk and dollars. Likewise, between all currency pairs there exists a price representing the exchange rate.

The currency *foreign exc*hange market, known as the *forex* market, began maturing in 1971 when major world economies adopted floating exchange rate systems. A floating exchange rate is one where supply and demand by traders determines currency price. Currency traders include multinational companies like General Electric or Toyota and financial institutions such as Compass Bank or J.P. Morgan Chase. Even some households trade currencies through internet accounts (an internet search for "forex" finds hoards of companies wanting your business). Other currency traders include government central banks such as the Federal Reserve Bank of the U.S.A. or the Bank of England or the European Central Bank or the Bank of Japan. Around the globe more than 50 central banks hold membership in the Bank for International Settlements (see www.bis.org) and exert significant influence on currency supply and demand.

Prior to 1971 exchange rates did not float. Instead, for the decades following World War II exchange rates were set at fixed prices in accordance with the Bretton-Woods Agreement of 1944 (not all governments became members of the system). This fixed exchange rate system forced currency exchanges at prices established by central banks through a committee within the newly established International Monetary Fund ("IMF"). U.S. companies making sales in France and receiving French francs, for example, exchanged francs into dollars at local banks with fixed prices set by the IMF. Banks and businesses around the world used these fixed exchange rates for converting currencies. Quite often, however, forces of supply and demand caused a currency's market price to diverge from the official government exchange rate.

Currencies are widely held by everybody (check your wallet) and even though government central banks exert significant influence other traders also affect supply and demand. A hotel in Paris, for example, would give a businessman a hotel bill denominated in francs. The hotel allowed the businessman to pay in either French francs or U.S. dollars. But the hotel was forced by law to use the official government exchange rate. Out on the street money-changers made a living by trading currencies at black-market floating exchange rates related to currency supply and demand. The hotel guest found advantageous prices for currency exchange in the black market. The businessman, and companies too, could rely on black-market money-changers to exchange currency and thereby reduce costs or increase revenue.

Currency black-markets grew. Governments increasingly had trouble holding the line on fixed currency prices. For a government to set the price of its currency is analogous to IBM setting the price of its stock - that's fine as long as everyone agrees but when supply and demand shift then economic forces cause the price to float away from its official fixed point. In 1971 the Bretton-Woods system of fixed prices disbanded and member central banks officially accepted free-market floating exchange rates. A flood of financial companies moved into the currency exchange line of business. The forex market flourished - and continues to do so. Currency prices in today's world, like prices for stocks, bonds, and milk, are set by competitive free-market forces of supply and demand.

The currency exchange market is the world's largest financial market. Table 12.5 shows that average trading volume for 2004 exceeds $1,800 billion dollars *per day*. Look back to chapter 7 and find that Table 7.1 shows average daily trading volume for the New York Stock Exchange in 2004 is $46 billion. Certainly the NYSE is huge and influential. But the difference between $46 billion and $1,800 billion (per day!) is a remarkable fact attesting to the power and pervasiveness of economic globalization. The forex market is by far the most liquid and active financial market in the world. Prices in this market float on global consensus estimates of currency values. It is impossible for any individual, company, central bank, or even any government, to persistently resist the free-market price for a dollar or dinar, rupee or ruble, yen or euro, or any other world currency.

TABLE 12.5
Average daily trading volume in the currency foreign exchange market (measured in billions of U.S. dollars).

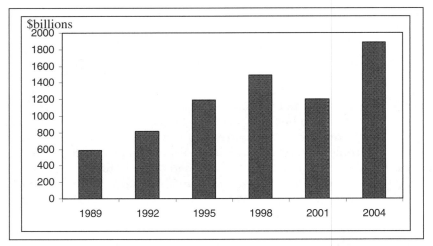

Source: Bank for International Settlements. http://www.bis.org/publ/qtrpdf/r_qt0412f.pdf

More than three-quarters of all forex activity involves the euro (EUR), Japanese yen (JPY), Australian dollar (AUD), Canadian dollar (CAD), Swiss franc (CHF), or British pound (GBP). Most trades involve the U.S. dollar (USD) on one side. Trading between two non-dollar currencies usually occurs by first trading one against the USD and then trading the USD against the second non-dollar currency. The USD is indeed the numeraire for measuring the price of all other currencies (this stems from the Bretton-Woods proclamation that $35 USD is "good-as-gold"). Direct and heavily traded non-USD currency pairs include GBP-to-EUR, EUR-to-CHF, EUR-to-JPY, and AUD-to-JPY.

Trading in the forex market is decentralized without exchanges or physical trading floors. Trades occur between any two counterparties agreeing to trade via telephone or electronic networks such as Reuters.com. Still, forex businesses concentrate geographically and London is site for about 30% of the market, New York handles 20%, Tokyo 12%, Zurich, Frankfurt, Hong Kong and Singapore each represent about 7% of the forex market, and Paris and Sydney host about 3% each.

4.A. Triangle arbitrage and currency prices

The term *cross-rate* refers to the price between two non-USD currencies. The currency price measured in British pounds for buying one Swiss franc, for example, is a cross-rate. Between the GBP, CHF, and USD there exist three currency pairs (GBP-to-USD, CHF-to-USD, and GBP-to-CHF) and three relative prices. Relations between prices for <u>any</u> 3 currencies abide by a triangle arbitrage equilibrium condition. Suppose for this lesson that numbers a and b measure prices in numeraire currency NC for one unit of foreign currencies FCA and FCB, respectively:

$$1\ FCA\ =\ a\ NC$$

and $1\ FCB\ =\ b\ NC$.

Rearrange and find that:

$$1/a\ FCA\ =\ 1/b\ FCB.$$

The preceding formula implies the equilibrium cross-rate for one unit of currency FCA as measured by FCB equals a/b. Formula 12.7 summarizes this lesson.

Prices for 1 unit of foreign currencies *FCA* and *FCB* as measured by numeraire *NC* equal *a* and *b* respectively. Equilibrium cross-rate between currencies *FCA* and *FCB* is given by:

$$\begin{pmatrix} equilibrium\ price \\ measured\ in\ FCB \\ for\ 1\ unit\ of\ FCA \end{pmatrix} = a/b.$$

Violation of formula 12.7 implies existence of arbitrage profits.

When the actual cross-rate for 1 unit of *FCA* differs from the no-arbitrage equilibrium cross-rate in formula 12.7 then arbitrage profit exists. Capture the arbitrage profit by executing three simultaneous trades between numeraire, *FCA*, and *FCB*. The exact sequence of trades depends on whether the actual cross-rate exceeds (overvalues) or is less (undervalues) than equilibrium. Rule 12.2 describes the triangle arbitrage trading strategy. The rule writes three trades involving three currency pairs wherein the middle trade is sale of overvalued and purchase of undervalued foreign currencies, respectively. First and last currency pairs involve the numeraire.

Prices for 1 unit of foreign currencies *FCA* and *FCB* as measured by numeraire equal *a* and *b* respectively. Equilibrium cross-rate for one unit of currency *FCA* as measured by *FCB* equals *a/b*. When actual cross-rate exceeds *a/b* then *FCA* is overvalued relative to *FCB* and vice versa. This trading strategy captures the arbitrage profit:

	TRADE 1		TRADE 2		TRADE 3

$$\begin{pmatrix} sell & buy \\ numeraire & overvalued \\ & FC \end{pmatrix} \begin{pmatrix} sell & buy \\ overvalued & undervalued \\ FC & FC \end{pmatrix} \begin{pmatrix} sell & buy \\ undervalued & numeraire \\ FC & \end{pmatrix}$$

Percentage profit from the arbitrage strategy equals percentage mispricing between actual and no-arbitrage cross-rates.

The example below illustrates why currency exchange rates must stay within rather tight tolerance limits.

EXAMPLE 12 Triangle arbitrage with USD as numeraire

The *Wall Street Journal* shows the following for currency exchange rates

COUNTRY	USD EQUIVALENT	CURRENCY PER USD
Britain (Pound, "GBP")	1.8879	0.5297
Switzerland (Franc, "CHF")	0.8433	1.1858

Suppose you begin with $10,000 USD.

    a. How much of each currency can you purchase?
    b. What does the table imply about the GBP-to-CHF cross-rate?
    c. Describe the possible triangle arbitrage if the actual cross-rate between GBP and CHF is 1 GBP = 2.50 CHF.

SOLUTION

    a. To find how much GBP equals $10,000 express the GBP-to-USD currency pair as an equation:

$$0.5297\ GBP = 1\ USD$$

The *Wall Street Journal*, like many other sources, reports two numbers between USD and GBP. The "USD equivalent" of 1.8879 is the price measured in dollars of 1 British pound. The "Currency per USD" of 0.5297 is reciprocal of 1.8879 and measures price in GBP of 1 USD. Multiply each side of the equation by 10,000.

$$5,297 \ GBP \ = \ 10,000 \ USD.$$

Computations for the CHF show

$$1.1858 \ CHF \ = \ 1 \ USD$$

or $11,858 \ CHF \ = \ 10,000 \ USD.$

$10,000 is equivalent in value to 11,858 Swiss francs or 5,297 British pounds.

b. Because one USD is the same as any other USD the following should hold true for the GBP-to-CHF currency pair:

$$0.5297 \ GBP \ = \ 1.1858 \ CHF.$$

Solve for price of British pound as measured by Swiss franc:

$$1 \ GBP \ = \ 2.2387 \ CHF.$$

2.2387 Swiss francs represents equilibrium cross-rate for 1 British pound. This result is consistent with formula 12.7 wherein prices in USD for 1 GBP is $a = \$1.8879$ and for 1 CHF is $b = \$0.8433$; equilibrium cross-rate a/b equals 2.2387.

c. The problem states that the actual cross-rate is:

$$1 \ GBP \ = \ 2.50 \ CHF.$$

The actual price for 1 GBP of 2.50 Swiss francs is bigger than the no-arbitrage price from part b of 2.2387. The GBP is overvalued relative to the CHF.

Actual and equilibrium cross-rates differ thereby signaling existence of arbitrage profit. Rule 12.2 says to sell overvalued GBP and buy undervalued CHF. First, however, exchange beginning wealth of 10,000 USD into GBP. Second, exchange GBP into CHF. And third, exchange CHF into USD. A successful strategy finishes with more than 10,000 USD. The increase equals arbitrage profit. Definition 12.1 states that arbitrage profit equals a certain return exceeding the risk-free return. These trades occur instantaneously and therefore the risk-free return is zero — any risk-free increase in wealth is therefore arbitrage profit.

The three trades are:

$$
\begin{array}{ccc}
TRADE\ 1 & TRADE\ 2 & TRADE\ 3 \\
\begin{pmatrix} sell & buy \\ USD & GBP \end{pmatrix} &
\begin{pmatrix} sell & buy \\ GBP & CHF \end{pmatrix} &
\begin{pmatrix} sell & buy \\ CHF & USD \end{pmatrix}
\end{array}
$$

Trade 1 exchanges 10,000 USD into 5,297 GBP. Trade 2 exchanges 5,297 overvalued GBP into undervalued CHF by using the actual cross-rate:

$$1 \ GBP \ = \ 2.50 \ CHF$$

or $5,297 \ GBP \ = \ 13,242 \ CHF.$

Trade 3 exchanges 13,242 CHF into USD by using the actual price of the CHF:

$$1 \ CHF \ = \ 0.8433 \ USD$$

$$13,242 \ CHF \ = \ 11,167 \ USD.$$

Ending wealth of 11,167 USD exceeds beginning wealth of 10,000 USD. Arbitrage profit therefore equals 1,167 USD. Notice that the percentage increase is 11.67%. This exactly equals the percentage by which the actual cross-rate overstates the equilibrium price (= 2.50 / 2.2387 - 1). If the arbitrageur were to begin with $100 million then arbitrage profit equals $11,670,000. Large multinational banks use arbitrage profit for maintaining global offices and staff for exploiting this type of transaction.

Triangle arbitrage is a powerful force that does not require the USD as numeraire. Among any three currencies, as the next example shows, exchange rates must align as formula 12.7 shows or else arbitrage profit exists.

EXAMPLE 13 Triangle arbitrage without the USD

The *Wall Street Journal* shows key cross-rates are

	EUR	CHF
European Union (euro "EUR")	...	0.6464
Japan (yen "JPY")	134.86	87.1720
Switzerland (franc "CHF")	1.5470	...

Each number is the amount of currency in each row that may be purchased by using one unit of the currency in the column heading.

a. Find the JPY-to-CHF cross-rate implied by EUR-to-JPY and EUR-to-CHF cross-rates. Is triangle arbitrage possible?

b. Suppose that European problems cause price of the EUR to depreciate 10% relative to the CHF. Relation between CHF and JPY, however, remains unchanged. Re-write the above table with resultant cross- rates.

SOLUTION

a. There are several ways to begin this answer, but all lead to the same place. Suppose you have 1 EUR. You may buy 1.5470 CHF or 134.86 JPY. Thus,

$$1.5470 \ CHF \ = \ 134.86 \ JPY.$$

This implies the following equilibrium cross-rate between JPY and CHF:

$$1 \ CHF \ = \ 87.1752 \ JPY.$$

The actual cross-rate in the table is that 1 CHF = 87.1720 JPY. Arbitrage profit exists because $87.1752 \neq 87.1720$. Notice though, that the percentage mispricing is less than one basis point. The arbitrage opportunity is so minuscule as to be practically unprofitable.

b. The table shows initial CHF-to-EUR cross-rate:

$$1 \ EUR = \quad 1.5470 \ CHF.$$

The statement "price of the EUR depreciates 10% relative to the CHF" implies a new cross-rate:

$$1 \ EUR \ = \ 1.5470 \ (1 - 0.10) \ CHF$$

$$\text{or} \quad 0.7182 \ EUR \ = \ 1 \ CHF.$$

Relation between CHF and JPY remains unchanged at 1 CHF = 134.86 JPY. Thus, equilibrium EUR-to-JPY cross-rate is:

$$0.7182 \ EUR \ = \ 134.86 \ JPY$$

$$\text{or} \quad 1 \ EUR \ = \ 187.77 \ JPY.$$

In summary, the new cross-rate table looks as follows:

	EUR	CHF
Euroland	...	0.7182
Japan	187.77	87.1720
Suisse	1.3923	...

4.B. Relative purchasing power parity

Why do currencies have different values? The answer depends fundamentally on the historical concept of purchasing power parity. Centuries ago political economists saw merchants trading gold across international borders. They also saw merchants trading currencies. Very quickly they realized that if an ounce of gold cost two British pounds in London and eight Danish krone in Copenhagen then the exchange rate tended to equate 2 British pounds with 8 krone; that is, the price of one krone in London approximately equaled one-quarter pound (5 shillings). Economists saw that exchange rates move in tandem with currency purchasing power. The concept of purchasing power parity argues that a currency's value depends on the quantity of goods that the currency buys.

Inflation erodes currency purchasing power. Rising prices in the U.S.A. means that one USD buys less milk, less gold, and less foreign currency. For this lesson suppose that today an ounce of gold costs $400 in New York. Also, say that today's spot price in USD for one Swiss franc is $0.8433.

$$1 \ CHF \ = \ 0.8433 \ USD$$

Strict purchasing power parity for gold worth $400 an ounce suggests this relation:

$$(400 \ / \ 0.8433) \ CHF \ = \ (400 \times 0.8433 \ / \ 0.8433) \ USD$$

$$\text{or} \quad \underbrace{474.33 \ CHF}_{\substack{\text{purchases one} \\ \text{ounce of gold} \\ \text{today in Geneva}}} = \underbrace{400 \ USD.}_{\substack{\text{purchases one} \\ \text{ounce of gold} \\ \text{today in New York}}}$$

Today an ounce of gold in Geneva probably costs about 474.33 Swiss francs.

Now suppose that over the next year inflation, that is the percentage change in prices of goods including gold, is 6% in the U.S.A. and 3% in Switzerland. Then next year the equality becomes

$$\underbrace{474.33 \ 3 \ (1 + 0.03) \ CHF}_{\substack{\text{purchases one ounce of gold} \\ \text{next year in Geneva}}} = \underbrace{400 \times (1 + 0.06) \ USD}_{\substack{\text{purchases one ounce of gold} \\ \text{next year in New York}}}$$

$$\text{or} \ 488.56 \ CHF \ = \ 424 \ USD, \ \text{or} \ 1 \ CHF \ = \ 0.8679 \ USD.$$

The spot price expected in one year for 1 Swiss franc is $0.8679 (= 424 / 488.56). Price of the CHF appreciates relative to the USD over the next year because inflation is bigger in the U.S.A. than Switzerland and the dollar erodes more than the franc.

Predicting price movements is important in any financial market, especially one as large as the foreign exchange market. Formula 12.8 summarizes the relation between today's currency spot price, expected inflation, and the expected currency spot price in the future.

FORMULA 12.8 Relative purchasing power parity ("PPP")

Let a equal initial price measured in numeraire currency called *NC* for one foreign currency called *FC*. The inflation rates applicable to *NC* and *FC* equal $inflation_{NC}$ and $inflation_{FC}$. Purchasing power parity pushes for this alignment of inflation rates with current and future currency spot prices:

$$\begin{vmatrix} \text{next year's} \\ \text{spot price for} \\ \text{1 unit of FC} \end{vmatrix} = a \times \left(\frac{1 + inflation_{NC}}{1 + inflation_{FC}} \right).$$

Formula 12.8 reveals that foreign currency price relates directly with inflation of the numeraire currency. As inflation in the U.S.A. increases, for example, the prices for all other currencies increase. From one perspective this suggests the values of other currencies increase. A more realistic perspective, however, is that inflation erodes numeraire currency value (after all, it buys less milk too).

EXAMPLE 14 Purchasing power parity and equilibrium cross-rates

A BigMac costs 3.90 Australian dollars ("AUD") in Sydney and 1.95 euros ("EUR") in Paris. Table 12.3 lists today's spot prices in USD for the AUD and EUR equal $0.7748 and $1.3046, respectively. Suppose that inflation is 9% down-under, 4% in Europe, and 6% in the U.S.A. Assume that strict purchasing power parity for BigMacs exists and that production costs for making them in Paris and Australia are identical. Find AUD and EUR currency prices expected next year and comment on movement in the AUD-to-EUR equilibrium cross-rate.

SOLUTION

Apply formula 12.8 to find next year's expected price of the euro given that European and U.S. inflation rates equal 4% and 6%, respectively:

next year's spot price for 1 EUR = *$1.3046 (1.06 / 1.04),*

= *1.3297 USD.*

Higher inflation in the U.S. than Europe means price of the euro appreciates almost 2% relative to the USD. Similar computation for the aussie dollar finds:

next year's spot price for 1 AUD = *$0.7748 (1.06 / 1.09),*

= *0.7535 USD.*

Higher inflation in Australia than U.S.A. means price of the AUD depreciates almost 3% relative to the USD.

Consider now the AUD-to-EUR equilibrium cross-rate. Apply formula 12.7 to today's spot prices and find:

today's price in EUR for 1 AUD = *$0.7748 / $1.3046,*

= *0.5939 EUR.*

Price today for 1 AUD is 59.39 European cents. Apply formula 12.7 with next year's spot prices.

next year's price in EUR for 1 AUD = *$0.7535 / $1.3297,*

= *0.5667.*

This price also obtains from application of formula 12.8 with inflation rates in the PPP relation:

next year's price in EUR for 1 AUD = *0.5939 EUR (1.04 / 1.09),*

= *0.5667 EUR.*

Higher inflation in Australia than Europe means price of the AUD depreciates almost 5% relative to the euro.

Currency prices float in response to forces of supply and demand. Inflation influences currency supply and demand. Inflation usually results from rapid growth in money supply and, just as for any other commodity, an increase in supply causes a fall in equilibrium price. Formula 12.8 for purchasing power parity captures powerful economic relationships.

Financial markets establish futures prices for currencies. For the preceding example today's spot price for one euro is $1.3046. Given U.S. and European inflation rates of 6% and 4%, respectively, strict adherence to PPP implies that next year's expected spot price for one euro is $1.3297. Suppose that today's futures price for one euro with delivery in one year differs from $1.3297. Does this signal an arbitrage opportunity? The answer is no.

Purchasing power parity is a fundamental relationship that for several reasons does not give rise to financial arbitrage opportunity. Foremost is ambiguity about *inflation*. A currency buys so many things from BigMacs to milk to gold to buildings to labor services, etc. Inflation is a general concept yet financial arbitrage requires contract specificity. Another reason that explains why PPP does not lead to a no-arbitrage equilibrium is incompleteness of financial markets. In the example that opens this chapter arbitrage with gold is possible because spot and futures markets for gold exist. Futures markets for most commodities do not exist - nobody wants a BigMac that's been in storage a year! Currencies store easier than BigMacs, however, and lessons in the next section explain how a similar parity relationship between currency prices and interest rates indeed gives rise to a no-arbitrage financial equilibrium.

4.C. Interest rate parity and covered interest arbitrage

Currency spot and futures markets exist and also interest rates link currency today with currency tomorrow. Currency prices and interest rates come together in a powerful parity relation constituting the biggest no-arbitrage financial equilibrium on the globe. Formula 12.9 summarizes the *interest rate parity* relationship.

FORMULA 12.9 Interest rate parity

Let a equal today's spot price measured in numeraire currency NC for one foreign currency FC. Let f_T equal today's futures price for 1 FC with delivery at time T. Interest rates applicable to NC and FC equal i_{NC} and i_{FC}. Interest rate parity pushes for this alignment of today's spot and futures currency prices with interest rates:

$$f_T = a \times \left(\frac{1 + i_{NC}}{1 + i_{FC}}\right)^T.$$

Violation of formula 12.9 implies existence of arbitrage profits.

Interest rate parity formula 12.9 is analogous to purchasing power parity formula 12.8 except that violation of 12.9 means arbitrage profit exists. There are five variables in formula 12.9. Usually length of futures contract T and interest rates i_{NC} and i_{FC} are known and predetermined. Supply actual value f_T for the futures price in formula 12.9 and solve for no-arbitrage spot price. If actual spot price a differs from no-arbitrage spot price then an arbitrage opportunity exists. Present value of arbitrage profit equals difference between actual and no-arbitrage spot prices.

Likewise in formula 12.9 supply actual value a for spot price and solve for no-arbitrage futures price. If actual futures price f_T differs from no-arbitrage futures price then an arbitrage opportunity exists. Future value of arbitrage profit equals difference between actual and no-arbitrage futures prices.

Capture arbitrage profit by exchanging NC and FC in the spot market, and by taking an opposite position in the futures market, and by borrowing and investing at interest rates i_{NC} and i_{FC}. Precise direction of transactions depends on whether FC is over or undervalued. Notice that formula 12.9 easily rearranges to solve for the no-arbitrage spot price:

$$\begin{pmatrix} no\text{–}arbitrage \\ spot\ price \\ for\ 1\ FC \end{pmatrix} = f_T \times \left(\frac{1 + i_{FC}}{1 + i_{NC}}\right)^T.$$

When actual spot price a exceeds no-arbitrage spot price then FC is relatively overvalued in the spot market and NC relatively undervalued. Rule 12.3 describes the *covered interest arbitrage* trading strategy for capturing arbitrage profit. The rule writes transactions in the top row that occur immediately at time 0 and in the bottom row transactions that occur at time T. At each time three steps occur.

For one unit of FC as measured by numeraire NC let a equal today's spot price and f_T today's futures price with delivery at time T. Credit market interest rates applicable to NC and FC equal i_{NC} and i_{FC}. When $a > f_T ((1+i_{FC})/(1+i_{NC}))^T$ then FC is overvalued in the spot market relative to NC and vice versa. This trading strategy captures arbitrage profit from the mispricing:

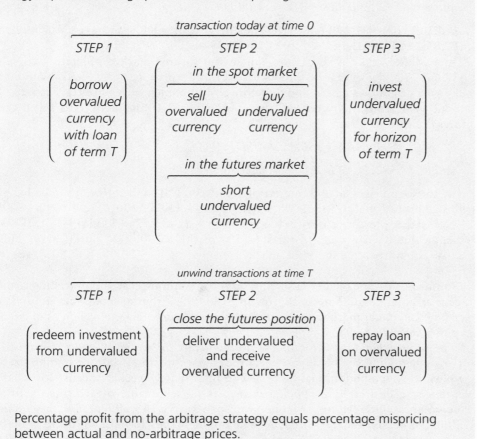

transaction today at time 0

STEP 1 — borrow overvalued currency with loan of term T

STEP 2 — *in the spot market*: sell overvalued currency / buy undervalued currency; *in the futures market*: short undervalued currency

STEP 3 — invest undervalued currency for horizon of term T

unwind transactions at time T

STEP 1 — redeem investment from undervalued currency

STEP 2 — *close the futures position*: deliver undervalued and receive overvalued currency

STEP 3 — repay loan on overvalued currency

Percentage profit from the arbitrage strategy equals percentage mispricing between actual and no-arbitrage prices.

The first step today identifies currency overvalued in the spot market and takes out a credit market loan for that currency. The loan principal and applicable interest rate are repayable at time T. Step 2 exchanges loan proceeds for currency undervalued in the spot market. Receive undervalued currency and invest at its applicable credit market interest rate. Also take a position in the futures market to deliver at time T currency that the investment promises to return.

Unwind the strategy at time T by receiving proceeds from the maturing investment and then by delivering the proceeds and exchanging them for currency originally overvalued by the spot market. Repay the loan and realize arbitrage profit. The example below implements the strategy.

EXAMPLE 15 Covered interest arbitrage

Table 12.3 shows today's price for one Australian dollar ("AUD") is $0.7748. Suppose the actual futures price for the AUD with delivery in one year is $0.8526. Applicable one year credit market interest rates equal 9.84% and 5.72% in Australia and U.S.A., respectively. Find the no-arbitrage spot price that *interest rate parity* implies and explain the trading strategy for capturing arbitrage profit.

SOLUTION

Actual spot price a for 1 AUD equals $0.7748. No-arbitrage spot price equals $0.8858 (= $0.8526 × (1.0984/1.0572)). Actual spot price for the aussie dollar is less than no-arbitrage price implying that the AUD is relatively undervalued and USD relatively overvalued: *sell USD and buy AUD in the spot market!*

First step is borrow overvalued currency, say, one million USD at 5.72% for one year. This obligates repayment of principal and interest next year equal to 1,057,200 USD (= 1,000,000 × 1.0572). Immediately exchange the million USD into AUD at the actual spot rate:

$$1 \ AUD \ = \ \$0.7748 \ USD,$$

and $\qquad 1,290,656 \ AUD \ = \ 1,000,000 \ USD.$

Immediately invest 1,290,656 AUD for one year at 9.84% and expect to receive 1,417,656 AUD next year (= 1,290,656 × 1.0984).

Immediately take a short position in the futures market obligating to sell 1,417,656 AUD next year at today's actual futures price f_1 of $0.8526. Note that today's net cash flows cancel and therefore cost of implementing arbitrage is zero.

One year from today redeem the 1,417,656 AUD and deliver to fulfill the futures obligation:

$$1 \ AUD \ = \ \$0.8526 \ USD,$$

and $\qquad 1,417,656 \ AUD \ = \ 1,208,694 \ USD.$

Repay the loan principal and interest of 1,057,200 USD and realize future value of arbitrage profit equal to $151,494 (= $1,208,694 - $1,057,200).

Notice that present value of arbitrage profit is $143,297 (= $151,494 ÷ 1.0572). Present value of arbitrage profit is 14.3% of the $1,000,000 initial loan. This exactly equals percentage spot market mispricing [= ($0.8858 - $0.7748) ÷ $0.7748].

Initial out-of-pocket net cash flow is zero. Without cost the preceding arbitrageur creates at time T net cash flow of $143,297. Arbitrage continues in foreign exchange and credit markets until interest rates and currency prices align as in interest parity formula 12.9.

The arbitrageur may capitalize arbitrage profit to "get it all and get it now." Borrow one million USD today to begin the covered interest arbitrage trading strategy plus borrow an additional $143,297 to immediately pocket and use for whatever purpose desired. This pocket money is present value of arbitrage profit. Principal plus interest for the one-year loan of $1,143,297 at 5.72% equals $1,208,694 (= $1,143,297 × 1.0572). Sell 1 million USD for AUD in the spot market, invest those AUD at 9.84%, take a short futures position on the expected AUD returns, and net cash flow upon unwinding at time T equals zero. The free pocket money is like currency lying on the sidewalk of the busiest street in town. And there is no risk (except counterparty) because the outcome is contractually guaranteed. Covered interest arbitrage induces globalization of financial markets with a force as powerful for financial science as is the force of a black hole for physical science - absolutely irresistible.

Volume in the forex market averages more than $1,800 billion *per day* during year 2004. Even tiny deviations from interest rate parity create huge profit potential. And unlike entrepreneurial factors driving hopeful profits in the company cash flow cycle, arbitrage profit is not a hope but a certainty. This powerful force binds wealth of nations, companies, and households, in a complex interdependent web. By linking our present and future wealth, financial markets spur creation and recognition of common interests. Perhaps from lessons about the structure of finance we can learn to pursue policies that maximize capitalized value of global wealth creation and that distribute economic profit in response to principal-agent and moral persuasions.

EXERCISES 12.4

Numerical quickies

1. Suppose a company in the USA has a chance to sell its product internationally for either (i) 36,000 bhat or (ii) 44,600 krone. Shipping and other costs are identical. The company bases its decisions on today's cur-

rency exchange rates: 1 USD = 4.10 bhat, and 1 USD = 3.15 krone. Which deal generates the most USD? ©CR1a

2. The table below indicates the quantity of currency in each row required to purchase 1 unit of the currency in each column.

	dinar	yuan
koruna	4.00	3.08
yuan	1.61	

2a. How much can you increase your wealth by executing a triangle arbitrage? ©CR3c

2b. Compare each pair of currencies and state which is overvalued. ©CR6

3. The company requires revenue of $175,000 USD on a particular export sale in order to cover costs and fair profit. The company accepts payment in the purchaser's local currency, which is peso. Today's spot rate is that 1 USD = 7.80 peso. Suppose the company makes a bid in peso to sell the product such that at today's spot rate the required revenue is obtained. The purchaser agrees to pay the bid. Several weeks later at time of delivery the purchaser makes the agreed upon payment in peso. By that time, however, price of the peso depreciates 8% relative to the USD. How much does the company receive in USD from the sale? ©CR4bm

4. A BigMac costs 21.3 yuan in China and 128.2 dinar in Bahrain. Suppose that business and other costs for the McDonalds in both countries are identical. Inflation over the next year is 24% in China and 31% in Bahrain. If exchange rate movements over the next year reestablish the Purchasing Power Parity relation, what is the exchange rate (dinar per yuan) for next year? ©PR2

5. Today's spot exchange rate is that 1 koruna = 6.90 zloty. Everybody correctly knows that over the next year inflation will equal 20% in Slovakia (koruna) and 26% in Poland (zloty). If exchange rate movements strictly adhere to the Purchasing Power Parity relation (PPP), complete the following statement:
PPP implies an exchange rate next year of _____(i)_____ zloty per koruna, and the price of the koruna is expected to _____(ii)_____ relative to the zloty. ©PR1b

Numerical challengers

6. The one-year risk-free interest rate is 7.25% in Slovakia (currency is the koruna) and 9.40% in Bahrain (currency is the dinar). Today's spot price for 1 koruna is 11.20 dinar. The futures price of 1 koruna with delivery in one-year is 9.52 dinar. Which currency is overvalued in the spot market and describe the trading strategy for capturing the arbitrage profit (assume complete futures markets)? ©PR3b

7. Listed below is the quantity of krone required today to purchase one unit of the currency in each column heading.

	peso	bhat
krone	5.30	7.58

Because of differences in economic prospects, the price of the peso is expected to depreciate 30% relative to the krone, and price of the bhat is expected to appreciate 20% relative to the krone.

7a. Find today's equilibrium peso-to-bhat cross-rate that is most consistent with the triangle arbitrage concept. (c)CR2am .

7b. Rewrite the table entries and explain movement in the peso-to-bhat cross-rate. ©CR2bm

ANSWERS TO CHAPTER 12 EXERCISES

EXERCISES 12.1

1. Use formula 12.1 to find the no-arbitrage spot price is $346.12 per ounce (= $370 / 1.069). Arbitrage profit equals absolute value of difference between actual and no-arbitrage spot prices. That equals $43.88 per ounce, or $43,882 for 1000 ounces. The actual spot overvalues the no-arb spot so short gold in the spot market, receive $390,000 (= 1000 x $390), go long in the futures obligating to buy 1000 ounces in one year for $370,000 (= 1000 x $370), immediately pocket the arbitrage profit of $43,882 for whatever purpose desired, and immediately invest the remaining $346,118 (= $390,000 - $43,882) for one year at 6.9%. In one year redeem the investment for $370,000 (= $346,118 x 1.069) and use the proceeds to purchase the 1000 ounces of gold, thereby satisfying the futures obligation and replacing the previously-sold gold.

2. The actual SP2 spot equals 88 (= 48 + 40). The no-arb SP2 spot equals 99.44 (= 110.58 / 1.112). The difference of $11.44 is the present value of arbitrage profits. Actual spot undervalues no-arb spot so take a long position in the spot market, short position in the futures market. Immediately borrow $99.44 at 11.2 percent for one year. Use $88 to buy the two stocks and immediately pocket the arbitrage profit of $11.44 for whatever purpose desired. In one year sell the stocks for $110.58 thereby satisfying the futures obligation. Use the proceeds to repay the loan principal plus interest (= $99.44 x 1.112).

EXERCISES 12.2

1. Compute with formula 12.4 that for a long position,
profit = ($3.71 - $3.90) x 1250; = $-238.
This represents a loss. Figuring the rate of return requires the margin. Compute with formula 12.3 that
margin = 0.0225 x $3.90 x 1250; = $110.
For a speculative position the margin represents initial cost of investment (even though it surely shall be returned). Rate of return equals profit divided by initial cost. The *ROR* is -217% (= -$238 /$110).

2a. $156,250 bid in USD= $125,000
The pretax cost is $110,000 and the company wants a 12% pretax rate of return. Thus,
0.12 = (Sales Bid - $110,000) ÷ Sales Bid
Sales Bid = $125,000
The bid should provide 157,895 USD.
 The problem tells us that the spot exchange rate today is 1 USD = 1.35 krone. Thus,
125,000 USD = 1.35 x 125,000 krone
           = 168,750 krone
If the company does the job for 168,750 krone and the exchange rate remains constant the pretax rate of return equals 12%.

2b. Find the original price of the krone as measured by the USD numeraire:
 1 krone = (1/1.35) USD.
The price of the krone appreciates by 10 percent so that the new price is:
 1 krone = (1/1.35) x (1 + 0.10) USD
         = 0.8148 USD.
The company receives 168,750 krone. Thus,
168,750 krone = 168,750 x 0.8148 USD
             = 137,500 USD.

The company exchanges its krone for $137,500 and the actual pretax profit is $27,500 (= $137,500 - $110,000). The pretax profit margin is 20% (= $27,500 / $137,500).

3. The price of the peso becomes:

1 peso = 0.7660 x (1 + 0.06) USD

= 0.8120 USD.

Use formula 12.4 for the short position and find

profit = ($0.7660 - $0.8120) x 100,000

= $-4,596.

This represents a loss. To find the rate of return requires finding the margin.

margin = 0.0175 x $0.7660 x 100,000

= $1,340.

ROR equals profit divided by cost and is -343% (= $-4,596 / $1,340).

4. Use formula 12.4 for the short position and find the profit on the futures contract is

profit = ($3.10 - $4.30) x 40,000

= $-48,000.

The company sends the futures exchange $48,000 (the margin is a wash and is irrelevant). They sell their soybeans for $160,000 (= 40,000 x $4.00). Net revenues therefore equal $112,000 (= $160,000 - $48,000). In this case the hedging strategy costs the company money ($48,000). That's because the price of soybeans rises. On the other hand, if the price had fallen the hedge would have saved money.

5. Find the June price of the sucre:

spot market: 1 sucre = 0.7420 (1 - 0.04) USD; = $0.7123,

futures market   1 sucre = 0.7450 (1 - 0.04) USD; = $0.7152.

The company sells sucre in the spot market for $85,478 (= 120,000 x $0.7123). The profit on the short futures position is

profit = ($0.7450 - $0.7152) x (5 x 24,000); = $3,576.

The net revenue is $89,054 (= $85,478 + $3,576).

EXERCISES 12.3

1. Intrinsic value of the call is $8.30 (= $10.80 - $2.50). That's the payoff at the current stock price and represents a lower bound on the option price. The arbitrage profit equals the amount by which actual option price is less than $8.30. The arbitrage profit is $3.30 (= $8.30 - $2.50).

2. Ending stock price is $83.49 (= $69.00 x 1.21). Payoff on the call is $13.49 (= $83.49 - $70). Rate of return is 1,249% (= $13.49 / $1 - 1).

3a. With stock price of $65.60 the profit is zero.

3b. Getting a 160% rate of return given a beginning investment of $5.60 requires an ending wealth of $14.56 (= $5.60 x (1 + 1.60)). Obtain a payoff of $14.56 when the stock price exceeds the strike by $14.56. A stock price of $74.56 (= $14.56 + $60) generates a 160% rate of return.

4. Apply a 21% rate of return to beginning wealth of $28.10 (= $20.35 + $7.75) and compute that ending wealth equals $34.00 (= $28.10 x 1.21). An ending stock price of $34.00 yields ending wealth of $34 (the put is out-of-the-money and worthless at that price).

5a. The initial investment is expenditure of $37.20 (= $33.20 + $4). Worst-case outcome is that the stock price ends below $35 in which case you exercise the put and sell the stock for $35. The rate of return for that outcome is -5.9% (= $35 / $37.20 - 1).

5b. Ending share price is $35.86 (= $33.20 x 1.08). The put is out-of-the-money and therefore ending wealth equals $35.86. Rate of return is -3.6% (= $35.86 / $37.20 - 1).

6. The cost of the put option is $168 (= 3,000 x $0.0560). The payoff equals $630 (= 3,000 x ($1.10 - $0.89)). The rate of return equals 275% (= $630 / $168 - 1).

7. An option with total cost of $705 (= 5,000 x $0.1410) provides the right to buy 5,000 bushels of corn at the strike of $2.08 each. The company buys 5,000 bushel for $10,400 with the option, much less than the cost of $12,750 (= 5,000 x $2.55) without the option. The net savings to the company of the strategy is $1,645 (= $12,750 - $10,400 - $705).

8a. For the worst-case outcome options expire out-of-the-money and are worthless. You still have, however, the 90% invested in the money market plus interest. The ending wealth for the worst-case outcome equals $13,190 (= 0.90 x $14,000 x (1 + .055/12)10. The rate of return is -5.79% (= $13,190/$14,000 - 1).

8b. For this case the ending wealth equals $13,190 from the money market investment plus the payoff on the options. Number of options purchased at $0.70 each is 2,000 (= 0.10 x $14,000 / $0.70). Ending share price is $32.26 (= $25.20 x 1.28). The payoff on 2,000 options with strike of 30 is $4,520 (= 2,000 x ($32.26 - $30)). Total ending wealth is $17,710 (= $13,190 + $4,520) and the rate of return is 26.5% (= $17,710 / $14,000 - 1).

9. You begin with $10,000 and the worst-case outcome is that ending wealth equals $8,000 (= $10,000 - $2,000). The future value of your money market investment equals $8,000 which means the present value is $6,766 (= 0.90 x $8,000 / (1 + .072/12)^{28}. You initially invest $6,766 in the money market and $3,234 in call options (= $10,000 - $6,766). Number of options purchased at $3.50 each is 924 (= $3,234 / $3.50). Ending share price is $50.18 (= $38.60 x 1.30). The payoff on 924 options with strike of $47.50 is $2,476 (= 924 x ($50.18 - $47.50)). Total ending wealth is $10,476 (= $8,000 + $2,476) and the rate of return is 4.8% (= $10,476 / $10,000 - 1).

10a. Purchase the stock and spend $40.65 and write the call option and receive $5.60. Your initial net investment therefore equals $35.05. In one year receive $2.85 plus proceeds from the stock. If the stock exceeds the strike of $50 then the short-side of the call option buys the stock from you for $50. For that best-case scenario your ending wealth is $52.85 and your annual rate of return is 50.8% (= $52.85 / $35.05 - 1).

10b. Ending share price is $45.12 (= $40.65 x 1.11). The call option expires out of the money and so that obligation disappears without cost. Ending wealth equals $47.97 (= $45.12 + $2.85). Rate of return equals 36.9% (= $47.97 / $35.05 - 1).

11. The cost of the put option is $172 (= 4,000 x $0.043). The intrinsic value at expiry equals $800 (= 4,000 x ($1.12 - $0.92)). The company receives $3,680 from selling the 4,000 Euros at the spot exchange rate (= 4,000 x $0.92). Total outflows equal $172, total inflows $4,480, and net cash flow from the transactions equal $4,308.

12a. Your initial investment cost equals $10.70 (= $9.80 + $0.90). For any stock price at expiry that is lower than $34.30 (= $45 - $10.70) then payoff on the put exceeds the investment cost and the strategy returns a profit (the call is worthless at those prices). For any stock price at expiry greater than $55.70 (= $45 + $10.70) then payoff on the call exceeds the investment cost and the strategy returns a profit (the put is worthless at those prices). For any stock price between $34.30 and $55.70 the straddle generates a loss. Maximum loss of $10.70 occurs at $45.

12b. Apply a 30% rate of return to beginning wealth of $10.70 and compute that ending wealth is $13.91. Two outcomes generate that amount of payoff. When the stock price at expiry equals $31.09 (= $45 - $13.91) then the put payoff is $13.91 and call is worthless. When the stock price at expiry equals $58.91 (= $45 + $13.91) then the call payoff is $13.91 and put is worthless.

12c. The put is in-the-money and generates a payoff of $8.40 (= $45 - $36.60). The call is worthless. The rate of return is -21.5% (= $8.40 / $10.70 - 1).

13. Initial cash flow equals the revenue of $7,200 (= 1,800 x $4.00) from writing the calls minus the expenditure of $13,500 from purchasing the put

options. Initial cash flow is $-6,300. Minimum ending wealth occurs when the stock price collapses in which case the put is in-the-money and you sell the stock for $35. The minimum ending wealth is $63,000 (= 1,800 x $35). Maximum ending wealth occurs when the stock price runs up in which case the call is in-the-money and you are forced to sell the stock for $45. The maximum ending wealth is $81,000 (= 1,800 x $45).

EXERCISES 12.4

1. Apply the exchange rates and find:
   (1 / 4.10) x 36,000 USD = 36,000 bhat; = 8,780 USD.
   (1 / 3.15) x 44,600 USD = 44,600 krone; = 14,159 USD.
   The company receives $5,378 more USD if they make the deal in krone.

2a. Rewrite the table as formulas for the price of 1 dinar:
   1 dinar = 4.00 koruna
   1 dinar = 1.61 yuan
   This implies that the no-arbitrage cross-rate between koruna and yuan:
   1 yuan = (4.00/1.61) koruna; = 2.4845 koruna.
   Equilibrium price for 1 yuan equals 2.4845 koruna. This is consistent with formula 12.7 wherein numeraire price a for 1 yuan equals (1/1.61) dinar and price b for 1 koruna equals 1/4 dinar. Equilibrium cross-rate a/b equals 2.4845 [= (1/1.61) ÷ 1/4].
   Actual cross-rate for 1 yuan from the table is 3.08 koruna. Actual price of one yuan exceeds the no-arb price. Percentage overvaluation is 24.0% (= 3.08/2.4845 - 1). Execution of triangle arbitrage increases wealth by 24.0%.

2b. The yuan costs more koruna than is consistent with no-arbitrage equilibrium. This means the yuan is overvalued relative to the koruna. Use rule 12.2 to write three currency pairs wherein middle pair is the sale of overvalued yuan and purchase of undervalued koruna. First and last currency pairs match the middle as shown by rule 12.2:

$$\begin{pmatrix} \text{sell} & \text{buy} \\ \text{dinar} & \text{yuan} \end{pmatrix} \quad \begin{pmatrix} \text{sell} & \text{buy} \\ \text{overvalued} & \text{undervalued} \\ \text{yuan} & \text{koruna} \end{pmatrix} \quad \begin{pmatrix} \text{sell} & \text{buy} \\ \text{koruna} & \text{dinar} \end{pmatrix}$$

Part a takes as given the dinar-to-yuan and koruna-to-dinar cross-rates and finds actual price of 1 yuan measured in koruna is bigger than equilibrium cross-rate. Within each currency pair, however, there is a relative mispricing - none of them is properly priced when one is mispriced. This is analogous to a triangle with 3 sides that don't connect and leave a gap at one corner, there is not just one side out of alignment - they are all misaligned.

Find relative mispricing between any currency pair by taking as given the other two. For example, take as given the yuan-to-koruna and koruna-to-dinar cross-rates. Find that the dinar is overvalued relative to the yuan. Between each currency pair the currency on left is relatively overvalued and currency on right relatively undervalued. Each of the three transactions involves selling the overvalued and buying the undervalued currency. An implication is that a specific currency is overvalued relative to one currency yet undervalued relative to the other. For example, the yuan is overvalued relative to the koruna and at the same time the yuan is undervalued relative to the dinar.

Another implication is that the triangle arbitrage trading strategy may rely on any one of three currencies as numeraire. Two trading sequences shown below work as well as the one shown above

$$\begin{pmatrix} \text{sell} & \text{buy} \\ \text{yuan} & \text{koruna} \end{pmatrix} \begin{pmatrix} \text{sell} & \text{buy} \\ \text{overvalued} & \text{undervalued} \\ \text{koruna} & \text{dinar} \end{pmatrix} \begin{pmatrix} \text{sell} & \text{buy} \\ \text{dinar} & \text{yuan} \end{pmatrix},$$

$$\text{or} \begin{pmatrix} \text{sell} & \text{buy} \\ \text{koruna} & \text{dinar} \end{pmatrix} \begin{pmatrix} \text{sell} & \text{buy} \\ \text{overvalued} & \text{undervalued} \\ \text{dinar} & \text{yuan} \end{pmatrix} \begin{pmatrix} \text{sell} & \text{buy} \\ \text{yuan} & \text{koruna} \end{pmatrix}.$$

Even though an arbitrageur holds only one of these currencies in inventory the trading strategy may be started with that currency in order to capture arbitrage profit. In summary, use formula 12.7 to find equilibrium cross-rate and overvalued currency. Use rule 12.2 to write the three currency pairs. Execute the strategy by proceeding rightward through the three transactions.

3. The company bid for the job is 1,365,000 pesos (= $175,000 x 7.80). Today's spot price for 1 peso is $0.1282 (= 1/7.80). Price of the peso depreciates 8% so that its new price is $0.1179. The company receives 1,365,000 pesos and sells them for $161,000 (= 1,365,000 x $0.1179). The revenue is 8 percent less than their target.

4. Write today's exchange rate
   21.3 yuan = 128.2 dinar or 1 yuan = 6.02 dinar.
   The dinar is numeraire NC measuring price of FC yuan. Apply formula 12.8 and find that next year's price for 1 yuan is 6.36 dinar [= 6.02 x (1.31/1.24)]. Price of the yuan appreciates 5.65% relative to the dinar (= 6.36/6.02 - 1).

5. The numeraire currency measuring price is zloty. Apply PPP formula 12.8 and find that next year's price for the koruna is 7.245 zloty [= 6.90 (1.26/1.20)]. Price for one koruna appreciates 5.0 percent relative to the zloty.

6. Apply interest rate parity formula 12.9 wherein dinar is NC and koruna FC. Solve for the no-arbitrage spot price for 1 koruna.

   no-arb spot price for 1 koruna = 9.52 (1.0940 / 1.0725) dinar,

   $$= 9.7108 \; dinar.$$

   Actual spot price of 11.20 overvalues by 15.33% (= 11.20/9.7108 - 1) the no-arb spot price implying the koruna is overvalued relative to the dinar: *sell overvalued koruna and buy undervalued dinar in the spot market!* Immediately borrow, say, 100,000 koruna at 9.40% for one year to start covered interest arbitrage. Also borrow an additional 15.33%, that is 15,330 koruna, to capitalize the arbitrage profit for whatever use desired. The loan of 115,330 koruna at 9.40% obligates repayment of principal and interest next year equal to 126,176 koruna (= 115,330 x 1.0940). Immediately exchange 100,000 koruna into dinar at the actual spot rate and receive 1,120,000 dinar (= 100,000 x 11.20). Invest the dinar at 7.25% and expect returns in one year of 1,201,200 dinar (= 1,120,000 x 1.0725). Immediately take a futures market position to exchange 1,201,200 dinar into koruna at the actual futures price of 9.52 dinar per koruna.
   Unwind the position next year and expect zero net cash flow. Exchange the 1,201,200 dinar into 126,176 koruna (= 1,201,200 ÷ 9.52). The strategy created wealth at time 0 of 15,330 koruna at absolutely no cost. Thereafter, project cash flows cancel and net cash flow at time T equals 0. Notice that this strategy is profitable even though it involves borrowing in koruna at relatively high 9.40% in order to invest in dinar at relatively low 7.25%.

7a. Rewrite the table entries as formulas:
   1 peso = 5.30 krone
   1 bhat = 7.58 krone

This implies that the no-arbitrage cross-rate between peso and bhat: (1/5.30) peso = (1/7.58) bhat.

Solve today's equilibrium price for 1 peso as measured in bhat: 1 peso = (5.30/7.58) bhat; = 0.6992 bhat.

This price is consistent with formula 12.7 wherein numeraire price a for 1 peso equals 5.30 krone and price b for 1 bhat equals 7.58 krone. Equilibrium cross-rate a/b equals 0.6992 bhat.

7b. Today's price for one peso measured in krone is 5.30. Depreciate the price 30% and find the new price for one peso is 3.71 krone (= 5.30 ×(1 - 0.30). This is the table entry for the first column. Today's price for one bhat measured in krone is 7.58. Appreciate the price 20% and find the new price for one bhat is 9.0960 krone (= 7.58 ×(1 + 0.20). This is the table entry for the second column.

The new equilibrium cross-rate a/b equals 0.4079 bhat (= 3.71 / 9.0960). Price for one peso measured in bhat begins at 0.6992 and ends at 0.4079 implying that the peso depreciates 41.7 percent relative to the bhat (= 0.4079 / 0.6992 - 1).

APPENDIX 1

Future and Present Value Factors of Annuities

PANEL A: FUTURE VALUE INTEREST FACTOR OF ANNUITIES (*FVIFA*).

Each entry is the future value of $1 deposits made for N consecutive periods that earn the periodic discount rate r computed with this formula:

$$FVIFA_{r, N} = \frac{(1 + r)^N - 1}{r}.$$

Column headings list periodic rate r, rows list N. The table omits entries larger than 10,000.

	0.5%	1.0%	3.0%	5.0%	7.5%	10.0%	12.5%	15.0%
1	1.0000	1.0000	1.0000	1.0000	1.0000	1.0000	1.0000	1.0000
2	2.0050	2.0100	2.0300	2.0500	2.0750	2.1000	2.1250	2.1500
3	3.0150	3.0301	3.0909	3.1525	3.2306	3.3100	3.3906	3.4725
4	4.0301	4.0604	4.1836	4.3101	4.4729	4.6410	4.8145	4.9934
5	5.0503	5.1010	5.3091	5.5256	5.8084	6.1051	6.4163	6.7424
10	10.2280	10.4622	11.4639	12.5779	14.1471	15.9374	17.9786	20.3037
20	20.9791	22.0190	26.8704	33.0660	43.3047	57.2750	76.3608	102.44
25	26.5591	28.2432	36.4593	47.7271	67.9779	98.3471	144.02	212.79
30	32.2800	34.7849	47.5754	66.4388	103.40	164.49	265.95	434.75
90	113.31	144.86	443.35	1594.60	8934.14			
120	163.88	230.04	1123.70	6958.23				
240	462.04	989.26						
360	1004.52	3494.96						

PANEL B: PRESENT VALUE INTEREST FACTOR OF ANNUITIES (*PVIFA*).

Each entry is the initial deposit earning interest at the periodic rate r that perfectly finances a series of N consecutive $1 withdrawals computed with this formula:

$$PVIFA_{r, N} = \frac{1 - (1 + r)^{-N}}{r}.$$

Column headings list periodic rate r, rows list N.

	0.5%	1.0%	3.0%	5.0%	7.5%	10.0%	12.5%	15.0%
1	0.9950	0.9901	0.9709	0.9524	0.9302	0.9091	0.8889	0.8696
2	1.9851	1.9704	1.9135	1.8594	1.7956	1.7355	1.6790	1.6257
3	2.9702	2.9410	2.8286	2.7232	2.6005	2.4869	2.3813	2.2832
4	3.9505	3.9020	3.7171	3.5460	3.3493	3.1699	3.0056	2.8550
5	4.9259	4.8534	4.5797	4.3295	4.0459	3.7908	3.5606	3.3522
10	9.7304	9.4713	8.5302	7.7217	6.8641	6.1446	5.5364	5.0188
20	18.9874	18.0456	14.8775	12.4622	10.1945	8.5136	7.2414	6.2593
25	23.4456	22.0232	17.4131	14.0939	11.1469	9.0770	7.5790	6.4641
30	27.7941	25.8077	19.6004	15.3725	11.8104	9.4269	7.7664	6.5660
90	72.3313	59.1609	31.0024	19.7523	13.3135	9.9981	7.9998	6.6666
120	90.0735	69.7005	32.3730	19.9427	13.3311	9.9999	8.0000	6.6667
240	139.5808	90.8194	33.3057	19.9998	13.3333	10.0000	8.0000	6.6667
360	166.7916	97.2183	33.3325	20.0000	13.3333	10.0000	8.0000	6.6667

APPENDIX 2
Glossary

AAII American Association of Individual Investors. A non-profit organization whose mission is to help individuals become smarter investors.

active management A money-management approach based on informed, independent investment judgment, as opposed to passive management (indexing) which seeks to match the performance of the overall market (or some part of it) by mirroring its composition or by being broadly diversified.

advance/decline line A technical analysis tool considered a good measure of the overall market's direction. Equal to the number of stocks which rose divided by the number of stocks which fell during some specified period. Considered bullish if greater than 1, or bearish if less than 1.

agency security A security, usually a bond, issued by a U.S. government agency. Agency securities are exempt from state and local taxes. also called U.S. Government Agency Security.

aggressive growth fund A mutual fund which aims for the highest capital gains and is not risk-averse in its selection of investments. Aggressive growth funds are most suitable for investors willing to accept a high risk-return trade-off, since many of the companies which demonstrate high growth potential can also show a lot of share price volatility. Aggressive growth funds tend to have a very large positive correlation with the stock market, and so they often produce very good results during economic upswings and very bad results during economic downturns. An aggressive growth fund might, for example, buy initial public offerings (IPOs) of stock from small companies and then resell that stock very quickly in order to generate big profits. Some aggressive growth funds may even invest in derivatives, such as options, in order to increase their gains.

alpha A coefficient measuring the risk-adjusted performance, considering the risk due to the specific security, rather than the overall market. A large alpha indicates that the stock or mutual fund has performed better than would be predicted given its beta (volatility).

American Depositary Receipt ADR. A negotiable certificate issued by a U.S. bank representing a specific number of shares of a foreign stock traded on a U.S. stock exchange. ADRs make it easier for Americans to invest in foreign companies, due to the widespread availability of dollar-denominated price information, lower transaction costs, and timely dividend distributions.

American option An option which can be exercised at any time between the purchase date and the expiration date. Most options in the U.S. are of this type. This is the opposite of a European-style option, which can only be exercised on the date of expiration. Since an American option provides an investor with a greater degree of flexibility than a European style option, the premium for an American style option is at least equal to or higher than the premium for a European-style option which otherwise has all the same features. also called American-style option.

American Stock Exchange AMEX. The second-largest stock exchange in the U.S., after the NYSE. In general, the listing rules are a little more lenient than those of the NYSE, and thus the AMEX has a larger representation of stocks and bonds issued by smaller companies than the NYSE. Some index options and interest rate options trading also occurs on the AMEX. The AMEX started as an alternative to the NYSE. It originated when brokers began meeting on the curb outside the NYSE in order to trade stocks that failed to meet the Big Board's stringent listing requirements, but the AMEX now has its own trading floor. In 1998 the parent company of the NASDAQ purchased the AMEX and combined their markets, although the two continue to operate separately. also called The Curb.

angel investor An individual who provides capital to one or more startup companies. The individual is usually affluent or has a personal stake in the success of the venture. Such investments are characterized by high levels of risk and a potentially large return on investment.

Annual Percentage Rate APR. The yearly cost of a mortgage, including interest, mortgage insurance, and the origination fee (points), expressed as a percentage.

Annual Percentage Yield APY. The rate of return on an investment for a one-year period. For an interest-bearing deposit account, such as a savings account, APY is equal to one plus the periodic rate (expressed as a decimal) raised to the number of periods in one year. Due to compounding, the APY will be greater than the periodic interest rate multiplied by the number of periods in the year.

annuity A contract sold by an insurance company designed to provide payments to the holder at specified intervals, usually after retirement. The holder is taxed only when they start taking distributions or if they withdraw funds from the account. All annuities are tax-deferred, meaning that the earnings from investments in these accounts grow tax-deferred until withdrawal. Annuity earnings are also tax-deferred so they cannot be withdrawn without penalty until a certain specified age. Fixed annuities guarantee a certain payment amount, while variable annuities do not, but do have the potential for greater returns. Both are relatively safe, low-yielding investments. An annuity has a death benefit equivalent to the higher of the current value of the annuity or the amount the buyer has paid into it. If the owner dies during the accumulation phase, his or her heirs will receive the accumulated amount in the annuity. This money is subject to ordinary income taxes in addition to estate taxes.

arbitrage Attempting to profit by exploiting price differences of identical or similar financial instruments, on different markets or in different forms. The ideal version is riskless arbitrage.

arithmetic mean Simple average, equal to the sum of all values divided by the number of values.

ascending bottoms Technical analysis term for a chart pattern in which each successive low price is higher than the previous one; considered a bullish indicator.

asset allocation The process of dividing investments among different kinds of assets, such as stocks, bonds, real estate and cash, to optimize the risk/reward tradeoff based on an individual's or institution's specific situation and goals. A key concept in financial planning and money management.

asset class A type of investment, such as stocks, bonds, real estate, or cash.

asset-backed security A bond or note backed by loan paper or accounts receivable originated by banks, credit card companies, or other providers of credit; not mortgages.

at the money A condition in which the strike price of an option is equal to (or nearly equal to) the market price of the underlying security.

balanced fund A mutual fund that buys a combination of common stocks, preferred stocks, bonds, and short-term bonds, to provide both income and capital appreciation while avoiding excessive risk. The purpose of balanced funds (also sometimes called hybrid funds) is to provide investors with a single mutual fund that combines both growth and income objectives, by investing in both stocks (for growth) and bonds (for income). Such diversified holdings ensure that these funds will manage downturns in the stock market without too much of a loss; the flip side, of course, is that balanced funds will usually increase less than an all-stock fund during a bull market.

balloon payment A large, lump-sum payment scheduled at the end of a series of considerably smaller periodic payments. A balloon payment may be included in the payment schedule for a loan, lease, or other stream of payments.

bank An organization, usually a corporation, chartered by a state or federal government, which does most or all of the following: receives demand deposits and time deposits, honors instruments drawn on them, and pays interest on them; discounts notes, makes loans, and invests in securities; collects checks, drafts, and notes; certifies depositor's checks; and issues drafts and cashier's checks.

bankruptcy A proceeding in a federal court in which an insolvent debtor's assets are liquidated and the debtor is relieved of further liability. Chapter 7 of the Bankruptcy Reform Act deals with liquidation, while Chapter 11 deals with reorganization.

basis point One hundredth of a percentage point (0.01%). Basis points are often used to measure changes in or differences between yields on fixed income securities, since these often change by very small amounts.

bear market A prolonged period in which investment prices fall, accompanied by widespread pessimism. If the period of falling stock prices is short and immediately follows a period of rising stock prices, it is instead called a correction. Bear markets usually occur when the economy is in a recession and unemployment is high, or when inflation is rising quickly. The most famous bear market in U.S. history was the Great Depression of the 1930s. The term "bear" has been used in a financial context since at least the early 18th century. While its origins are unclear, the term may have originated from traders who sold bear skins with the expectations that prices would fall in the future. opposite of bull market.

bearer bond An unregistered, negotiable bond on which interest and principal are payable to the holder, regardless of whom it was originally issued to. The coupons are attached to the bond, and each coupon represents a single interest payment. The holder submits a coupon, usually semi-annually, to the issuer or paying agent to receive payment. Bearer bonds are being phased out in favor of registered bonds. also called coupon bond.

best efforts offering An underwriting in which an investment bank, acting as an agent, agrees to do its best to sell the offering to the public, but does not buy the securities outright and does not guarantee that the issuing company will receive any set amount of money. Less common than a firm commitment offering.

beta A quantitative measure of the volatility of a given stock, mutual fund, or portfolio, relative to the overall market, usually the S&P 500. Specifically, the performance the stock, fund or portfolio has experienced in the last 5 years as the S&P moved 1% up or down. A beta above 1 is more volatile than the overall market, while a beta below 1 is less volatile.

block trade A large amount of securities being traded, typically at least 10,000 shares of stock or $200,000 in bonds. Normally, only institutional investors undertake such large trades. Block trades can affect the market price of the security, depending on the liquidity of the market.

Blue Chip Stock of a large, national company with a solid record of stable earnings and/or dividend growth and a reputation for high quality management and/or products. More generally, anything of very high quality.

Blue Sky Laws State regulations governing the sale of securities and mutual funds, designed to safeguard investors from being lured into fraudulent or unscrupulous deals.

Board of Directors Individuals elected by a corporation's shareholders to oversee the management of the corporation. The members of a Board of Directors are paid in cash and/or stock, meet several times each year, and assume legal responsibility for corporate activities. also called directorate.

bond A debt instrument issued for a period of more than one year with the purpose of raising capital by borrowing. The Federal government, states, cities, corporations, and many other types of institutions sell bonds. Generally, a bond is a promise to repay the principal along with interest (coupons) on a specified date (maturity). Some bonds do not pay interest, but all bonds require a repayment of principal. When an investor buys a bond, he/she becomes a creditor of the issuer. However, the buyer does not gain any kind of ownership rights to the issuer, unlike in the case of equities. On the hand, a bond holder has a greater claim on an issuer's income than a shareholder in the case of financial distress (this is true for all creditors). Bonds are often divided into different categories based on tax status, credit quality, issuer type, maturity and secured/unsecured (and there are several other ways to classify bonds as well). U.S. Treasury bonds are generally considered the safest unsecured bonds, since the possibility of the Treasury defaulting on payments is almost zero. The yield from a bond is made up of three components: coupon interest, capital gains and interest on interest (if a bond pays no coupon interest, the only yield will be capital gains). A bond might be sold at above or below par (the amount paid out at maturity), but the market price will approach par value as the bond approaches maturity. A riskier bond has to provide a higher payout to compensate for that additional risk. Some bonds are tax-exempt, and these are typically issued by municipal, county or state governments, whose interest payments are not subject to federal income tax, and sometimes also state or local income tax.

bond fund A mutual fund which invests in bonds, typically with the objective of providing stable income with minimal capital risk. also called debtholder.

bond rating A measure of the quality and safety of a bond, based on the issuer's financial condition. More specifically, an evaluation from a rating service indicating the likelihood that a debt issuer will be able to meet scheduled interest and principal repayments. Typically, AAA is highest (best), and D is lowest (worst).

book value A company's common stock equity as it appears on a balance sheet, equal to total assets minus liabilities, preferred stock, and intangible assets such as goodwill. This is how much the company would have left over in assets if it went out of business immediately. Since companies are usually expected to grow and generate more profits in the future, most companies end up being worth far more in the marketplace than their book value would suggest. For this reason, book value is of more interest to value investors than growth investors.

breakout Technical analysis term for a rise in a security's price above a resistance level (usually its previous high) or drop below a support level (usually its previous low).

broker An individual or firm which acts as an intermediary between a buyer and seller, usually charging a commission. For securities and most other products, a license is required.

brokerage account A customer's account at a brokerage. There are three kinds of brokerage accounts. The most basic kind is a cash-management account, into which investors place money in order to make trades. There must be enough money in the account to cover the trade at the time of its execution (including both the price of the security and the commission), or the investor must be able to pay for the trade within three days (which is called the settlement date). Some brokerage firms accept credit cards to fund cash accounts, but the most require cash or a personal check. Such an account is often a good substitute for a bank account. A second, more sophisticated kind of brokerage account is a margin account, which allows an investor to buy securities with money borrowed from the broker. The Federal Reserve limits margin borrowing to at most 50% of the amount invested, but some brokerages have even stricter requirements, especially for volatile stocks. Brokerages charge a relatively low interest rate on margin loans in order to encourage investors to buy on margin. A third kind of brokerage account is a discretionary account, which permits the broker to buy and sell shares for the investor without first contacting the investor for approval.

bull market A prolonged period in which investment prices rise faster than their historical average. Bull markets can happen as a result of an economic recovery, an economic boom, or investor psychology. The longest and most famous bull market is the one that began in the early 1990s in which the U.S. equity markets grew at their fastest pace ever. opposite of bear market.

buy and hold An investment strategy in which stocks are bought and then held for a long period, regardless of the market's fluctuations. The buy and hold approach to investing in stocks rests upon the assumption that in the very long term (over the course of, say, 10 or 20 years) stock prices will go up, but the average investor doesn't know what will happen tomorrow. Historical data from the past 50 years supports this claim. The logic behind the idea is that in a capitalist society the economy will keep expanding, so profits will keep growing and both stock prices and stock dividends will increase as a result. There may be short term fluctuations, due to business cycles or rising inflation, but in the long term these will be smoothed out and the market as a whole will rise. Two additional benefits to the buy and hold strategy are that trading commissions can be reduced and taxes can be reduced or deferred by buying and selling less often and holding longer.

buy and write A conservative options strategy in which stocks are bought and covered call options are written on them.

buy-side analyst An analyst employed by an entity, such as a mutual fund, that invests on its own accounts. Unlike that of the sell-side analysts employed by brokerage firms, research produced by buy-side analysts is usually unavailable outside of the firm that hired the analyst. A sell-side analyst's focus when analyzing possible investments is to see whether the investment should be recommended to the firm's clients, while a buy-side analyst would only be interested in analyzing whether the investment is suitable for the firm's investment strategy and portfolio. Thus, sell-side analysts structure their research such that it is usable for a wider audience than buy-side research. Buy-side analysts often source research from sell-side analysts, and then use this information as a base for their own research.

callable Able to be redeemed prior to maturity. The term usually applies to bonds and convertible securities. The issuer of a callable security has to state the conditions under which the security may be called at the time of issue. For most securities, there is a certain initial time period in which the security cannot be called. A bond will usually be called when market interest rates fall below the yield being paid on the bond (bonds are usually called when the price rises to a certain point). To reflect this risk, a callable security is usually priced lower than a non-callable security.

Capital Asset Pricing Model CAPM. An economic model for valuing stocks by relating risk and expected return. Based on the idea that investors demand additional expected return (called the risk premium) if asked to accept additional risk.

capital gain The amount by which an asset's selling price exceeds its initial purchase price. A realized capital gain is an investment that has been sold at a profit. An unrealized capital gain is an investment that hasn't been sold yet but would result in a profit if sold. Capital gain is often used to mean realized capital gain. For most investments sold at a profit, including mutual funds, bonds, options, collectibles, homes, and businesses, the IRS is owed money called capital gains tax. opposite of capital loss.

capital market A market where debt or equity securities are traded.

capital market line A graph relating risk (as represented by the market portfolio's beta) and the required return for the market portfolio. This is a positive, linear relationship that originates from the Capital Market Asset Pricing theory which states that all investors will own the market portfolio (as opposed to single securities). However, the amount of risk they will take on is positively correlated to expected return, where expected return = risk free rate + portfolio beta * (the difference between the expected return on the market as a whole and the risk-free rate).

capital structure The permanent long-term financing of a company, including long-term debt, common stock and preferred stock, and retained earnings. It differs from financial structure, which includes short-term debt and accounts payable.

capitalize To classify a cost as a long-term investment, rather than charging it to current operations. A capitalized cost does not appear on the income statement, but instead appears as a credit on the long-terms assets account and a debit on the cash account of the balance sheet. However, the depreciation expense related to the capitalized cost will appear as an expense on the income statement. Since the long-term assets account is larger due to the effect of capitalization, the depreciation costs are also proportionately larger. Thus, the timing of expense recognition is changed, but eventually all expenses do get recognized on the income statement.

carryback A technique for receiving a refund of back taxes by applying a deduction or credit from a current year to a prior year. also called tax loss carryback.

carryforward A technique for applying a loss or credit from the current year to a future year. also called tax loss carryforward.

carve-out A situation in which a parent company sells a minority share of a child company, usually in an IPO, while retaining the rest. The child company will have its own board of directors and financial statements, but will benefit from the parent company's resources and strategic support. Usually, the parent company will eventually sell the rest of the child company in the open market. also called partial spinoff.

cash budget A forecast of estimated cash receipts and disbursements for a specified period of time.

catastrophe bond A high-yield, insurance-backed bond containing a provision causing interest and/or principal payments to be delayed or lost in the event of loss due to a specified catastrophe, such as an earthquake.

CEO Chief Executive Officer. The executive who is responsible for a company's operations, usually the President or the Chairman of the Board.

Certificate of Deposit CD. Short- or medium-term, interest-bearing, FDIC-insured debt instrument offered by banks and savings and loans. CDs offer higher rates of return than most comparable investments, in exchange for tying up invested money for the duration of the certificate's maturity. Money removed before maturity is subject to a penalty. CDs are low risk, low return investments, and are also known as "time deposits", because the account holder has agreed to keep the money in the account for a specified amount of time, anywhere from three months to six years.

CFO Chief Financial Officer. The executive who is responsible for financial planning and record-keeping for a company.

Chartered Financial Analyst CFA. An individual who has passed tests in economics, accounting, security analysis, and money management, administered by the Institute of Chartered Financial Analysts of the Association for Investment Management and Research. Such an individual is also expected to have at least three years of investments-related experience, and meet certain standards of professional conduct. These individuals have an extensive economic and investing background and are competent at a high level of analysis. Individuals or corporations utilize their services as security analysts, portfolio managers or investment advisors.

charting The set of techniques used in technical analysis in which charts are used to plot price movements, volume, settlement prices, open interest, and other indicators, in order to anticipate future price movements. Users of these techniques, called chartists, believe that past trends in these indicators can be used to extrapolate future trends.

churning Excessive trading in a client's account by a broker seeking to maximize commissions regardless of the client's best interests, in violation of NASD rules. also called twisting or overtrading.

circuit breaker Any of a number of procedures implemented by a major stock or commodity exchange when a certain index falls a predetermined amount in a session, to prevent further losses. Examples include trading halts and restrictions on program trading.

clearinghouse An agency associated with an exchange, which settles trades and regulates delivery.

closed-end fund A fund with a fixed number of shares outstanding, and one which does not redeem shares the way a typical mutual fund does. Closed-end funds behave more like stock than open-end funds: closed-end funds issue a fixed number of shares to the public in an initial public offering, after which time shares in the fund are bought and sold on a stock exchange, and they are not obligated to issue new shares or redeem outstanding shares as open-end funds are. The price of a share in a closed-end fund is determined entirely by market demand, so shares can either trade below their net asset value ("at a discount") or above it ("at a premium"). also called closed-end investment company or publicly-traded fund.

collar The lowest rate acceptable to a buyer of bonds, or the lowest price acceptable to the issuer of an underwriting, or the lowest rate possible for an adjustable rate.

common stock Securities representing equity ownership in a corporation, providing voting rights, and entitling the holder to a share of the company's success through dividends and/or capital appreciation. In the event of liquidation, common stockholders have rights to a company's assets only after bondholders, other debt holders, and preferred stockholders have been satisfied. Typically, common stockholders receive one vote per share to elect the company's board of directors (although the number of votes is not always directly proportional to the number of shares owned). The board of directors is the group of individuals that represents the owners of the corporation and oversees major decisions for the company. Common shareholders also receive voting rights regarding other company matters such as stock splits and company objectives. In addition to voting rights, common shareholders sometimes enjoy what are called "preemptive rights". Preemptive rights allow common shareholders to maintain their proportional ownership in the company in the event that the company issues another offering of stock. This means that common shareholders with preemptive rights have the right but not the obligation to purchase as many new shares of the stock as it would take to maintain their proportional ownership in the company. also called junior equity.

consol A bond which never reaches maturity.

constant dollars Dollars as if in some base year, used to adjust for the effects of inflation.

corporate governance A generic term which describes the ways in which rights and responsibilities are shared between the various corporate participants, especially the management and the shareholders.

corporation The most common form of business organization, and one which is chartered by a state and given many legal rights as an entity separate from its owners. This form of business is characterized by the limited liability of its owners, the issuance of shares of easily transferable stock, and existence as a going concern. The process of becoming a corporation, call incorporation, gives the company separate legal standing from its owners and protects those owners from being personally liable in the event that the company is sued (a condition known as limited liability). Incorporation also provides companies with a more flexible way to manage their ownership structure. In addition, there are different tax implications for corporations, although these can be both advantageous and disadvantageous. In these respects, corporations differ from sole proprietorships and limited partnerships.

cost of capital The opportunity cost of an investment, i.e. the rate of return that a company would otherwise be able to earn at the same risk level as the investment that has been selected.

counterparty risk The risk that the other party in an agreement will default. In an option contract, the risk to the option buyer that the writer will not buy or sell the underlying as agreed. In general, counterparty risk can be reduced by having an organization with extremely good credit act as an intermediary between the two parties.

coupon rate The interest rate stated on a bond, note or other fixed income security, expressed as a percentage of the principal (face value). also called coupon yield.

credit rating A published ranking, based on detailed financial analysis by a credit bureau, of one's financial history, specifically as it relates to one's ability to meet debt obligations. The highest rating is usually AAA, and the lowest is D. Lenders use this information to decide whether to approve a loan.

current dollars Dollars in other time periods converted into present-day dollars, in order to factor out the effects of inflation.

current ratio Current assets divided by current liabilities. An indication of a company's ability to meet short-term debt obligations; the higher the ratio, the more liquid the company is.

current yield The annual rate of return on an investment, expressed as a percentage. also called yield.

debenture Unsecured debt backed only by the integrity of the borrower, not by collateral, and documented by an agreement called an indenture. One example is an unsecured bond.

default Failure to make required debt payments on a timely basis or to comply with other conditions of an obligation or agreement.

defined benefit plan A company retirement plan, such as a pension plan, in which a retired employee receives a specific amount based on salary history and years of service, and in which the employer bears the investment risk. Contributions may be made by the employee, the employer, or both.

defined contribution plan A company retirement plan, such as a 401(k) or 403(b), in which the employee elects to defer some amount of his/her salary into the plan and bears the investment risk.

demand deposit An account balance which can be drawn upon on demand, i.e. without prior notice.

derivative security A financial security, such as an option or future, whose characteristics and value depend on the characteristics and value of an underlying security.

dilution The change in earnings per share or book value per share that would result if all warrants and stock options were exercised and all convertible securities were converted.

discount bond A bond which is sold at a price below its face value and returns its face value at maturity. also called discounted bond.

discount broker A brokerage which executes buy and sell orders at commission rates lower than a full-service brokerage, but which typically provides fewer services such as research and advice.

discount rate The rate at which member banks may borrow short term funds directly from a Federal Reserve Bank. The discount rate is one of the two interest rates set by the Fed, the other being the Federal funds rate. The Fed actually controls this rate directly, but this fact does not really help in policy implementation, since banks can also find such funds elsewhere. also called Federal Reserve Discount Rate.

diversifiable risk The risk of price change due to the unique circumstances of a specific security, as opposed to the overall market. This risk can be virtually eliminated from a portfolio through diversification. also called unsystematic risk.

dividend A taxable payment declared by a company's board of directors and given to its shareholders out of the company's current or retained earnings, usually quarterly. Dividends are usually given as cash (cash dividend), but they can also take the form of stock (stock dividend) or other property. Dividends provide an incentive to own stock in stable companies even if they are not experiencing much growth. Companies are not required to pay dividends. The companies that offer dividends are most often companies that have progressed beyond the growth phase, and no longer benefit sufficiently by reinvesting their profits, so they usually choose to pay them out to their shareholders. also called payout.

Dividend Reinvestment Plan DRIP. An investment plan offered by some corporations enabling shareholders to automatically reinvest cash dividends and capital gains distributions, thereby accumulating more stock without paying brokerage commissions. Many DRIPs also allow the investment of additional cash from the shareholder, known as an optional cash purchase. Unlike with a Direct Stock Purchase Plan, with a DRIP the investor must purchase the first share in the company through a brokerage. After that, the company will take whatever dividends it would normally send as a check and instead it will reinvest them to purchase more shares in the company for you, all without charging a commission. The only drawback is that the investor has no control over when his/her money from the dividends is used to purchase new stock in the company, which means he/she might be buying new shares at sub-optimal times. also called Dividend Reinvestment Program.

dollar cost averaging An investment strategy designed to reduce volatility in which securities, typically mutual funds, are purchased in fixed dollar amounts at regular intervals, regardless of what direction the market is moving. Thus, as prices of securities rise, fewer units are bought, and as prices fall, more units are bought. also called constant dollar plan.

Dow Jones Industrial Average DJIA. The most widely used indicator of the overall condition of the stock market, a price-weighted average of 30 actively traded blue chip stocks, primarily industrials. The 30 stocks are chosen by the editors of the Wall Street Journal (which is published by Dow Jones & Company), a practice that dates back to the beginning of the century. The Dow was officially started by Charles Dow in 1896, at which time it consisted of only 11 stocks. The Dow is computed using a price-weighted indexing system, rather than the more common market cap-weighted indexing system. Simply put, the editors at WSJ add up the prices of all the stocks and then divide by the number of stocks in the index. (In actuality, the divisor is much higher today in order to account for stock splits that have occurred in the past.)

earnings surprise An earnings report that differs from the consensus forecast, i.e. what analysts were expecting. Often causes a substantial movement in the stock's price.

efficient frontier The line on a risk-reward graph comprised of all efficient portfolios.

Efficient Market Theory The (now largely discredited) theory that all market participants receive and act on all of the relevant information as soon as it becomes available. If this were strictly true, no investment strategy would be better than a coin toss. Proponents of the efficient market theory believe that there is perfect information in the stock market. This means that whatever information is available about a stock to one investor is available to all investors (except, of course, insider information, but insider trading is illegal). Since everyone has the same information about a stock, the price of a stock should reflect the knowledge and expectations of all investors. The bottom line is that an investor should not be able to beat the market since there is no way for him/her to know something about a stock that isn't already reflected in the stock's price. Proponents of this theory do not try to pick stocks that are going to be winners; instead, they simply try to match the market's performance. However, there is ample evidence to dispute the basic claims of this theory, and most investors don't believe it.

Electronic Communication Network ECN. An electronic system that brings buyers and sellers together for the electronic execution of trades. It disseminates information to interested parties about the orders entered into the network and allows these orders to be executed. Electronic Communications Networks (ECNs) represent orders in NASDAQ stocks; they internally match buy and sell orders or represent the highest bid prices and lowest ask prices on the open market. The benefits an investor gets from trading with an ECN include after-hours trading, avoiding market makers (and their spreads), and anonymity (which is often important for large trades).

emerging market A financial market of a developing country, usually a small market with a short operating history.

endowment A permanent fund bestowed upon an individual or institution, such as a university, museum, hospital, or foundation, to be used for a specific purpose.

equity Ownership interest in a corporation in the form of common stock or preferred stock. It also refers to total assets minus total liabilities, in which case it is also referred to as shareholder's equity or net worth or book value. In real estate, it is the difference between what a property is worth and what the owner owes against that property (i.e. the difference between the house value and the remaining mortgage or loan payments on a house). In the context of a futures trading account, it is the value of the securities in the account, assuming that the account is liquidated at the going price. In the context of a brokerage account, it is the net value of the account, i.e. the value of securities in the account less any margin requirements.

equity multiplier Total assets divided by common stockholder's equity. This is a measure of leverage. The higher the ratio is, the more the company is relying on debt to finance its asset base.

equity risk premium The extra return that the overall stock market or a particular stock must provide over the rate on Treasury Bills to compensate for market risk.

Eurodollar An American dollar held by a foreign institution outside the U.S., usually a bank in Europe, often as a result of payments made to overseas companies for merchandise.

European-style option An option which can only be exercised for a short, specified period of time just prior to its expiration, usually a single day. also called European option.

exchange rate Rate at which one currency may be converted into another. also called rate of exchange or foreign exchange rate or currency exchange rate.

exchange ratio The number of shares of the acquiring company that a shareholder will receive for one share of the acquired company.

Exchange Traded Fund ETF. A fund that tracks an index, but can be traded like a stock. ETFs always bundle together the securities that are in an index; they never track actively managed mutual fund portfolios (because most actively managed funds only disclose their holdings a few times a year, so the ETF would not know when to adjust its holdings most of the time). Investors can do just about anything with an ETF that they can do with a normal stock, such as short selling. Because ETFs are traded on stock exchanges, they can be bought and sold at any time during the day (unlike most mutual funds). Their price will fluctuate from moment to moment, just like any other stock's price, and an investor will need a broker in order to purchase them, which means that he/she will have to pay a commission. On the plus side, ETFs are more tax-efficient than normal mutual funds, and since they track indexes they have very low operating and transaction costs associated with them. There are no sales loads or investment minimums required to purchase an ETF. The first ETF created was the Standard and Poor's Deposit Receipt (SPDR, pronounced "Spider") in 1993. SPDRs gave investors an easy way to track the S&P 500 without buying an index fund, and they soon become quite popular.

ex-dividend A security which no longer carries the right to the most recently declared dividend; or the period of time between the announcement of the dividend and the payment. A security becomes ex-dividend on the ex-dividend date (set by the NASD), which is usually two business days before the record date (set by the company issuing the dividend). For transactions during the ex-dividend period, the seller, not the buyer, will receive the dividend. Ex-dividend is usually indicated in newspapers with an x next to the stock or mutual fund's name. In general, a stock's price drops the day the ex-dividend period starts, since the buyer will not receive the benefit of the dividend payout till the next dividend date. As the stock gets closer to the next dividend date, the price may gradually rise in anticipation of the dividend.

exercise price The specified price on an option contract at which the contract may be exercised, whereby a call option buyer can buy the underlier or a put option buyer can sell the underlier. The buyer's profit from exercising the option is the amount by which the spot price exceeds the exercise price (in the case of a call), or the amount by which the exercise price exceeds the spot price (in the case of a put). In general, the smaller the difference between spot and exercise price, the higher the option premium. also called strike price.

external financing Financing through the issuance of debt or equity. also called outside financing. opposite of internal financing.

factoring The selling of a company's accounts receivable, at a discount, to a factor, who then assumes the credit risk of the account debtors and receives cash as the debtors settle their accounts. also called accounts receivable financing.

family of funds A mutual fund company offering many mutual funds, for various objectives. Usually, investors can move assets between different funds of a family of funds at little or no cost, and can receive a single statement describing their holdings in all the funds in the family of funds. also called fund family or mutual fund family.

FASB Financial Accounting Standards Board. Independent agency which establishes GAAP.

Federal funds rate The interest rate that banks charge each other for the use of Federal funds. It changes daily and is a sensitive indicator of general interest rate trends. The Federal funds rate is one of the of two interest rates controlled by the Fed. While the Fed can't directly affect this rate, it effectively controls it in the way it buys and sells Treasuries to banks. This is the rate that reaches individual investors, though the changes usually aren't felt for a period of time.

Federal National Mortgage Association FNMA or Fannie Mae. A congressionally chartered corporation which buys mortgages on the secondary market, pools them and sells them as mortgage-backed securities to investors on the open market. Monthly principal and interest payments are guaranteed by FNMA but not by the U.S. Government.

Federal Open Market Committee FOMC. A 12-member committee which sets credit and interest rate policies for the Federal Reserve System. This committee consists of 7 members of the Board of Governors, and 5 of the 12 Federal Reserve Bank Presidents. This group, headed by the Chairman of the Federal Reserve Board, sets interest rates either directly (by changing the discount rate) or through the use of open market operations (by buying and selling government securities which affects the federal funds rate). The discount rate is the rate at which the Federal Reserve Bank charges member banks for overnight loans. The Fed actually controls this rate directly, but it tends to have little impact on the activities of banks because these funds are available elsewhere. This rate is set during the FOMC meetings by the regional banks and the Federal Reserve Board. The federal funds rate is the interest rate at which banks loan excess reserves to each other. While the Fed can't directly affect this rate, it effectively controls it through the way it buys and sells Treasuries to banks. There are 8 scheduled FOMC meetings during the course of each year. However, when circumstances dictate, the Fed can make inter-meeting rate changes.

Federal Reserve Bank One of 12 regional banks established to maintain reserves, issue bank notes, and lend money to member banks. The Federal Reserve Banks are also responsible for supervising member banks in their areas, and are involved in the setting of national monetary policy.

Federal Reserve Discount Rate The rate at which member banks may borrow short term funds directly from a Federal Reserve Bank. The discount rate is one of the two interest rates set by the Fed, the other being the Federal funds rate. The Fed actually controls this rate directly, but this fact does not really help in policy implementation, since banks can also find such funds elsewhere.

Federal Savings and Loan Association A federally chartered institution whose purpose is to collect savings deposits and provide residential mortgage loans.

financial leverage The degree to which an investor or business is utilizing borrowed money. Companies that are highly leveraged may be at risk of bankruptcy if they are unable to make payments on their debt; they may also be unable to find new lenders in the future. Financial leverage is not always bad, however; it can increase the shareholders' return on their investment and often there are tax advantages associated with borrowing. also called leverage.

firm commitment offering An arrangement in which an underwriter assumes the risk of bringing a new securities issue to market, by buying the issue from the issuer and guaranteeing sale of a certain number of shares to investors. More common than best efforts offering.

first mortgage The mortgage that has first claim in the event of a default.

fixed annuity An investment vehicle offered by an insurance company, that guarantees a stream of fixed payments over the life of the annuity. The insurer, not the insured, takes the investment risk. also called fixed dollar annuity.

fixed income A security that pays a specific interest rate, such as a bond, money market instrument, or preferred stock.

fixed-rate loan A loan in which the interest rate does not change during the entire term of the loan. For an individual taking out a loan when rates are low, the fixed rate loan would allow him or her to "lock in" the low rates and not be concerned with fluctuations. On the other hand, if interest rates were historically high at the time of the loan, he or she would benefit from a floating rate loan, because as the prime rate fell to historically normal levels, the rate on the loan would decrease. opposite of adjustable rate.

floating exchange rate Currency exchange rate which is determined by free market forces, rather than being fixed by a government.

floor broker An exchange member who executes orders on the floor of an exchange on behalf of others who do not have access to the trading area. also called pit broker.

flotation costs The costs of issuing a new security, including the money investment bankers earn from the spread between their cost and the price offered to the public, and the accounting, legal, printing and other costs associated with the issue.

foreign exchange Instruments, such as paper currency, notes, and checks, used to make payments between countries.

Form 10-K Audited document required by the SEC and sent to a public company's or mutual fund's shareholders at the end of each fiscal year, reporting the financial results for the year (including the balance sheet, income statement, cash flow statement and description of company operations) and commenting on the outlook for the future. The term sometimes refers to the glossy, colorful brochure and sometimes to Form 10-K, which is sent along with the brochure and contains more detailed financial information. All 10-Ks for public companies and mutual funds incorporated in the U.S. are available on the SEC's website for free. also called annual report.

forward contract A cash market transaction in which a seller agrees to deliver a specific cash commodity to a buyer at some point in the future. Unlike futures contracts (which occur through a clearing firm), forward contracts are privately negotiated and are not standardized. Further, the two parties must bear each other's credit risk, which is not the case with a futures contract. Also, since the contracts are not exchange traded, there is no marking to market requirement, which allows a buyer to avoid almost all capital outflow initially (though some counterparties might set collateral requirements). Given the lack of standardization in these contracts, there is very little scope for a secondary market in forwards. The price specified in a forward contract for a specific commodity. The forward price makes the forward contract have no value when the contract is written. However, if the value of the underlying commodity changes, the value of the forward contract becomes positive or negative, depending on the position held. Forwards are priced in a manner similar to futures. Like in the case of a futures contract, the first step in pricing a forward is to add the spot price to the cost of carry (interest forgone, convenience yield, storage costs and interest/dividend received on the underlying). Unlike a futures contract though, the price may also include a premium for counterparty credit risk, and the fact that there is not daily marking to market process to minimize default risk. If there is no allowance for these credit risks, then the forward price will equal the futures price.

forward exchange rate The exchange rate set today for a foreign currency transaction with payment or delivery at some future date.

forward price The price specified in a forward contract for a specific commodity. The forward price makes the forward contract have no value when the contract is written. However, if the value of the underlying commodity changes, the value of the forward contract becomes positive or negative, depending on the position held. Forwards are priced in a manner similar to futures. As with a futures contract, the first step in pricing a forward is to add the spot price to the cost of carry (interest forgone, convenience yield, storage costs and interest/dividend received on the underlying). However, unlike a futures contract, the price may also include a premium for counterparty credit risk, and there is not daily marking-to-market to minimize default risk. If there is no allowance for these credit risks, then the forward price will equal the futures price.

free cash flow Operating cash flow (net income plus amortization and depreciation) minus capital expenditures and dividends. Free cash flow is the amount of cash that a company has left over after it has paid all of its expenses, including investments. Negative free cash flow is not necessarily an indication of a bad company, however, since many young companies put a lot of their cash into investments, which diminishes their free cash flow. But if a company is spending so much cash, it should have a good reason for doing so and it should be earning a sufficiently high rate of return on its investments. While free cash flow doesn't receive as much media coverage as earnings do, it is considered by some experts to be a better indicator of a company's financial health.

friendly takeover Takeover which is supported by the management of the target company. opposite of hostile takeover.

full-service brokerage A brokerage which, in addition to executing trades for its clients, also provides them with research and advice. Significantly more expensive than discount brokers, which only execute trades.

fully diluted earnings per share Common stock earnings per share that would result if all warrants and stock options were exercised and all convertible bonds and preferred stock were converted. For a firm that has a lot of stock options, warrants, convertible bonds and preferred stock outstanding, the fully diluted earnings per share are the most appropriate way of looking at earnings on a per share basis.

fundamental analysis   A method of security valuation which involves examining the company's financials and operations, especially sales, earnings, growth potential, assets, debt, management, products, and competition. Fundamental analysis takes into consideration only those variables that are directly related to the company itself, rather than the overall state of the market or technical analysis data.

futures contract   A standardized, transferable, exchange-traded contract that requires delivery of a commodity, bond, currency, or stock index, at a specified price, on a specified future date. Unlike options, futures convey an obligation to buy. The risk to the holder is unlimited, and because the payoff pattern is symmetrical, the risk to the seller is unlimited as well. Dollars lost and gained by each party on a futures contract are equal and opposite. In other words, futures trading is a zero-sum game. Futures contracts are forward contracts, meaning they represent a pledge to make a certain transaction at a future date. The exchange of assets occurs on the date specified in the contract. Futures are distinguished from generic forward contracts in that they contain standardized terms, trade on a formal exchange, are regulated by overseeing agencies, and are guaranteed by clearinghouses. Also, in order to insure that payment will occur, futures have a margin requirement that must be settled daily. Finally, by making an offsetting trade, taking delivery of goods, or arranging for an exchange of goods, futures contracts can be closed. Hedgers often trade futures for the purpose of keeping price risk in check. also called futures.

futures price   The price at which the two participants in a futures contract agree to transact on the settlement date.

general partnership   A business partnership featuring two or more partners in which each partner is liable for any debts taken on by the business. Because the partners do not enjoy limited liability, all the partners' assets can be involved in an insolvency case against the company.

geometric mean   A measure of central tendency calculated by multiplying a series of numbers and taking the nth root of the product, where n is the number of items in the series. The geometric mean is often used when finding an average for numbers presented as percentages.

Glass-Steagall Act   1933 Congressional law which authorized deposit insurance and prohibited commercial banks from owning brokerages. The latter rule has softened, and many banks now own discount brokers, sell mutual funds, and participate in underwritings.

global fund   A mutual fund investing in stocks or bonds throughout the world, including the U.S. This differs from an international fund, which does not include the U.S. Global funds can provide more opportunities for diversification than domestic funds alone, but there can be additional risks associated with global funds, including currency fluctuations and political and economic instability. also called world fund.

golden parachute   A clause in an executive's employment contract specifying that he/she will receive large benefits in the event that the company is acquired and the executive's employment is terminated. These benefits can take the form of severance pay, a bonus, stock options, or a combination thereof.

Good Til Canceled   GTC. An order to buy or sell which remains in effect until it is either executed or canceled (although brokers usually set a limit of 30 to 60 days, after which the broker will automatically cancel it or ask the customer if he/she wants to keep it active). also called open order.

Government Securities Clearing Corporation   GSCC. An affiliate of the National Securities Clearing Corporation created to handle Treasury securities, including both new issues and resales.

growth fund   A mutual fund whose aim is to achieve capital appreciation by investing in growth stocks. They focus on companies that are experiencing significant earnings or revenue growth, rather than companies that pay out dividends. The hope is that these rapidly growing companies will continue to increase in value, thereby allowing the fund to reap the benefits of large capital gains. In general, growth funds are more volatile than other types of funds, rising more than other funds in bull markets and falling more in bear markets.

growth rate   Year-over-year change, expressed as a percentage.

Hang Seng Index   A market-value weighted index of the stock prices of the 33 largest companies on the Hong Kong market.

head and shoulders   A technical analysis term referring to a chart formation in which a price exhibits three successive rallies, the second one being the highest. The name derives from the fact that on a chart the first and third rallies look like shoulders and the second looks like a head. Believed by technical analysts to be a bearish indicator.

hedge fund   A fund, usually used by wealthy individuals and institutions, which is allowed to use aggressive strategies that are unavailable to mutual funds, including selling short, leverage, program trading, swaps, arbitrage, and derivatives. Hedge funds are exempt from many of the rules and regulations governing other mutual funds, which allows them to accomplish aggressive investing goals. They are restricted by law to no more than 100 investors per fund, and as a result most hedge funds set extremely high minimum investment amounts, ranging anywhere from $250,000 to over $1 million. As with traditional mutual funds, investors in hedge funds pay a management fee; however, hedge funds also collect a percentage of the profits (usually 20%).

high yield   Description of investments with high rates of return. Generally, a high yield bond will be ranked very low by a rating agency, because these are bonds which have a relatively high chance of default, and therefore have to offer higher returns. Similarly, a stock will offer a high dividend yield in order to compensate for lower expected capital gains, for example a large company in a mature industry which is no longer growing.

holding company   A company that owns enough voting stock in another firm to control management and operations by influencing or electing its board of directors. also called parent company.

home equity loan   A loan secured by a primary residence or second home to the extent of the excess of fair market value over the debt incurred in the purchase.

hurdle rate   The required rate of return in a discounted cash flow analysis, above which an investment makes sense and below which it does not. Often, this is based on the firm's cost of capital or weighted average cost of capital, plus or minus a risk premium to reflect the project's specific risk characteristics. also called required rate of return.

imputed interest   Interest considered by the IRS for tax purposes to have been paid, even if no interest was actually paid.

in the money   Situation in which an option's strike price is below the current market price of the underlier (for a call option) or above the current market price of the underlier (for a put option). Such an option has intrinsic value.

incentive stock option   ISO. A type of employee stock option which provides tax advantages for the employer that a non-qualified stock option does not, but which is subject to more stringent requirements. For ISOs, no income tax is due when the options are granted or when they're exercised. Instead, the tax is deferred until the holder sells the stock, at which time he/she is taxed for his/her entire gain. As long as the sale is at least two years after the options were granted and at least one year after they were exercised, they'll be taxed at the lower, long-term capital gains rate; otherwise, the sale is considered a "disqualifying disposition", and they'll be taxed as if they were nonqualified options (the gain at exercise is taxed as ordinary income, and any subsequent appreciation is taxed as capital gains). ISOs may not be granted at a discount to the current stock price, and they are not transferable, except through a will. Also called qualified stock option.

income fund A mutual fund which emphasizes current income in the form of dividends or coupon payments from bonds and/or preferred stocks, rather than emphasizing growth. Income funds are considered to be conservative investments, since they avoid volatile growth stocks. Income funds are popular with retirees and other investors who are looking for a steady cash flow without assuming too much risk.

incremental cost The cost associated with one additional unit of production. also called marginal cost.

indenture A written agreement between the issuer of a bond and his/her bondholders, usually specifying interest rate, maturity date, convertibility, and other terms.

index arbitrage A strategy designed to profit from temporary discrepancies between the prices of the stocks comprising an index and the price of a futures contract on that index. By buying either the stocks or the futures contract and selling the other, an investor can sometimes exploit market inefficiency for a profit. Like all arbitrage opportunities, index arbitrage opportunities disappear rapidly once the opportunity becomes well-known and many investors act on it. Index arbitrage can involve large transaction costs because of the need to simultaneously buy and sell many different stocks and futures, and so only large money managers are usually able to profit from index arbitrage. In addition, sophisticated computer programs are needed to keep track of the large number of stocks and futures involved, which makes this a very difficult trading strategy for individuals.

index fund A passively managed mutual fund that tries to mirror the performance of a specific index, such as the S&P 500. Since portfolio decisions are automatic and transactions are infrequent, expenses tend to be lower than those of actively managed funds.

index option An option whose underlying security is an index. If exercised, settlement is made by cash payment, since physical delivery is not possible.

Individual Retirement Account IRA. A tax-deferred retirement account for an individual that permits individuals to set aside up to $2,000 per year, with earnings tax-deferred until withdrawals begin at age 59 1/2 or later (or earlier, with a 10% penalty). IRAs can be established at a bank, mutual fund, or brokerage. Only those who do not participate in a pension plan at work or who do participate and meet certain income guidelines can make deductible contributions to an IRA. All others can make contributions to an IRA on a non-deductible basis. Such contributions qualify as a deduction against income earned in that year and interest accumulates tax-deferred until the funds are withdrawn. A participant is able to roll over a distribution to another IRA or withdraw funds using a special schedule of early payments made over the participant's life expectancy.

industrial revenue bond Bond used to finance the construction of manufacturing or commercial facilities for a private user.

inflation risk The possibility that the value of assets or income will decrease as inflation shrinks the purchasing power of a currency. Inflation causes money to decrease in value at some rate, and does so whether the money is invested or not.

inside information Material information about a company which is known by the company's board of directors, management, and/or employees but not by the public. The SEC forbids trading based on such information.

installment loan A loan that is repaid with a fixed number of periodic equal-sized payments.

institutional investor Entity with large amounts to invest, such as investment companies, mutual funds, brokerages, insurance companies, pension funds, investment banks and endowment funds. Institutional investors are covered by fewer protective regulations because it is assumed that they are more knowledgeable and better able to protect themselves. They account for a majority of overall volume.

interest rate risk The possibility of a reduction in the value of a security, especially a bond, resulting from a rise in interest rates. This risk can be reduced by diversifying the durations of the fixed-income investments that are held at a given time.

Intermarket Trading System ITS. A computer network that connects several major U.S. stock exchanges for the purpose of choosing the best market for a given transaction.

internal growth rate The maximum rate of growth a given company is able to achieve without outside sources of funding.

Internal Rate of Return IRR. The rate of return that would make the present value of future cash flows plus the final market value of an investment or business opportunity equal the current market price of the investment or opportunity. also called dollar-weighted rate of return.

international fund A mutual fund which invests in stocks and bonds of companies outside of the U.S.

intrinsic value The perceived actual value of a security, as opposed to its market price or book value.

investment bank An individual or institution which acts as an underwriter or agent for corporations and municipalities issuing securities. Most also maintain broker/ dealer operations, maintain markets for previously issued securities, and offer advisory services to investors. Investment banks also have a large role in facilitating mergers and acquisitions, private equity placements and corporate restructuring. Unlike traditional banks, investment banks do not accept deposits from and provide loans to individuals. also called investment banker.

Investment Company Act of 1940 A set of Federal laws which regulate the registration and activities of investment companies, enforced by the SEC.

investment policy A formal description of the investment philosophy that will be utilized for a given fund, retirement plan, or other investment vehicle.

IPO Initial Public Offering. The first sale of stock by a company to the public.

January Effect Tendency of the stock market to rise between December 31 and the end of the first week in January. The January Effect occurs because many investors choose to sell some of their stock right before the end of the year in order to claim a capital loss for tax purposes. Once the tax calendar rolls over to a new year on January 1st these same investors quickly reinvest their money in the market, causing stock prices to rise. Although the January Effect has been observed numerous times throughout history, it is difficult for investors to profit from it since the market as a whole expects it to happen and therefore adjusts its prices accordingly.

junk bond A high-risk, non-investment-grade bond with a low credit rating, usually BB or lower; as a consequence, it usually has a high yield. opposite of investment-grade bond.

large cap Over $5 billion capitalization. Companies are usually classified as either large cap, medium cap, small cap, or micro cap, depending on their market capitalization, but the dividing lines are somewhat arbitrary. As a general guideline, the market capitaliation is $5 billion or more for large caps, $1 billion to $5 billion for medium caps, $250 million to $1 billion for small caps, and less than $250 million for micro caps. When calculating the market caps of foreign companies who have issued ADRs in the US, only the outstanding ADR shares are considered, not the shares issued by that company in other countries.

LEAPS Long-Term Equity Anticipation Securities. Long-term stock options or index options, with expiration dates up to three years away. LEAPs are very similar to standard options except for the fact that they expire much further in the future. They can be safer than traditional options because it is somewhat easier to predict stock movement over longer periods. Like options, they allow an investor to lock in a fixed price for the underlying security. Therefore, like options, they can be effective for both leverage and insurance purposes. Expiration generally occurs 36 months after purchase, and LEAPs are American style, so they can be exercised at any time before expiration. Strike prices usually range around 25% above or below the price of the underlying stock when the LEAP is first offered.

lease A written agreement under which a property owner allows a tenant to use the property for a specified period of time and rent.

leverage The degree to which an investor or business is utilizing borrowed money. Companies that are highly leveraged may be at risk of bankruptcy if they are unable to make payments on their debt; they may also be unable to find new lenders in the future. Leverage is not always bad, however; it can increase the shareholders' return on their investment and often there are tax advantages associated with borrowing. also called financial leverage.

Leveraged Buyout LBO. Takeover of a company or controlling interest in a company, using a significant amount of borrowed money. Often the target company's assets serve as collateral for the borrowed money.

LIBOR London Inter-Bank Offer Rate. The interest rate that the banks charge each other for loans (usually in Eurodollars). This rate is applicable to the short-term international interbank market, and applies to very large loans borrowed for anywhere from one day to five years. This market allows banks with liquidity requirements to borrow quickly from other banks with surpluses, enabling banks to avoid holding excessively large amounts of their asset base as liquid assets. The LIBOR is officially fixed once a day by a small group of large London banks, but the rate changes throughout the day.

life insurance Insurance to be paid to a beneficiary when the insured dies.

limit order An order to a broker to buy a specified quantity of a security at or below a specified price, or to sell it at or above a specified price (called the limit price). This ensures that a person will never pay more for the stock than whatever price is set as his/her limit. This is one of the two most common types of orders, the other being a market order. opposite of no limit order.

Limited Liability Company LLC. A type of company, authorized only in certain states, whose owners and managers receive the limited liability and (usually) tax benefits of an S Corporation without having to conform to the S corporation restrictions.

limited partnership A business organization with one or more general partners, who manage the business and assume legal debts and obligations, and one or more limited partners, who are liable only to the extent of their investments. Limited partners also enjoy rights to the partnership's cash flow, but are not liable for company obligations.

liquidity risk The risk that arises from the difficulty of selling an asset. An investment may sometimes need to be sold quickly. Unfortunately, an insufficient secondary market may prevent the liquidation or limit the funds that can be generated from the asset. Some assets are highly liquid and have low liquidity risk (such as stock of a publicly traded company), while other assets are highly illiquid and have high liquidity risk (such as a house).

listed option An option authorized by an exchange for trading. also called exchange-traded option.

load A sales charge added to the purchase and/or sale price of some mutual funds and annuities. opposite of no-load.

lockbox A service offered by banks to companies in which the company receives payments by mail to a post office box and the bank picks up the payments several times a day, deposits them into the company's account, and notifies the company of the deposit. This enables the company to put the money to work as soon as it's received, but the amounts must be large in order for the value obtained to exceed the cost of the service.

lockup period An interval during which an investment may not be sold. In the case of an IPO, employees may not sell their shares for a period time determined by the underwriter and usually lasting 180 days.

MACRS Modified ACRS. Depreciation methods applied to assets placed in service after 1986. These are less favorable than the earlier ACRS system, but allow quicker write-offs for some types of assets. Useful method in the case of assets that quickly become obsolete.

margin buying A risky technique involving the purchase of securities with borrowed money, using the shares themselves as collateral. Usually done using a margin account at a brokerage, and subject to fairly strict SEC regulations. also called buying on margin.

market breadth The fraction of the overall market that is participating in the market's up or down move. Looking at this parameter allows investors to reduce the impact of the large cap stocks which influence market indices the most, and instead examine price trends of a diverse range of stocks. This parameter is important in the context of technical analysis, as a measure of market sentiment. Market breadth is also used to refer to the number of independently issued price forecasts for a certain number of stocks (less common). also called breadth.

market index An index which is designed to measure price changes of an overall market, such as the stock market or the bond market. An example is Vanguard's Total Bond Market Index.

market maker A brokerage or bank that maintains a firm bid and ask price in a given security by standing ready, willing, and able to buy or sell at publicly quoted prices (called making a market). These firms display bid and offer prices for specific numbers of specific securities, and if these prices are met, they will immediately buy for or sell from their own accounts. Market makers are very important for maintaining liquidity and efficiency for the particular securities that they make markets in. At most firms, there is a strict separation of the market-making side and the brokerage side, since otherwise there might be an incentive for brokers to recommend securities simply because the firm makes a market in that security.

market order A buy or sell order in which the broker is to execute the order at the best price currently available. also called at the market. These are often the lowest-commission trades because they involve very little work by the broker.

market portfolio A concept used in Modern Portfolio Theory which refers to a hypothetical portfolio containing every security available to investors in a given market in amounts proportional to their market values.

market risk   Risk which is common to an entire class of assets or liabilities. The value of investments may decline over a given time period simply because of economic changes or other events that impact large portions of the market. Asset allocation and diversification can protect against market risk because different portions of the market tend to underperform at different times. also called systematic risk.

market timing   Attempting to predict future market directions, usually by examining recent price and volume data or economic data, and investing based on those predictions. also called timing the market.

mark-to-market   Recording the price or value of a security, portfolio, or account on a daily basis, to calculate profits and losses or to confirm that margin requirements are being met.

merger   The combining of two or more entities into one, through a purchase acquisition or a pooling of interests. Differs from a consolidation in that no new entity is created from a merger.

mid cap $1 billion to $5 billion capitalization.

money market   Market for short-term debt securities, such as banker's acceptances, commercial paper, repos, negotiable certificates of deposit, and Treasury Bills with a maturity of one year or less and often 30 days or less. Money market securities are generally very safe investments which return a relatively low interest rate that is most appropriate for temporary cash storage or short-term time horizons. Bid and ask spreads are relatively small due to the large size and high liquidity of the market.

mortgage   A loan to finance the purchase of real estate, usually with specified payment periods and interest rates. The borrower (mortgagor) gives the lender (mortgagee) a lien on the property as collateral for the loan.

mortgage servicing   Administering a mortgage. Includes calculating principal and interest, collecting payments from the mortgagor, acting as an escrow agent, and foreclosing in the event of a default.

mortgage-backed security   MBS. Security backed by a pool of mortgages, such as those issued by Ginnie Mae and Freddie Mac. also called mortgage-backed certificate.

moving average   A technical analysis term meaning the average price of a security over a specified time period (the most common being 20, 30, 50, 100 and 200 days), used in order to spot pricing trends by flattening out large fluctuations. This is perhaps the most commonly used variable in technical analysis. Moving average data is used to create charts that show whether a stock's price is trending up or down. They can be used to track daily, weekly, or monthly patterns. Each new day's (or week's or month's) numbers are added to the average and the oldest numbers are dropped; thus, the average "moves" over time. In general, the shorter the time frame used, the more volatile the prices will appear, so, for example, 20 day moving average lines tend to move up and down more than 200 day moving average lines.

municipal bond   Bond issued by a state, city, or local government. Municipalities issue bonds to raise capital for their day-to-day activities and for specific projects that they might be undertaking (usually pertaining to development of local infrastructure such as roads, sewerage, hospitals etc). Interest on municipal bonds are generally exempt from federal tax. In the case that the bond is bought by a resident of the state that issued the bond, the interest payments are also exempt from state tax. Interest payments are further exempt from local tax if they are bought by residents of the locality that issued the bond. Capital gains however are taxable. Given the tax-savings they offer, municipal bonds are often bought by people who have large tax burdens. Yields on municipal bonds are often lower than corporate or Treasury bonds with comparable maturities, because of the important advantage of not being taxed at the federal level. In general, municipal bonds are considered safer than corporate bonds, since a municipality is far less likely to go bankrupt than a company. Some municipal bonds can also be insured by outside agencies. These companies will promise to pay the interest and principal if the issuer defaults. Both issuers and bondholders can carry this insurance, though a bondholder would need to have a large stake to get the coverage. There are two common types of municipal bonds: general obligation and revenue. General Obligation (GO) bonds are unsecured municipal bonds that are simply backed by the full faith and credit of the municipality. Generally, these bonds have maturities of at least 10 years and are paid off with funds from taxes or other fees. Revenue bonds are used to fund projects that will eventually create revenue directly, such as a toll road or lease payments for a new building. The revenues from the projects are used to pay off the bonds. In some cases the issuer is not obligated to pay interest unless a certain amount of revenue is generated. Municipal bonds usually come in $5,000 par values and usually require a minimum investment of $25,000 in order to get the best price. also called muni.

mutual fund   An open-ended fund operated by an investment company which raises money from shareholders and invests in a group of assets, in accordance with a stated set of objectives. Mutual funds raise money by selling shares of the fund to the public, much like any other type of company can sell stock in itself to the public. Mutual funds then take the money they receive from the sale of their shares (along with any money made from previous investments) and use it to purchase various investment vehicles, such as stocks, bonds and money market instruments. In return for the money they give to the fund when purchasing shares, shareholders receive an equity position in the fund and, in effect, in each of its underlying securities. For most mutual funds, shareholders are free to sell their shares at any time, although the price of a share in a mutual fund will fluctuate daily, depending upon the performance of the securities held by the fund. Benefits of mutual funds include diversification and professional money management. Mutual funds offer choice, liquidity, and convenience, but charge fees and often require a minimum investment. A closed-end fund is often incorrectly referred to as a mutual fund, but is actually an investment trust. There are many types of mutual funds, including aggressive growth fund, asset allocation fund, balanced fund, blend fund, bond fund, capital appreciation fund, clone fund, closed fund, crossover fund, equity fund, fund of funds, global fund, growth fund, growth and income fund, hedge fund, income fund, index fund, international fund, money market fund, municipal bond fund, prime rate fund, regional fund, sector fund, specialty fund, stock fund, and tax-free bond fund.

mutual life insurance company   A life insurance company owned by its policyholders, who share in the company's surplus earnings.

Mutual Savings Bank   A savings bank that is owned by, and operated for the benefit of, its depositors.

NAIC   National Association of Investors Corporation. A non-profit organization designed to help investors create or join investment clubs. This organization offers a variety of investment-related publications, online newsletters, software and videos that provide information on the investing process.

naked call   A short call option position in which the writer does not own the corresponding number of shares of the underlier, or has not deposited in a cash account an amount equal to the exercise value of the call. also called uncovered call. opposite of covered call.

NASD   National Association of Securities Dealers. A selfregulatory securities industry organization responsible for the operation and regulation of the Nasdaq stock market and overthecounter markets. The NASD investigates complaints against member firms and tries to ensure that all of its members adhere to both its own standards and those laid out by the SEC. The NASD has the power to expel its members from an exchange in the case of wrongdoing, but it cannot take legal action against a member other than by reporting it to the SEC. The association is run by a Board that takes half of its representatives from the securities industry and half from the public.

Nasdaq   A computerized system established by the NASD to facilitate trading by providing broker/dealers with current bid and ask price quotes on over-the-counter stocks and some listed stocks. Unlike the Amex and the NYSE, the Nasdaq (once an acronym for the National Association of Securities Dealers Automated Quotation system) does not have a physical trading floor that brings together buyers and sellers. Instead, all trading on the Nasdaq exchange is done over a network of computers and telephones. Also, the Nasdaq does not employ market specialists to buy unfilled orders like the NYSE does. The Nasdaq began when brokers started informally trading via telephone; the network was later formalized and linked by computer in the early 1970s. In 1998 the parent company of the Nasdaq purchased the Amex, although the two continue to operate separately. Orders for stock are sent out electronically on the Nasdaq, where market makers list their buy and sell prices. Once a price is agreed upon, the transaction is executed electronically.

National Securities Clearing Corporation   NSCC. Securities clearing organization owned jointly by the AMEX, NYSE and NASD through which brokerages reconcile accounts with one another.

NAV   Net Asset Value. The dollar value of a single mutual fund share, based on the value of the underlying assets of the fund minus its liabilities, divided by the number of shares outstanding. Calculated at the end of each business day.

negotiable certificate of deposit   A CD with a very large denomination, usually $1 million or more. These are usually bought by institutional investors who are interested in low-risk investments. Negotiable certificates of deposit are usually in bearer form, and have secondary markets that are highly liquid. also called jumbo CD.

Nikkei Index   Index of 225 leading stocks traded on the Tokyo Stock Exchange.

no-load fund   A mutual fund which doesn't impose a sales or redemption charge, selling and redeeming its shares at net asset value. opposite of load fund.

nominal rate   The stated interest rate on a bond, unadjusted for inflation.

nondiversifiable risk   Risk which is common to an entire class of assets or liabilities. The value of investments may decline over a given time period simply because of economic changes or other events that impact large portions of the market. Asset allocation and diversification can protect against nondiversifiable risk because different portions of the market tend to underperform at different times. also called systematic risk or market risk.

note   A short-term debt security, usually with a maturity of five years or less.

NOW   Negotiable Order of Withdrawal. An interest-bearing checking account at a bank or savings and loan.

NYSE   New York Stock Exchange. The oldest and largest stock exchange in the U.S., located on Wall Street in New York City. The NYSE is responsible for setting policy, supervising member activities, listing securities, overseeing the transfer of member seats, and evaluating applicants. It traces its origins back to 1792, when a group of brokers met under a tree at the tip of Manhattan and signed an agreement to trade securities. Unlike some of the newer exchanges, the NYSE still uses a large trading floor in order to conduct its transactions. It is here that the representatives of buyers and sellers, professionals known as brokers, meet and shout out prices at one another in order to strike a deal. This is called the open outcry system and it usually produces fair market pricing. In order to facilitate the exchange of stocks, the NYSE employs individuals called specialists who are assigned to manage the buying and selling of specific stocks and to buy those stocks when no one else will. Of the exchanges, the NYSE has the most stringent set of requirements in place for the companies whose stocks it lists, and even meeting these requirements is not a guarantee that the NYSE will list the company. also called Big Board.

odd lot   Less than 100 shares of a stock; or less than 10 shares of a very thinly traded stock. Some brokerages charge higher commissions for such transactions (often 1/8 of a point per share, called the differential). also called broken lot or uneven lot. opposite of round lot.

Office of Thrift Supervision   The agency of the U.S. treasury department which is responsible for overseeing and regulating the savings and loan industry.

offshore company   A company incorporated in a country where there is little government control and/or low tax rates.

open interest   The total number of futures contracts or option contracts that have not yet been exercised, expired, or fulfilled by delivery.

open-end fund   A fund operated by an investment company which raises money from shareholders and invests in a group of assets, in accordance with a stated set of objectives. Open-end funds raise money by selling shares of the fund to the public, much like any other type of company which can sell stock in itself to the public. Mutual funds then take the money they receive from the sale of their shares (along with any money made from previous investments) and use it to purchase various investment vehicles, such as stocks, bonds and money market instruments. In return for the money they give to the fund when purchasing shares, shareholders receive an equity position in the fund and, in effect, in each of its underlying securities. For most open-end funds, shareholders are free to sell their shares at any time, although the price of a share in an open-end fund will fluctuate daily, depending upon the performance of the securities held by the fund. Benefits of open-end funds include diversification and professional money management. Open-end funds offer choice, liquidity, and convenience, but charge fees and often require a minimum investment. Also called mutual fund.

operating leverage   Fixed operating costs divided by total (fixed plus variable) operating costs.

opportunity cost   The cost of passing up the next best choice when making a decision. For example, if an asset such as capital is used for one purpose, the opportunity cost is the value of the next best purpose the asset could have been used for. Opportunity cost analysis is an important part of a company's decision-making processes, but is not treated as an actual cost in any financial statement.

option   The right, but not the obligation, to buy (for a call option) or sell (for a put option) a specific amount of a given stock, commodity, currency, index, or debt, at a specified price (the strike price) during a specified period of time. For stock options, the amount is usually 100 shares. Each option has a buyer, called the holder, and a seller, known as the writer. If the option contract is exercised, the writer is responsible for fulfilling the terms of the contract by delivering the shares to the appropriate party. In the case of a security that cannot be delivered such as an index, the contract is settled in cash. For the holder, the potential loss is limited to the price paid to acquire the option. When an option is not exercised, it expires. No shares change hands and the money spent to purchase the option is lost. For the buyer, the upside is unlimited. Options, like stocks, are therefore said to have an asymmetrical payoff pattern. For the writer, the potential loss is unlimited unless the contract is covered, meaning that the writer already owns the security underlying the option. Options are most frequently as either leverage or protection. As leverage, options allow the holder to control equity in a limited capacity for a fraction of what the shares would cost. The difference can be invested elsewhere until the option is exercised. As protection, options can guard against price fluctuations in the near term because they provide the right acquire the underlying stock at a fixed price for a limited time. Risk is limited to the option premium (except when writing options for a security that is not already owned). However, the costs of trading options (including both commissions and the bid/ask spread) is higher on a percentage basis than trading the underlying stock. In addition, options are very complex and require a great deal of observation and maintenance. also called option contract.

option premium   The amount per share that an option buyer pays to the seller. The option premium is primarily affected by the difference between the stock price and the strike price, the time remaining for the option to be exercised, and the volatility of the underlying stock. Affecting the premium to a lesser degree are factors such as interest rates, market conditions, and the dividend rate of the underlying stock. Because the value of an option decreases as its expiration date approaches and becomes worthless after that date, options are called wasting assets. The total value of an option consists of intrinsic value, which is simply how far in-the-money an option is, and time value, which is the difference between the price paid and the intrinsic value. Understandably, time value approaches zero as the expiration date nears. also called option price.

Options Clearing Corporation   OCC. The organization that handles clearing of the options trades for the various options exchanges and regulates the listing of new options. It is regulated by the Securities and Exchange Commission, and is owned jointly by the U.S. stock exchanges that trade options (American Stock Exchange, Chicago Board Options Exchange, Pacific Exchange, and Philadelphia Stock Exchange). The fact that all listed options are cleared through OCC means that all options are free of default risk, since the OCC guarantees all option contracts. Therefore, the buyer or a seller of an option only faces the credit risk of the OCC (which is minimal), not the credit risk of the counterparty. In order to manage risk, the OCC imposes margin requirements on all options brokers. The margin requirement depends on the particulars of each specific contract.

origination fee   A fee charged by a lender for processing a loan application, expressed as a percentage of the mortgage amount.

out of the money   A call option whose strike price is higher than the market price of the underlying security, or a put option whose strike price is lower than the market price of the underlying security.

Over-the-Counter   OTC. A security which is not traded on an exchange, usually due to an inability to meet listing requirements. For such securities, broker/dealers negotiate directly with one another over computer networks and by phone, and their activities are monitored by the NASD. OTC stocks are usually very risky since they are the stocks that are not considered large or stable enough to trade on a major exchange. They also tend to trade infrequently, making the bid-ask spread larger. Also, research about these stocks is more difficult to obtain. also called unlisted.

owner of record   The name of an individual or entity that an issuer carries in its records as the registered holder (not necessarily the beneficial owner) of the issuer's securities. Dividends and other distributions are paid only to owners of record. also called stockholder of record or holder of record or shareholder of record.

par   The nominal dollar amount assigned to a security by the issuer. For an equity security, par is usually a very small amount that bears no relationship to its market price, except for preferred stock, in which case par is used to calculate dividend payments. For a debt security, par is the amount repaid to the investor when the bond matures (usually, corporate bonds have a par value of $1000, municipal bonds $5000, and federal bonds $10,000). In the secondary market, a bond's price fluctuates with interest rates. If interest rates are higher than the coupon rate on a bond, the bond will be sold below par (at a "discount"). If interest rates have fallen, the price will be sold above par. here also called face value or par value.

parent company   A company that owns enough voting stock in another firm to control management and operations by influencing or electing its board of directors. also called holding company.

partnership   A type of unincorporated business organization in which multiple individuals, called general partners, manage the business and are equally liable for its debts; other individuals called limited partners may invest but not be directly involved in management and are liable only to the extent of their investments. Unlike a limited liability company or a corporation, in a partnership the partners share equal responsibility for the company's profits and losses, and its debts and liabilities. The partnership itself does not pay income taxes, but each partner has to report their share of business profits or losses on their individual tax return. Estimated tax payments are also necessary for each of the partners for the year in progress. Partnerships must file a return on Form 1065 showing income and deductions. Estimated tax payments are also required if they expect their income to be greater than $1,000.

passive management   A money management strategy that seeks to match the return and risk characteristics of a market segment or index, by mirroring its composition. also called passive portfolio strategy.

payback period   The amount of time taken to break even on an investment. Since this method ignores the time value of money and cash flows after the payback period, it can provide only a partial picture of whether the investment is worthwhile.

payoff diagram   A chart of the profits and losses for a particular options strategy prepared in advance of the execution of the strategy. The diagram is plot of expected profit or loss against the price of the underlying security.

PEG ratio   A stock's price/earnings ratio divided by its year-over-year earnings growth rate. In general, the lower the PEG, the better the value, because the investor would be paying less for each unit of earnings growth.

penny stock   A stock which sells for less than one dollar per share (or in some cases, less than five dollars per share). Most penny stocks have only a few million dollars in net tangible assets and have a short operating history. Penny stocks are almost always small cap stocks, but the reverse isn't necessarily true.

Pension Benefit Guaranty Corporation   PBGC. A federal corporation established under ERISA which insures the vested benefits of pension plan participants.

pension fund   Fund set up for a pension plan.

permanent financing   Long-term debt or equity financing. In general, permanent financing is used to purchase or develop long-term fixed assets like factories and machinery. Since the payoff from a long-term asset tends to be over a period of time, financing through long-term options reduce the risk of principal payoff not being made (in the case of debt financing).

Personal Financial Specialist   PFS. A Certified Public Accountant who also offers financial planning services. Personal Financial Specialists must complete an exam, have at least three years of financial planning experience, and submit recommendations before certification. The title is authorized by the American Institute of Certified Public Accountants.

Pink Sheets   A daily listing of bid and ask prices for over-the-counter stocks not included in the daily Nasdaq over-the-counter listings, published by the National Quotation Bureau and used by brokerages.

point-and-figure chart   A chart which plots price movements only, without measuring the passage of time.

poison pill   Any tactic by a company designed to avoid a hostile takeover. One example is the issuance of preferred stock that gives shareholders the right to redeem their shares at a premium after the takeover.

portfolio   A collection of investments all owned by the same individual or organization. These investments often include stocks, which are investments in individual businesses; bonds, which are investments in debt that are designed to earn interest; and mutual funds, which are essentially pools of money from many investors that are invested by professionals or according to indices.

portfolio insurance   A strategy of hedging a stock portfolio against market risk by selling stock index futures short or buying stock index put options.

portfolio turnover   The rate of trading activity in a fund's portfolio of investments, equal to the lesser of purchases or sales, for a year, divided by average total assets during that year.

predatory lending   Any of a number of fraudulent, deceptive, discriminatory, or unfavorable lending practices. Many of these practices are illegal, while others are legal but not in the best interest of the borrowers.

preemptive right   The right of current shareholders to maintain their fractional ownership of a company by buying a proportional number of shares of any future issue of common stock. Most states consider preemptive rights valid only if made explicit in a corporation's charter. also called subscription privilege or subscription right.

preferred stock   Capital stock which provides a specific dividend that is paid before any dividends are paid to common stock holders, and which takes precedence over common stock in the event of a liquidation. Like common stock, preferred stocks represent partial ownership in a company, although preferred stock shareholders do not enjoy any of the voting rights of common stockholders. Also unlike common stock, a preferred stock pays a fixed dividend that does not fluctuate, although the company does not have to pay this dividend if it lacks the financial ability to do so. The main benefit to owning preferred stock is that the investor has a greater claim on the company's assets than common stockholders. Preferred shareholders always receive their dividends first and, in the event the company goes bankrupt, preferred shareholders are paid off before common stockholders. In general, there are four different types of preferred stock: cumulative preferred, non-cumulative, participating, and convertible. also called preference shares.

preliminary prospectus   The initial document published by an underwriter of a new issue of stock to be given to prospective investors. It is understood that the document will be modified significantly before the final prospectus is published. also called red herring.

primary market   The market for new securities issues. In the primary market the security is purchased directly from the issuer. This differs from the secondary market.

prime rate   The interest rate that commercial banks charge their most creditworthy borrowers, such as large corporations. The prime rate is a lagging indicator. also called prime.

principal-agent relationship   The arrangement that exists when one person or entity (called the agent) acts on behalf of another (called the principal). For example, shareholders of a company (principals) elect management (agents) to act on their behalf, and investors (principals) choose fund managers (agents) to manage their assets. This arrangement works well when the agent is an expert at making the necessary decisions, but doesn't work well when the interests of the principal and agent differ substantially. In general, a contract is used to specify the terms of a principal- agent relationship.

private placement   The sale of securities directly to institutional investors, such as banks, mutual funds, insurance companies, pension funds, and foundations. Does not require SEC registration, provided the securities are bought for investment purposes rather than resale, as specified in the investment letter.

program trading   Computer-driven, automatically-executed securities trades, usually in large volumes of a set (basket) of 15 or more stocks.

proprietary trading   Transactions made by a securities firm that affect the firm's account but not the accounts of its clients.

prospectus   A legal document offering securities or mutual fund shares for sale, required by the Securities Act of 1933. It must explain the offer, including the terms, issuer, objectives (if mutual fund) or planned use of the money (if securities), historical financial statements, and other information that could help an individual decide whether the investment is appropriate for him/her. also called offering circular or circular.

proxy   A written authorization given by a shareholder for someone else, usually the company's management, to cast his/her vote at a shareholder meeting or at another time.

public company   A company which has issued securities through an offering, and which are now traded on the open market. also called publicly held or publicly traded. opposite of private company.

purchasing power parity   The theory that, in the long run, identical products and services in different countries should cost the same in different countries. This is based on the belief that exchange rates will adjust to eliminate the arbitrage opportunity of buying a product or service in one country and selling it in another. For example, consider a laptop computer that costs 1,500 Euros in Germany and an exchange rate of 2 Euros to 1 U.S. Dollar. If the same laptop cost 1,000 dollars in the United States, U.S. consumers would buy the laptop in Germany. If done on a large scale, the influx of U.S. dollars would drive up the price of the Euro, until it equalized at 1.5 Euros to 1 U.S. Dollar—the same ratio of the price of the laptop in Germany to the price of the laptop in the U.S. The theory only applies to tradable goods, not to immobile goods or local services. The theory also discounts several real world factors, such as transportation costs, tarrifs and transaction costs. It also assumes there are competitive markets for the goods and services in both countries.

put   An option contract that gives the holder the right to sell a certain quantity of an underlying security to the writer of the option, at a specified price (strike price) up to a specified date (expiration date); here also called put option.

raider   An individual or entity attempting to acquire enough equity in a target company to assume a controlling interest, usually through a hostile takeover bid. Such an interest allows the raider to replace the existing management with his own representatives, completing the takeover. A raider would typically target a company with undervalued assets, which would be relatively inexpensive to take over. Once the raider has accumulated 5% of the shares in a company, he/she must report this fact to the SEC and the target company.

random walk theory An investment theory which claims that market prices follow a random path up and down, without any influence by past price movements, making it impossible to predict with any accuracy which direction the market will move at any point. In other words, the theory claims that path a stock's price follows is a random walk that cannot be determined from historical price information, especially in the short term. Investors who believe in the random walk theory feel that it is impossible to outperform the market without taking on additional risk, and believe that neither fundamental analysis nor technical analysis have any validity. However, some proponents of this theory do acknowledge that markets move gradually upward in the long run.

rating service A company that publishes ratings for securities such as preferred stock and debt issues based on the likelihood of consistent and timely payments. These rankings are arrived at by looking at a variety of balance sheet data. Some rating services are very influential, and an upgrade or downgrade can affect their borrowing costs significantly.

real estate agent A licensed salesperson working for a real estate broker. If the agent sells a house successfully, then he/she receives a portion of the sale price as a commission. In the U.S., all real estate agents have to be licensed by the state they work for.

real estate broker A person licensed to arrange the buying and selling of real estate for a fee.

real interest rate The current interest rate minus the current inflation rate.

rebalancing Making adjustments to counteract the fact that different assets have performed differently and now comprise different percentages of the portfolio than they were intended to.

receivership A form of bankruptcy in which a company can avoid liquidation by reorganizing with the help of a court-appointed trustee.

record date Date, set by the issuing company, on which an individual must own shares in order to be eligible to receive a declared dividend or capital gains distribution. The date is also used by the NASD to set the ex-dividend date. also called date of record.

red herring The initial document published by an underwriter of a new issue of stock to be given to prospective investors. It is understood that the document will be modified significantly before the final prospectus is published. also called preliminary prospectus. Its name comes from the warning, printed in red, that information in the document is still being reviewed by the SEC and is subject to change.

REFCORP Resolution Funding Corporation. The organization created by Congress in 1989 to bail out the savings and loan industry by offering debt to some companies. REFCORP also financed the Resolution Trust Company, which was responsible for liquidating and restructuring bankrupt or struggling savings and loans companies. The principal payments of the debt issued by REFCORP are guaranteed by zero-coupon Treasuries, so the chances of an investor losing his/her principal payment are very low.

refinancing Paying off an existing loan with the proceeds from a new loan, usually of the same size, and using the same property as collateral. In order to decide whether this is worthwhile, the savings in interest must be weighed against the fees associated with refinancing. The difficult part of this calculation is predicting how much the up-front money would be worth when the savings are received. Other reasons to refinance include reducing the term of a longer mortgage, or switching between a fixed-rate and an adjustable-rate mortgage. If there are prepayment fees attached to the existing mortgage, refinancing becomes less favorable because of the increased cost to the borrower at the time of the refinancing.

refunding Issuing a bond to retire an existing bond.

regional bank A bank that operates in one region of a country, as opposed to a money center bank, which operates nationally and globally.

regional exchange An SEC-registered stock exchange which focuses on listing stocks of corporations in its geographic region. The major U.S. regional exchanges are the Boston, Chicago, Cincinnati, Pacific, and Philadelphia stock exchanges. Regional exchanges are usually significantly smaller than exchanges that focus on listing stocks at the national level. Many stocks listed on regional exchanges are not listed on national exchanges. However, regional exchanges also feature stocks which list both on the regional and the national exchange.

Registered Investment Adviser RIA. Investment advisor registered with the SEC. No certification is required.

registered security Security that cannot be transferred or delivered to another party. opposite of negotiable security.

Regulation FD SEC regulation adopted in 2000 that eliminated the practice of selective disclosure. The rule requires that when a public company chooses to release any information, it must be done in such a way that the general public has access to it at the same time as institutional investors and analysts. If information is accidentally released to specific parties, the company must disseminate that information widely within 24 hours.

Regulation Q A Federal Reserve Board regulation that limits the interest rate that banks can pay on savings deposits.

Regulation Z A federal law requiring lenders to fully disclose in writing the terms and conditions of a mortgage, including the annual percentage rate and other charges. also called Truth in Lending.

reinsurance The sharing of insurance policies among multiple insurers, to reduce the risk for each.

reinvestment risk The risk resulting from the fact that interest or dividends earned from an investment may not be able to be reinvested in such a way that they earn the same rate of return as the invested funds that generated them. For example, falling interest rates may prevent bond coupon payments from earning the same rate of return as the original bond.

REIT Real Estate Investment Trust. A corporation or trust that uses the pooled capital of many investors to purchase and manage income property (equity REIT) and/or mortgage loans (mortgage REIT). REITs are traded on major exchanges just like stocks. They are also granted special tax considerations. REITs offer several benefits over actually owning properties. First, they are highly liquid, unlike traditional real estate. Second, REITs enable sharing in non-residential properties as well, such as hotels, malls, and other commercial or industrial properties. Third, there's no minimum investment with REITs. REITs do not necessarily increase and decrease in value along with the broader market. However, they pay yields in the form of dividends no matter how the shares perform. REITs can be valued based upon fundamental measures, similar to the valuation of stocks, but different numbers tend to be important for REITs than for stocks.

Relative Strength Index RSI. A technical analysis indicator which measures the magnitude of gains over a given time period against the magnitude of losses over that period. The equation is RSI = 100 - 100 / (1 + RS) where RS = (total gains / n) / (total losses / n) and n = number of RSI periods. The value can range from 1 to 100. Some technical analysts believe that a value of 30 or below indicates an oversold condition and that a value of 70 or above indicates an overbought condition.

repurchase agreement   A contract in which the seller of securities, such as Treasury Bills, agrees to buy them back at a specified time and price. also called repo or buyback.

required rate of return   The required rate of return in a discounted cash flow analysis, above which an investment makes sense and below which it does not. Often, this is based on the firm's cost of capital or weighted average cost of capital, plus or minus a risk premium to reflect the project's specific risk characteristics. also called hurdle rate.

reserve ratio   Amount of money and liquid assets that Federal Reserve System member banks must hold in cash or on deposit with the Federal Reserve System, usually a specified percentage of their demand deposits and time deposits. also called Federal Reserve requirement or reserve requirement.

restrictive covenant   A clause in a contract that requires one party to do, or refrain from doing, certain things. Often, a restriction on a borrower imposed by a lender. also called covenant.

revenue bond   Bond issued by a municipality to finance a specific public works project and supported by the revenues of that project. also called municipal revenue bond.

rights offering   Offering of common stock to investors who currently hold shares which entitle them to buy subsequent issues at a discount from the offering price.

risk adjusted return   A measure of how much an investment returned in relation to the amount of risk it took on. Often used to compare a high-risk, potentially high-return investment with a low-risk, lower-return investment.

risk premium   The reward for holding a risky investment rather than a risk-free one.

risk-free return   A theoretical interest rate that would be returned on an investment which was completely free of risk. The 3-month Treasury Bill is a close approximation, since it is virtually risk-free.

road show   A series of meetings with potential investors and brokers, conducted by a company and its underwriter, prior to a securities offering, especially an IPO.

rollover   A tax-free reinvestment of a distribution from a qualified retirement plan into an IRA or other qualified plan within a specific time frame, usually 60 days. These transfers can happen when leaving a job at an employer who offered a retirement plan such as a 401(k). The company can issue a check for the amount minus 20% in withheld taxes. To avoid this penalty, the rollover must be done trustee to trustee, meaning that the check is made out to the new trustee or custodian of the rollover IRA. The company will provide the check and the participant must deposit the check into the new account within 60 days. also called IRA rollover.

Rule 12b-1 fee   An extra fee charged by some mutual funds to cover promotion, distributions, marketing expenses, and sometimes commissions to brokers. A genuine no-load fund does not have Rule 12b-1 fees, although some funds calling themselves "no-load" do have Rule 12b-1 fees (as do some load funds). Rule 12b-1 fee information is disclosed in a fund's prospectus, is included in the stated expense ratio, and is usually less than 1%. also called 12b-1 fee.

Rule 13d   An SEC rule requiring disclosure by anyone acquiring a beneficial ownership of 5% or more of any equity security registered with the SEC. If the company is listed on an exchange, the form must be filed with the exchange, too.

Rule of 72   The estimation of doubling time on an investment, for which the compounded annual rate of return times the number of years must equal roughly 72 for the investment to double in value.

S&P 500   Standard & Poor's 500. A basket of 500 stocks that are considered to be widely held. The S&P 500 index is weighted by market value, and its performance is thought to be representative of the stock market as a whole. The S&P 500 index was created in 1957, although it has been extrapolated backwards to several decades earlier for performance comparison purposes. This index provides a broad snapshot of the overall U.S. equity market; in fact, over 70% of all U.S. equity is tracked by the S&P 500. The index selects its companies based upon their market size, liquidity, and sector. Most of the companies in the index are solid mid cap or large cap corporations. Like the Nasdaq Composite, the S&P 500 is a market-weighted index. Most experts consider the S&P 500 one of the best benchmarks available to judge overall U.S. market performance.

saucer   A technical analysis term used to describe a chart on which the price of a security has made a bottom and is moving up.

Savings and Loan   S&L. A federally or state chartered financial institution that takes deposits from individuals, funds mortgages, and pays dividends.

Savings Bond   A registered, non-callable, non-transferable bond issued by the U.S. Government, and backed by its full faith and credit. Savings bonds differ from other Treasury securities in several ways. Savings bonds are non-marketable, meaning that they cannot be bought and sold after they are purchased from the government; therefore, there is no secondary market for savings bonds. The tax benefits associated with savings bonds are significant. Like all treasury securities, they are exempt from state and local taxes, but in the specific case of savings bonds, all federal taxes may be deferred until the bond is redeemed. Therefore, even though interest will accrue, no taxes will be due until that money can be accessed. Additionally, if the money received at redemption is used to pay tuition expenses for the holder, a spouse or a dependent in the same year, the interest earned may be exempt from federal taxes as well. Face values range from $50 to $10,000. also called U.S. Savings Bond.

SCOR   Small Corporate Offering Registration. An over the counter sale of securities that allows for up to $1 million to be raised while avoiding the costs and formalities of an IPO. Used by small businesses to become publicly traded.

scorched-earth policy   A reaction to a takeover attempt that involves liquidating valuable assets and assuming liabilities in an effort to make the proposed takeover unattractive to the acquiring company.

second mortgage   A mortgage on real estate which has already been pledged as collateral for an earlier mortgage. The second mortgage carries rights which are subordinate to those of the first.

secondary market   A market in which an investor purchases a security from another investor rather than the issuer, subsequent to the original issuance in the primary market. also called aftermarket.

Section 529 plan   A state-sponsored program designed to help parents finance education expenses. Section 529 plans are administered by certain investment companies and subject to contribution requirements and investment guidelines. Withdrawals from the account are taxed at the child's tax rate, and anyone can contribute to a Section 529 plan, regardless of their income level. In most cases, the money is invested in a portfolio of stocks, bonds, or mutual funds. Most states offer Section 529 plans. The proceeds can be used only for education withdrawals for non-educational purposes trigger taxes and a 10% penalty. The investment company administering the account will be in control of how the money is invested, and will charge an ongoing free for its services.

sector fund   A mutual fund which invests entirely or predominantly in a single sector. Sector funds tend to be riskier and more volatile than the broad market because they are less diversified, although the risk level depends on the specific sector. Some investors choose sector funds when they believe that a specific sector will outperform the overall market, while others choose sector funds to hedge against other holdings in a portfolio. Some common sector funds include financial services funds, gold and precious metals funds, health care funds, and real estate funds, but sector funds exist for just about every sector.

Securities Act of 1933   First Congressional law regulating the securities industry. Required registration and disclosure and included measures to discourage fraud and deception.

securities analyst   An employee of a bank, brokerage, advisor, or mutual fund who studies companies and makes buy and sell recommendations, often specializing in a single sector or industry. Securities analysts use a wide variety of techniques for researching and making recommendations. The reports and recommendations they publish are often used by traders, mutual fund managers, portfolio managers and investors in their decision making processes. also called financial analyst or analyst.

Securities and Exchange Commission   SEC. The primary federal regulatory agency for the securities industry, whose responsibility is to promote full disclosure and to protect investors against fraudulent and manipulative practices in the securities markets. The Securities and Exchange Commission enforces, among other acts, the Securities Act of 1933, the Securities Exchange Act of 1934, the Trust Indenture Act of 1939, the Investment Company Act of 1940 and the Investment Advisers Act. The supervision of dealers is delegated to the self-regulatory bodies of the exchanges. The Securities and Exchange Commission is an independent, quasi-judiciary agency. It has five commissioners, each appointed for a five year term that is staggered so that one new commissioner is being replaced every year. No more than three members of the commission can be of a single political party. The Securities and Exchange Commission is comprised of four basic divisions. The Division of Corporate Finance is in charge of making sure all publicly traded companies disclose the required financial information to investors. The Division of Market Regulation oversees all legislation involving brokers and brokerage firms. The Division of Investment Management regulates the mutual fund and investment advisor industries. And the Division of Enforcement enforces the securities legislation and investigates possible violations.

Securities Exchange Act of 1934   The act which created the SEC, outlawed manipulative and abusive practices in the issuance of securities, required registration of stock exchanges, brokers, dealers, and listed securities, and required disclosure of certain financial information and insider trading.

Securities Industry Association   SIA. The principal trade association and lobbying group for broker/dealers. SIA members include most members of the New York Stock Exchange, and many members of other exchanges and the over-the-counter market.

Securities Investor Protection Corporation   SIPC. A non-profit membership corporation established by Congress which insures securities and cash in customer accounts up to $500,000 (up to $100,000 on cash) in the event of brokerage bankruptcy. The SIPC is funded by all of its member securities broker-dealers. While it insures the account in the event that a brokerage runs out of funds to cover its claims, it does not insure against investment losses.

securitization   The process of aggregating similar instruments, such as loans or mortgages, into a negotiable security.

security market line   Relationship between an investment's hurdle rate and its market risk.

sell limit order   An order to a broker to sell a specified quantity of a security at or above a specified price (called the limit price).

sell-side analyst   An analyst employed by a brokerage firm or another firm that manages client accounts. Unlike that of the buy-side analysts employed by mutual funds, research produced by sell-side analysts is usually available to the public.

senior debt   Debt that has priority for repayment in a liquidation.

settlement price   The closing range of prices after a trading session, used to calculate gains and losses, margin calls, and invoice prices for deliveries in futures market accounts.

shark repellent   Any corporate activity that is undertaken to discourage a hostile takeover, such as a golden parachute, scorched earth policy or poison pill.

shelf registration   A registration of a new issue which can be prepared up to two years in advance, so that the issue can be offered quickly as soon as funds are needed or market conditions are favorable.

short interest ratio   Short interest divided by average daily volume over some period, usually 30 days. Some investors believe that a high ratio is a bullish indicator, and a low ratio is a bearish indicator.

short position   In the case of a futures contract, the promise to sell a certain quantity of a good at a particular price in the future. Opposite of a long position.

short sale   Borrowing a security (or commodity futures contract) from a broker and selling it, with the understanding that it must later be bought back (hopefully at a lower price) and returned to the broker. Short selling (or "selling short") is a technique used by investors who try to profit from the falling price of a stock. For example, consider an investor who wants to sell short 100 shares of a company, believing it is overpriced and will fall. The investor's broker will borrow the shares from someone who owns them with the promise that the investor will return them later. The investor immediately sells the borrowed shares at the current market price. If the price of the shares drops, he/she "covers the short position" by buying back the shares, and his/her broker returns them to the lender. The profit is the difference between the price at which the stock was sold and the cost to buy it back, minus commissions and expenses for borrowing the stock. But if the price of the shares increase, the potential losses are unlimited. The company's shares may go up and up, but at some point the investor has to replace the 100 shares he/she sold. In that case, the losses can mount without limit until the short position is covered. For this reason, short selling is a very risky technique. SEC rules allow investors to sell short only on an uptick or a zero-plus tick, to prevent "pool operators" from driving down a stock price through heavy short-selling, then buying the shares for a large profit.

short-term gain or loss   A capital gain or loss on an investment which was held for less than some minimum amount of time (often a year and a day). A short-term gain usually results in a higher tax rate than a long-term gain.

simple interest   The interest calculated on a principal sum, not compounded on earned interest.

Single-Premium Deferred Annuity   SPDA. A tax-deferred investment plan in which an individual makes a single payment to a mutual fund or insurance company. Similar to an IRA, but having no annual contribution limit.

sinking fund   A fund into which a company sets aside money over time, in order to retire its preferred stock, bonds or debentures. In the case of bonds, incremental payments into the sinking fund can soften the financial impact at maturity. Investors prefer bonds and debentures backed by sinking funds because there is less risk of a default.

Small Business Administration   A Federal agency which makes loans to small businesses.

Small Business Investment Company   SBIC. A private investment company licensed by the Small Business Administration to provide small businesses with debt and equity financing.

small cap $250 million to $1 billion capitalization.

sole proprietorship   A business structure in which an individual and his/her company are considered a single entity for tax and liability purposes. A sole proprietorship is a company which is not registered with the state as a limited liability company or corporation. The owner does not pay income tax separately for the company, but he/she reports business income or losses on his/her individual income tax return. The owner is inseparable from the sole proprietorship, so he/she is liable for any business debts. also called proprietorship.

SPDR   Spider. Shares of a security designed to track the value of the S&P 500. Spiders trade on the American Stock Exchange under the symbol SPY. One SPDR unit is valued at approximately one-tenth of the value of the S&P 500. Dividends are distributed quarterly, and are based on the accumulated stock dividends held in trust, less any expenses of the trust. also called Standard & Poor's Depositary Receipt.

specialist   A stock exchange member who makes a market for certain exchange-traded securities, maintaining an inventory of those securities and standing ready to buy and sell shares as necessary to maintain an orderly market for those shares. Can be an individual, partnership, corporation or group of firms.

specialty fund   A mutual fund investing primarily in the securities of a particular industry, sector, type of security or geographic region. also called specialized fund.

spinoff   An independent company created from an existing part of another company through a divestiture, such as a sale or distribution of new shares.

split   An increase in the number of outstanding shares of a company's stock, such that proportionate equity of each shareholder remains the same. This requires approval from the board of directors and shareholders. A corporation whose stock is performing well may choose to split its shares, distributing additional shares to existing shareholders. The most common split is two-for-one, in which each share becomes two shares. The price per share immediately adjusts to reflect the split, since buyers and sellers of the stock all know about the split (in this example, the share price would be cut in half). Some companies decide to split their stock if the price of the stock rises significantly and is perceived to be too expensive for small investors to afford. also called stock split.

spot market   A market in which commodities, such as grain, gold, crude oil, or RAM chips, are bought and sold for cash and delivered immediately. also called cash market.

spread   The difference between the current bid and the current ask (in over-the-counter trading) or offered (in exchange trading) of a given security; also called bid/ask spread.

stakeholder   Any party that has an interest ("stake") in a firm.

Stock Clearing Corporation   SCC. The clearinghouse for the NYSE.

stock dividend   A dividend paid as additional shares of stock rather than as cash. If dividends paid are in the form of cash, those dividends are taxable. When a company issues a stock dividend, rather than cash, there usually are not tax consequences until the shares are sold.

stock fund   A mutual fund which invests primarily in stocks.

stop-limit order   An order to buy or sell a certain quantity of a certain security at a specified price or better, but only after a specified price has been reached. A stop-limit order is essentially a combination of a stop order and a limit order.

straddle   The purchase or sale of an equal number of puts and calls, with the same strike price and expiration dates. A straddle provides the opportunity to profit from a prediction about the future volatility of the market. Long straddles are used to profit from high volatility. Long straddles can be effective when an investor is confident that a stock price will change dramatically, but cannot predict the direction of the move. Short straddles represent the opposite prediction, that a stock price will not change.

street name   The term given to securities held in the name of a brokerage on behalf of a customer, usually done to facilitate subsequent transactions.

strike price   The specified price on an option contract at which the contract may be exercised, whereby a call option buyer can buy the underlier or a put option buyer can sell the underlier. The buyer's profit from exercising the option is the amount by which the strike price exceeds the spot price (in the case of a call), or the amount by which the spot price exceeds the strike price (in the case of a put). In general, the smaller the difference between spot and strike price, the higher the option premium. also called exercise price.

strip   Bond, usually issued by the U.S. Treasury, whose two components, interest and repayment of principal, are separated and sold individually as zero-coupon bonds. Strip is an acronym for Separate Trading of Registered Interest and Principal of Securities.

Student Loan Marketing Association   Sallie Mae. A federally established, publicly traded corporation which buys student loans from colleges and other lenders, pools them and sells them to investors. In this way, Sallie Mae is able to provide financing to providers of student loans.

Subchapter S Corporation   A form of corporation, allowed by the IRS for most companies with 75 or fewer shareholders, which enables the company to enjoy the benefits of incorporation but be taxed as if it were a partnership. also called S Corporation.

subordinated debt   Debt that is either unsecured or has a lower priority than that of another debt claim on the same asset or property. also called junior debt.

subsidiary   A company for which a majority of the voting stock is owned by a holding company.

sunk cost   Cost already incurred which cannot be recovered regardless of future events.

swap   An exchange of streams of payments over time according to specified terms. The most common type is an interest rate swap, in which one party agrees to pay a fixed interest rate in return for receiving a adjustable rate from another party.

sweep account   A brokerage account whose cash balance is automatically transferred into an interest-bearing investment, such as a money market fund.

target   Objective, goal.

tax deduction   An expense subtracted from adjusted gross income when calculating taxable income, such as for state and local taxes paid, charitable gifts, and certain types of interest payments. also called deduction.

tax equivalent yield   The yield that must be offered before factoring in taxes so that an investment pays off a certain after-tax yield. This measure is often necessary to compare taxable and tax-free investments, since tax-free issues tend have lower pre-tax yields due to the fact that the investment's proceeds will not be reduced by taxes. Tax equivalent yield is equal to required after-tax yield divided by (1 minus the tax rate).

tax-deferred   Income whose taxes can be postponed until a later date. Examples include IRA, 401(k), Keogh Plan, annuity, Savings Bond and Employee Stock Ownership Plan.

tax-exempt bond   A bond, issued by a municipal, county or state government, whose interest payments are not subject to federal income tax, and sometimes also state or local income tax.

technical analysis   A method of evaluating securities by relying on the assumption that market data, such as charts of price, volume, and open interest, can help predict future (usually short-term) market trends. Unlike fundamental analysis, the intrinsic value of the security is not considered. Technical analysts believe that they can accurately predict the future price of a stock by looking at its historical prices and other trading variables. Technical analysis assumes that market psychology influences trading in a way that enables predicting when a stock will rise or fall. For that reason, many technical analysts are also market timers, who believe that technical analysis can be applied just as easily to the market as a whole as to an individual stock.

tender offer   A takeover bid in the form of a public invitation to shareholders to sell their stock, generally at a price above the market price.

term life insurance   A life insurance policy which provides a stated benefit upon the holder's death, provided that the death occurs within a certain specified time period. However, the policy does not provide any returns beyond the stated benefit, unlike an insurance policy which allows investors to share in returns from the insurance company's investment portfolio.

thin market   A market with few bid and ask offers. Characterized by low liquidity, high spreads, and high volatility. Small changes in supply and/or demand can have a dramatic impact on market price. also called narrow market. opposite of liquid market.

time value   The amount by which an option's premium exceeds its intrinsic value. also called time premium.

time value of money   The idea that a dollar now is worth more than dollar in the future, even after adjusting for inflation, because a dollar now can earn interest or other appreciation until the time the dollar in the future would be received.

tombstone   An advertisement in a business newspaper or magazine, placed by an investment bank, announcing an offering and listing the syndicate members.

tracking error   When using an indexing or any other benchmarking strategy, the amount by which the performance of the portfolio differed from that of the benchmark. In reality, no indexing strategy can perfectly match the performance of the index or benchmark, and the tracking error quantifies the degree to which the strategy differed from the index or benchmark.

trade credit   A company's open account arrangements with its vendors.

Treasury Inflation-Protected Security   TIPS. A security which is identical to a treasury bond except that principal and coupon payments are adjusted to eliminate the effects of inflation.

Treasury Stock   Stock reacquired by a corporation to be retired or resold to the public. Treasury stock is issued but not outstanding, and is not taken into consideration when calculating earnings per share or dividends, or for voting purposes.

triple witching hour   The final hour of the stock market trading session on the third Friday of March, June, September, and December, when option contracts and futures contracts expire on market indexes used by program traders. The simultaneous expirations often set off heavy trading of options, futures and the underlying stocks, which can cause large fluctuations in the value of their underlying stocks.

U.S. Treasury Securities   Negotiable U.S. Government debt obligations, backed by its full faith and credit. Exempt from state and local taxes. U.S. Treasury Securities are issued by the U.S. government in order to pay for government projects. The money paid out for a Treasury bond is essentially a loan to the government. As with any loan, repayment of principal is accompanied by a specified interest rate. These bonds are guaranteed by the "full faith and credit" of the U.S. government, meaning that they are extremely low risk (since the government can simply print money to pay back the loan). Additionally, interest earned on U.S. Treasury Securities is exempt from state and local taxes. Federal taxes, however, are still due on the earned interest. The government sells U.S. Treasury Securities by auction in the primary market, but they are marketable securities and therefore can be purchased through a broker in the very active secondary market. A broker will charge a fee for such a transaction, but the government charges no fee to participate in auctions. Prices on the secondary market and at auction are determined by interest rates. U.S. Treasury Securities issued today are not callable, so they will continue to accrue interest until the maturity date. One possible downside to U.S. Treasury Securities is that if interest rates increase during the term of the bond, the money invested will be earning less interest than it could earn elsewhere. Accordingly, the resale value of the bond will decrease as well. Because there is almost no risk of default by the government, the return on Treasury bonds is relatively low, and a high inflation rate can erase most of the gains by reducing the value of the principal and interest payments. There are three types of securities issued by the U.S. Treasury (bonds, bills, and notes), which are distinguished by the amount of time from the initial sale of the bond to maturity. also called Treasuries.

underlier   A security or commodity which is subject to delivery upon exercise of an option contract or convertible security. Exceptions include index options and futures, which cannot be delivered and are therefore settled in cash.

underwriting   The procedure by which an underwriter brings a new security issue to the investing public in an offering. In such a case, the underwriter will guarantee a certain price for a certain number of securities to the party that is issuing the security (in exchange for a fee). Thus, the issuer is secure that they will raise a certain minimum from the issue, while the underwriter bears the risk of the issue.

uptick   A stock market transaction (or sometimes, a quote) at a price higher than the preceding one for the same security. Also called plus tick. Opposite of downtick.

value fund   A mutual fund that invests in companies which it determines to be underpriced by fundamental measures. Assuming that a company's share price will not remain undervalued indefinitely, the fund looks to make money by buying before the expected upturn. Value funds tend to focus on safety rather than growth, and often choose investments providing dividends as well as capital appreciation. They invest in companies that have low P/E ratios, and stocks that have fallen out of favor with mainstream investors, either due to changing investor preferences, a poor quarterly earnings report, or hard times in a particular industry. Value stocks are often mature companies that have stopped growing and that use their earnings to pay dividends. Thus value funds produce current income (from the dividends) as well as long-term growth (from capital appreciation once the stocks become popular again). They tend to have more conservative and less volatile returns than growth funds.

variable universal life   A form of whole life insurance which combines some features of universal life insurance, such as premium and death benefit flexibility, with some features of variable life insurance, such as more investment choices. Variable universal life adds to the flexibility of universal life by allowing the holder to choose among investment vehicles for the savings portion of the account. The differences between this arrangement and investing individually are the tax advantages and fees that accompany the insurance policy.

venture capital   VC. Funds made available for startup firms and small businesses with exceptional growth potential. Managerial and technical expertise are often also provided. also called risk capital.

vesting   An ERISA guideline stipulating that employees must be entitled to their benefits from a pension fund, profit-sharing plan or Employee Stock Ownership Plan, within a certain period of time, even if they no longer work for their employer.

volatility   The relative rate at which the price of a security moves up and down. Volatility is found by calculating the annualized standard deviation of daily change in price. If the price of a stock moves up and down rapidly over short time periods, it has high volatility. If the price almost never changes, it has low volatility.

volume   The number of shares, bonds or contracts traded during a given period, for a security or an entire exchange. Also called trading volume.

WACC   Weighted Average Cost of Capital. An average representing the expected return on all of a company's securities. Each source of capital, such as stocks, bonds, and other debt, is assigned a required rate of return, and then these required rates of return are weighted in proportion to the share each source of capital contributes to the company's capital structure. The resulting rate is what the firm would use as a minimum for evaluating a capital project or investment.

warrant   A certificate, usually issued along with a bond or preferred stock, entitling the holder to buy a specific amount of securities at a specific price, usually above the current market price at the time of issuance, for an extended period, anywhere from a few years to forever. In the case that the price of the security rises to above that of the warrant's exercise price, then the investor can buy the security at the warrant's exercise price and resell it for a profit. Otherwise, the warrant will simply expire or remain unused. Warrants are listed on options exchanges and trade independently of the security with which it was issued. also called subscription warrant.

white knight   A potential acquirer who is sought out by a target company's management to take over the company to avoid a hostile takeover by an undesirable black knight.

whole life   Life insurance which provides coverage for an individual's whole life, rather than a specified term. A savings component, called cash value or loan value, builds over time and can be used for wealth accumulation. Whole life is the most basic form of cash value life insurance. The insurance company essentially makes all of the decisions regarding the policy. Regular premiums both pay insurance costs and cause equity to accrue in a savings account. A fixed death benefit is paid to the beneficiary along with the balance of the savings account. Premiums are fixed throughout the life of the policy even though the breakdown between insurance and savings swings toward the insurance over time. Management fees also eat up a portion of the premiums. The insurance company will invest money primarily in fixed-income securities, meaning that the savings investment will be subject to interest rate and inflation risk.

World Trade Organization   WTO. An international agency which encourages trade between member nations, administers global trade agreements and resolves disputes when they arise.

Yankee bond market   Market for dollar-denominated bonds issued in the U.S. by foreign corporations, banks and governments.

Yellow Sheets   A daily bulletin from the National Quotation Bureau which provides updated bid and ask prices for over-the-counter corporate bonds along with a list of brokerages which make a market in those bonds.

yield curve   A curve that shows the relationship between yields and maturity dates for a set of similar bonds, usually Treasuries, at a given point in time.

yield to call   Yield that would be realized on a callable bond in the event that the bond was redeemed by the issuer on the next available call date.

yield to maturity   Yield that would be realized on a bond or other fixed income security if the bond was held until the maturity date. It is greater than the current yield if the bond is selling at a discount and less than the current yield if the bond is selling at a premium.

zero-coupon bond   A bond which pays no coupons, is sold at a deep discount to its face value, and matures at its face value. A zero-coupon bond has the important advantage of being free of reinvestment risk, though the downside is that there is no opportunity to enjoy the effects of a rise in market interest rates. Also, such bonds tend to be very sensitive to changes in interest rates, since there are no coupon payments to reduce the impact of interest rate changes. In addition, markets for zero-coupon bonds are relatively illiquid. Under U.S. tax law, the imputed interest on a zero-coupon bond is taxable as it accrues, even though there is no cash flow.

INDEX